Internationalization and Re-Confessionalization:
Law and Religion in the Nordic Realm 1945-2017

Internationalization and Re-Confessionalization: Law and Religion in the Nordic Realm 1945-2017

Edited by Pamela Slotte, Niels Henrik Gregersen, and Helge Årsheim

University Press of Southern Denmark

*Internationalization and Re-Confessionalization:
Law and Religion in the Nordic Realm 1945-2017*

© The authors and University Press of Southern
Denmark 2022
University of Southern Denmark Studies in History
and Social Sciences Vol. 621

Printed by Narayana Press
Cover by Dorthe Møller, Unisats Aps

ISBN 978-87-408-3288-4

University Press of Southern Denmark
55 Campusvej
DK-5230 Odense M
www.universitypress.dk

Distribution in the United States and Canada:
Independent Publishers Group
www.ipgbook.com

Distribution in the United Kingdom:
Gazelle Books
www.gazellebookservices.co.uk

Table of Contents

Note on Contributors 7

Acknowledgments 11

1. Introduction: Internationalization and Re-Confessionalization: Law and Religion in the Nordic Realm 1945-2017 13
Pamela Slotte, Niels Henrik Gregersen, and Helge Årsheim

I The Early Post-World War II Period

2. Nordic Lutheranism and Secular Law: The Role of Law in the Grundtvigian Creation Theologies of K.E. Løgstrup and Regin Prenter . . 41
Niels Henrik Gregersen

3. A Nordic Model of Democracy? Hal Koch and Alf Ross on Law and Religion in Nordic Societies 87
Tine Reeh

4. Christian Torchbearers in the Dark of Positivism: Survivors and Catalysts within Nordic Law and Religion 1950-2000 107
Kjell Å. Modéer

5. Sovereignty of the People or Sovereignty of God? The Transformation of Confessional Interpretations of the Democratic Principle in German Postwar Protestant Theology 131
Georg Kalinna

II Negotiations of the Secularity of Law

6. Neither Sacred nor Secular Law? The Self-Understanding of the Ecclesiastical Law in the Protestant Churches in Germany Before and After World War II 163
Hans Michael Heinig

7. Gender Equality Between Law and Religion in Norway: A Scandinavian Comparison 181
Aud V. Tønnessen

8. Minority, Media, and Law: Reality TV, Orthodox Canon Law, Finnish
and European Jurisprudence 203
Johan Bastubacka

9. Muslim Views on the Danish State and Law 233
Niels Valdemar Vinding

10. "By Law Established": The Nordic Lutheran Majority Churches in a
Comparative Perspective 259
Lisbet Christoffersen

11. Recognition, Religious Identity, and Populism: Lessons from Finland 315
Risto Saarinen and Heikki J. Koskinen

III Internationalization

12. Constitutional Identity in the Nordic Countries 1950-2015 339
Helle Krunke

13. A Minor Disturbance? Nordic Approaches to Minority Religion 363
Helge Årsheim

14. Moving Frontiers: Configuring Religion Law and Religious Law, and
Law-Religion Relations 385
Pamela Slotte

15. Freedom of Religion and Positive Duties of the State: The Case of
Sweden 419
Anna-Sara Lind

16. Making Religion Visible in Sweden: Secular Legislation Turns
Religious in the Name of Human Rights 447
Victoria Enkvist

Index of Subjects 465

Index of Names 471

Note on Contributors

Johan Bastubacka is Associate Professor (Docent) and senior university lecturer at the Faculty of Theology, University of Helsinki. Initially a researcher of Eastern Orthodox iconography, Bastubacka has widened the scope of his research to different topics of practical theology: religion and communication, liturgy and worship, and religion and law. Bastubacka currently works with issues of worship, mystagogues, and minorities in religious contexts.

Lisbet Christoffersen is Professor of Law & Religion at the Department of Society and Business Studies, Roskilde University, and Adjunct Professor of Ecclesiastical Law at the Faculty of Theology, University of Copenhagen. She holds a Ph.D. in constitutional law from the Faculty of Law at the University of Copenhagen. She is the PL of the HERA funded interdisciplinary comparative research project *Protestant Legacies in Nordic Law: Uses of the Past in the Construction of Secularity of Law* and has been a PI and PM of numerous other national, Nordic and European research projects on law and religion.

Victoria Enkvist is Senior Lecturer at the Faculty of Law at Uppsala University. She is affiliated to CRS. Her recent publications include *Freedom of Religion: An Ambiguous Right in the Contemporary European Legal Order* (co-editor, Bloomsbury Publishing 2020) and *Religionsfrihet—om rättsliga skiftningar och nyanser* (co-author, Iustus, *forthcoming*, 2020).

Niels Henrik Gregersen was Research Professor in Theology and Science at Aarhus University 2000-2004, and is since 2004 Professor of Systematic Theology at the University of Copenhagen. He was co-PI of the Excellence Center of *Naturalism and Christian Semantics* 2007-2013, co-PI of the Excellence Program *Changing Disasters* 2013-2016, and PI of the *Danish Reformation Project* 2014-2017, all at the University of Copenhagen. In science-and-religion, he is known for his work on theologies of self-organization and complexity theory, and in systematic theology for developing the concept of "deep incarnation" in the context of an evolutionary creation theology.

Hans Michael Heinig, Prof. Dr., holds the Chair of Public and Ecclesiastical Law at the Georg August University Goettingen and has a secondary appointment as Director of the Institute for Ecclesiastical Law of the EKD. Heinig has published extensively on the law of state-church relations, Protestant ecclesiastical law, constitutional law and the law of social security. See, for instance, *Öffentlich-rechtliche Religionsgesellschaften* (Duncker & Humblot 2003); *100 Begriffe aus dem Staatskirchenrecht* (co-editor, Mohr Siebeck 2012); *Handbuch des evangelischen Kirchenrechts* (co-editor, Mohr Siebeck 2016); *70 Jahre Grundgesetz: In welcher Verfassung ist die Bundesrepublik?* (co-editor, Vandenhoeck & Ruprecht 2019).

Georg Kalinna, Dr. Theol., studied theology and law in Bonn, Goettingen, and Berlin. He currently works as Assistant Professor at the Georg August University Goettingen, where he teaches systematic theology. His publications include a book about the development of Protestant interpretations of politics in Germany, *Die Entmythologisierung der Obrigkeit* (Mohr Siebeck 2019), as well as articles on political ethics and fundamental theology, with a special regard to the dialogue between continental and North American theology. His current work focuses on how to conceptualize change and innovation in the field of religious and theological language.

Heikki J. Koskinen, Docent of Theoretical Philosophy, Ph.D. His recent research has focused on systematic issues in contemporary recognition theory. Among other things, Koskinen has published the article "Antecedent Recognition: Some Problematic Educational Implications of the Very Notion" (*Journal of Philosophy of Education*, 2018), and co-edited the volumes *Recognition and Religion: Contemporary and Historical Perspectives* (Routledge 2019) and *Categories of Being: Essays on Metaphysics and Logic* (Oxford University Press 2012).

Helle Krunke is Professor of Constitutional Law at the Faculty of Law, University of Copenhagen, and First Vice President of the International Association of Constitutional Law. Her publications include *Transnational Solidarity: Concept, Challenges and Opportunities* (co-editor, Cambridge University Press 2020), *The Nordic Constitutions: A Comparative and Contextual Analysis* (co-editor, Hart Publishing 2018), and *Judges as Guardians of Constitutionalism and Human Rights* (co-editor, Edward Elgar 2016).

Anna-Sara Lind is Professor of Public Law at the Faculty of Law and the scientific leader of the Centre for Multidisciplinary Research on Religion and Society (CRS), Uppsala University. Her publications include *Reconsidering Religion, Law,* *and Democracy: New Challenges for Society and Research* (co-editor, Nordic Academic Press 2016) and *Transparency in the future—Swedish openness 250 years* (co-editor, Ragulka förlag 2017).

Kjell Å. Modéer is Professor Emeritus of Legal History, Lund University, guest professor in law at Luleå Technical University, Dr.iur.h.c. (Greifswald), Teol. dr.h.c. (Lund), Jur.dr.h.c. (Helsingfors). Research in the legal profession, legal cultures and legal traditions, law and religion. His recent publications include *Det förpliktande minnet* [The history of the Lund Law Faculty 1666—2016] (Santérus 2017), and the anthology *Law and The Christian Tradition in Scandinavia* (co-editor, Routledge 2020).

Tine Reeh is Associate Professor of Church History, University of Copenhagen. She has worked on Christianity and culture in a variety of projects and publications. Her book *Historie, kristendom, demokrati: Hal Koch 1932-1945* was published in 2012. Since 2018 she has held a grant for a research network exploring heritage from the UNESCO World Heritage Moravian colony in Christiansfeld. She is currently working on a book on the abolition of Mosaic Law in 18th century Denmark-Norway. Recent publications include "Cross Trade and Innovations: Judicial Consequenses of German Historical Exegesis" in *Deutschdänische Kulturbeziehungen im 18th Jahrhundert* (V&R unipress 2018).

Risto Saarinen is Professor of Ecumenics at the University of Helsinki and was the Director of "Reason and Religious Recognition" Centre of Excellence funded by the Academy of Finland from 2014 to 2019. He has written extensively on the Reformation, ecumenics, systematic theology, and history of philosophy. Saarinen's most recent books are *Recognition and Religion* (Oxford University Press 2016), and *Luther and the Gift* (Mohr Siebeck 2017). During the Spring of 2019, he participated actively in the Finnish public debate concerning the relationship between Finnish New Right and religious conservatives.

Pamela Slotte is Professor of Religion and Law at Åbo Akademi University and Vice-Director of the Centre of Excellence in Law, Identity and the European Narratives at the University of Helsinki. She is PI in the HERA funded interdisciplinary comparative research project *Protestant Legacies in Nordic Law: Uses of the Past in the Construction of Secularity of Law*. Recent publications include *Christianity and International Law: An Introduction* (co-editor, Cambridge University Press 2021), *Rights at the Margins: Historical, Legal and Philosophical Perspectives* (co-editor, Brill 2020), *Juridification of Religion?* (co-author, Brill

2017), and *Revisiting the Origins of Human Rights* (co-editor, Cambridge University Press 2015).

Aud V. Tønnessen is Professor of Contemporary Church History at the University of Oslo and dean at the Faculty of Theology. She has written the biography of the first female minister in Norway. She has also published extensively on church and the welfare state, including "The Church and the Welfare State in Postwar Norway: Political Conflicts and Conceptual Ambiguities" (2014) and "Christian Social Work in an Age of Crisis and Reform: The Case of Norway" (2017).

Niels Valdemar Vinding, BA in Theology (University of Copenhagen, 2006), MA in Islamic Studies (University of Copenhagen, 2009), Ph.D. in Islamic Studies (University of Copenhagen, 2013), LL.M. Canon Law (Cardiff, 2020). Postdoctoral researcher at the Department of Cross-Cultural and Regional Studies, University of Copenhagen. His general research is on Islam and Muslims in Denmark and Europe, currently as part of a research team working on mosques in Denmark, funded by the Independent Research Fund Denmark. Recent publications include *Annotated Legal Documents on Islam in Europe: Denmark* (Brill 2020).

Helge Årsheim is Research Editor at the Scandinavian University Press and researcher at the University of Oslo. He specializes in the relationship between law and religion, with a particular emphasis on transnational flows of laws on religion and the rise of "religion law" as an independent legal field. He is the author of *Making Religion and Human Rights at the United Nations* (De Gruyter 2018).

Acknowledgments

The present volume grew out of the research project "Protestant Legacies in Nordic Law: Uses of the Past in the Construction of the Secularity of Law" (ProNoLa), funded by "Humanities in the European Research Area" (HERA) during the period 2016-2019. A collaborative research group consisting of theologians and legal scholars from Copenhagen University, Göttingen University, the University of Helsinki, Oslo University, Uppsala University and Åbo Akademi University has undertaken a comparative study of Lutheran theology and secular law in the Nordic realm, comparing it to the German tradition of ecclesiastical law. The thesis of the project has been that Nordic Lutheranism has for centuries cultivated the idea of a comprehensive and shared secular law of the land, legitimized by a particular interpretation of Luther's two-regiments doctrine that opposed the idea of two distinct legal systems: secular law and canon law. German interpretations of the same doctrine, however, have emphasized the right of religious bodies to develop their own internal laws, since religious communities are seen as "Körper öffentlichen Rechtes". This volume shows that a similar trend is today visible in the Nordic realm, partly due to the re-establishment of Lutheran majority churches as relatively independent of the state, partly due to the increasing appeal to acknowledge the collective rights of religious minorities in a multicultural society. The thesis of this volume is thus that the internationalization of Nordic law, including of so-called religion law, goes hand in hand with a process towards a re-confessionalization of religious identities. Nonetheless, the religious communities in the Nordic region remain legally tied into the framework of the secular laws of the land, based on the national constitutions as well as international law.

Other aspects of Lutheran social ethics have been investigated as well, including different versions of the natural law tradition—some appealing to ethical fairness conditions, others to legal theories of natural law. Similarly, we have brought in the Lutheran doctrine of the three estates, seeing the Lutheran doctrine of the family household (*oeconomia*) as one source among many for ideas of a public household in the Nordic welfare societies that emerged after World War II.

While the present volume makes an independent argument concerning the mixed pattern of internationalization and re-confessionalization, especially in the 21st century, we stand on the shoulders of two other volumes coming out of the ProNoLa project: Tarald Rasmussen and Jørn Sunde, eds., *Protestant Legacies of Nordic Law: The Early Modern Period* (Brill-Schönningh, *forthcoming*), and Anna-Sara Lind and Victoria Enkvist, eds., *Constitutionalisation and Hegemonisation: Exploring the Boundaries of Law and Religion 1800-1950* (University Press of Southern Denmark, *forthcoming*).

We are indebted to HERA for generously funding the ProNoLa as part of its call "Joint Research Programme Uses of the Past" (grant number 15.050). We also wish to thank the five research teams for lively and inspiring discussions and collaborations, and Professor Lisbet Christoffersen, in particular, for taking the first steps to this project, and for being the Project Leader of our ProNoLa project. Finally, special thanks go to our research assistant, Master of Theology Niklas Antonsson, for his invaluable professional assistance throughout the process of producing this volume.

January 21, 2021
Pamela Slotte, Niels Henrik Gregersen, and Helge Årsheim

1. Introduction: Internationalization and Re-Confessionalization: Law and Religion in the Nordic Realm 1945-2017

Pamela Slotte, Niels Henrik Gregersen, and Helge Årsheim

This volume explores the interaction between law and religion in the Nordic region in the post-World War II period, up to about 2017 when five hundred years of the Protestant Reformation was publicly commemorated in the Lutheran countries. Across a broad range of empirical and historical settings, and applying different theories and methods, the contributors to this volume trace the interactions between law and religion in a comparative perspective that focuses on overarching, cross-regional perspectives. We offer case studies from different Nordic countries as well as Germany that explore how religion has been conceptualized and managed within "secular" law in this period, we examine the growing influence of international law on the regulation of religion in the region, and we discuss more recent renegotiations of theological positions with regard to the law of the land, including turns towards a revitalization of natural law and religious law in the Nordic and German region in conceptualizing collective religious rights.

The Nordic realm in the post-World War II period is generally characterized by a secular mentality, and this volume emphasizes the relationship between conceptions of secularity within law and theology, both with regard to the law of the land and the interaction between Nordic and international perspectives on this interrelationship. There is indeed a long prehistory for concepts of "the law of the land" in the Lutheran tradition that has shaped Nordic law and religion significantly. "Secular law" here means a law instituted by secular rulers (from kings to democratic governments). However, as several contributors point out in this volume, this organizational perspective does not rule out continuous interactions between religious and legal developments within the broader context of cultural and political developments. From a historical perspective, religion constitutes one source among others of legal teachings (e.g. against bigamy), and legislation and jurisprudence are henceforth created and exercised with the awareness that churches and religious communities and their doctrines continue to play major roles in the societies that the law aims to regulate.

In this chapter, we first clarify the specific historical conditions affecting the development of Lutheranism in the different parts of the Nordic realm, with a particular emphasis on the emergence of the Lutheran national churches that have developed across the region. Based on this "Nordic case", we present a more fine-grained analysis of three different dimensions of "secularization" in the Nordic realm: (1) the re-confessionalization of law, (2) the secularity of law, and (3) the internationalization of law. We argue that these aspects taken together provide a fertile ground for the formulation of a multidimensional perspective on the many entanglements between law and religion in the Nordic region.

A Longitudinal Perspective on Nordic Lutheranism

Nordic Lutheranisms share a number of common characteristics, not least due to the long history of Lutheran majority churches in the five Nordic countries. However, there are also notable differences between the countries, and particularly between the "West Nordic" (Iceland, Denmark and Norway) and the "East Nordic" (Sweden and Finland) realms.[1]

Comparatively speaking, the West Nordic realm has the longest and most continuous Lutheran history. In 1536, King Christian III declared Denmark-Norway to be a unified kingdom with a Lutheran faith, and in 1537 Martin Luther's (1483-1546) close collaborator, Johannes Bugenhagen (1485-1558), drafted the new Church Ordinance. Bugenhagen also installed the evangelical "superintendents" in place of the Catholic bishops who were now incarcerated, and he crowned King Christian III and his wife as king and queen of Denmark-Norway, and did so "as a true bishop" (as Luther proudly wrote).[2] At that time, Skåne,

---

1   For more detail, see the two other volumes of the ProNoLa project, covering earlier periods of the relations between law and religion in the Nordic realm: Tarald Rasmussen and Jørn Sunde, eds., *Protestant Legacies of Nordic Law: The Early Modern Period* (Paderborn: Brill-Schönningh, *forthcoming*), and Anna-Sara Lind and Victoria Enkvist, eds., *Constitutionalisation and Hegemonisation: Exploring the Boundaries of Law and Religion 1800-1950* (Odense: University Press of Southern Denmark, *forthcoming*).
2   Luther's Letter to Martin Bucer in Strasburg (December 6, 1537): "Pomeranus [Bugenhagen] is still in Denmark, and all things flourish which the Lord does through him. He has crowned the king and the queen as a true bishop, and restored the University." Luther, *WA Briefe* vol. 8, 158: "Pomeranus adhuc in Dania, & prosperantur omnia, quae facit Dominus per eum. Regem coronauit & reginam quasi verum Episcopus, Scholam instituit, etc."

Halland, and Blekinge in today's southern Sweden alongside Iceland and the Faroe Islands were also part of the kingdom, in addition to Schleswig-Holstein which were dukedoms under the Danish king and adopted a Lutheran Church Ordinance in 1542, also drafted by Bugenhagen.

Thus, Denmark-Norway was the first kingdom to break with Rome and adopt Lutheranism, and Denmark-Norway also shows the strongest continuity of Lutheran faith and social order compared with other Lutheran countries. Luther's own Saxony, by comparison, periodically became Catholic in alignment with Poland. Later, it was partly Reformed, partly Lutheran, and after World War II the region was part of the DDR and under communist rule between 1945 and 1991. Today, approximately 15% of the population of Sachsen-Anhalt are members of the Evangelical Lutheran Church.

Among the West Nordic countries, Lutheranism was established in Denmark in a fast and practically comprehensive way already by 1537. In Norway and Iceland, by contrast, there were only scattered Reformation movements from below among the citizens, so initially there was both a Catholic resistance against Lutheranism and a national resistance against the supremacy of the Danish king. Norway and Iceland, located as they were far away from the Danish capital region around Copenhagen and Malmö, were not Lutheranized at a societal level until the end of the 16th century, and in more remote regions probably even later.

Let us now look at the eastern part of the Nordic region. In Sweden and Finland, we find an early official embrace of Lutheranism by King Gustav Vasa at the Västerås Meeting in 1527. However, similar to the Reformation process in England, we also find periods of a return to Catholicism among later 16th century Swedish kings. Not until 1593 did Sweden formally adopt the Book of Concord of 1580. Already at that time, the Reformation of Sweden was a *fait accompli* and the Catholic-minded King Sigismund, also King of Poland and Lithuania, had to accept the Lutheran state church when he was crowned in Sweden. Accordingly, it was not until 1598, when Sigismund was expelled from the throne, that Lutheranism was firmly established in Sweden and Finland.

Thus, there are notable differences in the early 16th century development of Lutheranism between the eastern and western parts of the Nordic region. Nonetheless, the common net result was the long-term establishment of Lutheran majority churches, including a cultural program for school and education, and a social program for taking care of the sick and the poor. At the time of World War II, 98 % of all Danes were baptized members of the Evangelical Lutheran Church in Denmark, and similar numbers apply to the other Nordic countries. Today, despite a considerably diminishing membership across the region, some notable differences can be detected between the Danish "People's Church" (January 2017: 76%); and the Norwegian and Icelandic churches (Norway, December 2017: 71%; Iceland, 2017: 70%).

Subtler differences apply between Sweden and Finland. The Church of Sweden was a state church until 1952, but since 2000 the church and the state have been formally separated. In 2017, 59,3% of the population were members of the Church of Sweden, but it should be added that minority churches in Sweden are estimated to make up 5-7% of the population, comprising mainly a substantial number of Protestant free churches outside the Swedish church, in addition to the Roman Catholic Church. Finland was part of Sweden until 1809 and was a Grand Duchy under Russia from 1809 to 1917, when it finally won its independence. The Evangelical Lutheran Church of Finland is the majority church (2017: 69,89%). To this should be added the cultural and historical significance of the Orthodox Church of Finland (2017: 1,1%, under the Patriarch of Constantinople) and other Protestant free churches (many of which are not registered in the official statistics; they appear as non-affiliated).

From Confessionalization to Re-Confessionalization

The process of "confessionalism" has traditionally been used about the development towards inner dogmatic specificity in Lutheran, Reformed, and Catholic theology in the period between the 1555 Peace of Augsburg (with the principle *cuius regio ejus religio*) up to the conclusion of the Thirty Years' War in 1648. The age of confessionalism, in this sense, is a rather limited epoch in the history of theology. Since the 1970s, however, the German historians Wolfgang Reinhard and Heinz Schilling have developed the concept of a governmental process of "confessionalization" with long-term impact on early modern state building and social control.

This research paradigm has been fruitful, and the subsequent codifications of law in Nordic legislation such as the *Danish Code* (*Danske Lov*) of 1683, the amended *Norwegian Code* (*Norske Lov*) of 1687, and the *Swedish Code* (*Sveriges Rikes Lag*) of 1734 seem to fit well with the paradigm of a comprehensive state centralization. The confessionalization thesis, however, has also been criticized for taking a top-down approach to historical developments, which is not sufficiently attentive to parallel scientific developments, the decentralized revivalist movements in religion, and local practices of jurisdiction in the legal realm.[3]

---

3 See overview (with literature) in Ute Lotz-Heumann, "The Concept of 'Confessionalization': A Historiographical Paradigm in Dispute," *Memoria y Civilización* 4 (2001): 93-114.

Legal scholars, in particular, have pointed out that central aspects of Roman Law were continued from the age of the Reformation, and that Lutheran teachings on marriage were henceforth influenced by canon law while also locally adjusted to circumstances.[4] Similarly, the emergence of natural law tradition may suggest a root of early modern state building that was more secular, rather than only religious.[5] In Scandinavia, the natural law tradition was formulated by Samuel von Pufendorf (1632-1694) in *De iure naturae et gentium* (1672) when he was professor of law at Lund University, and later adapted by the Norwegian-Danish historian and jurist Ludvig Holberg (1684-1754) in his *Introduction til Naturens och Folkerettens Kundskab* (1716). Interestingly, both combined natural law tradition with the obligation of citizens towards their Creator, thus combining secular natural law with religious mindsets.

Schilling has been receptive to the critiques of the paradigm of confessionalization but has maintained the thesis that processes of confessionalization have laid the groundwork for early modern state building. In this process, he has been particularly attentive to the comparatively special case of the religiously more homogeneous Nordic countries even into the 1700s:

> The 'nations' in the center of Europe—the Netherlands, Germany, Switzerland—were not able to create similarly clear and monolithic confessional identities, but developed fragmented or multi-confessional identities. This was different in the North, where the Scandinavian societies developed close Lutheran confessional cultures and identities.[6]

The church historian Thomas Kaufmann has developed a parallel notion of "confessional cultures," aiming to be more attentive to the particular confessional cultures beginning already in the 1520s. While being skeptical about the macrohistorical thesis of a European-wide confessionalization process with

---

    For Scandinavian material, see Kaja Brilkman, "Confessionalisation, Confessional Conflict, and Confessional Culture in Early Modern Scandinavia," *Scandia* 82, no. 1 (2016): 93-106.

4 On marriage law, see John Witte Jr., *Law and Protestantism: The Legal Teachings of the Lutheran Reformation* (Cambridge: Cambridge University Press, 2002), 199-255. On the difference between legal norms and jurisdictional practices on divorce, see Mia Korpiola, "Lutheran Marriage Norms in Action: The Example of Post-Reformation Sweden, 1520-1600," in *Lutheran Reformation and the Law*, ed. Virpi Mäkinen (Leiden: Brill, 2006), 131-70.

5 Michael Stolleis, "'Konfessionalisierung' oder 'Säkularisierung' bei der Entstehung des frühmodernen Staates," *Ius Commune* 20 (1993): 1-23.

6 Heinz Schilling, "The Confessionalization of European Churches and Societies—an engine for Modernizing and for Social and Cultural Change," *Norsk Teologisk Tidsskrift* 110, no. 1 (2009): 10.

more or less the same functions and results, Kaufmann underlines the specifically theological character of distinct confessional cultures. He has thus offered a set of microhistorical analyses of the networks between different agents that together make up a confessional culture—from princes and professors at the universities to mayors, burghers, and local pastors, working in cities or in the countryside.[7]

As regards the general relation between law and Protestantism in the period up until the 17th century, we have available comprehensive studies by John Witte, Jr., Harold J. Berman (1918-2007), and Martin Heckel.[8] All of them underline the role of the Lutheran doctrine of the two regiments, which affirmed the legal framework of a secular government (*Obrigkeit*) with natural law as expressed in the Decalogue. While Witte and Heckel focus on the German context, Berman brings in English developments as well as glances at other European contexts, including Denmark. The perspectives of Heckel and Witte differ insofar as Heckel in his magnum opus barely mentions the Lutheran doctrine of the three estates (politics, church, and family life). Witte, by contrast, understands the legal program of the early Reformation as entailing a multifaceted social program, in which family life and educational programs play a central role.

Both Kaufmann and Witte's perspectives combine the Lutheran doctrine of the two regiments with the likewise important doctrine of the three estates (*ecclesia*, *politia*, and *oeconomia*). While the church is concerned with eternal salvation based on the gospel, the political realm focuses on the secular worldly order with the task of preventing disorder from taking over society. The estate of family life, by contrast, is as old as creation. Prior to the Fall as well as after the Fall, *oeconomia* is related to the goodness of ordinary life in the world of creation. While family life up until the mid-1800s encompassed larger households of workers, servants and others, family life was also connected to the schooling

---

7 Thomas Kaufmann, *Konfession und Kultur: Lutherischer Protestantismus in der zweiten Hälfte des Reformationsjahrhunderts* (Tübingen: Mohr-Siebeck, 2006); see also Kaufmann's overview of earlier discussions in "Die Konfessionalisierung von Kirche und Gesellschaft: Sammelbericht über eine Forschungsdebatte," *Theologische Literaturzeitung* 121 (1996): 1112-21.

8 Witte, *Law and Protestantism*; Harold J. Berman, *Law and Revolution*, Vol. 2: *The Impact of the Protestant Reformations* (Cambridge, MA: The Belknap Press of the Harvard University Press, 2003); Martin Heckel, *Martin Luthers Reformation und das Recht: Die Entwicklung der Theologie Luthers und ihre Auswirkung auf das Recht unter den Rahmenbedingungen der Reichsreform und der Territorialstaatsbildung im Kampf mit Rom und den 'Schwärmern'* (Tübingen: Mohr-Siebeck, 2016). See also Heikki Pihlajamäki and Risto Saarinen, "Lutheran Reformation and the Law in Recent Scholarship," in *Lutheran Reformation and the Law*, ed. Virpi Mäkinen (Leiden: Brill, 2006), 1-20.

of children. The field of education has a special role since it relates to all three estates. Organized by the state, education was carried out by the church but paid for by the parents. The idea of *oeconomia* as "the plant-school of love" (Niels Hemmingsen) may thus have advanced the idea of a "third-zone" Lutheranism, in which a society is to be guided by the ideals of ordinary communal life that underlie the more official institutions of state and church.

Kaufmann's content-specific approach of "confessional cultures" has been particularly helpful for the "Lutheran Mentality" research project at Aarhus University. A group around Bo Kristian Holm and Nina J. Koefoed has analyzed how social imaginaries regarding the family household (*oeconomia*) continued to shape Danish-Norwegian culture up until around 1800. Obviously, this was still a stratified society, in which parents (particularly fathers) ruled over children, and kings and magistrates over those who were subordinate to them. Yet at the same time, the model of the household spoke of networks of mutual obligations, thereby also shaping the ideals regarding a good and fair government, also in legislation.[9] With the introduction of democracy during the 1800s, kings and queens finally came to be ruled by parliaments elected by popular vote. Even so, to some extent Nordic democracies are still shaped by the view of society as a sort of "home" (in Swedish: *folkhemmet*), when the Nordic countries after World War II developed "welfare societies" upheld by the will of the people.[10]

Of course, we do not presume a religious homogeneity in the post-World War II setting of the Nordic countries. Confessional identities now operate in non-homogeneous and ever-shifting cultural climates. Already in the 19th century, we find considerable groups of secularist movements of freethinkers in all the Nordic countries, as well as, for example, a continuing historical presence of the Orthodox Church in the Grand Duchy of Finland. Nevertheless, after World War II, political lawmakers may still refer to what is perceived as socially shared "national" or "Nordic" values of partly secular, partly religious origin.

In the decades following the liberation from the German occupation of Norway and Denmark in 1945, and the settlement of a hard-won peace with Russia after the Finnish Winter War (1939-1940) and the Continuation War (1941-1944), there was still a high level of national homogeneity in the Nordic countries. This

---

9   This is the thesis of Bo Kristian Holm and Nina J. Koefoed, eds., *Lutheran Theology and the Shaping of Society: The Danish Monarchy as Example* (Göttingen: Vandenhoeck and Ruprecht, 2018). See in particular Bo Kristian Holm, "Dynamic Tensions in the Social Imaginaries of the Lutheran Reformation," 85-106, and Nina Javette Koefoed, "The Lutheran Household as Part of Danish Confessional Culture," 321-40.
10 Niels Henrik Gregersen, "From *oeconomia* to Nordic Welfare Societies: The Idea of a Third-Zone Lutheranism," *Theology Today* 76, no. 3 (2019): 234-41.

may be seen as an echo of an earlier religious homogeneity, but now a homogeneity drawing on a combination of secular and Christian values. Secularity became part of the religious mindset, but religious allegiance was the option still favored by a majority of the Nordic populations, though ordinarily without too much controversy. Rather than establishing a principal divide between religion and *laïcité*, we see a secularization pattern that involves zones of interaction between secular and religious realms.

The constellation of a secular law in Nordic countries–still relatively homogenous, though acknowledging differing worldviews among citizens—was shaped in this post-World War II cultural climate. However, due to a further secularization process at the individual level, especially since the 1970s, and due to immigration from non-Western countries, this cultural consensus increasingly came under challenge. Particularly after the year 2000, lawmakers came to acknowledge the fact that the world of religious communities in modern Nordic societies comprises not only the national majority churches of Lutheran origin (and in Finland also the Orthodox Church of Finland that holds the status of a "national church" alongside the Evangelical Lutheran Church of Finland) but also other Christian communities, as well as an increasing number of non-Christian religions, not least Muslim communities.

In this volume, we propose "re-confessionalization" as a theoretical concept to capture (1) the growing legal independence of the national churches and other religious communities from direct state involvement (Finland 1996, Sweden 2000, and Norway 2014), (2) the fact that legal thinking and national legislation has to deal with a considerable number of religious communities as part of a pluralistic society, and (3) the fact that religious communities begin to act as collectives based on specific confessional identities, Christian or non-Christian. In Finland, for example, the number of recognized religious communities grew from 49 to 110 in the period from 2000 to 2015. This new situation raises questions regarding the scope and limits of a re-confessionalization through law—both in terms of internal religious legislation and in terms of the secular recognition of internal religious legislation, in the "law of the land" as well as in international law.

The Secularity of Law and the Re-Confessionalization of Law and Religion

Recognizing the many meanings of "secularity" as a cross-cultural and cross-temporal concept, including numerous scholarly approaches,[11] the contributions to this volume approach the secularity of law in the Nordic region pragmatically, distinguishing mainly between its organizational, structural, and personal levels, and offering a slight adaptation of the tripartition of secularity suggested by Charles Taylor.[12] While a shift away from a "religious" orientation can be detected in some of the analytical levels, the ensuing understanding of what secularity means for lawmaking, jurisprudence, and legal theory differs substantially. For the *organizational level* (secularity^{meaning1}), the secularity of law denotes a move away from the duality of the medieval legal system, which saw all forms of secularity as a delegated power from Canon law under the authority of the one Church led by the Pope.[13] This notion of delegated power was transformed during the Protestant Reformations, which laid out a new conceptual framework

---

11 For the Nordic situation, see Inger Furseth, ed., *Religious Complexity in the Public Sphere: Comparing Nordic Countries* (London: Palgrave-MacMillan 2018). The international research literature on secularity, secularization, and secularism is substantial, and space only allows for a small selection of the many published surveys and works on this topic. For a selection of publications that touch upon the themes of this volume, see Philip S. Gorski and Ateş Altınordu, "After Secularization?", *Annual Review of Sociology* 34, no. 1 (2008): 55-85; Philip S. Gorski, "Historicizing the Secularization Debate: Church, State, and Society in Late Medieval and Early Modern Europe ca. 1300 to 1700," *American Sociological Review* 65, no. 1 (2000): 138-67; Mirjam Künkler and Yüksel Sezgin, "Diversity in Democracy: Accommodating Religious Particularity in Largely Secular Legal Systems," *Journal of Law and Religion* 28, no. 2 (2013): 337-40; Maia Carter Hallward, "Situating the 'Secular': Negotiating the Boundary between Religion and Politics," *International Political Sociology* 2, no. 1 (2008): 1-16; and Talal Asad, *Formations of the Secular: Christianity, Islam, Modernity* (Stanford, CA: Stanford University Press, 2003).

12 Taylor distinguishes between secularity 1 as the expulsion of religion from sphere after sphere of public life, secularity 2 as the decline of religious belief and practice, and secularity 3 as "the conditions of experience of and search for the spiritual" that make it possible to speak of ours as a "secular age". See Charles Taylor, *A Secular Age* (London: The Belknap Press, 2007).

13 On the shape of this doctrine, see Lester L. Field, *Liberty, Dominion, and the Two Swords: On the Origins of Western Political Theology* (Notre Dame, IN: Notre Dame University Press, 1998). On Danish material, Agnes S. Arnórsdóttir, Per Ingesman and Bjørn Poulsen, eds., *Konge, kirke og samfund: De to øvrighedsmagter i dansk senmiddelalder* (Aarhus: Aarhus Universitetsforlag, 2007) point to the reality of ongoing negotiations between different centers of power in Late Medieval epochs.

of law as a comprehensive system for both religious and secular life, but issued by earthly rulers rather than the Pope.[14]

For the level of *contents and structure* (secularity[meaning2]), on the other hand, the secular nature of law is less clear-cut. Even if the creation and management of legislation is organized within the secular realm, it may still be highly religious in content, as seen in the comprehensive *Danish Code* of 1683 and the corresponding *Norwegian Code* of 1687. Here, the first three of a total of six books follow the structure of the Lutheran doctrine of the three estates: Book I relates to the laws of the worldly regiment ("On Law and the Persons of Law"), Book II to the spiritual realm of the church ("On Religion and Clergy"), while Book III concerns the realm of the household and school ("On the Temporal and Domestic Estates").[15] In terms of content, central parts of these "secular" laws, even if organized by the secular realm, address religious life. This characteristic blend is not limited to 17th-century laws, but reappears in new forms in contemporary state legislation regarding church laws and laws for other religious organizations, either by securing a freedom of religion through non-interference, or by allowing religious communities to fulfill particular tasks, such as the right to conduct marriages. In such cases, we have a mixed case of something being "secular", insofar as it falls under the secular law of the land, while recognizing "lived religion" as a fact of life of people, communities and individuals. In addition, purely "secular" law, for example with regard to taxation, buildings, building safety and employment, regulates aspects of religious life.

The concrete sense of secularity[meaning1-2] can be even further specified by paying attention, as several authors do in this volume, to what Kaarlo Tuori has identified as different levels of law: a *surface level* (consisting of particular statutes and other legal regulations, court decisions, and statements of legal science); a *legal culture* (professional culture, general doctrines of different legal subfields, and the doctrine of the sources of law); and law's *deep structure* or "the *longue durée* of the law" (made up of basic categories, fundamental principles, as well as "a fundamental type of rationality").[16]

---

14 For a discussion of 'secularity' in relation to Luther's thoughts about law, secular authority, and political power, see Stefan Heuser, "The Contribution of Law to the Secularization of Politics: Impulses from Luther's Doctrine of the two Regimes," in *Lutheran Theology and Secular Law: The Work of the Modern State*, ed. Marie A. Fallinger and Roland W. Duty (Abingdon: Routledge, 2018), 3-13.

15 See Nina Javette Koefoed, "Authorities Who Care: The Lutheran Doctrine of the Three Estates in Danish Legal Development from the Reformation to Absolutism," *Scandinavian Journal of History* 44, no. 4 (2019): 430-53.

16 Kaarlo Tuori, *Critical Legal Positivism* (Aldershot: Ashgate 2002), 147, 150, 154-55, 157, 165-66, 169, 173-74, 177, 183-84, 186-88, 191-92.

At the *personal level* (secularity^{meaning3}), "having religion" has become optional. Particularly since the 19th century, and increasingly during the 20th century, having religion and being religious has become a personal matter largely outside the confines of legislation; being religious or not being religious, has no effect on the formal status of legal subjects in society. This form of secularity represents a mixed pattern, sometimes referred as a "post-secular" situation where wide-ranging secularization has taken place at both organizational and structural levels (secularity$^{meaning1-2}$) while at the same time agents and communities generate new religious commitments. Sometimes such commitment takes a more heated and radicalized form, sometimes a softer form, referred to as "cultural Christianity" or even "cultural Islam".

The contributions to this volume attest to the differences among these levels of secularity. However, the chapters often point to their mutual and sometimes conflictual interrelationship, too. Thus, the radical decoupling of law and jurisprudence from the management of personal religiosity (secularity^{meaning3}) has proven to be a fertile ground for controversies and public debates over the management of the religion-secular divide in the organizational and structural dimensions of social life (secularity$^{meaning1-2}$).

Intertwined with the potential decoupling of personal belief from organizational and structural constrictions, the majority churches in the Nordic region have attained an increasing autonomy and independence from state management.[17] Simultaneously, the organizations and communities representing religious minorities have gained additional recognition, attaining the status of "registered communities" across the Nordic region, securing so-called legal personality and access to state funding in the name of religious freedom and equality. These changes in the religious landscape can be grouped together under various monikers, from the "formatting" of Islam in Europe observed by Olivier Roy, to the "religion-making from above" identified by Markus Dressler and Arvind-Pal S. Mandair.[18] For this volume, however, we have selected the term "re-confessionalization", as it evokes the family resemblances between our present moment and the turbulent centuries of religio-political reorientations

---

17   We refer here to the helpful volume by Lisbeth Christoffersen, Kjell Å. Modéer and Svend Andersen, eds., *Law & Religion in the 21st Century—Nordic Perspectives* (Copenhagen: DJØF Publishing, 2010). See also Lisbet Christoffersen, "Towards Re-sacralization of Nordic Law?," in *Formatting Religion: Across Politics, Education, Media, and Law*, ed. Marius Timmann Mjaaland (London: Routledge, 2019), 175-204.

18   Oliver Roy, *Secularism Confronts Islam*, transl. by George Holoch (New York: Columbia University Press, 2009); Markus Dressler and Arvind-Pal S. Mandair, eds., *Secularism and Religion-Making* (Oxford: Oxford University Press, 2011).

to come out of the Protestant Reformations. The structural difference, however, is that the tendency towards re-confessionalization is spread across a broad set of different religious communities.

Internationalization of Law in the Nordic Region

From the time of their emergence as middle-range European powers in the wake of the Napoleonic Wars in the early 19th century, the countries of the Nordic region have been active proponents of a strong international order. Nordic churches contributed to international ecumenical work for peace, justice, and the promotion of international law and international institutions from the early 20th century onwards. Moreover, all of the countries of the region were among the founding members of the League of Nations and the United Nations, and Nordic statesmen like Dag Hammarskjöld (1905-1961) and Trygve Lie (1896-1968) were among the first Secretaries General of the United Nations. Despite minor differences in foreign policy orientation (Norway, Iceland, and Denmark are members of NATO, Sweden and Finland are not) and European policy (Norway and Iceland are outside of the European Union (EU), the rest of the region holds membership), the region has frequently acted in concert at the international level, promoting and supporting international order politically, materially, and economically. The ties and shared interests within the Nordic region are not limited to the political arena, but extend well into the cultural and social sphere. Especially in the second half of the 19th century, significant numbers of migrants from the region settled abroad (especially in the USA), seeking better fortunes in times of famine and poverty, in the process creating significant diasporic communities across the world that maintain active and vital links with the region of their forebears.

The strong propensity for international engagement and the maintenance of robust international order have been a significant influence on the development of the secularity of law in the Nordic region. In the early post-World War II era, the countries of the region were still strongly monoreligious, maintaining exceptionally high rates of membership in the national churches, promoting the Lutheran faith through the school system, in Sweden until 1969, in Denmark until 1975, in Norway until 1998. As a result of a comprehensive renewal of Finnish legislation on religious freedom at the turn of the 21st century, public schools provide for parallel non-confessional instruction "in the pupil's own religion."¹⁹ At this time, the Nordic countries provided very little to no recognition of religious minorities, apart from protecting religious groups through dormant, albeit still culturally significant, prohibitions against "defamation" and "blasphemy" (in Sweden until 1970, in Norway until 2015, in Denmark until 2017, while the current Finnish Criminal Code, Chapter 17, Section 10 still prohibits "the breach of the sanctity of religion"²⁰). As the countries of the region gradually engaged with international efforts to codify and implement human rights as a new "standard of civilization" through international treaties, the political and legal privileges afforded to the majority churches gradually became more controversial, prompting gradual legal reform.

Although reforms of the political and legal management of religion have differed across the countries of the region, the importance of the legal categories and taxonomies developed internationally has been notable. In particular, the legal frameworks of the Council of Europe and the EU have proven decisive for the management of religion in the Nordic region. The European Convention on Human Rights (ECHR, 1950), the main instrument created by the Council of Europe to protect human rights, entered into force on September 3, 1953. Today, acceptance of the ECHR is a prerequisite for membership in the Council of Europe. Since the establishment of the European Commission of Human Rights (1956) and the European Court of Human Rights (ECtHR, 1958) by the Council of Europe, member states of the Council of Europe have been obliged to abide by the judgments set by these monitoring bodies in cases brought against them. Over time, judgments that are binding in the case of a particular member state have also come to acquire more direct importance as interpretative precedents in relation to other member states. Norway, Denmark, and Sweden were among

---

[19] See further, Pamela Slotte, "Waving the 'Freedom of Religion or Belief' Card, or Playing it Safe: Religious Instruction in the Cases of Norway and Finland," *Religion and Human Rights* 3, no. 1 (2008): 33-69; Pamela Slotte, "'A Little Church, a Little State, and a Little Commonwealth at Once': Towards a Nordic Model of Religious Instruction in Public Schools?," in *Law and Religion in the 21st Century—Nordic Perspectives,* ed. Lisbet Christoffersen, Svend Andersen, and Kjell Å. Modéer (Copenhagen: Djøf Publishing, 2010), 239-73.

[20] Criminal Code of Finland (39/1889), Chapter 17, Section 10—*Breach of the sanctity of religion* (563/1998): "A person who (1) publicly blasphemes against God or, for the purpose of offending, publicly defames or desecrates what is otherwise held to be sacred by a church or religious community, as referred to in the Act on the Freedom of Religion (267/1922), or (2) by making noise, acting threateningly or otherwise, disturbs worship, ecclesiastical proceedings, other similar religious proceedings or a funeral, shall be sentenced for a *breach of the sanctity of religion* to a fine or to imprisonment for at most six months." Unofficial translation, Ministry of Justice, accessed June 29, 2020, https://www.finlex.fi/en/laki/kaannokset/1889/en18890039_20150766.pdf.

the founding members of the Council of Europe of 1949. Iceland became a member in 1950, but Finland only in 1989. However, in the early post-World War II decades very few cases were brought before the Commission and the ECtHR. The first judgment finding a violation of Article 9 of the ECHR on the freedom of thought, conscience, and religion was handed down only in 1993 (*Kokkinakis* v. *Greece*). Thus, in the early post-World War II decades, the obligation as member states to abide by the ECHR could be seen in practice as mainly political and moral. Still, member states were obliged to incorporate the ECHR into their domestic law, something which can take place automatically upon ratification or by enacting legislation that turns the provisions of the ECHR into binding domestic law, while also putting in place administrative procedures that secure the follow-up and assessment of the jurisprudence of the ECtHR.[21]

The EU has also developed a fundamental rights framework of growing importance. A signpost of this development is the Charter of Fundamental Rights of the European Union (2000) that entered into force and became binding for all member states when the Treaty of Lisbon entered into force (December 1, 2009). The charter includes both a prohibition of discrimination on the basis of religion and an article protecting the right to freedom of thought, conscience, and religion. Article 17 of the Treaty of Lisbon also addresses matters of religion, where it recognizes national "religion-state" arrangements and reaffirms a dialogue between EU institutions and religious, philosophical, and nonconfessional actors that has been ongoing since the early 1990s:[22]

1. The Union respects and does not prejudice the status under national law of churches and religious associations or communities in the member states.
2. The Union equally respects the status under national law of philosophical and nonconfessional organisations.

---

21 For an in-depth comparative analysis of how the different Nordic countries have incorporated international human rights norms, including the ECHR, into their domestic legal orders—and differences are detectable—see Tuomas Ojanen, "Human Rights in Nordic Constitutions and the Impact of International Obligations," in *The Nordic Constitutions: A Comparative and Contextual Study,* ed. Helle Krunke and Björg Thorarensen (Oxford: Hart, 2018), 133-66. Nor should it be forgotten that internationalization has also earlier affected Nordic law and enhanced Nordic legal collaboration. Pia Letto-Vanamo and Ditlev Tamm, "Nordic Legal Mind," in *Nordic Law in European Context,* ed. Pia Letto-Vanamo, Ditlev Tamm, and Bent Ole Gram Mortensen (Cham: Springer, 2019), 2-3.

22 See, e.g., Knox Thames, "Old Is New: Europe and Freedom of Religion or Belief," in *The Changing Nature of Religious Rights under International Law,* ed. Malcolm D. Evans, Peter Petkoff, and Julian Rivers (Oxford: Oxford University Press, 2015), 156-57.

3. Recognising their identity and their specific contribution, the Union shall maintain an open, transparent and regular dialogue with these churches and organisations.

As member states of the EU, Finland, Sweden, and Denmark are immediately bound by its laws, directives, and regulations, and by the rulings of the European Court of Justice. The hands-on effects of international rules and monitoring bodies are hard to trace, especially beyond the concrete binding rulings, for example, of the ECtHR. However, the *lingua franca* status of human rights norms, not only as "hard" law but as an enabling vocabulary for the discussion and criticism of social and cultural conditions, can be detected across all major legal and political changes in the Nordic region in the post-World War II era. The complex and multi-layered roles of state entities as overseers in managing and supporting majority churches have increasingly come to be discussed using the language and procedures offered by human rights norms. Importantly, in itself, the preponderance of human rights language infusing these discussions does not amount to a fixed resolution or unidirectional criticism of existing arrangements. Rather, the hegemony of human rights as a shared language has been effectively utilized by proponents and critics alike. Hence, religion-state arrangements have been discussed using terms and categories such as non-discrimination, the right to freedom of religion or belief, the distinctive rights of minorities, the right to education and, ultimately, the sovereign right to self-determination both on behalf of the nation-state and on behalf of subnational entities.

The introduction of human rights language, while not offering any single solutions or recommendations to religion-state arrangements in the countries of the Nordic region, has done much to alter the interrelationship between secularity^{meaning1} (organization), secularity^{meaning2} (content and structure) and secularity^{meaning3} (personal belief). In particular, the radical individualism offered by the freedom of religion or belief articulated in Article 9 of the ECHR offers a strong bulwark of protection for the individual to choose his or her belief freely, bolstering the effects of secularity^{meaning3}. Simultaneously, the same right offers protection for the free and unimpeded organization of communities of believers, further entrenching the division between religious and secular authority secured by secularity^{meaning1}. However, at the level of structure and content (secularity^{meaning2}), the infusion of human rights language into the countries of the Nordic region would appear to offer a fairly broad degree of autonomy. Each state can choose whether to regulate religion specifically or as a subset of more general provisions, as long as it stays within the boundaries offered by the ECHR. As seen above, EU law also pays heed to national arrangements on part of its member states, but not unreservedly so. Given the above, it is safe to say that the studies in this volume of the various Nordic countries and Germany make visible both divergences and common themes when it comes to regulating religion as part of the law of the land.[23]

Law and Religion in the Nordic Realm, 1945-2017

The contributions to this volume address a broad range of thematic and disciplinary specialties and approach the question of the relationship between law and religion in the Nordic region from different angles. The contributors have been given ample opportunity to explore different aspects of the re-confessionalization, secularity, and internationalization of law, resulting in a set of chapters grouped in three distinctive sections.

Section I: The Early Post-World War II Period

The first section is dedicated to the period during and immediately after World War II. The chapters assembled in this section show how actors in the field of theology, law, and politics felt a need to "locate" themselves as countries, as churches, and as legal professionals. *Niels Henrik Gregersen* shows how the Danish creation theologians K.E. Løgstrup (1905-1981) and Regin Prenter (1907-1990) viewed a nation ruled by secular law as a precondition for a proper rule of law. Seeing the violation of law as the basis for their theological resistance to the German occupation power, they referred to statutory Danish law alongside international law, while appealing to the moral sense of people living under occupation yet striving for Denmark as an independent nation in its own right. While Løgstrup and Prenter did not appeal to the early modern idea of *lex naturalis* at the legal level, they related a Lutheran concept of natural law to the pre-political level of social ethics as the only basis from which to criticize unjust laws.

Tine Reeh discusses the interesting collaboration between the Danish theolo-

---

23 This is in line with how Nordic law more generally and Nordic legal thinking both share common characteristics and differ internally, displaying distinct national features. While history plays an important role here, "only in the 19th century did the idea of a specific 'Nordic Law' become a current notion to substitute the old division between Danish-Norwegian law on the one hand and Swedish law (including Finland) on the other, and then especially as a tool to promote cooperation in the field of law". Letto-Vanamo and Tamm, "Nordic Legal Mind," 1-2, 5-6, as well as 14-18 for a more general overview of developments in the field of Nordic cooperation in the area of law.

gian Hal Koch (1904-1963) and the Danish proponent of legal realism, Alf Ross (1899-1979). Both argued for a Nordic model of democracy, rooted in a long legal culture of negotiation and conversation. While Koch argued that the spirit of Nordic democracy lies in the democratic "lifeforms" underlying democracy as a system, Ross was interested in shaping democracy as a political system with a clear legal structure. Nonetheless, both of them appealed to deep-seated legal cultures—some Hellenic, some Christian—that converge in the model of Nordic democracy.

Kjell Å. Modéer analyzes how particular "secular" and "rational" ways of thinking about law were resisted in the post-World War II era in the context of Swedish discussions on law and religion. As Modéer notes, beyond the surface level of the law, we encounter "a deep structure of Christian culture defending its declining position".[24] In his chapter, Modéer presents the jurist Göran Göransson (1925-1997) as an example of legal actors who during this period of critical rational modernity upheld the Church law as an autonomous discipline with its theological roots.

Analyzing the theological situation immediately after World War II, *Georg Kalinna*, in contrast, points to the need to offer new narratives for a democratic society in West Germany. The immediate past was to be built around—not least—an idea of "never again", but also to sort out what had happened and what could justifiably be learnt from the events in retrospect. These interpretations shaped ethics and helped actors make sense of their present. It led them to think anew about governance, democracy, and law, and the positive role of the churches in the new Constitution of 1949 is to be seen as part of this new theological narrative that relates to the well-being of democratic society as a whole.[25]

---

24 Kjell Å. Modéer, "Christian Torchbearers in the Dark of Positivism: Survivors and Catalysts within Nordic Law and Religion 1950-2000," in this volume.

25 For comparison, in his contribution to the recent volume *Lutheran Theology and Secular Law: The Work of the Modern State*, the American theologian Paul Hinlicky maintains that "Lutheranism is a conflicted tradition about the law," while the Swedish theologian Carl-Henric Grenholm, in turn, explores different strands of legal thought—legal positivism as well as natural law—that both feature in a Lutheran social ethics. As Grenholm also argues, while Lutheran tradition never imagined that positive laws could be deduced from natural law, ethical considerations may play a role in the legislative process, and statutory laws may be criticized from an ethical point of view. Marie A. Failinger and Ronald W. Duty, "Preface," in *Lutheran Theology and Secular Law: The Work of the Modern State*, eds. Marie A. Failinger and Roland W. Duty (Abingdon: Routledge, 2018), xiii. See, in particular, Carl-Henric Grenholm, "Legal Positivism in Lutheran ethics," 17-28, and Paul Hinlicky, "Antinomianism–the 'Lutheran' Heresy," 28-38.

Section II: Negotiations of the Secularity of Law

The chapters assembled in the second section of the book discuss the question of the secularity of law and the relationship between theological norms and the law of the land in a range of different thematic and historical settings across the Nordic region and Germany. *Hans Michael Heinig* analyzes in particular 20th-century German legal theological reflection on the nature, scope, role, and foundations of ecclesiastical law. This thought was shaped by and responded to contemporary trends in society and general legal thought, including legal positivism. Legal validity was seen as more or less detached from possible theological legitimations, ecclesiastical law as more or less dissimilar to strictly "secular" positive law. Not surprisingly, the experiences of World War II affected reflection on the criteria for judging whether positive law—including ecclesiastical law as "human law"—was "right".

Aud Tønnessen deals with the issue of democracy by turning to the theme of the inner dominium of the church in relation to the worldly legal order and rule of law. The immediate context of Tønnessen's discussion is the topic of female clergy, and the chapter traces shifts in vocabulary at a time where the frame of reference for worldly authorities decreasingly includes the notion of being governed by God. In parliamentary debates, self-confident theological reasoning on all sides is replaced by other, more secular vocabularies.

Where Tønnessen traces the tension between religious law and the law of the land to the legislative assembly, *Johan Bastubacka's* contribution approaches the boundaries between Orthodox canon law, Finnish secular law and European human rights law through the deposition of an Orthodox priest ("Father X") who remarried after becoming a widower. Pointing to the intertwined secular and religious legal orders governing the Orthodox Church of Finland, Bastubacka observes how the many-layered legal regulations concerning marriage challenges modernist distinctions by their entanglement of individuality and communality, thus mixing its faith-based and legal character.

Adding further perspectives, *Niels Valdemar Vinding's* chapter showcases the different strategies employed by Muslims seeking to find ways in which to locate themselves in Denmark by balancing out the strictures of religious law with the boundaries set by the secular legal order. *Lisbet Christoffersen*, in turn, shows how the Nordic Lutheran churches, despite their gradually diminishing numbers, have gained increased autonomy and self-rule, thus exemplifying processes of re-confessionalization. As the Swedish and Norwegian churches have been separated from the state, they have been granted privileges and entitlements that clearly set them apart from the organizations of minority religions, whose organization and recognition have become subject to increasing measures of control. Just as the Lutheran majority churches were once "established by law," in the 21st century they are also "re-established" by secular law, when they become autonomous legal subjects.

Hence, what we encounter in the Nordic countries at the present moment is a time of introspection, which takes place in a transition from modernity with its emphasis on "reason" to late modernity with an emphasis, among other things, on "identity" and "recognition" as well—key themes of the chapter by *Risto Saarinen* and *Heikki Koskinen* to this volume. We may call this a moment of introspection as far as the law of the land goes, a moment when in important ways this law is influenced by and reacts to the international and European legal regimes.

Section III: Internationalization

The chapters in the third section of the book all turn the gaze outwards, exploring how the countries in the Nordic region have been affected by the ever-increasing internationalization and Europeanization of law. As observed above, this volume investigates practices and patterns of thought concerning law and religion in a time when, in Europe, the general conditions for "having religion" have become optional and placed at a personal level (secularity$^{\text{meaning3}}$), without affecting one's formal legal status in society. For example, religious belonging does not affect whether someone is considered fit to hold public office or not, with the exception of the Nordic ruling monarchs. The principle of freedom of religion was already part of Nordic constitutions since the 1800s and, as shown by Christoffersen in her chapter, it was not a part that was remedied during the 1900s. However, *Helle Krunke's* chapter on Nordic constitutions in the postwar period shows that religion does not play the same role in the constitutional identities of the five Nordic countries, and if the countries want religion to play a role in relation to international law, it should be explicated at the constitutional level.[26]

Importantly, secularity$^{\text{meaning3}}$ has been rearticulated during the second half of the 20th century, concurrently with an increasing internationalization and Europeanization of Nordic law. Observing the effects of this rearticulation, *Helge Årsheim's* contribution examines how a wide selection of different, partly overlapping international legal frames have become available to minorities in the

---

26 For another recent comparative analysis of Nordic constitutions and "constitutional mentality", including the effects of internationalization, see Jaakko Husa, "Constitutional Mentality," in *Nordic Law in European Context*, ed. Pia Letto-Vanamo, Ditlev Tamm, and Bent Ole Gram Mortensen (Cham: Springer, 2019), 41-60.

Nordic region who are seeking to gain legal recognition. This situation invites a "strategic litigation" in which minorities can gain recognition by reinterpreting their religiosity according to the dictates of the legal framework that offers the most robust protections. While the availability of different legal frames may be viewed as indicative of secularity$^{\text{meaning3}}$, it can also be read as a sign of the dominance of state power, which sets clear boundaries regarding the forms of religiosity that are eligible for protection.

Another effect of internationalization and Europeanization is the widening of the gaze of Nordic religion law. For example, as *Pamela Slotte* points out in her contribution on the case of Finland, this internationalization and Europeanization has led to a broadening of the constitutional protective framework of freedom of religion. An effect of this broadening has been, for example, that the constitution now explicitly mentions the freedom to hold non-religious "convictions" alongside religious beliefs. It has also had the effect of strengthening the *positive* freedom of religion and conviction, also for collectives, something we identify earlier in this introduction as a facet of a legal "re-confessionalization".

Thus, a focus on the individual as a religious being *and* recognition of diversity in the area of religion and belief is discernable in Nordic law of the land (albeit with variations) at the turn of the 21st century. However, the focus is also not solely on individuals. It also concerns a politics of recognition of collectivities, including religious minorities, as well as to some limited extent the "identity politics" discussed by Saarinen and Koskinen. An identity politics can spill over into law when particular interests are allowed to dominate legislative practices and outcomes. In fact, Heuser proposes a Lutheran "re-secularization" of the law as a counterweight to the dangers of identity politics and a politization of law.[27]

It can be discussed whether such dangers are imminent in the case of the Nordic countries, and if so what kinds of emphases on collectives and identity politics through the medium of law need to be critically analyzed in the Nordic case. What is clear, as the contributors to this volume emphasize throughout, is that the relations between law and religion cannot be considered apart from the larger cultural, political, and institutional context with its values and ideas. For example, as *Anna-Sara Lind* points out in her contribution on Sweden, a strengthening of the constitutional protection of positive freedom of religion for individuals has not been supplanted by equal recognition of positive collective religious freedom. This situation is due to a narrow reading of the scope of the freedom and of "state neutrality", and a related limited understanding of the

---

[27] Heuser, "The Contribution of Law to the Secularization of Politics: Impulses from Luther's Doctrine of the Two Regimes," 4.

positive duties of the Swedish state in relation to human rights. In this context, Lind points to the influence of Scandinavian Legal Realism and the so-called Uppsala School of legal philosophy.

Adding to this diagnosis, *Victoria Enkvist* makes clear in her discussion of construction permits for religious buildings that the Swedish legal framework, due to its narrow focus with regard to religious freedom, provides few concrete tools for public officials and decision-makers in identifying matters as not solely "secular" in character, but rather as concerning matters of religious freedom, albeit perhaps only in an indirect sense. Lind and Enkvist note the resulting adverse impact of "neutral" Swedish legislation, its interpretation and application at multiple governance levels, on the possibilities for religious minorities to exercise their freedom of religion.

This points at an aspect worth highlighting as far as a simultaneous emphasis on collectives alongside a focus on individuals goes. Human rights law and thinking rest on the idea that all humans have something in common, including certain basic needs. Human rights law simultaneously maintains that most of these rights (for example, the right to freedom of religion or belief) can be limited precisely on the basis of recognized joint needs. This is expressed in international law, for example, via limitation clauses acknowledging that a right to freedom of religion or belief can be circumscribed for purposes of protecting other persons' rights and freedoms, public order, safety, and health. At least in the case of Finland, such international articulations of justified limits are normative when it comes to the legal interpretation of constitutionally enshrined fundamental rights.[28]

Here, at least in some sense, we are dealing with flexible concepts with changing content. For example, as Hussein Ali Agrama has noted with regard to the concept of "public order," such order conveys "the principles and sensibilities of particularist narratives, putatively rooted in majority sentiments, but that are also deemed foundational to the state."[29] Accordingly, the legal notion of public order "blurs division between legal equality and majority values".[30] Thus, formal equality before the law, an obviously key principle of all present-day Nordic constitutions, also in regard to matters of religion and boundaries of freedom of religion or belief, concretely assumes shapes influenced by majoritarian values and perceptions. What we end up with is an individualism/

28　See the chapter by Pamela Slotte, "Moving Frontiers: Configuring Religion Law and Religious Law, and Law-Religion Relations" in this volume.
29　Hussein Ali Agrama, *Questioning Secularism: Islam, Sovereignty, and the Rule of Law in Modern Egypt* (Chicago: University of Chicago Press, 2012), 38.
30　Agrama, *Questioning Secularism*, 98.

individualization, including that of religion, and indeed also a recognition of collective religious identities that still may be circumscribed by majoritarian religious notions or what could be called an "implicit theology". This is the case, despite the "declared" secularity of Nordic religion law. Is "common sense" really necessarily common to all citizens?

No wonder that religious minorities feel a need to negotiate with and partly perhaps outright resist parts of the Nordic law of the land, including that law in its Europeanized and internationalized form. The contours of this resistance can be seen throughout the volume, from the negotiations between religious and secular power in the management of the Orthodox Church in Finland as displayed in Bastubacka's chapter, and to the discussions among Muslims in Denmark, discussed by Vinding, on how to reconcile the demands of religious and secular law.

How are we to live with legal institutions that—while important for purposes of worldly order and peace—are imperfect, being located as they are in what Luther called the "*saeculum*"? In Heuser's reading of Luther, "secularity is not the result of a history of decay, but is an intended and at the same time highly contested mode of politics".[31] The chapters of this volume offer examples of how this co-existence with the law of the land has been and is interpreted and negotiated in the Nordic realm from a theological perspective, and from the perspective of religious agents beyond the majority churches as well.

Bibliography

Official sources
Strafflag (Criminal Code of Finland) (39/1889)

Literature

Agrama, Hussein Ali. *Questioning Secularism: Islam, Sovereignty, and the Rule of Law in Modern Egypt*. Chicago: University of Chicago Press, 2012.

Arnórsdóttir, Agnes S., Per Ingesman, and Bjørn Poulsen, eds. *Konge, kirke og samfund: De to øvrighedsmagter i dansk senmiddelalder*. Aarhus: Aarhus Universitetsforlag, 2007.

Asad, Talal. *Formations of the Secular: Christianity, Islam, Modernity*. Stanford, CA: Stanford University Press, 2003.

---

31 Heuser, "The Contribution of Law to the Secularization of Politics," 9.

Berman, Harold J. *Law and Revolution*, Vol. 2: *The Impact of the Protestant Reformations*. Cambridge, MA: The Belknap Press of the Harvard University Press, 2003.

Brilkman, Kaja. "Confessionalisation, Confessional Conflict, and Confessional Culture in Early Modern Scandinavia." *Scandia* 82, no. 1 (2016): 93-106.

Christoffersen, Lisbet. "Towards Re-sacralization of Nordic Law?" In *Formatting Religion: Across Politics, Education, Media, and Law*, edited by Marius Timmann Mjaaland, 175-204. London: Routledge, 2019.

Christoffersen, Lisbet, Kjell Å. Modéer, and Svend Andersen, eds. *Law & Religion in the 21st Century—Nordic Perspectives*. Copenhagen: DJØF Publishing, 2010.

Dressler, Markus, and Arvind-Pal S. Mandair, eds. *Secularism and Religion-Making*. Oxford: Oxford University Press, 2011.

Failinger, Marie A., and Ronald W. Duty. "Preface." In *Lutheran Theology and Secular Law: The Work of the Modern State*, edited by Marie A. Failinger and Roland W. Duty, xii–xv. Abingdon: Routledge, 2018.

Field, Lester L. *Liberty, Dominion, and the Two Swords: On the Origins of Western Political Theology*. Notre Dame, IN: Notre Dame University Press, 1998.

Furseth, Inger, ed. *Religious Complexity in the Public Sphere: Comparing Nordic Countries*. London: Palgrave-MacMillan 2018.

Gorski, Philip S. "Historicizing the Secularization Debate: Church, State, and Society in Late Medieval and Early Modern Europe ca. 1300 to 1700." *American Sociological Review* 65, no. 1 (2000): 138-67.

Gorski, Philip S., and Ateş Altınordu. "After Secularization?" *Annual Review of Sociology* 34, no. 1 (2008): 55-85.

Gregersen, Niels Henrik. "From *oeconomia* to Nordic Welfare Societies: The Idea of a Third-Zone Lutheranism." *Theology Today* 76, no. 3 (2019): 234-41.

Grenholm, Carl-Henric. "Legal Positivism in Lutheran Ethics." In *Lutheran Theology and Secular Law: The Work of the Modern State*, edited by Marie A. Failinger and Roland W. Duty, 17-28. Abingdon: Routledge, 2018.

Hallward, Maia Carter. "Situating the 'Secular': Negotiating the Boundary between Religion and Politics." *International Political Sociology* 2, no. 1 (2008): 1-16.

Heckel, Martin. *Martin Luthers Reformation und das Recht: Die Entwicklung der Theologie Luthers und ihre Auswirkung auf das Recht unter den Rahmenbedingungen der Reichsreform und der Territorialstaatsbildung im Kampf mit Rom und den 'Schwärmern'*. Tübingen: Mohr-Siebeck, 2016.

Heuser, Stefan. "The Contribution of Law to the Secularization of Politics: Impulses from Luther's Doctrine of the Two Regimes." In *Lutheran Theology and Secular Law: The Work of the Modern State*, edited by Marie A. Fallinger and Roland W. Duty, 3-13. Abingdon: Routledge, 2018.

Hinlicky, Paul. "Antinomianism–the 'Lutheran' Heresy." In *Lutheran Theology and Secular Law: The Work of the Modern State*, edited by Marie A. Failinger and Roland W. Duty, 28-38. Abingdon: Routledge, 2018.

Holm, Bo Kristian. "Dynamic Tensions in the Social Imaginaries of the Lutheran Reformation." In *Lutheran Theology and the Shaping of Society: The Danish Monarchy as Example*, edited by Bo Kristian Holm and Nina J. Koefoed, 85-106. Göttingen: Vandenhoeck and Ruprecht, 2018.

Holm, Bo Kristian, and Nina J. Koefoed, eds. *Lutheran Theology and the Shaping of Society: The Danish Monarchy as Example.* Göttingen: Vandenhoeck and Ruprecht, 2018.

Husa, Jaakko. "Constitutional Mentality." In *Nordic Law in European Context,* edited by Pia Letto-Vanamo, Ditlev Tamm, and Bent Ole Gram Mortensen, 41-60. Cham: Springer, 2019.

Kaufmann, Thomas. *Konfession und Kultur: Lutherischer Protestantismus in der zweiten Hälfte des Reformationsjahrhunderts.* Tübingen: Mohr-Siebeck 2006.

Kaufmann, Thomas. "Die Konfessionalisierung von Kirche und Gesellschaft. Sammelbericht über eine Forschungsdebatte." *Theologische Literaturzeitung* 121 (1996): 1009-25.

Koefoed, Nina Javette. "Authorities Who Care: The Lutheran Doctrine of the Three Estates in Danish Legal Development from the Reformation to Absolutism." *Scandinavian Journal of History* 44, no. 4 (2019): 430-53.

Koefoed, Nina Javette. "The Lutheran Household as Part of Danish Confessional Culture." In *Lutheran Theology and the Shaping of Society: The Danish Monarchy as Example,* edited by Bo Kristian Holm and Nina J. Koefoed, 321-40. Göttingen: Vandenhoeck and Ruprecht, 2018.

Korpiola, Mia. "Lutheran Marriage Norms in Action: The Example of Post-Reformation Sweden, 1520-1600." In *Lutheran Reformation and the Law*, edited by Virpi Mäkinen, 131-70. Leiden: Brill, 2006.

Künkler, Mirjam, and Yüksel Sezgin. "Diversity in Democracy: Accommodating Religious Particularity in Largely Secular Legal Systems." *Journal of Law and Religion* 28, no. 2 (2013): 337-40.

Letto-Vanamo, Pia, and Ditlev Tamm. "Nordic Legal Mind." In *Nordic Law in European Context,* edited by Pia Letto-Vanamo, Ditlev Tamm, and Bent Ole Gram Mortensen, 1-19. Cham: Springer, 2019.

Lind, Anna-Sara, and Victoria Enkvist, eds. *Constitutionalisation and Hegemonisation: Exploring the Boundaries of Law and Religion 1800-1950.* Odense: University Press of Southern Denmark, *forthcoming*.

Lotz-Heumann, Ute. "The Concept of 'Confessionalization': A Historiographical Paradigm in Dispute." *Memoria y Civilización* 4 (2001): 93-114.

Ojanen, Tuomas. "Human Rights in Nordic Constitutions and the Impact of International Obligations." In *The Nordic Constitutions: A Comparative and Contextual Study*, edited by Helle Krunke and Björg Thorarensen, 133-66. Oxford: Hart, 2018.

Pihlajamäki, Heikki, and Risto Saarinen. "Lutheran Reformation and the Law in Recent Scholarship." In *Lutheran Reformation and the Law*, edited by Virpi Mäkinen, 1-20. Leiden: Brill, 2006.

Rasmussen, Tarald, and Jørn Sunde, eds. *Protestant Legacies of Nordic Law: The Early Modern Period.* Paderborn: Brill-Schönningh, forthcoming.

Roy, Oliver. *Secularism Confronts Islam.* Translated by George Holoch. New York: Columbia University Press, 2009.

Schilling, Heinz. "The Confessionalization of European Churches and Societies—an Engine for Modernizing and for Social and Cultural Change." *Norsk Teologisk Tidsskrift* 110, no. 1 (2009): 3-22.

Slotte, Pamela. "'A Little Church, a Little State, and a Little Commonwealth at Once': Towards a Nordic Model of Religious Instruction in Public Schools?" In *Law and Religion in the 21st Century—Nordic Perspectives,* edited by Lisbet Christoffersen, Svend Andersen, and Kjell Å. Modéer, 239-73. Copenhagen: Djøf Publishing, 2010.

Slotte, Pamela. "Waving the 'Freedom of Religion or Belief' Card, or Playing it Safe: Religious Instruction in the Cases of Norway and Finland." *Religion and Human Rights* 3, no. 1 (2008): 33-69.

Stolleis, Michael. "'Konfessionalisierung' oder 'Säkularisierung' bei der Entstehung des frühmodernen Staates." *Ius Commune* 20 (1993): 1-23.

Taylor, Charles. *A Secular Age.* London: The Belknap Press, 2007.

Thames, Knox. "Old Is New: Europe and Freedom of Religion or Belief." In *The Changing Nature of Religious Rights under International Law*, edited by Malcolm D. Evans, Peter Petkoff, and Julian Rivers, 146-62. Oxford: Oxford University Press, 2015.

Tuori, Kaarlo. *Critical Legal Positivism.* Aldershot: Ashgate 2002.

Witte, John, Jr. *Law and Protestantism: The Legal Teachings of the Lutheran Reformation.* Cambridge: Cambridge University Press, 2002

I

The Early Post-World War II Period

2. Nordic Lutheranism and Secular Law: The Role of Law in the Grundtvigian Creation Theologies of K.E. Løgstrup and Regin Prenter

Niels Henrik Gregersen

The purpose of the present chapter is to reflect on the relations between Lutheran theology and secular law in the Nordic realm during and immediately after World War II.[1] I begin by pointing to the vastly different political situations of the five Nordic countries during wartime. Denmark and Norway were occupied by Germany on April 9, 1940, whereas Iceland declared its national independence from Denmark in 1944. Sweden kept its neutrality during the war, while Finland fought vehemently for retaining its independence in the Winter War against Russia 1939-1941.

Against this diverse Nordic background, I focus on the muddled Danish situation, which raised urgent questions on politics and law. How can one draw a line between the foreign politics during occupation and the domestic politics that in principle but not in reality were in the hands of the Danish government? How could the required political compromises be justified, if at all? In particular, in which sense can one appeal to law in a situation, where the Danish government issued new laws and regulations for Denmark under strong pressure from the German occupying power? These questions were not only political but also ethical in nature, and theologians contributed to the public debate regarding ethical dilemmas and the proper relation between politics, law, and the People's Church in Denmark.

My particular case will be a comparison between the views on law, justice, and politics of the philosopher-theologian K.E. Løgstrup (1905-1981) and the dogmatic theologian Regin Prenter (1907-1990). Løgstrup and Prenter were both members of the Danish resistance movement and worked as pastors, until

---

1   I wish to thank Lisbet Christoffersen and Mikkel Gabriel Christoffersen for carefully reading earlier drafts of this chapter, Jyrki Knuutila and Bengt Kristensson Uggla for offering highly valuable information about the Finnish and the Swedish situation during World War II, and Kees van Kooten Niekerk for advice on Løgstrup.

Løgstrup was named Professor of Ethics and Philosophy of Religion at Aarhus University in 1943, followed by Prenter as Professor of Dogmatics in 1945. Alongside their pastoral work and illegal activities, they took part in discussions on law and politics insofar as this was possible during the occupation. While Løgstrup and Prenter were later to become internationally renowned figures at the newly founded Faculty of Theology at Aarhus University (1942), their early writings exemplify two different positions within the spectrum of contemporary Lutheran and Grundtvigian understandings of church, culture, and law. While Prenter argued from the perspective of a confessing church, Løgstrup had a broader ethical concern regarding the conflicts between the Danish government and the Danish people. Nonetheless, both refer to the governmental violation of law as the only proper reason for resistance, while seeing lawfulness as the decisive criterion for the legitimacy of a government. While Prenter in *Church and Law* (1944) referred to positive laws at international political level (including the 1907 Hague Convention on warfare), Løgstrup based his view of law on pre-political "laws of life" that in his view were violated in the Danish appeasement politics vis-à-vis the German occupying power. Yet both Prenter and Løgstrup point to general principles of law as normatively binding for the rule of the state, not to a particular Christian view of right and wrong. Even though neither Løgstrup nor Prenter were secular (in the sense of being areligious), both of them referred to secular law as the basis for the integrity of a worldly government. Thus, the case of Prenter and Løgstrup contribute to the overall hypothesis of the ProNoLa project, which argues that Nordic Lutherans tend to appeal to the secular law and ethical principles and not to a particular Christological formation of legal order. For Løgstrup and Prenter, a creation theology that reflects on a world of gifts and demands shared by Christians and non-Christians alike constitutes the ultimate source of law. In this sense, they were promoting varieties of Lutheran "natural law" tradition, without deriving the specific contents of secular law from a *ius divinum* but also without deriving law and justice from universalist principles of human reasoning. The Lutheran emphasis on a *lex naturalis* centers on the demand of neighborly love, but since this demand is always refracted in different concrete contexts of life, the concern for the moral communities in which human beings are situated play a central role in their arguments. Accordingly, the Lutheran concept of natural law is, first and foremost, not a legal concept but an ethical concept of an other-directed behavior guided by reasonable principles of fairness.

This will lead us to our final question: How does this understanding of human beings as situated in already existing moral communities fit the distinction within Scandinavian legal philosophy between "idealistic" and "realistic" understandings of law? I argue that, from their own internal perspective, neither Løgstrup nor Prenter would describe their views on law as "idealistic," since they refer to a moral sense developed within existing human communities. Nonetheless, they argued that any positive law issued by German or Danish authorities will have to pass a test of reasonableness and fairness, which include moral considerations. From the perspective of a legal realism, such entanglement of moral and legal viewpoints would be classified as "idealistic" in orientation. So it may be: After World War II, the fundamental issue continued to be whether law is rooted only in positive laws plus state enforcement, or whether laws presuppose historically evolved legal cultures operating under the constraints of deep-seated human concerns.

East Norden and West Norden

Nordic Lutheranisms share a number of common characteristics, not least due to their shared history of Lutheran majority churches since the 1500s. Compared to the history of Germany, for example, the Nordic countries are unique in having a long history of intertwinement between nation-building and the Lutheran majority church. Nonetheless, there are also divergent theological cultures in the Nordic countries that have ramifications for the status of ecclesiastical law.

The Norwegian church historian Tarald Rasmussen has pointed to some historically developed differences between the *West Nordic* countries (Denmark, Norway, and Iceland) and the *East Nordic* countries (Sweden and Finland).[2] Until the 1520s, all Nordic countries were part of the Kalmar Union (1397-1523), but in the following centuries Denmark-Norway and Sweden-Finland went their separate ways in mutual warfare. Moreover, the confessional character differed between a more minimalist and congregation-centered oriented Lutheranism in Denmark and Norway, and a more high-church oriented development in Sweden and Finland, leading to what Rasmussen refers to as the "ambivalent legacy" of Swedish Lutheranism. Sweden and Finland retained Catholic elements such as archbishops, placing an emphasis on the apostolic succession of bishops back to Peter of Rome. Denmark and Norway thus represent a more "lean Lutheranism," while Sweden and Finland adopted a broader allegiance to the Lutheran confessions and retained a stronger continuity with the Catholic

---

2 Tarald Rasmussen, *Hva er protestantisme* [What is Protestantism?] (Oslo: Universitetsforlaget, 2017), 103-20. See also Lisbet Christoffersen, 'By Law Established': The Nordic Majority Churches in Comparative Perspective, in this volume.

heritage. These differences in confessional profile and leadership models have a material basis too: While the Church of Sweden retained much of its land and property after the Reformation, King Christian III took over the land of the Danish church with the Reformation in 1536, the last remnants being handed over to the democratic state in 1922.[3]

In all Nordic countries, the Lutheran Churches were established by the kings as "secular" lawgivers. During its time under Russian governance (1809-1917), however, the Lutheran Church in Finland established a synod with authority to propose internal laws for the governance of the church; in Sweden, a law of 1859 likewise established an internal governance structure for the church, until the full separation of state and church went through the Swedish parliament in 2000. These developments differ from the situation in West Norden. While the secular governments in Denmark and Norway established congregational councils at local level (in Denmark 1903; in Norway 1920), the parliaments retained their formal governance of the churches at national level. This is still today the case in the People's Church in Denmark; in Norway a representative Church Council was established in 1984, and the Norwegian Church became an independent legal subject in 2017, again established by secular law. By the mid-20th century, however, the Danish and Norwegian bishops were like kings and queens without land, and only in urgent circumstances did Norwegian and Danish church leaders take independent political steps. This is what happened during World War II, as we shall see.

Different Nordic Experiences during World War II

World War II impacted the Nordic countries in vastly different ways. *Finland* was attacked by the overwhelming Russian troops on November 30, 1939, and fought bravely against the Soviet troops until the Moscow Peace was agreed upon on March 13, 1940. Finland had to give away 9 % of its territory and about 20 % of its industrial capacity. For the Finns, the communist Soviet Union, and not Nazi Germany, was the main enemy. *Sweden* managed to keep its neutrality during World War II but also helped the German *Wehrmacht* by allowing the transport of iron and heavy water from occupied Norway through Sweden. Yet Sweden also became a safe haven for many fleeing Danes and Norwegians. In

---

[3] The history of this lean Lutheranism is told in Niels Henrik Gregersen, "Martin Luther in Denmark," *The Oxford Encyclopedia of Martin Luther*, ed. Derek R. Nelson and Paul R. Hinlicky, vol. 2 (New York: Oxford University Press, 2017), 256-70.

September-October 1943, the majority of Danish Jews and leading communists were thus transported at night from Denmark to Sweden via Øresund. After World War II, however, Sweden made no efforts to perform a transitional justice in relation to the Swedish collaborators with the Third Reich.[4]

By contrast, Denmark and Norway were occupied on the same morning of April 9, 1940. King Christian X and the Danish government capitulated to Germany after only a few hours of hopeless fight in the flat lands of Denmark. While Norway pursued a heroic resistance, Denmark surrendered "under protest" to the German troops, and the government saw a politics of negotiation as the only possible way forward, trusting the German "April promises" that the domestic government was still to be in the hands of Danish authorities. In the following years, the Danish government negotiated with the German authorities for retaining a continuous Danish government, a Danish police force, and a Danish rule, though with seemingly endless concessions regarding public order and the self-censorship of newspapers, books, and church publications. Cultural resistance, including national and political awareness of the values of the Danish democracy, constituted the main part of the Danish response. The outstanding figure here was the Danish church historian Hal Koch (1904-1963), who became leader of *Dansk Ungdomssamvirke*, an umbrella organization of Danish youth organizations established as early as June 25, 1940, in order to promote democracy and strengthen the popular sense of Danish culture. Alongside this broader strategy, illegal resistance groups began to be formed, and both Prenter and Løgstrup were active as couriers. While the official Danish politics of concession and appeasement (*eftergivenhedspolitik*) spared the lives of many Jews and communists in Denmark, it became the target for Løgstrup's uncompromising critique in The Life of the People and Foreign Policy (*Folkeliv og Udenrigspolitik*) in 1943. Finally, on August 29, 1943, popular general strikes began, and the Danish government resigned. The days of the negation politics were over. As a result, Jews, communists, and (in September 1944) also Danish police forces were now sent away to concentration camps in Germany, if they were not helped to Sweden.[5]

---

[4] So Anders Jarlert, "Sverige: Modernisering utan rättsuppgörelse," in *Nordiske folkekirker i opbrud: National identitet og international nyorientering efter 1945*, ed. Jens Holger Schjørring (Aarhus: Aarhus Universitetsforlag, 2001), 83: "Any real transitional justice did not take place in Sweden". Here, and in what follows, all translations from Nordic sources are mine.

[5] The historical literature on the five dark years 1940-1945 is ever burgeoning, with different emphasis between consensus-views and conflict views. A comprehensive overview is found in Bo Lidegaard, *Kampen om Danmark 1933-1945* [The Fight about Denmark 1933-45] (Copenhagen: Gyldendal, 2005), see 557-95 on the historiography. On the role of

Norway was able to resist for a longer period, both due to its geography and to the decisive will of the people. In consequence, the German forces dissolved the Norwegian parliament, and *Reichkommissar* Josef Terboven ruled Norway until the Norwegian Nazi Vidkun Quisling was put in charge of Norway in 1942. Already in April 1940 King Haakon VII and the government took refuge in Sweden, but were required to return with reference to the Swedish neutrality; thereafter the Norwegian king and government made a dangerous flight to England by boat, in June 1940. Due to the immediate regime change in Norway, the Norwegian army and resistance movement began from the onset of the occupation, and with a more undivided popular support than was the case in Denmark. In protest against celebrating the installation of Quisling in the Nidaros Cathedral on February 1, 1942, the seven bishops of the Church of Norway and more than 90 % of the pastors laid down their ministries. Together with lay people and the free churches, the Norwegian Church wrote the confession *The Foundation of the Church* (*Kirkens Grunn*) during Easter 1942. By comparison, the Danish bishops worked as far as possible in tandem with the government, as long as it was still in the hands of the Danish parliament. After that time, they began to issue independent statements such as the *Pastoral Letter of the Danish Bishops* of September 29, 1943, with its vocal support for "our Jewish brothers and sisters."

After the May 1945 liberation, both Denmark and Norway installed different procedures for the *transitional justice*. Norway carried out a comprehensive number of convictions, including as many as 2 % of the entire Norwegian population, with overall mild punishments.[6] While the Norwegian government in exile had prepared for legal procedures, the post-war government in Denmark had to proceed quickly in order to prevent vigilantism. In Denmark, only 0,3 % of the population were convicted but received hard judgments, especially in the first years after the war; the minimum punishment was 4 years' imprisonment. In Norway, 30 were convicted with capital judgment, 25 of them executed; in Denmark 103 were convicted, 46 executed.

---

the Danish church during the occupation, the main study is Erik Thostrup Jacobsen, *Som om intet var hændt: Den danske folkekirke under besættelsen* [As if nothing had happened: The Danish People's Church under the occupation] (Odense: Odense Universitetsforlag, 1991). Jacobsen's description is highly sensitive to the details and to the different ecclesiological positions within the Danish Church. His conclusion is that, even though anti-Nazism was overwhelming also within the church, the conflicts within the church reflected those in the Danish society at large. "Then as well as now, the church did not live an isolated life but was a mirror of society". Jacobsen, *Som om intet var hændt*, 245.

6   Numbers in Asbjørn Jaklin, *De Dødsdømte* (Oslo: Gyldendal, 2011), 305. On the transitional justice in Denmark, see Ditlev Tamm, *Retsopgøret efter besættelsen* (Copenhagen: Dansk Jurist- og Økonomforbund, 1984. The text of the Law Amendment is printed on 755-60.)

The Danish *Penalty Law Amendment* (*Straffelovstillæg*) of June 1, 1945, regarding treason, has remained a controversial issue, both legally and morally. Most importantly, the Law Amendment retroactively made criminal offences out of actions carried out even before August 29, 1943, while the Danish government still requested a peaceful co-operation with the German authorities, urged administrators to socialize with German representatives, etc. The theologian Koch's booklet, *I accuse the Parliament* (*Jeg anklager Rigsdagen*) from 1947 gained a widespread echo when he pointed out that the Law Amendment led to the prosecution of the little people, whereas the politicians promoting the collaboration were excused. This was a secular argument referring to fairness, presupposing a *lex naturalis* in the meaning of a shared moral sense.

The Nordic Bishops Meet in Postwar Copenhagen 1945

How did Nordic church leaders react to one another after World War II? The first official meeting of the Nordic bishops took place in Copenhagen after World War II, August 21-23, 1945, and tells a story of the conflicts between the Nordic countries during the war. One would imagine such a meeting to be cordial *rendez-vous* of Lutheran bishops finally being able to see one another face to face again and celebrate the liberation of May 1945 together. It was not so simple, though. The archbishop of Sweden, Erling Eidem (1880-1972), had earlier sent an invitation to such a reunion meeting in Sweden. However, the Oslo bishop Eivind Berggrav (1884-1959) refused to meet in Sweden, so the meeting took place in Copenhagen. Berggrav, a main drafter of the *The Ground of the Church* from 1942, took the upper moral position. He expressed his strong dismay with Sweden's allowance of the transit of iron from Norway through Sweden, a concession that was of central importance for the German warfare in addition to other Swedish supplies to the German *Wehrmacht*. In the same vein, Berggrav was upset by the Finnish cooperation with Germany during 1940-45, including the fact that the Finnish church had continued to cooperate with Nazified leaders of the German *Reichskirche*. The Copenhagen bishop Hans Fuglsang-Damgaard (1890-1979) (the initiator to the *Pastoral Letter of the Danish Bishops* of September 29, 1943) took a mediating position, expressing the need "to understand the difficult position of Finland." Fuglsang-Damgaard, on his side, critically asked the Icelandic bishop Sigurgeir Sigurðsson (1890-1953) why Iceland used the German occupation to declare the independence of Iceland in 1944 without prior consultations with Denmark. Bishop Sigurðsson replied that it was a matter of life and death for Iceland to do so in the given context. According to the official summary of the meeting, the bishops ended with an "agreement of will to continue the cooperation between the churches unhindered by what had happened in political regards." In addition, they committed to working collaboratively for a church aid to the ruined Europe. Only the archives inform about the underlying conflicts.[7]

The August 1945 meeting shows how geography matters in wartime, and how theological, political, and moral cultures influence one another. It also revealed the need to establish a Nordic Lutheran theology as an alternative to the reigning supremacy of German theology. Nordic Lutheranism was generally untainted by the Nazification of Lutheranism in Germany, with some exceptions in Finland and Sweden.[8] Among Danish and Norwegian pastors, the anti-Nazi stance was outspoken, especially in Norway but also in Denmark under censorship.[9] Professors of theology such as Prenter and Løgstrup gave another face to

---

7   I owe this case to the archival studies of Jens Holger Schjørring, "Introduction," in *Nordiske folkekirker i opbrud: National identitet og international nyorientering efter 1945*, ed. Jens Holger Schjørring (Aarhus: Aarhus Universitetsforlag, 2001), 11-15.

8   On the Finnish combination of patriotism and pietism, see Aila Lauha, "Finland: Ansvar för folket förblir kyrkans kallelse," in *Nordiske folkekirker i opbrud*, ed. Jens Holger Schjørring (Aarhus: Aarhus Universitetsforlag, 2001), 53-64. On the Swedish situation, see Martin Lind, *Kristendom och nazism* (Lund: Håkan Ohlssons förlag, 1975). Lind highlights the fact that leading voices of the Swedish church, particularly in the pietist Gothenburg diocese, approved of Nazism and even attacked the Norwegian *Kirkens Grunn* in the official organ of the diocese, *Göteborgs Stiftstidende*. In his auto-biography, *The Five Universities of my Life*, Gustaf Wingren recalls how the relation to Nazism was a divisive issue at Lund University too, see Gustaf Wingren, *Mina fem universitet: Minnen* (Lund: Proprius Forlag, 1991), 55-56. While Gustaf Aulén was outspokenly anti-Nazi (evident in Gustaf Aulén, *Kyrkan och nationalsocialismen: Kyrkan och statslivet* (Stockholm: Svenska kyrkans diakonistyrelses bokförlag, 1944), also illegally printed in Denmark 1945 under the name, "Andagtsbog for Hjem og Skole" [Devotional Book for Home and Church]!), Anders Nygren's concept of the pure agape-motif of Christian faith served the same purpose in the given situation. On the other side of the spectrum, however, we have the New Testament Professor Hugo Odeberg at the Faculty of Theology in Lund, who was president of *Riksförbundet Sverige-Tyskland* 1941-43, and worked in tandem with the Professor of Law at Lund, Karl Olivecrona, a strong proponent of legal realism of the Uppsala school. Olivecrona was pro-German based on the assumption that the power of positive law depends on strong political force. Wingren's unpublished diaries, "Johanneum Journal" from Berlin 1938, shows Wingren's keen awareness of these German sympathies at Lund University, see Bengt Kristensson Uggla, *Becoming Human Again: The Theological Life of Gustaf Wingren* (Eugene, OR: Cascade Books, 2016), 109-12. In the competition for the chair of ethics at Lund University in 1951, Wingren was finally chosen as professor above his own teacher, Herbert Olsson, who likewise combined an "old Lutheran characteristic" with "modern Nazi ideology", as Wingren put it in his diaries 1938, cited by Uggla, *Becoming Human Again*, 111.

9   See Arne Hassing, *Church Resistance to Nazism in Norway, 1940-1945* (Seattle, WA: University of Washington Press, 2014).

20th-century Lutheranism than did the proponents of the German Luther Renaissance such as Carl Stange (1870-1959) and Emanuel Hirsch (1888-1972). From the 1930s to the 1950s, Nordic Lutheran theology developed its own profile. In particular, Swedish Lutheran theology from the Lundensian school, marked by theologians such as Gustaf Aulén (1879-1977) and Anders Nygren (1890-1978), was internationally renowned, and after World War II also the creation theologian Gustaf Wingren (1910-2000) found international resonance in England and the US. The fact that the *Lutheran World Federation* was inaugurated in Lund 1947 under the leadership of Nygren shows the central role of the Swedish Church in international Lutheranism in the decades after World War II.

Consensus and Conflicts in Denmark 1933-1945: Political Backgrounds

We now turn to the Danish political situation that forms the background for Løgstrup's and Prenter's interventions in the Danish discussions on law and democracy. As we will see below, Løgtrup and Prenter were placed on opposite sides of the Lutheran-Grundtvigian spectrum, and with regard to their European influence, Løgstrup was inspired by the existentialist theology of Rudolf Bultmann (1884-1976), while Prenter was mainly influenced by Karl Barth (1886-1968) and shaped by his experiences with the Confessing Church in Germany.

On the very day of Adolf Hitler's *Machtübernahme* on January 30, 1933, a historic political settlement (*Kanslergadeforliget*) was reached in Denmark after 18 hours of negotiations in the home of prime minister Thorvald Stauning in Kanslergade. Stauning was prime minister in 1916-1924 and 1929-1942 for the Social Democratic Party, and he made a far-reaching agreement with the liberal parties *Venstre* and *Radikale Venstre.* The three parties decided upon extending the existing agreements on the working market by law (thus impeding the lockout warning issued by the industrial employers), and on providing better conditions for the important agricultural sector in Denmark. The settlement initiated a nationwide social reform too, which laid the ground for the postwar establishment of a welfare society in Denmark.

One year later, on May 23, 1934, Stauning issued the social democratic program *Danmark for Folket* (Denmark for the People), in which he called upon the Danish people as a shared community capable of withstanding the dangers of Nazism coming from the south and Communism coming from the east. Stauning did so in "an appeal to all forces who wish to maintain democracy and the rule by the people."[10] By implication, he thereby also called upon the cultural resources of the People's Church in Denmark (at that time its membership was 98 % of the population). At the subsequent election in 1935, Stauning won a significant victory under the dramatic slogan: "Stauning—or Chaos. Vote Socialdemocratic!"

The Copenhagen bishop Fuglsang-Damgaard was not a social democrat, but took basically the same stance on Denmark's political and geographic situation. In the first issue of the *Journal of the Pastor's Association* 1936, he discussed how to celebrate the 400 years of the Danish Reformation in 1536. Fuglsang-Damgaard, too, starts out by pointing to the dangerous situation of Denmark, placed between the threat from the south (Hitler) and the threat from the east (Stalin), before he addresses the threats to the church coming from secularism, partly indifferentist, partly Christophobic. In this context, Fuglsang-Damgaard states that the Lutheran church builds on the ideals of humanism in the vein of Immanuel Kant: No human person should to be treated as a mere instrument but always as a value and end in itself.[11]

Certainly, there were other voices in Denmark leading up to 1940. At the 1935-election the Communist party won 2 seats in the parliament (1,65 % of the votes), while the Nazi party did not even win one seat (0,99 % of the votes). The Social Democratic Party was the big winner of 68 seats (46,1 %).[12] The pressure from foreign authoritarian regimes like the Soviet Union may explain the relatively high degree of political consensus in Denmark across differences between left and right within the parliament. This consensus, however, was challenged by voices critical of the democratic system. On the right hand side of the Danish cultural spectrum, we find the prominent Professor of Law, Frederik Vinding Kruse (1880-1963), who argued for establishing an elitist, moral, and technic government consisting of "the best men of the kingdom" in order to withstand

---

10   Thorkil Stauning, "Danmark for Folket," *Socialisten* (1934): 214. See further Niels Henrik Gregersen, "Luther genopført, modsagt og genbrugt: Det 20. århundredes epoker," in *Reformationen i dansk kirke og kultur*, Vol. 3; 1914-2017, ed. Niels Henrik Gregersen and Carsten Bach-Nielsen (Odense: Syddansk Universitetsforlag 2017), 34-36.

11   Hans Fuglsang-Damgaard, "Anno 1936: Lutherdommens Opgave i den aktuelle Situation," *Præsteforeningens Blad*, no. 1 (1936): 1-12.

12   Pelle Mortensen and Astrid Øllgaard Christensen Scriver, "Folketingsvalget 1935," and Astrid Øllgaard Christensen Scriver, "Folketingsvalget 1935," danmarkshistorien.dk, Last modified March 23, 2018, https://danmarkshistorien.dk/leksikon-og-kilder/vis/materiale/folketingsvalget-1935/. At the elections in 1939, the Communist Party and the Danish National-Socialist Party (DNSAP) each won 3 seats (ca. 2 % of the votes each). In 1943, the Communist Party was forbidden but the DNSAP still only gained 3 seats.

the potential chaos of democratic divisions.[13] Vinding was highly critical of Nazism as well, however. Likewise, the anti-Nazi sentiment was strong in the small political party *Dansk Samling* (Danish Unity), an anti-modernist movement initiated by the young cultural critic Arne Sørensen (1906-1978) in 1936. This national party also expressed a critique of the parliamentary system in its wish for a strong social state based on the freedom of Danish people, albeit without pointing to alternatives to democracy.[14]

Prenter was part of the circle around *Dansk Samling* from its beginnings in October 1936, and from 1938 he wrote a series of articles in the cultural journal *Det Tredje Standpunkt* (The Third Position), edited by Sørensen.[15] In his *Memories*, Prenter says that he was initially skeptical about the new movement but after the German occupation in 1940 he became a member, since the party was against the official Danish politics of negotiation and cooperation with the German occupying power. *Dansk Samling* was a stronghold of the incipient Danish resistance movement, and after the liberation two seats were given to it in the *Danish Freedom Council* (Frihedsraadet), 1945. Prenter ran for election as a candidate of the party at the general elections in 1943 and 1945, though without success.[16] After World War II, Sørensen brought in Prenter as a co-editor of *Det Tredje Standpunkt*, but at that time the influence of the journal was fading, and the election in 1945 gave *Dansk Samling* only 4 seats (3,1 %). The party gave up its earlier anti-parliamentary rhetoric, but retained its criticism of the Danish politics of appeasement. Sørensen himself left the party in 1949, and the party was never again represented in parliament.

After World War II, there was no space left for voices critical of democracy and humanism, neither in the Nordic countries nor in Germany. In West Germany a new democratic constitution was established to be followed by a new democratic mentality, whereas the idea of a "Nordic democracy" was part of

---

13 On Vinding, see Esther Oluffa Pedersen, *Fremkaldte kulturrum: Diskussioner om diktatur, humanisme, ansvar og videnskab i tiden omkring Anden Verdenskrig* [Evoked Spaces of Culture: Discussions on Democracy and Dictatorship, Humanism, Responsibility and Science around World War II] (Copenhagen: Hans Reitzels Forlag, 2019), 41-58. Pedersen rightly argues that the antiparliamentary position of Frederik Vinding Kruse represents the foil against which one can understand the explicit support of democracy, developed during and after World War II. Pedersen, *Fremkaldte kulturrum,* 56.

14 See Henrik Lundbak, *Danish Unity: A Political Party between Fascism and Resistance 1936-47* (Copenhagen: Museum Tusculanums Forlag, 2003).

15 Five of his essays from *Det Tredje Standpunkt* are reprinted in Regin Prenter, *Ordets Herredømme* [The Reign of the Word] (Copenhagen: Det Tredje Standpunkts Forlag, 1941). Also K.E. Løgstrup wrote two articles on French personalism and on Ernst Jünger in *Det Trejde Standpunkt* in 1939 and 1940/1941.

16 Regin Prenter, *Erindringer* (Aarhus: Aros, 1985), 115-17.

a longer continuity with democratic institutions and mindsets.[17] In Denmark, the model of a collaborative democracy of the 1930s was continued within the framework of the Danish Constitution of 1849, now also securing some economic safety for all citizens. In the 1849 Constitution (§3, today §4) the Evangelical Lutheran Church in Denmark was called "the People's Church" (*Folkekirken*) in reference to its status as a comprehensive majority church. The Nordic model of a welfare state (initiated with the social reform after 1933 and developed between the 1950s and the 1970s) was in Sweden even called "the people's home" (*folkhemmet*). In the Nordic countries, the concept of "people" (in German: *Volk*) was untainted by associations with Nazism, and the emphasis on the freedom and law of the people even constituted a significant resource for resistance against Nazism. The inner relations between the welfare society as "the people's home" and "the People's Church" is still a matter of much scholarly discussion.[18]

Løgstrup and Prenter: Two Versions of Grundtvigianism

With the German occupation of Denmark on April 9, 1940, the overarching political consensus of the 1930s was further solidified, and earlier criticisms of the People's Church in Denmark receded and almost vanished during the war.

The wartime experiences gave a new public profile to the Grundtvigian movement in particular. In July 1940 began the "allsong" movement, with open air singing of national songs including many hymns by N.F.S. Grundtvig (1783-1872). On September 8, 1940, the majestic Grundtvig Church was opened, and in the fall of 1940, Koch began his open lecture series on Grundtvig in

---

17 Compare Tine Reeh, "A Nordic Model of Democracy: Hal Koch and Alf Ross on Law and Religion in Nordic Societies" in this volume and Georg Kalinna, "History as Argument: The Interpretation of National Socialist Rule and the Implications for Protestant Political Ethics in West Germany after World War II" in this volume.

18 The thesis of an affinity between the Lutheran majority churches and the development of Nordic welfare society is presented in Robert H. Nelson, *Lutheranism and the Nordic Spirit of Social Democracy: A Different Protestant Ethic* (Aarhus: Aarhus University Press, 2017); see also Niels Henrik Gregersen, "From *oeconomia* to Nordic Welfare Societies: The Idea of a Third-Zone Lutheranism," *Theology Today* 76, no. 3 (2019): 224-32. Many church leaders, however, expressed their criticism of the incipient welfare, including Eivind Berggrav, see Aud V. Tønnesen, "... *et trygt og godt hjem for alle"? Kirkelederes kritikk av velferdsstaten efter 1945* (Trondheim: Tapir Akademisk Forlag, 2000), 37-45. On the similar Danish situation, see Klaus Petersen and Jørn Henrik Petersen, "The Good, the Bad, or the Godless Society? Danish 'Church People' and the Modern Welfare State," *Church History* 82, no. 4 (2013): 94-140.

the overcrowded aula of the University of Copenhagen. Koch was also elected as leader of *Dansk Ungdomssamvirke* (Danish Youth Cooperation), covering many different political, cultural, and Christian youth organizations.[19] Inner Mission did not wish to enroll, however, since it worked for the conversion to Christ and not to Danish culture, and also YMCA (in Denmark: KFUM) was not officially a member of *Dansk Ungdomssamvirke*, though many of its local member organizations invited Koch to speak on cultural values of a democratic political culture. Nonetheless, Inner Mission always had a very pro-Jewish attitude too, and after 1942-1943, the movement expressed itself strongly against Nazism and favorably towards democracy, and began to talk about the need for a *Kirchenkampf*.[20]

Løgstrup and Prenter belonged to two opposite forces within the spectrum of Grundtvigianism. Prenter's view was based on Grundtvig's so-called Church View from 1825. The Church is a sacramental communion, constituted by the inviting words of Christ in Baptism and Eucharist. As a student of Ernst Wolf (1902-1971) in Bonn (a Lutheran member of the Confessing Church), Prenter already in 1934 (aged 27) presented Grundtvig's Church View to a German audience, emphasizing the need to rearticulate the presence of Christ in the sacraments, rather than centering an evangelical theology on the oral preaching of the gospel only.[21] Soon after, in 1936 (aged 29), he was also invited to contribute to the *Festschrift* to Barth. Writing on Grundtvig again, he brought in Grundtvig's broader cultural program by affirming the need to articulate not only "a primary theology" of revelation but also a "secondary theology" concerned with the "temporal well-being" of human society. On the one hand, Prenter hereby challenged Barth, who was always skeptical about the "both-and" theologies of liberal Protestantism.[22] On the other hand, Prenter followed Barth in arguing

---

19   On Koch's engagement in Dansk Ungdomssamvirke, see Tine Reeh, *Kristendom, historie, demokrati: Hal Koch 1932-1945* (Copenhagen: Museum Tusculanums Forlag, 2012), 470-516.

20   See Jacobsen, *Som om intet var hændt*, 129-30 and 212-13, who points out the increasing influence from Barthians in Inner Mission, alongside with the inspiration from *Kirkens Grunn* 1942 in Norway. In contrast to the official view of Inner Mission, quite a few center and right-wing theologians appealed to the need to establish a stronger ecclesial leadership in line with the widely read book from Sweden, *En Bok om Kyrkan*, edited by Gustaf Aulén (Stockholm: Svenska Kyrkans diakonistyrelses bokförlag, 1942). Both Tidehverv and the Grundtvigians were against any such structures; among the Grundtvigians, Prenter was almost alone in supporting the high church views coming from Lutheran Sweden and from Anglican theology.

21   Regin Prenter, "Die sogenannte 'Kirchliche Anschauung' N.F.S. Grundtvigs als Frage die evangelische Theologie von heute," *Evangelische Theologie* 1, no. 7 (1934): 278-88.

22   At his visit to Copenhagen and Aarhus in March 1933, Barth gave his famous lecture on "The first commandment as the axiom of theology," later translated in *The Way of*

that it is on the basis of the primary theology that the secondary task of theology is to be pursued. Accordingly, the church has a two-fold ministry but "the task of 'the enlightenment of life' is based in the incarnation".[23] Prenter had hereby given a space to Grundtvig's cultural program, albeit a subordinate one.

Grundtvig's cultural program from 1832 was expressed in his famous motto from 1837: "Human comes first, and Christian next, for that is life's true order."[24] The motto (*Menneske først, Christen saa*) means that every human being is a "divine experiment of dust and spirit," created in the image and likeness of God (cf. Genesis 1:26-28). Løgstrup's Grundtvigianism is based on this cultural program of 1832 that had guided his own philosophical work since the 1930s. Løgstrup argued that one cannot understand the Christian gospel without presupposing a prior understanding of the world as continuously created by God, and that the gospel is to be of benefit to a true human living.[25] The fact that human experiences are both the beginning and the end of theological work explains why Løgstrup never had the quarrels with humanism that we find in Prenter. Biographically, Løgstrup himself began in the Copenhagen YMCA (and still wrote in its journals until 1934), but he soon left the movement and turned to the Danish version of dialectical theology, *Tidehverv* (established 1926). After 1937, Løgstrup was part of forming what has later been called

---

Theology in Karl Barth: Essays and Comments, ed. H. Martin Rumscheidt (Allison Park, PA: Pickwick Publications, 1986), 63-78. Herein, Barth criticized the both-and theologies of liberal Protestantism up to Bultmann and Emil Brunner (1889-1966).

23 Regin Prenter, "Die Frage nach einer theologischen Grundtvig-interpretation," in *Theologische Ausätze: Karl Barth zum 50. Geburtstag*, ed. Ernst Wolf (München: Chr. Kaiser Verlag, 1936), 507, 510. In his doctoral thesis on Prenter, Ådne Njaa views Prenter's early articles as belonging to his "Barthian-Grundtvigian phase," which I think is an apt characterization, see Ådne Njaa, *"Det ånder himmelsk over støvet": Faser i Regin Prenters grundtvigske pagtsteologi* (Oslo: Unipub, 2007), 142-47. I would argue, however, that Prenter actually challenged the one-sided preaching-theology of dialectical theology in 1934, just as he challenged Karl Barth in his 1936 article. The differences between Prenter and Barth, comes clearer forth in Regin Prenter, "Die Einheit von Schöpfung und Erlösung: Zur Schöpfungslehre Karl Barth," *Theologische Zeitschrift* 2, no. 3 (1946): 161-82. Reprinted in Regin Prenter, *Theologie und Gottesdienst: Gesammelte Aufsätze* (Aarhus:Aros/Göttingen: Vandenhoeck & Ruprecht, 1977), 9-27. Prenter here criticizes the docetic traits in Barth's view of the creation as a mere "analogy" to Christ. This article falls within what Njaa designates as "the Lutheran-Grundtvigian phase" of Prenter's theology, beginning in 1944.

24 On the continuities and differences between Grundtvig's Church View of 1825 and his cultural program after 1832, see Niels Henrik Gregersen, "Church and Culture in Living Interaction: Grundtvig the Theologian," in *Human Comes First: The Christian Theology of N.F.S. Grundtvig*, ed. Edward Broadbridge (Aarhus: Aarhus University Press, 2018), 22-54.

25 On this program, see K. E. Løgstrup, "Die humanen Erfahrungen als Verständnishorizont für das Evangelium," in *Dem Menschen zugute: Christliche Existenz und humane Erfahrung*, ed. K.E. Løgstrup and Ernst Wolf (München: Chr. Kaiser Verlag, 1970), 9-27.

the Tidehverv-Grundtvigian movement.[26] Together with his impulses from Grundtvigianism with its emphasis on the life of the people, Løgstrup followed Bultmann's view that the meaning of the Christian message has to be intelligible and accessible from a human perspective, even though the Christian message also contradicts the false preconception that we are in control of our lives. Connectivity and conflict (*Anknüpfung und Widerspruch*) belong together. In this vein, Løgstrup developed his many micro-phenomenological analyses of interhuman relations. Moreover, Løgstrup also fully endorsed Bultmann's method of historical criticism, here expressing a strong criticism of the theology of Barth, including the Barthian-Grundtvigian position of Prenter.[27] At the same time, Løgstrup followed *Tidehverv's* low-church oriented theology and its cultural criticism, highly critical of pharisaic tendencies in the established church but also critical of the light hearted bourgeois mentality of not taking the demands of the day seriously. To Løgstrup, the role of the philosophy is to explicate the human condition with its heavy demands, while the role of the church is to proclaim the gospel in the awareness that the Christian is a sinner but also shares the same world of creation with people of other faiths, or no faith. At this place, the theologians of *Tidehverv* adopted Nietzsche's appeal of being "faithful to the earth."

Only later, around 1960, Løgstrup took issue with Bultmann's restrictive and anthropocentric view of human existence, and worked out a broader theology of creation based on the interplay between humanity and cosmic aspects of reality. In this phase, Løgstrup and Prenter came closer to one another theologically, and a later generation has seen them as two founding figures of the movement of "Scandinavian creation theology." The third founding figure of Scandinavian creation theology, Wingren at Lund University, was an independent theologian as well, but a mediator who embraced Løgstrup's philosophy of religion and understood the doctrinal work of Prenter. However, the methods of Løgstrup

---

26 Løgstrup himself wrote the entry on "Tidehverv" in *Religion in Geschichte und Gegenwart*[3], of which he was a co-editor. On its development, he wrote: "Anfangs stützte man sich kurze Zeit auf die Theologie von Karl Barth, entdeckte aber bald, dass hier eine Mesalliance vorlieg. Bleibend wichtig würde für [Tidehverv] die theologische Arbeit R. Bultmanns." Løgstrup also states that the Kierkegaardian orientation after World War II did not redeem the promise of a Grundtvigian theology concerned with contemporary culture. See *RGG*[3], vol. 6 (Tübingen: Mohr-Siebeck, 1962), 885-86. In 1964, Løgstrup left *Tidehverv* because of fundamental disagreement.
27 K.E. Løgstrup, *Prædikenen og dens Tekst* [The Sermon and its Text], ed. Niels Henrik Gregersen and Jan Nilsson (Copenhagen: Gyldendal, 1999), accusing Barthian theology of subscribing to a theophany Christology that transforms Christianity into a mystery religion. Rather, we need to understand the reign of God that Jesus preached, and that he himself realized, in and through our own humanity.

and Prenter remained vastly different, they hardly socialized and did not work on common projects, as Løgstrup did with Wingren.[28]

Compared with Prenter, Løgstrup did not spend much time reading Grundtvig himself (his personal copy of Grundtvig's works is mostly unread). Rather, the young Løgstrup studied intensely the central works of Martin Luther (1483-1546), especially his social ethics, together with the works of Søren Kierkegaard (1813-1855). In his early years he was likewise inspired by Friedrich Gogarten's (1887-1967) *Politische Ethik* from 1932 in combination with personalism and the I-Thou philosophy of Martin Buber (1878-1965).[29] Løgstrup's main philosophical inspirations, however, came from the phenomenologists Hans Lipps (1889-1941) (Løgstrup's teacher in Göttingen, 1932-1933) and Martin Heidegger (1889-1976) (Løgtrup's teacher in Freiburg, 1933-1934).

While Prenter brought with him the Confessing Church credentials when entering the World War II discussions on church, state, and law, some of Løgstrup's theological and philosophical inspirations were, as a matter of fact, coming from intellectual circles with affinity to Nazism. Gogarten spoke in favor of the German Christians for a short period from 1933-1934 (though discovering his mistake already in 1934), but Heidegger was a famous member of the Nazi party in the mid-1930s, and Løgstrup was fully aware of this problematic fact.[30] Against this background, it is a historical irony that Løgstrup persistently expressed anti-establishment ideas during the war and always understood Christian faith as fully aligned with humanism, whereas Prenter, at least in 1937, could express a criticism of democracy as a self-absolutizing humanity putting itself in the place of God.

---

28   Niels Henrik Gregersen, Bengt Kristensson Uggla, and Trygve Wyller, eds., *Reformation Theology for a Post-Secular Age: Løgstrup, Prenter, Wingren, and the Future of Scandinavian Creation Theology* (Göttingen: Vandenhoeck & Ruprecht, 2017).
29   Kees van Kooten Niekerk, "Vejen til den etiske fordring," in *Livtag med den etiske fordring*, ed. David Bugge and Peter Aaboe Sørensen (Aarhus: Klim, 2007), 39-41, has pointed to no less than six excerpts of Gogarten's *Politische Ethik* in Løgstrup's archives (altogether more than 100 pages). On the relation between Gogarten and Løgstrup, see Svein Aage Christoffersen, "Friedrich Gogartens 'Politische Ethik' og Knud E. Løgstrups 'Den etiske fordring'—en systematisk analyse," *Norsk Teologisk Tidsskrift* 83, no. 3 (1982): 203-17. Christoffersen shows how Gogarten and Løgstrup shared an interest in developing a social ethics based on creation theology, both being critics of idealism and individualism. As Christoffersen also points out, however, Gogarten argues from revelation and faith, whereas Løgstrup argues for a philosophical interpretation of creation theology. To this can be added that Løgstrup, unlike Gogarten, shows no interest in arguing for a strong state.
30   See K.E. Løgstrup, "Nazismens filosof," *Dagens Nyheder*, April 14, 1936. Whether Løgstrup also knew that Lipps later enrolled as medical officer in the SS (and died in a battle in 1941) is uncertain.

Løgstrup on the "Orders of Creation" 1934-1939: Between Barth and Heidegger

Løgstrup began as a phenomenologist in the tradition of Edmund Husserl (1859-1938) and Heidegger, aiming to overcome the Kantian split between the human observer and the observed world, a split that he saw returning in Husserl's conception of the transcendental Ego but helpfully overcome by Heidegger in his *Sein und Zeit* from 1927.[31] Indeed, for Løgstrup the social conception of human existence is part of his theological project from the beginning.

Applying for a position at Copenhagen University in 1934, Løgstrup had to present three lectures, one of which reflected on whether a Christian ethics can acknowledge the autonomy (*Eigengesetzlichkeit*) of social life. Løgstrup answered in the positive, arguing that "the Christian ethics does acknowledge the autonomous laws of society, because it is the immanent law in God's orders of creation." Løgstrup, however, does not relate the idea of orders of creation to anything like an absolute obedience towards the state. Rather, he refers to social life as "one stream", in which we find the basic forms of human conviviality— "marriage, work-life, people, state, and culture"—while adding that it is always a human responsibility to shape the orders of creation, for example, for or against monogamy or polygamy. Yet the orders of creation give evidence that "a human being does always already rely on others."[32] These two arguments, (1) the interdependence of human existence and (2) the need to take responsibility for a moral shape of the shared life conditions, reappear in Løgstrup's main work in ethics, *The Ethical Demand* from 1956.

In the era of Nazism, however, the concept of the "orders of creation" had become associated with a Lutheran obedience culture and with the idea of a strong state. When Barth visited Denmark in 1939, Løgstrup gave a lecture in German, in which he incidentally used the term *Schöpfungsordning*. According to Prenter's *Memories*, Barth reacted with rage, assuming a German *Blut and Boden* ideology in Løgstrup. Prenter writes that Løgstrup himself was utterly surprised, and that Prenter had to take Barth aside and calm him down, trying to explain him that no such meaning was associated with the term as used by

---

31 This was the main argument in Løgstrup's first doctoral proposal (rejected), which carried the title *Det religiøse Motiv i den erkendelsesteoretiske Problemstilling* (unpublished manuscript, 1933).
32 K.E. Løgstrup, "Kan den kristne Etik anerkende Tanken om Samfundslivets egen Lovmæssighed?", (unpublished manuscript, 1934), 2, 6, 10 and 16-17. See also van Kooten Niekerk, "Vejen til *Den etiske fordring*," 12-13.

Løgstrup.³³ Perhaps because of this incidence, Løgstrup later refrained from using the term of the "orders of creation." Instead, he used the more dynamical and ethical concept of "laws of life" (*Livslove*) during World War II.

Otherwise, Løgstrup was well informed about the German situation, having studied in Freiburg with Heidegger. Løgstrup agreed with Heidegger's emphasis on the engaged decision and on criticizing the attitude of the indifferent observer (*das Man*). Much like Bultmann, he used his existential analysis for theological purposes, too. Yet Løgstrup also knew that Heidegger had put himself in the service of Nazism as rector of the University in Freiburg. Having married his half-Jewish wife Rosemarie (born Pauly) in 1935, and returning to Denmark in 1936 to become a pastor on Funen, Løgstrup wrote a long newspaper essay on Heidegger entitled "The philosopher of Nazism," followed by two other essays on the German distinction between a *Führer* (who wishes to define a people) and a dictator (who uses sheer power). In these latter essays, Løgstrup was fully aware of the watershed that divided the top-down view of society in the idea of a *Führer* and the model of democracy.³⁴ Yet he was also critical of the pragmatist laid-back attitude of letting things happen as swiftly as possible without taking a personal moral stance.

The Illness of Anti-Judaism and the Role of Law

After the occupation, Løgstrup appeared with a moral voice going beyond his phenomenological method, taking strong positions against the view that Danish society should merely carry on as if nothing had happened. In the Christmas

---

33 Prenter, *Erindringer,* 102-3. When asked by the Danish pastors what Denmark should do in the given situation (1939), Barth replied, "Beten—Kanonen kaufen" ("Pray—and buy cannons"), Prenter, *Erindringer,* 104. Denmark did not do so out of fear of German revenge for the northern part of Schleswig having been voted back to Denmark in 1920.

34 K.E. Løgstrup, "Nazismens Filosof," *Dagens Nyheder,* April 14, 1936, and "Førerskab og Diktatur I–II," *Dagens Nyheder,* June 24-25, 1936. As always, Løgstrup gives a congenial interpretation of the views under investigation, before indicating his own view. As a phenomenologist, Løgstrup refrains from issuing moral statements before explicating the positions that he is elucidating (so also in his books on Immanuel Kant, with whom he disagreed). This phenomenological method has recently caused consternation by contemporary readers. Oluffa Pedersen, *Fremkaldte kulturrum,* 263-64, even argues that Løgstrup in 1936 was "fascinated" by Heidegger's Nazism. However, there is no such fascination expressed in Løgstrup's essay on Heidegger as the philosopher of Nazism, he simply indicates his disagreement without spelling it out. In "Førerskab og diktatur," by contrast, he issues a clear criticism of the political idea of a *Führer* in light of democracy, without involving himself in further discussions on democracy.

issue of a church letter from December 1941, Løgstrup wrote the article "What is hatred of Jews?" Here, Løgstrup sees anti-Semitism partly as a result of a scapegoating mechanism, which only reveals that "one is not able to solve one's own problems," partly as a result of a "modern version of the Medieval belief in the devil." The hatred against Jews is like a psychosis that "lies in the air as a contamination." It is rare to see Løgstrup involving himself in psychological explanations, but his principal view of the legal and moral situation of the Danish people is expressed as follows: "The Danish people should, based on its Enlightenment (*Oplysning*) and legal awareness (*Retsbevidsthed*) be inoculated against the sickness of the hatred to the Jews... Shame be on us if we allow ourselves to be contaminated by the contaminators, who due to the unfortunate situation are currently making a noise."[35] Naturally, the article evoked strong reactions from the editor of the Nazi newspaper *Kamptegnet*, who wrote threatening letters. Indeed, Løgstrup expressed himself on the brink of what was allowed under censorship, but he did not mention Germany or Nazism by name.

Løgstrup's views on anti-Semitism were shared by the vast majority of Danish theologians, if not by all, and Koch was probably the single most effective communicator among the theologians. In *Lederbladet* (the journal of *Dansk Ungdomssamvirke*) on January 7, 1942, he pointed out that there was no basis for a continuation of the cultural work of the organization, if the German promises of April 9 were trampled down. The urgency of the matter concerns "the truth and lawfulness (*Ret*) in relation to the Jews" but also "the lawfulness and the freedom of the life of the Danish people".[36]

1940-45: Løgstrup's "Laws of Life" and the Letter Exchange with Koch

Against this background, it is interesting to follow the heated exchange of letters between the two friends, Koch and Løgstrup.[37] Koch represented the cultural resistance (under censorship), while Løgstrup's work was mostly legal (under

---

35   K.E. Løgstrup, "Hvad er Jødehad?," *Kirkeblad for Sandager-Holevad,* no. 10 (1941), also printed in at least five other church letters. Here cited from Sofie Lene Bak, *Dansk antisemitisme 1930-1945* (Copenhagen: Ascheoug, 2004), 377-78, who also refers to the strong reactions from Nazi circles to Løgstrup's article.
36   Bak, *Dansk antisemitisme 1930-1945*, 375-76, who shows that that the content of Koch's article was published in no less than eight Danish newspapers.
37   Henrik S. Nissen, ed., *Kære Hal, Kære Koste: Breve 1940-43 mellem K.E. Løgstrup og Hal Koch* (Copenhagen: Gyldendal, 1992). Løgstrup was called "Koste" ("Broomy") because of his hair.

censorship) but also involved illegal activities in the Danish resistance movement. The exchange between Løgstrup and Koch falls into four different phases of the Danish politics during the occupation:

(1) The Danish surrender on April 9, 1940, marks the beginning of the first phase. Neither Koch nor Løgstrup saw alternatives to the Danish surrender, given the very limited military resources in Denmark, and both saw the Danish surrender "under protest" as a humiliation of the Danish people.

(2) A new phase began with the German demand to incarcerate Danish communists in June 1941 (followed by the official Danish subscription to the Anti-Comintern Pact in November 1941, also required by Germany); it was followed by the downfall of the collaborative government (*Samlingsregeringen*) on November 9, 1942, after which the former minister of foreign affairs, Erik Scavenius (*Radikale Venstre*), was named prime minister, as explicitly required by Germany. The phase ended when the Danish government resigned on August 29, 1943, after general strikes. The official Danish appeasement politics between 1941 and 1943 was the divisive issue between Løgstrup and Koch. Løgstrup made public his critique of Koch in his booklet *The Life of the People and Foreign Politics* from 1943, written before the resignation of the Danish government.

(3) The third phase goes from the resignation of the Danish government August 29, 1943, to the liberation on May 5, 1945. In this period, governmental issues were regulated among jurists, mainly between the departmental chief in the Danish governance system Niels Svenningsen and the SS-Officer Dr. Jur. Werner Best. In this period, we see a rapprochement between the two friends—Løgstrup feeling somewhat uneasy about having targeted Koch publicly while insisting that "friendship is not an association of mutual admiration," Koch declaring that he and Løgstrup were "in agreement on basic matters".[38] Koch was imprisoned between August and November 1943, and barely survived an attempted clearing murder in 1944. For the German authorities, the national role of Koch constituted the bigger danger, whereas Løgstrup was just one of many pastors speaking up against the Danish politics of compliance.

(4) After the liberation on May 5, 1945, a new round of discussions began regarding the nature of the transitional justice of the armed collaborators with Germany, followed by Koch's famous book, *What is Democracy?*, from 1945.

The main bulk of the letters relate to phase (2), that is, the time between June 1941 and August 1943. Løgstrup chastizes the Danish government for signing the Anti-Ckomintern Pact. In Løgstrup's view, Koch and *Dansk Ungdoms-*

---

38 See Nissen ed., *Kære Hal, Kære Koste*, 111-14 (Letter from Løgstrup to Koch of August 9, 1943, and from Koch to Løgstrup of August 12, 1943).

samvirke were wrong in supporting an official Danish politics of appeasement that allowed Danes to pursue a relatively comfortable life in wartime. As he argued, this is neither statesmanship nor genuine democracy: "Democracy—especially now—is not about concerning oneself with the backwards, cowardly, comfortable part of the people, those who want nothing but money and being comfortable ..."[39] In the same letter Løgstrup presupposes that the majority of the Danish population did indeed retain a will to resistance. Most people have an instinctual sense of honor and shame, which impels them to act according to the "laws of life" (*Livslovene*). Løgstrup accuses Koch of being a weak and ever accommodating ethical relativist, even an "unbeliever" (*vantro*), who thinks that he can estimate the positive consequences of giving in to the endless German requirements. Against the consequential argumentation of Koch, Løgstrup refers to the absoluteness of the laws of life: "it is all about being obedient to the Laws of Danish life, and take the consequences of our obedience to the absoluteness of our life."[40]

We may interpret the reference to "absoluteness" in Løgstrup's view as having three interdependent claims. (1) The moral *evidence* of the laws of life (epistemological level). (2) The *existence* of immanent laws of creation prior to, and independent of, our acknowledgement of them (ontological level). (3) The absoluteness of God the creator as the *source* of the laws of life (theological level). In the years after 1941, Løgstrup argues that Denmark should follow Norway and the Netherlands, no matter the consequences, and leave it up to God to take care of the consequences, such as deportations.

In his comparatively calm response, Koch argues that Løgstrup has not at all understood the consequences of the Danish surrender of April 9. Moreover, there is in the sphere of the political realms no such thing as absoluteness: "Stay away from me with all your crap about absoluteness and Danish politics. This does not concern the absolute. It is only about one thing; building up the [cultural] strengths (*Kræfter*), which perhaps are still there, to enable us to fight in the future. And that fight begins the day when we encounter a victorious Germany."[41] In 1941, Koch seems to have anticipated the possibility of Germany winning the war.

In 1943, the debate between Koch and Løgstrup became a public affair, when Løgstrup published *The Life of the People and Foreign Politics* (prefaced June 28 1943), targeting an article by Koch from May 1943 entitled 'The Office of States-

---

39 Letter to Hal Koch of December 1, 1941, *Kære Hal, Kære Koste*, 44.
40 Letter to Hal Koch of December 6, 1941, *Kære Hal, Kære Koste*, 56.
41 Letter to Løgstrup of December 14, 1941, *Kære Hal, Kære Koste*, 60-61.

men—and Ours'. Here, Koch seems to have reapplied the Lutheran doctrine of the two regiments on the new situation, making a distinction between the role of the Danish government as a secular, diplomatic, cunning, and anything but absolutist affair, whereas the task of *Dansk Ungdomssamvirke* is to tell the truth and stick to the cause of law and justice. The task of the government and the administration is to "clear the peas" (*klare ærterne*), that is, to work things out in a swift manner, to the best of their capacity and judgment in the given situation. Koch gives a long leash to this office:

> Sometimes it [the government] must use measures that violate the law (*Retten*), sometimes it must make interventions that despise freedom, sometimes it must make pronouncements that are not in harmony with truth. It is the task of this office—within the framework of the parliament—to find ways out (*Udveje*), not to find the truth. But for us [in *Ungdomssamvirke*] the obligation is to make sure that the cause of truth and law is not silenced.[42]

Løgstrup's booklet begins in phenomenology before he launches his attack on Koch. Interpreted in terms of Lutheran theology, Løgstrup uses inspiration from the doctrine of the three estates by arguing that we do not only live in the civil estate (*politia*) and in the spiritual estate of the church (*ecclesia*), but beneath the worldly government and the office of the church, we also live in the sphere of everyday human life (*oeconomia*). What Løgstrup calls the "life of the people" belongs to this latter category, referring to the needs of the hour in the occupied Danish nation.

Løgstrup starts out with the problem of loneliness (*Ensomhed*), and he argues that becoming a member of the mass is a misguided solution (cf. Heidegger's term of *Das Man*). Rather, a first part of the solution is to understand that "our life is bigger than our ego". We have not created life; it is there prior to me and my enterprises—life is a gift given to us prior to ourselves. A second part of the solution is to understand that there are "laws of life" that constitute our living together. We should trust one another, and we should honor and respect one another. Løgstrup mentions two examples: (1) "It is a law for our life as parents that we should raise our children to obedience"—otherwise the living relation between the giving and taking between parents and children will be damaged, to the detriment of both children and parents. Similarly, (2) "The law for one another as employee and employer is justice and fairness (*Retfærdighed*)"—oth-

---

[42] Hal Koch, "Statsmændendes Embede—og vort," *Lederbladet* no. 5, May 1943, reprinted in *Kære Hal, kære Koste*, 95-99, citations at 98-99.

erwise the relation between employer and employee is dead and mechanical, so that the employee becomes a wage slave (*Lønslave*).[43] We are always part of structured, social relations.

It is worth noting that Løgstrup—neither in his 1943 book nor in his earlier 1934 lecture—views the obedience to the power as part of the "laws of life." The reason, in my interpretation, is that Løgstrup is not primarily interested in *politia* but in *oeconomia*, that is, in the *pre-political* basis for state governance and legislation. Everyday life is the realm in which the basic ethical phenomena live and thrive, unless they are violated. Løgstrup uses the parallel between the laws of life and being part of a game:

> It is with life as it is with a game. Every game has its rules, and the game consists in following them. The rules are even the essence of the game. If you break them, the game breaks down and becomes cheating.[44]

Moreover, while a defeat in a game is honorable, cheating is dishonorable, and this brings Løgstrup to the problem that he is after: Are the spokespersons for the Danish people like cheaters who do what they do in the hope of not being caught cheating? Løgstrup admits, however, that the game of foreign politics (cf. *politia*) is different from the laws of life (cf. *oeconomia*), insofar as politics has to be to be pursued cynically, without sentimentality and without being naïve, "unless one wants to commit suicide." There is indeed a difference between foreign politics vis-à-vis Germany (that is, a politics without trust) and the everyday life of the people (a life in trust in one another). Yet there is also a mutual interpenetration (*Vekselvirkning*) between the two. Accordingly, the tactics of foreign politics has a limit since it must be pursued "for the sake of the life of the people—and only that!"[45]

In this context, Løgstrup uses the catchword *Vekselvirkning*, which plays a central role in Grundtvig's view of the mutual and critical relation between church and culture. Hereby, Løgstrup shows that Koch's separation of the two offices—that of the politician and that of the inner cultural resistance—is much too simple. Any such neat distinction between the two offices is utterly unrealistic and misses the point of politics, which is to stand in the service of the trusting relations within the life of the people. "The art of statesmanship is

---

43 Løgstrup, *Folkeliv og Udenrigspolitik* (Copenhagen: Tidehvervs Forlag, 1943), 10. Reprinted in *Kære Hal, kære Koste*, 146-72, at 148-49.
44 Løgstrup, *Folkeliv og Udenrigspolitik*, 14; *Kære Hal, kære Koste*, 151.
45 Løgstrup, *Folkeliv og Udenrigspolitik*, 15-17; *Kære Hal, kære Koste*, 152-53.

not only to find ways out but also to know the boundary set for the political solutions."[46]

This principal view led Løgstrup to pursue a public criticism of Koch in the second half of the booklet. "One is not allowed to make a neat principle and seemingly clear distinction between offices, tasks, and responsibility out of one's own indecisiveness."[47] According to Løgstrup, it is insufficient to speak eloquently about truth and law in public lectures in a situation where "the inviolability of the home and the independence of the courts" are not respected by the German authorities.[48]

During 1944, Løgstrup and Koch did not really reach out to one another, but after the liberation on May 5, 1945, they were able to reconcile. In Løgstrup's contribution to the *Tidehverv*-book *The Necessity of Settling a Justice* (*Opgørets Nødvendighed*) from the summer of 1945, he took issue—like Koch did two years later—with transitional justice in more demanding ways. Løgstrup here points to three phases of the Danish occupation, as laid out above.[49] The military occupation on April 9, 1940, was so overwhelming that only a cultural resistance was possible in the first phase.[50] However, as soon as the Danish government, as a further concession to the German occupying power, agreed to cut the diplomatic ties to Russia and sign the Anti-Comintern Pact of March 26, 1941, while allowing the Danish police to incarcerate communists, Denmark eventually went into the war on the German side, which is inexcusable. Only when the government finally resigned on August 29, 1943, did Denmark break with Germany and place itself on the side of the Allied. To Løgstrup, the Danish politicians were nonetheless dishonest when after the liberation they placed themselves on par with the resistance movement.[51] The idea of a unified Danish people during the occupation is a self-delusion to be controverted.

In his 1943 book, Løgstrup had pointed to the principal ethical right of a resistance against a government not exercising law in respect for people, leaving the fateful consequences over to God. Now, in 1945, he is concerned about the attribution of guilt to human parties—the German authorities as well as the Danish collaboration. All the same, he continues to refer to a necessary

---

46 Løgstrup, *Folkeliv og Udenrigspolitik*, 23; *Kære Hal, kære Koste*, 157.
47 Løgstrup, *Folkeliv og Udenrigspolitik*, 27; *Kære Hal, kære Koste*, 160.
48 Løgstrup, *Folkeliv og Udenrigspolitik*, 20-21; *Kære Hal, kære Koste*, 155.
49 Løgstrup, "Opgør eller Selvbedrag [Controversy or Self-delusion]," in *Opgørets Nødvendighed*, ed. Vilhelm Krarup, K.E. Løgstrup, and H. Østergaard-Nielsen (Copenhagen: Tidehvervs Forlag, 1945), 30-48.
50 Løgstrup, "Opgør eller Selvbedrag," 31.
51 Løgstrup, "Opgør eller Selvbedrag," 24 and 41.

obedience towards the laws of human life since such "basic laws" (*Grundlove*) are not created by human beings but given by the creator.[52] In 1945, however, Løgstrup no longer relegates the question of the consequences of our actions to divine care. Rather, German authorities carry the guilt, and only if the German people admits its guilt and understands that Nazism constituted a break with the idea of a state ruled by law (*Retsstat*) will there be a future for Germany in Europe. During the occupation, it was necessary to hate (*hade*) the Germans, since Germany wished to eliminate Denmark. After 1945, however, it is no longer appropriate to hate the Germans, who are now impoverished, nor is it correct for Danes to exult and despise the Germans, who now need our material help. The Germans should not be pitied either, however, for they urgently need enlightenment to combat the delusions of Nazism. Their "inner Nazism" needs to be controverted in order to bring back the sense not only of Germany belonging squarely within the shared European culture, but also of the role of the state as protector of legal institutions and cultures. "Neither hate nor pity is the solution, but enlightenment (*Oplysning*) and settlement of scores (*Opgør*)."[53] Likewise, the Danish politicians should at least concede their complicity in iniquity during their politics of appeasement up to the resignation of the Danish government in August 1943. The comfortable idea that there was an implicit agreement between the Danish government and the resistance movement is a falsification of history (*Historieforfalskning*). Among Danes, too, "a ruthless self-criticism is required for the sake of honesty".[54]

Prenter's Views on the Status of the State and its Laws

While Løgstrup's philosophical approach to ethics and law focused on the pre-political aspects of law, Prenter took a stronger interest in the institutions

---

52 Løgstrup, "Opgør eller Selvbedrag," 56-57. While Løgstrup refers to the pre-political laws of life as *Grundlove* ("basic laws"), he does not conceive of the Danish Constitution of 1849 (*Grundloven*) as given by divine law. Put in classic Lutheran terms, political legislation (*politia*) is a secular affair, though it must stand in the service of communal life (*oeconomia*).
53 Løgstrup, "Opgør eller Selvbedrag," 17-30, on 26.
54 Løgstrup, "Opgør eller Selvbedrag," 45-55, on 46. Løgstrup even highlights the much despised Scavenius for standing up, at least for his dispositions as prime minister during 1942-1943, on 47. The same criticism was levelled at the politicians from *Tidehverv*, and very directly by pastor Thorkild Glahn at the official service opening the parliament in 1945, leading to many reactions, see Martin Schwarz Lausten, *Politikere og prædikanter* [Politicians and Preachers] (Copenhagen: Anis, 2014), 187-96.

of society: the church and the state. In his early Barthian-Grundtvigian phase, however, Prenter was critical of the idea of state and law as autonomous spheres of society (unlike Løgstrup), and unlike Løgstrup he was critical of anything smacking of humanism. This comes to the fore in his early booklet from 1937, *Christianity and Culture*, in which he argued that the modern democratic state makes the citizens the superiors of the government, while making the government a subordinate under the democratic voters. From a contemporary perspective, it is shocking to read the following quotation from 1937 that shows how the young Prenter shared the anti-democratic sentiments of the political party *Dansk Samling*:

> This is the modern democratic state, one of the clearest examples of the modern will of culture. There is no room for a responsibility towards God, since the political forms of the modern world are decided by the majority vote. This is humanism in its purest cultural form (*Humanisme i Renkultur*), humanity placing itself on God's throne.[55]

During and after World War II, Prenter became a convinced democrat, as evidenced in his book, *Protestantism in Our Time*, in which he declares: "At a time, when totalitarian and democratic systems around the world duel to the death, Protestant Christianity can *only* support democracy."[56] Prenter, however, retains a sense that the system of democracy must be part of a bigger package. Any political system needs to cultivate "a reasoned judgment" (*sagligt skøn*) against a pure politics of power.[57] Prenter's view of the state remains guided by the concept that any state needs to know its own boundaries in order not to absolutize itself. Likewise, Protestantism can and should endorse secularization and a genuine worldliness of society, but not a self-absolutizing secularism that either erects "a heathen-theocratic" system or slides into a "pseudo-scientific" culture.[58] In an article on "The Church and the State" from 1941, Prenter makes a similar argument, while also distancing himself from the idea of a Christian theocracy. The self-limitation of the state is expressed in being ruled by law and giving room to the independent voice of the church:

---

55 Prenter, *Kristendom og Kultur* (Ringkøbing: De Unges Forlag, 1937), 18.
56 Prenter, *Protestantismen i vor tid* (Copenhagen: Hirschsprungs Forlag, 1957), 78. Italics in original.
57 Prenter, *Protestantismen i vor tid*, 78.
58 Prenter, *Protestantismen i vor tid*, 80-81. Prenter certainly had in mind his experiences with Nazism, and probably contemporary ideas of a socio-technocratic concept of rule (e.g., Alva and Gunnar Myrdal in Sweden).

> Hereby narrow limits of the state are set. The state *cannot* and *should* not testify for or against the truth. It should neither be a church state (*Kirkestat*) nor an anti-church bully state (*Tyranstat*). It should be a state ruled by law (*Retsstat*), which makes room for the church.[59]

A secular state, ruled by law and knowing its own boundaries, is Prenter's view of a good state. This ideal is typical of Prenter but is in no way special to him. We have seen how Løgstrup, too, emphasized the awareness of the boundaries of politics and the importance of law, but Løgstrup had nothing to say about the institutions of church and state. Prenter, by contrast, had much to say about the church, and something about the legal institutions, too.

German, Norwegian, and Danish Inspirations Behind "The Church and the Law", 1944

Coming with his experiences from the Confessing Church during his studies in Germany 1933-1935, Prenter was familiar with the Barmen Declaration of May 29-31, 1934. Drafted mainly by Prenter's teacher Barth, this Protestant confession spoke about the proper relation between church and state. In its Article 5, a version of the doctrine of the two regiments is affirmed on the basis of 1 Peter 2:17: "Fear God. Honor the emperor." The Barmen declaration sees the state as "a divine arrangement (*Anordnung*)" which Christians should see as a good institution "in thanks and reverence towards God." Its primary task is to be a provider of justice and peace (*Recht and Frieden*). This positive task, however, is overstepped if a government absolutizes itself, and even demands that the church itself should become an institution within the state and an instrument for the purposes of a state too. Article 5 therefore ends with two rejections:

> We reject the false doctrine, as though the State, over and beyond its special commission, should and could become the single and totalitarian order of human life, thus fulfilling the Church's vocation as well. We reject the false doctrine, as though the Church, over and beyond its special commission, should and could appropriate the characteristics, the tasks, and the dignity of the State, thus itself becoming an organ of the State.[60]

---

59 Prenter, "Kirken og Staten," in *Ordets Herredømme* (Copenhagen: Det tredje Standpunkts Forlag, 1941), 115. Italics in original. Prenter does not reflect on the state giving room to religious groups other than the church, but the same argument could well be made since the state does not harbor the truth.

60 The English translation of the Barmen Declaration is from Arthur C. Cochrane, ed., *The Church's Confession Under Hitler* (Philadelphia, PA: Westminster Press, 1962), 237-42.

The Barmen Declaration was occasioned by the Arian Paragraph proposed by the German Christians already in September 1933 to the effect that no Jew should be allowed to hold an office in the German Church. Against this background, it is telling that the Barmen Declaration does not address the Jewish question. The declaration was meant to clarify the status of the evangelical churches and protect them from external intrusion by the Nazified German Christians, but the declaration did not utter a critique against the Nazi politics on the Jews.

Something similar applies to the important Norwegian confession, *The Foundation of the Church*. In October 1940, Norwegian churches, across the divide between state church and free churches, formed the *Christian Consultative Council* (*Kristent Samråd*). The document itself was drafted by Berggrav, a young pastor (Olav Valen Sendstad) and a layperson (Kristian Hanson), and it was read aloud in all Norwegian Churches on Easter Day 1942 when all seven bishops and 797 of the 858 Norwegian pastors resigned from their positions within the state church due to the Quisling regime.[61]

In its first two articles, the document appears to be a standard tract on the nature of the Lutheran Church as based on scripture (Article 1) and on the ordination within the believing community (Article 2), adding a clear emphasis on the independence of the church from earthly powers and principalities. What is more characteristic is Article 3 on the body of the church, which states that the Church comprises "not only servants of the Word—laypeople and theologically trained—but everyone who in his [or her] calling works in accordance with God's will." A special emphasis is put on the Christian school, the Christian home and the social work of church members and organizations. This comprehensive view of the "holy connectedness" (*hellige samhørighed*) within the Church is followed up in Article 4: "On the rights and duties of parents and Church in the education of children." The role of Christian parents (an element of the *oeconomia*) was highlighted in order to counteract the compulsion to enroll all children as youth members of the Norwegian Nazi party. "By baptism the Church has received the approval of the parents to follow the obligation [of an education of their children into the Christian faith]." Without using the term, the education of children, based on baptism, is seen as a *status confessionis*, a question of the essence of the church: one cannot be both a Christian and a Nazi. Articles 5 and 6 relate to the worldly authorities. While the doctrine of

---

61 On the historical background, see Hassing, *Church Resistance to Nazism in Norway, 1940-1945*, 158-60. On the theology of the confession, see Thorleiv Austad, *Kirkens Grunn: Analyse av en kirkelig bekendelse fra okkupasjonstiden 1940-45* (Oslo: Luther Forlag, 1974).

the two regiments is affirmed, the distinction between the two regiments is so much more underlined. Citing Luther, Article 5 states that "the worldly regiment shall not rule over the conscience," and that Christians owe no obedience to a worldly regiment that attempts to do so.[62] This is followed up in Article 6, "On the State Church," which clarifies that the "order of the State Church has only come into being, because the State has declared that it will serve the cause of the Church and guard the Christian faith." In its conclusion, the document states with a remarkable amount of self-confidence: "The Evangelical Lutheran Church is today, as it was in the generations before us, our spiritual homeland in Norway."

The *Foundation of the Church* was issued in a situation in which Quisling's Norwegian Nazi regime infringed the essence of the church, including the upbringing of children into the Christian faith. This is similar to the background of the Barmen Declaration. The difference is that the Norwegian Church spoke on behalf of the majority of the Norwegian people, which was not the case in Germany where the Confessional Church constituted a minority. Both declarations, however, concerned the internal independence of the church, without challenging the general Nazi politics against people outside the church, in particular the Jews.

In Denmark, by contrast, the government was still in charge until August 1943 and had managed to protect the Danish Jews. Soon after the resignation of the Danish government on August 29, 1943, German authorities promulgated new laws against Jews, leading to the intended nationwide arrest and deportation of all Jews in Denmark on October 1-2, 1943.[63] The *Pastoral Letter by the Danish Bishops of September 29* was issued in this situation, to be read aloud in all Danish churches on Sunday, October 3.[64] This pastoral letter was not concerned with the inner affairs of the church but addressed the Danish public (and indirectly the

---

62 With reference to Martin Luther, *Weimarer Ausgabe* (WA) 12, 334.
63 Out of the c. 7000 Danish Jews, only 474 were transported to Theresienstadt after September-October 1943, and less than 100 died during the German occupation. By comparison, about 40 % of the c. 1800 Norwegian Jews died, and about 75 % of the Dutch Jews, numbers in Lidegaard, *Kampen om Danmark,* 406. Secretly, a leading German representative warned the Danish authorities about the upcoming arrest of the Jews, which is part of the explanation behind the successful flight of most Danish Jews to Sweden.
64 On the hectic background of this letter, see Jacobsen, *Som om intet var hændt*, 147-53, text at 264-65. The Copenhagen bishop had commissioned two Copenhagen pastors (Thorkild Glahn and N.J. Rald from the *Unofficial Pastors Organization*) to write a draft, received September 15, 1943; Fuglsang-Damgaard strongly urged his bishop colleagues to support the text collectively, and do it quickly, due to the urgency of the situation of the Jews. However, the Pastoral Letter was received and carried forward in different forms by the bishops. For example, some omitted the reference to "The Position of the Church on

German occupying power via the Church Department) with respect to the situation of the Jews. The letter begins as follows: "The position of the Danish Church to the Jewish question. Wherever a persecution of Jews is initiated for reasons of race or religion, it is the duty of the Christian Church to protest". Referring to Galathians 3:28 ("here is no Jew and no Greek"), it is emphasized that every human life is precious and God makes no distinction between persons. In the third and final paragraph, we find the reference to the "sense of law" (*Retsbevidsthed*), which has "grown in the Christian culture through the centuries." The Pastoral Letter even refers to the Constitutional Law of 1849 with its emphasis on "the equal right and responsibility for the law."[65] Herein is mentioned also the full civil rights of Danish citizens, regardless of faith,

> so that race and religion can never in itself lead to the infringement of right, freedom, and possessions. Despite differing religious views we will fight for (*kæmpe for*) our Jewish brothers and sisters maintaining the same freedom that we cherish higher than life.

The Pastoral Letter thus refers to the secular law of the land in its expressions of being fully on the side of the Jewish co-citizens of Denmark, addressed as "brothers and sisters."

Also later, in February 1944, the bishops (after many negotiations) issued a new pastoral letter occasioned by the clearing murders of several Danes, including the famous playwright, pastor Kaj Munk (1898-1944).[66] The bishops did not want to single out Munk in particular, but broadened the perspective to fundamental issues of law: "we condemn the fact that principles of law, which Christianity has anchored in the Danish people, are sidelined and transgressed."[67] Here, as also in the previous pastoral letter, one notices the view that the "secular law" of the land is perceived as rooted in a deeper Christian culture.

---

the Jewish Question," in order to maintain that the church can only speak unanimously regarding the gospel. In substance, however, agreement was maintained on the basic text.

65 On the freedom clause in the Danish Constitution of 1849, see Lisbet Christoffersen and Niels Henrik Gregersen, "Shaping the Danish People's Church in the Context of Freedom of Religion: A.S. Ørsted (1778-1860) and N.F.S. Grundtvig (1783-1872)," in *Law and the Christian Tradition in Scandinavia: The Writings of Great Nordic Jurists*, ed. Kjell Å. Modéer and Helle Vogt (London: Routledge, 2020, 206-41).

66 Munk was among the harshest and most direct critics of the German occupying power, he was assassinated by Gestapo on January 4, 1944. Celebrated nationwide for his authorship, including his poems and plays at the Royal Theatre, Danes were in uproar about his assassination. His undialectical understanding of the imitation of Christ, however, was criticized by *Tidehverv* and leading Grundtvigians for seeking martyrdom.

67 Text in Jacobsen, *Som om intet var hændt*, 283-84.

We have at least one reaction from the *Reichsbevollmächtige* in Denmark, Best, showing a German perception of this Pastoral Letter. Best was under pressure from Berlin to adopt a stricter approach to the Danish church. In his response to Berlin, he downplays the role of the Pastoral Letter. He assures the Foreign Office in Berlin that that he is closely surveying the activities of the church; but there is no need to intervene, since the anti-German views of most pastors, and the bishops in particular, are already well known; moreover, the churches have only a very minor influence on the views of the population and on the political situation in general.[68] This is hardly an accurate description of the role of Danish church at the time, but whether it was an honest perception by Best, or rather an elegant excuse for remaining passive in anticipation of the near downfall of the Third Reich (with the consequences of justice), we cannot know.

Prenter's Declaration on "The Church and the Law," 1944

The *Unofficial Pastors Association* (*Præsternes Uofficielle Forening*) was in principle a legal association, though with ties to the resistance movement. This association was impatient about the slow and internally divided collegium of bishops that did not mention Nazism by name and did not declare its ideology to be a confessional issue, as was the case with the Norwegian *The Foundation of the Church*. In Dalum, Funen, the association held a meeting on February 7-8, 1944, in which they decided to ask Prenter to formulate an appropriate declaration to be read through also by Løgstrup. We do not know anything about their collaboration but the voice and style of argumentation of *The Church and the Law in the contemporary situation* (*Kirken og Retten i den aktuelle Situation*) reveals the hand of Prenter. Eventually, the pamphlet was sent out in 20.000 copies via *Dansk Samling's* illegal journal, *People and Freedom* (*Folk og Frihed*), issued March 1944.[69]

---

68 Werner Best, Letter of April 28, 1944: "An das Auswärtige Amt, Berlin … Ich bemerke aus diesem Anlass, dass ich von jedem Eingriff in das dänische Kirchenwesen abgesehen habe, obwohl mir die deutschfeindliche Einstellung der meisten Geistlichen und insbesondere der Bischöfe durchaus bekannt ist. Denn von der Kirche, bzw von den Kirchen, wird tätsächlich nur ein sehr geringer Einfluss auf die Meinungsbildung der Bevölkerung und damit auf die politische Lage im Lande ausgeübt … Ich werde deshalb auch weiter die Tätigkeit der Kirchen und der Geistlichen zwar kontrollieren, aber mich Eingriffs in das Kirchenwesen enthalten," reprinted in Jacobsen, *Som om intet var hændt*, 285-86. The complex personality of Dr. Jur. Werner Best may have served Denmark better than other potential alternatives within the ranks of the SS. Best was sentenced to capital punishment after 1945 but pardoned and released in 1951.

69 See Jacobsen, *Som om intet var hændt*, 205-10, text at 288-94. See also Lisbet Christoffersen, "Prenter: Kirken og Retten, 1944," in *Lidenskab og stringens: Festskrift til Svend Andersen*, ed. Kees van Kooten Niekerk and Ulrik Nissen (Copenhagen: Anis, 2008), 301-17.

As rightly pointed out by Danish theologian Christine Svinth-Værge Põder, *The Church and the Law* can be seen as "the Danish parallel to the Barmen Declaration of the Confessing Church in Germany".[70] In a brief essay, written immediately after the liberation, Prenter indeed saw the Unofficial Pastors Association as "an association, which was prepared to take over and lead a *Kirchenkampf*, if our bishops were to be removed from their positions."[71] Yet in terms of context and content, important differences remain. Like the Norwegian confession, the Danish declaration was written within a nationwide consensus against Nazism. Moreover, as we shall see, the internationally oriented Prenter referred to the international regulations of the Hague Convention from 1907, that is, to a piece of positive secular law, as the criterion on which to judge the injustice of the German government. Finally, Prenter and the Danish bishops did not shy away from explicating the central issue of Jewish deportations. In effect, *The Church and the Law* may well be read as an argument for the legitimacy of an armed resistance against the German occupation power.

The Church and the Law[72] takes its point of departure in the Pastoral Promise (*Præsteløftet*) to which all Danish pastors subscribe formally before their ordination. The first and foremost obligation is to preach the gospel, but the gospel "sheds a light on all human relations". Since God is the sovereign Lord of all human affairs, the Pastoral Promise includes the "relation of Christians to the state and its lawful order (*Retsorden*), and to the distress of our co-citizens regarding earthly needs." In this sense, the church cannot avoid speaking about the government and the needs of one's neighbor.

While this Article 1 takes a somewhat Barthian approach (by moving from gospel to law), Article 2 takes issue with the question of lawfulness *per se*. The declaration clarifies that the obligation of obedience towards the worldly government is made extremely difficult in the present situation of the church, since "the state of law is for the time being in such a shape that it is difficult to judge whether we really have a lawful government to obey." A state ruled by law is the prerequisite for any obedience to the worldly government. The

---

70 Christine Svinth-Værge Põder, "Regin Prenter and Scandinavian Creation Theology," in *Reformation Theology for a Post-secular Age: Løgstrup, Prenter, Wingren and the Future of Scandinavian Creation Theology*, ed. Niels Henrik Gregersen, Bengt Kristensson Uggla, and Trygve Wyller (Göttingen: Vandenhoeck & Ruprecht, 2017), 71.

71 Regin Prenter, "Kirken og Modstandskampen" [The Church and the Resistance Fight], in *Fem Aar: Indtryk og oplevelser*, ed. Christian Refslund and Max Schmidt, vol II (Copenhagen: Hagerup, 1945), 221-25. Here cited from Christoffersen, "Prenter: Kirken og Retten, 1944," 303.

72 The *Church and the Law in its contemporary situation* is reprinted in Jacobsen, *Som om intet var hændt*, 288-94. In what follows, I refer to its four articles in my own translation.

text gives many examples of obvious injustices, which call for "a change of the legal condition (*Retstilstanden*)." Those working for the German cause as well as those active in sabotage have placed themselves in the frontline of war, with all the associated risks. But when innocent Danish men and women are targeted, when illegal arrests and methods of interrogation are used "in conflict with Danish law and Nordic customary laws", and "when Danish men and women are, without indictment and trial, deported due to their national engagement or race only," the sense of law and order is obviously blurred. The "dissolution of the legal order" is indeed ravaging in the present situation; accordingly, there is no lawful authority to obey in the given situation. Prenter is referring to the apparent (dis)order of law, which neglects Danish law and the legal traditions of the Nordic countries.

On this basis, it is important to note that Prenter in Article 3 makes a further secular move when he argues that Denmark is an occupied territory involved in war. Prenter brings in the international law of the Hague Convention. As a matter of fact, when General von Hanneken on August 29, 1943, declared Denmark in a state of emergency, he did so with reference to Articles 42-56 of the Hague Convention concerning the laws and customs of war.[73] Even if this state of emergency was cancelled in October 1943, Prenter argued that whether or not this view is still upheld by German authorities, a state of war "is the only acceptable description of the relation between Germany and Denmark." A territory is occupied, when it is *de facto* under the authority of a foreign army. Prenter is now citing several Articles from the Hague Convention of 1907, such as:

> Article 43. The authority of the legitimate power having in fact passed into the hands of the occupant, the latter shall take all the measures in his power to restore, and ensure, as far as possible, public order and safety, while respecting, unless absolutely prevented, the laws in force in the country.
>
> Article 45. It is forbidden to compel the inhabitants of occupied territory to swear allegiance to the hostile Power.

---

73 Jacobsen, *Som om intet var hændt*, points out two complicating issues. First, the state of emergency was declared by Germany "im Sinne der Landkriegsordnung", which may translated as "under the law of war between countries" or "in analogy to" the law of war, on 334. Second, the state of emergency was lifted again by October, 1943, on 141. As argued by Ditlev Tamm, from a purely legal perspective, Denmark's situation may well be described as an "*occupatio pacifica*, in which the rules of law did not find immediate application," *Retsopgøret*, 37.

> Article 46. Family honor and rights, the lives of persons, and private property, as well as religious convictions and practice, must be respected. Private property cannot be confiscated.
>
> Article 50. No general penalty, pecuniary or otherwise, shall be inflicted upon the population on account of the acts of individuals for which they cannot be regarded as jointly and severally responsible.
>
> Article 56. The property of municipalities, that of institutions dedicated to religion, charity and education, the arts and sciences, even State property, shall be treated as private property. All seizure of, destruction or wilful damage done to institutions of this character, historic monuments, works of art and science, is forbidden, and should be made the subject of legal proceedings.

Prenter is aware that the interpretation of the Hague Convention may be controversial among the warring parties. However, "the principal view must be that the *military* German authorities have the superior power, but that this power as far as possible should be exercised in accordance with the current Danish law." Thus, it cannot be required (Hague Convention, Article 43) that the violation of Danish law should take place regarding the deportation of Danish Jews. Indeed, "arbitrariness" (*Vilkårlighed*) has replaced law and order so that "lawlessness and chaos" rule. It is notable that Prenter refers here to the *positive law* of the Hague Convention as well as to the *existing* statutory Danish law (*gældende dansk lov*).[74] From Prenter's own perspective, divine law does not prescribe particular positive legislation, which is left to the worldly regiment.

In Article 4, *The Church and the Law* restates the point of the Lutheran two-regiment doctrine that church and state each have their function, and that the church does not wish to "mix with the affairs of the state," but "respects the state in its sovereignty as the servant of God" (with reference to Romans 13:4). Yet as soon as the state "abandons the ground of the law (*Rettens Grund*) and dissolves itself in the arbitrariness of autocracy (*Despoti*), it is the duty of the church to call for a protection of the law." In this context, we find the sentence:

---

74 Christoffersen sees Prenter as representing "an idealistic position" in contrast to a legal realism. Christoffersen, "Prenter," 301. Insofar as the term "idealistic" refers to something beyond what can be identified in a space-time continuum (a substantive naturalism), Prenter is no doubt an "idealist," since he speaks of God the creator as the final source of love, and about law being intrinsically related to ethical concerns regarding one's neighbor. Nontheless, Prenter appeals to existing positive laws as the basis for his argument. It seems to me that he moves from an emphasis on divine sovereignty (Article 1) to a discussion of the ethical undercurrents of positive Danish law and Nordic customary law (Article 2), and further on to the positive laws of the Hague Convention which, in turn, require the respect for statutory Danish law during wartime (Article 3).

"The church is passionately interested in the maintenance of law" followed by the practical point that *"The church cannot be a silent spectator of the dissolution of the order of law"* (both italicized in original). Before coming to these principal points, Prenter notes that the church can live under many forms of state order (as it has done in its history), "except for a form of state that makes itself at one with lawlessness." In a situation in which a state *requires* of their citizens to execute a brutal selfishness (Prenter: "sin"), the Augsburg Confession rightly states that "you should obey God more than human beings" (Augsburg Confession, Article 16). Implicitly, Prenter argues that open revolt (as in the Danish resistance movement) is the last resort, but is legitimate if a state identifies itself with a lawless arbitrariness.

The whole gist of Prenter's argument is that a Lutheran ethics does not demand obedience to state power *per se*, but only obedience to a state ruled by law. This explains Prenter's point that "revenge and hatred shall be extinguished not only by mercy but by law." In a sense, this is a restatement of the Lutheran view of the political order's preventive function in holding down ruthless expressions of human selfishness. From this perspective, *The Church and the Law* concludes with the following statement: "For the Church, the law is God's gift and benefaction." Note that it is not the state that is God's gift and benefaction, but a state ruled by law!

In this interpretation of *The Church and Law*, I have seen Prenter's text as making up a compound argument that brings together different layers within the concept of law. Prenter moves from a somewhat Barthian emphasis on the commitment of the gospel to address the distress of Danish people suffering under a lawless regime (Article 1). From there, the declaration discusses the ethical undercurrents of positive Danish and Norwegian law, ethical principles that are evidently violated in the current situation (Article 2). Implicitly, Prenter here appeals to a sense of fairness as an aspect of the natural law tradition in a Lutheran ethics. A law is not something to be promulgated by brute state power only, but a proper law must regulate ordinary life in such ways that it helps and relieves the needs of the suffering neighbor. Prenter then moves on to the positive laws of the Hague Convention which, in turn, support the operation of positive Danish law during the occupation by a foreign war power (Article 3). This Article 3 shows the significance of positive law for Prenter's argument. Finally, Prenter argues that a state with arbitrary laws is *not* a state to be obeyed by Christians (Article 4). Therefore, it is not state power that is the divine gift but law and justice, the two aspects of law combined in the Danish word *Retten*.

Concluding Perspectives: Scandinavian Creation Theology and Scandinavian Legal Realism

We have seen how Løgstrup and Prenter used aspects of Lutheran and Grundtvigian creation theology as the theological background from which they engaged in the discussion on law and politics in the 1940s. Their shared assumption was that the world of creation constitutes an immanent, ethical realm common to Christians and non-Christians alike. The sense of right and wrong depends on the existence of communities, which share a moral sense that is convergent with but not derived from the church. This orientation is particularly clear in Løgstrup who in 1943 focused on the *pre-political* laws of life. We have seen that Løgstrup after 1945 extended his view of laws of life from the Danish situation to European culture as a whole. Germany had belonged to this European legal culture until 1933, and Løgstrup argued that Germans after 1945 urgently needed to return to their roots in European culture and law. Prenter differed from Løgstrup in paying more attention to the church and state as social institutions, arguing that the church supports a secular worldly state ruled by law and justice (*Retsstat*).

Løgstrup and Prenter did not view themselves as moral idealists. Rather, they argued that basic ethical phenomena (Løgstrup) and legal institutions (Prenter) are part of the shared human realm of existing moral communities. In this sense, they saw themselves as moral realists, assuming that human interactions cannot be described properly without taking into account the moral concerns present within the immanent frame of the world of creation. Prenter is particularly interesting by making what I have called a "compound argument" for law and order, moving from ethical principles of human conduct to the statutory laws of Danish and Nordic legislation, and even further on to the Hague Convention at an international level.

This raises the wider question of how Løgstrup's and Prenter's positions fit with the standard distinction between "legal idealism" and "legal realism" in Nordic philosophy of law. The first generations of so-called Scandinavian Legal Realism were strongly committed to a *metaphysical naturalism*, arguing that only things in the spatio-temporal world exist. This commitment was central to the Uppsala philosopher Axel Hägerström (1868-1939) and shared by two of his students, the Lund Professor of Law Karl Olivecrona (1897-1980) and the Copenhagen Professor of Law Alf Ross (1899-1979). On the account of a metaphysical naturalism, Løgstrup and Prenter are "idealists" by definition insofar as they refer to God the creator as the final source of ethics, even though none of them derived positive laws from divine law. As noticed by philosophers Brian Leiter and Matthew X. Etchemendy, the strong commitment to a substantive naturalism in Scandinavian Legal Realism "is today viewed as an intellectual-historical museum piece rather than as a live contender in jurisprudential debate."[75] Contemporary jurists usually bracket metaphysical commitments in order to deal with the more tractable problems of jurisprudence, and the wide spectrum of social ontologies in contemporary philosophy of law means that only few philosophers of law today need to support a strict metaphysical naturalism.

In addition, the Scandinavian legal realists were *moral anti-realists*, that is, committed to the view that morality does not refer to real features of reality. Accordingly, neither moral intuitions nor references to the common good should play a role in legal philosophy. Rather, jurisprudence reflects on what is "established by law," to be decided solely by the political authorities. On this view, all statutory laws are by definition "valid laws" (Ross), and the question of the legitimacy of law cannot be raised within legal philosophy.

As we saw, Prenter likewise made his arguments on right and wrong with reference to statutory laws in Danish, Nordic, and international law. Yet Prenter also referred to a moral substructure of law, indicating that a state could not indict innocent people, thereby implying that discriminatory laws are not "in order," simply by virtue of being "established by law." Prenter, we may say, argued for a *state rule of law* (Retsstat), which is a more demanding view than speaking only of a state *ruled by law*.[76] Thus, the Scandinavian creation theologians reused elements of Luther's concept of *lex naturalis,* understood as an *ethical concept* related to the demands of neighborly love in everyday life. At the same time, the Lutheran doctrine of the two regiments acknowledges that the political government cannot build directly on the Golden Rule, since a state cannot operate without an enforcement of law ("the sword"). Still so, the Scandinavian creation theologians argued that governments are accountable if they are not in allegiance with lawfulness and fairness (what Luther referred to as *Recht und Billigkeit*) in their exercise of political power.

The purely procedural concept of laws being valid simply by being issued by a legislator, irrespective of the contents of law, is not an entirely harmless affair. Eventually, we see very divergent political views in the two leading proponents of Scandinavian Legal Realism: Olivecrona and Ross. Ross was a convinced democrat, who wanted the "directives" of law to be issued by a democratically

---

75 Brian Leiter and Matthew X. Etchemendy, "Naturalism in Legal Philosophy," in *Stanford Encyclopedia of Philosophy*, last modified March 27, 2017, https://plato.stanford.edu/entries/lawphil-naturalism/, section 5.1.

76 I owe this distinction from discussions with my colleague in law, Professor Lisbet Christoffersen. On the possibility of "false laws," see Hans Michael Heinig, "Neither secular nor sacral law" in this volume.

elected government. The Nazi-minded Olivecrona, by contrast, had hoped for a Nazi-German victory during World War II, arguing that a German hegemony over Europe would give governments the necessary strength to motivate a compelling law in a population.[77] While Olivecrona's pro-German views were rarely known in England ant the US, the possibility of a state absolutism is already opened by his *Law as Fact* from 1939, also in the amended second edition from 1971: "Legal language is not a descriptive language. It is a directive influential language serving as an instrument of social control".[78]

The moral anti-realism of Scandinavian Legal Realism was thus amenable to democratic as well as absolutist views of the statehood. Similarly, repeating its attacks on natural law, the Scandinavian Legal Realists were highly skeptical regarding the United Nations' concept of human rights in the post-World War II discussions.[79] My point here is not to suggest that only a strong concept of natural law (either as endowed by God or as evident by human reasoning) can lead to the affirmation of human rights in international and national law. But my point is that a separation between established laws, on the one hand, and issues of fairness and justice, on the other, is untenable in democratic and pluralistic societies, especially if the former is relegated to the happenstance of state power and the latter reduced to private emotions.

In Koch's important book: *What is Democray?* from 1945, he argued that such a separation is against the spirit of democracy. Koch advanced the view that democracy cannot be captured as a system or doctrine but only as a "form of life" which involves dialogue and conversation in the wider civil society. "Democracy never lives by virtue of laws and paragraphs. It lives in and through living human beings. It is the mentality of the People (*Folkets Sind*) that matters, not the regulations only that are written into laws and put on paper."[80] In this context, Koch reformulated parts of Løgstrup's view from 1943 by saying that there are "some general basic laws (*Grundlove*) of human life that must be respected if a shared life of coexistence is to be realizable." Like Løgstrup,

---

77 See Roger Cotterrell, "Northern Lights: From Swedish Realism to Sociology of Law," *Journal of Law and Society* 40, no. 4 (2013): 657-69. In 1940, Olivecrona wrote the Swedish pamphlet, *England or Germany*, translated into German and printed in 80.000 copies in Berlin (and in eight continental languages but not English), followed up by another pamphlet in 1943 with the title *Europe and America*, likewise translated and published in Berlin, see Cotterrell, "Northern Lights," 665.
78 Karl Olivacrona, *Law as Fact*, 2nd ed. (London: Stevens & Sons, 1971), 253.
79 See Johan Strang, "Scandinavian Legal Realism and Human Rights: Axel Hägerström, Alf Ross and the Persistent Attack on Natural Law," *Nordic Journal of Human Rights* 36, no. 3 (2018): 202-18.
80 Hal Koch, *Hvad er Demokrati?* (Copenhagen: Gyldendal, 1945), 50.

Koch argued that such basic laws (*Grundlove*) of human coexistence are placed at a deeper level than the Danish democratic Constitution of 1849 (*Grundloven*). Laws of life are operative as a pre-political condition for a democracy that brings together striving parties in a democratic conversation. Koch furthermore argues that a society cannot be shaped and ruled in just any manner, and he adds a theological interpretation to this view: "Life is not an unformed matter that is up to everyone to give form and shape according to their own head. Life is something specific—created by God, given to human beings as gift."[81]

From the perspective of Scandinavian Legal Realism such arguments are to be seen as "idealistic," insofar as Koch and Løgstrup argue that a democratic system is rooted in a democratic mindset, which presupposes the existence of a civil society involving moral communities, even if people only rarely agree with one another on the political level.[82] Working as a philosopher, Løgstrup's postwar considerations on the relation between ethical phenomena, social norms, and political ideas are particularly revealing in terms of the difference between his phenomenological concept of moral realism versus the moral anti-realism of Scandinavian Legal Realism.

After 1945, Løgstrup gave up the term "laws of life", just as he gave up speaking about "orders of creation." Løgstrup's ethical perspective continued, however. In *The Ethical Demand* from 1956, he focused again on the phenomenon of trust, claiming that it is rooted in the prior fact of human interdependence. Conversation is born as an ethical phenomenon, since the truster trusts the trustee, and conversation is neither an ethics-free nor a power-free zone.[83] From the fact of power that I have something of another person's life in my hand follows the ethical requirement of caring for the vulnerability of the other person: "In its basic sense trust is essential to every conversation. In conversation as such we deliver ourselves over into the hands of another.

---

81 Koch, *Hvad er Demokrati?*, 52-53. See Tine Reeh, *Kristendom, historie, demokrati: Hal Koch 1932-1945* (Copenhagen: Museum Tusculanum, 2012), 671-78. Reeh does not mention Koch's indebtedness to the basic arguments in K.E. Løgstrup's work, *Den erkendelsesteoretiske Konflikt mellem den transcendentalfilosofiske Idealisme og Teologien* (Copenhagen: Samlerens Forlag, 1942) and his 1943 book, *The Life of the People and Foreign Politics*.

82 Eventually, this view leads to a more minimalist conception of the role of the state as providing freedom and security under the law, while the civil society, building on moral communities, must tolerate a good deal of dissent. So Hendrik Munsonius, *Öffentliche Religion im säkularen Staat* (Tübingen: Mohr-Siebeck, 2016), 2: "In der Gewährleistung von Freiheit und Sicherheit findet der Staat seine Rechtfertigung und nicht in irgendeinem religiös-weltanschaulichen System".

83 Løgstrup's phenomenology of communication here differs from Jürgen Habermas' theory of communicative action, in which there are power-free zones of discursive communication.

This is evident in the fact that in the very act of addressing a person we make a certain demand of him".[84]

Løgstrup hereby criticized exactly the separation between "is" and "ought" in the prevailing contemporary philosophy, repeated in the separation between descriptive and directive utterances within Scandinavian Legal Realism. Human life is not an ethics-free zone but rather a field of reciprocal interactions in which unspoken demands come up, rooted in the expectation of being taken seriously by the other party in a communication. Not responding to the needs of the other means devaluating the one who has approached me. In interhuman communication there is no divide between what is and what ought to be. In his "Rejoinder" from 1962 to the criticisms levelled at *The Ethical Demand*, Løgstrup put it as follows:

> We must accept that we cannot merely describe and theorize, leaving it at that. We cannot exist without taking a position and intervening. We are, first and last, enterprising and emotional beings who therefore live though goals, actions, and decisions. It is therefore impossible in a given situation to recognize that the other person's life has been surrendered to one without taking a position in respect of that circumstance. Between fact and demand there is the most intimate connection. The demand arises directly out of the fact.[85]

According to Løgstrup, the ethical demand is thus a feature of life rooted in the prior fact of human interdependence, neither the result of a social contract between two independent partners, nor a divinely imposed external command. This being the case, the fact of being ethically demanded is always refracted by a personal adjudication of the circumstances and always guided by moral norms that may differ markedly from epoch to epoch.

On this basis, Løgstrup did not see human rights as part of natural law, but as an important regulative idea, a construction of law though rooted in ethical phenomena, acknowledging the painful fact that also human selfishness is part of human life together: "'[B]eneath' the social-political life lies what is natural and is not natural, compassion alongside sadism."[86] Løgstrup is fully aware, of course, that there was a time, when torture was still a part of the general administration of justice in society, so that sadism was socially recognized. Yet

---

84 Løgstrup, *The Ethical Demand* (Notre Dame, IN: Notre Dame University Press 1997), 14.
85 Løgstrup, *Beyond the Ethical Demand* (Notre Dame, IN: Notre Dame University Press 2007), 8.
86 Løgstrup, "Torturen breder sig [Torture expands]," in *Solidaritet og kærlighed og andre essays* [Solidarity and Love and other Essays] (Copenhagen: Gyldendal, 1987), 77.

he argues that sadism stands in opposition to the prior ethical phenomenon of trust and compassion, from which our legal decisions should be evaluated at normative level. In Løgstrup's view, human rights are not derived from an abstract concept of "natural law" but is a human convention. Nonetheless, human rights are of immense cultural importance, as it shields powerless individuals from ruthless state powers. In this sense, human rights are to be affirmed, neither as a foreign divinely imposed law nor as a law derived from human reasoning, but as a regulative human construction that is "good", because it is legally concerned with the pre-legal sense of morality and fairness, by which any laws are to be measured.

Nowhere do Løgstrup and Prenter appeal to *legal concepts* of natural law, as we find it in early modern thinkers such as Hugo Grotius (1583-1645) and Samuel von Pufendorf (1632-1694). As shown in an insightful article by Olivecrona from 1977, both Grotius and Pufendorf referred to "nature" as an immanent framework without reference to a superior lawgiver. Moreover, they defined justice negatively, from what is unjust; what is *iniustum,* in turn, is defined by that which violates that which belongs to the *suum* ("what is mine") of citizens. A *suum* is that which is properly in the hands of the individual, such as one's life, body, limbs, liberty, reputation, and honor.[87]

With historical hindsight, some noticeable aspects of what Grotius and Pufendorf saw as "unjust" resurfaced in the arguments of Løgstrup, Prenter, and Koch, for example when they criticized the German occupying power for violating innocent individuals and not keeping to their promises. The framework of Løgstrup, however, is social in its orientation. The ethics of political life is rooted in the phenomenon of responsibility of human beings living under circumstances of inequality, where the stronger has to care for the weaker—prior to and independent of any social and legal contracts. The sociality of human interdependence is prior to individual powers and social contracts.

Interestingly, however, Olivecrona points to a difference between Grotius and Pufendorf: the former viewed the state of nature as a state of potential warfare, whereas Pufendorf saw peace as the more basic phenomenon. Again, in historical hindsight, the Scandinavian creation theologians are more in line with Pufendorf who occasionally did refer to sociality as a fundamental human

---

[87] Karl Olivecrona, translated with an introduction by Thomas Mautner, "The Two Levels in Natural Law Thinking," *Jurisprudence* 1, no. 2 (2010): 197-224; originally published as Karl Olivecrona, "Die zwei Schichten im naturrechtlichen Denken," *Archiv für Rechts- und Sozialphilosophie* 63 (1977): 79-103.

inclination on the ethical level.[88] In a historical reconstruction, there are thus some convergences between the Scandinavian creation theology and the early modern tradition of natural law, even if the former never appeals to legal concepts of natural law, but rather to ethical principles of a moral sense—given in, with, and under human communities.

Bibliography

Literature

Aulén, Gustaf, ed. *En Bok om Kyrkan*. Stockholm: Svenska Kyrkans diakonistyrelses bokförlag, 1942.

Aulén, Gustaf. *Kyrkan och nationalsocialismen: Kyrkan och statslivet*. Stockholm: Svenska kyrkans diakonistyrelses bokförlag, 1944.

Austad, Thorleiv. *Kirkens Grunn: Analyse av en kirkelig bekendelse fra okkupasjonstiden 1940-45*. Oslo: Luther Forlag, 1974.

Bak, Sofie Lene. *Dansk antisemitisme 1930-1945*. Copenhagen: Aschehoug, 2004.

Barth, Karl. "The First Commandment as the Axiom of Theology." In *The way of Theology in Karl Barth: Essays and Comments*, edited by H. Martin Rumscheidt, 63-78. Allison Park, PA: Pickwick Publications, 1986.

Christoffersen, Lisbet. "Prenter: Kirken og Retten, 1944." In *Lidenskab og stringens: Festskrift til Svend Andersen*, edited by Kees van Kooten Niekerk and Ulrik Nissen, 301-17. Copenhagen: Anis, 2008.

Christoffersen, Lisbet, and Niels Henrik Gregersen. "Shaping the Danish People's Church in the Context of Freedom of Religion: A.S. Ørsted (1778-1860) and N.F.S. Grundtvig (1783-1872)." In *Law and the Christian Tradition in Scandinavia: The Writings of Nordic Jurists*, edited by Kjell Åke Modéer and Helle Vogt. London: Routledge, 2020, 206-241.

Christoffersen, Svein Aage. "Friedrich Gogartens 'Politische Ethik og Knud E. Løgstrups 'Den etiske fordring': en systematisk analyse." *Norsk Teologisk Tidsskrift* 83, no. 3 (1982): 203-17.

Cochrane, Arthur C. ed. "Barmen Declaration." In *The Church's Confession Under Hitler*. Philadelphia, PA: Westminster Press, 1962.

Cotterrell, Roger. "Northern Lights: From Swedish Realism to Sociology of Law." *Journal of Law and Society* 40, no. 4 (2013): 657-69.

Fuglsang-Damgaard, Hans. "Anno 1936: Lutherdommens Opgave i den aktuelle Situation." *Præsteforeningens Blad*, no. 1 (1936): 1-12.

---

88 Olivecrona, "The Two Levels in Natural Law Thinking," refers to Samuel von Pufendorf, *De jure naturae et gentium libri octo* (Lund: Adam Junghans, 1672) 2.3.15: "By sociality (*socialitas*) I understand a disposition towards every other person such that one feels that there are bonds in relation to them of benevolence, peacefulness, love, and even through reciprocal obligations." This could have been expressed by Løgstrup as well.

Gregersen, Niels Henrik. "Luther genopført, modsagt og genbrugt: Det 20. århundredes epoker." In *Reformationen i dansk kirke og kultur: Bind 3; 1914-2017*, edited by Niels Henrik Gregersen and Carsten Bach-Nielsen, 11-47. Odense: Syddansk Universitetsforlag 2017.

Gregersen, Niels Henrik. "Martin Luther in Denmark." In *The Oxford Encyclopedia of Martin Luther*, vol. 2, edited by Derek R. Nelson and Paul R. Hinlicky, 256-70. New York: Oxford University Press, 2017.

Gregersen, Niels Henrik. "Church and Culture in Living Interaction: Grundtvig the Theologian." In *Human Comes First: The Christian Theology of N.F.S. Grundtvig*, edited by Edward Broadbridge, 22-54. Aarhus: Aarhus University Press, 2018.

Gregersen, Niels Henrik. "From oeconomia to Nordic Welfare Societies: The Idea of a Third-Zone Lutheranism." *Theology Today* 76, no. 3 (2019): 224-32.

Gregersen, Niels Henrik, Bengt Kristensson Uggla, and Trygve Wyller, eds. *Reformation Theology for a Post-Secular Age: Løgstrup, Prenter, Wingren, and the Future of Scandinavian Creation Theology*. Göttingen: Vandenhoeck & Ruprecht, 2017.

Hassing, Arne. *Church Resistance to Nazism in Norway, 1940-1945*. Seattle, WA: University of Washington Press, 2014.

Jacobsen, Erik Thostrup. *Som om intet var hændt: Den danske folkekirke under besættelsen*. Odense: Odense Universitetsforlag, 1991.

Jaklin, Asbjørn. *De Dødsdømte*. Oslo: Gyldendal, 2011.

Jarlert, Anders. "Sverige: Modernisering utan rättsuppgörelse." In *Nordiske folkekirker i opbrud: National identitet og international nyorientering efter 1945*, edited by Jens Holger Schjørring, 78-88. Aarhus: Aarhus Universitetsforlag, 2001.

Koch, Hal. *Hvad er Demokrati?* Copenhagen: Gyldendal, 1945.

Koch, Hal. "Statsmændendes Embede—og vort." *Lederbladet* no. 5, May 1943. Reprinted in *Kære Hal, kære Koste: Breve 1940-43 mellem K.E. Løgstrup og Hal Koch*, edited by Henrik S. Nissen, 95-99. Copenhagen: Gyldendal, 1992.

van Kooten Niekerk, Kees. "Vejen til den etiske fordring." In *Livtag med den etiske fordring*, edited by David Bugge and Peter Aaboe Sørensen, 9-46. Aarhus: Klim, 2007.

Kristensson Uggla, Bengt. *Becoming Human Again: The Theological Life of Gustaf Wingren*. Eugene, OR: Cascade Books, 2016.

Lauha, Aila. "Finland: Ansvar för folket förblir kyrkans kallelse." In *Nordiske folkekirker i opbrud, National identitet og international nyorientering efter 1945*, edited by Jens Holger Schjørring, 53-64. Aarhus: Aarhus Universitetsforlag, 2001.

Leiter, Brian and Matthew X. Etchemendy. "Naturalism in Legal Philosophy." In *Stanford Encyclopedia of Philosophy*. Last modified March 27, 2017. https://plato.stanford.edu/entries/lawphil-naturalism/.

Lidegaard, Bo. *Kampen om Danmark 1933-1945*. Copenhagen: Gyldendal, 2005.

Lind, Martin. *Kristendom och nazism*. Lund: Håkan Ohlssons förlag, 1975.

Lundbak, Henrik. *Danish Unity: A Political Party between Fascism and Resistance 1936-47*. Copenhagen: Museum Tusculanums Forlag, 2003.

Løgstrup, K.E. "Det religiøse Motiv i den erkendelsesteoretiske Problemstilling." Unpublished manuscript, 1933.

Løgstrup, K.E. "Kan den kristne Etik anerkende Tanken om Samfundslivets egen Lovmæssighed?" Unpublished manuscript, 1934.

Løgstrup, K.E. "Nazismens filosof." *Dagens Nyheder*, April 14, 1936.

Løgstrup, K.E. "Førerskab og Diktatur I–II," *Dagens Nyheder*, June 24-25, 1936.

Løgstrup, K.E. "Hvad er Jødehad?" *Kirkeblad for Sandager-Holevad* no. 10 (1941).

Løgstrup, K.E. *Den erkendelsesteoretiske Konflikt mellem den transcendentalfilosofiske Idealisme og Teologien*. Copenhagen: Samlerens Forlag, 1942.

Løgstrup, K.E. *Folkeliv og Udenrigspolitik*. Copenhagen: Tidehvervs Forlag, 1943. Reprinted in *Kære Hal, kære Koste: Breve 1940-43 mellem K.E. Løgstrup og Hal Koch*, edited by Henrik S. Nissen, 146-72. Copenhagen: Gyldendal, 1992.

Løgstrup, K.E. "Opgør eller Selvbedrag." In *Opgørets Nødvendighed*, edited by Vilhelm Krarup, Knud Ejler Løgstrup, and H. Østergaard-Nielsen, 17-57. Copenhagen: Tidehvervs Forlag, 1945.

Løgstrup, K.E. "Tidehverv." In *Religion in Geschichte und Gegenwart*[3] (RGG[3]), vol. 6, 885-86. Tübingen: Mohr-Siebeck, 1962.

Løgstrup, K.E. "Die humanen Erfahrungen als Verständnishorizont für das Evangelium." In *Dem Menschen zugute: Christliche Existenz und humane Erfahrung*, edited by K.E. Løgstrup and Ernst Wolf, 9-27. München: Chr. Kaiser Verlag, 1970.

Løgstrup, K.E. "Torturen breder sig." In *Solidaritet og kærlighed og andre essays*, 74-77. Copenhagen: Gyldendal, 1987.

Løgstrup, K.E. *The Ethical Demand*. Notre Dame, IN: Notre Dame University Press 1997.

Løgstrup, K.E. *Prædikenen og dens Tekst*, edited by Niels Henrik Gregersen and Jan Nilsson. Copenhagen: Gyldendal, 1999.

Løgstrup, K.E. *Beyond the Ethical Demand*. Notre Dame, IN: Notre Dame University Press 2007.

Munsonius, Hendrik. *Öffentliche religion im säkularen Staat*. Tübingen: Mohr-Siebeck, 2016.

Nelson, Robert H. *Lutheranism and the Nordic Spirit of Social Democracy: A Different Protestant Ethic*. Aarhus: Aarhus University Press, 2017.

Nissen, Henrik S. ed. *Kære Hal, Kære Koste: Breve 1940-43 mellem K.E. Løgstrup og Hal Koch*. Copenhagen: Gyldendal, 1992.

Njaa, Ådne. *"Det ånder himmelsk over støvet": Faser i Regin Prenters grundtvigske pagtsteologi*. Oslo: Unipub, 2007.

Olivecrona, Karl. *Law as Fact*. 2nd ed. London: Stevens & Sons, 1971.

Olivecrona, Karl. "Die zwei Schichten im naturrechtlichen Denken," *Archiv für Rechts- und Sozialphilosophie* 63 (1977): 79-103. Translated with an introduction by Thomas Mautner. "The Two Levels in Natural Law Thinking." *Jurisprudence* 1, no. 2 (2010): 197-224.

Oluffa Pedersen, Esther. *Fremkaldte kulturrum: Diskussioner om diktatur, humanisme, ansvar og videnskab i tiden omkring Anden Verdenskrig*. Copenhagen: Hans Reitzels Forlag, 2019.

Petersen, Klaus, and Jørn Henrik Petersen. "The Good, the Bad, or the Godless Society? Danish 'Church People' and the Modern Welfare State." *Church History* 82, no. 4 (2013): 94-140.

Põder, Christine Svinth-Værge. "Regin Prenter and Scandinavian Creation Theology." In *Reformation Theology for a Post-secular Age: Løgstrup, Prenter, Wingren and the Future of Scandinavian Creation Theology*, edited by Niels Henrik Gregersen, Bengt Kristensson Uggla, and Trygve Wyller, 67-90. Göttingen: Vandenhoeck & Ruprecht, 2017.

Prenter, Regin. "Die sogenannte 'Kirchliche Anschauung' N.F.S. Grundtvigs als Frage die evangelische Theologie von heute," *Evangelische Theologie* 1, no. 7 (1934): 278-88.

Prenter, Regin. "Die Frage nach einer theologischen Grundtvig-Interpretation." In *Theologische Ausätze: Karl Barth zum 50. Geburtstag*, edited by Ernst Wolf, 505-13. München: Chr. Kaiser Verlag, 1936.

Prenter, Regin. *Kristendom og Kultur*. Ringkøbing: De Unges Forlag, 1937.

Prenter, Regin. "Kirken og Staten." In *Ordets Herredømme*, 103-19. Copenhagen: Det tredje Standpunkts Forlag, 1941.

Prenter, Regin. *Ordets Herredømme*. Copenhagen: Det tredje Standpunkts Forlag, 1941.

Prenter, Regin. "Kirken og Modstandskampen." In *Fem Aar: Indtryk og oplevelser*, vol. 2, edited by Christian Refslund and Max Schmidt, 221-25. Copenhagen: Hagerup, 1945.

Prenter, Regin. *Protestantismen i vor tid*. Copenhagen: Hirschsprungs Forlag, 1957.

Prenter, Regin. "Die Einheit von Schöpfung und Erlösung: Zur Schöpfungslehre Karl Barth." *Theologische Zeitschrift* 2, no. 3 (1946): 161-82. Reprinted in Regin Prenter. *Theologie und Gottesdienst: Gesammelte Aufsätze*, 9-27. Aarhus: Aros/Göttingen: Vandenhoeck & Ruprecht, 1977.

Prenter, Regin. *Erindringer*. Aarhus: Aros, 1985.

Pufendorf, Samuel von. *De jure naturae et gentium libri octo*. Lund: Adam Junghans, 1672.

Rasmussen, Tarald. *Hva er protestantisme*. Oslo: Universitetsforlaget, 2017.

Reeh, Tine. *Kristendom, historie, demokrati: Hal Koch 1932-1945*. Copenhagen: Museum Tusculanums Forlag, 2012.

Schjørring, Jens Holger. "Introduction." In *Nordiske folkekirker i opbrud: National identitet og international nyorientering efter 1945*, edited by Jens Holger Schjørring, 11-46. Aarhus: Aarhus Universitetsforlag, 2001.

Schwarz Lausten, Martin. *Politikere og prædikanter*. Copenhagen: Anis, 2014.

Stauning, Thorkil. "Danmark for Folket." *Socialisten* (1934): 214.

Strang, Johan. "Scandinavian Legal Realism and Human Rights: Axel Hägerström, Alf Ross and the Persistent Attack on Natural Law." *Nordic Journal of Human Rights* 36, no. 3 (2018): 202-18.

Tamm, Ditlev. *Retsopgøret efter besættelsen*. Copenhagen: Dansk Jurist- og Økonomforbund, 1984.

Tønnesen, Aud V. "… et trygt og godt hjem for alle"? *Kirkeledres kritikk av velferdsstaten efter 1945*. Trondheim: Tapir Akademisk Forlag, 2000.

Wingren, Gustaf. *Mina fem universitet: Minnen*. Lund: Proprius Forlag, 1991.

Webpages

Mortensen, Pelle and Astrid Øllgaard Christensen Scriver. "Folketingsvalget 1935." Danmarkshistorien.dk. Last modified March 23, 2018. https://danmarkshistorien.dk/leksikon-og-kilder/vis/materiale/folketingsvalget-1935/.

3. A Nordic Model of Democracy? Hal Koch and Alf Ross on Law and Religion in Nordic Societies

Tine Reeh

Introduction

In 1946, professor of theology Hal Koch and professor of law Alf Ross published a book by the title of *Nordic Democracy*. In the book's preface, they state that the purpose of their work is "to capture the spirit and way of life that is the core of Nordic democracy".[1] The historical context for this publication was an intense debate concerning the construction of society after World War II. Interconnected with this debate was the beginning of the Cold War and the precarious geopolitical situation of the Nordic countries, situated as they were between the so-called economic democracy of Soviet Union and the liberal democracies of Western Europe. In this situation, Koch and Ross claimed, "between New York and Moscow is a Nordic area, where human life has created political and social structures, which have not been taken over from either side. Instead, these political and social structures have grown harmonious from the everyday life in the region, and this kind of democracy gives better and more decent conditions of life than you find most places."[2]

The following will introduce Koch and Ross and their work. We shall look at how the theologian Koch and the jurist Ross characterize what they conceive of as a "Nordic" democracy. Furthermore, we shall explore their work as a case of the relationship between Lutheran theology and a secular democratic form of government and law.

---

1 Hal Koch and Alf Ross, *Nordisk Demokrati* (Copenhagen: Westermann, 1949), XV.
2 Koch and Ross, *Nordisk Demokrati*, XVI.

Hal Koch

Hal Koch (1904-1963) was one of the Danish theologians who had the broadest impact on the general public in the 20th century. It was, however, not his theology but rather his work on democracy that made him an influential opinion maker. Nevertheless, Lutheran theology was his point of departure also when it came to his work on democracy and the construction of society. More specifically, it was a specific form of Lutheran theology that was decisive for his way of thinking.

Koch was born into a well-known Danish family of theologians and was deeply rooted in the traditions of Nordic Lutheran theology as well as a tradition for social commitment. His grandfather, the theologian L. Koch (1837-1917), published several important studies in church history.[3] His father, Hans Koch (1867-1949), was also a Lutheran pastor and renowned for his contributions to the public debate on social developments and his socially minded commitment. He was allegedly the first Danish theologian to declare himself a Social Democrat in public. Therefore, it was no surprise that the 17-year-old Koch began to study theology and decided to specialize in church history, in particular the relation between church and society in the past. When he graduated in 1926 with top marks, he received grants to attend lectures on Plato at the Sorbonne and began his work on a doctoral dissertation on the nexus of culture and theology in early Christianity. He interrupted his stay in Paris to return home to marry Bodil Thastum (1903-1972). They had been fellow students at the Faculty of Theology in Copenhagen, and she was later to become a member of parliament for the Social Democrats for more than twenty-five years and the first female Minister of Ecclesiastical Affairs in Denmark.[4] The newlyweds went to Italy where Hal and Bodil encountered totalitarianism for the first time. From their letters home, it is clear that the encounter made a strong impression on the young couple. In one of his letters to his academic patron, Professor Jens Nørregaard, Koch describes how he and Bodil had passed by a beautiful Renaissance palace and looked into the atrium only to see a large banner with the words: "Mussolini ha sempre ragione": "Mussolini is always right."[5] How could an old, civilized

---

3 L. Koch was made *doctor honoris causa* at the University of Copenhagen.
4 In addition, she became the person holding that office for the longest period in Denmark since the time of absolutism. See Birgitte Possing, *Uden omsvøb: Portræt af Bodil Koch* (Copenhagen: Gyldendal, 2007); Tine Reeh, "Borgerlig Indretning—Kristi Kirke: Bodil Kochs stilling til folkekirkens tilpasning til det danske samfund efter Anden Verdenskrig," in *Kirkeretsantologi*, ed. Svend Andersen et al., 49-66 (København: Selskab for Kirkeret, 2012).
5 Letter from Hal Koch to Jens Nørregaard May 14, 1930, Danish National Archives, *Personal Archives, Jens Schoubo Nørregaard (06073)*.

society with a rich tradition of art, literature, and philosophical thought come to that conclusion? After living in Italy for a while, the couple moved to Tübingen where they lived from 1929-1931. The letters from this period bear witness to their attention to the political dynamics of their surroundings. They describe how the milieu at the university was gradually poisoned by increasing political uncertainty. Free speech was under pressure, and self-censorship escalated. In addition, it became clear to them how the youth in Germany as well as in Italy constituted a strong resource and power base for political changes in the direction of totalitarianism.

In 1932, Koch defended his doctoral thesis, in 1937 he became Professor of Church History at the University of Copenhagen.[6] After Nazi Germany occupied Denmark on April 9, 1940, he decided to use his position to give a series of lectures on the Danish theologian N.F.S. Grundtvig for students from all faculties. The aim of the lectures was to immunize the academic youth against totalitarianism; they were immensely successful and made the young professor widely known outside the university.[7] In the fall of 1940, a group from the political elite wished to create an organization to strengthen the youth against the dangers of Nazism. They turned to Koch to be the nonpolitical chairman of the association named *Dansk Ungdomssamvirke*. Koch accepted becoming the figurehead but insisted that the mission must be to combat not the national, but the democratic, crisis.

Koch's reluctance towards nationalism during the occupation has been subject to criticism, but his work to prevent the Danish youth from absorbing totalitarian sympathies was a success.[8] In the summer of 1945, he published the book *What is Democracy?*, still a classic in the Danish debate on the construction

---

6   Hal Koch, *Pronoia und Paideusis: Studien über Origenes und sein Verhältnis zum Platonismus* (Berlin/Leipzig: Walter de Gruyter, 1932). The book, still a standard within the field of Origen studies, treats the relationship between Christianity and culture through a study of Origen's way of rethinking Christianity in a Hellenistic context. Over the following years Koch worked intensively on the theme of state and church, or *Regnum* and *Sacerdotium*, in the Middle Ages. This enabled him to best his rivals for the vacant chair in church history at the University of Copenhagen in 1937.
7   Jes Fabricius Møller, *Hal Koch: En biografi* (Copenhagen: Gads Forlag, 2009), 88-89.
8   Henrik S. Nissen and Henning Poulsen, *På dansk friheds grund: Dansk Ungdomssamvirke og De ældres Råd 1940-1945* (Copenhagen: Gyldendal, 1963); Hans Sode-Madsen, "Hal Koch og ungdommens opdragelse til demokrati," in *Fra mellemkrigstid til efterkrigstid*, ed. Henrik Dethlefsen and Henrik Lundbak (Copenhagen: Museum Tusculanums Forlag, 1998), 297-331; Ove Korsgaard, "Hal Koch: En republikaner i grundtvigiansk klædedragt," in *Poetisk demokrati: Om personlig dannelse og samfundsdannelse*, ed. Ove Korsgaard (Copenhagen: Gads Forlag, 2001), 63-82.

of society, and the latest edition is from 2015.⁹ This publication was not meant as a theological work. However, in the following we shall see how a specific Lutheran theology could be said to be the point of departure for Koch's argumentation for, and his understanding of, a secular democratic organization of society.

Hal Koch's Lutheran Theology[10]

The core of Koch's understanding of Christianity is Luther's idea of justification *sola fide*. In this, Koch is not particularly original but should rather be viewed as an early representative of a widespread theological tendency within Danish and Nordic theological circles of his generation as well as in the postwar period. The principal line of Koch's theology can be characterized as follows: God is the origin of life, and human beings therefore owe him everything. This is expressed in the law as articulated in the Decalogue and the Sermon on the Mount. However, as both the reality of everyday life and the biblical narratives show, it is part of the human condition that, along with the capacity to do good, all human beings bear a natural inclination to become selfish and thereby turn against God. Augustine calls this inclination original sin; Luther terms it *incurvatus in se*. This is a life-destroying inclination, a self-centered disposition that leads to destruction and death. The Gospel is perceived as the good news of how God meets the human being when it has destroyed its own life and the life of others. The New Testament texts are read as a kerygma or proclamation of how God meets the human being not with judgment but with infinite love, and restores life. This is the fundamental message of the biblical narrative. In the life, death, and resurrection of Jesus, God meets the human being with love and a new life. All human beings are given life or salvation, not by their own means and actions but by the love of God.

In Koch's understanding of Christianity, the Lutheran idea of justification by faith alone is pivotal, and it entails that Christianity is to be understood as an existential connection or relationship between the individual human being and a life-giving God. TIn other words: The human being is neither condemned by his wrongdoing, nor *saved* by his good works. This means that Christianity

---

9   Hal Koch, *Hvad er Demokrati?* (Copenhagen: Gyldendal, 1945/2015).
10   The following section builds on Koch's sermons located in the Danish National Archives: *Personal Archives, Hans Harald (Hal) Koch (07280)*. For a more detailed reading of the material, see Tine Reeh, *Kristendom, historie, demokrati: Hal Koch 1932-1945* (Copenhagen: Museum Tusculanums Forlag, 2012), 270-326 and 593-613.

is not and should not be understood as a question of good works, be it practical actions, prayers, or thoughts. According to this theological perspective, there is no such thing as a particularly Christian code of conduct or Christian material ethics. In other words, Christianity is not a matter of morals, since that would be reliance on or confidence in good works and thus a papist heresy.

However, according to Koch, this does not mean that the Christian person may do whatever he pleases. The good news of the love of God sets the individual human being free from his self-centered concern for his own happiness and salvation. By doing so, the human being is also set free, radically free, to turn his attention to his neighbor.[11] And this is what the Christian should do. He should turn his attention to the world around him and to the needs of his neighbor. These needs are contextual and relative; therefore, once again, it is not possible to create general Christian rules, laws, or ethics. Christianity or the Gospel entails only one absolute ethical demand: to live a life in service to your neighbor. Any talk of specific Christian ethics, morals, or politics makes no sense. That would be to elevate something contextual or relative to the category of the absolute.

In Koch's view, human beings will always be inclined to absolutize their own situation, be it morals, nationality, or politics. This could be called an "urge to absolutize", (*absoluteringsdriften*), which disturbs the relation between the human being and God; this is the basis for heresy.[12] According to Koch, this was the case with totalitarianism and the reason why he risked his life to combat it.[13]

However, after the Nazi occupation ended in 1945, Koch still felt an obligation as a Christian to engage in public life in service to his neighbor. Therefore, he continued to be an active player in the public political debate on the organization of society.

---

11   Koch explicitly draws on Martin Luther's *Tractatus de libertate christiana*; it constitutes a key text in his reception of Luther, as is also seen in Hal Koch, *Martin Luther* (Copenhagen: Gads Forlag, 1958).

12   Jakob Balling, "Hal Koch som dansk historiker under besættelsen," in *Historisk kristendom: Artikler og afhandlinger i udvalg* (Copenhagen: Anis, 2003), 293-304.

13   Koch never mentioned the attempts on his life in public, but from police records and newspapers we know of one bomb attack on his house in June 1942, in which part of his house was blown up. In December 1944, Bodil Koch reported an attempted assassination; finally, on April 10, 1945, Koch barely survived a new attack in which he broke his back, was severely injured, and was hospitalized for four months. Møller, *Hal Koch*, 144-49; 188-91. Possing, *Uden omsvøb*, 75.

Hal Koch's *What is Democracy?*

In 1945, Koch edited some of his contributions to the public debate into a book, published under the title *What is Democracy?*. The context of the book was the then debate on how to organize society in a time of governmental vacuum. Quite a few people argued for a reinstatement of a pre-liberal "old order" monarchy as a more genuine type of "Christian rule". Others, among these many young people and people from academia, were inclined to see this point in time as a chance to introduce "economic democracy", also known as communism.

Koch took advantage of his experience in church history and set out to influence the perception of the fundamental concepts for the foundation of the postwar community. He had seen how the definition of the basis of a social structure, be it in a church or another social unit, could be decisive for the life lived within it. In parallel with his theological work, he now sought to combat a dogmatic, absolutizing understanding of democracy. Democracy, Koch claims, does not have an absolute character; it is a relative, human creation and a concrete way of life. One can stimulate but never guarantee or secure a democracy with dogmas and formal structures. In order to illustrate this, Koch drew attention to the fact that the majority of voters in pre- and possibly also postwar Germany would have voted in favor of restrictions for Jews and their right to own property. Nevertheless, even though it might formally be a democratic decision, such a decision would in fact be a majority dictatorship, not democracy.

As an alternative, Koch pleads for an understanding of democracy as a way of life rather than a legal form of government. An early expression of this idea reads:

> the decisive issue is not what goes on in parliament. That only mirrors what goes on in the free life of civil society (*frie folkelige liv*). This is the important battlefield ... The forum (*tingmøde*) for you and me is not likely to be parliament ... but rather every time we are to settle matters within the municipality, when we pay tax, when we serve the community. In other words, every time we meet and interact within our community and this happens many times a day for each of us ...[14]

After the interwar period, it was a painful lesson to Koch that democracy could not be secured by means of laws and constitutions. In 1945 he formulated his view on the insufficiency of mere trust in democratic institutions: "Democracy

---

14   Hal Koch, *Dagen og Vejen* (Copenhagen: Westermann, 1942), 39.

cannot be captured in a formula. It is not a system or a doctrine."[15] Koch repeatedly pointed to England as one of the oldest democracies, and yet one without a democratic constitution. By accentuating democracy as a way of life, Koch wished to draw attention away from the political candidates to the political subject matter, away from the self-interest of the citizen to what was better for the community. To Koch, what is pivotal in a democracy is not the casting of the ballots but rather the debate preceding the vote.[16]

Koch did not target Ross and other law professionals who had worked with jurisprudential aspects of democracy. Rather, his appeal to democracy as a way of life was a warning against the dictatorship of a populist majority or a proletariat. He stressed that every citizen had the obligation to be aware of his or her responsibility for the well-being of not only themselves and their kind, but also the well-being of their neighbor in the minority party. Democracy was not accomplished by the establishment of a particular voting system, it was a duty to each and every member of a human community.

Anthropology and the ontology of a community are important parts of Koch's understanding of democratic living, and again we find significant references to his theological background. Koch begins one of the central chapters of the book as follows: "When two, three or more—possibly an entire people—are to make a decision about the future or lay down a law for their communal dealings, one can rest assured that there will be disagreements."[17] Koch's description of some kind of natural law of social units alludes to Matthew 18:20, but at the same time he emphasizes the difference between the social situation in the Christian church and in society. In the Christian church, the divine intrudes in the worldly sphere and creates a kind of unity out of numerous individuals.

The secular community has no such nature. Here, conversely, it is only natural that conflicts of interest occur. The crucial element is how a society handles these natural conflicts. One possible way is by the law of nature or the law of the jungle, in which it is everyone for themselves and the survival of the strongest, superiority of brute force and self-interest.

Koch claimed that in order to avoid the law of the jungle and in order to establish civilization, the state must exercise power and justice. When determining the right way to construct society or state, or when finding the right solutions to societal problems or conflicts, Koch was reluctant about the use

---

15   Koch, *Hvad er demokrati?*, 11-12.
16   Mogens Herman Hansen, *Demokrati som styreform og som ideologi* (Copenhagen: Museum Tusculanum Forlag, 2010), 29-30.
17   Koch, *Hvad er demokrati?*, 14; Reeh, *Hal Koch*, 655.

of natural law. He was aware of German theologians' use of creation theology (*Schöpfungsordnungen*) in the interwar period, and this also made him hesitant about accentuating these elements in N.F.S. Grundtvig's work, as he feared they might be misinterpreted.[18] The few times when Koch refers to natural law, he expresses caution and strong reservation. Instead, he prefers to call on the Golden Rule as an expression of ancient thought, or the Gospel according to Matthew.

To Koch, another possible—and preferable—way is to keep raw power in check through dialogue. In dialogue, the members of society engage in conversation based on respect for their fellow human being. Here, the person is not only occupied with his or her own interest but is also concerned for the well-being of the neighbor.

According to Koch, this way of conduct is not a specialty of Lutherans or a Lutheran creation, but is the least evil way of exercising power in the worldly sphere. It accords with the Lutheran anthropology and the Christian demand for attention to one's fellow man. By making "dialogue" the nature of democracy, Koch dismisses contemporary communists' claims to be true democrats, since they were arguing for restrictions on the freedom of speech and the free press. Koch first aired his thoughts on dialogue and democracy in a polemical feature article against the propaganda of his communist colleagues Professor Jørgen Jørgensen and Professor Mogens Fogh, who had argued strongly for the limitation of free speech and supported military action in order to accomplish a true democracy, namely "economic democracy".[19]

When Koch makes dialogue the nature of democracy, he also claims that politics and law have a relative character. In an authoritarian regime—a dictatorship or a theocracy—the word of a law can be considered the final say in the matter. There is no dialogue after the leader or the vote has determined the word of the law. In a true democracy, Koch asserts, the dialogue about how to find the best solution possible continues after the vote on a law, since all laws and decisions have a relative or temporal character. Morals and sentiments of justice are cultural and historical.

---

18   Hal Koch, *Grundtvig* (Copenhagen: Gyldendal, 1943), see also Niels Henrik Gregersen, "Nordic Lutheranism and Secular Law: The Role of Law in the Grundtvigian Theologies of K.E. Løgstrup and Regin Prenter," this volume.

19   Henrik S. Nissen, "Demokratidebatten efter befrielsen," in *Fra mellemkrigstid til efterkrigstid*, ed. Henrik Dethlefsen and Henrik Lundbak (Copenhagen: Museum Tusculanum, 1998), 163-77. See also Søren Hein Rasmussen and Niels Kayser Nielsen, *Strid om demokratiet: Artikler fra en dansk debat 1945-46* (Århus: Aarhus Universitetsforlag, 2003).

Alf Ross

Alf Ross (1899-1979) was a Danish professor of law. Unlike Koch, he was not from a family of academics. His father was a civil servant who had worked his way up in social status, and Ross and his two sisters were raised in an upper middle-class home in Copenhagen. In 1922, Ross completed his law degree with remarkable academic distinctions. He was inclined to do more philosophical studies but took up employment in a barrister's office.[20] In 1923, he married Else-Merete Helweg-Larsen (1903-1976), who later became a high-school teacher and a member of parliament for the social liberal party, *Radikale Venstre*, during 1960-1973. The practical work with law did not satisfy him, and he decided to continue his academic work instead.[21] He easily received a scholarship, and went abroad to learn with an open mind. In Vienna he was inspired by Hans Kelsen (1881-1973), and this led to his book *Theorie der Rechtsquellen*.[22] He submitted it as a doctoral thesis it to the Faculty of Law at the University of Copenhagen in 1926, but it was not accepted. He then went to Uppsala, where he studied practical philosophy with Axel Hägerström (1868-1939), and his doctoral dissertation was finally accepted at the Faculty of Philosophy in 1929.

Ross's first work was occupied with questions regarding law as social reality and normative validity, *Sein* and *Sollen*. His philosophical bent is also present in his second, impressive volume, *Kritik der sogenannten praktischen Erkenntnis: Prolegomena zu einer Kritik der Rechtswissenshaft* (1933). In this publication dedicated to Hägerström, Ross argues that normative statements in morals and law are assertions about human values, wishes, and emotions but not cognitive expressions or objective conclusions. To put it another way, moral philosophy can be a science about values, but never a science that establishes values.[23] In his next opus, *Reality and Validity in Jurisprudence* (1934), he developed this line of thought with what has been called "a historical socio-psychological model of the phenomenon of law".[24] This is not the place to explicate this important work, but for the theme of this chapter it is important that Ross continued his work on the difference between and consequences of *Sein* and *Sollen* with regard to law. The validity of law cannot rest on *Sollen* but the validity itself is part of reality, or *Sein*.

---

20 Knud Waaben, "Alf Ross 1899-1979: A Biographical Sketch," *European Journal of International Law* 14, no. 4 (2003): 661-74, 661.
21 Jens Evald, *Alf Ross: Et liv* (Copenhagen: Jurist og Økonomforbundets Forlag, 2010), 39-41.
22 Alf Ross, *Theorie der Rechtsquellen: Ein Beitrag zur Theorie des positiven Rechts auf Grundlage dogmenhistorischer Untersuchungen* (Leipzig: Franz Deuticke, 1929).
23 Waaben, "Alf Ross 1899-1979," 663.
24 Waaben, "Alf Ross 1899-1979," 663.

In 1934, Ross published *Virkelighed og Gyldighed*, which at last earned him a doctoral degree in law from the University of Copenhagen. The title of the English edition is *Towards a Realistic Jurisprudence*.[25] In 1935, he was appointed Reader at the Faculty of Law in Copenhagen with constitutional law as his responsibility, and in 1938, he was appointed Professor of International Law. As a member of the faculty, he continued to work towards what has been called "Nordic Reality", and the law as social reality. It has been pointed out that a line can be discerned between Ross and the founder of the faculty, Anders Sandøe Ørsted (1778-1860), who was not a protagonist of natural law at the university, but instead regarded law as a phenomenon of this world that is determined by time and place.[26] In other words, law is time-bound and relative, an expression of ideas of justice and moral values embodied in statutes. Ross took up and developed Ørsted's line of thought and became part of the so-called Scandinavian legal realism movement.

Alf Ross' *Credo*

In 1974, Ross wrote the essay *Credo* in which he expressed some of his thoughts on religion and law.[27] He begins with reflections on how to understand the words "believe in". They can mean that you assume or expect something that you cannot know. But they can also signify an unfounded certainty that is elevated beyond doubt without proof or rational reasoning. This "certainty" identifies itself with knowledge and is in opposition to doubt or disbelief. One could also say it represents a belief beyond or despite reason.

The third way to understand the words to "believe in" regards what one holds not to be true but good and valuable. Ross quotes Luther's catechism, in which he believes in God in the sense that he has trust in him and expects all good things to come from him. As a parallel, Ross mentions how millions of Germans believed in Hitler and regarded him as a god. In this manner, one could also believe in a cause: for instance, feminism or temperance, an ideal such as justice or love, or an ideology like Nazism, Marxism, or democracy.

Moving on to the question of what he himself believes in, Ross declares that

---

25 The English appeared as *Towards a Realistic Jurisprudence: A Criticism of the Dualism in Law* (Copenhagen: Einar Munksgaard, 1946).
26 Waaben, "Alf Ross 1899-1979," 664.
27 *Weekendavisen* 21. juni 1974. It was republished as "Credo" in Alf Ross, *Ret som teknik, kunst og videnskab—og andre essays*, ed. Isi Foighel, Hans Gammeltoft-Hansen, and Henrik Zahle (Copenhagen: Jurist- og Økonomforbundets Forlag, 1999), 383-90.

he will not defend his confession. He can only state that like everyone else he assumes and presupposes a number of things, but:

> It is more important to state that all certainty of faith is unfamiliar to me. To hold something true without good reason is meaningless to me. We do not have the slightest reason to believe that a "God" exists. And thoughts on his existence easily lead to contradictions ... And we do not have the slightest reason to assume that our life should continue after death.[28]

A dualism of body and soul is a delusion, and Ross considers the concept of the soul a fable. In other words, he refuses to confess a metaphysical reality. Instead, he declares:

> I believe in the creative force of thought, fantasy, and will expressed in the individual human being's contribution to science, art, philosophy, and politics ... The societal framework can make it more or less difficult for the individual human being to blossom and express their personal freedom. That is why I believe in democracy. For that is the state form that gives the best conditions possible for individual liberty and autonomy.[29]

Ross declares that he believes in the moral freedom and responsibility of the individual as well as in the boundless selfishness of human beings. He elaborates upon his anthropology with statements on the desire for power and supremacy as fundamental characteristics of being human. Therefore, he cannot believe in love or justice. However, Ross believes in justice as a willingness to judge fairly in a conflict, but it must be considered an ideal that can never be fulfilled. Ross has been described as a moral nihilist and a moral sceptic, and he denies that moral claims express anything that may be called truth.[30] One could connect this to his views on legal realism and the perception that norms are set by people in a cultural and historical context. At the same time, Ross' *Credo* highlights his anti-metaphysical perception of law, his endeavor to work empirically with it and his fundamental view that values cannot be debated on purely rational grounds. This is also evident in Ross's texts on democracy where he says: "I know very well what I believe in [i.e. democracy] and would

---

28 Alf Ross, "Credo," 385.
29 Alf Ross, "Credo," 387.
30 Jes Bjarup, "Jens Evald, Alf Ross: Et Liv," (review of *Alf Ross: Et liv* by Jens Evald) in *Tidsskrift for Rettsvitenskab* 127, no. 2 (2014): 270.

fight for if it comes to that. But I do not fancy that it can be proven by science nor that my position is the 'right' one."[31]

Ross' *Credo* leaves the reader with a clear picture of his reluctance towards old school metaphysical Christianity as well as natural law. How, then, does he then understand democracy which he claims to "believe in"? Is there a connecting principle or coherence between his philosophy of life and his work on democracy?

Alf Ross' *Why Democracy?*

In 1946, Ross published *Why Democracy?* He began working on it during the Nazi occupation of Denmark, and some of the preliminary work is visible in the pamphlet *Communism and Democracy,* from the Social Democratic publishing house, *Fremad*. Ross states that the aim of his book is to stimulate an awareness regarding democracy and dictatorship, and to defend against the threat of communism.

Ross distinguishes among three basic understandings of the term "democracy". He himself is occupied with democracy as a form of government of state, "political democracy". This means that the people as a whole (not only a section of the population or a single individual) is the supreme sovereign of the state. Political democracy is a judicial and formal concept that expresses a procedure and practice for the establishment of the political will of the state. It is the rule of the state *by* the people. It does not concern the goals nor the means of the state.

So-called "economic democracy" (the model of the German Democratic Republic), on the other hand, has the goal of government as its point of departure. It is the rule of the state, not by but *for* the people. According to Ross, communists misuse the goodwill of the concept of democracy when they apply it to their autocratic form of government or dictatorship of the proletariat.

A third and perfectly legitimate way of speaking about democracy is as a mentality, a way of life. Ross refers to and endorses the work of Koch. In fact, Ross speaks of Koch's understanding as the heart of the concept of democracy.[32] However, as a professor of law he concentrates his work on democracy on its constitutional and legal aspects.

Ross defines democracy as a form of state in which the inhabitants judicially are the political sovereign of the state. Such a democracy can be operational-

---

31 Alf Ross, *Hvorfor demokrati?* (Copenhagen: Munksgaard, 1946), 182.
32 Ross, *Hvorfor Demokrati?*, 165.

ized through the principle of representativeness. However, there are different degrees of representativeness; an absolute monarch or dictator can sometimes claim to represent the people. This means that one must also take effective representativeness into account. Direct elections give the viewpoints of the inhabitants more effect, whereas the strength of a representative democracy rests on the control the inhabitants have over their representatives. One must also consider the extent of the democracy, how far the influence and control of democratic elections reaches within the state. In other words, different forms of representative democracy may have different degrees of democratic intensity, effect, and extent.

In order to establish a solid political democracy, one needs a democratic constitution. Here, one could draw a parallel to Ross' legal philosophy and his focus on legal positivism. But according to Ross, representative democracy also builds on what he labels an ideology. Direct democracy is based on independence, while dictatorship is based on the need for leadership: the two meet in a harmonious way in representative democracy. The leadership is under the control of the people and dependent on upholding the trust of citizens on the basis of free expression of opinion and critique. In Ross' opinion, education or *Bildung* is a necessary part of a representative democracy.[33]

In addition, it is of fundamental importance to Ross that there is what he terms a "democratic mentality" present outside the formal field of governance and judicial organization. Whenever power is exercised in a human relationship, one can talk of a democratic—or non-democratic—mentality.[34] Ross uses the relationship between parents and children as an example of a human relation that can build on either autocratic or democratic principles. A democratic upbringing is characterized by "respect for the child's own personality and striving for the best conditions of growth for the youth. It stimulates self-independence and self-determination; by means of conversation, it seeks to explain the reasons for the viewpoint of the adult in order to gain the understanding and approval of the child."[35] Ross goes on to show how democratic relations between humans also can be vital in other areas of society: for example between teacher and pupil, husband and wife, employer and employee, priest and congregation, in an association, in management, and in social society. In other words, the idea of fundamental equality or *egalitet* is vital to Ross' concept of democracy both as a formal principle of governance and as a mentality intimately connected to

---

33   Evald, *Alf Ross*, 184-85; Reeh, *Hal Koch*, 669-70.
34   Ross, *Hvorfor Demokrati?*, 228-30.
35   Ross, *Hvorfor Demokrati?*, 229.

religion and Christianity. He does not investigate the theological arguments, as Koch does. Instead, he is occupied with the formal structure of governance in different churches. He describes the Roman Catholic Church as a typical and distinct autocratic body. By contrast, Ross characterizes Protestant churches as "relatively democratic"[36] and he stresses that democratic ideas in England emerged due to a wish for a new constitution for the Church.

Just like his theological colleague, Ross also emphasizes the need in democracy for "a readiness to listen to others" and a willingness to submit to a common understanding out of respect for the other party. In other words, Ross is not at all blind to factors that are not strictly part of constitutional law and political government, but as a professor of law, he primarily concentrates on these issues.

Nevertheless, he was well aware of and interested in other perspectives. Ross and his wife were members of a private study group that debated the issues. The other members of the group were the Social Democrat and later Cabinet Minister Lis Groes and her husband Ebbe Groes, head of department in the Ministry of Finance Erik Ib Schmidt and his wife, the pedagogical pioneer Anne-Marie Nørvig, and last but not least Bodil and Hal Koch. All were strong figures in the public debate and very much occupied with the organization of postwar society in Denmark.

Koch and Ross' *Nordic Democracy*

The reorganization of postwar Nordic societies was the main motivation for Koch and Ross's joint anthology, *Nordic Democracy* (1949). In its preface, Koch and Ross evoke the experience of World War II with "the battle for democracy and freedom"[37] and the subsequent Cold War chasm between the postwar societies in East and West as the incentive for this almost 500-page volume. The authors wish to draw attention to the way of the Nordic countries, as they thought that their democratic anatomy could be an alternative to the East-West dichotomy.[38] Through their history, social structure, and cultural approach, the Nordic countries were knit together and created their own political and social development. They established political and social forms that were not copied from Eastern or Western ideals, but rather constituted a third, Nordic framework

---

36 Ross, *Hvorfor Demokrati?*, 230.
37 Koch and Ross, *Nordisk Demokrati*, XIV.
38 It was originally the plan of Koch and Ross to have the book published in English, but it has not been possible to establish why the two, internationally well connected and otherwise efficient, editors failed in this regard.

for human life. These societies constitute a type of "democracy in the middle" that includes the Western respect for personal and political freedom along with the Eastern ideals of economic and social equalization.

The book falls in two parts. After introductions and recommendations from the prime ministers Tage Erlander, Einar Gerhardsen, and Hans Hedtoft, the first part is called "The History of Nordic Democracy." A sizeable chapter depicts early Nordic legacies of freedom, and this is followed by three chapters with expositions of "The Technique of Democracy", "Political Parties", and "Peoples Movements." All three contain subdivisions covering developments in Sweden, Norway, and Denmark, thereby taking the specific historical and national situation as a point of departure but also stimulating comparative perspectives and allowing a transnational Nordic structure to emerge. The historical section concludes with statistics on the number of votes from the Nordic countries' elections 1918-1948.

The second part of the volume is "systematic," as the editors label it. It is not their intention to display "the pure doctrine of democracy" or a democratic "orthodoxy".[39] Rather, their wish is to have 18 Nordic intellectuals and academics investigate problems connected with life in a democratic society "seen from a Nordic background but with universal perspectives." In the following, we shall concentrate on the subjects of law and religion as they appear in this part of the book, and in particular on the two independent contributions by Koch and Ross.

The title of Ross' article is "What is Democracy?"—the same as Koch's book from the year before. Like Koch, he enters the debate about the definition and understanding of the concept. From the very start, it is clear that it is of key importance to him to dismiss or repudiate the communist use of the term. To Ross, democracy is a judicial line of procedure and form of organization, a method for the execution of public authority; communist states cannot be considered democratic.

After explaining his concept of democracy as a form of government, Ross moves on to a passage on the ideas that are fundamental to his judicial concepts. He accentuates the idea of respect for "the moral personality of the human being," rooted in a humanist and Christian tradition, and especially the idea that every human being has infinite value in the eyes of God.[40] According to Ross, a fellow human being should not be treated as a means to an end, but an end in itself. This is part of the Christian heritage in Europe, he claims, but it is not uniquely Christian: it is the mental foundation for a democratic government in

---

39 Koch and Ross, *Nordisk Demokrati*, XV.
40 Koch and Ross, *Nordisk Demokrati*, 202.

secular society as well. Respect for the moral personality of the human being is a recognition of its autonomy, its freedom of self-determination, and it is the philosophical basis for the legitimacy of any majority rule.

Ross moves on to emphasize what can be termed "democratic manners" or a "democratic culture." Here, again, he mentions the Catholic Church as having a pronounced autocratic culture, while the egalitarian and anti-hierarchical ideas of Protestant Christianity have stimulated democratic ways of life. However, the nexus between religion and democracy is not the topic of Ross' contribution, and he concludes his text with a praise of dialogue and a renewed rejection of the communist claim to qualify as democratic.

Koch's contribution is called "Democracy and Religion." The theological professor points out that the role of religion, especially Christianity, for the development of modern democracy is contested. Some have seen Christianity as an enemy of democracy, stressing that the church has often been on the side of authoritarian rulers and reactionary elements, and that it has been used as the "opium of the people." Others have claimed that only Christianity can "make the world safe for democracy." From the beginning of civilization, religion and power, including political power, have been closely connected. Koch locates in ancient Greece an important break with theocracy, in which mythos and logos were partly separated, creating a space for rational political debate. In the Roman Republic, religion was in many cases a private matter. The foundations of the Republic were *lex*, *libertas*, and *iustitia*—and political thought was based on arguments and reason rather than on the authority of priesthood. However, the imperial cult and devotion to the emperor turned things in a different direction and became an example of the human inclination to elevate the relative and earthly into something absolute or divine. In some ways, the Roman idea of power and authority extended into the Middle Ages, where *regnum* and *sacerdotium* were closely connected and the idea of theocracy was supported by both. At the time of the Renaissance and the Protestant Reformation, there was a new rupture in intellectual history in which human reason was detached from religion. Within the field of political science, reason became an authority that gradually separated from religion and itself replaced religious authorities. According to Koch's narrative, this is clearly an improvement.

In his article, Koch repeats his consistent position that, just like there is no such thing as a Christian math, there is no such thing as a Christian politics.[41] Politics must build on reason, as it is expressed in the political debate, and is

---

41 Compare Gregersen, "Nordic Lutheranism and Secular Law: The Role of Law," in this volume.

embedded—and limited—in a cultural and relative, historical context. Here, we find an intellectual fellowship between the theology of Koch and the legal positivism of Ross. Consequently, one could say that, from this perspective, there is no particular connection between Christianity and democratic government as Koch and Ross both see it.

However, if the concept of democracy is expanded from the narrow meaning of a formal way of government to that of a general way of life, a connection with Christianity emerges. Koch repeats his claim that, as a consequence of holding a Christian faith in salvation or justification *sola fide*, the Christian is responsible for and committed to his neighbor or fellow citizen. This is an ethical demand, here and now, but it cannot be fixed in a general political principle or by law. If one attempts to create specific laws out of the gospel, it is no longer gospel but law. Instead, this ethical demand calls the Christian to engage in dialogue with his neighbor and to pay attention to his or her problems—also when the neighbor is an opponent or constitutes a minority in society.

Koch thus comes to the same result as Ross: that the true Nordic (Lutheran) form of government is a secular democracy—even though secular democracy was unthinkable to Luther himself.

Concluding Remarks

As illustrated above, one can identify strong parallels between the concepts of secularity as conceived by the theology professor Koch and the law professor Ross. They shared a reluctance towards metaphysics—in theology and law respectively—and favored a secular law and constitution of society. Both rejected the idea of a God-given pattern, law, or regulation of society. Both dismissed the use of natural law as well as metaphysical arguments for law and the construction of society. All laws and constitutions of society must be considered relative and historical.

There are other parallels between Koch and Ross. Both felt a strong inclination to use their academic disciplines and platforms in the university to fight totalitarian regimes and ways of thought, be the right-wing or left-wing. In the eyes of both, totalitarianism could be seen as a false "belief" or idolatry. Both shared a pessimistic anthropology and emphasized the human instinct to usurp power. Moreover, their anthropology prevented them from assuming that an ideal society was a realistic option. Instead, both tried to warn against postwar idealism and utopias. At the same time, both supported the contemporary social democratic egalitarianism and vision for a welfare state as a realistic and responsible goal. The wives of both became members of parliament and driving forces in the creation of the postwar welfare state. Koch as well as Ross were elitist, academic professors who made a remarkable and very effective effort to communicate to the public and to be active agents in the development of society in general.

Ross obviously did not subscribe to a classical metaphysical Christianity. But there is a coherence between his philosophy of life and anthropology and his work on law and democracy. Even though it may seem a contradiction, Koch's struggle for secular democracy and political arguments was deeply rooted in his concept of Christianity.

Koch's *What is Democracy?* and Ross' *Why Democracy?* were translated into several languages and were published in numerous editions. Their collective opus, *Nordic Democracy*, became an immediate standard in postwar Denmark, and was of key importance for the perception of democracy and self-understanding among Danes. Throughout the second half of the 20th century, it was part of the mandatory curriculum for all schoolteachers and left its mark on the education and socialization of children. In 2008, the work of Koch and Ross became part of the official "Danish Canon of Democracy" published by the Danish Ministry of Education.[42]

However, it would not be loyal to their way of thinking to see their perception of democracy as something normative or as an ideal. It is, rather, to be understood as an expression of thought and a historical reality, which we may learn from in order to take better care of the development of the society of our own time.

Bibliography

Literature

Balling, Jakob. "Hal Koch som dansk historiker under besættelsen." In *Historisk kristendom: Artikler og afhandlinger i udvalg*, 293-304. Copenhagen: Anis, 2003.
Bjarup, Jes. "Jens Evald, Alf Ross: Et Liv." *Tidsskrift for Rettsvitenskab* 127, no. 2 (2014): 268-85.
Danish Ministry of Education. *The Danish Democracy Canon*. Copenhagen, 2008.
Evald, Jens. *Alf Ross: Et liv.* Copenhagen: Jurist og Økonomforbundets Forlag, 2010.
Hansen, Mogens Herman. *Demokrati som styreform og som ideologi.* Copenhagen: Museum Tusculanum Forlag, 2010.

---

42   Danish Ministry of Education, *The Danish Democracy Canon* (Copenhagen, 2008).

Koch, Hal. *Pronoia und Paideusis: Studien über Origenes und sein Verhältnis zum Platonismus*. Berlin/Leipzig: Walter de Gruyter, 1932.
Koch, Hal. *Dagen og Vejen*. Copenhagen: Westermann, 1942.
Koch, Hal. *Grundtvig*. Copenhagen: Gyldendal, 1943.
Koch, Hal. *Hvad er Demokrati?* Copenhagen: Gyldendal, 1945/2015.
Koch, Hal. *Martin Luther*. Copenhagen: Gads Forlag, 1958.
Koch, Hal, and Alf Ross. *Nordisk Demokrati*. Copenhagen: Westermann, 1949.
Korsgaard, Ove. "Koch: En republikaner i grundtvigiansk klædedragt." In *Poetisk demokrati: Om personlig dannelse og samfundsdannelse*, edited by Ove Korsgaard, 63-82. Copenhagen: Gads Forlag, 2001.
Møller, Jes Fabricius. *Hal Koch: En biografi*. Copenhagen: Gads Forlag, 2009.
Nissen, Henrik S. "Demokratidebatten efter befrielsen." In *Fra mellemkrigstid til efterkrigstid*, edited by Henrik Dethlefsen and Henrik Lundbak, 163-77. Copenhagen: Museum Tusculanums Forlag, 1998.
Nissen, Henrik S., and Henning Poulsen. *På dansk friheds grund: Dansk Ungdomssamvirke og De ældres Råd 1940-1945*. Copenhagen: Gyldendal, 1963.
Possing, Birgitte. *Uden omsvøb: Portræt af Bodil Koch*. Copenhagen: Gyldendal, 2007.
Rasmussen, Søren Hein, and Niels Kayser Nielsen. *Strid om demokratiet: Artikler fra en dansk debat 1945-46*. Århus: Aarhus Universitetsforlag, 2003.
Reeh, Tine. "Borgerlig Indretning—Kristi Kirke: Bodil Kochs stilling til folkekirkens tilpasning til det danske samfund efter Anden Verdenskrig." In *Kirkeretsantologi*, edited by Svend Andersen, Peter Christensen, Peter Garde, Peter Lodberg, and Anders Jørgensen, 49-66. Copenhagen: Selskab for Kirkeret, 2012.
Reeh, Tine. *Kristendom, historie, demokrati: Hal Koch 1932-1945*. Copenhagen: Museum Tusculanums Forlag, 2012.
Ross, Alf. *Theorie der Rechtsquellen: Ein Beitrag zur Theorie des positiven Rechts auf Grundlage dogmenhistorischer Untersuchungen*. Leipzig: Franz Deuticke, 1929.
Ross, Alf. *Hvorfor demokrati?* Copenhagen: Munksgaard, 1946.
Ross, Alf. *Towards a Realistic Jurisprudence: A Criticism of the Dualism in Law*. Copenhagen: Einar Munksgaard, 1946.
Ross, Alf. "Credo." In *Ret som teknik, kunst og videnskab—og andre essays*, published by Isi Foighel, Hans Gammeltoft-Hansen and Henrik Zahle. Copenhagen: Jurist- og Økonomforbundets Forlag, 1999.
Sode-Madsen, Hans. "Hal Koch og ungdommens opdragelse til demokrati." In *Fra mellemkrigstid til efterkrigstid*, edited by Henrik Dethlefsen and Henrik Lundbak, 297-331. Copenhagen: Museum Tusculanums Forlag, 1998.
Waaben, Knud. "Alf Ross 1899-1979: A Biographical Sketch." *European Journal of International Law* 14, no. 4 (2003): 661-74.

Other Sources

Danish National Archives, Personal Archives, Jens Schoubo Nørregaard (06073).
Danish National Archives, Personal Archives, Hans Harald (Hal) Koch (07280).

4. Christian Torchbearers in the Dark of Positivism: Survivors and Catalysts within Nordic Law and Religion 1950-2000

Kjell Å. Modéer

Prologue

The period of time we deal with in this volume is very dramatic and turbulent from the perspective of intellectual history.[1] In the postwar period, the paradigm of modernity, the social welfare state, positivism, pragmatism, secularization, and decolonialization were dominant. The period of the "social" was succeeded by a paradigm dominated by the human rights revolution. It evolved from the end of World War II, and that period continued into that of "late modernity".[2] Today, we live in a post-secular period of time in which transparent geographical and cultural borders and a turn towards history and tradition have appeared on the scene, perhaps not as a dominant factor but as a significant part of the intellectual discourses regarding law, politics, and religion.

This period of time has been described as "The Fall of the Priests and the Rise of the Lawyers," indicating the fall of the traditional professional calling and the rise of the market and its corporate lawyers.[3] When the Nordic countries left the traumas of World War II behind them, secularization became a keyword for postwar modernity. In Sweden, the 1951 Freedom of Religion Act introduced the negative freedom of religion—the citizen's right not to have a religion. It opened the door not only to individual freedom, but also to the eroding secularization of the Christian culture which for centuries had dominated Nordic society.

---

1 Duncan Kennedy, "Three Globalizations of Law and Legal Thought: 1850-2000," in *The New Law and Economic Development: A Critical Appraisal*, ed. David M. Trubek and Alvaro Santos (Cambridge: Cambridge University Press, 2006), 19-73.
2 Ulrich Beck, Anthony Giddens, and Scott Lash, *Reflexive Modernisierung: Eine Kontroverse* (Frankfurt: Suhrkamp, 1996); Kjell Å. Modéer, *Juristernas nära förflutna: Rättskulturer i förändring* (Stockholm: Santérus Förlag, 2009), 327ff.
3 Philip R. Wood, *The Fall of the Priests and the Rise of the Lawyers* (London: Hart Publishing, 2016).

During this period of time, the majority state churches in the Nordic countries also faced many challenges. Critical perspectives regarding the concepts of metaphysics, the arrival of foreign religions as well as internal conflicts within Christianity in an increasingly secularized context all made it necessary for the churches to defend their positions. A cultural analysis from a Christian perspective, however, yields the picture of a tenacious tradition, a deep structure of Christian culture defending its declining position.[4] The aim of this chapter is to identify this deep structure and how it survived critical, secular, and rational ways of thought from 1950 up until the implementation of the new relationship between the Swedish church and the state beginning in 2000.

The Renaissance of the Concept of *Rechtstheologie*

The most important perspective for this topic is that of how the two classical concepts of law and justice, traditionally regarded as Siamese twins, were dramatically separated from each other during the modernity of the postwar period. Only the law survived in the postwar anti-metaphysical paradigm. In a seminar during my law studies at the Faculty of Law of the University of Lund in the early 1960s, one of my fellow students asked a question of the professor regarding the importance of "human rights" within civil law. He received the following answer: "It's not a topic we discuss in the law. Such matters you can discuss in the coffee break".

In 1995, Göran Göransson (1925-1998), the most prominent lawyer within Swedish church law of the postwar period, published the article "Om rätten och rättsteologin" ("On Law and the Theology of Law"). It was based on the lecture he held at a seminar when he received an honorary degree from the Faculty of Theology at the University of Lund.[5] Göransson underlined in this article, that church law is not only administrative law, it has an underlying theology, a *Rechtstheologie*, which belongs to the borderless, deep structures of European law.

Göransson passed away in 1998, so he never experienced the new relationship between church and state in Sweden in 2000, a work he had been deeply involved in since the 1950s. This chapter can be regarded as my tribute to him

---

4   Kaarlo Tuori, "Towards a Multilayered View of Modern Law," in *Justice, Morality and Society: A Tribute to Aleksander Peczenik on the Occasion of his 60th Birthday 16 November 1997*, ed. Aulis Arnio, Robert Alexy, and Gunnar Bergholz (Lund: Juristförlaget i Lund, 1997), 432ff.

5   Göran Göransson, "Om rätten och rättsteologin," *Svensk Teologisk Kvartaltidskrift* 71, no. 3 (1995): 111ff.

as a torchbearer and to his great contributions to law and theology as well as law and religion.

In this chapter, Göransson will serve as an informative example of the contextual transition from modernity to late modernity within the field of law and religion. It will describe the dominant discourses within this field, the different constitutional concepts in the Nordic countries arising from a pragmatic view related to the secularization of family law, and to Göransson's professional networks—especially his affiliation with Nordic and international relations. This narrative will portray Göransson as a catalyst in the Nordic Christian legal culture which was changing during the period 1950-2000.

Göransson was born in Gothenburg in 1925 and passed away in Stockholm in 1998.[6] He was raised in a bourgeois family (his father was the city statistician in Gothenburg) in the interwar period and was confirmed by the Bishop of Härnösand (northern Sweden) Torsten Bohlin (1889-1950), a close friend of Göransson's father. Bohlin was one of the great Swedish theologians of his time and one of Archbishop Nathan Söderblom's (1866-1931) devoted supporters during the first part of the 20th century. As Göransson once remarked, the bishop talked with his confirmand about the difficulties and richness of Christian belief "from his own experiences and in a vocabulary [he] understood".[7] It was Bohlin who made it possible for Göransson to "observe the essentials in Christianity and dare to *start* to believe". "He helped us with the first steps, the most difficult ones and those one hesitates the most to take".[8]

Göransson began his academic studies with a B.A. in foreign languages at the University of Gothenburg and in 1946 moved to Uppsala where he began his law studies. The intellectual debates in Uppsala in the postwar years were very much related to the Uppsala School of Law (Scandinavian legal realism).[9]

---

6   Kjell Å. Modéer, "Göran Göransson 1925-1998: A Post-Secular Catalyst in Modern Swedish Church Law," in *Law and the Christian Tradition in Scandinavia: The Writings of Great Nordic Jurists*, ed. Kjell Å. Modéer and Helle Vogt (London: Routledge, 2020). See also Kjell Å Modéer, "Kyrkans rätt framför dess lag: Europé och jurist i den svenska folkkyrkans tjänst; Göran Göransson (1925-1998)—en kyrkorättshistorisk biografi," *Kyrkohistorisk Årsskrift* 119 (2019): 153-73.

7   Göran Göransson, "Min konfirmationslärare," in *En bok om Torsten Bohlin av 40 författare*, ed. Bo Bengtson and Gunnar Åkerstedt (J.A. Lindblads Förlag: Uppsala 1950), 307.

8   "[H]an underlättade för andra att se till det väsentliga i kristendomen och att våga *börja* tro. Så hjälpte han oss de första stegen, de som är de svåraste och som man tvekar mest inför." Göransson, "Min konfirmationslärare," 310.

9   Kjell Å. Modéer, "From Classical Legal Thought into a Human Rights Paradigm: Law and Religion in Three Different Contexts 1809-1950," in *Constitutionalisation and Hegemonisation: Exploring the Boundaries of Law and Religion 1800-1950*, ed. Anna-Sara Lind and Victoria Enkvist (Odense: University Press of Southern Denmark, *forthcoming*).

From a theological perspective, there was a parallel radical modern discourse during the years after the war. In 1946, the social-democratic parliamentarian Stellan Arvidson (1902-1997) together with the bishop (and former professor of theology) Bohlin published a widely read and discussed book on *Christianity—Against and pro (Kristendomen. Mot—för)*. When the Uppsala professor of philosophy Ingemar Hedenius (1908-1982) published his provocative work *Tro och vetande (Belief and Knowledge)* in 1949, he initiated an extensive debate on contemporary religion and presented a critical view regarding the role of the state church in the modern and democratic Swedish *folk-home* (*folkhemmet*). During his years at Uppsala, Göransson took intensively part in discussions on Hedenius' book.

Lawyers and Clergy during World War II in the Nordic Countries

During the war, there were several great individuals in all the Nordic countries who were identified with resistance, liberty, and Christian faith. They were lawyers, judges, and law professors—but also clergymen. In Denmark it was Kaj Munk, in Norway bishops Eivind Berggrav and Henrik Aubert Seip, and in Sweden bishops Gustaf Aulén and Tor Andræ. In neutral Sweden there were clergymen who resisted or avoided applying the German Nazi legislation, even though Sweden had international obligations to do so due to its ratification of the 1904 Hague Convention. Due to this ratification, the Swedish clergy were to implement the Nuremburg laws regarding the Jews who had emigrated to Sweden and wanted to marry here.[10]

National law and a patriotic church were the signs of the Nordic legal culture at a time when totalitarian states increasingly threatened the Nordic culture.

Societal cooperation between the Nordic countries was substantive and also continued from the interwar period onward. The foundation of the Nordic Association (*Föreningen Norden*) in 1919 marked the beginning of an inter-state organization independent of religious affiliation, and it attained great cultural importance and created impressive networks, which were of great importance during the war. This emphasis on Nordic cooperation underwent a renaissance in the postwar years with the foundation of the Nordic Council and the emphasis on cooperation had its parallels among the clergy.

---

10 Anders Jarlert, *Judisk "ras" som äktenskapshinder i Sverige: Effekten av Nürnberglagarna i Svenska kyrkans statliga funktion som lysningsförrättare 1935-1945* (Malmö: Sekel, 2006).

Apart from Sweden, the geopolitical situation of all the Nordic countries involved in the war activities created a special dichotomy between those who participated in war activities and those who did not. This situation became a modern deep structure which persisted throughout the period concerned in this book.[11]

The modernization of the Nordic Lutheran folk churches began already in the interwar period. In 1936, Sweden received a new diocese law, which mandated a new role between the clergy and the laity.[12]

In addition, idealists within the judiciary articulated their criticism not only of the un-law of the occupied entities but also of those who rigidly adjusted to legal positivism. The Norwegian Supreme Court's justices collectively declined to follow the laws of the Terboven regime 1940[13] and the decision of Andreas Cervin (1888-1972), a judge at the city court of Gothenburg, refused to adjust to the political regime and made a new translation into Swedish of Rudolf von Jhering's pamphlet *Der Kampf ums Recht* (*The Struggle for Law*), published in 1941.[14]

The international and ecumenical trend during the interwar period gradually changed into a more nationalistic and patriotic trend. For many Christians, their belief played an important role during the war. From a religious standpoint, the term "Second Religiousness" was used by the German philosopher Oswald Spengler (1880-1936) in his great meta-historical study published in 1918, *The Decline of the West (Der Untergang des Abendlandes)*. Spengler described the final phase in the spiritual development of a civilization, and he referred to a time when the primordial religion comes back: holy people, holy law, holy places overshadow the theological systems that the civilization create earlier in its history, as well as the skepticism that briefly replaces religion among the educated.[15] "Second Religiousness" became a term well-suited to the *Zeitgeist* of the modernity of the 20th century.

In modern democratic societies there was no longer any great divide between popular and elite opinion on these matters. The Swedish poet Hjalmar

---

11   Kjell Å. Modéer, "'Den kulan visste var den tog!': Om svenska juristers omvärldssyn 1935-1955," in *Festskrift till Per Henrik Lindblom*, ed. Torbjörn Andersson and Bengt Lindell (Uppsala: Iustus förlag, 2004), 443ff.
12   SFS 1936:567 Lag om domkapitel.
13   Hans Petter Graver, *Okkupasjonstidens Høyesterett* (Oslo: Pax Forlag, 2019), 21ff.; "Krigsstart 9. april 1940—høyesterett under krigen," Lovdata, accessed September 10, 2019, https://lovdata.no/artikkel/krigsstart_9__april_1940_-_hoyesterett_under_krigen/1532.
14   Rudolf von Jhering, *Striden för rätten*, trans. Andreas Cervin (Stockholm: Natur och kultur, 1941).
15   Oswald Spengler, *The Decline of the West* (New York: Knopf, 1926-1928).

Gullberg (1898-1961) is just one example. He debuted in 1933 with a widely read volume, *Kärlek i tjugonde seklet* (*Love in the 20th Century*). It was a brave collection of poems embracing an undogmatic religiosity. "With love and religion the poet conquered his audience, a big audience".[16] During World War II, Gullberg's nationalistic and religious poems became part of the literary canon of the time. This religous poetic paradigm of his endured up until 1951. That year, the Swedish daily *Svenska Dagbladet* published a poem of his with the Nietzschean message *Gott ist tot*, "God is dead." This statement became a symbolic message of its time. Gullberg had adjusted to postwar modernity and its irreligious character.[17]

The Young Post-World War II Generation as Catalyst for Christian Faith

The paradigmatic new start for the young postwar generations also included a revitalization of the religious life. It actually was a continuous process from the wartime when the Nordic folk churches had served as a secure place for national collectivism with regard to historical, patriotic, and religious values.

Göransson became emblematic of the legal culture of the autonomous church in the modern welfare state. His generation developed from the nation state with open borders. The younger generations of the World War II had been raised with closed borders. Even if Göransson was situated in a very national Swedish legal context, he became an internationally oriented jurist. This orientation started immediately after the war.

In contrast to the Swedish national legal culture during the war, the international contexts of the intellectual debates in Uppsala in the late 1940s were much more colorful, rich, and engaged regarding the foundations of the law "in the ruins of a perverted legal system, whose consequences had raised abomination and against which one wanted to create guarantees for the future".[18] The European postwar legal and constitutional discourses were connected to the concept of *human dignity* and *natural law*, especially in the canon law of the Roman Catholic Church. The modern Swedish jurists, trained in the Uppsala School of Law, were extremely reluctant regarding this revival of natural law.[19]

---

16 Olle Holmberg, *Hjalmar Gullberg: En vänbok* (Stockholm: Bonniers, 1966), 162.
17 Holmberg, *Hjalmar Gullberg*, 160ff.
18 Göransson, "Om rätten," 112.
19 Modéer, "'Den kulan visste var den tog!'," 443ff.

In addition, after World War II, the churches became important institutions for restoring belief in human dignity. The concept of human dignity engaged theologians as well as jurists. As early as 1942, Bishop Bohlin had published an article entitled "Kampen för människovärdet" ("The Struggle for Human Dignity"), in which he formulated Christ as our incomparably best spiritual asset. "He is the only great hope for our ill-fated generation. In that sign the struggle for human dignity sometime in the future will be turned into victory."[20]

Immediately after the war, international Christian organizations were reorganized. In the Lutheran World Foundation as well as the World Council of the Churches the Nordic representation was remarkable. The Lutheran World Federation was founded at a conference in Lund, Sweden, held from June 30 to July 6, 1947.[21] Under the theme "The Lutheran Church in the World Today," 200 delegates from 26 countries participated and elected Professor Anders Nygren (1890-1978), Lund, as the first president of the federation. It was hailed as a new start after the war, although there was no debate in the media on this event in the Swedish church.[22] From July 22 to 31, the World Student Christian Federation (WSCF) met in Oslo, and the 22-year-old law student Göransson participated together with about 50 internationally engaged Swedish students, among them Olof Sundby (1917-1996), later Archbishop of Sweden. To many of them, including Göransson, this meeting with young Christians from all over the world became of "vital importance".[23]

Students had not had the possibility to travel abroad in wartime. When the borders opened up in the summer of 1945, they made up for this lack of experience. Many of them became internationalists. The Christian students were also included in the ecumenical Christian work, which had begun before the war with a 1939 conference in Amsterdam and had resulted in an "emergency committee" for international Christian organizations.

Göransson became involved in the work of the WSCF, founded in Vadstena (Sweden) in 1895. This organization had already played an important role in the ecumenical debate during the Great War. After World War II, this international organization together with the Young Men's Christian Association and the Young

---

20 Torsten Bohlin, "Kampen för människovärdet," in *En bok om människan: Av tjugofem författare,* ed. Natanael Beskow (Stockholm: Norstedts, 1942), 25.
21 Jens Holger Schjørring et al., eds., *From Federation to Communion: The History of the Lutheran World Federation* (Minneapolis, MN: Fortress Press, 1997).
22 Jens Holger Schjørring, ed., *Nordiske folkekirker i opbrud: National identitet og internationell nyorientering efter 1945* (Århus: Aarhus Universitetsforlag: 2001), 417.
23 Göran Göransson, "Kristna världsungdomsmötet i Oslo—ett femtioårsminne," *Svensk Kyrkotidning* (1991), 89-92.

Women's Christian Association met in Oslo at the World Conference on Christian Youth in July 1947.²⁴ 1,200 young Christians from 75 countries participated in the Oslo conference under the motto "Jesus Christ is Lord." For the Nordic participants, this conference became the starting-point for a comprehensive ecumenical engagement in the years to come.²⁵

The Norwegian bishop Eivind Berggrav (1884-1959) initiated this conference to which famous Christian church leaders were invited, such as Reinhold Niebuhr from New York, and Martin Niemöller from Frankfurt am Main. Niebuhr stated that this conference had impressed him: "the usual differences between American and European Christians were not nearly as wide as in previous years".²⁶ The Oslo meeting became a catalyst for the young generation. Göransson wrote an article on this important event for a Swedish daily in which he referred to the speeches given by Niebuhr and Niemöller.²⁷ He told his readers how Niebuhr had underlined how "God had used human institutions, movements, or nations to claim justice and law to crush the Nazi regime". The difficulties "to claim justice but avoid oppression, to abolish or punish obvious injustice within social and international life, but not revert into self-righteousness" had become a new postwar problem. "Only by being permanently open to repentance and a will to change for the better could a human institution avoid this danger."

Even 50 years after the Oslo meeting, Göransson recalled its importance for contemporary young Christians. The 1947 law student from Uppsala had experienced how "the dominion of Christ in each area of individual and societal life is the road to the solution of the problems of its time". Each of the participants got a sense of what it would be like to live in a world under the dominion of Christ. "It's a matter for us in thoughts and life to bear witness to that dominion, for only in this do we see the possibility for a more blessed future for this world, which seems to be doomed to chaos, as long as it's serving other masters."²⁸ This quotation demonstrates the frustration of the young, idealistic postwar generation, who dreamed of a future of human rights and

---

24 *Oslo-1947: World Conference of Christian Youth. Conference papers and programmes* (1947). At the private boardingschool of Lundsberg in Sweden the WSCF also held a summer school in August 1-9, 1947. Yale Divinity Library, YMCA—Student Division Records: RG 58, *Delegate list and morning prayer service for WSCF Lundsberg Conference, Aug. 1-9, 1947.*

25 Gunnar Heiene, "Den norske kirke og økumenikken i etterkrigstiden," in *Nordiske folkekirker i opbrud: National identitet og internationell nyorientering efter 1945,* ed. Jens Holger Schjørring (Århus; Aarhus Universitetsforlag, 2001), 392.

26 Charles C. Brown, *Niebuhr and His Age: Reinhold Niebuhr's Prophetic Role and Legacy* (Harrisburg, PA: Trinity Press, 2002), 142.

27 Göran Göransson, "Oslo 1947," *Göteborgs-Posten* (September 9, 1947), 2.

28 Göransson, "Oslo," 2.

human dignity and at the same time were surrounded by the real world with its Iron Curtain and threat of nuclear war.

The Oslo meeting became a prologue for the establishment of the World Council of Churches (WCC), which took place in Amsterdam in August 1948. Several of the leading theologians who participated in the Oslo meeting were instrumental for the Amsterdam conference. Due to his language skills, Göransson was also sent as a youth delegate to this meeting. His participation in this ecumenical event became an important experience for him. The foundation of this world organization had already been decided before the war. The motto of the meeting was "Man's Disorder and God's Design". Göransson was part of the active Youth Department, with the task of being the liaison for all the youth organizations participating in the WCC. In Amsterdam the saying was that "the youth can be the most explosive power in the WCC".[29]

Back in Sweden, Göransson published a report dedicated to his experiences in Amsterdam. In his discussions at the Amsterdam meeting he observed fragmentation as well as unity. As a member of the WCC each church had to make its own walk to Canossa. The plural form "churches" became a reminder for all that this organization was an emergency solution "due to the sin of fragmentation." He also got the strong impression that the churches were aligned with a distinct group, class, race, or nation. He observed, however, that in that respect there had been a recent improvement, perhaps related to the advance of secularization. "When you become less and less (without any undertone of irony) able to talk about the West, the middle class, and the people of Sweden as carriers of Christian belief and ethos, the consequence will be that the Church is increasingly aware of its singular task of being the salt and light in a neo-pagan world."[30]

His most powerful experience at the Amsterdam conference, however, was his encounter with a "penitent Christendom". "We intend to stay together" was the message to all Christians and to "those who want to listen". Historical organizations, national prejudices, racial antagonism, "denying the unity of the Christian, or a self-satisfied patronized attitude to 'young' churches and 'colored' people", were to him all false concepts in the new context. There is only one position, he stated: "the one and only loyalty, the loyalty to the Lord." He felt the existence of unity—"deep under the confessional barriers." He recalled meeting one of the many youth delegates he got to know, a young student from Ceylon who was in Europe for the first time. In his conversations

---

29 Göran Göransson, "Amsterdam: Splittring eller enhet?," *SKS: Organ för Sveriges Kristliga Studentrörelse*, no. 4 (1948): 50ff.
30 Göransson, "Amsterdam," 52.

with this young student, Göransson realized that "he had more in common in terms of belief and ethos" with this stranger from another corner of the world, than he had with "most of [his] friends in [his] boardinghouse in Uppsala".[31]

His involvement in the WCC included his participation twice (1952 and 1964) in legal conferences held at the Château Bossey ecumenical institute near Geneva.[32]

His meetings with international Christian students affected Göransson strongly, and they meant a lot to his professional work in ecclesiastical law in postwar Europe.[33] Consequently, he strengthened his skills in international public law and made study trips to war-torn European countries, to The Hague in 1948 and to Bonn in 1950. There was strong political engagement at those meetings. "Christians and Power Politics" was a strong discourse within the WSCF during those years.[34]

This intense international activity among the Swedish Christian jurists after World War II came to be of great importance to their future professional work. It was not only internationalism that characterized their postwar years. It was also ecumenical work, which in the Swedish church had been emphasized since Söderblom was Archbishop of Sweden. Two of his successors, Yngve Brilioth (1891-1959)[35] and Sundby,[36] firmly placed the Swedish church into that international and ecumenical context. In that respect, the jurist Dag Hammarskjöld (1905-1961), Secretary General of the UN, is a relevant figure. His deep religiosity was made public after his death in his posthumous diary *Vägmärken* (*Markings*). This book with its Christian mysticism has had a great impact on the younger generation of theologians since the late 1960s.[37]

These international relations also meant influences from theological dis-

---

31 Göransson, "Amsterdam," 53.
32 Göransson, "Om rätten," 113. He also seems to have participated in the important 1950 conference of the WCC in Treysa.
33 Carl Gustaf Andrén to Kjell Å. Modéer, email message, March 24, 2017. Copy by the author.
34 "Christians and Power-Politics," Special Issue, *The Student World* 41, no. 3 (1948); William Wylie-Kellerman, "Naming the Powers: William Stringfellow as Student and Theologian," *Student World: Power and Principalities; Ecumenical Review* 247 (2003): 28-29.
35 Carl Fredrik Hallencreutz and Katharina Hallencreutz, *Yngve Brilioth: Svensk medeltidsforskare och internationell kyrkoledare* (Uppsala: Svenska institutet för missionsforskning, 2002).
36 Oloph Bexell, "Olof Sundby," in *Svenskt biografiskt lexikon*, ed. Åsa Karlsson, vol. 6 (Stockholm: Riksarkivet, 2014), 233.
37 Dag Hammarskjöld, *Vägmärken* (Stockholm: Bonniers, 1963). English translation: *Markings* (Ballantine: New York, 1983).

courses in foreign countries. For Göransson, Karl Barth's postwar works became an important source of inspiration. In Amsterdam in 1948 he purchased Karl Barth's 1938 booklet *Rechtfertigung und Recht*, [*Justification and Justice*], which he read extensively.[38] In this article, Barth articulated his opposition against Hitler's politicised church, which was divided between the German Christians, who supported the Hitler regime and its "fundamental antichristian Anti-Church" (*grundsätzlich antichristliche Gegenkirche*), and the Confessing Church.[39] Secular law is the ordinance that secures the church's teaching, Barth argued. Therefore the church may not refuse ecclesiastical law, but shall secure it by "proclaiming divine justification".[40]

The human rights revolution, initiated at Hour Zero (*Stunde Null*) 1945, became instrumental for legal thinking in the West for the following 50 years. In Germany, the renaissance of natural law became a very important discourse for theologians as well as for jurists. The important dichotomy between law and legislation—*Recht und Gesetz*—between a natural law-based legal system and a positivistic one, was made public. The continuity in this discourse from the early 20th century was evident.[41]

After World War II, the reconstruction of the relationship between an autonomous church and the democratic state made Barth's analysis of the New Testament important. The renaissance of natural law in the early postwar period contributed to this justification. In addition, in the late 1940s the justification of the sinful human being became a counterpoint to the most important discourse regarding human dignity.[42] Several other European jurists and theologians contributed to this discourse, among these the Calvinist theologian Erik Wolf (1902-1977), who in the 1947 work *Rechtsgedanke und biblische Weisung* demonstrated an easier way to formulate a Christian rationale for the law. In the Bible, Wolf argued, there are directives and instructions for societal and legal frame-

---

38 Karl Barth, *Rechtfertigung und Recht: Theologische Studien Heft 1*, 2nd ed. (Zollikon-Zürich: Evangelischer Verlag A.G, 1944).
39 Andreas Pangritz, *Politischer Gottesdienst: Zur theologischen Begründung des Widerstands bei Karl Barth,* 12, accessed September 10, 2019, https://www.etf.uni-bonn.de/de/ev-theol/einrichtungen/systematische-theologie/personen/prof.-dr.-phil.-a.-pangritz-1/texte-zum-download/politischer-gottesdienst.pdf.
40 Alice Lorber, "Divine Power and Human Politics: Karl Barth's Understanding of Church and State in His Writings from 1926-1946: An Investigation of the Consistency of His Thought," in *Perspectives on Power: An Inter-Disciplinary Approach*, ed. Heather M Morgan, Jerner Letnar Černič, and Lindsay Milligan (Newcastle: Cambridge Scholars, 2010), 175.
41 Lena Foljanty, *Recht oder Gesetz: Juristische Identität und Autorität in den Naturrechtsdebatten in der Nachkriegszeit* (Tübingen: Mohr Siebeck, 2013).
42 See Torsten Bohlin, "Kampen för människovärdet," in *Kristendomen: Mot—för*, ed. Stellan Arvidsson and Torsten Bohlin (Stockholm: Natur och Kultur, 1947).

work. These were not to be interpreted as legal rules, but rather as directives and guidelines for legislators, judges, and administrators.[43] Karl Barth's concept of *Rechtstheologie* articulated a keyword for the Swedish Christian jurist Göransson.

The Barmen Declaration (1934) became the reaction of Christian opponents such as Dietrich Bonhoeffer (1906-1945) and Karl Barth to the politically totalitarian regime in Germany. In the Nordic countries as well, it became an important document for political resistance. However, in Sweden Karl Barth never became a prophet for the theologians. As Ola Sigurdson has demonstrated in his 1996 doctoral dissertation, Karl Barth's *Rechtstheologie* never was the Swedish theologians' cup of tea.[44]

None of the great postwar Nordic theologians based their theology directly on Karl Barth, neither Gustaf Wingren (1910-2000) in Sweden[45] nor Regin Prenter (1907-1990) and Knud Løgstrup (1905-1981) in Denmark. Prenter, and to some extent Wingren, were originally inspired by Barth, but over the course of time they moved closer to "the theological neighborhood of Løgstrup".[46] Even if in his early career Prenter characterized himself as a "Barthian"—he contributed to Barth's 1936 *Festschrift*—he indicated his distance from Barth later in his career.[47] Gustaf Wingren, another representative of the Scandinavian creation theology, based his theology on Martin Luther, especially the concept of vocation.[48]

This theological discussion on law and justice provides an explanation for the secularization and transformation of church law into purely administrative law, a transformation dominant in the Nordic countries, especially in Sweden.

Torchbearers versus Positivists

Who were the torchbearers of law and theology-based church law in the increasingly secularized Nordic countries? Did they participate in the natural law-based, metaphysical movement, and how did they react to the strictly rational

---

43 Göransson, "Om rätten," 115.
44 Ola Sigurdson, *Karl Barth som den andre: En studie i den svenska teologins Barth-reception* (Stehag: Brutus Östlings bokförlag Symposion, 1996).
45 Bengt Kristensson Uggla, *Gustaf Wingren: människan och teologin* (Stehag: Brutus Östlings bokförlag Symposion, 2010).
46 Christine Svinth-Værge Põder, "Regin Prenter and Scandinavian Creation Theology," in *Reformation Theology for a Post-Secular Age: Løgstrup, Prenter, Wingren, and the Future of Scandinavian Creation Theology,* ed. Niels Henrik Gregersen, Bengt Kristensson Uggla, and Trygve Wyller (Göttingen: Vandenhoeck & Ruprecht, 2017), 70.
47 Svinth-Værge Põder, "Regin Prenter and Scandinavian Creation Theology," 21ff.
48 Gustaf Wingren, *Luthers lära om kallelsen* (Lund: Gleerups, 1942).

concept related to the negative freedom of religion articulated in the Swedish 1951 Freedom of Religion Act?

This legislation was a necessary reform for Sweden to be able to ratify the European Convention on Human Rights (ECHR). On the other hand, the Swedish skepticism toward the "natural law" based human rights concept was well articulated by the jurists of the Uppsala School of Law, the Scandinavian version of legal realism.[49] One of the harshest opponents of the Swedish ratification of the ECHR in 1952 was the foreign minister and professor of law Östen Undén (1886-1974).[50] He was a member of the social-democratic party and had served as a professor of civil law at the University of Uppsala when the first generation of the Uppsala School was established. Immediately after he left his position as foreign minister 1966, Sweden ratified the protocol on accepting the jurisdiction of the European Court of Human Rights.

When in 1951 the Swedish government in its bill to parliament asked for religious freedom, it also made a statement regarding the nature of the Swedish church. The Swedish church had not been established as a part of the functions of the state. "The church is a spiritual community, a religious community (*trossamfund*) … and its character and activities were defined by its confession". In Göransson's eyes, the Swedish state church, like the free churches and the Roman Catholic Church, must have the right to "design and shape its own work". He argued for a new platform for the church in Sweden.[51] Together with his friend and contemporary in Uppsala, the theologian Carl Strandberg (1926-2013),[52] he argued for the reform making baptism rather than birth that which constitutes membership of the Swedish church.

The negative freedom of religion became a sort of icon for the Swedish secularized legal culture of the post-war period, just like Gullberg's position in his poetry from 1951 and onwards, mentioned above.

Even if the number of jurists specialized in church law also decreased in the postwar period, several distinguished Swedish jurists participated in the many commissions which succeeded each other with the aim of reforming the relation between state and church. One of the few skilled Swedish

---

49   Legal realism is a version of legal positivism. It seeks a strict separation between law and politics and law and morality. See Max Lyles, *A Call for Scientific Purity: Axel Hägerström's Critique of Legal Science* (Stockholm: Institutet för rättshistorisk forskning, 2006).
50   Lennart Petri, *Sverige i stora världen: Minnen och reflexioner från 40 års diplomattjänst* (Stockholm: Atlantis, 1996), 241.
51   Göran Göransson, "Riksdag och kyrkomöte," *Kristen student*, ed. Sveriges kristliga studentrörelse, no. 5 (1951): 3ff, 6.
52   Oloph Bexell, "Carl Strandberg 1926-2013," *Svensk Pastoraltidskrift* 55, no. 20 (2013): 593ff.

jurists with European perspectives and knowledge in church law was Sture Petrén (1908-1976), president of the Svea Court of Appeal and chairman of the Commission for Human Rights of the European Council.[53] His cousin, the Administrative Supreme Court Justice Gustaf Petrén (1917-1990) was one of the few human rights activists during a period of time when the Swedish legal and political culture were predominantly affected by rational and secular law.[54] The official Swedish attitude to human rights as late as the early 1980s was articulated by Prime Minister Olof Palme, who in one of his speeches talked about the European Court of Human Rights as "Gustaf Petrén's playhouse". The contradiction between law and human rights among Swedish jurists during this period was distinct.

In 1954, Göransson was recruited to the Ministry of Education and Religion (*Ecklesiastikdepartementet*), where he served for ten years. In the ministry he wanted to take a more active part in matters related to ecclesiastical law but was prevented from doing so due to his publicly demonstrated faith. In the social-democratic political environment in the postwar period he was regarded as being too ecclesiastical (*kyrklig*). For him this was an annoying situation.[55]

Göransson's career in ecclesiastic law in postwar Sweden ran parallel to the period of increased secularization of the society. In 1956, just a few years after the Freedom of Religion Act, the parliament initiated the separation between the state and the church. This resulted in an expert investigation (1958), which delivered several proposals and in 1968 concluded its work.[56] Another committee was appointed in 1956 by the Swedish church and worked parallel to the state committee: the Church Organization Committee (*Kyrkoorganisationskommittén* 1956-1964).[57] Göransson was recruited as a member of this committee from its beginning. He also served as an expert to the State-Church-Council (*Stat-Kyrka-beredningen* 1968-1972) chaired by a member of the social-democratic government, Alva Myrdal (1902-1986).[58]

---

53 Sten Rudholm, *Sture Petrén* (Stockholm: Norstedts, 1977).
54 Kjell Å. Modéer, "Gustaf Petrén," in *Svenskt biografiskt lexikon*, ed. Göran Nilzén, vol. 29 (Stockholm: Riksarkivet, 1995-1997), 189.
55 During all these years he was an active participant in Christian youth organizations: Riksförbundet kyrklig ungdom (Chair), Kristliga studentförbundet i Göteborg resp. Uppsala (Chair), Ekumeniska nämnden (Member).
56 SOU 1968:11 Svenska kyrkan och staten: Slutbetänkande.
57 Sören Ekström, *Kyrkan och staten: Förteckning omfattande utredningarnas sammansättning 1956-1999*, 9. Accessed March 27, 2011, www.sorenekstrom.se/Documents/StatOchKyrka.pdf.
58 SOU 1971:29 Kyrkan kostar: en ekonomisk studie av Svenska kyrkans församlingar 1969; SOU 1972:36 Samhälle och trossamfund: Slutbetänkande; Fredrik Sterzel, "Staten och kyrkan," *Svensk Juristtidning*, no. 1 (1974): 269ff.

In 1979, Göransson became assistant undersecretary at the Ministry of Civil Affairs with primary responsibility for the church law reform. Swedish church law at that time had to be adapted (and adjusted) to the new 1974 Instrument of Government (*Regeringsformen*), which in its first paragraph emphasized the democratic imperative that all public power emanates from the state.

Göransson's combined skills in law and church law became essential to him as a Christian jurist. He became one of the foremost experts in Swedish church law. As a member of the ongoing legal reform within the Swedish state church in the 1990s, Göransson also published frequently in this field of law.

Göransson was not only instrumental when the new Church Law was prepared and adopted in 1992,[59] he also wrote the necessary substantial commentary to this legislation.[60] It was the first handbook in Swedish church law since Halvar Sundberg's in 1948, and it marked a new trend in the post-positivist Swedish legal culture. In this book, *Svensk kyrkorätt* (*Swedish Church Law*), he also made his great reverence for the theological aspects apparent. In the chapter on the essence of the understanding of ecclesiastical law he wrote:[61] "But if one limits the field of view to solely the state acquis, one risks losing sight of what is the specific essence of the church law. In such a view, the church would be an institution, which would be a creation wholly of the Swedish legal framework and which depends exclusively on the existence of a state church legislation."

In the continuous work on the changes in the relation between the Swedish state and its church, a new commission resulted in an opening for the new relation adopted in 1998. Göransson took part in the investigation related to the property of the church.[62]

Göransson's contributions to church law from an academic as well as a more pragmatic and realistic perspective resulted in 1995 in an honorary degree given to him by the Faculty of Theology at Lund University. In its justification for granting the degree, the faculty emphasized that Göransson "in his practical deed and in his theoretical work with ecclesiastical law acquired deep insights

---

59 SFS 1992:300 Kyrkolag (Church law).
60 Göran Göransson, *Svensk kyrkorätt: En översikt* (Stockholm: Norstedt, 1993).
61 "Men begränsar man synfältet till enbart det statliga regelverket, riskerar man att förlora blicken för vad som utgör kyrkorättens specifika väsen. Kyrkan skulle med ett sådant synsätt vara en institution som helt och hållet vore en skapelse av den svenska rättsordningen och som står och faller med förekomsten av en statlig kyrkolagstiftning." Göransson, *Svensk kyrkorätt*, 18.
62 Göran Göransson and Robert Schött, *Kyrklig egendom: En kommentar* (Stockholm: Norstedts Juridik, 1996).

and reported knowledge characterized by qualified analytical overview and valuable educational ability".[63]

In 1995, Sweden became a member of the European Union and incorporated the ECHR into Swedish law. Göransson wanted to regard the church law from a more contextual perspective upholding the contextual deep structures of ecclesiastical law. The theological principles, so special for ecclesiastical law, had to be observed, he said in his 1995 lecture. Church law is not only a set of administrative legal rules, *Verwaltungsrecht*, it has also an underlying theology, a *Rechtstheologie*, that belongs to the transnational borderless deep structures of European law. In that sense he connected to the concept of Barth and the debates he had met on the spirit and fundamental common values in the early 1950's.

Göransson was the Swedish interpreter of the intertwining of law and theology in the secularized modern society of Sweden, and his theological positions came to be of great importance for the new role of the Swedish church after 2000.

Göransson passed away in 1998, the same year the new relationship between the state and the autonomous Swedish church was decided in parliament.[64] During his lifetime he became an important catalyst for the transformation of Swedish church law. In a time dominated by secularization, throughout the decades he consistently upheld, aided by a historical argumentation, the deep structures related to European Christian theology and law. In the new millennium this transformation has resulted in new perspectives on this field of law—as a result of a *desecularization* of the modern concept of administrative church law. One example of this transition can be found in the new Swedish Church Order (*Kyrkoordningen*) of 1999, which was implemented after the change of relations between the state and church in 2000. In this church order for the Swedish church as an autonomous entity in relation to the state, each chapter has a preamble containing the theological arguments for the administrative legal rules to follow.

Nordic Legal Actors as Visible Christian Lawyers

There were also several Nordic legal actors who contributed to the upholding of the traditional metaphysical relation between law and human rights, law and justice, and law and theology.

---

63 Lunds universitet: *Doktorspromotionen 24.5.1995. Hedersdoktorer 1995*, Teologiska fakulteten. "Göransson har i sin praktiska gärning och i sitt teoretiska arbete med kyrkorättsproblem förvärvat djupa insikter och redovisat kunskaper präglade av kvalificerad analytisk överblick och värdefull pedagogisk förmåga."
64 Law regarding the Swedish Church (SFS 1998:1591 *Lag om Svenska kyrkan*).

Contemporaries of Göransson, they created a Nordic network which from the 1970s onward interacted in study groups and on the international scene Göransson's contemporary in Norway was the professor of church history at the Norwegian School of Theology Andreas Aarflot (b. 1928), from 1978 to 1998 Bishop of the Oslo Diocese. Over the years, he was a defender of an autonomous Norwegian church, and he supported the reform which in 2012 resulted in the new constitutional reform. In an article in the Festschrift for Aarflot, Göransson completely agreed with Aarflot's imperative statement: "Let the Church be the Church" (*La kirken være kirke*).[65] The possibilities for influencing state legislation and judicature have to be accomplished in the preaching of the gospel and participation in Christian organizations, and in an autonomous congregation. In postwar Sweden, a secularized and from a religious perspective neutral welfare state, the possibilities for attaining this form of idealistic Christian community were small. Göransson quoted an anonymous German theologian: "How should theology help at the foundation of legal science, if the jurist does not participate in the decline of its last binding, of that to God.[66]

In the late 1970s, Aarflot came to be as a spider in the net for a progressive network of Nordic theologians and jurists, in which also Per-Otto Gullaksen (b. 1953), senior counselor in the Church Department, participated on the Norwegian side, and who wrote a book in Aarflotian style, *State and Church in Norway: Church law between Theology and Politics* (2000).[67] On the Swedish side, the later Bishop of Lund Per Olov Ahrén (1926-2004), an old friend of Göransson's, also participated. Ahrén was also a member of several state-church commissions from that time up until the new church law and the 1998 Law of the Swedish Church.

If Göransson and Aarflot had similar views regarding the theological importance of church law, other Nordic church lawyers had a more positivist attitude toward their profession and law. The Finnish representative Gunnar Träskman (1929-2007) was a contemporary of Göransson. He served as a private lawyer for a couple of years but was recruited already in 1959 as a judge in the Chapter of Turku where he served for decades. Due to his knowledge of church law, he was engaged in many Finnish commissions where he served as the only Swedish-

---

65 Andreas Aarflot, *Let the Church be the Church: The Voice and Mission of the People of God* (Minneapolis, MN: Augsburg Fortress, 1988). Norwegian edition: *La kirken være kirke* (Oslo: Cappelen, 1990).
66 "Wie soll die Theologie bei der Grundlegung der Rechtswissenschaft helfen, wenn der Jurist den Rückgang auf die letzte Bindung, auf Gott nicht mitmacht?" Göransson, "Om rätten," 115.
67 Per-Otto Gullaksen, *Stat og kirke i Norge: Kirkerett mellom teologi og politikk* (Oslo: Verbum, 2000).

speaking representative. He played an important role in the reformation of the 1980-1988 Finnish Church Law. Träskman was also a teacher of Church Law at the Swedophone Royal Academy of Åbo where, in 1988, he also received an honorary degree from the Theological Faculty at Åbo Akademi University.[68]

Göransson totally agreed with his colleague Träskman when, in an article inspired by the contemporary Finnish church law reform in 1993, he emphasized that church law had to be attached to "divine law, i.e. the constitutive elements of the church, evangelism and the sacrament". Confession defined the commitment.[69] He referred to this article and related it to the new Swedish Church Law adopted in 1992. He also published an article on the necessity of a theological dimension on the church law.[70]

In Denmark, Preben Espersen (1931-2007) was Göransson's contemporary. He was an employee in the Ministry of Ecclesiastical Affairs and head of the department. For many years he was the authoritative representative for Danish church law; he also wrote important handbooks on Danish church law. He became an expert on the internal and external matters in the Danish folk church. Espersen was a loyal traditional Danish civil servant and held more of a positivist position.[71] The professor of constitutional law at Copenhagen University, Henrik Zahle (1943-2006), who in a very active way wanted to link to the relation between church and state, became more of a torchbearer in that respect.[72] However, Zahle was not a religious person. His interest was based on his fundamental interest in culture and societal problems in contemporary society. Up until the time of his early death in 2006, he was a very active and productive colleague in the field of law and religion.

Epilogue

Throughout modernity, there were clashes of norms with the Bible related to the modern drafts of legislation regarding the female clergy and the law on abortion. In the postwar period, both of these reforms resulted in important discussions between believers of tradition and modern reformists. In this respect, secular law had no room for religion.

---

68 Gunnar Grönblom, "Gunnar Träskman," *SFV-Kalendern* 122 (2008): 158-59.
69 Gunnar Träskman, "Kyrkorätten som teologi," *Svensk Pastoraltidskrift* 33, no. 16 (1991): 269-73.
70 Göran Göransson, "Kyrkolag och rättsteologi," *Svenska Kyrkans tidning* (Summer 1991).
71 Bente Clausen, "Ret skal være ret," *Kristeligt Dagblad,* September, 12, 2007.
72 Kjell Å. Modéer, "Henrik Zahle in memoriam," *Svensk Juristtidning*, no. 10 (2006): 1000f.

This chapter demonstrates not only a new relation between state and church, it is also an example of a post-secular era, to which Göransson contributed to a great extent from the post-World War II years up until the changed relationship between state and church in Sweden in 2000. His views on *Rechtstheologie* and *Law and Religion* are also brought into focus within contemporary Swedish interdisciplinary legal research.[73]

From the time of his experiences in the WCC in Amsterdam in 1948, Göransson increasingly utilized his international networks among European Christian jurists and became the Swedish communicator to Lutheran scholars and networks on Swedish church-state relations from the 1950s up until the late 1990s. This chapter thus demonstrates the internationalization of Scandinavian discourses on law and theology as well as on ecumenism to a great extent, upheld by the young postwar generation of theologians and jurists.

In this respect, Göransson can be perceived as a torchbearer of the idealistic view of the law. He regarded the law as principles and norms, not only as pragmatic legal rules.

In the new millennium, law and religion have a quite new position in relation to the paradigm of modernity of the post-war period. The return of legal values within law and the contextualization of law as well as religion, are just two phenomena which make the torchbearers in this field especially important and interesting.

Bibliography

Official Sources

SFS 1936:567 Lag om domkapitel
SFS 1992:300 Kyrkolag (Church law)
SFS 1998:1591 Lag om Svenska kyrkan (Law regarding the Swedish Church)
SOU 1968:11 Svenska kyrkan och staten: Slutbetänkande
SOU 1971:29 Kyrkan kostar: en ekonomisk studie av Svenska kyrkans församlingar 1969
SOU 1972:36 Samhälle och trossamfund: Slutbetänkande

Literature

Aarflot, Andreas. *Let the Church Be the Church: The Voice and Mission of the People of God*. Minneapolis, MN: Augsburg Fortress, 1988.

---

[73] Kjell Å. Modéer, "Religionens plats i det offentliga rummet: Rättshistoriska och rättskulturella perspektiv," *Svensk Teologisk Kvartaltidskrift* 81, no. 1 (2005): 2ff.

Barth, Karl. *Rechtfertigung und Recht: Theologische Studien Heft 1*. 2nd ed. Zollikon-Zürich: Evangelischer Verlag A.G, 1944.

Beck, Ulrich, Anthony Giddens, and Scott Lash. *Reflexive Modernisierung: Eine Kontroverse*. Frankfurt: Suhrkamp, 1996.

Bexell, Oloph. "Carl Strandberg 1926-2013." *Svensk Pastoraltidskrift* 55, no. 20 (2013): 593-601.

Bexell, Oloph. "Olof Sundby." In *Svenskt biografiskt lexikon*, vol. 6, edited by Åsa Karlsson, 233. Stockholm: Riksarkivet, 2014.

Blückert, Kjell. "Svenska kyrkan och ekumeniken: 1947-70." In *Nordiske folkekirker i opbrud: National identitet og internationell nyorientering efter 1945*, edited by Jens Holger Schjørring, 413-25. Århus; Aarhus Universitetsforlag, 2001.

Bohlin, Torsten. "Kampen för människovärdet." In *En bok om människan: Av tjugofem författare*, edited by Natanael Beskow, 19-25. Stockholm: Norstedts, 1942.

Brown, Charles C. *Niebuhr and His Age: Reinhold Niebuhr's Prophetic Role and Legacy*. Harrisburg, PA: Trinity Press, 2002.

"Christians and Power-Politics," Special Issue, *The Student World* 41, no. 3 (1948).

"Christians and Power-Politics," Special Issue, *The Student World* 41, no. 3 (1948); William Wylie-Kellerman, "Naming the Powers: William Stringfellow as Student and Theologian," *Student World: Power and Principalities; Ecumenical Review* 247 (2003): 28-29.

Clausen, Bente. "Ret skal være ret." *Kristeligt Dagblad*, September 12, 2007.

Ekström, Sören. *Kyrkan och staten: Förteckning omfattande utredningarnas sammansättning 1956-1999*. Accessed March 27, 2011. www.sorenekstrom.se/Documents/StatOchKyrka.pdf.

Foljanty, Lena. *Recht oder Gesetz: Juristische Identität und Autorität in den Naturrechtsdebatten in der Nachkriegszeit*. Tübingen: Mohr Siebeck, 2013.

Graver, Hans Petter. *Okkupasjonstidens Høyesterett*. Oslo: Pax Forlag, 2019.

Gregersen, Niels Henrik, Bengt Kristensson Uggla, Bengt, and Trygve Wyller, eds. *Reformation Theology for a Post-Secular Age: Løgstrup, Prenter, Wingren, and the Future of Scandinavian Creation Theology*. Göttingen: Vandenhoeck & Ruprecht, 2017.

Grönblom, Gunnar. "Gunnar Träskman." *SFV-Kalendern* 122 (2008): 158-59.

Gullaksen, Per-Otto. *Stat og kirke i Norge: Kirkerett mellom teologi og politikk*. Oslo: Verbum, 2000.

Göransson, Göran. "Oslo 1947." *Göteborgs-Posten*, September 9, 1947, 2.

Göransson, Göran. "Amsterdam: Splittring eller enhet?" *SKS: Organ för Sveriges Kristliga Studentrörelse*, no. 4 (1948): 50-53.

Göransson, Göran. "Min konfirmationslärare." In *En bok om Torsten Bohlin av 40 författare*, edited by Bo Bengtson and Gunnar Åkerstedt, 307-11. Uppsala: J.A. Lindblads Förlag, 1950.

Göransson, Göran. "Riksdag och kyrkomöte." *Kristen student*, edited by Sveriges kristliga studentrörelse, no. 5 (1951): 3-6.

Göransson, Göran. "Kyrkolag och rättsteologi." *Svensk Kyrkotidning* (Summer 1991).

Göransson, Göran. *Svensk kyrkorätt: En översikt*. Stockholm: Norstedt, 1993.

Göransson, Göran. "Om rätten och rättsteologin." *Svensk Teologisk Kvartaltidskrift* 71, no. 3 (1995): 111-18.

Göransson, Göran, and Robert Schött. *Kyrklig egendom: En kommentar*. Stockholm: Norstedts Juridik, 1996.

Göransson, Göran. "Kristna världsungdomsmötet i Oslo: Ett femtioårsminne." In *En hälsning till församlingarna i ärkestiftet*, 89-92. Uppsala: Ärkestiftet 1998-1999.

Hallencreutz, Carl Fredrik, and Katharina Hallencreutz. *Yngve Brilioth: Svensk medeltidsforskare och internationell kyrkoledare*. Uppsala: Svenska institutet för missionsforskning, 2002.

Hammarskjöld, Dag. *Vägmärken*. Stockholm: Bonniers, 1963.

Heiene, Gunnar. "Den norske kirke og økumenikken i etterkrigstiden." In *Nordiske folkekirker i opbrud: National identitet og internationell nyorientering efter 1945*, edited by Jens Holger Schjørring, 385-98. Århus: Aarhus Universitetsforlag, 2001.

Holmberg, Olle. *Hjalmar Gullberg: En vänbok*. Stockholm: Bonniers, 1966.

von Jhering, Rudolf. *Striden för rätten*. Translated by Andreas Cervin. Stockholm: Natur och kultur, 1941.

Jarlert, Anders. *Judisk "ras" som äktenskapshinder i Sverige: Effekten av Nürnberglagarna i Svenska kyrkans statliga funktion som lysningsförrättare 1935-1945*. Malmö: Sekel, 2006.

Kennedy, Duncan. "Three Globalizations of Law and Legal Thought: 1850-2000." In The New Law and Economic Development: A Critical Appraisal, edited by David M. Trubek and Alvaro Santos, 19-73. Cambridge: Cambridge University Press, 2006.

Kristensson Uggla, Bengt. *Gustaf Wingren: människan och teologin*. Stehag: Brutus Östlings bokförlag Symposion, 2010.

Lorber, Alice. "Divine Power and Human Politics: Karl Barth's Understanding of Church and State in His Writings from 1926-1946; An Investigation of the Consistency of His Thought." In *Perspectives on Power: An Inter-Disciplinary Approach*, edited by Heather M Morgan, Jerner Letnar Černič, and Lindsay Milligan, 172-88. Newcastle: Cambridge Scholars, 2010.

Lyles, Max. *A Call for Scientific Purity: Axel Hägerström's Critique of Legal Science*. Stockholm: Institutet för rättshistorisk forskning, 2006.

Modéer, Kjell Å. "Gustaf Petrén." In *Svenskt biografiskt lexikon*, vol. 29, edited by Göran Nilzén, 189. Stockholm: Riksarkivet, 1995-1997.

Modéer, Kjell Å. "'Den kulan visste var den tog!': Om svenska juristers omvärldssyn 1935-1955." In *Festskrift till Per Henrik Lindblom*, edited by Torbjörn Andersson and Bengt Lindell, 443-68. Uppsala: Iustus förlag, 2004.

Modéer, Kjell Å. "Religionens plats i det offentliga rummet: Rättshistoriska och rättskulturella perspektiv." *Svensk Teologisk Kvartaltidskrift* 81, no. 1 (2005): 2-13.

Modéer, Kjell Å. "Henrik Zahle in memoriam." *Svensk Juristtidning*, no. 10 (2006): 1000-1.

Modéer, Kjell Å. *Juristernas nära förflutna: Rättskulturer i förändring*. Stockholm: Santérus Förlag, 2009.

Modéer, Kjell Å. "Kyrkans rätt framför dess lag: Europé och jurist i den svenska folkkyrkans tjänst; Göran Göransson (1925-1998)—en kyrkorättshistorisk biografi." *Kyrkohistorisk Årsskrift* 119 (2019): 153-73.

Modéer, Kjell Å. "Göran Göransson 1925-1998: A Post-Secular Catalyst in Modern Swedish Church Law." In *Law and the Christian Tradition in Scandinavia: The*

Writings of Great Nordic Jurists, edited by Kjell Å. Modéer and Helle Vogt. London: Routledge, 2020.

Modéer, Kjell Å. "From Classical Legal Thought into a Human Rights Paradigm: Law and Religion in Three Different Contexts 1809-1950." In *Constitutionalisation and Hegemonisation: Exploring the Boundaries of Law and Religion 1800-1950*, edited by Anna-Sara Lind and Victoria Enkvist. Odense: University Press of Southern Denmark, *forthcoming*.

Pangritz, Andreas. *Politischer Gottesdienst: Zur theologischen Begründung des Widerstands bei Karl Barth*. Accessed September 10, 2019. https://www.etf.uni-bonn.de/de/ev-theol/einrichtungen/systematische-theologie/personen/prof.-dr.-phil.-a.-pangritz-1/texte-zum-download/politischer-gottesdienst.pdf.

Petri, Lennart. *Sverige i stora världen: Minnen och reflexioner från 40 års diplomattjänst*. Stockholm: Atlantis, 1996.

Põder, Christine Svinth-Værge. "Regin Prenter and Scandinavian Creation Theology," in *Reformation Theology for a Post-Secular Age: Løgstrup, Prenter, Wingren, and the Future of Scandinavian Creation Theology*, ed. Niels Henrik Gregersen, Bengt Kristensson Uggla, and Trygve Wyller (Göttingen: Vandenhoeck & Ruprecht, 2017), 70.

Põder, Christine Svinth-Værge. "Regin Prenter and Scandinavian Creation Theology," 21ff.

Rudholm, Sten. *Sture Petrén*. Stockholm: Norstedts, 1977.

Schjørring, Jens Holger, Prasanna Kumari, Norman A. Hjelm, and Viggo Mortensen, eds. *From Federation to Communion: The History of the Lutheran World Federation*. Minneapolis, MN: Fortress Press, 1997.

Schjørring, Jens Holger, ed., *Nordiske folkekirker i opbrud: National identitet og internationell nyorientering efter 1945* (Århus: Aarhus Universitetsforlag: 2001), 417.

Sigurdson, Ola. *Karl Barth som den andre: En studie i den svenska teologins Barth-reception*. Stehag: Brutus Östlings bokförlag Symposion, 1996.

Spengler, Oswald. *The Decline of the West*. New York: Knopf, 1926-1928.

Sterzel, Fredrik. "Staten och kyrkan." *Svensk Juristtidning*, no. 1 (1974): 269-94.

Träskman, Gunnar. "Kyrkorätten som teologi." *Svensk Pastoraltidskrift* 33, no. 16 (1991): 269-73.

Tuori, Kaarlo. "Towards a Multilayered View of Modern Law." In *Justice, Morality and Society: A Tribute to Aleksander Peczenik on the Occasion of His 60th Birthday 16 November 1997*, edited by Aulis Arnio, Robert Alexy, and Gunnar Bergholtz, 432-42. Lund: Juristförlaget i Lund, 1997.

Uggla, Bengt Kristensson. *Gustaf Wingren: människan och teologin*. Stehag: Brutus Östlings bokförlag Symposion, 2010.

Wingren, Gustav. *Luthers lära om kallelsen*. Lund: Gleerup, 1942.

Wylie-Kellerman, William. "Naming the Powers: William Stringfellow as Student and Theologian." *Student World* 247 (2003): 24-35.

Wood, Philip R. *The Fall of the Priests and the Rise of the Lawyers*. London: Hart Publishing, 2016.

Webpages

Lovdata. "Krigsstart 9. april 1940—høyesterett under krigen." Accessed September 10, 2019. https://lovdata.no/artikkel/krigsstart_9__april_1940_-_hoyesterett_under_krigen/1532.

Other Sources

Delegate list and morning prayer service for WSCF Lundsberg Conference, Aug. 1-9, 1947. Yale Divinity Library. YMCA—Student Division Records RG 58.

Doktorspromotionen 24.5.1995. Hedersdoktorer 1995, Teologiska fakulteten. Lunds universitet.

Oslo-1947: World Conference of Christian Youth. Conference papers and programmes (1947) (Unpublished material: Google books).

5. Sovereignty of the People or Sovereignty of God? The Transformation of Confessional Interpretations of the Democratic Principle in German Postwar Protestant Theology

Georg Kalinna

Introduction

In one form or another, legal legitimacy in modern democratic systems rests on the assumption that laws, including the constitution, are expressions of the will of the people. The term "sovereignty of the people" sums up this idea as it has been historically advanced by liberal thinkers since the 18th century. Christian churches in Europe have long struggled to accept the idea that political power and legal structures are based on the will of the people, arguing that legitimate authority must be rooted in a transcendent power. When a society abandons the pre-modern assumption of a transcendent source of legal legitimacy in favor of the principle of the sovereignty of the people, religious traditions are forced to reconsider their traditions in light of the seemingly secular notion of a popular sovereignty. If one wishes to understand how a religion deals with secular law, it is crucial to trace the transformations that have taken place within confessional traditions which used to see the sovereignty of God and the sovereignty of the people as opposing principles.

Although I will confine myself to a case study within a brief period in German history,[1] it is my contention that it is for different reasons an especially interesting case study for the endeavor of this volume. Firstly, Christian traditions in Germany were particularly skeptical towards secular forms of legal and political legitimacy. The German case is therefore a case in which

---

1   The following chapter has grown out of the work on the author's dissertation: Georg Kalinna, *Die Entmythologisierung der Obrigkeit: Tendenzen der evangelischen Ethik des Politischen in der frühen Bundesrepublik der 1950er und 1960er Jahre* (Tübingen: Mohr Siebeck, 2019).

the conflict between secular forms of legitimacy and religious traditions is more visible than elsewhere. Secondly, the end of World War II was a delicate turning point in the legal, social, and religious history in that it was marked by continuities and discontinuities that were interwoven in complex relationships. A fourth reason has to do with the relationship between German and Nordic thinkers. The Nordic Lutheran tradition, most notably the Norwegian Bishop Eivind Berggrav (1884-1959), furnished Lutheran theologians in Germany with a language that could make cautious steps toward the acceptance of the secular notion of authority possible. I will argue that the confessional traditions of that time period are to be understood as the attempt to transform the idea of the sovereignty of God so as to find a new place within a secular notion of a popular sovereignty as it was enshrined in Article 20 of the West German constitution of 1949.

Nowadays, many German theologians and historians tend to emphasize the deficits of the political ethics during the 1950s and 60s. In this view, the history of theological ethics in postwar Germany is written as the story of a reluctant adaption to democracy; it is seen as a process of appropriation *(Aneignung)* with a clear aim: the "acceptance" of the democratic system, including the principle of the sovereignty of the people.[2] Many scholars argue that Protestant thought remained stuck in pre-democratic patterns. To them, the Protestant stance seemed like a continued re-enactment of the church struggle, the *Kirchenkampf,* thereby implying that their theological predecessors or opponents lack a proper understanding of a democratic and pluralistic society.[3] After all, the Barmen Declaration of May 31, 1934, probably the most influential text of the 20th century on political ethics in Germany, was a reaction to totalitarianism, not a document on religious engagement in a democratic society. This led many theologians to be skeptical about its ongoing applicability. For instance, Trutz Rendtorff (1931-2016), the most important proponent of a liberal Protestant ethics in the 1970s and 80s, criticized his theological opponents and claimed they perpetuated conflicts of the 1930s instead of embracing the democratic

---

2 See Arnulf von Scheliha, "'Aneignung'—Der lange Weg zur Demokratie" ("'Appropriation'—The Long Way to Democracy"), in *Protestantische Ethik des Politischen* (Tübingen: Mohr Siebeck, 2013), 214: "Ihren Abschluss findet die theologische Bewegung hin zum freiheitlich-demokratischen Rechtsstaat in der 'Demokratie-Denkschrift' der EKD". "The theological movement towards the liberal democratic state reaches a conclusion *(Abschluss)* in the 'Democracy Memorandum' *(Demokratie-Denkschrift)* of the Evangelical Church in Germany".

3 See Falk Wagner, *Zur gegenwärtigen Lage des Protestantismus* (Gütersloh: Gütersloher Verlagshaus, 1995), 158-79.

structures of the Federal Republic.[4] Friedrich Wilhelm Graf even went so far as to describe the Protestant political ethics of the 1950s and 60s as a rehash of pre-modern ideas.[5] In the 1980s and 90s, some scholars contributed to a more balanced depiction of the political thought in Protestant ethics. Most notable are the works of Martin Honecker and Joachim Inacker.[6] In recent years, ethicists such as Reiner Anselm and Arnulf von Scheliha have written lengthy discussions on the topic.[7] But still, the theological work on political ethics of the 1950s and 60s is portrayed as rudimentary and backwards-looking when compared with the *Demokratiedenkschrift* (1985). The *Demokratiedenkschrift,* an official memorandum on the Protestant view of democracy issued by the Evangelical Church in Germany, is widely regarded as the decisive step in the Protestant acceptance of democracy. Consequently, the political thought before 1985 seems to lack a proper understanding of democracy. I would like to suggest a different approach and propose that the ethics of that time was not stuck in outdated forms of thinking. Instead, it used the interpretation of historical experience to understand its present. In this view, the acceptance of a secular notion of legal authority is not so much a fixed goal that a philosophical or a theological tradition can "get used" to.[8] Rather, its acceptance needed historical experience and a transformed vocabulary.[9] So, instead of asking if or when Protestant ethicists

---

4   Trutz Rendtorff, "Demokratieunfähigkeit des Protestantismus? Über die Renaissance eines alten Problems," *Zeitschrift für Evangelische Ethik* 27, no. 3 (1983): 253-56.
5   Friedrich Wilhelm Graf, "Königsherrschaft Christi in der Demokratie: Karl Barth und die deutsche Nachkriegspolitik," *Evangelische Kommentare* 23 (1990): 735-38.
6   See Martin Honecker, "Protestantismus und Politik," in *Kirche und Politik: Ein notwendiges Spannungsfeld in unserer Demokratie*, ed. Hans F. Zacher (Düsseldorf: Patmos, 1982), 118-31; Michael Inacker, *Transzendenz, Totalitarismus und Demokratie: Die Entwicklung des kirchlichen Demokratieverständnisses von der Weimarer Republik bis zu den Anfängen der Bundesrepublik (1918-1959)* (Neukirchen-Vluyn: Neukirchener Verlag, 1994).
7   Reiner Anselm, "Politische Ethik," in *Handbuch der evangelischen Ethik*, ed. Wolfgang Huber, Torsten Meireis, and Hans-Richard Reuter (Munich: Mohr Siebeck, 2015), 195-263; Arnulf von Scheliha, *Protestantische Ethik* (Tübingen: Mohr Siebeck, 2013).
8   Modern political theory alone shows that it is highly doubtful whether it is possible to "arrive at" a concept such as democracy. Instead, it reveals a variety of ever-changing concepts. See David Held, *Models of Democracy,* 3rd ed. (Cambridge: Polity, 2006), 1-8.
9   This view ows a great deal to the works of Hans Joas, who himself draws upon the tradition of American pragmatism and continental historicism, especially George Herbert Mead and Ernst Troeltsch. Joas criticizes teleological concepts of history. History, in his view, is not a teleological process in which certain aspects culminate in logical conclusions, but a field in which contingency and human creativity play a crucial role. History is a sequence of reactions or responses to given challenges, not a linear process. See especially Hans Joas, *The Creativity of Action,* trans. Jeremy Gaines and Paul Keast (Chicago: University of Chicago Press, 1996) and Hans Joas, *The Sacredness of the Person: A New Genealogy of Human Rights,* trans. Alex Skinner (Washington D. C.: Georgetown University Press, 2013).

embraced or understood democracy, it might be fruitful to look for the specific use of historical narratives that served to rewrite the acceptance of secular forms of legal legitimacy. One example can illustrate how historical narratives help to develop and support a normative claim that is brought forward as response to a specific challenge.

During the early 1980s, Protestantism was polarized. Liberal-conservative advocates of democratic procedures warned against using the faith to legitimize political action.[10] Left-leaning representatives of the peace movement, on the other side, saw the conciliatory stance of their opponents as a lack of Christian conviction.[11] In a famous article, the Munich-based ethicist Rendtorff, the most important proponent of a liberal-conservative approach to theological ethics in the late 20th century, attacked the left-leaning activists. To Rendtorff, their political engagement seemed to be yet another sign of a Protestant democratic deficit. According to him, it showed that parts of Protestantism in Germany were still *demokratieunfähig*, "incapable of democracy", because they sought to discredit their political opponents by invoking the *status confessionis*, thereby saying that the strict opposition towards nuclear armament was the only viable Christian option.[12] In addition to that, some of the Protestant clergy actively supported or spoke in favor of actions of civil disobedience such as blockades of nuclear power plant sites.[13] In order to support his claim, Rendtorff compared these activists' attitudes to those held by Protestants during the Weimar Republic, who had justified and promoted the rise of National Socialist rule over Germany. To Rendtorff, both fell under the category of "fundamentalists."[14]

Accusations such as these might not serve to further a sober discussion.

---

10   Trutz Rendtorff, "Die Autorität der Freiheit," in *Vielspältiges: Protestantische Beiträge zur ethischen Kultur* (Stuttgart: Kohlhammer, 1991), 81-100, especially 99-100.
11   See Helmut Gollwitzer, *Reich Gottes und Sozialismus bei Karl Barth* (Munich: Christian Kaiser, 1972); Wolfgang Huber, "Prophetische Kritik und demokratischer Konsens," in *Charisma und Institution,* ed. Trutz Rendtorff (Gütersloh: Gütersloher Verlagshaus 1985), 110-531. See also Werner G. Jeanrond, "From Resistance to Liberation Theology: German Theologians and the Non/Resistance to the National Socialist Regime," *Journal of Modern History* 64 (1992): S187-203.
12   See Sebastian Kalden and Jan Ole Wiechmann, "The Churches," in *The Nuclear Crisis: The Arms Race, Cold War Anxiety, and the German Peace Movement of the 1980s,* ed. Christoph Becker-Schaum, et al. (New York/Oxford: Berghahn, 2016), 242-57.
13   See Michael L. Hughes, "Civil Disobedience in Transnational Perspective: American and West German Anti-Nuclear-Power Protesters, 1975-1982," *Historical Research* 39, no. 1 (2014): 247. Hughes especially emphasizes the differences with regards to the religious character of the American and the German traditions of civil disobedience.
14   Rendtorff, "Demokratieunfähigkeit," 254.

Given the horrific nature of National Socialism, it might seem offensive to use such a strong comparison more than a generation after World War II. Nonetheless, it is noteworthy to register the fact: To understand his opponents, Rendtorff used this analogy deliberately. His argument rests on a specific interpretation of the rise of National Socialism. It serves as a cognitive grid that allows for an analogy between patterns of the past and the present.

Rendtorff's use of a specific narrative and its application says much about a core narrative of political ethics in Germany that is still valid today. This core narrative could be summarized as "never again". The important thinkers of the 1950s and 60s were united in the experience of the autocratic mechanisms of political rule; consequently, they shared an interest in the assessment of the past as well as conclusions for the present, with the following question in mind: How is it possible to ensure that totalitarian rule will "never again" rise in Germany? A driving force behind not only political ethics in postwar Germany but also behind the drafting of the constitution of West Germany were questions such as these: What exactly had gone wrong? What were the causes of the rise of National Socialism? What could have been done to prevent it? Which of the present developments resemble the circumstances of that part of the past, and which do not? If we look at the political ethics of the 1950s and 60s with these questions in mind, I think we will have a better grasp of what they thought about politics than if we assess their understanding of democratic procedures in comparison to that of the 1980s. Questions such as these helped to transform the traditional unwillingness to accept the sovereignty of the people as a basis for the legitimacy of legal authority.

Values do not form in an ahistorical void. They are creative responses to challenges and work by constructing or reconstructing historical narratives—they form around narrative responses to profound experiences.[15] We defend our attachments to values by expressing in words how we got to these values and what happens if one violates these values. Narratives serve to sort out what happened, and what we can justifiably learn from them in retrospect. The present article argues that this is exactly what Protestant ethicists did after the collapse of Germany in 1945: they established new narratives, rooted in the past, that were built around the idea of "never again". This chapter seeks to describe how these interpretations shaped their ethics, including their stance toward the state's law, and how they helped them to make sense of their present.

---

15 For a further elaboration of these brief remarks, see Hans Joas, *The Genesis of Values*, trans. Gregory Moore (Chicago: Polity Press, 2000), 20-34; Joas, *Sacredness*, 97-139.

Of course, not all appeals to the past are the same. The construal of the past can be implicit or explicit; that is to say, it can be a historically oriented account of what happened, or it can use terms that implicitly carry the meaning of "this is the same as back then". It can be used simply to discredit a theological or political opponent, or to legitimize or rehabilitate one's own tradition. This was especially important to Lutheran theologians of the time who were facing attacks levelled against their political conservatism.[16] It can also be used to criticize political institutions in the present. In short, historical narratives, be they implicit or explicit, can be a reflective account of *what happened,* a mode of criticizing *what is happening at the moment* or a prospective view of *what could happen.* In any case, the view of what exactly it is that went wrong has an enormous influence on the contemporary evaluation of politics.

Many of those explanations for the fall of the Weimar Republic in 1933 that were given in the 1950s were a mixture of honest analysis, rationalization, self-justification, and denial.[17] Many subsequent interpreters replaced former explanations for the causes of the rise of National Socialism with new ones. For instance, many experts in the late 1940s and 50s thought that the failure of the German democracy had largely been caused by a dysfunctional legal framework. They considered constitutional deficiencies to be a main factor in the decline of democracy and concluded that it was necessary to weaken the president's authority in order to strengthen the authority of the Chancellor and to give the Constitution a number of unalienable norms.[18] Although several legal ramifications are still part of the constitutional framework of Germany up to the present time, many historians now tend to favor socio-economic as well as cultural reasons in explaining the stability of the *Bonner Republik* as opposed to "Weimar".[19] A similar story could be told about the theological

---

16 See Ernst Wolf, "Politia Christi: Das Problem der Sozialethik im Luthertum (1948/9)," in *Peregrinatio: Studien zur reformatorischen Theologie und zum Kirchenproblem,* vol. 1, 2nd ed. (Munich: Christian Kaiser, 1962), 214-42; Karl Barth, "Ein Brief nach Frankreich (1939)," in *Eine Schweizer Stimme 1938-1945* (Zollikon-Zurich: Evangelischer Verlag, 1945), 108-17, especially 113-14.

17 See Axel Schildt, *Deutsche Kulturgeschichte: Die Bundesrepublik von 1945 bis zur Gegenwart* (Munich: Hanser Verlag, 2009), 43-67.

18 Peter Graf Kielmansegg. "The Basic Law: Response to the Past or Design for the Future?," in *Fourty Years of the Grundgesetz (Basic Law),* ed. Hartmut Lehmann and Kenneth F. Ledford. (Washington D. C.: German Historical Institute, 1990) 5-18, accessed April 8, 2019, https://www.ghi-dc.org/fileadmin/user_upload/GHI_Washington/PDFs/Occasional_Papers/Forty_Years_of_the_grundgesetz.pdf.

19 See Sebastian Ulrich, *Der Weimar-Komplex: Das Scheitern der ersten deutschen Demokratie und die politische Kultur der frühen Bundesrepublik* (Göttingen: Wallstein Verlag, 2009); Christian Waldhoff, "Folgen—Lehren—Rezeptionen: Zum Nachleben des Verfassungswerks von

debates on politics and the state after World War II. Of course, the religious or theological view towards totalitarian rule is only one aspect. Other social scientific or historical theories, not to say prejudices, informed the theologians' answer. They held implicit or explicit ideas on the legal, economic, and social reasons why democracy had failed. In order to comprehend and criticize their present, they brought their experiences and interpretations of what had happened into the discussion.

The aim of this chapter is not to ask whose interpretation of the rise of the Nazi reign was "truer" to the events, but to identify different theological interpretations of the dangers of totalitarianism and their implications for political ethics. This approach objects to the idea that the political ethics of the 1950s and 60s are nothing but reiterations of earlier debates or even of pre-modern ideas. The different context reframes and alters the content and purpose of the arguments. The descent into political chaos during the 1920s and the implementation of the Nazi rule was now a worst-case scenario with a tremendous impact on the interpretation and normative outlook on political values and institutions.

Before I continue, it might be advisable to say a word about the use of the terms "Lutheran" and "Barthian". Although I believe that these categorizations are problematic because they lump together very diverse thinkers and because they blur many common features,[20] I will use them for the sake of convenience in this chapter. Lutherans and Barthians are usually considered to be the most important theological schools of political ethics in the mid-20th century.[21] When I speak of Lutherans, I will refer mainly to Helmut Thielicke and Wolfgang Trillhaas—as well as on occasion to the more conservative-leaning Walter Künneth and to Otto Dibelius.[22] Their theology stresses continuity with the writings of

---

Weimar," in *Das Wagnis der Demokratie: Eine Anatomie der Weimarer Reichsverfassung*, ed. Horst Dreier and Christian Waldhoff (Munich: C. H. Beck, 2018), 289-316.

20 See Georg Kalinna, "Zurück in den 'Irrgarten' der Zwei-Reiche-Lehre? Ein Vorschlag zur Differenzierung im Umgang mit der Zwei-Reiche-Lehre anhand von Helmut Thielickes Theologischer Ethik," in *Angewandtes Luthertum? Die Zwei-Reiche-Lehre als theologische Konstruktion in politischen Kontexten des 20. Jahrhunderts*, ed. Jürgen Kampmann and Hans Otte (Gütersloh: Gütersloher Verlagshaus, 2017), 121-40.

21 The dichotomy between Lutherans and Barthians rests on their respective self-descriptions. See already Erwin Wilkens, "Grenzen des Gehorsams: Der evangelische Christ vor der Obrigkeit," *Die politische Meinung* 69 (1962): 23; Anselm, *Ethik*, 215-20.

22 Helmut Thielicke (1908-1986), nowadays widely neglected by German academic theology, used to be one of the most famous and important Lutheran theologians of the early Federal Republic. Not only did he write two impressive integral systems of theology (The *Theological Ethics*, published in four volumes between 1951 and 1964, and his systematic theology, *The Evangelical Faith*, published in three volumes between 1968 and 1978). He also gathered crowds at his sermons and speeches given in the St. Michael's Church in Hamburg, and he influenced the academic landscape as Rector of the University of

Martin Luther (1483-1546) and his successors; they begin their ethical thinking with the doctrine of justification by faith alone, and they tend to differentiate between God's call upon the individual Christian and God's calling in social structures. When I write about Barthians in the context of this chapter, I am referring to Helmut Gollwitzer, Ernst Wolf, and Wolfgang Schweitzer, who emphasize a Christological foundation of ethics and stressthe applicability of God's Law to all spheres of life.[23]

> Hamburg. His popularity beyond academia is attested to by the fact that Tielicke was only the second theologian next to Karl Barth (1886-1968) to appear on the front cover of the weekly newspaper *Der Spiegel*. His theology rests on a confessional Lutheranism, especially a moderate reformulation of the doctrine of the two kingdoms. For further information on Thielicke, see John T. Pless, "Helmut Thielicke (1908-1986)," *Lutheran Quarterly* 23, no. 4 (2009): 439-64. Wolfgang Trillhaas's (1903-1995) significance stems especially from his influential *Ethics* (first published in 1959) and his *Dogmatics* (first published in 1962). Both of these textbooks were widely used by a whole generation of theology students. Theologically, Trillhaas can be seen as the attempt to combine the interests of a moderate Lutheranism with the philosophical school of phenomenology and Schleiermacher. See Dietz Lange, "Wolfgang Trillhaas (1903-1995)," in *Stiftsgeschichte(n)*, ed. Bernd Schröder (Göttingen: Vandenhoeck und Ruprecht, 2015), 277-89. Walter Künneth (1901-1997) stands in the tradition of a conservative Lutheranism that he had encountered during his studies in Erlangen. His benevolent view towards the rise of Hitler changed only when his post at the *Apologetische Centrale*, a church institution based in Berlin, came into question. After World War II, Künneth found himself more and more on the outskirts of mainline Lutheranism. Thus, in 1966 he supported the campaign *No Other Gospel (Kein anderes Evangelium)* that openly opposed the content and influence of Rudolf Bultmann's demythologization of the Christian message. See Nathan Howard Yoder, "Erhaltungsordnungen: A Trinitarian Answer to Ideology. Walter Künneth (1901-1977)," in *"Ordnung in Gemeinschaft": A Critical Appraisal of the Erlangen Contribution to the Orders of Creation* (New York/Bern: Peter Lang, 2016), 163-210. Otto Dibelius (1880-1967) was one of the most important, albeit controversial, figures of German Protestantism between the 1920s and the 1950s. Dibelius did not technically belong to the Lutheran tradition in the specific sense. Instead, he was an offspring of the national-conservative Prussian United Church. His initial stance toward National Socialism had been conciliatory, to say the least, and his legacy is heavily tainted by his antisemitism. A recently published article refers to him as a "successful opportunist" (*erfolgreicher Opportunist*). See Thomas Klatt, "Der erfolgreiche Opportunist: Otto Dibelius," *Evangelisch.de*, May 15, 2017, accessed April 12, 2019, https://www.evangelisch.de/inhalte/142177/15-05-2017/ekd-ratsvorsitzender-otto-dibelius-antisemit-predigt-zu-hitlers-machtergreifung-vor-dem-bundestag. Gradually, his view towards the regime grew more ambivalent. After World War II, Dibelius became one of the most important figures among the architects of the Evangelical Church in Germany (EKD) as well as one of the most prominent proponents of the Ecumenical Movement. For further information on Dibelius, see Albrecht Beutel, "Otto Dibelius: Ein Promemoria zum 40. Todestag des preußischen Kirchenfürsten," *Theologische Literaturzeitung* 132, no. 1 (2007): 3-16. For a recent overview, see Mark C. Mattes, ed., *Twentieth-Century Lutheran Theologians* (Göttingen: Vandenhoeck und Ruprecht, 2013), especially 7-16.
> 23 The names of this list already indicate the difficulty of pinning down confessional specifics along the lines of Lutherans and Barthians. Both Helmut Gollwitzer (1908-1993) and Ernst Wolf (1902-1971) were prominent students and outspoken scholarly companions of Barth.

In using the term "totalitarianism," I do not refer to a specific technical definition of the word. Instead, I will use it in a broad sense, following the Encyclopedia Britannica, which states that totalitarianism delineates a "strong central rule that attempts to control and direct all aspects of individual life through coercion and repression."[24] In the context of this chapter, it refers to the perceived "other" of the desired political order and the threat to its flourishing.

Secularization as the Main Problem?

In 1945 Germany lay in ruins—literally, but also figuratively. While the majority of the population struggled to cope with the material hardships at hand, the moral and political bankruptcy of the society was hardly addressed or in many cases actively suppressed. The war and the atrocities that Nazi Germany had wrought throughout Europe ended in the occupation and the division of the German territory.[25] At the same time, it was clear that the political system had to undergo significant changes. In this situation, a re-Christianization seemed to many to be a viable candidate for the reconstruction of the political culture and the society.[26]

These factors played a role in a powerful interpretation of National Social-

---

Nontheless, both of them drew heavily on the works of Martin Luther. Not only did they formulate their theological viewpoints with specific reference to the texts of Luther, they also engaged in the study of church history in the period of the Protestant Reformation. Gollwitzer, who sympathized with the student revolt of the late 1960s, formulated his theological insights with a growing interest in Marxism and Socialism. Wolf, also heavily indebted to the theological insights of Barth, did not influence postwar Protestantism so much through his writings as through his role as an organizer of academic institutions and as a publisher of key journals in the field of theology. For a helpful English introduction to Gollwitzer, see W. Travis McMaken, *Our God Loves Justice: An Introduction to Helmut Gollwitzer* (Minneapolis, MN: Fortress Press, 2017). For Wolf, see Heinz Schmidt, "Herrschaft Christi als Legitimationsgrundlage für gesellschaftlichen Wandel: Die Bedeutung Ernst Wolfs für das politische Engagement des deutschen Protestantismus," in *Glaube—Freiheit—Diktatur in Europa und den USA*, ed. Katarzyna Stokłosa (Göttingen: Vandenhoeck und Ruprecht, 2007), 201-18.

24 *Encyclopedia Britannica Online*, s.v. "Totalitarianism (Government)," accessed April 12, 2019, https://www.britannica.com/topic/totalitarianism.
25 See Konrad Jarausch, *After Hitler: Recivilizing Germans, 1949-1995* (New York: Oxford University Press, 2006), 3-18.
26 See Reiner Anselm, "Verchristlichung der Gesellschaft?," in *Christentum und politische Verantwortung: Kirchen im Nachkriegsdeutschland*, ed. Jochen-Christoph Kaiser and Anselm Döring-Manteuffel (Stuttgart: Kohlhammer, 1990), 63-87.

ism which viewed National Socialism as an offspring of *secularism*.²⁷ While most commentators today disagree with this assumption, the thrust of the argument is understandable. A person who professes a sympathy to the Christian faith and its tenets is inclined to show that there are reasons *inherent in Christianity* that are counter to National Socialism. In postwar Germany, theological justifications of totalitarian rule were discredited. The rise and the tight grip of totalitarian rule, many argued, could not be attributed to Christianity. Instead, most theologians made the loss of a Christian grounding of society responsible for the rise of National Socialism. The logical solution to the problem at hand was the revival of a Christian society.

More specifically, the idea was that the political power had emancipated itself from its moral roots, which are necessarily bound to religious sources. It is worth pointing out that this idea was by no means peculiar to Germany. Indeed, the ecumenical contacts fostered a lively debate within Lutheran circles, including Berggrav, the Primate of the Church of Norway. His resistance and imprisonment during the Nazi occupation of Norway reinforced his moral authority. The German translations of his publications on the Lutheran theory of civil disobedience were an important influence on German Lutheran theologians.²⁸ In his book *Staten og mennesket*, translated as *Man and State*, Berggrav dealt with the party program of the National Socialist Party of Vidkun Quisling.²⁹ According to Berggrav, power and its extension became the only purpose of the state, since the state had disengaged itself from morals and religion. It had become totalitarian by penetrating into every corner of society.³⁰ In this view, National Socialism was not a specific historical phenomenon of the early 20th century but rather the conclusion of a development that began in the 15th century when Nicholo Macciavelli wrote his book, *The Prince*, which, according to Berggrav, might as well be called *Der Führer* because it promoted the idea that

---

27 It is difficult to place the idea of secularization that authors such as Berggrav or Dibelius had in mind within the framework of this volume. With regard to their political ethics, it seems that they mainly referred to the legal-cultural dimension of secularity (see the Introduction to this volume by Pamela Slotte, Niels Henrik Gregersen and Helge Årsheim). However, they also saw a deep connection between secularity[meaning2] and secularity[meaning3]. To them, the level of society's religiousness seemed to be deeply connected with moral roots of the law. Needless to say, that secularization was, at least until the 1950s, a pejorative word that was deeply tainted by the idea that National Socialism was an offspring of atheism.

28 See Hans Dombois and Erwin Wilkens, eds., *Macht und Recht: Beiträge zur lutherischen Staatslehre der Gegenwart* (Berlin: Lutherisches Verlagshaus, 1956).

29 Eivind Berggrav, *Der Staat und der Mensch*, trans. Walter Lindenthal (Hamburg: Neuer Verlag, 1946).

30 Berggrav, *Der Staat und der Mensch*, 7.

political power followed its own logic.[31] Modern ideologies are mere means to the end of disguising the detachment of the state from its moral roots. In his view, the violence of the French Revolution is not a coincidence but its logical and necessary companion.[32] In this narrative, "liberal paganism"[33] is the precursor to the National Socialist state.

To Berggrav, legal positivism is an expression on the same tendency. A secular legitimation of law seems dangerous to him because the law hereby becomes a tool for power and particular interests. A deeper respect for the law is needed, Berggrav insists, which must be rooted in "eternal and unchangeable principles"[34] In this way, the judiciary becomes more important to Berggrav than the principle of popular sovereignty. Indeed, he thinks that the American Supreme Court is a good example for generating real legitimacy. The "Supreme Court," he writes, is "deeply democratic" in that it acts as a "successor to the constitutional convention."[35] This connection between the judiciary and legislative competence shows how Berggrav tries to point to social embodiments of the idea that legitimacy must rest in eternal principles, not in the "volatile" will of the people.

The strategy for renewal and healing corresponds to this diagnosis. The goal is to contain the state. Berggrav contended that this was to be achieved by harnessing the resources of Christianity, especially Christianity's sense of awe and its recognition of sacred boundaries. Both were supposed to counterbalance the power-hungry state.[36] On the political level, Berggrav recommends the principle of federalism, not only as a relation between geographical political units but as a foundational principle governing all power relations.[37] In addition to that, Berggrav wishes to implement authority as a conception of power that combines trust, freedom, and equality. This is only possible if the state allows decentralized smaller institutions to be centers and sources of authority.[38]

As stated above, not only were similar positions popular among Lutheran theologians during the first years of the Federal Republic; they were also entertained by prominent leaders of the Evangelical Church in Germany. Dibelius, Bishop of Berlin and Chairman of the Council of the Evangelical Church

---

31   Berggrav, *Der Staat und der Mensch*, 13.
32   Berggrav, *Der Staat und der Mensch*, 18-23.
33   Berggrav, *Der Staat und der Mensch*, 62.
34   Berggrav, *Der Staat und der Mensch*, 175.
35   Berggrav, *Der Staat und der Mensch*, 176.
36   Berggrav, *Der Staat und der Mensch*, 54-62.
37   Berggrav, *Der Staat und der Mensch*, 93.
38   Berggrav, *Der Staat und der Mensch*, 102.

in Germany (EKD), shared Berggrav's pessimism with regard to the modern state.[39] To him, the modern state was the epitome of "a reality that breaks away from God."[40] One of the results was that the law does not rest on an objective and firm foundation, in Dibelius's view one of the main factors for the disastrous consequences of National Socialism. When politics instrumentalizes law, it becomes destructive. However, Dibelius does not confine those totalitarian tendencies to totalitarian systems in our sense. To him, the Nuremburg Trials belong to the same category of instrumentalization of the law as Hitler's rule.[41] The secularization of values such as the sanctity of marriage and the loss of "metaphysical limitations" makes the state into something destructive.[42] The "total" state is not merely a degeneration of an otherwise desirable political way of organizing political authority. Instead, it is identical with statehood itself. Part of the solution is the Christian church and Christians who work in politics while acknowledging its limitations. The church, he writes, is "the firm bulwark against the tyranny of the state's authority", the "shelter for human freedom and humaneness."[43] Next to the church, the judicial system seems to him more trustworthy than political procedures. Thus, Dibelius favors a strong judicial branch, as does Berggrav, including a supreme court that imposes restrictions on the political process. To him, the law functions as a bulwark against the totalitarian tendencies intrinsic to every state. In that way, the law issued and enforced by the state gains a sacred quality that is sharply distinguished from democratic procedures. Thus, Dibelius can say that the law is "something independent, something majestic, something holy."[44]

This strong emphasis on sacred barriers against the state's power derived its plausibility at the time from the specific context of the period shortly after the breakdown of National Socialist power. One of them was the idea that the churches were *victims* of the totalitarian systems of the mid-20th century. While this view has been widely refuted by historical research, it did seem plausible

---

39 See William McGuire King, "Prelude to the German Church Struggle: Otto Dibelius and 'The Century of the Church'," *Journal of Church and State* 24, no. 1 (1982): 53-71; Hartmut Fritz, *Otto Dibelius: Ein Kirchenmann in der Zeit zwischen Monarchie und Diktatur* (Göttingen: Vandenhoeck und Ruprecht, 1998).
40 Quoted from Dorothee Buchhaas-Birkholz, *Zum politischen Weg unseres Volkes: Politische Leitbilder und Vorstellungen im deutschen Protestantismus 1954-1952; Eine Dokumentation* (Düsseldorf: Droste Verlag, 1989), 17.
41 Otto Dibelius, *Grenzen des Staates* (Tübingen: Wichern-Verlag, 1949), 45.
42 Dibelius, *Grenzen des Staates*, 53-63.
43 Dibelius, *Grenzen des Staates*, 84.
44 Dibelius, *Grenzen des Staates*, 101.

to many people at the time.⁴⁵ The megatrend of secularization seemed to be a satisfying explanation for the political failures of the 20th century. However, Dibelius's assessment paints with a broad brush, to say the least. It rests on the assumption that there is something inherently wrong with political power itself. In doing so, he draws together very different political systems and their distinct features and does not shy away from comparing the anti-religious actions of the Nazi regime with policies of the Weimar Republic. This, of course, obscures the actual responsibility for the breakdown of a free society in 1933.

While most theologians of that time agreed with the assumption that, in its essence, the Christian faith should or could not legitimately be used to justify a dictatorship, they tended to give more distinct reasons. Again, the intention to show that the Christian faith, at its core, opposes totalitarianism, is understandable. Most theologians, however, tried to show more precisely what it was *about* the Christian faith that spoke against totalitarianism.

A representative statement in this direction had already been issued in 1945. In the so-called Stuttgart Declaration of Guilt, which helped to reestablish the partnership with the churches worldwide, the freshly-founded Evangelical Church in Germany acknowledged its shortcomings and its guilt.⁴⁶ The crucial paragraph reads as follows: "[W]e accuse ourselves of not witnessing more courageously, of not praying more faithfully, of not believing more joyously, and of not loving more ardently."⁴⁷ One important aim of this document was to initiate a healthy relation with international partners in the Ecumenical Council of Churches.⁴⁸ The Declaration shares one important conviction with the statements of Dibelius, who was involved in drafting the text: a conviction that the catastrophes of National Socialist rule and the war were consequences of a lack of Christianity. Yet, there is a marked difference between Dibelius and the Declaration. Whereas Dibelius accuses the megatrend of secularization, the Declaration accuses the Church itself. The perpetrator is not an anonymous force outside of Christianity, but forces within Christianity itself. This narrative presupposes that

---

45 See Schildt, *Kulturgeschichte*, 64-67.
46 See Roger Newell, "The Stuttgart Declaration of 1945: A Case Study of Guilt, Forgiveness and Foreign Policy," in *Trinity and Transformation: J. B. Torrance's Vision of Worship, Mission, and Society,* ed. Todd Speidell (Eugene, OR: Wipf and Stock, 2016), 157-74. The text of the Stuttgart Declaration is printed in, and from here on quoted from, Newell, "The Stuttgart Declaration of 1945," 173. See also John S. Conway, "How Shall the Nations Repent? The Stuttgart Declaration of Guilt, October 1945," *Journal of Ecclesiastical History* 38, no. 4 (1987): 596-622.
47 Newell, "Stuttgart Declaration," 173.
48 Martin Greschat, *Der Protestantismus in der Bundesrepublik Deutschland* (Leipzig: Evangelische Verlagsanstalt, 2011), 16-18.

the lack of Christian conviction and action contributed to the political failures of the 1930s. Instead of arguing that there is a correlation between secularization and tyranny or that power is inherently demonic, the Declaration presupposes a sense of agency on the part of the church. It is *the church* itself that did something wrong and that should do better in the future. I will now turn to the following question: If totalitarian rule is said to be caused by the lack of right conviction and practice—what convictions and practice are these?

The Example of Romans 13

To engage with this question, I would like to draw attention to the famous—or infamous—chapter 13 of Paul's letter to the Romans.[49] The King James Version which is closer to the German translation by Martin Luther, renders Romans 13, 1 as follows: "Let every soul be subject unto the higher powers. For there is no power (Luther: *Obrigkeit*) but of God: the powers that be are ordained of God."[50] A lot of the discussion about the reorientation of Protestant ethics in Germany revolved around this verse, the reason being that Romans 13 was used to legitimize authoritarian rule. The theology of orders of creation, as they were put forward by reactionary theologians such as Emanuel Hirsch, rested upon a particular interpretation of Romans 13.[51] While some theologians began doubting whether Romans 13 could be used as a basis for political ethics, virtually all of them took up a position with regard to Romans 13. In a heated debate in the late 1950s, Dibelius used Romans 13 to deny that the German Democratic Republic rightfully claimed to be instituted by God, a controversy that came to be known as the *Obrigkeitsdebatte*.[52] Dibelius doubted whether the term *Obrigkeit* was applicable to the modern state.[53] He emphasized the radical difference

---

49 To be sure, this approach does not argue that political ethics is grounded solely on interpretations of Scripture. When I draw upon the different interpretations of Romans 13, my aim is to identify exemplary patterns of argumentation.
50 The New Revised Standard Version translates this verse as follows: "Let every person be subject to the governing authorities; for there is no authority except from God, and those authorities that exist have been instituted by God."
51 See John Stroup, "Political Theology and Secularization Theory in Germany, 1918-1939: Emanuel Hirsch as a Phenomenon of His Time," *Harvard Theological Review* 80, no. 3 (1987): 321-68.
52 See Martin Greschat, "Römer 13 und die DDR: Der Streit um das Verständnis der 'Obrigkeit' (1957-1961)," *Zeitschrift für Theologie und Kirche* 105, no. 1 (2008): 63-93.
53 Otto Dibelius, "Obrigkeit? Eine Frage an den 60jährigen Landesbischof," in *Kirchliches Jahrbuch für die Evangelische Kirche in Deutschland,* ed. Joachim Beckmann, vol. 86, 1959 (Gütersloh: Gütersloher Verlagshaus, 1960), 123-29.

between the 16th-century context of the term and the political and social reality of the present. The main issue here lies in the idea that the administration is subject to the majority of a parliamentary body. Thus, the *Obrigkeit* was now ordained or instituted by the majority of a parliament.[54] The opposition, he contended, strove to replace the respective holder of power.[55] However, the decisive problem, Dibelius wrote, was not the difference between the 16th and the 20th century; that is to say, between a pre-modern and a modern conception of authority. Instead, it was the fact that the "total" state expands its grip on every part of life.[56]

After World War II, the debates on the applicability of Romans 13 had at least three purposes: the *first* was to re-evaluate the shortcomings of Protestant ethics before and during the Nazi rule. Romans 13 had been used to legitimize the National Socialist system. The most striking expression of this ideological use of Romans 13 is found in the Ansbach Memorandum (1934). Right-leaning theologians drafted this document as a reaction to the Confessing Church's Barmen Declaration (1934). It stated: "As believing Christians, we thank God the Lord that he has given to our *Volk,* in its moment of need, the Führer as a 'devout and loyal ruler,' and that he brings forth through the National Socialist state a 'good government,' a government with 'discipline and honor.'"[57] After 1945, Protestant theologians, especially Lutheran theologians, went to great lengths to show that this use of Romans 13 had been misguided. The *second* purpose of the debates on Romans 13 was to make its content relevant for a modern political ethics. After analyzing the shortcomings of outdated interpretations of Romans 13, they wanted to show what could be inferred from these shortcomings—what had to be done in order to prevent similar tendencies in the future. The *third* purpose of these debates was to discriminate between the political systems of East and West. This is where the *Obrigkeitsdebatte* gained its attention and relevance.

Romans 13 can be used to illustrate the tendencies of Protestant political ethics in postwar Germany. I would like to stress here the main points. If one focuses on the last part of the verse, "ordained of" (KJV) or "instituted by God" (NRSV), the main issue is that of *legitimate authority or the legitimacy of legal arrangements.* What, the theologians asked, does it mean to say that

---

54   Dibelius, "Obrigkeit?," 123-29
55   Dibelius, "Obrigkeit?," 126.
56   Dibelius, "Obrigkeit?," 126.
57   Quoted from James M. Stayer, *Martin Luther, German Saviour: German Evangelical Theological Factions and the Interpretation of Luther, 1917-1933* (Montreal: McGill Queen's University Press, 2000), 132.

the "powers" or the "governing authorities" are "ordained" or "instituted by God"? Is it possible to apply this idea to a democratic order? And was it correct to assume, as the German Christians had done, that the Nazi regime was "ordained" or "instituted" by God? The obvious answer after World War II had to be "no". The National Socialist regime, so Thielicke argued, did not constitute a legitimate order of God but something else entirely.[58] What is ordained is the fact of statehood itself, not the form of government.[59] There are no specifics of a given political system that can claim that they are ordered by God. What *is* instituted by God, though, is politics, understood as a necessary form of human conduct, and the necessity of participating in politics on grounds of political reason.

Another way to look at the verse is to focus on its first part. One could then ask: What does it mean for a citizen in a democracy to "be subject unto the higher powers" or to be "subject to the governing authorities"? Wolf, especially, refused to speculate on the ontological foundation of legal or political legitimacy, in his view a dire relic of the fateful errors of the 1930s. "Metaphysics of the state", as he called it, was to be avoided.[60] According to him, this metaphysics of the state had played a fateful role in the uncritical acceptance of dictatorial rule. Instead, the proper question to ask of Romans 13 is: Which conduct is to be required of a Christian in a given political system? At least it cannot simply mean being obedient to political rulers. Instead, it should be interpreted as meaning to be co-responsible in advancing the welfare of the state and all its citizens. Co-responsibility encompasses the right to criticize those in power and to work towards attaining justice within political institutions.

Most theologians tried to strike a balance between reaffirming the normative assertions of Romans 13 while also raising the possibility of criticizing and amending its content. Gollwitzer's statements on the topic are typical. According to him, there is a continuity between the political ethics of the Reformation and the modern state. Luther's and Jean Calvin's (1509-1564) doctrines of political authority may seem pre-modern to us. Yet their aim, Gollwitzer writes, was to guarantee the subjects' freedom.[61] At the same time, he argues that the change

---

58 See Helmut Thielicke, *Theologische Ethik: Ethik des Politischen,* vol. II/2 (Tübingen: Mohr Siebeck, 1958), 27.
59 Thielicke, *Theologische Ethik*, 20.
60 Ernst Wolf, "Die Königsherrschaft Christi und der Staat," in *Königsherrschaft Christi: Der Christ im Staat*, ed. Ernst Wolf and Werner Schmauch (Munich: Christian Kaiser Verlag, 1958), 20-61.
61 Helmut Gollwitzer, "Bürger und Untertan," in *Forderungen der Freiheit: Aufsätze und Reden zur politischen Ethik,* ed. Helmut Gollwitzer (Munich: Christian Kaiser Verlag, 1964), 79;

in the political context also requires a modification and update of this doctrine. Against conservative Lutherans, he specifically denied the church's ability to serve as a counter agent to keep the state's power at bay.[62] Democracy, he writes, is the only way to control and restrict power in the present.[63] Only an uncritical application of the Reformation doctrine leads to a form of tyranny. In his view, the *Führerstaat* of National Socialism was a "bizarre endeavor that our forefathers of the Reformation could not have dreamed of."[64]

With these options to interpret Romans 13 in mind, I will arrange the following remarks as follows: The first part will deal with *the source of legitimacy*, the second part will deal with *political practice within the boundaries of the law*.

The Source of Legitimacy

With regards to the source of legitimacy, there was a broad consensus in the German theology that it was important to stress the fact that the purpose of the state is entirely this-worldly. Keeping in mind the overall topic of this volume, however, it is noteworthy that the way of describing this fact was only in exceptional instances the term "secular" (*säkular*). More often the theologians of the time used the term *weltlich* ("worldly" or "profane") to describe in what way political institutions and practices are legitimately non-Christian or non-religious.[65] With reference to the terms as they are used in the introduction to this volume,[66]

---

originally published in *Libertas Christiana: Friedrich Delekat zum 65. Geburtstag*, ed. Ernst Wolf (Munich: Christian Kaiser Verlag, 1957), 30-56.

62 Gollwitzer, "Bürger und Untertan," 79.
63 Gollwitzer, "Bürger und Untertan," 79.
64 Gollwitzer, "Bürger und Untertan," 79.
65 See, e.g., Wolfgang Trillhaas, *Ethik* (Berlin: Töpelmann, 1959), 348: "Die 'Weltlichkeit' des Staates hat eine theologische Bedeutung ... Weltlichkeit bedeutet, daß es vor unserem Blick verborgen ist, wie sich Gott, der Schöpfer und Herr der Welt, zur Regierung dieser Welt der staatlichen Macht bedient. Der christlich verstandene Staat ist der 'weltliche' Staat." "The 'profaneness' of the state has theological significance ... Profaneness means that the way in which God, the Creator and Lord of the world, uses the state's power to rule the world, is concealed from us. The state, understood in a Christian way, is the 'profane' state." Thielicke explicitly uses the term "secularity" when he analyzes the relationship between authority and freedom, arguing that "secularism" is to be interpreted as "a gigantic experiment" that helps theology to deepen its understanding of freedom. Thielicke, *Ethik,* 244. According to Heinz-Dietrich Wendland (1900-1992), one of the founding fathers of "social ethics" as a distinct academic field within theological ethics, politics is "a practice with *worldly* powers." Heinz-Dietrich Wendland, *Einführung in die Sozialethik* (Berlin: De Gruyter, 1963), 53, 85.
66 See Slotte, Gregersen, and Årsheim, "Introduction: Internationalization and Re-Confessionalization: Law and Religion in the Nordic Realm 1945-2017," in this volume.

one could say that it seemed self-evident to the theological mainstream in Germany during the 1950s and 60s to affirm secularity[meaning1] and secularity[meaning2], but only up to a certain point. Secularity[meaning3], if taken into account at all,[67] was seen rather as a threat to secularity[meaning1-2]. Thus, religion or the Christian traditions was a means of keeping the state profane, especially of protecting society from the ideological abuse of political power. Wolfgang Schweitzer (1916-2009), co-founder of the *Zeitschrift für Evangelische Ethik*, one of the most notable publication organs in the field of Protestant ethics, could refer to Luther when he wrote that the political ethics of Protestantism meant the "liberation of reason to real profaneness wherever this profaneness is threatened."[68] Not least, this was in line with a general tendency in Western political theory after World War II to emphasize soberness as a political virtue and to delegitimize ideologies.[69] The state's function was to further benefits such as peace, order, and humaneness and not to indoctrinate its population.[70] From this perspective, totalitarianism was an attempt to sacralize politics and to sanctify finite realities.

Against the danger of imbuing the state with theological dignity, theologians such as Heinz-Dietrich Wendland and Trillhaas emphasized that the profane character of political institutions was not a compromise with political liberalism, but a legitimate expression of Christianity itself.[71] Political institutions are "worldly entities" (*weltliche Gebilde*) that are to be organized by reason.[72] Schweitzer calls them "profane-human shells" and continues: "it is our task to furnish them for our children in order for them to live in."[73] According to Trillhaas, the state is to be understood as a profane institution because it is the sphere of "God's mysterious work of creation"—not of his plan of salvation. The "Christian state", properly understood, is nothing other than the "profane (*weltlicher*) state."[74]

---

67 After all, in 1970, 93,6 % of the population still belonged to one of the two main churches in Germany, the Roman Catholic Church and the Evangelical Church in Germany (EKD). See Carsten Frerk, "Deutschland: Die Konfessionen," Forschungsgruppe Weltanschauungen in Deutschland, January 15, 2018, accessed May 26, 2019, https://fowid.de/meldung/deutschland-konfessionen.
68 Wolfgang Schweitzer, *Der entmythologisierte Staat: Studien zur Revision der Ethik des Politischen* (Gütersloh: Gütersloher Verlagshaus, 1968), 61.
69 See Jan-Werner Müller, *Contesting Democracy: Political Ideas in Twentieth-Century Europe* (New Haven, CT: Yale University Press, 2011), 125-70.
70 As Thesis 5 of the Barmen Declaration says, the purose of political power consists in "providing for justice and peace."
71 See Wendland, *Einführung*, 53.
72 Wendland, *Einführung*, 31.
73 Wendland, *Einführung*, 31.
74 Trillhaas, *Ethik*, 348.

This theological line of thought led to a new appreciation of the study of law and social sciences from the late 1950s onward. Thus, Schweitzer drew on the sociological works of contemporary sociologists such as Ralf Dahrendorf (1929-2009) and Helmut Schelsky (1912-1984), while also rediscovering some of the "classics" such as Max Weber (1864-1920) and Ferdinand Tönnies (1855-1936).[75] Wolf could appeal to the influential legal scholar Rudolf Smend (1882-1975) when he interpreted Article 1 of the German constitution, the *Grundgesetz*, as a major point of contact between a theological and a legal interpretation of the powers of the state.[76] This is the point where human rights begin to play a crucial role for political ethics in German Protestantism. However, it was not until the 1970s that this affiliation with the causes of human rights is seen as a genuine theological task.[77] The legitimacy of the political system and legislation is thereby derived from the idea of human dignity. This idea helped to reconcile the traditional theological notion of a "higher" source of legitimacy with the secular notion of the sovereignty of the people. The act of deliberation is thereby bound by the idea of human dignity as it was stated in Article 1 of the constitution, which says that "[h]uman dignity shall be inviolable. To respect and protect it shall be the duty of all state authority." Non-religious knowledge is required, since the state is entirely profane. This dialogue fosters the idea that the political order is changeable. The state is not—as it had been to former generations of theologians—an organism,[78] its purpose is not to fend off evil,[79] the source of its legitimacy is decisively not God.[80] Rather, political action and state power have the purpose of protecting dignity[81] and freedom[82] or simply protecting human life.[83] Flourishing in an immanent sense is the aim and the purpose of politics, not salvation.

---

75 See Schweitzer, *Der entmythologisierte Staat*, 299-305.
76 See Ernst Wolf, "Die rechtsstaatliche Ordnung als theologisches Problem," in *Der Rechtsstaat, Angebot und Aufgabe: Eine Anfrage an Theologie und Christenheit heute* ed. Ernst Wolf, Theo Immer, and Karl Linke (Munich: Christian Kaiser Verlag, 1964), 47ff.
77 This reorientation was especially promoted by the Heidelberg theologians and ethicists Wolfgang Huber (*1942) and Heinz Eduard Tödt (1918-1991). See Wolfgang Huber and Heinz Eduard Tödt, *Menschenrechte: Perspektiven einer menschlichen Welt* (Berlin: Kreuz Verlag, 1977), but also Martin Honecker, *Das Recht des Menschen: Einführung in die evangelische Sozialethik* (Gütersloh: Gütersloher Verlagshaus, 1982).
78 Honecker, *Das Recht des Menschen*, 256.
79 Walter Künneth, *Politik zwischen Dämon und Gott: Eine christliche Ethik des Politischen* (Berlin: Lutherisches Verlagshaus, 1954), 157.
80 Künneth, *Politik zwischen Dämon und Gott*, 183.
81 Wolf, "Königsherrschaft," 58.
82 Wendland, *Einführung*, 75.
83 Schweitzer, *Staat*, 94.

Theologically, the totalitarian state is seen as *idolatry*. While most theologians were keen on showing that Western democratic systems are in harmony with the legitimate authority of Romans 13, many of them denied that Romans 13 was applicable to the totalitarian state. The "total state", so Thielicke's argument goes, is not within the boundaries that are set by the theological tradition of the Reformation. The reason is that total states are not even states in the strict sense of the word. Instead, they are "pseudo churches,"[84] "institutions of salvation" that compete with religious institutions, not with political institutions. The total state is characterized by its attempt to determine its citizens as a whole. The total state denies the freedom and individuality of the person. Instead, the person seems to be an object instead of a "partner" who is qualified by autonomy.[85] Thielicke interprets human rights as the endeavor to preserve the idea that there are authoritative values beyond the disposition of the people.[86] Totalitarianism is the result of a process whereby human beings attempt to take God's place. In absolutizing the finite, religious, moral, and political fanaticism become the main problems.[87] Compromise is seen as a necessary tool to overcome the dangers of fanaticism and ideologies, interpreted as idolatry. Structurally, checks and balances are the most important features for fending off totalitarian tendencies. The uncontrolled or uncontrollable accumulation of power was an important concern of the theologians, especially Lutheran theologians. Thielicke recommends a permanent distrust of power; he interprets this distrust as a conscious or unconscious knowledge of the Fall which posits that human beings are susceptible to the abuse of power.[88] The separation of powers especially functions as a guard against this threat to individual freedom.[89] This assessment rests on a deeper conviction that the distribution and control of power are more important than the question of what or who *constitutes* power. In contrast to Wolf, for example, Thielicke does not introduce the separation of powers as a constitutional concept. Thus, the German equivalent to the concept of the rule of law, the *Rechtsstaat*, does not play a systematic role in his discussion of the separation of powers. This deliberate distancing from actual legal frameworks leads Thielicke to a peculiar interpretation of human rights. In his view, they are another expression of the distrust of power, a "protest against the state's trend

---

84 Thielicke, *Ethik*, 27
85 Thielicke, *Ethik*, 61.
86 Thielicke, *Ethik*, 83.
87 Trillhaas, *Ethik*, 335.
88 Thielicke, *Ethik*, 255.
89 Thielicke, *Ethik*, 264ff.

toward omnipotence."[90] He is interested in the function of human rights, which he defines as containing power, not so much in the idea that human rights are the expression of a deliberate decision. In other words, he is more interested in what to do with political power instead of what constitutes political power in the first place.

Political Practice

Another common feature was the assumption that Christians were called to participate in politics—not because democracy requires them to, but because their religious convictions allegedly compel them to do so. To sacralize political action or political structures is one danger, to remain politically passive is another. While this may seem trivial in our contemporary context, the call to participate in political procedures and institutions was a crucial step beyond the shortcomings of the 1920s. "Co-responsibility" (*Mitverantwortung*) is the most important term used to describe this form of participation. Political inaction and passivity were seen as major factors in the failure of the Weimar Republic.

One key theological symbol was the idea that Jesus Christ had deprived this-worldly realities of their power, according to the Letter to the Philippians (Phil 1:9-11).[91] Politics may not be seen as a fight between God and anti-godly powers, since Christ had already gained victory over those powers. Totalitarianism in its Christian form is the attempt to derive political power from God's power. Jesus Christ frees one to participate in politics.

These theologians accentuated the *malleability* of human institutions. Activity instead of passivity, freedom instead of obedience, dynamism instead of stasis is what is to be demanded by theology. God's activity is not to be separated from Christians' participation in politics. What is of interest is the "Christian's behavior within the concrete reality of the state,"[92] not the search for an "essence of the state". Political involvement is seen as one of the "worldly forms of Christian love."[93] Thus, Christians contribute to the foundations of politics, to the "building of a moral climate for democracy."[94]

---

90 Thielicke, *Ethik*, 284.
91 Wolf, "Königsherrschaft," 23.
92 Wolf, "Königsherrschaft," 39.
93 Wendland, *Einführung*, 87.
94 Wolf, "Königsherrschaft," 60.

It is important to point out that the recommendation of active commitment in politics was a common feature of *all* theological groups. Until recently, some scholars held that only Barthian theologians were able to come to terms with political commitment.[95] Others argued that only Lutheran theologians avoided the pitfalls of fundamentalist politics.[96] While there certainly are differences with regard to *what* this political commitment was to look like, the fact *that* there was an obligation to engage in politics was uncontroversial.

What *was* controversial, though, was what a proper Christian participation in politics should look like. Lutheran theologians tended to emphasize the strengths of the compromise, the virtue of a sober, detached reasoning and agency in politics. In the words of Thielicke, "salvation also means salvation towards sobriety (*Nüchternheit*)". He criticizes the tendency to cling to absolute positions as being a form of "utopian idolatry" and requires objectivity and the avoidance of prejudices as fruits of the faith. "Realism"[97] is an important watchword for Thielicke and Trillhaas. This is not to say that Barthian theologians championed an unquestioned, rigid religious foundation for Christian politics. Wolf, for example, writes that ideology is "moral self-justification."[98] The content of a Christian political commitment is to be determined by reason, albeit a "reason that is illuminated by faith."[99] Schweitzer points out that the Christian law of love takes the shape of reason when applied to political action. The Christian witness aims at freeing reason to "real worldliness, wherever this worldliness is threatened."[100] Thielicke assumed, with many others, that the sacralization of relative institutions had been at least partly responsible for the downfall of the Weimar Republic.

In addition to that, moderate conservative theologians of the 1950s assumed that the inability to make compromises had been a key problem of theological ethics before 1945. Thielicke justified the duty to make compromises with the argument that God himself makes a compromise by entering the flesh in Jesus Christ. Thus, the willingness to make compromises is not a weakness or a vice. It is a way of imitating God's own behavior, necessary for sustaining the fabric of society. Furthermore, Thielicke emphasizes the necessity of distinguishing

---

95 Wolfgang Huber, "Protestantismus und Demokratie," in *Protestanten in der Demokratie. Positionen und Profile im Nachkriegsdeutschland*, ed. Wolfgang Huber (München 1990), 11-36.
96 Inacker, *Transzendenz*, 287-91.
97 Thielicke, *Ethik*, 612; Trillhaas, *Ethik*, 70.
98 Wolf, "Königsherrschaft," 59.
99 Wolf, "Königsherrschaft," 59.
100 Schweitzer, *Staat*, 61.

between a person and substantive matters. He favors an education that aims at reducing ideological tendencies and the ethical appreciation of reason.[101]

Trillhaas makes another argument for compromise. According to him, the future is the common horizon of every member of society. The most radical solution for resolving problems is to eliminate opposing views. In order to ensure that citizens shape their shared future, it is necessary to make compromises. To him, compromise is identical with politics. "Politics", he writes, "is nothing but the struggle to make a compromise."[102] According to Trillhaas, the lack of a proper theory of compromise had been a major lacuna in Protestant ethics. He stresses the importance of compromise by observing that "our own fate, our own future, is interconnected with the future of other people."[103] This makes compromise necessary for ensuring a common future as well as peace.[104]

Barthian theologians tended to emphasize the exemplary role of the church in political matters.[105] In their view, Christian political commitment mainly consisted in the affirmation and advocacy of a politics in accordance with the gospel. In their view, the Christian community plays a crucial role in shaping a Christian commitment. Here, God is not so much understood as a necessary barrier against the danger of absolutizing the relative, but rather as an enabling and empowering source. The particular community of the church points to the universality of God's rule in Jesus Christ and thereby reflects the Gospel by mirroring his good will in political activity. Christ is Lord of *every* realm of existence. Wolf develops this idea by promoting a "Protestant theory of political virtues"[106] as a guide to Christian political action. Barthian theologians identified political inactivity and passivity as the main reasons for the Christian susceptibility to National Socialism, and they found this weakness in the individual as well as in the Christian community. In order to prevent Christianity from ever falling prey to totalitarianism, they favored a strong communal sense of political principles. The Christian community, Wolf and Gollwitzer concluded, is responsible for being an example, for showing what freedom and equality look like. As a result, political responsibility becomes a necessary consequence of faith; the main task of the Christian is to be a witness to the gospel by participating in politics. In this reading, the problem in advance of the rise of National Socialism had not

---

101 Thielicke, *Ethik*, 616ff.
102 Thielicke, *Ethik,* 616ff.
103 Trillhaas, *Ethik*, 408.
104 Trillhaas, *Ethik*, 408.
105 For a concise portrayal of Barth's political ethics, see William Werpehowski, "Justification and Justice in the Theology of Karl Barth," *Thomist* 50, no. 4 (1986): 623-42.
106 Wolf, "Königsherrschaft," 53.

been the unwillingness to make compromises, but quite the opposite: the eager willingness to make compromises with "the world" and, consequently, with the Hitler regime.

Conclusion

To be sure, there are substantial shortcomings in the political ethics of the time when compared to what we know about the sources of totalitarian rule. I will only note the major ones in a short aside. One of the most notable issues is the lack of any serious mention of the Holocaust.[107] In this respect, the theologians were an exemplary part of a society that chose to repress its own guilt. In their theories they dealt with threats to freedom, with the violent or even murderous tendencies of totalitarianism, but they mentioned neither the victims nor identified the horrors of the Holocaust as the root of the importance of the norm of human dignity. The theological scene began to change in the late 1960s, when new historical narratives called into question more conservative readings of the past. Civil rights and democratization transformed the basic assumptions about the fundamentals of society.[108]

Nevertheless, it is noteworthy that the different interpretations of the political worst case had a lasting and transforming impact on the Christian view of the legitimacy of the constitutional state in German postwar society, and that the historically conditioned assumptions about the totalitarian threat impacted the theological symbols that were being used to understand politics. The experiences and interpretations of past events raised the awareness of certain dangers and shaped the response to political institutions and events. The tendency to use past experiences and their interpretation for grasping the political reality of the present can be seen as a liability, because it can easily become a backwards-looking, untenable historical analogy. But this pitfall can be avoided only through reflection.

---

107 See Edgar Wolfrum, *Die geglückte Demokratie: Geschichte der Bundesrepublik Deutschland von ihren Anfängen bis zur Gegenwart* (Stuttgart: Klett Cotta Verlag, 2007), 169-81.

108 Especially notable are the works of Tödt, Huber, and Rendtorff. See Huber and Tödt, *Menschenrechte*; Trutz Rendtorff, *Politische Ethik und Christentum: Möglichkeit und Unmöglichkeit christlicher Politik; Macht und Gewalt heute* (Munich: Christian Kaiser Verlag, 1978). Theologians such as Dorothee Sölle and Jürgen Moltmann proposed more radical and new forms of political ethics. See Dorothee Sölle, *Politische Theologie: Auseinandersetzung mit Rudolf Bultmann* (Stuttgart: Kreuz Verlag, 1971); Jürgen Moltmann, *Theologie der Hoffnung* (Munich: Christian Kaiser Verlag, 1966).

A current analysis of the weaknesses of Protestant political ethics and its responsibility in the ascent of National Socialism runs as follows. According to this view, reactionary theologians used Luther's talk of two kingdoms or realms to establish the priority of a religiously grounded claim over the increasingly secular society.[109] This interpretation posits that the purpose of the doctrine of two kingdoms, established in the early 20th century, had never been to separate religion and politics, but to ground politics in religion. Ultimately, this is supposed to have led to the uncritical affirmation of the status quo that helped to legitimize the National Socialist regime. Contrary to the hope of reintegrating the whole of society under a Christian umbrella, political elites took note of the over-legitimization of their rule, without conforming to Christian or churchly values. The idea that the state was ordained and instituted by God encouraged an understanding of politics in which the acts of political elites were construed as expressions of God's will. Hence, the only viable political option was obedience.[110]

Note how that narrative runs counter to the standard explanations that were put forward during the 20th century, especially by Karl Barth and his followers. To them, the idea of the two kingdoms weakened the link between Christian morals and political action. They argued that the doctrine of two realms established double standards that robbed genuinely Christian norms of their impact.[111] The problem, most theologians in the 1950s concluded, had been a lack of a religious grounding of morals. Contemporary commentators argue the other way around. To the theologians of the 1950s and 60s, the problem did not seem to lie in a religious commitment in politics but in the lack of implementation of religious tenets. To them, the problem was not a lack of a religious grounding but rather an *overly* religious grounding. To many contemporaries, the problem seems to be the "dose" of religion: "too much" religion seems to be intolerant and dehumanizing. In contrast to earlier generations of theologians, it is not the

---

109 For a helpful introduction to the use of the two kingdoms doctrine in the 20th century, see Richard V. Pierard, "The Lutheran Two-Kingdoms Doctrine and Subservience to the State in Modern Germany," *Journal of the Evangelical Theological Society* 29, no. 2 (1986): 193-203.
110 For such a narrative, see Reiner Anselm, *Ethik,* 211-14.
111 See Ulrich Duchrow, "Luther und der Gebrauch und Missbrauch der 'Zweireichelehre' in Theologie, Praxis und Institution lutherischer Kirchen: Einige geschichtliche Beispiele und Perspektiven," in *Zwei Reiche und Regimente: Ideologie oder evangelische Orientierung?,* ed. Ulrich Duchrow (Gütersloh, 1977), 9-32. Wolfgang Huber, "'Eigengesetzlichkeit' und 'Lehre von den zwei Reichen'," in *Gottes Wirken in seiner Welt: Zur Diskussion um die Zweireichelehre,* ed. Niels Hasselmann, vol. 2 (Hamburg: Lutherisches Verlagshaus, 1980), 27-51.

5. Sovereignty of the People or Sovereignty of God?

"wrong application" that leads to social or political disaster, but "too much" religion. In my view, it is necessary to reflect on implicit assumptions such as these; they, too, are rooted in specific historical contexts, and it seems likely to me that a lot of political ethics of our time is implicitly shaped by unquestioned notions of religious "fundamentalism" and assumptions about its nature. It would surely prove helpful to take a closer look at our own assumptions about threats to democracy and to be sensitive to the symbols that we use.

The assessment of the past may be seen as a motivation for questioning and analyzing the narratives that shape our own ethical beliefs. Many political developments in our present time cause commentators to compare the present with the mid-20th century threats to a free society. The theological-historical approach helps to understand and criticize overly simplified analogies. For one thing, it shows how our own evaluations change over time; for another, they encourage us to constantly update our culture of remembrance and to question our own assumptions which we bring to the table when we evaluate our political commitments.

Bibliography

Literature

Anselm, Reiner. "Politische Ethik." In *Handbuch der evangelischen Ethik*, edited by Wolfgang Huber, Torsten Meireis, and Hans-Richard Reuter, 195-263. Munich: Mohr Siebeck, 2015.

Anselm, Reiner. "Verchristlichung der Gesellschaft?" In *Christentum und politische Verantwortung: Kirchen im Nachkriegsdeutschland*, edited by Jochen-Christoph Kaiser and Anselm Döring-Manteuffel, 63-87. Stuttgart: Kohlhammer, 1990.

Barth, Karl. "Ein Brief nach Frankreich (1939)." In *Eine Schweizer Stimme 1938-1945*, 108-17. Zollikon-Zurich: Evangelischer Verlag, 1945.

Berggrav, Eivind. *Der Staat und der Mensch*. Translated by Walter Lindenthal. Hamburg: Neuer Verlag, 1946.

Beutel, Albrecht. "Otto Dibelius: Ein Promemoria zum 40. Todestag des preußischen Kirchenfürsten." *Theologische Literaturzeitung* 132, no. 1 (2007): 3-16.

Buchhaas-Birkholz, Dorothee. *Zum politischen Weg unseres Volkes: Politische Leitbilder und Vorstellungen im deutschen Protestantismus 1954-1952; Eine Dokumentation*. Düsseldorf: Droste Verlag, 1989.

Conway, John S. "How Shall the Nations Repent? The Stuttgart Declaration of Guilt, October 1945." *Journal of Ecclesiastical History* 38, no. 4 (1987): 596-622.

Dibelius, Otto. *Grenzen des Staates*. Tübingen: Wichern-Verlag, 1949.

Dibelius, Otto. "Obrigkeit? Eine Frage an den 60jährigen Landesbischof." In *Kirchliches Jahrbuch für die Evangelische Kirche in Deutschland*. Vol. 86 (1959), edited by Joachim Beckmann, 123-29. Gütersloh: Gütersloher Verlagshaus, 1960.

Dombois, Hans, and Erwin Wilkens, eds. *Macht und Recht: Beiträge zur lutherischen Staatslehre der Gegenwart.* Berlin: Lutherisches Verlagshaus, 1956.

Duchrow, Ulrich. "Luther und der Gebrauch und Missbrauch der 'Zweireichelehre' in Theologie, Praxis und Institution lutherischer Kirchen: Einige geschichtliche Beispiele und Perspektiven." In *Zwei Reiche und Regimente: Ideologie oder evangelische Orientierung?*, edited by Ulrich Duchrow, 9-32. Gütersloh: Mohn, 1977.

Encyclopedia Britannica Online, s.v. "Totalitarianism (Government)," accessed April 12, 2019, https://www.britannica.com/topic/totalitarianism.

Fritz, Hartmut. *Otto Dibelius: Ein Kirchenmann in der Zeit zwischen Monarchie und Diktatur.* Göttingen: Vandenhoeck und Ruprecht, 1998.

Gollwitzer, Helmut. "Bürger und Untertan." In *Forderungen der Freiheit: Aufsätze und Reden zur politischen Ethik*, 70-97. Munich: Christian Kaiser Verlag, 1964.

Gollwitzer, Helmut. "Bürger und Untertan." In *Libertas Christiana: Friedrich Delekat zum 65. Geburtstag*, edited by Ernst Wolf, 30-56. Munich: Christian Kaiser Verlag, 1957.

Gollwitzer, Helmut. *Reich Gottes und Sozialismus bei Karl Barth.* Munich: Christian Kaiser, 1972.

Graf, Friedrich Wilhelm. "Königsherrschaft Christi in der Demokratie: Karl Barth und die deutsche Nachkriegspolitik." *Evangelische Kommentare* 23 (1990): 735-38.

Greschat, Martin. *Der Protestantismus in der Bundesrepublik Deutschland.* Leipzig: Evangelische Verlagsanstalt, 2011.

Greschat, Martin. "Römer 13 und die DDR: Der Streit um das Verständnis der 'Obrigkeit' (1957-1961)." *Zeitschrift für Theologie und Kirche* 105, no. 1 (2008): 63-93.

Held, David. *Models of Democracy.* 3rd ed. Cambridge: Polity, 2006.

Honecker, Martin. "Protestantismus und Politik." In *Kirche und Politik: Ein notwendiges Spannungsfeld in unserer Demokratie*, edited by Hans F. Zacher, 118-31. Düsseldorf: Patmos, 1982.

Honecker, Martin. *Das Recht des Menschen: Einführung in die evangelische Sozialethik.* Gütersloh: Gütersloher Verlagshaus, 1982.

Huber, Wolfgang. "'Eigengesetzlichkeit' und 'Lehre von den zwei Reichen'." In *Gottes Wirken in seiner Welt: Zur Diskussion um die Zweireichelehre.* Vol. 2, edited by Niels Hasselmann, 27-51. Hamburg: Lutherisches Verlagshaus, 1980.

Huber, Wolfgang. "Prophetische Kritik und demokratischer Konsens." In *Charisma und Institution*, edited by Trutz Rendtorff, 110-31. Gütersloh: Gütersloher Verlagshaus, 1985.

Huber, Wolfgang. "Protestantismus und Demokratie." In *Protestanten in der Demokratie: Positionen und Profile im Nachkriegsdeutschland*, edited by Wolfgang Huber, 11-36, Munich: Christian Kaiser Verlag, 1990.

Huber, Wolfgang, and Heinz Eduard Tödt. *Menschenrechte: Perspektiven einer menschlichen Welt.* Berlin: Kreuz Verlag, 1977.

Hughes, Michael L. "Civil Disobedience in Transnational Perspective: American and West German Anti-Nuclear-Power Protesters, 1975-1982." *Historical Research* 39, no. 1 (2014): 236-53.

Inacker, Michael. *Transzendenz, Totalitarismus und Demokratie: Die Entwicklung des kirchlichen Demokratieverständnisses von der Weimarer Republik bis zu den Anfängen der Bundesrepublik (1918-1959)*. Neukirchen-Vluyn: Neukirchener Verlag, 1994.

Jarausch, Konrad. *After Hitler: Recivilizing Germans, 1949-1995.* New York: Oxford University Press, 2006.

Jeanrond, Werner G. "From Resistance to Liberation Theology: German Theologians and the Non/Resistance to the National Socialist Regime." *Journal of Modern History* 64 (1992): S187-203.

Joas, Hans. *The Creativity of Action.* Translated by Jeremy Gaines and Paul Keast. Chicago: University of Chicago Press, 1996.

Joas, Hans. *The Genesis of Values.* Translated by Gregory Moore. Chicago: Polity Press, 2000.

Joas, Hans. *The Sacredness of the Person: A New Genealogy of Human Rights.* Translated by Alex Skinner. Washington, D.C.: Georgetown University Press, 2013.

Kalden, Sebastian, and Jan Ole Wiechmann. "The Churches." In *The Nuclear Crisis: The Arms Race, Cold War Anxiety, and the German Peace Movement of the 1980s,* edited by Christoph Becker-Schaum, Philipp Gassert, Wilfried Mausbach, Martin Klimke, and Marianne Zepp, 242-57. New York/Oxford: Berghahn, 2016.

Kalinna, Georg. *Die Entmythologisierung der Obrigkeit: Tendenzen der evangelischen Ethik des Politischen in der frühen Bundesrepublik der 1950er und 1960er Jahre.* Tübingen: Mohr Siebeck, 2019.

Kalinna, Georg. "Zurück in den 'Irrgarten' der Zwei-Reiche-Lehre? Ein Vorschlag zur Differenzierung im Umgang mit der Zwei-Reiche-Lehre anhand von Helmut Thielickes Theologischer Ethik." In *Angewandtes Luthertum? Die Zwei-Reiche-Lehre als theologische Konstruktion in politischen Kontexten des 20. Jahrhunderts,* edited by Jürgen Kampmann and Hans Otte, 121-40. Gütersloh: Gütersloher Verlagshaus, 2017.

Kielmansegg, Peter Graf. "The Basic Law: Response to the Past or Design for the Future?" In *Fourty Years of the Grundgesetz (Basic Law),* edited by Hartmut Lehmann and Kenneth F. Ledford, 5-18. Washington, D.C.: German Historical Institute, 1990. Accessed April 8, 2019. https://www.ghi-dc.org/fileadmin/user_upload/GHI_Washington/PDFs/Occasional_Papers/Forty_Years_of_the_grundgesetz.pdf.

King, William McGuire. "Prelude to the German Church Struggle: Otto Dibelius and 'The Century of the Church'." *Journal of Church and State* 24, no. 1 (1982): 53-71.

Künneth, Walter. *Politik zwischen Dämon und Gott: Eine christliche Ethik des Politischen.* Berlin: Lutherisches Verlagshaus, 1954.

Lange, Dietz. "Wolfgang Trillhaas (1903-1995)." In *Stiftsgeschichte(n),* edited by Bernd Schröder, 277-89. Göttingen: Vandenhoeck und Ruprecht, 2015.

Mattes, Mark C, ed. *Twentieth-Century Lutheran Theologians.* Göttingen: Vandenhoeck und Ruprecht, 2013.

McMaken, W. Travis. *Our God Loves Justice: An Introduction to Helmut Gollwitzer.* Minneapolis, MN: Fortress Press, 2017.

Moltmann, Jürgen. *Theologie der Hoffnung*. Munich: Christian Kaiser Verlag, 1966.

Müller, Jan-Werner. *Contesting Democracy: Political Ideas in Twentieth-Century Europe.* New Haven, CT: Yale University Press, 2011.

Newell, Roger. "The Stuttgart Declaration of 1945: A Case Study of Guilt, Forgiveness and Foreign Policy." In *Trinity and Transformation: J. B. Torrance's Vision of Worship, Mission, and Society,* edited by Todd Speidell, 157-74. Eugene, OR: Wipf and Stock, 2016.

Pierard, Richard V. "The Lutheran Two-Kingdoms Doctrine and Subservience to the State in Modern Germany." *Journal of the Evangelical Theological Society* 29, no. 2 (1986): 193-203.

Pless, John T. "Helmut Thielicke (1908-1986)." *Lutheran Quarterly* 23, no. 4 (2009): 439-64.

Rendtorff, Trutz. "Die Autorität der Freiheit." In *Vielspältiges. Protestantische Beiträge zur ethischen Kultur,* 81-100. Stuttgart: Kohlhammer, 1991.

Rendtorff, Trutz. "Demokratieunfähigkeit des Protestantismus? Über die Renaissance eines alten Problems." *Zeitschrift für Evangelische Ethik* 27, no. 3 (1983): 253-56.

Rendtorff, Trutz. *Politische Ethik und Christentum: Möglichkeit und Unmöglichkeit christlicher Politik; Macht und Gewalt heute.* Munich: Christian Kaiser Verlag, 1978.

Scheliha, Arnulf von. "'Aneignung'—Der lange Weg zur Demokratie." In *Protestantische Ethik des Politischen,* 154-218. Tübingen: Mohr Siebeck, 2013.

Scheliha, Arnulf von. *Protestantische Ethik des Politischen.* Tübingen: Mohr Siebeck, 2013.

Schildt, Axel. *Deutsche Kulturgeschichte: Die Bundesrepublik von 1945 bis zur Gegenwart.* Munich: Hanser Verlag, 2009.

Schmidt, Heinz. "Herrschaft Christi als Legitimationsgrundlage für gesellschaftlichen Wandel: Die Bedeutung Ernst Wolfs für das politische Engagement des deutschen Protestantismus." In *Glaube—Freiheit—Diktatur in Europa und den USA,* edited by Katarzyna Stokłosa, 201-18. Göttingen: Vandenhoeck und Ruprecht, 2007.

Schweitzer, Wolfgang. *Der entmythologisierte Staat: Studien zur Revision der Ethik des Politischen.* Gütersloh: Gütersloher Verlagshaus, 1968.

Stayer, James. *Martin Luther, German Saviour: German Evangelical Theological Factions and the Interpretation of Luther, 1917-1933.* Montreal: McGill Queen's University Press, 2000.

Stroup, John. "Political Theology and Secularization Theory in Germany, 1918-1939: Emanuel Hirsch as a Phenomenon of His Time." *Harvard Theological Review* 80, no. 3 (1987): 321-68.

Sölle, Dorothee. *Politische Theologie: Auseinandersetzung mit Rudolf Bultmann.* Stuttgart: Kreuz Verlag, 1971.

Thielicke, Helmut. *Theologische Ethik: Ethik des Politischen.* Vol. II/2. Tübingen: Mohr Siebeck, 1958.

Trillhaas, Wolfgang. *Ethik.* Berlin: Töpelmann, 1959.

Ulrich, Sebastian. *Der Weimar-Komplex: Das Scheitern der ersten deutschen Demokratie und die politische Kultur der frühen Bundesrepublik.* Göttingen: Wallstein Verlag, 2009.

Wagner, Falk. *Zur gegenwärtigen Lage des Protestantismus.* Gütersloh: Gütersloher Verlagshaus, 1995.

Waldhoff, Christian. "Folgen—Lehren—Rezeptionen: Zum Nachleben des Verfassungswerks von Weimar." In *Das Wagnis der Demokratie: Eine Anatomie der Weimarer Reichsverfassung*, edited by Horst Dreier and Christian Waldhoff, 289-316. Munich: C. H. Beck, 2018.

Wendland, Heinz-Dietrich. *Einführung in die Sozialethik*. Berlin: De Gruyter, 1963.

Werpehowski, William. "Justification and Justice in the Theology of Karl Barth." *Thomist* 50, no. 4 (1986): 623-42.

Wilkens, Erwin. "Grenzen des Gehorsams: Der evangelische Christ vor der Obrigkeit." *Die politische Meinung* 69 (1962): 23-33.

Wolf, Ernst. "Die Königsherrschaft Christi und der Staat." In *Königsherrschaft Christi: Der Christ im Staat*, edited by Ernst Wolf and Werner Schmauch, 20-61. Munich: Christian Kaiser Verlag, 1958.

Wolf, Ernst. "Politia Christi: Das Problem der Sozialethik im Luthertum (1948/9)." In *Peregrinatio: Studien zur reformatorischen Theologie und zum Kirchenproblem*, vol. 1, 214-42. 2nd ed. Munich: Christian Kaiser, 1962.

Wolf, Ernst. "Die rechtsstaatliche Ordnung als theologisches Problem." In *Der Rechtsstaat, Angebot und Aufgabe: Eine Anfrage an Theologie und Christenheit heute,* edited by Ernst Wolf, Theo Immer, and Karl Linke, 28-63. Munich: Christian Kaiser Verlag, 1964.

Wolfrum, Edgar. *Die geglückte Demokratie: Geschichte der Bundesrepublik Deutschland von ihren Anfängen bis zur Gegenwart*. Stuttgart: Klett-Cotta Verlag, 2007.

Yoder, Nathan Howard. "Erhaltungsordnungen: A Trinitarian Answer to Ideology. Walter Künneth (1901-1977)." In *"Ordnung in Gemeinschaft": A Critical Appraisal of the Erlangen Contribution to the Orders of Creation*, 163-210. New York/Bern: Peter Lang, 2016.

Webpages

Frerk, Carsten. "Deutschland: Die Konfessionen." Forschungsgruppe Weltanschauungen in Deutschland, January 15, 2018. Accessed May 26, 2019. https://fowid.de/meldung/deutschland-konfessionen.

Klatt, Thomas. "Der erfolgreiche Opportunist: Otto Dibelius." *Evangelisch.de*, May 15, 2017. Accessed April 12, 2019. https://www.evangelisch.de/inhalte/142177/15-05-2017/ekd-ratsvorsitzender-otto-dibelius-antisemit-predigt-zu-hitlers-machtergreifung-vor-dem-bundestag.

II

Negotiations of the Secularity of Law

6. Neither Sacred nor Secular Law? The Self-Understanding of the Ecclesiastical Law in the Protestant Churches in Germany Before and After World War II

Hans Michael Heinig

Introduction

Can there be "wrong" law? Is "wrong" law even law? What kind of criteria can be used to assess the "wrongness"—moral, religious, or simply legal? Is the catalogue of possible criteria limited to positive norms (in the sense of a hierarchy of norms) or is the legal order as set by the legislator itself under the provision of extra positive norms? What do those higher principles of law look like, how are they determined and enforced? Does legal thinking like that not endanger the fundamental functions of modern law — legal certainty, protection of the individual self-determination, legitimisation of secular law through democratic procedures?

Questions like these are the big themes of jurisprudence in all kinds of legal regimes. They revolve around the center of our legal understanding. To Germany in particular, this question posed itself with a certain urgency: From 1945 onwards, there was intensive debate regarding the role of law in the Nazi barbarity and on what lessons were to be drawn. Generals, Gauleiters, Adolf Eichmann, commanders of concentration camps — all of these people tried to legally exculpate themselves after 1945: They were simply following orders. In light of these horrendous crimes committed by the state, more than one legal scholar was looking for reassurance in natural law.[1] Later on, after 1989, the

---

1   Cf. for the debate the collection of sources Werner Maihofer, ed., *Naturrecht oder Rechtspositivismus?* (Darmstadt: Wissenschaftliche Buchgesellschaft, 1962); for an overview Hasso Hofmann, *Rechtsphilosophie nach 1945: Zur Geistesgeschichte der Bundesrepublik Deutschland* (Berlin: Duncker & Humblot, 2012), 10ff.; comprehensively: Lena Foljanty, *Recht oder Gesetz: Juristische Identität und Autorität in den Naturrechtsdebatten der Nachkriegszeit* (Tübingen: Mohr Siebeck, 2013).

question of whether state functionaries could invoke the chain of commands and an ideological understanding of law contrary to that of the liberal constitutional view when dealing with grave human rights violations raised itself in a completely different way.[2]

The question of "wrong" law does not, however, only pose itself in "secular" legal systems but also in ecclesiastical or religiously shaped ones. As the actions and the organisation of religious groups are always related to the religious question of truth, the question of "wrong" law poses itself in religiously coined or ecclesiastical legal orders in a more poignant way: Where divine law is postulated, the question of legal finding is always one of revelations and divine knowledge. Right law and true belief are in reference to each other: religious law is part of the divine law and adherence to this law can be considered worship.

Even in religious cultures that, like Protestantism, abstain from the notion of a *ius divinum*, the question of how to understand ecclesiastical law loses itself: Is ecclesiastical law like secular law? And what would that mean considering the debates on the relationship between positive legal enactment and extrapositive linkage of secular law? Are there particularities when concerned with ecclesiastical law? The protestant ecclesiastical legal cultures of Central and Northern Europe give different answers to the posed questions, depending on the historical coining of the relationship between state and church. In Germany, the debates on the theological basis of ecclesiastical law in the 20th century can give an impression of how these questions are dealt with. They can be seen as a special case of the question of "wrong" law. The core of these debates is the theological legitimisation of ecclesiastical law: Why and under which preconditions can ecclesiastical law be of legal validity in churches? When does ecclesiastical law lose its claim to observance? Often, this central question of legitimisation is reformulated as a problem of adherence to and coinage by scripture and creed. Because of this adherence the protestant ecclesiastical law gets into a rather maverick floating position: it considers itself neither a sacral or divine law, nor a purely secular law in the sense that nowadays it is simply part of the *secular ius publicum*.

Up until today, this debate gained crucial impulses through the experiences of the *Kirchenkampf* in the Nazi Era and its processing in the postwar time. This chapter wishes to give an overview over these long-term dynamics.[3]

---

2   See, e.g., Bernhard Schlink, "Rechtsstaat und revolutionäre Gerechtigkeit," in Bernhard Schlink, *Vergangenheitsschuld und gegenwärtiges Recht* (Frankfurt am Main: Suhrkamp, 2002), 38ff.

3   The term "overview" is to be stressed here: a more detailed work would have to give more depth of focus in differentiating between the individual debates concerning Natural

Legal Positivism and Beyond: The Debates Before and during the Weimar Republic

According to the standardised tales of the history of Protestant ecclesiastical law in Germany, the thoughts behind said law in the beginning of the German imperial period were shaped by legal positivism.[4] The spiritual foundation and legitimization of ecclesiastical law only played a marginal role. A representative starting point for reconstructions of the history of ecclesiastical law in the 20th century is the dictum of Rudolf Sohm (1841-1917) that ecclesiastical law is contrary to the nature of church. "The nature of the Church is spiritual, the nature of law is worldly and mundane", Sohm wrote in 1892.[5] He was working on and criticizing the fact that the rulers of the states in the German Empire were also heads of the churches in their states (the so-called *Landesherrliches Kirchenregiment*). While the influence of the state on the Protestant Church did diminish in the course of the 19th century and administration of state and church started to go separate ways, for Sohm the church was an utterly spiritual occurrence that was to be strictly separated from the legal authority over human societies, clubs and such, and in particular from state sovereignty. According to Sohm the legally constituted, in this sense perceptible, church is "not the Church of Christ, but a part of the (mundane) world".[6]

With this strict separation of the spiritual church on the one hand and of the mundane and worldly church on the other hand, Sohm brought about a legal positivism in ecclesiastical jurisprudence of its own on the verge of the 20th century.[7] To Sohm, the law was "a born heathen".[8] The worldly order of the

---

Law and positive law, secular and non-secular law, by which ecclesiastical body the law was set, and, finally, by the adherence to scripture and creed.

4 See, e.g., Michael Germann, "Die Diskussion über die Grundlagen des evangelischen Kirchenrechts," in *Handbuch des evangelischen Kirchenrechts*, ed. Hans Ulrich Anke, Heinrich de Wall, and Hans Michael Heinig (Tübingen: Mohr Siebeck, 2016), 46ff.

5 Rudolf Sohm, *Kirchenrecht*, vol.1: *Die geschichtlichen Grundlagen* (Leipzig: Duncker and Humblot, 1892),1, 700.

6 Sohm, *Kirchenrecht*, 699.

7 The constitutional law, too, was governed by legal positivism; defining in particular was Paul Laband, for whom "all historical, political and philosophical views" were "without relevance" for constitutional dogmatics, Paul Laband, *Das Staatsrecht des Deutschen Reiches*, vol. 1, 2nd ed. (Freiburg im Breisgau: Mohr, 1888), VII. See further for the constitutional positivism in the German Imperial Era, e.g., Michael Stolleis, *Geschichte des öffentlichen Rechts in Deutschland*, vol. 2: *Staatsrechtslehre und Verwaltungswissenschaft 1800-1914* (Munich: Beck, 1992), 337ff.; Christoph Schönberger, *Das Parlament im Anstaltsstaat: Zur Theorie parlamentarischer Represantation in der Staatsrechtslehre des Kaiserreichs (1871-1918)* (Frankfurt am Main: Klostermann, 1997), 21ff., esp. 83ff.

8 Quoted from Wolfgang Huber, *Kirche und Öffentlichkeit*, 2nd ed. (Munich: C.E. Beck, 1991), 91.

church appears to be spiritually irrelevant in the light of Sohm's remarks. Then, however, it can take on arbitrary forms. Thus, the question of "wrong" ecclesiastical law does not even arise. The ecclesiastical law is irrelevant for the being of the church. Ecclesiastical law simply is a human product of entirely pragmatical decisions. Legal validity and theological legitimization are completely unlinked, and Sohm's critical view of ecclesiastical law turns into an understanding of ecclesiastical law that can do without any theological legitimization.[9] This is the starting point of the traditional narrative in Germany concerning the end of the 19th and the beginning of the 20th century.

It seems worthwhile to pursue the question further of whether this canonized story of the Protestant ecclesiastical law in the beginning of the 20th century really is true — or whether it would at least need a supplementary explanation and a further placement in the academical discourse. Pursuing this point of interest would, however, push the boundaries of this chapter. The following suggestion must therefore suffice: Whoever states that the jurisprudence of Protestant ecclesiastical law around the turn of the 20th century was strongly coined by legal positivism should not only point towards Sohm but also take into account the *Historische Rechtsschule* (the German Historical School of Jurisprudence) as precursor and concomitant. With that, the prologue on the debates of the ecclesiastical legal positivism is much more multi-layered than commonly assumed.

The Historical School of Jurisprudence superseded the Natural-Law based thinking not only in the legal scholarship generally but also in that of ecclesiastical law. Not reason and revelation as part of a timeless truth but the variable historical consciousness of the legal community became the pivotal point of legal enactment. The forefront figure of the Historical School of Jurisprudence par excellence was Friedrich Carl von Savigny (1779-1861).

It was greatly disputed between the followers of Savigny whether these guiding themes are transferable to ecclesiastical law.[10] With the rejection of Natural

---

9   See the accusation from Rudolf Smend, "Zweihundert Jahre Göttinger Kirchenrechtswissenschaft," in Rudolf Smend, *Abhandlungen zum Kirchen- und Staatskirchenrecht*, ed. Hans Michael Heinig, Hendrik Munsonius, and Jens Reisgies (Tübingen: Mohr Siebeck, 2019), 251 (255); Rudolf Smend, "Wissenschafts- und Gestaltungsprobleme im evangelischen Kirchenrecht," *Zeitschrift für evangelisches Kirchenrecht* 6 (1957/58): 243 (247ff.).

10 The ecclesiastical law historian Ulrich Stutz remarked at the beginning of the 20th century that the ecclesiastical jurisprudence did not really manage to bring together the fact of a codified ecclesiastical law with the major trend of the Historical School of Jurisprudence. While he then, as a legal historian, pleaded for the positivists to let go of the historical method, his analysis of the deficit touches on a nerve nonetheless. That goes in particular because his plead seemed to be more of a makeshift solution; see further Ulrich Stutz, *Die Kirchliche Rechtsgeschichte: Rede zur Feier des 27. Januar 1905 gehalten in der Aula der Universität zu Bonn* (Stuttgart: F. Enke, 1905).

Law by the Historical School of Jurisprudence came the understanding that law is variable and dependent on historical context. The national character (*Volksgeist*) postulated by Savigny and his pupils as the source of law, however, is actually very foreign to the church. Some of the foremost scholars of ecclesiastical law at the end of the 19th century wrote great historical editions on ecclesiastical law which were influenced by the Historical Jurisprudence while working on the prevailing ecclesiastical law completely in the fashion of legal positivism.[11] Georg Friedrich Puchta (1798-1846), for instance, denied the ability of the church to set legal orders based on the *Volksgeist* and with that the ability to cultivate customary law.[12] The ecclesiastical legal positivism of the 19th and early 20th centuries is therefore also an emanation of this jurisprudential setting.[13] Others, like Adolf von Scheurl (1811-1893), did on the other hand see room for the possibility of cultivating a collective consciousness of the church that is comparable to a *Volksgeist*. If this consciousness differs from the will of Christ, it would, however, cease to be a holistic ecclesiastical consciousness.[14] The question of "wrong" ecclesiastical law did therefore already pose itself at the turn of the 20th century.[15]

In today's understanding, these multi-faceted and complex conditions on which the legal ecclesiastical positivism was built have been forgotten. The perception of the ecclesiastical jurisprudence of the Weimar Republichas been devised by its critics in the postwar time right up to this day. The only laudable exceptions who are referred to are Günther Holstein (1892-1931) and Hans Lier-

---

11 Peter Landau, "Evangelische Kirchenrechtswissenschaft im 19. Jahrhundert," in Peter Landau, *Grundlagen und Geschichte des evangelischen Kirchenrechts und des Staatskirchenrechts* (Tübingen: Mohr Siebeck, 2010), 253ff.
12 Georg Friedrich Puchta, *Das Gewohnheitsrecht,* vol. 2 (Erlangen: Palm, 1837), 270; see in more depth Peter Landau, "Die Theorie des Gewohnheitsrechts im katholischen und evangelischen Kirchenrecht des 19. und 20. Jahrhunderts," in Peter Landau, *Grundlagen und Geschichte des evangelischen Kirchenrechts und des Staatskirchenrechts* (Tübingen: Mohr Siebeck, 2010), 45 (55ff.).
13 Whereby the ecclesiastical law, in contrast to the other areas of law which were discussed more closely by the Historical School of Jurisprudence, was looking back at a long history of codification.
14 Adolf von Scheurl, "Kirchliches Gewohnheitsrecht," in Adolf von Scheurl, *Sammlung kirchenrechtlicher Abhandlungen* (Erlangen: Deichert, 1873), 169-230; concerning von Scheurl more closely cf. for instance Christoph A. Stumpf, *Kirchenrecht als Bekenntnisrecht: die Verbindung von Erlanger Theologie und geschichtlicher Rechtswissenschaft im Leben und Werk von Adolf von Scheurl* (Ebelsbach: Aktiv Druck & Verlag, 1999); Landau, "Evangelische Kirchenrechtswissenschaft im 19. Jahrhundert," 253 (258ff.).
15 The Historical School lost its influence over the Protestant ecclesiastical jurisprudence at the end of the 19th century; as was the case with constitutional law, the imperatives theory ("Imperativentheorie") prevailed, which can be shown for example in Sohm. Consequently, territorialism gained ground compared to the more collegialistic approaches in ecclesiastical law; cf. Peter Landau, "Die Theorie des Gewohnheitsrechts," 45 (76ff.).

mann (1893-1976), who did preliminary work on the overcoming of the legal positivism in ecclesiastical jurisprudence. Holstein, who took inspiration from Friedrich Schleiermacher, interrelated the spiritual with the worldly church in his work *Die Grundlagen des evangelischen Kirchenrechts* ("The Basics of Protestant Ecclesiastical Law"),[16] which was in very stark contrast to Sohm. Hans Liermann followed his example with the account *Deutsches Evangelisches Kirchenrecht* ("German Protestant Ecclesiastical Law"), which was published in 1933. The law, according to Liermann, "is limited to the church as a sociological group".[17] The Bible contains "religious norms, not legal ones".[18] Therefore, the ecclesiastical law only touches on the external order of the church. At the same time, however, there are boundaries to be recognized when designing ecclesiastical law. It can only be considered binding and in force "insofar as it is not contrary to the nature of the church".[19] Similarly it says in Holsteins work: "It is not the Legal Church (*Rechtskirche*) that moulds the Spiritual Church (*Geistkirche*) — which would mean putting the human will above God's free mercy as sovereignly prevailing by Jesus Christ, but that, whenever the two magnitudes collide, the Legal Church will be confined by the Spiritual Church and is so affirmed in its validity."[20]

Insights in the "Kirchenkampf" after 1933

Under the influence of the *Kirchenkampf* (lit. "church struggle") the theologian Friedrich Brunstädt (1883-1944) went one step further than Holstein and Liermann. He writes: "The Church is the origin of a distinct and specific ecclesiastical law".[21] This way of thinking was to shape the self-image of Protestant ecclesiastical law for a long time: Where Sohm established a twofold and strictly divided concept of church, now a twofold concept of law was to

---

16   Günther Holstein, *Die Grundlagen des evangelischen Kirchenrechts* (Tübingen: Mohr, 1928). More detailed concerning Holstein see, for instance, Otto von Campenhausen, *Günther Holstein: Staatsrechtslehrer und Kirchenrechtler in der Weimarer Republik* (Pfaffenweiler: Centaurus-Verlagsgesellschaft, 1997); Stefan Korioth, "Geisteswissenschaftliche Methode" und Rückwendung zum Rechtsidealismus: Günther Holstein (1892-1931)," in *Greifswald—Spiegel der deutschen Rechtswissenschaft 1815 bis 1945*, ed. Joachim Lege (Tübingen: Mohr Siebeck, 2009), 285-302.
17   Siegfried Grundmann, *Abhandlungen zum Kirchenrecht* (Köln: Böhlau, 1969), 22ff.
18   Hans Liermann, *Deutsches Evangelisches Kirchenrecht* (Stuttgart: Enke, 1933), 21.
19   Liermann, *Deutsches Evangelisches Kirchenrecht*, 23.
20   Holstein, *Die Grundlagen des evangelischen Kirchenrechts*, 228.
21   Friedrich Brunstädt, *Die Kirche und ihr Recht* (Halle: Niemeyer, 1935), 19.

govern.[22] Ecclesiastical law was to be understood utterly different from state and secular law. It is not only autonomous but also of a different kind, with a different nature or essence.

The historical context of this legal thinking is to be found in the *Kirchenkampf* of 1933 and 1934.[23] After Hitler's seizure of power, a range of people from throughout the loosely federated Protestant territorial churches (*Landeskirchen*) formed the group *Deutsche Christen* ("German Christians") which was open to the ideology of National Socialism. Intermittently, they were able to gain popularity in church elections. The Nazi government was eager to establish a unified Protestant national church in the Reich that would take on the notion of the *Führerprinzip* ("Führer-principle") and break radically with the constitutional principles of the church from the 19th century. In July 1933, a constitution like that was passed for the German Evangelical Church. Hitler's candidate for the newly introduced office of *Reichsbischof* (Bishop of the Empire), Ludwig Müller (1883-1945), was elected in September 1933. Subsequently, the German Christians aspired to integrate the territorial churches into the German Evangelical Church and to have them subordinated under the primate of the German *Reichsbischof*.

Soon resistance formed itself against this theological, church political, and ecclesiastical jurisprudence of the German Christians. Prominent manifestation of this revolt against the *völkisch* (ethnic) remodelling of the Christian gospel and the enforced coordination of the church is the *Barmer Theologische Erklärung* (*Barmen Declaration of Faith*). It was passed by the so called Confessing-Synod (*Bekenntnissynode*) of Barmen in late May of 1934. At the same time the synod passed the "Declaration concerning the legal situation" (*Erklärung zur Rechtslage*). Shortly after, in October 1934, a second Confession-Synod took place in Berlin-Dahlem. There, for a second time, it was declared why, based on an "ecclesiastical emergency law", no obedience was owed to the new German Christian leadership of the Church.

The followers of the Confessing Church referred to the fact that ecclesiastical law could not take on any arbitrary form but were in fact, as was already being noted in the Protestant church constitutions from the mid-19th century

---

22 Even though Brunstädt himself did not advocate a twofold notion of law. For more concerning the concept of a species-specific ("arteigen") law lately, see Jens Reisgies, *Evangelische Kirchenrechtssetzung: Staatliche und kirchliche Anforderungen* (Göttingen: Universitätsverlag Göttingen, 2017), 38ff.

23 For an overview, see Kurt Meier, *Kreuz und Hakenkreuz* (Munich: Deutscher Taschenbuch-Verlag, 2001); Christoph Strohm, *Die Kirchen im Dritten Reich* (Munich: C.H. Beck, 2011).

onwards, tied to scripture and confessions of faith.[24] The Constitution of the German Evangelical Church also had a similar preamble on which the Synod of Barmen recurs in the Declaration of Faith. The Gospel, according to the representatives of the Confessing Church, forbids the remodelling of the witnessing community divinely ordained through Jesus Christ into a neo-pagan cultic community as imagined by the German Christians. Consequently, the third thesis of the Declaration of Faith stated:

> The Christian church is the congregation of the brethren in which Jesus Christ acts presently as the Lord in word and sacrament through the Holy Spirit. As the church of pardoned sinners, it has to testify in the midst of a sinful world, with its faith as with its obedience, with its message as with its order, that it is solely his property, and that it lives and wants to live solely from his comfort and from his direction in the expectation of his appearance. We reject the false doctrine, as though the church were permitted to abandon the form of its message and order to its own pleasure or to changes in prevailing ideological and political convictions.[25]

The Confession Synod gets more concrete in the "Declaration Concerning the Legal Situation". There it is written that:

> only those can speak and act in the name of the German Evangelical Church, who adhere to the Holy Scripture and Confession of the Church as its sacrosanct foundation and who aspire to reinstate their authoritative standing in the German Evangelical Church ... There can be no separation of the external order from the confession. Thus the division of the German Evangelical Church into several territorial churches (*Landeskirchen*) is founded in the confession. Territorial Churches bound by confession must not be deprived of their autonomy through absorption by administrative means, as their external order must always be justified

---

24 Concerning the history of the confession clauses in the preambles of church constitutions, see Joachim Mehlhausen, "Schrift und Bekenntnis," in *Das Recht der Kirche*, ed. Gerhard Rau, Hans-Richard Reuter, and Klaus Schlaich, vol. 1 (Gütersloh: Gütersloher Verlagshaus, 1997), 417 (432ff.).

25 "Theologische Erklärung zur gegenwärtigen Lage der Deutschen Evangelischen Kirche vom 31.5.1934," in *Die erste Bekenntnissynode der Deutschen Evangelischen Kirche zu Barmen*, vol. 2: *Text—Dokumente—Berichte*, ed. Gerhard Niemöller (Göttingen: Vandenhoeck & Ruprecht, 1959), 200. The English translation can be found at https://www.ekd.de/en/The-Barmen-Declaration-303.htm, accessed June 8, 2020.

by their confession. The incorporations of the Imperial Church Administration (*Reichskirchenregierung*) are therefore without legal effect.²⁶

In the same manner it was said in Dahlem a few weeks later: "On the grounds of the ecclesiastical emergency law of the Churches, parishes, and holders of spiritual office bound by scripture and confession, the Confession Synod creates new governing bodies."²⁷

The fact of being bound by scripture and confession acted as the prevailing argument for the legitimisation of their own church and theology-related political positions. This was their way of denying the leadership of the German Christians both in spiritual and in legal ecclesiastical matters. "Wrong", as in contrary to the faith, law was deprived of its validity; conformity to the faith therefore became *conditio sine qua non* for validity. Notabene: this was not an "invention" of the Confessing Church, but it came in the preambles of the newly founded territorial churches that were released into autonomy from the regional rulers' church rule (*Landesherrliches Kirchenregiment*) in 1919 and even the constitution of the German Evangelical Church of 1933 knew a similar confession clause.²⁸ Those ecclesiastical constitutional clauses of creed in the 19th and 20th centuries were a manifestation of the separation of state and church even in a time where throne and altar were supposedly still a unity. Up until 1933, however, it was far from obvious what consequences a breach of the preambles of the ecclesiastical constitutions containing a commitment to the faith would have. The Confessing Church drew, owing to the circumstances, quite far-reaching consequences: the break of confession executed by the German Christians dispensed from any claim of legal obedience: in the "true" church, "spiritually based" law was to govern. Contemporaries like the mentioned Brunstädt used this background in order to unseat the positivism in ecclesiastical law and instead put new emphasis on ecclesiastical theory. This way, a new notion of vis-à-vis between a new distinct ecclesiastical law and the secular law was established owing to the concrete historical situation of conflict (*Kirchenkampf*) between the German Christians and the Confessing Church.

---

26 "Theologische Erklärung zur gegenwärtigen Lage der Deutschen Evangelischen Kirche vom 31.5.1934," 202-3.
27 "Botschaft der Bekenntnissynode der Deutschen Evangelischen Kirche vom 20.10.1934," in *Die zweite Bekenntnissynode der Deutschen Evangelischen Kirche zu Dahlem: Text, Dokumente, Berichte,* ed. Wilhelm Niemöller (Göttingen: Vandenhoeck & Ruprecht, 1958), 38.
28 Cf. proof in fn. 21.

Basic Principles Enthusiasm after 1945

In light of the Nazi rupture of civilization, the criticism of legal positivism already visible in the Weimar Republic intensified in the discussion of ecclesiastical law, likewise in secular law. Rudolf Smend (1851-1913) for instance considered his predecessor in Göttingen, Paul Schoen (1867-1941), as the grandmaster of ecclesiastical legal positivism and as such spoke of him with mild mockery.[29]

The debates in ecclesiastical jurisprudence display a remarkable similarity to that of the general jurisprudential discussion concerning legal positivism, which was influenced by a renaissance of Natural Law.[30] Both lines of thought shared the conviction of Gustav Radbruch[31] (1878-1949) that the legal positivism rendered the lawyers defenceless against National Socialism, which is why the validity of law was to require extra-legal preconditions. The protagonists did, however, conceal and suppress the fact that some of the most poignant critics of legal positivism tendered their services to the Nazi regime in particular with and because of their anti-positivistic stance (which was the case for Carl Schmitt [1888-1985] as well as for Johannes Heckel[32] [1889-1963]). The legal profession was not necessarily defenceless in the years that led from Weimar to the Nazi regime but for a big part it lacked the liberal-democratic ethos, or in the language of the church, a mindset that was true to the faith.[33]

An accurate accounting for the immediate past was impossible for the general jurisprudence as well as the ecclesiastical one in the first years of the Bonn Republic. Instead, the perception of an autonomous, spiritually conditioned and coined ecclesiastical law took on a life of its own contrary to the historical circumstances. The history of the *Kirchenkampf* was rewritten for this in a rather idiosyncratic fashion. The legal positivism in ecclesiastical jurisprudence was held well-nigh completely accountable for the Nazi exertion of influence on the church. Nothing indeed could have been further from the truth for the German

---

29 See foot note 9.
30 See foot note 1.
31 Gustav Radbruch, "Gesetzliches Unrecht und übergesetzliches Recht," *Süddeutsche Juristenzeitung* 1, nr. 5 (1946): 105 (107).
32 E.g. Johannes Heckel, "Der Einbruch des jüdischen Geistes in das deutsche Staats- und Kirchenrecht durch Friedrich Julius Stahl," *Historische Zeitschrift* 155, no. 1 (1937): 506ff.
33 Manfred Walther, "Hat der juristische Positivismus die deutschen Juristen wehrlos gemacht? Zur Analyse und Kritik der Radbruch-These," in *Recht und Justiz im "Dritten Reich,"* ed. Ralf Dreier and Wolfgang Sellert (Frankfurt am Main: Suhrkamp, 1989), 323ff.

Christians than to be followers of legal positivism in ecclesiastical law.[34] After all, the whole Nazi jurisprudence was in harsh contrast to legal positivism. It was coined by the Nazi ideology that felt nothing but contempt for the liberal rule of law, individualism, and the formality and technicity of law. At best (or worst), the Nazi jurisprudence can be understood as power-positivism.

Heckel, Erik Wolf (1902-1977) and Hans Dombois[35] (1907-1997) can be understood as proponents for fundamental theological discussions of law. They presented comprehensive blueprints with the aspiration to overcome legal positivism in ecclesiastical law. For that they drew on remarkable anti-positivistic stereotypes. It is not worthwhile going into the particulars of these outlines in this chapter. For an impression, the following will suffice: Johannes Heckel relied on a reconstruction of the Lutheran doctrine of two kingdoms (*Zwei-Reiche-Lehre*) as a legal doctrine. An "order of divine love" governs in God's Kingdom.[36] This is why the title of the magnum opus of Heckel is *Lex charitatis*. The faithful Christian, freed of the original sin through the justification of a true relationship with God, fulfils the divine law due to its spiritual realization. In stark contrast to that, Heckel draws the picture of the worldly kingdom. Here, the divine will act as a *lex irae et mortis*.[37] He allocates the role of ecclesiastical law in this dichotomy of kingdoms through the interlacing of twofold legal terms and threefold ecclesiastical terms. Heckel draws complex systems of reference in the forcefield of church and law, spiritual and mundane, integrated into the Lutheran theological schools of thought of the two kingdoms and two regiments.

A potent alternative ecclesiastical law was developed that leaned on the theology of Karl Barth (1886-1868). With the moral certainty of the winners of history, they postulated a Christologically based, avowing ecclesiastical law. Ecclesiastical law in this reading was not just bound by scripture and creed but was, itself, creedal. A leading exponent of this view, Erik Wolf, was, however, aware of the danger of over-theologizing ecclesiastical law and was

---

34   Cf. for the legal thinking in the Nazi dogmatics Bernd Rüthers, *Die unbegrenzte Auslegung: Zum Wandel der Privatrechtsordnung im Nationalsozialismus*, 4th ed. (Heidelberg: C. F. Müller, 1991), 91ff; Ralf Dreier and Wolfgang Sellert, eds., *Recht und Justiz im "Dritten Reich"* (Frankfurt am Main: Suhrkamp, 1989); Michael Stolleis, *Recht im Unrecht: Studien zur Rechtsgeschichte des Nationalsozialismus* (Frankfurt: Suhrkamp, 1994).
35   Reviewed in a very comprehensive fashion by Wilhelm Steinmüller, *Evangelische Rechtstheologie: Zweireichelehre, Christokratie, Gnadenrecht*, 2 vols. (Köln: Bohlau, 1968).
36   Johannes Heckel, *Lex charitatis: Eine juristische Untersuchung über das Recht in der Theologie Martin Luthers* (Munich: Beck, 1953), 61.
37   Heckel, *Lex charitatis*, 133.

looking for a way out through increasing complexity in creating a paradox.[38] Dombois, lastly, construed "the ecclesiastical law as a complex of instances, through which the relationship between God and man consummates itself unmediatedly".[39] In his work "The Law of Mercy" (*Das Recht der Gnade*)[40] he was trying to juridificate God's mercy and focalize the liturgical rites. With this aspiration Dombois tried to develop an ecumenical ecclesiastical law that could be connected to canon law.

The Current Double Perspective: Ecclesiastical Law—Constitutionally Embodied and Theologically Accountable

The legal development in the ecclesiastical legal practice (i.e. norm-setting, norm-executing, and norm-control) remained curiously unaffected by these fundamental scholarly debates. While it did not commit itself completely to one of the drafts that had become classics by that time, it did take on its fundamental concern: ecclesiastical law must answer to theology and cannot take an arbitrary form. The ecclesiastical jurisprudence follows suit — it developed pragmatic approaches to the fundamental questions.[41]

A similar development unfolded in secular law under the German Basic Law (*Grundgesetz*). The Jurisprudence of Natural Law was soon stretched to its limits.[42] Increasingly, human rights (as guaranteed in basic constitutional rights or in international human rights and the norms of human dignity) introduced to the legal system became the basis for justice.[43] The condition for validity, that

---

38   Erik Wolf, *Ordnung der Kirche: Lehr- und Handbuch des Kirchenrechts auf ökumenischer Basis* (Frankfurt am Main: Klostermann, 1961), 7.
39   Germann, "Die Diskussion über die Grundlagen des evangelischen Kirchenrechts," 46 (66).
40   Hans Dombois, *Das Recht der Gnade: Ökumenisches Kirchenrecht*, vol. 1 (Witten: Luther-Verlag, 1961).
41   An overview is found in Michael Germann, "Der Status der Grundlagendiskussion in der evangelischen Kirchenrechtswissenschaft," *Zeitschrift für evangelisches Kirchenrecht* 53, no. 4 (2008): 375ff; Wolfgang Huber, *Gerechtigkeit und Recht: Grundlinien christlicher Rechtsethik*, 3rd ed. (Gütersloh: Gütersloher Verlagshaus, 2006), 501ff.
42   An overview is found in Ulfried Neumann, "Rechtsphilosophie in Deutschland seit 1945," in *Rechtswissenschaft in der Bonner Republik*, ed. Dieter Simon (Frankfurt am Main: Suhrkamp, 1994), 145ff.; Foljanty, *Recht oder Gesetz*, 349ff.
43   Hans Michael Heinig, "Was ist so attraktiv an der Radbruchschen Formel," in *Recht, Gesellschaft, Kommunikation—Festschrift für Klaus F. Röhl*, ed. Stefan Machura and Stephan Ulbrich (Baden Baden: Nomos, 2003), 321ff.

any positive law must adhere to the fiats of transjuridic normativity, was itself postulated in the Basic Law, namely in Art. 1 §1 and Art. 79 §3.

At the same time, the wiser circles in law, politics, and the church are aware that any value-committed legal system can only influence the factual conditions of its actual implementation in a very limited fashion. The Freiburg Professor of constitutional law and judge at the Federal Constitutional Court Ernst-Wolfgang Böckenförde encapsulated it clearly: The law cannot ensure the ethos of the legal applicant in a legal manner.[44] Art. 79 §3 of the Basic Law is no guarantee of perpetuity against revolutions, and clauses of confessions are unable to rule out the comeback of the German Christians or other confusions of Christian existence. But positivized references to trans-juridical stipulations for validity do of course interfere with pretensions of legality and distribute burdens of proof, which is a good starting point.

On this bedrock, the ecclesiastical jurisprudence and legal theology can make their peace with a legal positivism that reflects its own prerequisites and limits:

- The technicity, malleability, and formality of law are not foreign to the church. Ecclesiastical law is law and as such not of a wholly different quality from secular law.
- The ecclesiastical law knows its limits set by secular law: constitutionally, ecclesiastical law is protected as an expression of religious freedom. Art. 140 of the Basic Law in connection with Art. 137 §3 of the Weimar Imperial Constitution (*Weimarer Reichsverfassung*) decrees a certain civil potency while setting limits in the secular legal sphere under the consideration of concerns of public interest (within the limits of the law that applies to all as a weighing of interests enriched with considerations of equality under the law).[45]
- Ecclesiastical law as human law can be set and shaped, it cannot therefore be derived solely as an act of faith from theological sources.
- In light of the mission of proclamation (*Verkündungsauftrag*), law in its mundane form is an instrument of coordinating acts of evangelical freedom and is therefore not contrary to the "nature" of the church.

---

44 Ernst-Wolfgang Böckenförde, "Die Entstehung des Staates als Vorgang der Säkularisation," in Ernst-Wolfgang Böckenförde, *Recht, Staat, Freiheit*: Studien zur Rechtsphilosophie, Staatstheorie und Verfassungsgeschichte (Frankfurt am Main: Suhrkamp, 1991), 92 (112); with revisions Ernst-Wolfgang Böckenförde, *Der säkularisierte Staat: Sein Charakter, seine Rechtfertigung und seine Probleme im 21. Jahrhundert* (München/Berlin: Carl Friedrich Siemens Stiftung, 2007), 11ff.

45 Cf. Hans Michael Heinig, *Öffentlich-rechtliche Religionsgesellschaften: Studien zur Rechtsstellung der nach Art. 137 Abs. 5 WRV korporierten Religionsgesellschaften in Deutschland und in der Europäischen Union* (Berlin: Duncker & Humblot, 2003), 142ff.

- The attachment of ecclesiastical law to scripture and creed realizes itself in legal procedures, particularly in synodal legislative procedures, when the ecclesiastical statute is given precedence over ecclesiastical administrative acts and the binding to scripture and creed is mediated by statutory law.[46]
- When the leadership of the church is being described as a "spiritually and legally indispensable unity" in the "pathos formulas"[47] of church constitutions of several territorial churches, the spiritual and legal dimensions do not just blend into each other in this description but they refer to each other in their difference. The differentiation becomes the "prerequisite for unity".[48]

It is on this line that Michael Moxter is approximating himself to the positivity of law, including ecclesiastical law, in a substantial legal-theological study. He emphasizes that "one can only interfere with the sovereignty of the legislating process or into subordinated accountabilities on the basis of the existing law and for the nature of the Church".[49] It was not by chance that the Barmen Declaration referred to in Art. 1 of the Constitution of the German Evangelical Church, which postulated the loyalty to the confession. Moxter therefore warns against an "over-interpretation" of the third thesis of the Barmen Declaration: The order of the church could not be deduced from scripture and creed. It also is not creed itself. Barmen III only states that the order gives testimony to the character of the church. A testimony like that does not, however, provide the ecclesiastical order either sacrosanct qualities or irreversibility.

After World War II and under the experiences of the Church Struggle, confession-clauses were being introduced into preambles and basic articles of the ecclesiastical constitutions, but one should not prematurely take that as a sacralization of the ecclesiastical law. Here, human action is being normatively coordinated. Rules of law for ensuring spiritually substantial action of the church are "not themselves spiritual law".[50]

---

46 In more detail to this approach cf. Michael Germann, "Die Bindung der kirchlichen Gerichte an Schrift und Bekenntnis," *Zeitschrift der Savigny-Stiftung für Rechtsgeschichte: Kanonistische Abteilung* 91, no. 1 (2005): 499 (551).

47 Hendrik Munsonius, "'… geistlich und rechtlich in unaufgebbarer Einheit': Das Leitungsdogma als Pathosformel," *Zeitschrift für evangelisches Kirchenrecht* 64, no. 1 (2019): 47ff.

48 Munsonius, "'… geistlich und rechtlich in unaufgebbarer Einheit'," 47 (58); for the same question cf. also Hans Michael Heinig, "Geistlich leiten—aus kirchenrechtlicher Perspektive betrachtet," *Kirche & Recht* 17, no. 1 (2011): 1ff.

49 Michael Moxter, "Die Kirche und ihr Recht: Perspektiven einer theologischen Annäherung an den Rechtspositivismus," *Zeitschrift für evangelisches Kirchenrecht* 56, no. 2 (2011): 113 (136).

50 Moxter, "Die Kirche und ihr Recht," 113 (138).

Protestant ecclesiastical law in this sense does not nowadays understand itself as either "secular" (as it is not simply part of the general *ius publicum*, but based on ecclesiastical will of law, which is respected by the state) or as sacred (as it is manmade and variable, oriented towards the biblical order but not itself an immediate expression of a Christian truth of beliefs, but just serving the latter).

Bibliography

"Botschaft der Bekenntnissynode der Deutschen Evangelischen Kirche vom 20.10.1934." In *Die zweite Bekenntnissynode der Deutschen Evangelischen Kirche zu Dahlem: Text, Dokumente, Berichte,* edited by Wilhelm Niemöller, 38. Göttingen: Vandenhoeck & Ruprecht, 1958.

Brunstädt, Friedrich. *Die Kirche und ihr Recht*. Halle: Niemeyer, 1935.

Böckenförde, Ernst-Wolfgang. "Die Entstehung des Staates als Vorgang der Säkularisation." In Ernst-Wolfgang Böckenförde, *Recht, Staat, Freiheit: Studien zur Rechtsphilosophie, Staatstheorie und Verfassungsgeschichte*, 92-114. Frankfurt am Main: Suhrkamp, 1991.

Böckenförde, Ernst-Wolfgang. *Der säkularisierte Staat: Sein Charakter, seine Rechtfertigung und seine Probleme im 21. Jahrhundert*. München/Berlin: Carl Friedrich Siemens Stiftung, 2007.

Campenhausen, Otto von. *Günther Holstein: Staatsrechtslehrer und Kirchenrechtler in der Weimarer Republik*. Pfaffenweiler: Centaurus-Verlagsgesellschaft, 1997.

Dombois, Hans. *Das Recht der Gnade: Ökumenisches Kirchenrecht*. Vol. 1. Witten: Luther-Verlag, 1961.

Dreier, Ralf, and Wolfgang Sellert, eds. *Recht und Justiz im "Dritten Reich"*. Frankfurt am Main: Suhrkamp, 1989.

Foljanty, Lena. *Recht oder Gesetz: Juristische Identität und Autorität in den Naturrechtsdebatten der Nachkriegszeit*. Tübingen: Mohr Siebeck, 2013.

Germann, Michael. "Die Bindung der kirchlichen Gerichte an Schrift und Bekenntnis." *Zeitschrift der Savigny-Stiftung für Rechtsgeschichte: Kanonistische Abteilung* 91, no. 1 (2005): 499-555.

Germann, Michael. "Die Diskussion über die Grundlagen des evangelischen Kirchenrechts." In *Handbuch des evangelischen Kirchenrechts*, edited by Hans Ulrich Anke, Henrich de Wall, and Hans Michael Heinig, 46-80. Tübingen: Mohr Siebeck, 2016.

Germann, Michael. "Der Status der Grundlagendiskussion in der evangelischen Kirchenrechtswissenschaft." *Zeitschrift für evangelisches Kirchenrecht* 53, no. 4 (2008): 375-407.

Grundmann, Siegfried. *Abhandlungen zum Kirchenrecht*. Köln: Böhlau, 1969.

Heckel, Johannes. "Der Einbruch des jüdischen Geistes in das deutsche Staats- und Kirchenrecht durch Friedrich Julius Stahl." *Historische Zeitschrift* 155, no. 1 (1937): 506-41.

Heckel, Johannes. *Lex charitatis: Eine juristische Untersuchung über das Recht in der Theologie Martin Luthers.* Munich: Beck, 1953.

Heinig, Hans Michael. "Geistlich leiten—aus kirchenrechtlicher Perspektive betrachtet." *Kirche & Recht* 17, no. 1 (2011): 1-12.

Heinig, Hans Michael. "Was ist so attraktiv an der Radbruchschen Formel?" In *Recht, Gesellschaft, Kommunikation—Festschrift für Klaus F. Röhl,* edited by Stefan Machura and Stephan Ulbrich, 321-33. Baden Baden: Nomos, 2003.

Heinig, Hans Michael. *Öffentlich-rechtliche Religionsgesellschaften: Studien zur Rechtsstellung der nach Art. 137 Abs. 5 WRV korporierten Religionsgesellschaften in Deutschland und in der Europäischen Union.* Berlin: Duncker & Humblot, 2003.

Hofmann, Hasso. *Rechtsphilosophie nach 1945: Zur Geistesgeschichte der Bundesrepublik Deutschland.* Berlin: Duncker & Humblot, 2012.

Holstein, Günther. *Die Grundlagen des evangelischen Kirchenrechts.* Tübingen: Mohr, 1928.

Huber, Wolfgang. *Gerechtigkeit und Recht: Grundlinien christlicher Rechtsethik.* 3rd ed. Gütersloh: Gütersloher Verlagshaus, 2006.

Huber, Wolfgang. *Kirche und Öffentlichkeit.* 2nd ed. Munich: C.E. Beck, 1991.

Korioth, Stefan. "'Geisteswissenschaftliche Methode' und Rückwendung zum Rechtsidealismus: Günther Holstein (1892-1931)." In *Greifswald—Spiegel der deutschen Rechtswissenschaft 1815 bis 1945,* edited by Joachim Lege, 285-302. Tübingen: Mohr Siebeck, 2009.

Laband, Paul. *Das Staatsrecht des Deutschen Reiches.* Vol. 1. 2nd ed. Freiburg im Breisgau: Mohr, 1888.

Landau, Peter. "Evangelische Kirchenrechtswissenschaft im 19. Jahrhundert." In Peter Landau, *Grundlagen und Geschichte des evangelischen Kirchenrechts und des Staatskirchenrechts,* 253-268. Tübingen: Mohr Siebeck, 2010.

Landau, Peter. "Die Theorie des Gewohnheitsrechts im katholischen und evangelischen Kirchenrecht des 19. und 20. Jahrhunderts." In Peter Landau, *Grundlagen und Geschichte des evangelischen Kirchenrechts und des Staatskirchenrechts,* 45-79. Tübingen: Mohr Siebeck, 2010.

Liermann, Hans. *Deutsches Evangelisches Kirchenrecht.* Stuttgart: Enke, 1933.

Maihofer, Werner, ed. *Naturrecht oder Rechtspositivismus?* Darmstadt: Wissenschaftliche Buchgesellschaft, 1962.

Mehlhausen, Joachim. "Schrift und Bekenntnis." In *Das Recht der Kirche,* vol. 1, edited by Gerhard Rau, Hans-Richard Reuter, and Klaus Schlaich, 417-47. Gütersloh: Gütersloher Verlagshaus, 1997.

Meier, Kurt. *Kreuz und Hakenkreuz.* Munich: Deutscher Taschenbuch-Verlag, 2001.

Moxter, Michael. "Die Kirche und ihr Recht: Perspektiven einer theologischen Annäherung an den Rechtspositivismus." *Zeitschrift für evangelisches Kirchenrecht* 56, no. 2 (2011): 113-39.

Munsonius, Hendrik. "'… geistlich und rechtlich in unaufgebbarer Einheit': Das Leitungsdogma als Pathosformel." *Zeitschrift für evangelisches Kirchenrecht* 64, no. 1 (2019): 47-67.

Neumann, Ulfrid. "Rechtsphilosophie in Deutschland seit 1945." In *Rechtswissenschaft in der Bonner Republik*, edited by Dieter Simon, 145-87. Frankfurt am Main: Suhrkamp, 1994.

Puchta, Georg Friedrich. *Das Gewohnheitsrecht.* Vol. 2. Erlangen: Palm, 1837.

Radbruch, Gustav. "Gesetzliches Unrecht und übergesetzliches Recht." *Süddeutsche Juristenzeitung* 1, nr. 5 (1946): 105-8.

Reisgies, Jens. *Evangelische Kirchenrechtssetzung: Staatliche und kirchliche Anforderungen.* Göttingen: Universitätsverlag Göttingen, 2017.

Rüthers, Bernd. *Die unbegrenzte Auslegung: Zum Wandel der Privatrechtsordnung im Nationalsozialismus*, 4th ed. Heidelberg: C. F. Müller, 1991.

Scheurl, Adolf von. "Kirchliches Gewohnheitsrecht." In Adolf von Scheurl, *Sammlung kirchenrechtlicher Abhandlungen*, 169-230. Erlangen: Deichert, 1873.

Schlink, Bernhard. *Vergangenheitsschuld und gegenwärtiges Recht.* Frankfurt am Main: Suhrkamp, 2002.

Schönberger, Christoph. *Das Parlament im Anstaltsstaat: Zur Theorie parlamentarischer Repräsentation in der Staatsrechtslehre des Kaiserreichs (1871-1918).* Frankfurt am Main: Klostermann, 1997.

Smend, Rudolf. "Wissenschafts- und Gestaltungsprobleme im evangelischen Kirchenrecht." *Zeitschrift für evangelisches Kirchenrecht* 6 (1957/58): 225-40.

Smend, Rudolf. "Zweihundert Jahre Göttinger Kirchenrechtswissenschaft." In Rudolf Smend, *Abhandlungen zum Kirchen- und Staatskirchenrecht*, edited by Hans Michael Heinig, Hendrik Munsonius, and Jens Reisgies, 243-50. Tübingen: Mohr Siebeck, 2019.

Sohm, Rudolf. *Kirchenrecht*, vol.1: *Die geschichtlichen Grundlagen.* Leipzig: Duncker & Humblot, 1892.

Steinmüller, Wilhelm. *Evangelische Rechtstheologie: Zweireichelehre, Christokratie, Gnadenrecht*, 2 vols. Köln: Bohlau, 1968.

Stolleis, Michael. *Geschichte des öffentlichen Rechts in Deutschland,* vol. 2: *Staatsrechtslehre und Verwaltungswissenschaft 1800-1914.* Munich: Beck, 1992.

Stolleis, Michael. *Recht im Unrecht: Studien zur Rechtsgeschichte des Nationalsozialismus.* Frankfurt: Suhrkamp, 1994.

Strohm, Christoph. *Die Kirchen im Dritten Reich.* Munich: C.H. Beck, 2011.

Stumpf, Christoph A. *Kirchenrecht als Bekenntnisrecht: die Verbindung von Erlanger Theologie und geschichtlicher Rechtswissenschaft im Leben und Werk von Adolf von Scheurl.* Ebelsbach: Aktiv Druck & Verlag, 1999.

Stutz, Ulrich. *Die Kirchliche Rechtsgeschichte: Rede zur Feier des 27. Januar 1905 gehalten in der Aula der Universität zu Bonn.* Stuttgart: F. Enke, 1905.

"Theologische Erklärung zur gegenwärtigen Lage der Deutschen Evangelischen Kirche vom 31.5.1934." In *Die erste Bekenntnissynode der Deutschen Evangelischen Kirche zu Barmen*, vol. 2*: Text—Dokumente—Berichte*, edited by Gerhard Niemöller. Göttingen: Vandenhoeck & Ruprecht, 1959.

"Theologische Erklärung zur gegenwärtigen Lage der Deutschen Evangelischen Kirche vom 31.5.1934," in Die erste Bekenntnissynode der Deutschen Evangelischen Kirche zu Barmen, vol. 2: Text—Dokumente—Berichte, ed. Gerhard Niemöller (Göttingen: Vandenhoeck & Ruprecht, 1959), 200. The English translation can be found at https://www.ekd.de/en/The-Barmen-Declaration-303.htm, accessed June 8, 2020.

Walther, Manfred. "Hat der juristische Positivismus die deutschen Juristen wehrlos gemacht? Zur Analyse und Kritik der Radbruch-These." In *Recht und Justiz im "Dritten Reich,"* edited by Ralf Dreier and Wolfgang Sellert, 323-54. Frankfurt am Main: Suhrkamp, 1989.

Wolf, Erik. *Ordnung der Kirche: Lehr- und Handbuch des Kirchenrechts auf ökumenischer Basis.* Frankfurt am Main: Klostermann, 1961.

7. Gender Equality Between Law and Religion in Norway: A Scandinavian Comparison

Aud V. Tønnessen

Introduction

In 1948, the first three women were ordained as ministers to the Evangelical Lutheran Church of Denmark, also referred to as the Danish Folk Church. The Church of Sweden followed in 1960 and the Church of Norway in 1961. In all three Scandinavian countries, access to the ministry of the church was regulated by the state and negotiated in the parliaments. The integration of ecclesial law into the constitution led to parliamentary debates in which political and theological arguments were merged, and in which the relation between law and theology was negotiated. The case of women's access to the ministry of the Lutheran churches is therefore well suited to the investigation of the relation between theology, politics, and law in the otherwise secular Nordic realm.

As laid out in the introductory chapter, re-confessionalization can serve as an analytical tool for understanding the growing legal independence of the national churches from the state. The strong reactions from dominant layers of the Church to the legal changes that made it possible for women to seek ordination can be interpreted as early pressures towards a re-confessionalization. In what follows, re-confessionalization will be read from a gender-critical perspective too. What meaning did gender have in the processes that took place?

The main focus of this chapter will be on the Norwegian situation, but comparative perspectives will be drawn from the other Scandinavian countries. In particular, the comparison between Norway and Sweden is interesting: the first ordinations of female ministers to the Evangelical Lutheran state churches in these countries took place at about the same time. Iceland and Finland followed significantly later than the Scandinavian countries, with the first female ministers being ordained in the Evangelical Lutheran Church of Iceland in 1974.

In Finland, the Evangelical Lutheran Church opened its ministry to women in 1986; the first ordinations took place in 1988.[1]

I have limited my chapter to the discussions regarding the Scandinavian constitutional state churches. In Norway, the first female minister in the Methodist Church was ordained in 1954. The Methodist Church was a registered free church, and the ministry not a state ministry. Therefore, the ordination took place within a different context. The relation between church and state, between theology and the law of the land, did not come into play in this case.

Women's access to the ministry of the Church of Norway had been highly contested up until 1961 (and even beyond that), and prior to the debates in parliament, the majority of bishops and ministers opposed any change. To them, access to the ministry was an ecclesial affair that had to be handled with reference to theological premises. The inherent tension within the legal and political system with the integration of state and church facilitated debates in which politicians turned into theologians. As Synnøve Hinnaland Stendal has pointed out, with the state being confessional by constitution, the parliament functioned as a synod.[2]

I will start with a presentation of significant legal changes concerning women's access to the ministry of the state church, before going deeper into the political and theological discussions concerning these changes. This chapter will focus on the concept of gender, as well as on the understanding of the relationship between church and state. The primary sources are debates in parliament, consultations, and responses to the revisions of the laws in question.

Historical background: Closing the Gender Gap

By the Constitution of 1814, the Church of Norway was a state church. §2 declared that "(t)he Evangelical Lutheran Religion shall be maintained and constitute the established Church of the Kingdom. The inhabitants who profess the said religion are bound to educate their children in the same".[3] The king was head of the church and ordained "all public worship and divine service, all meetings and congregations concerning religion and superintends the public teachers'

---

[1] Kati Niemelä, "Female Clergy as Agents of Religious Change?," *Religions* 2, no. 3 (2011): 358-71.

[2] Synnøve Hinnaland Stendal, "*…under forvandlingens lov": En analyse av stortingsdebatten om kvinnelige prester i 1930-årene* (Lund: Arcus, 2013), 380.

[3] *The Constitution of the Kingdom of Norway: Translated Pursuant to Order of the Government* (Christiania: Printed by Jacob Lehmann, 1814).

adherence to the norms prescribed for them" (§16).⁴ Decisions concerning liturgy, Sunday services, and appointments were therefore on his table. From §2 followed the regulation in §93 (later §92) that the offices of the state could only be employed by "those Norwegian citizens who profess the Evangelical Lutheran religion". "Citizen" referred to males. Women's access to the ministry of the Church of Norway was thus historically regulated by the constitution and its confessional demands on the state's civil servants.

In the course of the 19th century, legal rights were gradually extended to new groups. Confession, income, and gender were the main obstacles to full legal rights. The requirement of adherence to the Lutheran confession was a general requirement for being able to hold offices of the state until 1892. In 1884, women were admitted to the University of Oslo (at that time named *Det Kongelige Frederiks Universitet*). In 1888, married women were granted the right to own separate property. In 1901, women won the right to vote in municipal elections, based on their income. This was extended to the general election for the small group of women paying a minimum amount of tax. The breakthrough came in 1913 with the decision of parliament to extend suffrage to all women, the same right that men had earned in 1898. With the extension of women's rights educationally, professionally, and politically, there was a need to revise the law regulating access to the offices of the state. In 1912, women were included in the offices of the state with the exception of the following areas: police, military, government, foreign affairs, and the Church. A 1916 revision allowed women to take up office in the government.

Women's access to all the ministries of the state was a major issue for the women's movement. The movement, or rather movements, as it involved a number of organizations and associations, was comprehensive and included women from political parties, academia, and also Christian associations. They pushed for a change that would allow women the same right to the state's offices as men. In 1921, the Ministry of Church Affairs asked the bishops and theological professors about their opinion on women and the pastoral ministry. It was already known that increasingly more of the professors held a positive view, but the bishops with one exception unanimously argued against women's ordination based on the Bible and the Christian tradition. In 1926, the parish councils were asked by the Ministry of Church Affairs about their opinion on women's ministry. Out of 1000 responses, only 43 were indisputably positive.⁵ Despite the reluctance of the leaders and laypeople of the Church, the question of women's access to all

---

4   *The Constitution of the Kingdom of Norway*.
5   *Ot.prp.nr.6* (1936) Om adgang til å ansette kvinner i statens embeter, 3.

the ministries of the state, including that of the state church, became an increasingly pressing issue throughout the 1930s, with propositions by the government to change the law being advanced in 1930, 1934, 1936, and 1938.

Similar processes took place at the same time in Sweden and Denmark; the role of the women's movement played a significant role in them. As in Norway, women originally had no access to the state's ministries. In Denmark in 1919 and Sweden in 1925, most ministries of the state were opened up to women with a few exceptions, the church ministry being one.[6]

The insistent push for change from various women's movements impacted the internal ecclesial debates about the role of women in the Church. For example, in 1919, the Swedish Bishop's Conference had identified the need for a specialized vocation for women, one that would focus on the education of children and youths within congregations.[7] This initiative was followed up in 1938 by a motion presented by Manfred Björkquist from Sigtunastiftelsen arguing for a specialized ministry for women.[8] In Norway, the 1937 Bishop's Conference presented a program for a new ministry for women.[9] In both Norway and Sweden, a basic motivation behind the programs was to provide women with an alternative to the pastoral ministry of the Church, one that would also be attractive to female theologians. Diaconical work and education were listed as its main tasks and responsibilities.

The Parliament Acting as Church Synod

The initiatives taken in Norway and Sweden to establish a complementary vocation for women came as responses to the ever more active and insistent political efforts to change the law and make all the ministries of the state available to women. There was a fear among church leaders that women's ordination could be forced upon them by the politicians. Making new space for women was therefore a strategical move intending to halt the political initiatives, and to ensure that the Church (neither the politicians nor the women's movement)

---

6   Lis Bisgaard, "Debatten om kvindelige præster," in *Se min kjole: De første kvindelige præsters historie*, ed. Else Marie Wiberg Pedersen (Copenhagen: Samleren, 1998), 144-88; Göran Lundstedt, "Vägen fram till kyrkomötets beslut att öppna prästämbetet för kvinnor," in *Äntligen stod hon i predikstolen! Historiskt vägval 1958*, ed. Boel Hössjer Sundman (Stockholm: Verbum, 2008), 127-39.
7   Lundstedt, "Vägen fram," 128.
8   Lundstedt, "Vägen fram," 129.
9   *Om en særskilt kvinnelig tjeneste: Utgreeing av en av bispemøtet opnevnt komité* (Oslo: H. Aschehoug & co, 1938).

controlled such ecclesial developments. In addition, it was meant to satisfy those women who studied theology and who expressed a wish to become ministers in the Church. They were not many and they were moderate in their approach, but they were still there.

The Norwegian bishops' meeting in 1936 issued a warning to the government. Although the state had the right to give "anyone" access to its civil ministries, the ministry of the Church was of a different kind. A trustful relationship between state and church presupposed that the state respected the unique character of the Church.[10] In other words, women's ordination could prove harmful to the institution of the state church.

The proposals for a new ecclesial ministry for women came too late to change the political course. Already in 1938, the Norwegian parliament voted to change the law and give women access to the state's ministries, including that of the Church. The worries and warnings from the Church had made an impact. Johan Ludwig Mowinckel, former prime minister and at that time the parliamentary leader of the Liberal Party, *Venstre*, argued that the opposition voiced by the congregations had to be taken into consideration. It was solid liberal politics to hear them out on this, he argued. Mowinckel therefore proposed an amendment to the main sentence, "Based on the same conditions as men, women can be appointed to the state's ministries". This would secure the freedom of the congregations: "When appointing to office in the church, one ought not to employ women as ministers in congregations that on principle grounds oppose this".[11] The amendment passed and would be referred to as the *lex Mowinckel*.

The parliamentary debate provides an interesting picture of how the politicians negotiated law and theology on a question that was highly controversial to the church leaders and active laypeople. Knowing the opposition and acknowledging that the ministry of the Church was different from other state ministries, all politicians, more or less, sought to base their arguments on theology and biblical texts, acting in the way one would expect a church synod to do. The politicians rejecting a legal change leaned on theology when arguing that women's ministry was an internal affair of the Church, not to be implemented against the will of the church leaders. But change was also legitimated through lengthy and informed discussions of biblical passages, their interpretations as well as translations. Although secular arguments played a certain role, not

---

10   Kristin Molland Norderval, *Mot strømmen: Kvinnelige teologer i Norge før og nå* (Oslo: Land og kirke/Gyldendal Norsk Forlag, 1982), 67.
11   *Ot.prp.nr.* 12 (1956) Om oppheving av lov av 24. juni 1938 om adgang til å ansette kvinner i statens embeder, 2.

least in connection with the rights-based approach by the women's movement, the extent of theological argumentation is striking. This is an indication of the close identification of the state with the Church, as well as the extent to which theological arguments were accepted as politically reasonable.

Already in the 1934 debate, theology had been dominant. With reference to the Gospel of Matthew, Gulla M. Grundt from the Conservative Party, *Høyre*, had announced that the women already at Jesus' tomb had been appointed ministers. The women who on Easter morning met the risen Jesus outside his grave had been commissioned to preach the Gospel to the whole world that Christ had been raised from the dead: "In other words, it is Jesus who has installed her as priest".[12] This theological argumentation was followed up in the later debates, including the crucial debate of 1938. For example, Erling Bjørnson of the Farmers' Party, *Bondepartiet*, gave a lengthy lecture on modern exegesis, drawing on the expertise of international professors. Citing Galatians 3, that all are one in Christ and that there is neither Jew nor Greek, neither slave nor free, neither man nor woman, as well as calling upon Paul's references to Phoebe being called "sister" and "a servant of the Church," Bjørnson argued that there was nothing in Paul's writings that discriminated against women exercising the ministry of the Church.[13] Anna J. Henriksen of the Liberal Party referred to the parable about the use and misuse of talents, arguing that "the most important gift we get when we are born, is our capacities. To let them lie unused is against the will of Jesus".[14] In other words, preventing women from using their talents and capacities for church ministry would be sinful.

The message of these politicians was clear: neither the Bible nor theology spoke against the new law. The proposed legal reform did not harm nor disrespect the uniqueness of the Church. The politicians spoke to the church leaders, using Biblical language when trying to reassure them that the proposed legal change did not contradict the theology of the Church. It was also clear that they did not see the change merely as a legal reform for the sake of the state, but one that would be to the advantage of the Church. From a political point of view, the legal change could have been seen as a strictly secular act securing women the same rights as men, furthering and expanding the developments of 1913 when women received the right to vote. Instead, they also argued that women's ministry had a legitimate place within the Church and was for its best.

---

12 *Innst. O. Nr. 4* (1934) *Indstilling fra justiskomiteen om lov om adgang til å ansette kvinner i statens embeder*. Odeltingstidende, 15.
13 *Storthingstidende* (1938) Indeholdende den syvogåttiende ordentlige Stortings forhandlinger. Forhandlinger i Odelstinget, 679.
14 *Storthingstidende* (1938), 690.

On a secular legal basis, the ministry of the Church could have been understood as being no different from the other state ministries, and the Church as being equal to state institutions such as the post or the transport, but that was not the case. The politicians identified with the Church and recognized it as unique. They also respected the fact that the question of women's access to the ministry of the Church was of a different order than their access to other state offices. Therefore, both adherents and opponents of the revision presented arguments based on theological reflections.

The amendment proved to be a Solomonic solution. The law passed, but with an amendment giving concessions to the opposition from church leaders as well as lay Christians. What the amendment regulated was legally disputed. What did the phrase "ought not to employ" mean, and what was the effect of it? Did it mean an unconditional 'must not employ', as professor in law and church law Knut Robberstad insisted?[15] Or did it primarily imply that the congregations had the right to be heard before an appointment took place, as they had with bishops and provosts? The meaning and implication of the amendment were never tested, since no woman applied for a ministry. In any case, with the concession to the congregations, support for the new law, which in §1 firmly stated that women could be appointed to offices of the state, under the same conditions as men was secured. At the same time, the amendment symbolically emphasized that the ministry of the Church was different from other offices of the state, and that the Church's relation to the state was of another kind than, for example, the military.

Internationalization Triumphs Theology

In the long run, the 1938 amendment was unsatisfactory. The women's movement would not settle for a law that discriminated based on gender. The question was brought up again after World War II, and this time the women's movement was assisted by international legal processes.

In 1948, Norway voted for the Universal Declaration of Human Rights of the United Nations. Article 21 in it read, "Everyone has the right of equal access to public services in his country". This was understood by politicians as contradicting the 1938 amendment, because of its discrimination on the basis of gender. Furthermore, in 1952, the General Assembly of the United Nations further approved, and adopted in 1953, the Convention of the Political Rights of Women.

---

15   *Ot.prp.nr.* 12 (1956), 3.

This stimulated the Norwegian government to invite bishops and the theological faculties to a new hearing where they were asked if they could approve the removal of the amendment. The government's view was that the amendment contradicted the Convention. This view was not shared by the majority of the bishops. They warned that annulling the amendment would cause unrest and conflicts. They also found that the amendment's regulation of women's employability in the Church had a direct impact on the question of ordination.

According to Bishop Johannes Smemo of Oslo, the amendment dealt with an internal matter of the Church that had to be decided based on the authority of the Bible. His concern was the freedom of the Church as a religious institution. If the state were to treat the question at hand merely as a legal matter concerning equal rights for men and women, the freedom of the Church would be harmed.[16] Bishop Bjarne Skard of Tunsberg warned that opening the ministry to women had no foundation at all, neither in the Bible nor in Christian tradition, and argued that the law should, if possible, state "even clearer" that the ministry of the Church was a divine office instituted by Christ himself.[17] The Bishop of Kristiansand, Johannes Smidt, defended the amendment as a democratic regulation that secured the autonomy of the congregations.[18] Bishop Ragnvald Indrebø of Bergen warned that what was at stake was no less than the freedom of faith and conscience but, like Smemo, he referred not to the individual, but to the collective conscience of the Church. He argued that if the state now were to become the master and guardian in theological questions and use the law to implement a new ecclesial order, the prerequisite for the state church order was broken. After all, the Church had only one authority, the Bible, and the state could not overrule this authority without causing conflict and division.[19]

From 1938 to the beginning of the 1950s, the debate on women's ministry had been transformed into a discussion on the relation between state and church. This was not so much a result of the international legal developments as it was a consequence of the experience of the Nazi occupation. When the bishops and the majority (about 93%) of the pastors in 1942 broke with the Nazi state, at the same time they stated that they would continue their office in the Church.[20] From 1942-1945, they organized themselves as a free church. After the war, the Church was immediately reinstituted as the state church it had been

---

16 Ot.prp.nr. 12 (1956), 9.
17 Arne Fjelberg, *Kvinnelige prester?* (Oslo: Land og kirke, 1958), 135.
18 Fjelberg, *Kvinnelige prester,* 138.
19 Ot.prp.nr. 12 (1956), 11.
20 Torleiv Austad, *Kirkens Grunn: Analyse av en kirkelig bekjennelse fra okkupasjonstiden 1940-1945* (Oslo: Luther forlag, 1974).

before, but a government-appointed committee was tasked with a mandate to propose reforms, and within the Church there were great expectations regarding the outcome of this work. The committee was led by Bishop Eivind Berggrav of Oslo, who had been one of the leaders of the Church's civil resistance. During his three-year arrest he had written extensively on state and church relations, arguing for a reform of the Norwegian state church.[21] Distinguishing between the external and internal church, he argued that legal, economical and administrative affairs should still be placed within the remit of the state and the parliament, distancing himself from those wanting the Church of Norway to be reorganized as a free church.[22] What was important was to secure the internal freedom of the Church. It had to possess the freedom to preach, the freedom of confession, and the freedom of vocation, that is, appointment to positions. The first freedom was secured within the old order, he said, but what belonged to the confession was regulated by §16 and had to be changed. With the king as head of the Church, this paragraph instituted him as responsible for the provision of worship and the supervision of the public teachers of the state religion, including the bishops and professors. Berggrav proposed an amendment to the law, one that would give the Church a veto in confessional questions. With regard to the appointment of church ministers and bishops, he proposed a model similar to the one in Denmark and Sweden, in which the king was obligated to appoint a person who had been promoted by the Church.

The church order committee included these demands and in addition proposed a new organisation within the Church with the synod as its head. The synod would have the power of veto in matters that concerned the spiritual life of the church.

The committee submitted its recommendations in 1947, but it would take another five years before parliament in 1953 finally held a vote over the proposed reforms. By then, the recommendations from the committee had been heavily reduced, to the great disappointment of the bishops. The church synod was still included but reduced to a consultative body. Despite the downscaling, the reforms were voted down. The Labour Party's politicians argued that it was a reform of the church and not of the state, and that the state's interests had been neglected. The Labour Party held a supreme majority in the parliament at that time; thus, when the proposed church reforms were rejected, it was in fact the Labour Party that went against its own government, whereas the other parties voted in favour of the government. After this long process, the result did not

---

21 Eivind Berggrav, *Kirkens ordning i Norge: Attersyn og framblikk* (Oslo: Land og kirke, 1945).
22 Berggrav, *Kirkens ordning i Norge,* 47.

come as surprise to church leaders. Instead, it rather reinforced old patterns of mistrust between church and the Labour Party.²³

Given this background, the warnings raised by the majority of the bishops a few years later against removing the 1938 amendment can be understood as expressions of a fear that the state would use its power to overrule the church and install a new church order that to them contradicted the Word of God. This can explain the strong words on schism and conflict expressed by several bishops. The amendment had a symbolic meaning as a fence protecting the freedom of the church. Legal experts had been divided about the actual meaning and importance of the amendment, whether "ought" meant a noncommittal recommendation to the government, or if a congregation with its statement could bind the government. However, the amendment seemed to guarantee the state's recognition of the unique character of the church and functioned as a bulwark against the expanding power of the state.

The motion to the parliament presented by the Ministry of Legal Affairs in February 1956 aimed at keeping theology and law apart. The theological concerns raised by the bishops were mostly overlooked or dismissed, but the disagreements between the bishops were noted.²⁴ Two of the bishops (Alf Wiig of Nord-Hålogaland and Kristian Schjelderup of Hamar) had positively welcomed the change. Bishop Schjelderup dismissed the arguments of his colleagues that the Bible spoke against women's ministry.²⁵ He also questioned the validity of arguments that referred to the Christian tradition. Bishop Skard had underlined that the church had no tradition for female ministers. According to Schjelderup, it was historically possible that women had served as ministers. But even if Skard were right, tradition should not hinder a progress that stemmed from life itself, Schjelderup argued. It was both timely and right that the law should be changed as soon as possible and that equality between men and women should be implemented in the church. The same kind of argument was used by the state: the law of the land had to accommodate to the principle of gender equality.

The amendment did not conform to the principles of equality basic to Norwegian democracy, the Ministry of Legal Affairs stated.²⁶ The ministry found it particularly problematic that of all the features and qualifications a candidate had to have, gender was emphasized as the only discriminatory principle. In addition, the ministry emphasized, the amendment prevented the government

---

23 For more on this, see Aud Tønnessen, "*...et trygt og godt hjem for alle?*" *Kirkeledere's kritikk av velferdsstaten etter 1945* (Trondheim: Tapir forlag, 2000).
24 *Ot.prp.nr.* 12 (1956), 16.
25 *Ot.prp.nr.* 12 (1956), 9-10.
26 *Ot.prp.nr.* 12 (1956), 18.

from unconditionally ratifying the international Convention of the Political Rights of Women.[27] The adaptation of Norwegian law to international commitments demanded that the amendment be annulled. Despite these secular legal and political arguments, even the Ministry of Legal Affairs could not prevent itself from engaging in a debate about theological arguments and argued that neither the Bible nor the Christian tradition would be weakened by a revocation of the law.[28]

In the parliamentary discussion of the amendment, several politicians raised doubts as to whether the ratification argument was valid at all. After all, Sweden had ratified the international Convention on the Political Rights of Women and still did not allow women to become ministers in the Church. But more importantly, the amendment was interpreted as protecting the ecclesial and spiritual freedom of the congregations and the Church, a guard that kept them safe from state intervention. If the amendment were annulled, congregations could be forced to compromise their conscience. Deprived of the option to reject a woman as minister, the state could intervene unhindered and appoint women to congregations, even those who objected to it on a principled theological basis. If so, the argument went, the state would then have taken over an authority that belonged only to God. This theological line of reasoning was then translated into legal arguments. After having presented his theological understanding of the problem, Arne Askildsen of the Christian Democratic Party, *Kristelig Folkeparti*, declared that the result would be a violation of human rights principles.[29] And, he added, it would be "undemocratic" and an "abuse" by the "tyranny of the majority".[30]

The shift from explicitly debating women's ministry to a more general state church debate also led to a shift from predominantly theological arguments to a much more rights-based approach. The amendment discriminated on the basis of gender alone, the spokespersons for its revocation argued, but removing it was not an attack on the autonomy of the Church. To give women the same rights as men was to meet their rightful demand for justice, the Labor Party's representative Jakob Pettersen said.[31] Should the congregations have a greater power over the female applicants than over male applicants? asked Hjalmar Storeide, a minister in the Church of Norway, also representing the Labour

---

27 *Ot.prp.nr.* 12 (1956), 18.
28 *Ot.prp.nr.* 12 (1956), 18.
29 *Stortingstidende* (1956) 100. ordentlige Stortings forhandlinger. Odelstinget, 272.
30 *Stortingstidende* (1956), 273.
31 *Stortingstidende* (1956), 280.

Party.³² Ola Høyland of the Farmers' Party called the amendment a politics of devaluation of women. The law made them inferior to men, and that could not be tolerated.³³ The same point was made by Rakel Seweriin of the Labour Party; the key question, she said, was whether the state should uphold a law that made women subordinate to men.³⁴ The Farmers' Party's Karen Grønn-Hagen noted sarcastically that the reactions by the opposition against the law seemed to indicate that the church needed to be protected against women, and that that was their main reason for wanting to retain the amendment.³⁵

Lost in Translation: Women Between Law and Theology

A clear majority voted for the revocation of the amendment. But, as in 1938, the 1956 change did not immediately lead to women entering the ministry. In 1956, 34 women had received their theology degree, and of these eight had in addition the practical theological training needed to qualify for a ministry. Whereas the legal change in Denmark in 1947 relatively soon resulted in three women being ordained, the Norwegian female theologians hesitated.³⁶ Why? Had Bishop Smidt in Kristiansand been right when he said that women did not apply because they shared the same understanding as the rest of the church, namely, that women's ministry was unwanted?³⁷ When asked about their vocations, female theologians answered that they did not want to force themselves upon the church. Ordination had to come as something facilitated by God, one of them, Agnes Vold, said.³⁸ Changing the law was simply not enough, and by no means any indication of God's intervention. Instead, they adapted to the situation and waited for a change within the church. More precisely, they waited for an invitation from the bishops. Before that, they would not act on the law.

In 1958, the organization *Norsk Kvinnelig Teologforening* (Association of Norwegian Female Theologians) had been established. Symptomatic of the situation, there was no mention of women's ordination in its mission statements. The association aimed to bridge the gap between the special interests of the

---

32 *Stortingstidende* (1956), 283.
33 *Stortingstidende* (1956), 281.
34 *Stortingstidende* (1956), 299.
35 *Stortingstidende* (1956), 295.
36 Bisgaard, "Debatten om kvindelige præster."
37 *Odeltingsproposisjon* no. 12 (1956), 11.
38 Fjelberg, *Kvinnelige prester?*, 169.

members and not siding with one over the others.[39] Women's ordination was a non-question for the female theologians of that time, something that was not to be brought to the table. The changed situation after 1956 had no effect on them. One wonders why, and the most likely explanation seems to lie in the understanding of the relevant jurisdiction that was dominant within the church. Here, the legal changes were not recognized as theologically relevant. The legal order may have instituted a potential shift in practice, but as long as this was not accepted by those in power, acting upon the law could only mean failing the test of faithfulness to the church. It would mean politicizing and secularizing theology and church. Women's ordination was a strictly theological matter and had nothing to do with the state's law or politics, least of all with women's rights. This was accepted as the true interpretation and internalized by most female theologians at that time. Three young female theology students were asked by a journalist in 1961 about their opinion on female ministry. At first, they denied having any opinion at all on the subject, but then changed their mind and said that one thing was clear: this question had nothing to do with the women's rights movement. It was a matter only the church could resolve.[40]

The female theologians were trapped between a law that their professors and bishops judged as secular and a threat to the ecclesial autonomy and freedom of conscience, and a hegemonic theology that did not accept women's ordination. The freedom the law gave was not something they were free to use.

Comparison with Denmark and Sweden

In Denmark the situation was different. In 1946, before the employment law for state offices was changed, the theologian Johanne Andersen had been elected as minister by a free Grundtvigian congregation within the Danish Folk Church (in Danish: *valgmenighed*). The election had to be approved by the Ministry of Church Affairs, but the law prevented it from doing so. In addition, two years earlier, another female theologian, Ruth Vermehren, had been employed to serve among female prisoners, but as a lay person. Whereas in Norway the question of women's ministry had been treated as a strictly hypothetical reality, the parliamentary debate in Denmark 1947 related to concrete cases, which

---

39 Anne Dalen, *Norsk kvinnelig teologforenings historie 1958-2008: Interesseforening, plogspiss og vaktbikkje* (Oslo: Pax forlag, 2008).
40 Aud V. Tønnessen, *Ingrid Bjerkås. Motstandskvinnen som ble vår første kvinnelige prest* (Oslo: Pax forlag, 2014), 73.

made it clear that the push for change came from within the church and from below. It came from the congregation that had elected Andersen, and it came from women like Andersen and Vermehren who had accepted positions that traditionally had been reserved for men. In turn, they were actively supported by other female theologians, as well as by the women's movement. The resistance came from the church elite, bishops, and ordained ministers, what the ministry of Church Affairs in 1919, Thorvald Poulsen, had called "the organized men's Church".[41] The new law was approved in June 1947, but the pertinent bishops denied ordination.[42] A new law gave bishops, under certain conditions, the freedom from supervising a congregation and their ministers, and instead let this be taken up by a colleague. In reality, this meant that a bishop colleague was given the freedom to ordain women, as well as to supervise them. The law was approved in March 1948, and already on April 28 three women were ordained: Vermehren, Andersen, and Edith Brenneche-Petersen.[43]

In Sweden, first in 1957 and then again in 1958, the church synod was asked by the government to approve a change in the law that would allow women access to the ministry of the church. The synod held the power of veto in matters of ecclesial concern. The request was rejected in 1957, but when it was brought up again the next year, it passed. According to Margareta Brandby-Cöster, the decision by the church synod was no real decision, as it was followed by a number of restrictions that guaranteed male pastors extended rights based on reference to their conscience.[44] A so-called "conscience clause" guaranteed male pastors the right not to serve and minister *in sacris* together with female colleagues. This law went further than what the Danish regulation had done. The Danish law gave bishops the right not to participate in the ordination of women and supervise them, whereas the Swedish law included the entire community of colleagues, stating that no male minister had to serve together with a female minister. This was, Brandby-Cöster says, a "declaration of war" leading to a long-lasting war-like conflict that for many years would place women in an inferior position in which they had to defend their vocations and rights.[45]

---

41 Bisgaard, "Debatten om kvindelige præster," 151.
42 Bisgaard, "Debatten om kvindelige præster," 141.
43 Bisgaard, "Debatten om kvindelige præster," 143.
44 Margareta Brandby-Cöster, "Dubbla budskap—vilket skall firas?," in *Äntligen stod hon i predikstolen! Historiskt vägval 1958,* ed. Boel Hössjer Sundman (Stockholm: Verbum, 2008), 162-80.
45 Brandby-Cöster, "Dubbla budskap," 162.

Gender Equality and Re-Confessionalization

When viewing the debates in the Scandinavian countries in a longer historical perspective, we can see that they place themselves within a complex narrative about the church and women's rights. In the final decades of the 19th century, most church leaders in Scandinavia had been firm opponents of women's fight for liberation. For example, Norwegian bishops and theology professors had almost unanimously opposed the right of married women to own property, and had fought women's suffrage. One of the leading professors of theology, Fredrik Petersen, who was considered to be both modern and moderate, denounced the women's movement as sinful and based on disbelief.[46] Rights-based claims for liberation were incompatible with theology.

The same skepticism about a rights-based approach was inherited by Petersen's successors and resurfaced in the discussions about women's ministry in the 1930s and onward. Church leaders dismissed as invalid the arguments that equal rights for women meant that women could become ministers. The same view was shared by most female theologians at that time. As noted above, they argued that references to secular rights were irrelevant to theology and church; such rights were even hostile to the church. The same was the case in Sweden. Bo Giertz, bishop of Gothenburg from 1949-1970, declared in a debate in 1939 that female ministry had nothing to do with rights. "We do not fight for 'rights' of any kind. None of us, neither woman nor man, has any right at all to an office in the service of God," he said, underlining, as Maria Södling has shown, an opposition in principle between women's rights and Christian faith, between feminism and church.[47] Rights-based claims had no place whatsoever within the church. Demands for gender equality stood in direct opposition to theology and church. Gender equality became, says Södling, a matter of ideology and politics, far removed from theology.[48]

The same perspective also dominated the Norwegian debate and was internalized by very many young women. To take advantage of the legal opening that had been created in 1956 was unthinkable. That would mean acting in contradiction to the needs of the church. Claims that women earned the right to equality also within church was interpreted as a secular attempt by an expanding

---

46 Bente Nilsen Lein, *Kirken i felttog mot kvinnefrigjøring: Kirkens holdning til den borgerlige kvinnebevegelsen i 1880-årene* (Oslo/Bergen/Trondheim: Universitetsforlaget, 1981), 81.
47 Maria Södling, "Inga kvinna synes än: En historia om kvinnliga präster," in *Äntligen stod hon i predikstolen! Historiskt vägval 1958*, ed. Boel Hössjer Sundman (Stockholm: Verbum, 2008), 181-92.
48 Södling, "Inga kvinna synes än," 187.

state to subject the church to its will. This state was understood as an unfaithful partner to the church, having no respect for its inner autonomy. Thus, for a woman to seek ordination under such premises would mean alienating herself from the Christian community. It would further mean that she had become an instrument of the state intended to secularize it from within. Given such a perspective, it is no surprise that, in Norway, it would take 23 years from the law was changed in 1938 until the first woman was ordained in 1961.

Breaking with the massive condemnations of feminism as anti-ecclesial and anti-theological required courage. A great deal of pressure was placed on the female theologians. The reactions and sanctions against them were strong and even aggressive. In Sweden, the new law of 1958 led to the formation of *Kyrklig samling kring Bibel och bekännelsen* (Ecclesial consolidation around the Bible and confession), with Bishop Giertz as its primary leader, and with a 17-point program for opposing the new order of female pastors. This attempt at re-confessionalization also had a clear anti-feminist character. For example, in the program articles one can read that, since a woman was not commissioned by Christ to become pastor, a pastor cannot administer the office together with her, and also, a pastor should avoid participating in all ecclesial affairs, whether legal or voluntary, where a woman partakes as a pastor.[49] Being a pastor was exclusively defined with respect to gender, not age nor theology. As Södling shows, "male" was thus coined as something positive and theologically valid, whereas "female" was the opposite. In this way, the vocation of the female ministers was invalidated.[50]

In Norway, conservative theologians and church leaders were inspired by the firm opposition in Sweden. Norwegian female theologians were told that if they acted upon the new law, they would bear responsibility for throwing the church into conflicts that could split the community. The employability that had been made possible had no legitimate place within the church. It was said to be in opposition to both the Bible and the Christian tradition. Therefore, to seek a position as a minister was tantamount to admitting a total lack of respect for the church and its life. In addition, the fact that women's movements had been active in the processes leading to legal change further underlined the secularity of the legal system and its lack of respect for the order of the church. Women's rights were neither compatible with the church nor with theology.

---

49   Södling, "Inga kvinna synes än," 169.
50   Södling, "Inga kvinna synes än," 186-87.

Acting Upon the Law—Rebelling Against the Hegemony

The first woman to be ordained in Norway 1961 was Ingrid Bjerkås. She had begun to study theology at the age of fifty, at that time already a grandmother. During the years of the occupation of Norway by the German Nazi state (1940-1945), she had been arrested several times for acts of resistance and had been imprisoned for a year in the German concentration camp Grini outside of Oslo. After the war, she had been a teacher in a local Sunday school, and she began studying theology to learn more. Soon, she declared that she would use her education to become a minister in the church. She finished her degree and practical training in 1960 and immediately began to apply for positions, but getting hired proved more difficult than expected. As her bishop noted, the campaign against her secured a surprising number of applicants for the positions.[51]

Her open agenda to seek office attracted the interest of the media. In an interview she claimed that the ordination of women was a women's rights issue. This was akin to cursing in church. She said:

> One cannot hide that it is a women's rights issue that we are allowed to preach and be rightly called. But it is not degrading that it is a women's rights issue. Rather, it is my hope that many young women will study theology. The church needs women, and women need the church. It is very important, though, that women are not reduced to assistants, but are rightly called, just like men, to preach the word of God and administer the sacraments.[52]

Such an approach to ordination and ministry was a provocation to most church leaders as well as other female theologians. Bishop Kristian Schjelderup asked for example two female theologians if they would consider ordination and maybe do it together with Bjerkås. From his perspective, it would be good if the three of them could share the historical moment together. He was also concerned with the negative attention the ordination of the first woman would attract, and also for that reason he thought it would be positive if the first ordination included more women. He asked Vold and Agnethe Fischer who already held offices in the church and had been outspoken in their vocation to seek ordination, but both of them turned down the invitation. The time was not right, they said, but most of all they did not want to be identified or allied with Ingrid Bjerkås and

---

51 Tønnessen, *Ingrid Bjerkås*, 86.
52 Tønnessen, *Ingrid Bjerkås*, 73.

her women's rights arguments.[53] To them, ordination was strictly ecclesial and theological and had nothing to do with either legal processes or rights. To take advantage of the law and defy the majority of church leaders, as in their view Bjerkås did, represented to them a secularization of the ministerial vocation and ordination. In their view, her ordination took place on the basis of false premises. Her statement about women's ministry as a women's rights issue only proved her lack of understanding of theology and its relation to the law. It was not the law, but theology, that should open the door to the ministry. Referring to law and women's rights only proved how wrong her theological mindset was. The ministry was a strictly internal cause for the church and had to treasured as such.

By 1961, Vold had waited 24 years for ordination. She had completed her education in 1937. She had a conservative theological background, but also a clear understanding that her vocation was to become a minister in the church. But to her, neither the legal openings nor the fact that another woman was about to be ordained were received as invitations from the church and an indication that the time was finally right. Instead, she waited another two years, thereby also distancing her ordination from that of Bjerkås, thus signaling that her ordination was of a different kind, not one based on women's rights, but on God's calling.[54]

Re-Confessionalizing Gender

As in Sweden, there was a massive mobilization against women's ordination. When Bjerkås was appointed minister to Berg and Torsken in Senja, an island in the far north, six out of nine bishops issued a warning that this would cause great suffering and divisions in the church.[55] Women's ministry had been promoted by other interests than ecclesial and had unjustly been inflicted upon the church, they declared. They encouraged everyone to follow his or her conscience and reject any collaboration that could lead to women's ministry. Thus, the tone for the following debate had been set. A woman had no legitimate vocation, but had instead been misled. If she sought ordination, she acted on interests that had nothing to do with the church, interests that were secular.

A few days after Bjerkås' appointment, Leiv Aalen, the chairman of the conservative theological organization *Prestelaget for Bibel og Bekjennelse* (Priestly

---

53 Tønnessen, *Ingrid Bjerkås*, 97.
54 Tønnessen, *Ingrid Bjerkås*, 97.
55 Tønnessen, *Ingrid Bjerkås*, 92.

Brotherhood for the Bible and confession), who also happened to be a professor of dogmatics at the MF School of Theology and Religion and a teacher to many future female theologians, declared that women's ministry was un-Christian and unbiblical. Women's ministry had been imposed on the church from the outside. Aalen's aim and hope were that Bjerkås would be the first and only woman to be ordained. He told the press that other female theologians were unhappy with the situation and that they had no plans to seek ordination. Even if they failed in understanding how unbiblical the ordination was, a reality check would tell them that the only one cheering for the forthcoming ordination was the radical press. He thought that the situation could hardly have become more shameful.[56]

More strongly than they had done before, the opposition against women's ministry now presented their theology. It was a theology of women's subordination. From creation, women were subordinate to men. This order had been established by God from the beginning and was eternal and objective. Because she was subordinate, Christ had forbidden her to speak in the church. When Paul commanded women to be silent, this was a commandment given to him directly by Christ. Therefore, the commandment was valid beyond its historical time and space. Further, the tradition said that Jesus had only male disciples. In conclusion, women's ministry contradicted creation, the New Testament, and church history. Only groups that were hostile to the church could have an interest in promoting women's ministry.[57]

The rather aggressive arguments against women's ministry dismissed any reference to women's rights and legal regulations as being secular and anti-church. With their vocation, women were placed outside of the gates of the church. A process of re-confessionalization took place: the only true church was one that rejected women's ministry. The freedom of conscience that was necessary for defending the church from the secular threat posed by women's ministry was also gendered. Only a male ministry could guarantee ecclesial autonomy over the secular state and its law of the land.

Concluding remarks

The process of re-confessionalization had a clear gender dimension. As this chapter has shown, in this case to defend the Church's autonomy from state intervention was a defense against women's entry into ministry. When bishops

---

56 Tønnessen, *Ingrid Bjerkås*, 91-92.
57 Tønnessen, *Ingrid Bjerkås*, 94.

and others warned against conflicts and division and referred to hostile interests that threatened the unity and uniqueness of the church, the hostility they found wore a woman's face. With such a narrative, female theologians who referred to rights or argued on the basis of legal regulations were placed outside of the church. They implemented a secularization in the church that the law of the land had made possible.

Processes for securing freedom for conscience for those who did not accept women's ministry also focused on gender. In the case of Bjerkås, a petition was sent by a group of members in one of her congregations to the Ministry of Church Affairs and the bishop, demanding that a male pastor should be sent to help them out, since they could not accept her services.[58] When a liberal male minister served during her summer vacation, only praise could be heard: even from the most conservative members. Even though they did not agree with his theological views, he was accepted because of his gender, whereas she was not.

Women's ministry was identified with secularity, whereas men's freedom of conscience expressed a true understanding of church. This freedom of conscience represented a re-confessionalization that had a male expression and content. In Sweden, the freedom of conscience for male ministers was instituted with the "conscience clause" and in Norway with the so-called "driving rules" (in Norwegian: *kjøreregler*).[59] These gave men the right to reject participation and collaboration with a female colleague based on conscience and theological principles. Both the "conscience clause" and the "driving rules" express how re-confessionalization impacted the developments of the Scandinavian churches, and how this was related to a gendered agenda in which theology and law were played against each other.

Bibliography

Official Sources

Innst. O. Nr. 4 (1934) *Indstilling fra justiskomiteen om lov om adgang til å ansette kvinner i statens embeder*. Odeltingstidende.

Ot.prp.nr. 6 (1936) *Om adgang til å ansette kvinner i statens embeter*.

Ot.prp.nr. 12 (1956) *Om oppheving av lov av 24. juni 1938 om adgang til å ansette kvinner i statens embeder*.

Storthingstidende (1938) Indeholdende den syvogåttiende ordentlige Stortings forhandlinger. Forhandlinger i Odelsthinget.

---

58 Tønnessen, *Ingrid Bjerkås*, 147.
59 Dalen, *Norsk kvinnelig teologforenings historie 1958-2008*.

Stortingstidende (1956) 100. ordentlige Stortings forhandlinger. Odelstinget.

Om en særskilt kvinnelig tjeneste: Utgreeing av en av bispemøtet opnevnt komité. Oslo: H. Aschehoug & co., 1938.

The Constitution of the Kingdom of Norway: Translated Pursuant to Order of the Government. Christiania: Printed by Jacob Lehmann, 1814.

Literature

Austad, Torleiv. *Kirkens Grunn: Analyse av en kirkelig bekjennelse fra okkupasjonstiden 1940-1945.* Oslo: Luther forlag, 1974.

Berggrav, Eivind. *Kirkens ordning i Norge: Attersyn og framblikk.* Oslo: Land og kirke, 1945.

Bisgaard, Lis. "Debatten om kvindelige præster." In *Se min kjole: De første kvindelige præsters historie,* edited by Else Marie Wiberg Pedersen, 144-88. Copenhagen: Samleren, 1998.

Brandby-Cöster, Margareta. "Dubbla budskap—vilket skall firas?" In *Äntligen stod hon i predikstolen! Historiskt vägval 1958,* edited by Boel Hössjer Sundman, 162-80. Stockholm: Verbum, 2008.

Dalen, Anne. *Norsk kvinnelig teologforenings historie 1958-2008: Interesseforening, plogspiss og vaktbikkje.* Oslo: Pax forlag, 2008.

Fjelberg, Arne. *Kvinnelige prester?* Oslo: Forlaget Land og kirke, 1958.

Lundstedt, Göran. "Vägen fram till kyrkomötets beslut att öppna prästämbetet för kvinnor." In *Äntligen stod hon i predikstolen! Historiskt vägval 1958,* edited by Boel Hössjer Sundman, 127-39. Stockholm: Verbum, 2008.

Molland Norderval, Kristin. *Mot strømmen: Kvinnelige teologer i Norge før og nå.* Oslo: Land og kirke/Gyldendal Norsk Forlag, 1982.

Niemelä, Kati. "Female Clergy as Agents of Religious Change?" *Religions* 2, no. 3 (2011): 358-71.

Nilsen Lein, Bente. *Kirken i felttog mot kvinnefrigjøring: Kirkens holdning til den borgerlige kvinnebevegelsen i 1880-årene.* Oslo/Bergen/Trondheim: Universitetsforlaget, 1981.

Stendal, Synnøve Hinnaland. *"…under forvandlingens lov": En analyse av stortingsdebatten om kvinnelige prester i 1930-årene.* Lund: Arcus, 2013.

Södling, Maria. "Inga kvinna synes än: En historia om kvinnliga präster." In *Äntligen stod hon i predikstolen! Historiskt vägval 1958,* edited by Boel Hössjer Sundman, 181-92. Stockholm: Verbum, 2008.

Tønnessen, Aud V. *"…et trygt og godt hjem for alle?" Kirkelederes kritikk av velferdsstaten etter 1945.* Trondheim: Tapir forlag, 2000.

Tønnessen, Aud V. *Ingrid Bjerkås: Motstandskvinnen som ble vår første kvinnelige prest.* Oslo: Pax forlag, 2014.

8. Minority, Media, and Law: Reality TV, Orthodox Canon Law, Finnish and European Jurisprudence

Johan Bastubacka

Introduction—Primarily Orthodox?

His Eminence Archbishop Leo reminded the Finnish Orthodox commmunity in a newspaper-interview in 2015 that their primary responsibility was to understand their identity and loyalties firstly with respect to Orthodoxy and only secondly to their nationality as Finns, as members of the national community. "The members of our Church, as for their identity, are firstly Orthodox, and only secondly Finnish."[1] The statement was his response to the media coverage of the controversial issue of a Lutheran female bishop's visit to the sanctuary of the Ouspensky Cathedral during the Divine Liturgy.[2]

By publishing this statement in the media, the Archbishop also publicly raised certain significant problems relating to the interpretation and jurisprudence of religious law. How can the two legal cultures that define Orthodoxy in Finland—Orthodox canon law and Finnish legislation on the Orthodox minority—be connected to one another? Moreover, what does it mean to be "primarily Orthodox"?

This question has become current specifically in those cases in which Orthodox legal understanding and jurisprudence have publicly appeared to be or been represented as appearing to be in tension or contradiction with evolving notions of peoples' equal rights. They primarily concern the principles of human rights agreements and the relationship of national and European legislation to these agreements. The internationalization and Europeanization of Finnish (and

---

1 Martti Ripaoja, "Kirkkomme jäsenet ovat identiteetiltään ensisijaisesti ortodokseja ja vasta sitten suomalaisia," *Savon Sanomat*, March 3, 2015, https://www.savonsanomat.fi/kotimaa/Arkkipiispa-Leo-%C3%A4r%C3%A4hti-piispa-Irjasta-alttarilla/530291.
2 See also Katarina Baer and Marjo Valtavaara, "Ortodoksien oppiriita pahenee pääsiäisen alla," *Helsingin Sanomat*, April 4, 2015, A14-15.

Nordic) law in the post-World War II era have become discernible in these issues. Moreover, the notion of "Nordic secularity" is also significant in this context.

Several cases have been covered in the Finnish media during the past ten years. The three best-known of them demonstrated problems related to aspects of priestly life: political rights, second marriage, and the above-mentioned liturgical and ecumenical openness concerning ecumenism and a female Lutheran bishop.[3]

This chapter analyzes one of these media-cases or media events in terms of aspects of Orthodox legal culture: the deposition of one Orthodox priest ("Father X") who remarried after becoming a widower. How was that "problem" or "event" represented and framed on Finnish nationwide TV? And how was the minority's legal culture framed and reflected in the one, most prominent media product concerning this one case? What was understood, omitted, and misunderstood, and how? Finally, I also consider how media publicity was related to the different aspects of the jurisprudence of the case.

By studying one case in terms of both media analysis[4] and legal analysis, I want to shed light on the framing of minority religion in contemporary media, and specifically the framing of the minority religion's legal culture and its different aspects. One legal case that involved Eastern canon law, national legislation, European agreements, ecclesiastical and secular and national jurisprudence was reflected in nationwide media-publicity. This "event" may be interpreted as highlighting the diverse components of a legal culture in formation, the connections of and boundaries between Orthodox canon law, Finnish secular law, and European human rights law.

Kevin Glynn has said: "Tabloid television is often taken to task for ostensibly ignoring issues around party politics and government policy making. What the tabloid media may lack in attention to the official political system, however, they make up for with their intense interest in the gender politics of everyday life."[5] Even though it was written for other contexts, this analysis is also largely

---

3   See Jussi Pullinen, "Mitro Repo hakee KHO:sta kieltoa pappipannalleen," *Helsingin Sanomat*, May 30, 2009, https://www.hs.fi/kotimaa/art-2000004656051.html; Bishop Ambrosius, "Piispa Irja Askolan vierailu Uspenskissa oli kaunis ekumeeninen ystävyyden ele," *Helsingin Sanomat*, March 14, 2015, https://www.hs.fi/mielipide/art-2000002808409.html. The second-mentioned case is analyzed in this chapter.
4   See the analytical ideas presented by John Fiske according to Henry Jenkins's introduction "Why Fiske Still Matters," to *Introduction to Communication Studies,* by John Fiske (New York: Routledge, 2011), esp. XXV–XXVII; John Fiske, *Introduction to Communication Studies* (New York: Routledge, 2011) esp. 80-106.
5   Kevin Glynn, *Tabloid Culture, Trash Taste, Popular Power, and the Transformation of American Television* (Durham NC: Duke University Press, 2000), 132.

fitting with regard to this Finnish case. Moreover, the strategies of representation and media production could be conceptualized in terms of sensationalism, a striving to present the ordinary as extraordinary.[6] But, 21st-century reality TV can also be understood as epitomizing certain characteristics that in detail are also meaningful for this one Finnish example:

> The driving force of reality TV shows was thus broadened from competition to challenge, a term which can equally mean an oppositional encounter, a test of one's abilities, or a stimulating task with a set goal. All three of these aspects are folded into second-generation reality TV shows, with US formats tending more heavily to goal-orientation as the basis for personal growth and UK formats tending more to the test as the basis of sociological experimentation. In either case, the challenge as a stimulating task—whether this involves scaling a wall or solving one's personal problems—underwrites the bulk of these formats.[7]

Yet, as Misha Kavka points out, while producers and audiences seem to know relatively clearly what reality TV is, the academic circumscribing and defining of the phenomenon suffers from the complexity of the genre or, more precisely, changing genres.[8]

This mixture of peering into one's personal relationship problems and the representation of efforts to "solve" or reconcile people with local societies was clearly one of the motivations for creating and broadcasting this one media-product—apart from purely economic and other media-productional interests. For example, a somewhat similar reality TV format was found in Sweden in the series "Priests Looking for Love" that was broadcast on April 6, 2017.[9] The tone of that later production was, however, much lighter and dealt less, if at all, with obstacles and ostracizing.

Ethical Issues and the Focus of the Chapter

Since I am writing on one particular contemporary media case involving actual, living persons, their relatives, and people close to them, as well as the theme of ostracizing people, I want to consider carefully the protection of their privacy

---

6   Chris Frost, *Media Ethics and Self-Regulation* (Harlow: Longman, 2000), 19.
7   Misha Kavka, *Reality TV* (Edinburg: Edinburgh University Press, 2012), 112.
8   Kavka, *Reality TV*, 2, 5-6.
9   *Tro, Hopp och Kärlek: Präster letar efter kärleken*, Sveriges Television, April 4, 2017, https://www.svt.se/tro-hopp-och-karlek/.

and their well-being. I will focus on those aspects that they themselves have decided to make public in terms of one reality TV program. As far as legal and administrative documents are concerned, no personal information concerning the people involved will be published in this chapter, including the name of the priest involved and his close people. The judicial documents in the case will be used primarily to point out the this-far-procedure of the case. Some of them, moreover, have been designated as secret.[10] Regarding these documents, my analysis reveals nothing that was not already known publicly.

Even though they are private persons, the main characters of the reality TV episode have decided to reveal certain aspects of their private lives to the media. Thus, in my interpretation, they have been involved in a process of creating publicity that in itself is the subject of my research. Because the Finnish Orthodox community comprises a relatively small minority (some 60,000 people), including a network of acquaintances, friendships, and family ties, even a full anonymization does not hide the fact that the case took place. It was presented and discussed on public media both locally and nationally, and many people know the main characters.

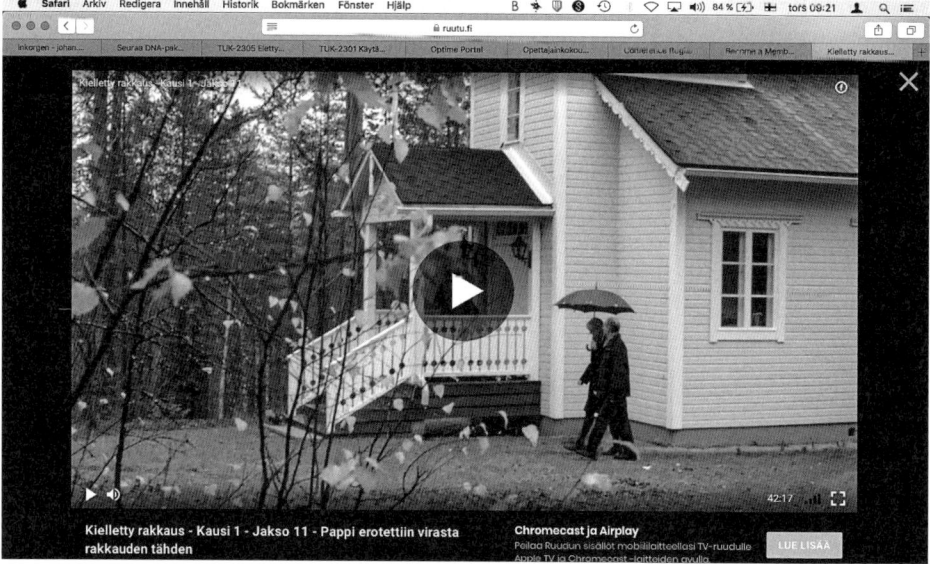

Picture 1. The webpage of episode 11 of the reality TV-program "Forbidden Love"

---

10 Esp. the document: Eduskunnan oikeusasiamiehen kanslia, Dnro 810/4/13 Res.fin Salaiset asiakirjat.

The Framework, Broadcasting, and Main Theme of a Reality TVProgram

In terms of Finnish reality TV programs, a new series emerged in national broadcasting on a commercial TV channel on March 19, 2016. The program *Kielletty rakkaus* (Forbidden Love) began featuring stories on difficult, contradictory love stories that were in one way or another despised or problematical in the eyes of the local community. The program format is of local, Finnish origin, but bears a definite resemblance to certain contemporary soap operas that feature socially ostracized or difficult love stories.[11] The show is still being broadcast as of 2019.

Each episode consists of segments in which the program host meets and interviews or talks with a couple, usually in their home and places significant to them, arranges for them to have contact with potentially estranged family or friends, and sets up a reunion (if possible). These events are framed by interventions by the program host and a psychotherapist. The role of the therapist is to describe, in a compassionate and understanding manner, the psychological and emotional stress and processes the couple and those close to them have gone through. She gives general and specific advice on how to cope in demanding psychological situations. The therapist actually acts as an absent counsellor (she only comments on the situation, never encountering the couple in person) but can also subtly take a moral stand by explaining and interpreting the difficult or impossible situation of the people involved. She speaks on their behalf and creates understanding for them. The overall mode of presentation is one of psychologizing, understanding, and supporting the individual against all community and structural hindrances of their "unusual love"—a notion that is thus actually outlined by this reality television program.[12]

Each episode is a tightly edited unit usually consisting of four larger sections, separated by commercials, beginning and interluding inserts. An episode is made to fit into an approximately 40-minute timeframe. Taken together, commercial breaks occupy several minutes. Musical elements provide color and frame the show.

The program series was launched on March 14, 2016 on the Finnish com-

---

11 *Kielletty Rakkaus*, Nelonen, accessed January 18, 2019 https://www.nelonen.fi/ohjelmat/kielletty-rakkaus/2132545-camilla-auttoi-miestaan-tulemaan-jessicaksi-han-auttoi-minua-vapautumaan.
12 *Kielletty Rakkaus*, Nelonen, accessed January 18, 2019 https://www.nelonen.fi/ohjelmat/kielletty-rakkaus/2132545-camilla-auttoi-miestaan-tulemaan-jessicaksi-han-auttoi-minua-vapautumaan.

mercial TV channel 4 (*Nelonen*). Within this framework, the story of one former Orthodox priest was broadcast as episode 11. It was rebroadcast several times and still remains (as of June 2019) in the digital archives of the Nelonen TV channel. There it can easily be viewed online.[13]

The main theme of the program can be defined as the obstacles to love and the right to remarry involving one Finnish Orthodox priest—now a former priest, since he was deposed and laicized.

Characters, Roles, and Scenes

In the program, the former "Father X" (always called by first name only) was presented together with his second partner in marriage, an elderly woman, who was presented in a similar manner by her first name as Y. They were undeniably the two lead characters of the program. "Y, age, and X, age, from the region of Z."[14]

In order of appearance, the characters and their main roles in the episode were: the program host Anni Hautala (female, a known radio host), X (male, ex-priest, widower), Y (female, his wife, widow), the psychotherapist Maaret Kallio (female, expert, absent from the meetings with the couple), V and W (obviously a couple, friends of Y and X, Orthodox parish members), Professor Jukka Korpela (expert, University of Eastern Finland[15], in a skype-interview). It is a well-known fact within the Orthodox community that Korpela is also a deacon in the Orthodox Church of Finland, but this knowledge of his dual role was not revealed in the show.

Of these, the host, Y, and X regularly interacted in the show, whereas their friend couple were briefly interviewed, and the expert professor appeared only once via a web-camera interview organized by the host. The psychotherapist always spoke directly only to the TV viewers and appeared on the show four times in total. In the promotion video, the host and the therapist claimed that they strove to support all the couples. Thus, the perspective of the show and the roles of the two lead figures was firmly set already at the beginning: both

---

13 "Kielletty rakkaus (2016)," Elonet, Kansallisfilmografia, accessed January 18, 2019, https://www.elonet.fi/fi/elokuva/1571913.
14 The episode was initially broadcast 2on March 25, 2016 at 16:15 h. See "Pappi erotettiin virasta rakkauden tähden: Kausi 1—jakso 11," *Kielletty Rakkaus*, Nelonen/ruutu.fi, accessed January 18, 2019, https://www.ruutu.fi/video/2625166.
15 Jukka Korpela, see "Jukka Korpela (historioitsija)," *Wikipedia*, accessed January 20, 2019, https://fi.wikipedia.org/wiki/Jukka_Korpela_(historioitsija).

the host and the therapist wanted to support and defend the couple—their togetherness and love.

No officials or bishops of the local or any Orthodox church, nor any (other than the ex-priest) Orthodox theologians were among the characters or interviewees. The Metropolitan of Oulu[16] was mentioned (not by name) as was Leo, at the time Archbishop of Karelia and all of Finland[17]. Yet, since their actions were reflected in the show, ecclesiastical law and jurisprudence framed the entire display.

The roles of these characters functioned in different ways. X and Y were depicted and presented as victims and as suffering individuals. The role of the program host was specifically one of raising questions, emphasizing, and directing the focus of the episode. The figure of the host was necessary to create a storyline and to keep the story going, whereas the experts created reflective pauses and lacunae for consideration. The experts were portrayed as authoritative professionals who had the power to interpret the good of the people and the course of history.

V and W, a couple and friends of Y and X, were also interviewed in the episode. Their role in the casting of the episode was to support the deposed priest as parish members. V related that he had asked during the local bishop's visitation about the potential restoration of X's priesthood, but never got any response to his questions—even in the minutes of the visitation. The role of V and W was one of representing and personifying supporting, confused, and also dissatisfied parish members.

Anonymous aggressive co-workers and parish members were mentioned in dialogue, but they did not appear in person in the show. They were described as aggressive and ruthless opponents. The whole setting of characters was relatively dualist: the suffering individuals versus the harassing and pressing church members. Thus, the program gave the TV viewer little space to critically ponder the whole setting or the viewpoints and fragments of stories presented, but instead created a setting that was predetermined to be in support of the suffering individual and to lament the non-understanding ecclesiastics and laypeople.

The main scenes and locations that feature as background, create moods, and provoke thought in the encounters of this reality TV show are: 1) outdoors, river, road and courtyard (host arriving), 2) the home or living room of Y and X

---

16 "Panteleimon Oulun emeritus metropoliitta," Ortodoksi.net, accessed June 24, 2019, http://www.ortodoksi.net/index.php/Panteleimon_Oulun_emeritus_metropoliitta.
17 "Henkilötiedot," Archbishop of Helsinki and All Finland, accessed June 24, 2019, https://ort.fi/arkkipiispa/info/henkilotiedot.

(cozy, homely space), 3) the psychologist on a living room sofa, 4) a home altar (icon corner of the home), 5) the outdoors, W and Z together, 6) on the road, in Sweden, local Lutheran parish church exterior in Sweden, 7) a cemetery, 8) a beach, 9) in nature, in darkness, 10) images of Skype video calls, 11) arriving at a wooden Orthodox church (outside the building), and 12) an Orthodox cemetery. The show ends in the couple's home living room as they lovingly hold each other.

In terms of this imagery, home is juxtaposed with the place of death, while the church exterior (closed reality) is juxtaposed with the open home, with its icon corner. Finally, nature, road, forest, and water functioned in a very typical Finnish manner as the great canvas for human existence. This "staged authenticity"[18] was constructed as a frame for the representation of the second layer: human emotion, loss, struggle and, specifically, love. As presented above, in a typical reality TV manner, personal struggle was portrayed as a challenge to be overcome.

Orthodox Religion as an Obstacle to Love— A Peculiarity to be Observed

The two widowed people, Y and X, had encountered each other on "social media" and met in person due to their common hobby: photography in the wild nature of Lapland. They began dating and were married in 2013. The program gave no more precise description of their wedding—whether it was ecclesiastical or civil.[19]

In terms of the narration of the program, everything took place within an apparent time frame of three years. X's wife passed away, the couple met and started to date, parish members and colleagues reacted negatively, the bishop suspended the priest in the autumn of 2011, and the local Finnish synod of bishops deposed the priest in 2012.

In the broadcast episode, X related that he wanted to remarry and to keep or rather to be reinstated in his clerical position and duties. The TV show created a documentary perspective and an impression of authenticity concerning highly personal, yet simultaneously societal, and also legal and ecclesiastical issues.

The emotional pain of the ex-priest caused by the loss of his priesthood, ecclesiastical position, certain social relationships, and the lifestyle of a priest

---

18   Kavka, *Reality TV*, 160.
19   "Pappi erotettiin virasta," at 8:25, 9:20, 14:50 min.

were depicted in a lamenting atmosphere. The ex-priest was anxious about the possibility he had lost to perform sacred services for family members and friends, and the couple were portrayed as critical and utterly dissatisfied with the decisions of the church officials. Affliction and sorrow were caused by the comments of certain parish members and the breaking of relationships with them. Worst of all was a prohibition from joining the Easter night service. The person or persons issuing this prohibition were not identified.

The main point of the episode was pointing out the unfairness of the process, the invaluable nature of new love after personal loss, and the problem created by a religious tradition that could hinder people from loving each other and living together openly. Institutional religion was basically depicted as an outdated set of systems that needed renewal—although this conclusion was never directly articulated in the show. It can, however, be easily recognized as a more indirect and subtler message of the program. This perspective was established and emphasized especially by the interventions and questions of the program host. For example, she would say: "Apparently the reason [of the turmoil] is that Orthodox priests are not allowed to remarry", or "What!", or "Are you disappointed?"[20]

The former priest stated modestly that the initial meeting with his new spouse was "proper and nice", whereas subsequent meetings with parish members when he was in the company of his new beloved could be "surprising and shocking", and colleagues could give "unprintable comments" and "relatively cruel text," even during the conduct of the Divine Liturgy. According to the episode narrative, an "additional difficulty" was the concurrent administrative process of transferring X's priestly and pastoral office from the countryside to the largest city of the region. He did not want to leave his beloved rural surroundings. "It has been decided that the office is to be transferred to --. Given this, it doesn't matter, what I do," he stated.[21]

The critique made by X had to do with the administrative decisions made by the local metropolitan and the Finnish Orthodox Bishops' Synod. X related that he had opposed the metropolitan on the occasion of his suspension, saying: "This is your view, others may do what they like." The bishop was said to have replied: "You have made your decision, I wish you all the best." According to X, as priest he had thus committed "the worst act of all"—criticizing and opposing episcopal authority.[22]

---

20 "Pappi erotettiin virasta, at 2:20, 12:15, 16:30 min
21 "Pappi erotettiin virasta," at 11:30, 12:50, 27:00 min.
22 "Pappi erotettiin virasta," at 13:20 min.

The sharpest tones and critical voices came from X and Y in the middle of and near the end of the episode; thus, the program was constructed to create an effective drama out of the stories of the people. Y went on to state that it would have been easier to have a gay relationship in the church with a priest than a heterosexual one. According to her, such relationships were more tolerated. When the program host asked for evidence of what she had said, she plainly let the host (and viewers) understand that there were other people who had broken their celibacy.[23]

According to X, only "certain people," not the church, had turned their backs on him. He still wanted to ask the bishops to show "love that goes beyond laws and paragraphs" and "forgiveness, love, and compassion".[24] The program host conducted a Skype conversation with the other expert appearing in the episode, Korpela, Professor of General History at the University of Eastern Finland, who gave an online mini-lecture about the development of marriage law and the idea of sacramental marriage in Eastern and Western Europe. Korpela concluded by pointing out that episcopal jurisprudence should not depend on "the mood one [the bishop] happens to be in [at the moment of decision-making]".[25]

The couple related that they had also been harassed, avoided, and ostracized as heretics. The program host concluded the climax of the show by stating that the otherwise totally absent or excluded part of the issue, church administration and leadership, the archbishop in person, had forbidden anyone to comment on the issue. The host stated: "As far as I understand, Archbishop Leo has forbidden anyone to comment."[26]

The final minutes of the show consisted of more peaceful reflections on the significant constructive issues of life. The show ended with the pair holding each other lovingly in their home. Orthodox jurisprudence concerning the boundaries for priestly love and intimacy were depicted as being peculiar in contemporary modern society, and specifically the hindrances it created for priests' second marriages were portrayed as an outdated demand that had already been violated numerous times.[27]

However, some consideration was given to the Orthodox tradition and the meaning of the limitation of the number of priests' marriages. Professor Korpela's presentation emphasized the significance of the emerging, historical

---

23 "Pappi erotettiin virasta," at 14:30, 24:20 min.
24 "Pappi erotettiin virasta," at 28:40 min.
25 "Pappi erotettiin virasta," at 30:40 min.
26 "Pappi erotettiin virasta," at 38:10 min.
27 "Pappi erotettiin virasta," at 25:10, 38:40 min.

idea of sacramental marriage and its impact on the regulation of the lives of those people who conducted sacramental marriages. In addition, the host, Hautala, actually critically pointed out the complexity of the setting of the program by either stating to X or posing a question to him in the middle of one conversation: "You knew well the stipulations of the church[?]".[28]—The interpretation of the host's intention depends on the interpretation of the nuances of the utterance.

Legal, Jurisprudential, and Theological Dimensions of the Episode

Orthodox Tradition

This brief statement of the host cited above referred to the fact that all candidates for the Orthodox priesthood basically know that if they want to marry, marriage will have to take place before their ordination to the office of deacon, and that marriage can take place only once in a priest's life.[29] When discussing the stipulation on marrying, X did not actually criticize the stipulation itself as somehow alien or dysfunctional. What he did criticize was the strictness (*akribeia*[30]) with which the stipulation was applied to him. The sharp commentaries by Y especially reveal this aspect: honesty in public relationships was—in their experience—rewarded with public punishment.

While the issue was presented in the program as not open to discussion, the issue has actually been discussed in the meetings of Orthodox primates. The 1923 Pan-Orthodox Congress in Constantinople had prepared to discuss the issue of deacons' and priests' second marriages, but the theme was deleted from the schedule of the meeting. Yet, according to Anne Jensen, it may still have been discussed under another title, "hindrances for marriage".[31] At the second pre-

---

28 "Pappi erotettiin virasta," at 26:50 min.
29 *Ortodoksisen kirkon kanonit selityksineen [Pravila pravoslavne crkve s tumačenjima][Canons of the Orthodox Church and Interpretations]*, trans. Antti Inkinen (Helsinki: Ortodoksisen kirjallisuuden julkaisuneuvosto, 1980), 64-66 (canons 17 an 18 of the Apostles and *hermeneia*), 370 (in Trullo 26 and *hermeneia*), 372-73 (in Trullo 30 and *hermeneia*); Panteleimon Rodopoulos, *An Overview of Orthodox Canon Law* (Rollinsford, NH: Orthodox Research Institute, 2007), 126-27.
30 On the significant Orthodox legal hermeneutic concepts akribeia and economy, see Jérôme Kotsonis, *Problèmes de l'économie ecclésiastique* (Gembloux: Éditions J. Duculot, 1971), 33-36, 97-99. See also Frank Gavin, *Some Aspects of Contemporary Greek Orthodox Thought* (New York: AMS Press, 1970), 262-63.
31 Anne Jensen, *Die Zukunft der Orthodoxie, Konzilspläne und Kirchenstrukturen* (Zürich: Benziger, 1986), 25-26.

conciliar meeting in Chambésy in 1982, the preparatory committee had created texts that also included a draft text from 1971. The first part examined marriage between Orthodox people as well as the question of the marriage of priests. The commission that prepared the text proposing marriage after ordination as well as second marriage for priests. The 1971 recommendations were accepted for the 1982 preconference, but they did not gain support: only a minority spoke in favor of these reformulations.[32]

The canonical basis for discussion is challenging and requires scholarship concerning Orthodox canonical hermeneutics. Canon 17 of the Canons of the Apostles laconically stipulates that, after baptism, a second marriage makes a person unsuited for priesthood. Canon 18 forbids functioning as a priest if one has married a widow, an abandoned wife, a prostitute, maidservant, or actress. Thus, the text is archaic and historical. The Finnish 1980 translation of the canons gives also a translation of an 1895 and 1896 Serbian commentary. Concerning canon 17, the text refers to the council in Trullo canon 3 (held in the year 692) and the Canons of St. Basil the Great (329-379), canon 12, and discusses the issue in light of the 18th-century compilation the *Pedalion* the "Rudder"[33], in particular Theodore Balsamon's (c. 1130/40–c. 1195) interpretations. The intent of the commentary is to illuminate prohibitions and emphasize their meaning, not so much to discuss or question the principles of their interpretation.[34]

In view of these canons and their *hermeneia*, the TV program subtly introduced the major theological discussion about the principles of *oikonomia* and *akribeia* in traditional Orthodox jurisprudence, and also pointed out that in Eastern Canon Law not all members of the church were subject to the same rights and responsibilities. Moreover, it presented critical perspectives on the Orthodox way of life and its ideal and practical solutions in terms of realizing family life and sexuality.

In the Orthodox tradition, bishops are expected to be celibate, which means being either monks or widowed, and priests and deacons are required either to remain celibate or to marry before ordination. For the most part, the parish clergy are not celibate. A widowed priest is supposed to live a single and celibate life. Kyprian Kern says: "the union of the priest with his flock is a lasting union, just as the principle of marriage; neither can be dissolved … But there is yet another, a more important characteristic to this sacrament: priesthood—as

---

32   Jensen, *Die Zukunft der Orthodoxie*, 43.
33   On the "History and Character of the *Pedalion*", see David Heith-Stade, *The Rudder of the Church: A Study of the Theory of Canon Law in the Pedalion* (Lund: Lund University, Centre for Theology and Religious Studies, 2014), 16-24.
34   *Ortodoksisen kirkon kanonit*, 64-66.

taught by Roman Catholics, is ingrained. The Greek theologians hold the same opinion."[35]

Ascesis, "exercise," is also theologically an integral part of the idea of marriage: in marriage, people are supposed to refrain from time to time from sexual contact, for example, in times of preparation to receive the Eucharist, on the day of receiving the Sacrament, and during (deep) Lent. Weddings are never conducted during Great Lent or any deeper Lent, which in the Eastern calendar makes up a great part of the ecclesiastical year.[36] Everybody is supposed to practice faithfulness and to seek to avoid the power of enslaving passions, whether of a sexual or of some other nature. In Byzantium, it was customary for elderly couples to enter monasteries by joint decision in the latter part of their lives.[37]

However, these actions are usually not closely supervised or controlled, but are rather modes of conduct and ideals that are regarded as built-in to an Orthodox way of life. Theological presentations of the priestly office and life can be surprisingly idealistic and focused on the theological-sacramental aspect of the office.[38]

Nicholas Afanasiev has written: "If the power founded upon love is insufficient in actual life, which has lost the principle of love, it is on the contrary completely sufficient in the Church, where love is the first and the last principle. Judicial power is a substitute for love in actual social life."[39]

For laypeople, the more lenient Greek and Byzantine tradition, in which a layperson, after repentance, is allowed to enter into a second or potentially even third marriage, has its counterpart in the stricter Russian practice, in which it is more difficult to receive a divorce in ecclesiastical court. Traditionally, the second or even third wedding services have been conducted in the Eastern rite with a

---

35   Kyprian Kern, "Pastoral Christian Ministry," in *Called to Serve, Readings on Ministry from the Orthodox Church*, ed. William C. Mills (St. Paul, MN: OCABS Press, 2016), 121; Helen L. Parish, *Clerical Celibacy in the West, c. 1100-1700* (Farnham: Ashgate, 2010), 59, 75-76.
36   See instructions, "Paastoajat," Ortotoksi.net, accessed June 24, 2019, http://www.ortodoksi.net/index.php/Paastoajat.
37   See Gavin, *Some Aspects*, 378-79, 386; Hilarion Alfejev, *Trons Mysterium: En introduktion till den ortodoxa kyrkans troslära och andlighet* (Skellefteå/Södertälje: Artos & Norma, 2002), 224-25; Thomas Bremer, Hacik Rafi Gazer, and Christian Lange, eds., *Die orthodoxen Kirchen der byzantinischen Tradition* (Darmstadt: WBG, 2013), 129-30. See also "Sakramentit eli mysteeriot," Suomen ortodoksinen kirkko, accessed January 19, 2019, https://ort.fi/tutustu-ortodoksiseen-kirkkoon/sakramentit-eli-mysteeriot. On the "ascetic impulse" in the early church and its impact in the East, and yet the continuous practice of married Orthodox clergy, see Parish, *Clerical Celibacy*, 60-86.
38   See, e.g., Nicholas Afanasiev, *The Church of the Holy Spirit* (Notre Dame, IN: University of Notre Dame Press, 2007), 273-74.
39   Afanasiev, *The Church*, 274.

different ritual in comparison to the first wedding: without crowning and with asking for forgiveness and a new beginning. However, even a second or third marriage has been regarded as sacramentally valid.[40]

As to how a required code of conduct has been realized in practice, this code has often been subject to local conditions, personal solutions, and decisions. This was also one of the core issues in the deposed Father X's complaint, as we shall see below.[41] In the Orthodox tradition, the church actually very late, if ever, gained a position from which it could regulate the conduct of married life with the same efficiency as in Western Christendom.[42] In contemporary Orthodox thought, it is customary to hear statements about the supposed "realism" of Orthodox thinking in terms of people's sexual lives. The ideals can be high, yet the lack of realization of these ideals in human efforts can be understood, however, with empathy. Kern says: "the Orthodox priest must be inspired by faith in man ... Characteristically, pastoral counseling should strive to overcome the evil in the world and in man with goodness and love rather than with accusations and condemnations."[43]

The reality TV program gave minimal room to the reflection of these principles. It questioned the significance of the traditional Orthodox way of life as juxtaposed with contemporary Western individualism and, in addition, juxtaposed bishops' ecclesiastical jurisprudence with people's personal decisions over their life issues. It also made the decision of the ecclesiastical court a matter of public discussion.

However, in the program, the former priest remained loyal to the church and its canons in the sense that he criticized episcopal jurisprudence and called for leniency (*oikonomia*), but did not openly juxtapose the canons with Finnish legislation or contemporary agreements on human rights. Interestingly, the canons and the tradition of the church were mentioned in the program, but not Finnish or any contemporary legislation or legal culture as if in contrast to *the*

---

40 See, e.g., Gavin, *Some Aspects*, 385-86. Bremer, Gazer, and Lange, *Die orthodoxen Kirchen*, 129-30; Jelisei Heikkilä, *Canonical Development through Dialogue: Marriage and Divorce in the Pre-Conciliar Period and in the All-Russian Church Council of 1917-1918* (Helsinki: University of Helsinki, Faculty of Theology, 2015), 17-19. See also the Finnish-language *Euhologion* online: "Euhologion (käsikirja)," Ortodoksi.net, accessed January 18, 2019, http://www.ortodoksi.net/index.php/Euhologion_(käsikirja).

41 See the chapter below: *Jurisprudence: Deposition of a Priest and the Response of the Ombudsman*.

42 Especially among the Slavs, where the tradition of common law marriage without church blessing was usual and prominent in the medieval era up to the 17th century. See Eve Levin, *Sex and Society in the World of the Orthodox Slavs, 900-1700* (Ithaca, NY: Cornell University Press, 1989), 83-88.

43 Kern, "Pastoral Christian Ministry," 103.

complaint made to the Ombudsman by X. In the complaint, however, these perspectives emerged as a major focus.[44] Probably, this was a question of strategic choices relevant in the situation: in which arena to make argumentation and on what basis, in view of the possibility of success.

Finnish Legislation on the Orthodox Church

Canon law was incorporated into Finnish legislation concerning the Orthodox Church in the 19th and 20th centuries. Initially in 1918, and in more detail in 1925 government decrees, the new nation-state wanted both to cooperate with the nationalist section of the church and to integrate the institution into the republic by creating for it a position as the second, minority national church. In accordance with the Tomos given by the Patriarch of Constantinople in 1923, canon law was not to be in open contradiction to Finnish legislation, but there existed an effort to merge different legal cultures and traditions. Government decrees on the church contained numerous direct and indirect references to the canons.[45] To what extent this effort was successful and in what manner is a question open to scholarly discussion.

Chapter 5 of the no. 206 Government Decree on the "Orthodox Denomination" (issued May 15, 1953), presents the essentials, institutions, and practices of ecclesiastical jurisprudence. In terms of the 1953 decree, no direct or indirect references are to be found on the issue of priestly marriages. Chapter 5 §85 denotes with no further exactness the potentially "indecent life" of priests, deacons, and monks (nuns are not on the list), of which the punishment was to be deposition from office. In the case of these accusations and issues, the upper ecclesiastical court was to act as the only court level: no lower ecclesiastical court ruling was necessary.[46]

The 8.8.1969/521 Law on the Orthodox Denomination (hereafter LOC1969), the first ever Finnish law on the minority state church, continued in a similarly scant manner concerning the issue. Chapter 6 on "correction proceedings" also presented the "correction board" with more detailed prescriptions for its work.[47] It now took the place and functions of the previous lower ecclesiastical court

---

44 X's complaint, Dnro 810/4/13, Office of the Ombudsman.
45 Johan Bastubacka, "Mirroring the Majority? The Emerging Legal Understanding on Finnish Orthodoxy in terms of the 1925 Government Decree" (article submitted for publication, 2018).
46 The 1953 Decree on the Orthodox Denomination, §85, 455-56.
47 Finnish *ojennusmenettely*, and *ojennuslautakunta*. See 8.8.1969/521 Law on the Orthodox Denomination (abolished), ch. 6, §42, Finlex Data Bank, accessed January 21, 2019, https://finlex.fi/fi/laki/ajantasa/kumotut/1969/19690521.

and was also to judge in cases of priestly actions that were regarded as contradicting the obligations of the priestly office or as indecent behavior. No more specific regulations regarding what was to be considered "indecent" appear in the stipulation. The board could depose a priest, and one could appeal its decisions to the upper ecclesiastical court, but otherwise no specific guidelines for judging indecency were prescribed.

In the next stipulation, the 10.11.2006/985 Law on the Orthodox Church (hereafter LOC2006), §109, on "the general obligations of priest, deacon, and cantor," stated that a priest may not teach against the doctrine of the church, either in a sermon or otherwise spread opinions that are "contradictory to the confession and canonical structure of the church". The demeanor of a priest must be "in work assignments and also outside of them realized in a manner proper to his position". Moreover, §111 stipulated that a violation of the principles of §109 could lead to suspension or deposition depending on the seriousness of the offence. Deposition or a long suspension were defined to be issued by the local bishops' meeting, which was to act as the upper level ecclesiastical court.[48]

The 2007 Church Order of the Orthodox Church complements certain aspects concerning the LOC2006. Paragraph 2 states that "the priesthood of the church is based on the requirements given in the canons and a sacramental consecration". According to §63, the bishop of a diocese oversees that priests act according to LOC2006 §109.[49]

Altogether, the Finnish legislation on the issue of indecency or acting against traditional Orthodox notions regarding marriage, celibacy, and how a priest should conduct his life in terms of these issues, is sketched out in an elementary manner. The punishments are clearly defined, but the offences are not specified in the law or in the church order. Thus, infrequent and general references to canon law—not to specific canons—became very significant in terms of these stipulations. After 2006, the interpretation of the canons then took place only in the jurisdiction and jurisprudence of the diocesan bishop and also the Local Bishops' Synod. It remained their obligation and task to define what was deemed indecent for a priest, in accordance with traditional Orthodox jurisprudence and previous interpretations.

---

48   10.11.2006/985 Law on the Orthodox Church, §109, §111, Finlex Data Bank, accessed January 20, 2019, https://www.finlex.fi/fi/laki/ajantasa/2006/20060985.
49   12.12.2006/174 v. 2007 the Church Order of the Orthodox Church, §2, §63, Finlex Data Bank, accessed January 20, 2019, https://www.finlex.fi/fi/laki/ajantasa/2007/20070174?search%5Btype%5D=pika&search%5Bpika%5D=ortodoksisen%20kirkon%20kirkkojärjestys.

Consequently, Finnish national legislation provided an open, relatively autonomous space for the minority's own jurisprudence that can be compared to the legal requirements stipulated concerning state officials in their offices. Chapter 4 of the 19.8.1994/750 Law on State Officials defines the obligations of the state official in the following manner: to promote equality, freedom to join associations, to enjoy pertinent salary, rights, and advantages, to perform dutifully, to act in accordance with one's position, to avoid one's own benefit in duty (against bribery), and to avoid contradictions in certain positions in public life with one's office and its obligations. There are also stipulations on publicity about the official and side businesses, health, and moving offices to other places.[50] Moreover, a potential deposition of the official is strictly regulated in § 25, which also protects the freedom of political, religious, and other opinions.

"To act in accordance with one's position", is an expression that resembles the wording of the legislator of the Orthodox stipulations. Regarding these, the effort has obviously been both to create a legal basis for jurisprudence and potential deposition and, simultaneously, to oblige the ecclesiastical courts and pertinent officials to develop the necessary interpretation for each case and context.

However, after 2006, the 1994 law no longer regulated the priests of the Orthodox Church of Finland. From the time of the 1925 Decree to the LOC1969, they were regarded as state officials, but after the LOC2006 only as employees of the church. The position was removed, and the offices of the Orthodox church in Finland thus became more than before the church's own matter and a matter of its own canonical interpretation, in particular.

Jurisprudence: Deposition of a Priest and the Response of the Ombudsman

The documents of the office of the Parliamentary Ombudsman of Finland and the protocol of the Bishops' Synod[51] shed light on the process of deposition that X was subjected to. He had worked as a priest in a parish for approximately 30 years. After becoming widowed, he started a new relationship, was harassed by co-workers and parish members, and decided to resign from his office "due to the intolerable situation". The local bishop proposed to the Bishops' Synod that he be suspended from exercising the priestly ministry for the following

---

50   19.8.1994/750 Law on State Officials, § 11–§ 22, Finlex Data Bank, accessed January 1, 2019, https://www.finlex.fi/fi/laki/ajantasa/1994/19940750?search%5Btype%5D=pika&search%5Bpika%5D=Virkamieslaki.

51   Dnro 220/2012, Ote piispainkokouksen pöytäkirjasta 6/12, Istunto 27.11.2012 klo 9.10-9.45 Valamon Kristuksen kirkastumisen luostarissa.

year and, after a year had passed, decided to depose X from the priesthood on the basis of his "changed life situation". According to the document, all these occurrences took place in the timespan of only approximately two years.[52]

The content of the complaint to the ombudsman by X emphasized the following proposed deficiencies with respect to the bishops' rights to interpret canons case by case, the restriction of appeals and, finally, the view of the Law on the Orthodox Church and ecclesiastical administration as being in contradiction with the other core elements of Finnish legislation and, specifically, people's fundamental rights, especially the Universal Declaration of Human Rights 1948, Article 16:

1. Men and women of full age, without any limitation due to race, nationality or religion, have the right to marry and to found a family. They are entitled to equal rights as to marriage, during marriage and at its dissolution.
2. Marriage shall be entered into only with the free and full consent of the intending spouses.
3. The family is the natural and fundamental group unit of society and is entitled to protection by society and the State.[53]

Canons and their interpretation by the traditional episcopal authority were viewed as an outdated practice that could not guarantee equal rights and unbiased ecclesiastical jurisprudence to the clergy. Finally, the complaint appealed to the ombudsman to take action to correct both the law and the ecclesiastical jurisprudence. "…I respectfully ask you to acquaint yourself with this issue and investigate the necessary actions in order to renovate the Finnish law on the Orthodox Church and its administrative culture for the benefit of guaranteeing the rights of Orthodox clergy and their families."[54] This request meant, in close reading, not only a petition to help correct administrative defects but actually a demand to the ombudsman to act on the very edge of or even beyond the powers and authority of a public servant. These aspects concerning the tone and content of the complaint probably reflected the writer or writers' desperation

---

52 X's complaint, Dnro 810/4/13; Ombudsman's Office, Dnro 810/4/13, Response to complaint.
53 United Nations General Assembly, *Universal Declaration of Human Rights*, 10 December 1948, 217 A (III).
54 "… pyydän teitä kunnioittavasti perehtymään asiaan ja ryhtymään tarvittaviin toimenpiteisiin Suomen ortodoksisen kirkon lain ja hallintokulttuurin korjaamiseksi sekä ortodoksisen papiston ja heidän perheidensä oikeuksien turvaamiseksi." X's complaint, Dnro 810/4/13.

and unfamiliarity with the legal system. The Parliamentary Ombudsman Act defines the remit of the official, especially in Section 11, as follows:

1. In a matter within the Ombudsman's remit, he or she may issue a recommendation to the competent authority that an error be redressed or a shortcoming rectified.
2. In the performance of his or her duties, the Ombudsman may draw the attention of the Government or another body responsible for legislative drafting to defects in legislation or official regulations, as well as make recommendations concerning the development of these and the elimination of the defects.[55]

The entire complaint was supplemented with detailed descriptions of occurrences, including meetings and citations from discussions with various people and the local bishop, and a number of appendices, of which only the statement of a local Lutheran hospital pastor has been preserved. All of the ecclesiastical documents were absent from the file.[56]

Altogether, the complaint portrayed the Finnish law system as deficient and basically inadequate with regard to the subject of Orthodox priesthood, which was a huge difference in comparison to the human life aspect and relatively mild criticism of the reality TV program. Different strategies were employed on different stages.

The response of the ombudsman started with an abbreviated review of the essential occurrences, references to the constitution and its essential application concerning the matter, the jurisprudence of the ombudsman and the obligations, powers, and limitations of the institution. Moreover, the law on administration, and the LOC2006 and its relevant paragraphs were reviewed: § 1, on the foundation of the church, § 26, on the obligations of the Bishops' Synod, § 39, on the bishop as the leader of the dioceses, § 106, on the restriction of appeals, § 109, on priestly (and other parish workers') obligation in their offices, and finally § 111, on punishments.[57]

The discussions of the Constitutional Law Committee from the years 1997 and 2006 were also reviewed. In terms of these excerpts, the committee had considered the relationship of the intended statute in the law on the Orthodox Church and specifically the obligations of the priest to teach according to the

---

55 Law on the Ombudsman 14.3.2002/197, Finlex Data Bank, accessed June 26, 2019, https://www.finlex.fi/sv/laki/ajantasa/2002/20020197.
56 X's complaint, Dnro 810/4/13; Ombudsman's Office, Dnro 810/4/13, Response to complaint; Appendix Dnro 810/4/13.
57 Ombudsman's Office, Dnro 810/4/13, Response to complaint.

doctrine of the church. The relationship of these restrictions to the constitutional freedom of speech came under examination. The committee pointed out that offence had to be serious and continuing, and that the bishop needed to warn the offender prior to punishments. However, it regarded the intended paragraphs as belonging to the "inner autonomy" of the church, its doctrines and confession.[58]

The ombudsman pondered the interpretation of the European Convention on Human Rights (ECHR) and selected decisions of the European Court of Human Rights (ECtHR) as related to the case in Finland. These cases included Turkey (Islam), Finland (Adventism), Germany (Catholicism), and Germany (Mormonism). As a specific, Finnish Orthodox comparison, the decision of the Supreme Administrative Court of Finland made on December 14, 2009 concerning the rights of one Orthodox priest to retain his priesthood while taking (potentially uncanonical) part in political campaigning and elections was presented. In that case, the decision of the bishops' council to suspend the priest form holy offices was regarded as valid.[59] However, the ombudsman did not reflect on the issue in relation to EU legislation.

In the actual assessment of the case, the ombudsman contemplated the position of Finnish Orthodoxy as belonging to two different realms simultaneously: that of worldwide Orthodoxy and that of Finnish public law. The autonomous Archbishopric of Finland belongs to the Patriarchate of Constantinople, and according to Finnish legislation, its practices concerning priesthood were based on canons and the notion of sacramental ordination. The constitutional freedom of religion means that a priest uses his freedom of religion while in the process of becoming ordained but cannot "hereafter appeal to his own, personal conviction as a basis for diverging from the confession of a denomination." A bond of loyalty had been created to the ecclesiastical employer, and that reality emerged as a significant fact in the assessment.[60]

The complaint called for an assessment of the legitimacy and rightfulness of the episcopal decisions. In terms of the response of the ombudsman, that too was to be regarded a matter of the inner autonomy of the church and a canonical question. This interpretation was in line with the discussions of the Constitutional Law Committee in 2006. Hence, no need to take further action concerning the complaint existed.[61]

---

58 Ombudsman's Office, Dnro 810/4/13, Response to complaint.
59 Ombudsman's Office, Dnro 810/4/13, Response to complaint.
60 Ombudsman's Office, Dnro 810/4/13, Response to complaint.
61 Ombudsman's Office, Dnro 810/4/13, Response to complaint.

Finally, complaints concerning the administrative handling of harassment in the parish, deficient or superficial hearing by a superior, and even delayed information to X (caused by human error) concerning the decision of the local Bishops' Synod were regarded as not acceptable in view of future actions by the ombudsman. Yet, the ombudsman wanted to point out the need to perform a hearing in a professional manner, not as a mere formality. In these sentences, a critical undertone can be regarded, a tone that is in accord with the previous rulings of the ECtHR as well.[62]

The ombudsman's rulings had an interesting and even concurrent parallel dating from June 2014. In the case of *Fernandez Martinez* v. *Spain*[63], the ECtHR stated that it had to be possible to appeal rulings and have them examined by national authorities. The latter cannot obviously have legitimacy concerning dogma, but their role was to examine the terms of employment and its possible termination. Domestic courts (for example, the office of the ombudsman) had to take all factors of comparable cases into account and weigh up the interest involved in detail and in depth, affording due weight to the principle of autonomy of religious groups.

In the case of *Fernandez Martinez* v. *Spain*, the court in the Grand Chamber finally ruled in favor of Spain and also of the Catholic Church, largely on the basis of the idea of religious autonomy that could be interpreted as significant in the case. Slotte and Årsheim describe, among other aspects, the decision in the following manner:

> Thus, religious autonomy is presented as a principally vital part of Article 9 and is connected with the overarching idea of religious pluralism as one of the cornerstones of the democratic society that the ECHR protects. Religious communities are, with few exceptions, allowed freely to determine their doctrines and the ways in which they wish to communicate them. They may independently choose and exclude members, and this also includes those persons whom they wish to entrust with religious tasks. Religious autonomy presupposes state neutrality in certain respects. The ECtHR here simply summarized its earlier case law.[64]

---

62 Ombudsman's Office, Dnro 810/4/13, Response to complaint.
63 A Spanish Catholic married priest, whose teaching contract in public school was not renewed. See *Fernández Martínez* v. *Spain* [GC], application 56030/07, 12 June 2014.
64 Pamela Slotte and Helge Årsheim, "The Ministerial Exception: Comparative Perspectives", *Oxford Journal of Law and Religion* 4, no. 2 (2015): 18-19.

This Spanish case also had its own, local, media dimension.[65] In that case, media publicity was also used as a tool for promoting married priests' visibility in public, but initially prior to the court cases, and it also became an aspect that was used in the jurisprudence to weigh the actions of the complainant in relationship to the Catholic Church and its dogmatic teaching.[66] A significant aspect was also the question of whether "[i]n the case of Mr. Fernández Martínez, the trust between the ecclesiastical authorities and the applicant had been broken. With reference to religious autonomy, the ecclesiastical authorities had a right to act as they did, and thus, the Spanish High Court of Justice and Constitutional Court had made the right assessment."[67] This aspect was recognized also in other research concerning the case.[68]

The verdict of the ombudsman was critically reviewed in the national newspaper *Helsingin Sanomat* in April 2015. In the story by Katarina Baer that was published together with another story on the quarrels of the Orthodox minority (and with pictures of the ex-priest and his wife) on pages A14-15, Professor of Labor Law Seppo Koskinen (currently retired)[69] and the above-mentioned Professor Korpela criticized the decision for positioning religious law in contradiction and into autonomous position with the "basic principles of the society"[70]. The third interviewee, Associate Professor of Public Law Juha Lavapuro,[71] considered in a more nuanced manner the relationship of religious autonomy to current Finnish legislation and the decisions of the ECtHR in the newspaper article.[72]

Conclusion—Religious Law and Autonomy Contested

In terms of these findings, the media case of one defrocked Finnish priest can be regarded as exceptional. The openness of the involved people was unprecedented, as was the built-in media production that transformed human interest

---

65 Javier Martínez-Torrón, "Fernández Martínez v. Spain," in *When human rights clash at the European Court of Human Rights: Conflict or harmony?*, ed. Stijn Smeet and Eva Breems (Oxford: Oxford University Press, 2017), 193, 204.
66 *Fernández Martínez v. Spain*.
67 Slotte and Årsheim, "The Ministerial Exception," 18.
68 Martínez-Torrón, "Fernández Martínez v. Spain," 209.
69 "Seppo Koskinen, työoikeuden professori," *Wikipedia*, accessed June 6, 2019, https://fi.wikipedia.org/wiki/Seppo_Koskinen_(työoikeuden_professori).
70 Katariina Baer, "Käveleekö uskonnollinen autonomia perusoikeuksien yli?," *Helsingin Sanomat*, April 4, 2015, A14-15.
71 "Juha Lavapuro," Tutkimusportaali, Turun Yliopisto, accessed June 25, 2019, https://research.utu.fi/converis/portal/Person/1087954?auxfun=&lang=fi_FI.
72 Baer, "Käveleekö uskonnollinen autonomia perusoikeuksien yli?," A14-15.

into commercial broadcasting. In the process, both personal integrity and notions of ecclesiastical autonomy were to a degree compromised. The TV production defended what they regarded as "unusual love," and questioned religious tradition and institutions that were depicted as outdated and detached from reality. The constructed reality of the program reflected society. Kavka describes the celebrity phenomenon in reality TV with the following notions: "While the celebrification of 'everyday people' may be most visible—and most derided—on reality TV, no television genre operates in a vacuum. Rather, discourses about ordinariness and celebrity traverse reality, cultural and political value."[73] This was also what took place in Father X's case. Even if on a minor scale, visibility and even celebrity was gained and, simultaneously, hierarchies were challenged by means of popular culture.

An Orthodox way of life and, specifically, Orthodox legal culture were predominantly questioned in the program, and Orthodox imagery was represented mostly as a romantic background for peoples' individual life choices. In terms of these representations, the minority's legal culture was largely dismissed as if it did not exist. Professor Korpela's learned commentaries were used in support of the case of the deposed priest, but the interesting position of the minority in terms of its traditions, dogma, canons, and Finnish legislation was not raised, not even to a minor degree. Minority religion and questions concerning the realizations of religious freedom were not raised in any comparative perspective, whereas in the jurisprudence of the ombudsman all these aspects were scrutinized. Media publicity in this case was related to the jurisprudence of the case in an odd manner, almost as diametrical opposites in terms of the chosen strategies. In different fields the issue was approached from different angles, and the issue came to be framed differently. The reality TV program could even be regarded as a disappointed claimant's last nationwide effort to change or challenge the situation. Hence the sadness and the subtle tone of desperation, which can also be interpreted as strategic choices, however.

In itself, the case is by no means singular in the Orthodox world. Moreover, it raises huge questions that cannot be easily answered simply by utilizing the notions of contemporary Western individuality and secularity. The sacrament of marriage challenges modernist distinctions by its mere entanglement of individuality, communality, faith-based character, and legal character. Specifically, in the Orthodox canonical realm, it is a mixture of all these aspects.[74] And in

---

73 Kavka, *Reality TV*, 157.
74 Afanasiev, *The Church*, 220-28. "Under de första kristna århundradena ansågs det [äktenskpet] höra hemma i den civila rätten snarare än den kanoniska rätten—det fanns ingen

terms of the tradition, Orthodox theology and canonical interpretation cannot simply denote certain historical developments as a starting point and escape to a certain idealized past. Its hermeneutics are more challenging. A significant hermeneutical horizon is, moreover, to ponder whether formally legitimate canonical decisions—that follow strictly the letter of a stipulation—can be regarded as rightful and humane when all relevant contextual aspects are considered in a coherent manner. Where can the lines between *akribeia* and *oikonomia* and all the pertinent in-between shades be drawn, and by whom?

Finnish marriage law—surprisingly never explicitly discussed in the case—still remains in tension with the canons of the Orthodox Church: the secular notion of marriage as opposed to the sacramental union, the openness of remarrying to basically everyone versus the restrictions and different positions of clergy and the laypeople. According to the interpretation of the ombudsman, by joining the Orthodox Church and specifically by joining the ordained priesthood, people renounce some of their constitutional freedoms or, perhaps more accurately, these freedoms are suspended or limited or given specific interpretations as a consequence of them taking up a specific office of trust and membership in a specific organization. But does this apply only to priesthood? What is the position of laypeople, in comparison? It seems to be utterly significant to consider how religious law actually can regulate marriage and living together in a country in which the legacy of Nordic secularity remains prevalent in marriage legislation, and now lately also regarding same-sex marriages.[75]

Another issue is the deep relationship between law and religious perceptions in general. Slotte and Årsheim have pondered their potentially common undercurrents in an interesting manner:

> Looking more closely, however, the dividing line between law and religion is complex: while no other sector of society in the West may have been so thoroughly 'secularized', law simultaneously shares many of its defining structural characteristics with religion. Indeed, several scholars of law and religion today argue that the relation between law and religion in the Western tradition is symbiotic, with religion furnishing the law with spirit, morals, and meaning and the law providing religion with structure and institutional coherence.[76]

---

särskild vigsel i den kristna kyrkan." Afanasiev, *The Church*, 221.
75 See Äktenskapslag, 13.6.1929/234, Finlex Data Bank, accessed June 26, 2019, https://www.finlex.fi/sv/laki/ajantasa/1929/19290234.
76 Slotte and Årsheim, "The Ministerial Exception," 3.

There is no way to avoid the issue that the members of the Orthodox minority have to figure out primarily by themselves: What is the place and manner of the interpretation of the holy canons in a contemporary, basically non-religious and non-confessional nation state in which, however, many citizens are religious and practice a variety of religions and other beliefs, and in which the highest institutions, the parliament, the president, and the government, gather in common for ecumenical worship services twice a year?

People may belong to churches and religious organizations, but in a fundamental manner, they are still considered as enjoying rights to privacy, freedom of speech, and freedom of religion according to the constitutional human rights clauses and related international agreements. Specifically, after the horrors of World War II, this emerging human rights discourse has become increasingly significant in ecumenical work and in the life of local churches and for Christians in general. How the human rights, understood and defined as fundamental, are related to the dogma and practices of religious communities remains a question largely still unanswered. The individual and collective dimensions of religious freedom interact and become juxtaposed in different ways.[77] This Finnish media and legal case can also be regarded as one aspect of that discourse, in terms of both media and jurisprudence.

In her meeting with different denominations during the past 400 years, Orthodoxy has experienced certain developments that can be conceptualized as confessionalization, in this context meaning counteraction as well as application of presuppositions and notions given by Western theologians.[78] In order to maintain and preserve one's own uniqueness, one needs to make distinctions with regard to perceptible otherness, in this case the Western denominations and their written confessions. But while engaging with these discussions, the dominant forms used by the opponent were also, seemingly unintentionally, mirrored and put to use. Much of contemporary Orthodox thinking can still be conceptualized as a reaction against the assessed Westernization of the past centuries. In view of this horizon, it will be necessary in the future to study the effect of these developments on local Orthodox communities and on their marriage theology and praxis.

---

77 Slotte and Årsheim, "The Ministerial Exception," 4, 13.
78 E.g., Patriarch Mētrophanēs Kritopoulos' 1624 published "Confessio". Regarding this significant development, the discussions with Reformation theologians, influences from the Protestant and Catholic sources and the entire setting, new at the time in the West, see Robert Hotz, *Sakramente: Im Wechselspiel zwischen Ost und West* (Gütersloh: Gütersloher Verlagshaus, 1979), 117-30. See also the broad description in Georges Florovsky, *Ways of Russian Theology, Part I* (Belmont, MA: Nordland Publishing, 1979), 46-85.

Specifically, the meeting of émigré Orthodox theologians with the West and its religious traditions in the 20th century highlighted this development.[79] The comments by Balanos and Florovsky at the Athens 1936 congress, for example, are specifically illustrative. They "called for a return to the Fathers, not a return to the letter of the patristic texts, in a blind, servile repetition; but rather a further development of the patristic teaching, homogenous with the corpus of teaching and yet creative enough to be meaningful for our modern age."[80] Notions like these unavoidably also imply canonical perspectives.

In the case of Orthodoxy, these succeeding, and even contemporary developments blur the image. Inescapably, the predominant move over the past centuries has been towards presentations of Orthodoxy as a specific confession within the contexts of different nation states, a move which can be seen as being in contradiction with the notion of the one, holy, apostolic, Catholic, and universal Orthodox Church. However, confessional and nationalist self-presentations have been challenged, in particular by the theological ideas of the Orthodox tradition understood as a continuum of faith and practice that emerges in time and through time, a continuum that both encounters and transcends local idiosyncrasies as a living stream of the Holy Spirit.[81]

In this volume, the proposed notion of "'re-confessionalization' as a theoretical concept to capture (1) the growing legal independence of the national churches and other religious communities from direct state involvement (Finland 1996, Sweden 2000, and Norway 2014), (2) the fact that legal thinking and national legislation has to deal with a considerable number of religious communities as part of a pluralistic society, and (3) the fact that religious communities begin to act as collectives based on specific confessional identities, Christian or non-Christian"[82] is actually quite fitting with regard to this specifically Orthodox context in all these three aspects. The growing legal independence and emphasis on solutions regarded as autonomous can be discerned as being in tune with efforts to develop, express, and defend "authentically Orthodox" principles and practical

---

79   George A. Maloney, *A History of Orthodox Theology since 1453* (Belmont, MA: Nordland, 1976), 203. See also the description of the "taint" of Protestantism, in Florovsky, *Ways*, 50, and esp. the notion of Pseudomorphosis, 85.
80   Maloney, *A History*, 204.
81   See the interestingly paradoxical representation concerning the notion of tradition by Lossky, in Vladimir Lossky, "Tradition and Traditions," in *The Meaning of Icons* (Crestwook, NY: St Vladimir's Seminary Press, 1999), esp. p. 16: the "vertical and horizontal" lines of the "Truth possessed by the Church".
82   Pamela Slotte, Niels Henrik Gregersen and Helge Årsheim, "Introduction: Internationalization and Re-Confessionalization: Law and Religion in the Nordic Realm 1945-2017," in this volume.

solutions in terms of canonical and doctrinal views—all this within and as a part of shifting landscapes of legal culture in a more pluralist society. Contemporary discussions on the sacrament of marriage are not unattached to these settings.

Altogether, the specific case of Father X illustrates in miniature how the relationships of law and religion emerge and are shaped within the complex network of theological interpretations, political structures, law of the land and religious law, their jurisprudence, human rights discourses, and—last but not least—contemporary media.

Epilogue

An interesting twist concerning the issue of the remarriage of Orthodox priests took place during the summer of 2018, as this chapter was already in preparation. The Patriarchate of Constantinople announced that it was going to create a specific procedure for priests who have been widowed or whose wives have left them, in order to give them a possibility to enter into a second marriage. As to how this procedure is going to be realized in practice remains to be seen in the future. However, it is evident that this issue remains disputable and one of specific interest and urgency to this day. New action by the Patriarchate may potentially change the situation of many defrocked priests altogether,[83] and recent development in Finland right before the printing of this article confirmed that changes are going to take place.[84]

Bibliography

The European Court of Human Rights
Fernández Martínez v. Spain [GC], application 56030/07, 12 June 2014

---

83 See the following Finnish articles: Antti Berg, "Konstantinopolin ekumeeninen patriarkaatti sallimassa ortodoksipappien uudelleen avioitumisen tietyin ehdoin," *Kotimaa24*, September 5, 2018. https://www.kotimaa24.fi/artikkeli/konstantinopolin-ekumeeninen-patriarkaatti-sallimassa-ortodoksipappien-uudelleen-avioitumisen-tietyi/; Maria Hattunen ja Vladimir Sokratilin, "Kirkon eheys vahvasti esillä Konstantinopolissa," Suomen Ortodoksinen kirkko, September 7, 2018, https://ort.fi/uutishuone/2018-09-07/kirkon-eheys-vahvasti-esilla-konstantinopolissa.
84 Piispainkokouksen 21.4.2021 pöytäkirja 3/21, §22. Lähteisiin, Official Sources: Piispainkokouksen 21.4.2021 pöytäkirja 3/21, Orthodox Church of Finland. https://ort.fi/sites/default/files/2021-04/Piispainkokouksen%20pöytäkirja_3_21_21.4.2021.pdf

Official Sources

The Church Order of the Orthodox Church 12.12.2006/174 v. 2007. Finlex Data Bank. Accessed January 20, 2019. https://www.finlex.fi/fi/laki/ajantasa/2007/20070174?search%5Btype%5D=pika&search%5Bpika%5D=ortodoksisen%20kirkon%20kirkkojärjestys.

Excerpt of the minutes of the Finnish Orthodox Bishops council. Dnro 220/2012, Ote piispainkokouksen pöytäkirjasta 6/12, Istunto 27.11.2012 klo 9.10-9.45 Valamon Kristuksen kirkastumisen luostarissa.

Finnish Acts and Decrees, Decree n:o 206 On the Orthodox Denomination. 15.5.1953.

Law on the Ombudsman 14.3.2002/197. Accessed January 21, 2019. https://www.finlex.fi/sv/laki/ajantasa/2002/20020197.

Law on the Orthodox Denomination 8.8.1969/521, repealed. Finlex Data Bank. Accessed January 21, 2019. https://finlex.fi/fi/laki/ajantasa/kumotut/1969/19690521.

Law on the Orthodox Church 10.11.2006/985. Finlex Data Bank. Accessed January 20, 2019. https://www.finlex.fi/fi/laki/ajantasa/2006/20060985.

Law on State Officials 19.8.1994/750. Finlex Data Bank. Accessed January 1, 2019. https://www.finlex.fi/fi/laki/ajantasa/1994/19940750?search%5Btype%5D=pika&search%5Bpika%5D=Virkamieslaki.

Office of the Ombudsman, Eduskunnan oikeusasiamiehen kanslia-Dnro 810/4/13 Res.fin Salaiset asiakirjat. Dnro 810/4/13, Response to complaint, Appendix Dnro 810/4/13. X's complaint, Dnro 810/4/13.

Ortodoksisen kirkon kanonit selityksineen [Pravila pravoslavne crkve s tumačenjima] [Canons of the Orthodox Church and Interpretations]. Translated by Antti Inkinen. Helsinki, 1980.

United Nations General Assembly. *Universal Declaration of Human Rights*, 217 A (III), 10 December 1948.

Äktenskapslag, 13.6.1929/234. Finlex Data Bank. Accessed June 26, 2019. https://www.finlex.fi/sv/laki/ajantasa/1929/19290234.

Literature

Afanasiev, Nicholas. *The Church of the Holy Spirit.* Notre Dame, IN: University of Notre Dame Press, 2007.

Alfejev, Hilarion. *Trons Mysterium: En introduktion till den ortodoxa kyrkans troslära och andlighet.* Skellefteå/Södertälje: Artos and Norma, 2002.

Ambrosius (Bishop). "Piispa Irja Askolan vierailu Uspenskissa oli kaunis ekumeeninen ystävyyden ele." *Helsingin Sanomat*, March 14, 2015. https://www.hs.fi/mielipide/art-2000002808409.html.

Baer, Katariina. "Käveleekö uskonnollinen autonomia perusoikeuksien yli?" *Helsingin Sanomat*, April 4, 2015, A14-15.

Baer, Katarina, and Marjo Valtavaara. "Ortodoksien oppiriita pahenee pääsiäisen alla." *Helsingin Sanomat*, April 4, 2015, A14-15.

Bastubacka, Johan. "Mirroring the Majority? The Emerging Legal Understanding on Finnish Orthodoxy in terms of the 1925 Government Decree." Article submitted for publication, 2018.

Berg, Antti. "Konstantinopolin ekumeeninen patriarkaatti sallimassa ortodoksipappien uudelleen avioitumisen tietyin ehdoin." *Kotimaa24*, September, 5, 2018. https://www.kotimaa24.fi/artikkeli/konstantinopolin-ekumeeninen-patriarkaatti-sallimassa-ortodoksipappien-uudelleen-avioitumisen-tietyi/.

Bremer, Thomas, Hacik Rafi Gazer, and Christian Lange, eds. *Die orthodoxen Kirchen der byzantinischen Tradition*. Darmstadt: WBG, 2013.

Fiske, John. *Introduction to Communication Studies*. New York: Routledge, 2011.

Florovsky, Georges. *Ways of Russian Theology, Part I*. Belmont, MA: Nordland Publishing, 1979.

Frost, Chris. *Media Ethics and Self-Regulation*. Harlow: Longman, 2000.

Gavin, Frank. *Some Aspects of Contemporary Greek Orthodox Thought*. New York: AMS Press, 1970. First published 1923.

Glynn, Kevin. *Tabloid Culture, Trash Taste, Popular Power, and the Transformation of American Television*. Durham, NC: Duke University Press, 2000.

Heikkilä, Jelisei. *Canonical Development through Dialogue: Marriage and Divorce in the Pre- Conciliar Period and in the All-Russian Church Council of 1917-1918*. Helsinki: University of Helsinki, Faculty of Theology, 2015.

Heith-Stade, David. *The Rudder of the Church: A Study of the Theory of Canon Law in the Pedalion*. Lund: Lund University, Centre for Theology and Religious Studies, 2014.

Hotz, Robert. *Sakramente: Im Wechselspiel zwischen Ost und West*. Gütersloh: Gütersloher Verlagshaus, 1979.

Jenkins, Henrik. "Why Fiske Still Matters." Introduction to *Introduction to communication studies*, by John Fiske. New York: Routledge, 2011.

Jensen, Anne. *Die Zukunft der Orthodoxie, Konzilspläne und Kirchenstrukturen*. Zürich: Benziger, 1986.

Kavka, Misha. *Reality TV*. Edinburg: Edinburgh University Press, 2012.

Kern, Kyprian. "Pastoral Christian Ministry." In *Called to Serve, Readings on Ministry from the Orthodox Church, e*dited by William C. Mills, 99-127. St. Paul, MN: OCABS Press, 2016.

Kotsonis, Jérôme. *Problèmes de l'économie ecclésiastique*. Gembloux: Éditions J. Duculot, 1971.

Levin, Eve. *Sex and Society in the World of the Orthodox Slavs, 900-1700*. Ithaca, NY: Cornell University Press, 1989.

Lossky, Vladimir. "Tradition and Traditions." In *The Meaning of Icons,* 9-22. Crestwook, NY: St Vladimir's Seminary Press, 1999.

Maloney, George A. *A History of Orthodox Theology since 1453*. Belmont, MA: Nordland, 1976.

Martínez-Torrón, Javier. "Fernández Martínez v. Spain." In *When Human Rights Clash at the European Court of Human Rights: Conflict or Harmony?*, edited by Stijn Smeet and Eva Breems. Oxford: Oxford University Press: 2017.

Parish, Helen L. *Clerical Celibacy in the West, c. 1100-1700*. Farnham, Ashgate, 2010.

Pullinen, Jussi. "Mitro Repo hakee KHO:sta kieltoa pappipannalleen." *Helsingin Sanomat*, May 30, 2009. https://www.hs.fi/kotimaa/art-2000004656051.html.

Ripaoja, Martti. "Kirkkomme jäsenet ovat identiteetiltään ensisijaisesti ortodokseja ja vasta sitten suomalaisia." *Savon Sanomat*, March 3, 2015. https://www.

savonsanomat.fi/kotimaa/Arkkipiispa-Leo-%C3%A4r%C3%A4hti-piispa-Irjasta-alttarilla/530291.

Rodopoulos, Panteleimon. *An Overview of Orthodox Canon Law*. Rollinsford, NH: Orthodox Research Institute, 2007.

Slotte, Pamela, and Helge Årsheim. "The Ministerial Exception: Comparative Perspectives." *Oxford Journal of Law and Religion* 4, no. 2 (2015): 1-28.

Slotte, Pamela, Niels Henrik Gregersen, and Helge Årsheim. "Introduction: Internationalization and Re-Confessionalization: Law and Religion in the Nordic Realm 1945-2017," in this volume.

Webpages

Archbishop of Helsinki and All Finland. "Henkilötiedot." Accessed June 24, 2019. https://ort.fi/arkkipiispa/info/henkilotiedot.

Elonet, Kansallisfilmografia. "Kielletty rakkaus (2016)." Accessed January 18, 2019. https://www.elonet.fi/fi/elokuva/1571913.

Hattunen, Maria, ja Vladimir Sokratilin. "Kirkon eheys vahvasti esillä Konstantinopolissa." Suomen Ortodoksinen kirkko, September 7, 2018. https://ort.fi/uutishuone/2018-09-07/kirkon-eheys-vahvasti-esilla-konstantinopolissa.

Nelonen. *Kielletty Rakkaus*. Accessed January 18, 2019. https://www.nelonen.fi/ohjelmat/kielletty-rakkaus/2132545-camilla-auttoi-miestaan-tulemaan-jessicaksi-han-auttoi-minua-vapautumaan.

Nelonen/ruutu.fi. "Pappi erotettiin virasta rakkauden tähden: Kausi 1— jakso 11." *Kielletty Rakkaus*, Accessed January 18, 2019. https://www.ruutu.fi/video/2625166

Ortodoksi.net. "Euhologion (käsikirja)." Accessed January 18, 2019. http://www.ortodoksi.net/index.php/Euhologion_(käsikirja).

Ortotoksi.net. "Paastoajat." Accessed June 24, 2019. http://www.ortodoksi.net/index.php/Paastoajat.

Ortodoksi.net. "Panteleimon Oulun emeritus metropoliitta." Accessed June 24, 2019. http://www.ortodoksi.net/index.php/Panteleimon_Oulun_emeritus_metropoliitta.

Suomen ortodoksinen kirkko. "Sakramentit eli mysteeriot." Accessed January 19, 2019. https://ort.fi/tutustu-ortodoksiseen-kirkkoon/sakramentit-eli-mysteeriot.

Sveriges Television. *Tro, Hopp och Kärlek: Präster letar efter kärleken*. Accessed April 4, 2017. https://www.svt.se/tro-hopp-och-karlek/.

Turun Yliopisto. "Juha Lavapuro." Tutkimusportaali. Accessed June 25, 2019. https://research.utu.fi/converis/portal/Person/1087954?auxfun=&lang=fi_FI.

Wikipiedia. "Jukka Korpela (historioitsija)." Accessed January 20, 2019. https://fi.wikipedia.org/wiki/Jukka_Korpela_(historioitsija).

Wikipedia. "Seppo Koskinen, työoikeuden professori." Accessed June 25, 2019. https://fi.wikipedia.org/wiki/Seppo_Koskinen_(työoikeuden_professori).

9. Muslim Views on the Danish State and Law

Niels Valdemar Vinding

Introduction: The Question of Muslim Conformity

Well into the 21st century, the significant presence of very heterogeneous groups of Muslims in Denmark and the other Nordic countries seems to question established understandings of religion in our secular democratic states, known for vast political and civic freedoms and a sound secular legal frame governing the historical majority churches. Regarding responsible government, the question of governing Islam has become a central issue in legislation, in administration, and in adjudication. To paraphrase Anne Norton, "the Muslim question", for better or worse, has become the great question of our time.[1] From the perspective of this volume, this question adds a measure of "fuzz and ferment" to the longstanding discourse on state and religion.

In many ways, Islam and Muslims constitute a distinct "other" for the particularities of the "secular" Nordic states and law. As ongoing debates have demonstrated, on the one hand, *some* interpretations of Islam and *some* groups of Muslims present a counter-narrative of religion, social justice, and political identity that is critical and challenging to the secular order. In public and political discourse, such counter-narratives are seen, for example, in hot-button questions of migration, integration, and multiculturalism. This is arguably the case of Hizb ut-Tahrir in the Danish debates. On the other hand, in many ways Islam and Muslims conform very well to the secular and liberal ideals and values about freedom of expression, freedom of religion, and freedom of thought voiced in the Danish constitution and law. In light of current value-political discourse and recent legislation that seeks to alienate or even disintegrate Islam and Muslims in Denmark,[2] this apparent conformity to Danish state and law seems surprising and may even counter or deflate the governing political prejudices.

---

1 Anne Norton, *On the Muslim Question* (Princeton: Princeton University Press, 2013).
2 Niels Valdemar Vinding, *Annotated Legal Documents on Islam in Denmark* (Leiden: Brill, 2020).

This chapter will explore such seeming discord regarding the compatibility or conformity of Muslims to secular rule. To what extent do Muslims in their diverse expressions of religion, law, and theology conform to the deeply rooted Danish expressions of a distinct secularity negotiated through centuries of Protestant Lutheran theology and ecclesiology converging with state and law? Kjell Åke Modéer would ask, do Islam and Muslims converge with or diverge from the principles of secular, Nordic states?[3] How do Muslims in Denmark, as the case may be, see themselves, address themselves to and negotiate with the "secular" Danish state and law? How does Danish secularity cope with Islamic law, practice, and ethics, and how do Muslim communities deal with their position in relation to national law? The overall question of this paper is: how do Muslims view, understand, and think of state and law in Denmark?

Not surprisingly, the answers to these questions depend on whom amongst Danish Muslims we seek to study. In the particular case of Islam and Muslims in Denmark, there are very diverse points of view among the 256,000 Muslims out of a Danish population of 5.8 million, as estimated as of January 1, 2020.[4] In Denmark, we have no precise numbers on Muslims, because it is illegal to register people according to confession and political convictions. However, we do know that Muslims are a tremendously diverse group. The ethnic and national origins as well as the history of these minorities reflect the global conflicts, instabilities and migratory push-and-pull effects of the second half of the 20th and the 21st centuries more than it reflects anything else.[5]

Theologically, Muslims in Denmark follow the diversity of Islamic schools through greatly varying degrees of orthodoxy and orthopraxy. This ranges from outspoken secularist and everyday lived Islam[6] with its mixed syncretism, to the ultra-orthodoxy and hyper-purism of the Salafists.[7] Some even follow the

---

3   Kjell Å. Modéer, "Internal Convergence—External Divergence. Religion in Nordic Legal Culture and Tradition at the Threshold of the Third Millenium," in *Law & Religion in the 21st Century: Nordic Perspectives,* ed. Lisbet Christoffersen, Kjell Å. Modéer, and Svend Andersen (Copenhagen: DJØF Publishing, 2010), 61-78.
4   Brian Arly Jacobsen and Niels Valdemar Vinding, "Denmark," in *Yearbook of Muslims in Europe* 10, ed. Egdunas Racius et al. (Leiden: Brill, 2021), 207.
5   See Jørgen S. Nielsen, ed., *Islam in Denmark: The Challenge of Diversity* (Lanham: Lexington Books 2012). Also, Marianne Holm Pedersen and Mikkel Rytter, eds., *Islam og muslimer i Danmark: Religion, identitet og sikkerhed efter 11. september 2011* (Copenhagen: Museum Tusculanum Press, 2011).
6   Nadia Jeldtoft, "Lived Islam: Religious identity with 'Non-Organized' Muslim Minorities," *Ethnic and Racial Studies* 34, no. 7 (2011): 1134-51.
7   Lene Kühle, "Radikalisering: Ekstremisme eller vækkelse? En undersøgelse af aarhusianske muslimers holdninger," *Islam og muslimer i Danmark: Religion, identitet og sikkerhed efter 11. september 2011,* ed. Marianne Holm Pedersen and Mikkel Rytter (Copenhagen:

neo-fundamentalist ideas of the Islamic State in Iraq and Syria with its nihilistic terror regime of arbitrary violence that actively seeks to invoke the end of days.[8]

In general—both in the so-called Islamic world and the global West—Muslims face significant crises and challenges regarding how to interpret and communicate their values, identity, and message to their contemporary world.[9] This challenge is as old as Islam itself and one that most theologies recognize. How are muslims to understand the eternal and divine message of God in the ever-changing realm of mortal being and limited understanding? Specifically, Islam's current crisis can be traced through the second half of the 19th, the whole of the 20th, and well into the 21st century. In simple terms, this crisis has two interrelated aspects. First, how to make the message of Islam resonate with the challenges that Muslims face with the advent of modernity and secularism and, second, how to reconcile the many different understandings of Islam currently competing for authority? Especially in the 20th century, we have seen many competing solutions, including nationalism, pan-Arabism, Arab socialism, modernistic traditionalism, Islamism, and Islamic revolutions, yet none of these have been satisfactory or lasting. Considering this, it seems obvious that Muslims in Denmark do not comprise one uniform group nor have one unanimous view of law in Denmark. Rather, Muslims are an ethnically, religiously, demographically, and politically diverse group with almost every conceivable view of law and society represented to some extent.

For the purposes of the present study, the scope may be reduced considerably. Our interest is in Muslim views on state, law, and society, allowing us to focus on the Muslims in Denmark who actively, openly, and deliberately identify, perceive, criticize, or in other ways address state, law, and society. Following international political science on political Islam,[10] this chapter presents a frame for understanding where the Danish Muslim voices are coming from, and presents four major socio-religious categories of (a) secular, (b) modernist, (c) traditional, and (d) fundamentalist Muslims in Denmark. This categorization

---

Museum Tusculanum, 2011), 89-114; Shiraz Maher, *Salafi-Jihadism: The History of an Idea* (London: Hurst & Company, 2016).

8   Anthony Bubalo and Greg Fealy, *Between the Global and the Local: Islamism, the Middle East, and Indonesia* (Washington, D.C.: Brookings Institution, 2005).

9   Olivier Roy, *The Failure of Political Islam* (Cambridge: Harvard University Press, 1994); Bernard Lewis, *The Crisis of Islam: Holy War and Unholy Terror* (New York: Random House Incorporated, 2004).

10 Cheryl Benard et al., *Civil Democratic Islam: Partners, Resources, and Strategies* (Santa Monica, CA: Rand Corporation, 2004); Asef Bayat, *Making Islam Democratic: Social Movements and the Post-Islamist Turn* (Stanford: Stanford University Press, 2007); Peter Mandaville, *Global Political Islam* (London: Routledge, 2010).

resonates with a well-demonstrated distinction in sociology and political science between different Muslim groups and their understanding of the Islamic view on state, society, law, and democracy. With minor methodological and epistemological reservations, we may group Danish Muslims into these four overall ideal-typical groups and provide a few key examples of voices from their midst.[11]

Drawing on Danish research and recent evidence from public discourse within the Muslim community, each of these four categories is represented by means of a significant public figure amongst Danish Muslims. For the secular position, Iranian-born polemicist Jaleh Tavakoli in her recent book *The Public Secrets of Islam* (2018) stresses the paramount dichotomy between a mainstream Islam, which she equates with Islamism, and secular society. Speaking from a modernist and reformist position, Sherin Khankan in her memoir, *Women are the Future of Islam* (2018), sets forth a critical, equal and progressive Islam. A traditionalist voice is found in Tarek Ziad Hussein's recent book *The Black Beard* (2018), where he criticizes from an internal and traditional position the lazy assumptions and weak cultural idiosyncrasies of his fellow coreligionists in Denmark. The chapter's presentation of the fundamentalist position is based on an exhaustive survey of ten years' worth of press releases and media material from Hizb ut-Tahrir in Scandinavia, and analysis of their views on state, law, society, and democracy.

The conclusion makes key, overall observations regarding the diversity of Muslim positions, between conformities and counter-narratives. In light of the overall theme of this volume, the conclusion considers the wider implications for understanding the secularity of law and state from a Muslim perspective, and discusses in particular how the four positions view secularity at different levels of the Danish state and law.

Secularist Muslim Views of Law, State, and Society

Muslim secularism might sound like a contradiction in terms. However, analysis revels it to be a fitting term. Most secularists, Muslims included, regard religion as a private, not merely a civil, matter separate from politics and state. Some, more uncompromising, voices argue for entirely abandoning religion in favor of a secular worldview. As a matter of principle for both hard and soft secularist positions, the state should not interfere in religion, but should establish a framework for public order and regulation of religion. In this light, all religion

---

11 Following Benard et al., *Civil Democratic Islam*.

must adhere to and subject itself to democracy, the law of the land, and human rights. Should conflict arise between Islamic and democratic principles, Muslims must unequivocally follow democratic ideals and law.[12] Elsewhere in this volume, Pamela Slotte discusses with Hussain Ali Agrama the crucial importance of the idea of "public order" as a basis for the rule of law, and criticizes how public order confirms majoritarian sentiments.

For the purpose of the present analysis of Muslim secularist positions, it is appropriate to distinguish between mainstream secularists and more radical secularists. The former maintain that Islam may give rise to legitimate input and a place in society outside the state, whereas the latter argue that social justice and equality call for democracy to extraordinarily set aside its principles of freedom of religion and belief in regulating Islam or even abandoning Islam completely.[13] A frequent example of Muslim secularism can be found in the Kemalist ideas of 20th-century Turkey as inspired by the French laicist model.[14] More radical secularists include, for example, the activist Ayaan Hirsi Ali, who promotes a somewhat alarmist view of Islam, even to the extent of being unable to distinguish between different interpretations, worldviews, and practices in Islam.[15]

In Denmark, we find many of the more outspoken secular Muslim voices amongst the refugee communities that have left Islamist regimes in the Middle East, and in socialist-atheist communities that argue for a secular humanism "after faith."[16] Significantly, two ethnic groups appear to be well represented. One is the minority of Iranian refugees and succeeding generations, whose secularity is a reaction against the Iranian Revolution and regime since 1979. The other comprises the groups of Turkish origin, who have brought a Kemalist, secular view with them. Without manhandling these categories too much, a rule of thumb would be that many Iranian secularists take a hard secularist position, while the Turkish secularists take a soft secularist stance.

One of the voices from the Muslim community that is decidedly secularist and very critical of Islam and Muslims in Denmark is Iranian-born Tavakoli. Born in 1982, her father was a communist; she grew up reading Marxist literature and engaging in political activism amongst the most left-wing political

---

12 Benard et al., *Civil Democratic Islam*, 26.
13 Benard et al., *Civil Democratic Islam*, 13, 25ff.
14 Emir Kaya, *Secularism and State Religion in Modern Turkey: Law, Policy-Making and the Diyanet* (London: Bloomsbury Publishing, 2018).
15 Merijn Oudenampsen, "Deconstructing Ayaan Hirsi Ali: On Islamism, Neoconservatism, and the Clash of Civilizations," *Politics, Religion & Ideology* 17, no. 2-3 (2016): 227-48.
16 Anders Stjernholm, *Eftertro: Lad os tale om tro, tvivl og det svære valg at forlade en religion* (Copenhagen: Gyldendal, 2017); Philip Kitcher, *Life after Faith: The Case for Secular Humanism* (New Haven, CT: Yale University Press, 2014).

parties in Denmark. She is an avid opinion maker, spokesperson for Free Iran in Denmark and vocally Islam-critical or even polemicist. She sees herself as an atheist or non-believing Muslim who has "defected" from Islam.

In an interview following the release of her self-published book titled *The Public Secrets of Islam*, Tavakoli states her view plainly: "Islam has a problem with democracy and peaceful coexistence."[17] "Islam is the problem," she continues, and "today we are only discussing secularism in relation to Islam as a political religion and a law-religion," which is relevant, "because Islam as a religion has a great theological problem with secularism and the universal rights and freedoms."[18] While the details of the argument in her book reveal that her view on Islam and Muslims is informed by the fundamentalisms of a politicized Islam, she maintains a rather generalizing attitude to Islam and Muslims. Tavakoli appears to superimpose her experiences and analysis of the post-1979 Iranian regime onto most of Islam. Counter to most presentations of Islam and Muslims, she uses her own neologism of "Mainstream Islam" as a concept for both Islamism and Jihadism, and identifies Mainstream Islam as working against integration and promoting literalism in interpreting the Qur'an. Such criticism of Islam quickly becomes too broad and generalizing, setting up a straw man, utterly skewing the nuances in different Muslim positions. As the four Muslim positions presented in this chapter demonstrate, conflating modernist, traditionalist, and fundamentalist Islam into one catchall category destroys meaningful and analytical difference. However, such conflations resonate well with conservative and nationalist right-wing opinion makers and politicians in the current Danish debate, where Tavakoli serves as a voice that confirms, authenticates, and validates their biases and agendas.

In explicit contrast to "Mainstream Islam," Tavakoli promotes secularism and critique of religion,[19] but has a surprisingly uncritical and idealized understanding of secularism. She argues: "The greater separation there is between religions and the state and all other types of authorities, organizations, communities and not least our democratic conversation, the greater the guarantee that we all speak and understand the same language."[20]

Although it is unclear what she means by "language," she clearly under-

---

17 Inge Haandsbæk Jensen, "Jaleh Tavakoli: Jeg byder reformvillige muslimer velkommen," *Religion.dk,* October 8, 2018, https://www.religion.dk/jaleh-tavakoli-reformislam-soeges.
18 Jaleh Tavakoli, *Islams offentlige hemmeligheder* (Copenhagen, Self-published, 2018). Vinding's translations through out.
19 Jaleh Tavakoli, "Kampen om værdierne: Sekularisme," *Information*, May 14, 2016, https://www.information.dk/debat/2016/05/kampen-vaerdierne-sekularisme.
20 Tavakoli, "Kampen om værdierne."

stands state, public authority, and democracy itself as standing in clear contrast to—and even as detrimental—to religion. "Secularism is exactly a bulwark against radicalization, because secularism offers a common and inclusive alternative."[21] Tavakoli argues for secularism as a great solution to the problems of society in general and to the problems of Islam in particular. In her understanding, secularism is not radical, extreme, or fundamentalist, but remains inclusive and the antithesis of everything she considers Islam to be. From University of Copenhagen, Associate Professor Birgitte Schepelern Johansen debates Tavakoli on this point, and warns against such idealization of secularism which, historically, has also transformed itself into a very radical idea.[22]

Tavakoli unwaveringly continues to promote the conflation of Islam and Islamism and has been welcomed by Danish right-wing politicians, who champion her as a voice of truth. She has been compared to Hirsi Ali.[23] Amongst other contrasts embedded in her profile and, perhaps, reflecting some of the political and populist trends defined by the "Muslim Question," Tavakoli has moved completely across the political spectrum from being a far left-wing activist to being a supporter of a clearly right-wing agenda on this particular topic.

Modernist and Reformist

Modernists seek change and reform in Islam, and challenge both the fundamentalist and orthodox understandings and practices of Islam. They are prepared to move much further beyond the strict adherence to Islamic legal-deductive reasoning of the traditional schools.[24]

Theologically, modernists tend to identify an essential core of Islamic belief through a process of induction and speculation on the "universal principles" of the Qur'anic message, concretely in the iterations of the superior goals of sharia (*maqasid as-shariah*): Religion (*din*), Life (*nafs*), Lineage (*nasl*), Intellect (*'aql*), and Property (*mal*). If the concrete rulings of Islamic law, state, or the public and private morals of Muslims go against these goals or principles, then such hu-

---

21 Tavakoli, "Kampen om værdierne."
22 Birgitte Schepelern Johansen, "Kampen om værdierne: Sekularisme," *Information*, May 14, 2016, https://www.information.dk/debat/2016/05/kampen-vaerdierne-sekularisme.
23 Marie Høgh, "Her er den altoverskyggende årsag bag voldtægterne," *BT*, July 1, 2018, https://www.bt.dk/debat/her-er-den-altoverskyggende-aarsag-bag-voldtaegterne.
24 Benard et al., *Civil Democratic Islam*, 37ff.

man rulings must be wrong.²⁵ Modernists therefore see the principles of Islam and democracy as completely compatible and mutually helpful to each other's prosperity. Muslims should fully participate in democratic and public life, for the benefit of all citizens. In general, we find modernists all over the world, but of particular interest are the reforming and rethinking ideas found on the margins of the Muslim world. For example, in Europe, America, South Africa, and South East Asia, we find Muslim feminists' voices speaking in favor of equality between the genders and equal responsibly in Islamic law and institutions. There have been other modernist voices, but examples of the position from the late 1990s and after can be found in the thinking of Nasr Hamid Abou Zayd (2018), Tariq Ramadan (2003) and many others.²⁶

Of significant international fame and renown, female imam and mosque organizer Khankan stands front and center in the modernist and reformist segment of the Danish Muslim community. After years of increasing media and international attention, Khankan recently published her memoir, *Women Are the Future of Islam* (Rider publishers, 2018). Khankan famously established the women's Mariam Mosque and is leading Friday prayers as *Imamah*. She is easily labelled reformist, progressive, moderate, feminist, and so on. Most likely, such outsiders' characteristics are appropriate. However, systematically going through her own statements and writings, such as her 2018 memoir, manifests, op-eds, and newspaper interviews, it seems that many external agents have an interest in producing the figure "Sherin Khankan."²⁷

In her book, Khankan outlines her journey towards a more equal, more tolerant and reformed understanding of Islam. Explicitly inspired by the Sufism of Ibn Arabi (1165-1240) and very much a product of her parents' interfaith marriage, Khankan seems to be drawing the obvious conclusions for a reform of a European Islam, but without necessarily being able to argue for her positions in strict scholastic or hermeneutic terms. Khankan looks to be on a trajectory of attracting further fame and attention. In the spring of 2019, a documentary

---

25 Jasser Auda, *Maqasid al-Shariah as Philosophy of Islamic Law: A Systems Approach* (Herndom: International Institute of Islamic Thought, 2008); Jasser Auda, "Rethinking Islamic Law for Europe," in *Imams in Western Europe: Developments, Transformations and Institutional Challenges*, ed. Mohammed Hashas, Jan Jaap de Ruiter, and Niels Valdemar Vinding (Amsterdam: Amsterdam University Press, 2018).

26 Tariq Ramadan, *Western Muslims and the Future of Islam* (Oxford: Oxford University Press, 2003); Nasr Hamid Abu Zayd, *Critique of the Religious Discourse*, trans. Jonathan Wright (New Haven, CT: Yale University Press, 2018); Mohammed Hashas, *The Idea of European Islam: Religion, Ethics, Politics and Perpetual Modernity* (London: Routledge, 2018).

27 Jesper Petersen, "Media and the Female Imam," *Religions* 10, no. 3 (2019), https://doi.org/10.3390/rel10030159.

premiered, presenting her as a "Reformist,"[28] that is, one who seeks reform. Aptly named, Khankan seems to remain exactly that: a reformist, one who seeks reform, rather than a reformer, who brings about reform in her own intellectual capacity.

Khankan has much experience with the media and public exposure and in one way or the other has been working explicitly as a Muslim voice in the interaction with society. A few weeks before 9/11 2001, Khankan launched the *Forum for Critical Muslims* precisely in an attempt to further the dialogue between Muslims and the rest of society.[29] With this forum, Khankan highlighted critique and self-criticism as virtues in the search for understanding and interpretation of what it means to be Muslim. In the manifesto of the forum that she wrote, Khankan emphasizes the renewal and reform of Islam amongst Muslims in the West.

She and the *Forum for Critical Muslims* are "working to reform the Muslim understanding of the Qur'an"[30] and have a "wish to re-establish the active role women have played in the history of Islam."[31] Directly, she highlights that "One of our visions is a mosque with a female *khatiba*, a woman leading the sermon (*khutba*) for men and women during Friday prayers."[32]

In Khankan's memoir, the forum is remembered as a reformist, activist movement. Effectively, however, Khankan emerged front and center as spokeswoman for the project, making it difficult to see any movement behind her.[33] In the following years, the *Forum for Critical Muslims* became a platform from which Khankan was able to develop these ideas further. In late 2014, Khankan spoke at a conference on interreligious dialogue in Istanbul and was interviewed for the Danish weekly *Weekendavisen*, where she presented the idea that Islam and secularity were not at all incompatible. Already in the manifesto, Khankan had carved out a middle position between the political wings, stating that Islam and democracy were compatible. This was unfolded at the conference in Istanbul, as she says, appropriately self-critically, that "most Muslims see Islam and secularism as incompatible, because they think that the Turkish or French form of secularism are the only viable models, and that these leave no place

---

28 Marie Skovgaard, dir., *The Reformist: A Female Imam*, TV documentary, 2019, Filmdatabasen, accessed October 3, 2019, https://www.dfi.dk/en/viden-om-film/filmdatabasen/film/reformisten-den-kvindelige-imam.
29 Sherin Khankan, *Women are the Future of Islam* (New York: Random House, 2018).
30 Sherin Khankan, "A Muslim Manifesto," Forum for kritiske muslimer, accessed October 3, 2019, http://www.kritiskemuslimer.dk/?page_id=245.
31 Khankan, "A Muslim Manifesto."
32 Khankan, "A Muslim Manifesto."
33 Khankan, *Women are the Future of Islam*, 61.

for religion."³⁴ Rather, Khankan references Jürgen Habermas and Abdol Karim Sorouch for the view that

> secularism is a dialogue between religion and politics. Religion is seen as a strength to society, but the idea is rather that religion and religious arguments do not have primacy nor special status in society or in the political debate.³⁵

She further argues her point by highlighting that "in a secular society, all citizens are equal," and that "if you emphasize that a dimension of faith is to be maintained, then most Muslims do see compatibility between Islam and secularism."³⁶

In her memoir, she develops her understanding of secularism somewhat further, arguing that "religion must not impose itself on political decisions, only inspire them. Reciprocally, politics must not dictate its requirements to religions. In every case, politics and religion must be separate. But at the same time, religion can inspire societies."³⁷ While not very clear as to the degrees of separation and inspiration among religion, politics, and society, the idea seems to be that "Muslim faith" on the one hand and "opening up to a democratic secular society" on the other are neither contradictory nor incompatible notions.³⁸

In 2015, shortly after the Charlie Hebdo shootings on January 7 and the Copenhagen shootings on the night of February 14, Khankan presented the viability of female imams, a women-led mosque and interreligious marriage, effectively transforming the *Forum for Critical Muslims* by setting up a committee called FEMIMAM. In a March 3, 2015 interview,³⁹ and in an op-ed in March 2015,⁴⁰ Khankan set the ideas of the committee in motion and announced that, during the summer, they would set up a mosque with inter-gender prayer led by female imams. Anticipating much of the criticism, Khankan's argument remains that legitimate readings of the Qur'an, the tradition and legal schools, as well as select modern thinkers, allow equal rights and female religious leadership.⁴¹ The op-ed is titled "We need female imams," and unfolds her criticism of the

---

34 Pernille Bramming, "Vejen Frem," *Weekendavisen*, November 21, 2014.
35 Bramming, "Vejen Frem."
36 Bramming, "Vejen Frem."
37 Khankan, *Women are the Future of Islam*, 61.
38 Khankan, *Women are the Future of Islam*, 63.
39 "Danmarks næste iman?," *Information*, March 3, 2015, https://www.information.dk/indland/2015/03/danmarks-naeste-iman.
40 Sherin Khankan, "Vi har brug for kvindelige imamer," *Politiken*, March 5, 2015.
41 "Danmarks næste iman?," *Information*

more conservative voices within Islam, in both Europe and the Middle East. She does not call for a revolution, but rather for a renewal or return that abolishes the male monopoly on prayer leadership and the patriarchal state of Qur'anic interpretations, but recognizes the legitimate and well-established pluralism within Muslim traditions.

Although she promotes a strategy of not causing enough animosity to divide the Muslim community as she puts her ideas forward,[42] Khankan is steadfast in her convictions: "Many imams in this country belong to a traditional school and do not recognize the culture that we are part of."[43]

Khankan's position seems a difficult one. While she clearly wants to present female imams as well-established in the tradition, at the same time she is very critical of that same tradition for failing to cultivate equality. As much as she is critical of tradition, she needs its legitimacy and that of the legal and theological arguments of the legal schools of Islam in order to continue arguing for female prayer leadership as legitimate. A further hindrance to Khankan's project is her limited qualifications in that same legal and theological scholasticism, which she overcomes by highlighting spiritual and Sufi ideals. Relatively mainstream, traditionally educated leaders such as Waseem Hussain, or then-spokesman of the United Muslim Council, Sami Kücükakin, distanced themselves from Khankan's views and activism. They found that Khankan's promotion of female prayer leaders did not take the sources seriously and that her position was not coherently argued in terms of Islamic theology or law.[44]

While the strict coherence of her theology may be wanting, she almost opportunistically needs to operationalize and utilize the legitimacy of the legal tradition to bring about her project, not just in terms of equality, but also in terms of law and justice. In a programmatic statement in the op-ed she says, "Justice and equality cannot survive in a patriarchal structure, and without equality there is no democracy. Equality must be ensured everywhere. The idea of women and men as opposites is a modern construction and does not have its origins in the Qur'an or in modern *fiqh*."[45] She gives such statements an activist flavor by promoting provisions in Islamic marriage (*nikah*) that disallow polygamy, grant women equal access to divorce and make sure that an Islamic marriage automatically ends if the couple receives a civic divorce.[46] In this way, she uses

---

42 "Danmarks næste iman?," *Information*
43 "Danmarks næste iman?," *Information*
44 "Danmarks næste iman?," *Information.*
45 Khankan, "Kvindelige imamer."
46 Khankan, "Kvindelige imamer."

her interpretation of the Qur'an and her understanding of equality in Islam to tie Islamic law much closer to contemporary, secular Danish law.

Traditionalists

The third category includes the very conservative orthodox, the mainstream traditionalists[47] as well as those of more critical reformist inclination. As opposed to both the most outspoken secularists and fundamentalists, traditionalists follow the Islamic schools of law, they adhere to the teachings of history and the accumulated wisdom of the Islamic sciences, and they very much support the grand institutions of Islam.[48] They consider the great Caliphal dynasties as legitimate yet historical rulers, and recognize their states, law, and administration as mediated by human attempts at just rule.[49]

Traditionalists see significant room for democratic practice and legislation within the governing paradigm of the authority of the tradition of the Qur'an and Sunnah, and they see much law and administration that is necessary, yet not directly rooted in scripture, as for example in the Ottoman Empire.[50] Rights and freedoms, including human rights, are not derived from human agreement on common dignity, but from God. Therefore, under a just Muslim rule, the conditions for human flourishing are optimal. Under such rule, a poor understanding or application of Islamic principles will lead to injustice, indignity, loss of rights, and freedoms. Some reformist traditionalists recognize in *shura* (Arabic, "consultation") a kind of council or parliament equivalent to democratic institutions and regard the community of believers as just rulers (in this world). In general, we find traditionalists among the ranks of the established *ulama*—the learned ones in the community of scholars. This includes graduates of the al-Azhar University in Cairo like Yousuf al-Qaradawi and the scholars of the Islamic universities in Sarajevo, Kuala Lumpur and elsewhere around the

---

47   The word "tradition" may be the cause of some confusion. Here, "tradition" refers analytically to the tradition of Islam based on scholarship, the schools of law and rationalistic Islamic thought. The term "traditionalist theology," however, is also associated with *the tradition of the Prophet or Sunnah of the Prophet* as transmitted through hadith, and in turn is literalist.
48   For example, the Ulama of Al-Azhar, the Grand Muftis, the Shaykh ul-Islam and the imams of the Mosque of the Kaaba.
49   Benard et al., *Civil Democratic Islam*, 29ff.
50   Roger Ballard, "Changing Interpretations of Shari'a,'Urf and Qanun," *Electronic Journal of Middle Eastern Law* 1 no. 6 (2013): 115-59.

globe—including, surprisingly, many places in the Islamic Republic of Iran.[51] In Denmark, we find examples of conservative traditionalists in the Islamic Faith Community, most iconically personified in the late Imam Abu Laban who became notorious during the Danish Cartoon Crisis of 2005-2006.

The reformist traditionalists in Denmark make an interesting study in themselves. Following the migration trends of the second half of the 20th century, understandings and interpretations of Islam were not very rigorous or intellectually grounded, and levels of religiosity were low.[52] However, as the children of the first generation grew up, some took upon themselves to return to an explicit and qualified understanding and practice of traditional Islam. Such a traditional Islam is characterized by moderation, humility, and faith as well as a strong emphasis on Islamic knowledge and a high regard for the particularities and arguments of the particular legal and theological schools of Islam. Legally and theologically accounting for the history, arguments, and positions of Islamic scholasticism and drawing the appropriate directions for faith, they consider worship and practice to be the virtues of traditional Islam. Amongst Danish Muslims, we see a number of examples of young men and women, well-trained and educated, who speak and work to their coreligionists in contemporary Denmark with an authority derived from tradition. Some are leaders in mosques, some are imams and chaplains, while others are intellectuals, educators, and teachers. To this category belongs Ziad Hussein, lawyer and author of *The Black Beard—On Being a Danish Muslim* from 2018.[53] Such positions have also been discussed in recent scholarly literature, amongst others by Malik Larsen in his master's degree thesis *Balancing God and Country: On Denmark's New Muslim Intellectuals* from 2016.[54]

Whereas Khankan promotes a progressive re-interpretation of Islam, Ziad Hussein vocally argues for a return to the more comprehensive, critical, and qualified understanding and practice of the principles of Islam in the everyday life of Danish Muslims. His book addresses his fellow Muslims as much as a general readership. He sees himself as a layman who is highly critical of the religious elite that have remained detached from a new generation of young

---

51 Bettina Gräf and Jakob Skovgaard-Petersen, *Global Mufti: the Phenomenon of Yusuf al-Qaradawi* (London: Hurst & Company, 2009).
52 Jørgen Bæk Simonsen, *Det retfærdige samfund: Om islam, muslimer og etik* (Copenhagen: Samleren, 2001).
53 Tarek Ziad Hussein, *Det sorte skæg: Om at være dansk muslim* (Copenhagen: Gyldendal, 2018).
54 Malik Larsen, *At balancere gud og fædreland: Om Danmarks nye muslimske intellektuelle* (MA thesis, Aarhus Universitet, 2016).

Muslims. They have failed to integrate and cultivate a sustainable Islam for the future. Equally, he is critical of the political establishment in Denmark, who have sought insincerely to gain political capital and prominence by alienating ordinary Muslims. To many of his Muslim peers and to the public, Ziad Hussein challenges the idea that being both Muslim and Danish is a contradiction, which both the political right wing and radical Islamism argue in unison.[55] In many ways, the existence of right-wing political parties rests on the fact that Islam and Muslims are present in society.[56] In his own way, the "black beard" is an illustration of Ziad Hussein's middle and mediating position, demonstrating to the Islamists that their claim to a monopoly on Islam and their interpretation of tradition is unwarranted, but also showing the right-wing politicians that the "black beard" counters their problematic prejudice.

Being a traditional and practicing Muslim is an important premise for Ziad Hussein in writing his book. It gives him an insider position that makes his criticism much more legitimate and palpable to his peers, and he sees it as his mission to "unite an identity as a faithful and practicing Muslims with his identity as Danish."[57] Expressly, his book is a counter-argument against the identity politics championed by both the right wing and the radical Islamists, who seek to be the ones who decide what a Muslim really is. This is the core of much identity politics with regard to Islam and Muslims. To challenge such politics, Ziad Hussein unfolds his arguments, his analysis, and his solutions "from within a framework of a traditional, Islamic theology," in the deep conviction that "we as Muslims must interpret our faith in a contemporary context."[58] He repeatedly refers to scholarly disagreements and positions within the Islamic schools of thought. This makes his traditional positioning increasingly nuanced and intra-Islamically critical. He speaks much about the problems within Islam: from radical Islamists, from ISIS, from Salafists, and from Muslims who do not apply themselves, but instead rely on internet-trolls-turned-muftis, whom he calls "google Imams."[59]

In considering state, society, and law, Ziad Hussein is also critical. He is a trained jurist who has worked for the Danish Institute for Human Rights for several years. He argues for Muslim political participation, for an informed civil society under the rule of law, absolutely affirming the sovereignty of the democratic state, for the great integration and professionalization of Islamic

---

55 Ziad Hussein, *Det sorte skæg*, 16-17.
56 Ziad Hussein, *Det sorte skæg*, 46.
57 Ziad Hussein, *Det sorte skæg*, 17.
58 Ziad Hussein, *Det sorte skæg*, 14-15.
59 Ziad Hussein, *Det sorte skæg*, 69ff.

chaplaincy in public institutions, for the public responsibility of Muslims, and for civic rights and duties in the modern welfare state.[60] However, he is also critical of state and society from an intellectual, civic and expressly traditional Islamic point of view. His position is a criticism of the polarization on the issues of Islam, migration, rule of law, identity politics, and so forth. His position is well-aligned with that of many traditionalists who consider themselves mainstream, centrists, moderate, or on "the middle path," as they would say.[61]

One of the telltale signs of a traditionalist position, as opposed to Islamist or fundamentalist arguments, is that traditionalists do not alienate culture. As argued below, Olivier Roy has shown precisely how Islamic fundamentalism is a radical response to a loss of culture, history, and identity. In this context, fundamentalism and, more predominantly, the fundamentalisms of the 21st century, seek to "vindicate the loss of cultural identity and allow a pure religion to be conceptualized independently of all its cultural variations and influences."[62] This means that they substitute Islam in its many manifestations into the voids left by the purification of elements of local cultures, such as history, cuisine, and language. This is Islamization or Arabization, such as fatwas and opinions on quite mundane things, Arabic vocabulary and perceivable Islamic identifiers, such as headscarves, beards, and so on. Roy points to the Taliban in Afghanistan and their restrictions on kite-flying and music.[63]

Clearly in opposition to this, Ziad Hussein and other traditionalists seek the proper place in life for religion and seek to bring the relevant aspects of religion into life and everyday practice. Part of the problem is mistaking culture for religion, or religion for culture.[64] In contemporary public debate on Islam, it seems everything Muslims do is understood and interpreted in terms of religion. Muslims, obviously, he says "are human beings like all others, who consider religion, culture, history, socio-economics, upbringing, environment, education, psychology, and much more."[65] Implicit in this argument is both a critique of the national-conservative antagonists who might assume on behalf of Muslims that they only follow a certain culture, but also against those who insist on importing cultural traits from a particular Middle Eastern or South East Asian culture and claim that alone to be Islam. However, he does not

---

60 Ziad Hussein, *Det sorte skæg*, 42-44, 66-68, 116, 169.
61 Benard el al., *Civil Democratic Islam*, 33.
62 Olivier Roy, "Islam in Europe: Clash of religions or convergence of religiosities?," *Eurozine*, May 3, 2007, www.eurozine.com/islam-in-europe.
63 As portrayed in Khaled Khosseini, *The Kite Runner* (New York: Riverhead Books, 2003).
64 Ziad Hussein, *Det sorte skæg*, 91ff.
65 Ziad Hussein, *Det sorte skæg*, 91.

go as far as criticizing the deeply embedded culture in Danish secular law or democracy for the particular Danish tradition of mingling together culture and religion.

Fundamentalists

The final category includes groups of fundamentalists, literalists, Islamists, Salafists, and so on, who reject democratic values and contemporary Western law, society, and culture.[66] Their alternative is an authoritarian Islamic state for implementing what they consider Islamic law and morals, while they apply completely modern technology and innovations to achieve this. They consider democracy entirely wrongful, in that only God holds legislative power and has given his law in revelation. An Islamic state should be global and supranational, organizing the Ummah in one community and, in lieu of a legislature, human beings are delegated the tasks of policing and adjudication. A variation of this argues that God has given Islam as a form of human government stewardship through the *khilafa*: the Caliphate state. Hizb ut-Tahrir boasts a very comprehensive doctrine of government. Similarly, society in all its aspects should be thoroughly Islamized, with little to no toleration of religious minorities and dissidents, who should convert.[67]

General examples of this includes Hizb ut-Tahrir, Wahhabi-Salafis, and sympathizers with the Islamic State in Iraq and Syria. In Denmark, we find (quietist-)Salafi sympathizers in the Grimhøj Mosque in Aarhus and Hizb ut-Tahrir in the Masjid al-Faruq. As briefly discussed above, Olivier Roy's fundamental analysis is an excellent opening for understanding of fundamentalists and in particular the political fundamentalists as they come to expression in the political Islamism of Hizb ut-Tahrir.

Hizb ut-Tahrir is a global, Islamist, and fundamentalist political party that was founded in Jerusalem in 1953. It was founded by Taqiuddin al-Nabhani, who was an Islamic scholar and appeals court judge. Hizb ut-Tahrir considers itself a political party that builds on Islam as a political ideology. Its mode of operation is political activism and can be classified as extra-parliamentary opposition. The party defines the Islamic Ummah ("community") as its political goal and works for a return to a true Islam and to reestablish the Khilafa

---

66 Benard et al., *Civil Democratic Islam*, 27.
67 Olivier Roy, *Globalized Islam: The Search for a New Ummah* (New York: Columbia University Press, 2006).

state, justice executed according to the revealed commandments of Allah, and to punish those Muslims who neglect their duties.[68] Al-Nabhani has written extensively on the *khilafa*-state doctrine of Hizb ut-Tahrir, including a full political program, a constitution for the Caliphate as well as complete monographs, such as *The Islamic State*.[69]

Hizb ut-Tahrir was established in Denmark in 2000. While there has been significant political criticism of Hizb ut-Tahrir, and many of its key figures violated Danish legislation on racism and hate speech, it remains a legally permitted political organization. The Danish attorney general, chief prosecutors and Ministry of Justice have explored the possibility of dissolving the party through the courts, but have found that it works within the legitimate frame of the constitution. After 2005, national Hizb ut-Tahrir organizations have gained more independence, and the organization is now working as Hizb ut-Tahrir Scandinavia.[70]

Hizb ut-Tahrir is a relevant and significant voice to consider in a study on Muslim views on state, society and law. While they are quite marginal and are estimated at about 1,000 core members and sympathizers, they remain one of the most vocal organizations on these precise issues for two reasons. One is that they have very controversial and far-reaching opinions on the matter of Islam in relation to state, society, law, and secularism. Another is that they are significantly better organized than most other Muslim groups in Denmark, and they organize and communicate like an activist political party. In comparison to the three other positions and voices studied here, so far we have identified one key Muslim author as an ideal-typical representative of a broader position, each with a major recent book and additional interviews, op-eds or newspaper articles. For this section on Hizb ut-Tahrir, a systematic approach has been applied in analyzing the views on state, society, law, and politics in 74 press releases and 54 flyers published online from January 2010 to May 2019. They have been coded and analyzed in terms of statements about and views on law and democracy, politicians and politics, government and authorities, society and secularism, media, and Islam and Hizb ut-Tahrir itself. Naturally, the material is much too vast—in print, about 300 pages—to be covered exhaustively here, but recent and ample examples will be provided to illustrate the position of Hizb ut-Tahrir.

Both their press releases and flyers have developed into very specific genre pieces and follow the same communicative and rhetorical scheme, adapted for

---

68 "Hizb ut-Tahrir Definitionen," Hizb ut-Tahrir Skandinavien, accessed October 3, 2019, http://www.hizb-ut-tahrir.dk/content.php?contentid=102.
69 Taqi al-Din Nabhani, *The Islamic State* (London: Al-Khilafah Publications, 1998).
70 Kirstine Sinclair, "Hizb ut-Tahrir i Danmark og Storbritannien: Samtidige transnationale og nationale tendenser," *Tidsskrift for Islamforskning* 6, no. 1 (2012): 37-53.

a Danish audience on the basis of the press material of the international main organization.

On September 7, 2018, in a broad campaign on the occasion of the Swedish elections, Hizb ut-Tahrir advocated for not voting, but rather speaking out against democracy. Through their criticism of the general election and the Swedish authorities, their view on democracy and secularism as opposed to their view of Islam, reveals itself. A press release of September 7, 2018 stated:

> The centre of the campaign has been to argue how Muslims may be active in society without compromising their Islamic identity." They continue, "Hizb ut-Tahrir does not recognize democracy as a form of government because it is based on secularism, which is against Islam. Democracy assumes that man legislates, while according to Islam, it is only Allah, the All-Mighty creator, who has the right to legislate. Additionally, we consider democracy a system that predominantly serves the holders of capital and the interests of business through changing governments.[71]

Naturally, Hizb ut-Tahrir is met with significant criticism. The Swedish authorities' attempt to limit Hizb ut-Tahrir's campaign only made them rail even more vocally against the authorities:

> This panic reaction reveals the Swedish authorities' fear of Islamic political thought and our work to protect the identity of Muslims and to cultivate a consciousness about solely thinking and acting on the basis of Islam as a collective. Such desperate endeavors are clear evidence of the withering ability to intellectually debate the ideas of Islam, and thus they seek by force to limit the expression of Islamic ideas.[72]

Generally, Hizb ut-Tahrir seeks to expose the hypocrisy and inability of governments and democracies to argue their own values and virtues against Islamist ideas. Recent Danish legislation has tightened anti-radicalization efforts and public authorities are forbidden from supporting associations that counteract

---

71 "Hizb ut-Tahrirs kampagne i Sverige: Brug din stemme, men ikke til valget!," Hizb ut-Tahrir Skandinavien, Press release, September 7, 2018, http://www.hizb-ut-tahrir.dk/content.php?contentid=877.

72 "De svenske myndigheders håbløse forsøg på at hindre Hizb ut-Tahrirs kald," Hizb ut-Tahrir Skandinavien, Press release, August 31, 2018, http://www.hizb-ut-tahrir.dk/content.php?contentid=874.

or undermine democracy and basic freedoms and human rights.[73] For Hizb ut-Tahrir, this means that, as of November 14, 2018, the Municipality of Copenhagen declined their request to rent a public gym hall for their event. In a press release of November 16, 2018, titled "The Liberal Tyranny of Prohibitions are undermining the Danish Democracy," Hizb ut-Tahrir complains against the series of tightenings and clampdowns on immigration, integration, and—as they see it—Islam and Muslims. Their view of law and democracy reflects what they see as an overarching struggle between Islam and the West, and they rhetorically ask, "How frail and fragile is the foundation of this democracy and these values, if it is undermined by criticism and Islamic attitudes?"[74] They continue to "expose" the anti-Islamic sentiment they perceive to be behind such legislative tightening. In a way, while in principle Hizb ut-Tahrir is against democracy as they view it as usurping Allah's legislative prerogative, they express significant concern for the well-being of that same democracy:

> The amendment is a part of the flared struggle against Islam in this country, which is led by the government and parliament and trumpeted by the so-called 'free' media. Ministers and significant politicians are frantically championing one raving and subversive suggestion after the other, in order to appear 'tough on Muslims,' and strangle Islamic expressions in a panic fear that Islam might be normalized and grow stronger roots in this country.[75]

Also more broadly in Europe, Hizb ut-Tahrir identifies other secular democratic and legal institutions as illegitimate. On March 14, 2017, the Grand Chamber of the Court of Justice of the European Union ruled that employers had the right to forbid employees from wearing religious symbols, including the Islamic headscarf as some Muslim women wear. This, of course, was provided that certain conditions were fulfilled as spelled out in the judgment. This ruling was viewed by Dr. Nazreen Nawaz, the director of the women's wing of Hizb ut-Tahrir's central media office, as discrimination promoted by the European Court of Human Rights:[76]

---

73 L 13, *Proposal for a law amending the Public Education Act and the Taxation Act*, 2016.
74 "Det liberale forbudstyranni underminerer det danske demokrati," Hizb ut-Tahrir Skandinavien, Press release, November 16, 2018, http://www.hizb-ut-tahrir.dk/content.php?contentid=892.
75 Hizb ut-Tahrir Skandinavien, "Det liberale forbudstyranni."
76 CJEU, 14 March 2017, C-157/15, *Samira Achbita, Centrum voor gelijkheid van kansen en voor racismebestrijding V G4S Secure Solutions NV*, ECLI:EU:C:2017:203. It seems Dr. Nazreen Nawaz mistakes the judicial bodies, taking the European Court of Human Rights for the Court of Justice of the European Union.

> The European Court of Human Rights ruled on 14 March 2017 that employers have the right to forbid employees from wearing religious symbols, including the Islamic headscarf, as Muslim women wear … In the same way as it has become tradition with the secular governments and institutions, the European Court of Human Rights chooses to adopt and legitimate the populist intolerance against Muslims, rather than fighting it. The Court reveals the dangers of the flakey secular system, where one cannot predict the outcome, because minorities are at the mercy of those intolerant ones, who rule and judge, which makes rights annullable according to the damaging whims of these people … The secular design of society, which tries to force Muslim women to surrender their Islamic convictions and adopt a secular identity, is nothing but the latest phase in a series of desperate measures put in motion by Western governments and their institutions to fight the overwhelming and significant presence of Muslims …[77]

As recently as January 3, 2019, Hizb ut-Tahrir restated their highly critical view on the relationship between politics and (their view on) Islam:

> While they hastily undermine their own values of freedom, the politicians demonstrate an obvious intellectual impotence against the strong ideas of Islam. A vast political majority has in effect given up faith on democracy and secular values, as they promote sanctions, thought control, and the full power of law to forcefully assimilate Muslims.[78]

Comparisons and Conclusions

While Muslims might agree on the virtues of Islam and on some of the recent critique of government overreach, there is very little agreement on any of the relevant issues concerning state and law, as seen in the points raised by the different Muslim positions, primarily Hizb ut-Tahrir and others. For all the four main arguments exemplified here, it seems that all demonstrate to a greater or lesser degree their inability to correctly, analytically, or even relatively clearly understand the other positions. This speaks to the level of polemicism at play among them.

---

77 "Den europæiske menneskerettighedsdomstol legitimerer diskrimination mod muslimske kvinder på grund af deres islamiske påklædning," Hizb ut-Tahrir Skandinavien, Press release, March 20, 2017, http://www.hizb-ut-tahrir.dk/content.php?contentid=806.

78 "Berlingske afslører sin uhæderlighed og politikernes agenda med artikel om Hizb ut-Tahrir," Hizb ut-Tahrir Skandinavien, Press release, January 3, 2019, https://www.hizb-ut-tahrir.dk/content.php?contentid=912.

For the two extreme positions presented here, the question of convergence between state, law, and society, on the one hand, and Islam and Muslims on the other, must be answered in the negative. For both the opposite and uncompromising positions represented by Tavakoli and Hizb ut-Tahrir, it seems that, however much they disagree, they confirm each other's points of view. To Tavakoli, Islam is extreme, intolerant, and fundamentalist, and Hizb ut-Tahrir seems to confirm this view. In contrast, Hizb ut-Tahrir sees secularism as the antithesis of Islam and the core of a political agenda against the views, thoughts and ideas of Muslims, which in turn, Tavakoli promotes.

While both Khankan and Ziad Hussein present their points of view with greater nuance and thought, their understanding and analysis of the extreme positions leave much to be desired. Even among themselves, the modernist and traditionalist positions seem to get into a bit of trouble, perhaps because of the details in the distinction.

Khankan's view of the secular seems sober and balanced. She is not as uncompromising as neither the secularists, who have little sympathy for Islamic identity, nor the fundamentalists, who see secularism as the end of Islam. She speaks about the possibility of being both Muslim and secular and argues for a separation of both. Sufi attitudes and worldviews are influential on Khankan's interpretation of Islam, which might even seem to converge with a secular, if not secularist, position. Khankan does not evince a strict adherence to doctrine and has no concern for the "purity" of Islam; quite the contrary. However, Khankan seems to conflate a conservative, yet mainstream, understanding of traditional Islam with those holding more expressly Islamist or even fundamentalist positions.

Compared with the other positions within Islam presented here, Ziad Hussein shares many views and principled positions with Khankan. He too argues for an increased critical hermeneutics and the need for 21st-century, modern interpretations. However, he does so to a much more profound degree. In order for it to make sense, he needs his arguments to resonate with the Islamic schools and with the traditional Islamic environments. He calls for a new and younger generation to present informed arguments that will continue the conversations of the faithful into the future.

This volume discusses three different layers of secularity. Based on the material surveyed in this chapter and the four main positions presented, all four recognize the deep structural levels of secularity in Denmark (secularity$^{meaning1\text{-}2}$), but only Hizb ut-Tahrir seems actively to resist and work against such influences. Considering the personal level, in which religion is seen as optional (secularity^{meaning3}), only the two middle positions, exemplified by Khankan and

Ziad Hussein, recognize such secularity as indeed personal and optional. Where Tavakoli sees such secularity as mandatory (as secular*ism*), Hizb ut-Tahrir sees it as dangerous and something to be completely rejected. Both represent a radical decoupling of personal religiosity from the governing Danish law and jurisprudence—each in their distinct and opposite direction—and both seem to seek to re-confessionalize their position. The re-confessionalization of the Islamism of Hizb ut-Tahrir speaks to the growing efforts to cast off the influence and power of the state, and to restore an anti-democratic independence. With "religious fervor," the secularist voices can be viewed as a direct and opposite reaction to this Islamist position. They argue for a growing legal dependence and involvement of state in religious issues. Such a "re-confessionalization" of secularism would in effect result in a "de-confessionalization" of the state.

Considering the overall problem of the chapter of what Muslims think of state and law in Denmark, there seems to be the potential for maintaining justice and the rule of law in both the modernist and traditional identities. Both recognize the deep structural secularity in Denmark and allow for individual choice in an optional religiosity. In opposition to this view, the polarized and marginal voices of hardline secularists and Hizb ut-Tahrir actively work to make a balanced understanding of justice and the rule of law impossible.

Bibliography

Court of Justice of the European Union
CJEU, 14 March 2017, C-157/15, *Samira Achbita, Centrum voor gelijkheid van kansen en voor racismebestrijding V G4S Secure Solutions NV*, ECLI:EU:C:2017:203.

Official Sources
L 13. *Proposal for a law amending the Public Education Act and the Taxation Act*, 2016. Ministry of Cultural Affairs.

Literature
Auda, Jasser. *Maqasid al-Shariah as Philosophy of Islamic Law: A Systems Approach*. Herndom: International Institute of Islamic Thought, 2008.
Auda, Jasser. "Rethinking Islamic Law for Europe." In *Imams in Western Europe: Developments, Transformations and Institutional Challenges*, edited by Mohammed Hashas, Jan Jaap de Ruiter, and Niels Valdemar Vinding. Amsterdam: Amsterdam University Press, 2018.
Ballard, Roger. "Changing interpretations of Shari'a,'Urf and Qanun." *Electronic Journal of Middle Eastern Law* 1, no. 6 (2013): 115-59.

Bayat, Asef. *Making Islam Democratic: Social Movements and the Post-Islamist turn.* Stanford: Stanford University Press, 2007.

Benard, Cheryl, Andrew Riddile, Peter A. Wilson, and Steven W. Popper. *Civil Democratic Islam: Partners, Resources, and Strategies.* Santa Monica, CA: Rand Corporation, 2004.

Bramming, Pernille. "Vejen Frem." *Weekendavisen*, November 21, 2014.

Bubalo, Anthony and Greg Fealy. *Between the Global and the Local: Islamism, the Middle East, and Indonesia.* Washington, D.C.: Brookings Institution, 2005.

Gräf, Bettina, and Jakob Skovgaard-Petersen. *Global Mufti: The Phenomenon of Yusuf al-Qaradawi.* London: Hurst & Company, 2009.

Hashas Mohammed. *The Idea of European Islam: Religion, Ethics, Politics and Perpetual Modernity.* London: Routledge, 2018

"Hizb ut-Tahrirs kampagne i Sverige: Brug din stemme, men ikke til valget!," Hizb ut-Tahrir Skandinavien, Press release, September 7, 2018, http://www.hizb-ut-tahrir.dk/content.php?contentid=877.

Høgh, Marie. "Her er den altoverskyggende årsag bag voldtægterne." *BT*, July 1, 2018. https://www.bt.dk/debat/her-er-den-altoverskyggende-aarsag-bag-voldtaegterne.

Information. "Danmarks næste iman?" March 3, 2015. https://www.information.dk/indland/2015/03/danmarks-naeste-iman.

Jacobsen, Brian Arly, and Niels Valdemar Vinding. "Denmark." In *Yearbook of Muslims in Europe* 12, edited by Egdunas Racius, Stephanie Müssin, Samim Akgönül, Ahmet Alibašić, Jørgen S. Nielsen, and Oliver Scharbrodt, 199-216. Leiden: Brill, 2021.

Jeldtoft, Nadia. "Lived Islam: Religious identity with 'Non-Organized' Muslim Minorities." *Ethnic and Racial Studies* 34, no. 7 (2011): 1134-51.

Johansen, Birgitte Schepelern. "Kampen om værdierne: Sekularisme." *Information*, May 14, 2016. https://www.information.dk/debat/2016/05/kampen-vaerdierne-sekularisme.

Kaya, Emir. *Secularism and State Religion in Modern Turkey: Law, Policy-Making and the Diyanet.* London: Bloomsbury Publishing, 2018.

Khankan, Sherin. "Vi har brug for kvindelige imamer." *Politiken*, March 5, 2015.

Khankan, Sherin. *Women are the Future of Islam.* New York: Random House, 2018.

Khosseini, Khaled. *The Kite Runner.* New York: Riverhead Books, 2003.

Kitcher, Philip. *Life after Faith: The Case for Secular Humanism.* New Haven, CT: Yale University Press, 2014.

Kühle, Lene. "Radikalisering: Ekstremisme eller vækkelse? En undersøgelse af aarhusianske muslimers holdninger." *Islam og muslimer i Danmark: Religion, identitet og sikkerhed efter 11. september 2011*, edited by Marianne Holm Pedersen and Mikkel Rytter, 89-114. Copenhagen: Museum Tusculanum, 2011.

Larsen, Malik. *At balancere gud og fædreland: Om Danmarks nye muslimske intellektuelle.* MA diss., Aarhus Universitet, 2016

Lewis, Bernard. *The Crisis of Islam: Holy War and Unholy Terror.* New York: Random House Incorporated, 2004.

Maher, Shiraz. *Salafi-Jihadism: The History of an Idea.* London: Hurst & Company, 2016.

Mandaville, Peter. *Global Political Islam*. London: Routledge, 2010.

Modéer, Kjell Å. "Internal Convergence—External Divergence: Religion in Nordic Legal Culture and Tradition at the Threshold of the Third Millenium." In *Law & Religion in the 21st Century: Nordic Perspectives,* edited by Lisbet Christoffersen, Kjell Å. Modéer, and Svend Andersen, 61-78. Copenhagen: DJØF Publishing, 2010.

Nabhani, Taqi al-Din. *The Islamic State*. London: Al-Khilafah Publications, 1998.

Nielsen, Jørgen S., ed. *Islam in Denmark: The Challenge of Diversity*. Lanham: Lexington Books, 2012.

Norton, Anne. *On the Muslim Question*. Princeton: Princeton University Press, 2013.

Oudenampsen, Merijn. "Deconstructing Ayaan Hirsi Ali: On Islamism, Neoconservatism, and the Clash of Civilizations." *Politics, Religion & Ideology* 17, no. 2-3 (2016): 227-48.

Pedersen, Marianne Holm, and Mikkel Rytter, eds. *Islam og muslimer i Danmark: Religion, identitet og sikkerhed efter 11. september 2011*. Copenhagen: Museum Tusculanum Press, 2011.

Petersen, Jesper. "Media and the Female Imam." *Religions* 10, no. 3 (2019). https://doi.org/10.3390/rel10030159.

Ramadan, Tariq. *Western Muslims and the Future of Islam*. Oxford: Oxford University Press, 2003.

Roy, Olivier. *Globalized Islam: The Search for a New Ummah*. New York: Columbia University Press, 2006.

Roy, Olivier. "Islam in Europe: Clash of religions or convergence of religiosities?" *Eurozine*, May 3, 2007. www.eurozine.com/islam-in-europe.

Roy, Olivier. *The Failure of Political Islam*. Cambridge: Harvard University Press, 1994.

Simonsen, Jørgen Bæk. *Det retfærdige samfund: Om islam, muslimer og etik*. Copenhagen: Samleren, 2001.

Sinclair, Kirstine. "Hizb ut-Tahrir i Danmark og Storbritannien: Samtidige transnationale og nationale tendenser." *Tidsskrift for Islamforskning* 6, no. 1 (2012): 37-53

Stjernholm, Anders. *Eftertro: Lad os tale om tro, tvivl og det svære valg at forlade en religion*. Copenhagen: Gyldendal, 2017.

Tavakoli, Jaleh. *Islams offentlige hemmeligheder*. Copenhagen: Selfpublished, 2018.

Tavakoli, Jaleh. "Kampen om værdierne: Sekularisme." *Information*, May 14, 2016. https://www.information.dk/debat/2016/05/kampen-vaerdierne-sekularisme.

Vinding, Niels Valdemar. *Annotated Legal Documents on Islam in Denmark*. Leiden: Brill, 2020.

Zayd, Nasr Hamid Abu. *Critique of the Religious Discourse*. Translated by Jonathan Wright. New Haven, CT: Yale University Press, 2018.

Ziad Hussein, Tarek. *Det sorte skæg: Om at være dansk muslim*. Copenhagen: Gyldendal, 2018.

Webpages

Hizb ut-Tahrir Skandinaven. "Den europæiske menneskerettighedsdomstol legitimerer diskrimination mod muslimske kvinder på grund af deres islamiske påklædning." Press relearse, March 20, 2017. http://www.hizb-ut-tahrir.dk/content.php?contentid=806.

Hizb ut-Tahrir Skandinaven. "De svenske myndigheders håbløse forsøg på at hindre Hizb ut-Tahrirs kald." Press release, August 31, 2018. http://www.hizb-ut-tahrir.dk/content.php?contentid=874.

Hizb ut-Tahrir Skandinaven. "Det liberale forbudstyranni underminerer det danske demokrati." Press release, November 16, 2018. http://www.hizb-ut-tahrir.dk/content.php?contentid=892.

Hizb ut-Tahrir Skandinaven. "Berlingske afslører sin uhæderlighed og politikernes agenda med artikel om Hizb ut-Tahrir." Press release, January 3, 2019. https://www.hizb-ut-tahrir.dk/content.php?contentid=912.

Hizb ut-Tahrir Skandinaven. "Hizb ut-Tahrir Definitionen." Accessed October 3, 2019. http://www.hizb-ut-tahrir.dk/content.php?contentid=102.

Jensen, Inge Haandsbæk. "Jaleh Tavakoli: Jeg byder reformvillige muslimer velkommen." *Religion.dk*, October 8, 2018. https://www.religion.dk/jaleh-tavakoli-reformislam-soeges.

Khankan, Sherin. "A Muslim manifesto." Forum for kritiske muslimer. Accessed October 3, 2019. http://www.kritiskemuslimer.dk/?page_id=245.

Skovgaard, Marie, dir. *The Reformist: A Female Imam*, TV documentary, 2019. Filmdatabasen. Accessed October 3, 2019. https://www.dfi.dk/en/viden-om-film/filmdatabasen/film/reformisten-den-kvindelige-imam.

10. "By Law Established": The Nordic Lutheran Majority Churches in a Comparative Perspective

Lisbet Christoffersen[1]

The old Lutheran majority churches in the five Nordic countries are regularly referred to as *state churches*. This is no longer a relevant concept for at least four of the five churches. Rather, relevant concepts to identify the legal status for these churches is *by law established* or maybe *by law re-established* into ever new formats.

The aim of this chapter is to analyze the post-World War II impact of internationalization on the Nordic changes from state churches to churches established by law. This analysis will lead to a discussion of the legitimacy behind these changed formats of regulation as well as a discussion of the extent to which these changes open for a re-confessionalization of the Nordic Lutheran (majority) churches.

The concept *by law established* describes the majority model in the Nordic countries. In 2017, Norway celebrated the 500 year anniversary of the beginning of the Lutheran Reformation by changing the Church of Norway into an independent legal subject, an Evangelical Lutheran *folkekirke*, which is no longer part of the state hierarchy.[2] As per January 1, 2017, the Church of Norway is no longer a state church. The church has, however, been re-established or re-organized by law. Legally speaking, the Church of Norway is still not equivalent to other religious communities in Norway. The same is true for the Evangelical

---

[1] This paper builds on research provided within the research projects *What Money Can't Buy* (funded by the Independent Research Fund Denmark) and the HERA-funded research project *Protestant Legacies in Nordic Law*. I wish to express my gratitude for funding and for precise and relevant comments. To earlier versions of the paper, presented at guest lectures and seminars in all Nordic countries. Legal papers are updated as per May 2020.

[2] https://lovdata.no/dokument/LTI/lov/2016-05-27-17, Lov om endringer i kirkeloven (omdanning av Den norske kirke til eget rettssubjekt m.m.). See, e.g., Lisbet Christoffersen, "Towards Re-Sacralisation of Nordic Law?," in *Formatting Religion: Across Politics, Education, Media, and Law*, ed. Marius Timmann Mjaaland (London/New York: Routledge, 2020), 175-204, for a detailed analysis of this change, with a bibliography including Norwegian literature and original legal sources.

Lutheran Church of Finland, the Church of Sweden, and the Icelandic Evangelical Lutheran Church: They are all more or less independent from the state hierarchies and their legal statuses have been re-settled through constitutional changes and legislation during the last 30 years, but their legal foundation is still statutory parliamentary law. This legal status is different from being a state church, and it sets these Nordic churches in a legal position different from other religious communities in the region.

Also the Danish Evangelical Lutheran *folkekirke* is organized by state legislation, albeit in a manner different from the other Nordic majority churches. This church remains partly interwoven into the administrative hierarchy of the state-governance system, which implies that the Danish *folkekirke* also retains more of the old state-church characteristics with a certain role of not only executive powers, but also a larger role for the legislative powers and a clear role for the judiciary.

Only the Lutheran majority churches, but no other religious community, have their organizational structure and their legal status established by law. Instead, other religious communities base their legal identity on other sources: the Catholic Church, for example, is established by what one could identify as a religio-legal tradition in Canon Law, not by state law, and so are Orthodox Churches (in the Nordic region as well as in other parts of the world). Another group of religious communities, such as the United Methodist Church, derive their legal basis from a transnational religio-legal order.[3] Finally, churches such as the Baptists and other evangelical churches derive their legal legitimacy from being organizations based on decisions by the members.

These different models are also present in these five countries, since they have freedom of religion and belief enshrined in law. Formally speaking, Norway was the last of these countries to constitutionally acknowledge freedom of religion and belief in a constitutional change of 1964.[4] In practice, however,

---

3   For a detailed analysis of the legal order of the United Methodist Church, see Lisbet Christoffersen, "Transnational Religious Law: Exemplified by the United Methodist Church," in *Transnationalisation and Legal Actors: Legitimacy in Question*, ed. Bettina Lemann Kristiansen et al. (London/New York: Routledge, 2019), 201-16. The UMC, which a generation ago was one of the most liberal churches in the world, supporting human rights protection against discrimination on the basis of gender, race, sexuality etc., is currently splitting on grounds of theological conflicts regarding female priesthood and homosexual praxis among the ordained bishops. For a while, the united legal and economic structure of UMC has functioned as a "cover-up" for the splits but is now becoming part of the conflict.

4   The original constitution of the Kingdom of Norway (dating from 1814) contained a clause preventing Jews, monastic orders, and Jesuits from entering the kingdom. Limited freedom of religion and belief was introduced by law in 1845 (the law on dissenting communities), after which the Catholic Church and other Christian communities could

the entire 20th century has been a century of freedom of religion and belief in all Nordic countries. Other religious communities are accepted and many of them are acknowledged by law or by administrative decision. Until now, however, full legal equality between the Nordic Lutheran majority churches and other religious communities is not established.

Freedom of religion and belief cannot be said to favor any of the legal structures mentioned. The point of departure in the thinking of human rights is that all religious communities must *organize themselves* within the framework of the law of the land, unless state legislation relieves the religious communities from their organizational freedom of religion and belief. In this picture, both state churches and by-law establishment of churches, which previously was the North-European normal, becomes the exception. Increasing implementation of human rights in the field of religion and law thus leads to more organizational freedom within the majority churches, too. The question for this chapter is the extent to which more organizational freedom also entails more freedom for the individual as well as more legitimacy behind the regulation of the national churches.

In section 1, I present the legal background for the development of the Nordic churches with legal legitimacy in statutory law. In section 2, I compare the concept of being by law established with the theoretical concept of church autonomy, well known from the literature. Section 2 then provides an empirical comparative analysis of how the laws in the Nordic churches have established rights for individual church members and staff, such as accession rights to the rituals, rights of equal treatment etc. and thereby shows the impact of law on the rights of individuals in these churches. Section 3 is a conclusion on the role of legal establishment in ensuring rights for individuals in the Nordic churches. In section 4, the impact of internationalization on the changes of Nordic religion law and ecclesiastical law is discussed regarding the Nordic Lutheran majority churches. While focus in sections 1-3 is on the current (2020) valid law of the Nordic Lutheran majority churches, section 4 deals with the most recent change of Nordic religion law, namely the new Norwegian law on

---

re-establish themselves in Norway. The prohibition against Jews settling in Norway was lifted by a change of the constitution in 1851. From 1892, civil servants were no longer bound to be members of the Church of Norway. Monastic orders were allowed in 1897, and Jesuits, allowed after the European Convention of Human Rights of 1953, followed by a change of the Norwegian constitution in 1956. Finally, in 1964, a general rule on freedom of religion was incorporated into the constitution. The occasion for the change to the constitution in 1964 was, according to Johannes Andenæs and Arne Fliflet. *Statsforfatningen i Norge*, 10th ed. (Oslo: Universitetsforlaget, 2006), 388, the 150-year celebration of the constitution.

religious communities, including the Church of Norway. This law was passed in parliament on April 24, 2020, and is in force from January 1, 2021. It marks a milestone in the change of not only the legislation, but also the legitimacy behind the legislation on the Nordic Lutheran majority churches. Finally, in section 5, I discuss how the increasing change of legal legitimacy behind the Nordic Lutheran majority churches contributes to re-confessionalization in the sense discussed in this book.

Legal Developments of by Law Established Churches from the Reformation to the 21st Century

The Reformation impacted ecclesiastical law differently in the East-Nordic realm and in the West-Nordic realm. These differences formed the basis of the legislation and constitutional changes in the 19th and 20th centuries, and thus form the point of departure also for understanding how the legislative changes occurring at the beginning of the 21st century differed in the Nordic countries. The following paragraphs provide a short overview of the particular national legal contexts.

In the East-Nordic realm, the *Swedish* Reformation started in Västerås in 1527 when the upcoming king, Gustav Vasa, called a meeting in order to establish unity in religious matters, based on the tenets of the Lutheran Reformation. Gustav Vasa also needed money for the wars against Denmark, which led to a first round of expropriation of ecclesiastical land. Different theological opinions and practices were still allowed, partly also due to a period in which there was a Polish Catholic king in Sweden/Finland. A church meeting in Uppsala in 1593, however, confirmed that the church was to be Lutheran and that no civil servants with other faiths were allowed. After a short internal war, the king also became obliged to follow the Lutheran confession. Around 1600, the second period of secularization of ecclesiastical land took place, monasteries were closed, and Canon Law was formally rendered illegitimate. The confessional obligation of the king was further confirmed when Queen Kristina (reigning from 1644) abdicated at the end of the European wars of religion in 1654, left the country, and shortly afterwards converted to the Catholic faith. However, even though the Church of Sweden was in 1593 confirmed as Lutheran, the traditional internal structure of an archbishop, chapters, and dioceses was retained. Likewise, the church hierarchy remained in charge of internal matters regarding matters of faith, albeit under royal supervision.[5]

This national structure for the Church of Sweden survived through absolutism (1680) with a re-establishment of the church under a new ecclesiastical law of 1686, ensuring uniformity of the church organization. This legislation finally gave the king full influence over the internal matters of the church, such as the appointment of clerics, including bishops. The ordinary courts were at the same time given control over ecclesiastical matters. A constitutional reform of 1809 kept the king loyal to the Lutheran confession, but opened the way for freedom of religion.[6] New legislation from 1859 onwards cemented this freedom, also for other religious communities. At the same time, the Church of Sweden was again reorganized by constitutional law in 1866, when a national Church Assembly was added to the surviving structure with an archbishop at its top. The Church Assembly was designed to be responsible for the internal, theological decisions of the Church of Sweden. Any legislative change concerning the Church of Sweden, which was still to be decided by the legislative institutions of the state, also had to be confirmed by the Church Assembly in order to become legitimate. Full freedom of religion and belief, including the right not to belong to any religious community, was finally approved by law in Sweden in 1952. In 1982, the state delegated all decisions concerning internal affairs to the Church Assembly and a central governance structure of the Church of Sweden was also established by law.

In 2000, the Swedish government (re-)established the Church of Sweden by law as an Evangelical Lutheran church, structured with an ecclesiastical hierarchy and democratic organization at all levels and with the obligation to cover all geographical parts of Sweden.[7] Besides the brief and specific law

---

5 Further on the legal dimensions of the Swedish Reformation history, see, e.g., Kjell Å. Modéer, "The Long Way towards Traditional Autonomy," in *Law & Religion in the 21st Century—Nordic Perspectives*, ed. Lisbet Christoffersen, Kjell Å. Modéer, and Svend Andersen (Copenhagen: DJØF Publishing, 2010), 81-88; Martin Berntson, Bertil Nilsson, and Cecilia Wejryd. *Kyrka i Sverige: Introduktion till svensk kyrkohistoria* (Skellefteå: Artos & Noma Bokförlag, 2012), 119-200, 273-350; Henrik Meinander, *Finlands historia: Linjer, strukturer, vändpunkter* (Helsingfors: Schildt & Söderströms, 2006), 44; and Per Pettersson, "State and Religion in Sweden: Ambiguity between Disestablishment and Religious Control," in "Legal Regulation of Religion in the Nordic Countries," Special Issue, edited by Lene Kühle, *Nordic Journal of Religion and Society* 24, no. 2 (2011): 121-22, especially for the last period.
6 Victoria Enkvist provides a very good historical overview in chapter 3 of her doctoral thesis, *Religionsfrihetens rättsliga ramar* (Uppsala: Iustus förlag, 2013).
7 Lag (1998:1591) om Svenska kyrkan, https://www.riksdagen.se/sv/dokument-lagar/dokument/svensk-forfattningssamling/lag-19981591-om-svenska-kyrkan_sfs-1998-1591

on the Church of Sweden, its affairs are also covered by the general law on religious communities, supplemented by a law on economic support to religious communities.[8] Supplementing the secular laws, the Church of Sweden developed an internal body of ecclesiastical governance norms via the Church Ordinance, *Kyrkoordningen*.[9] This internal regulation is either decided directly by the Church Assembly as such or indirectly legitimized by delegation from the Church Assembly.

As part of the Swedish kingdom, the *Finnish* church was reformed in the same way as the Swedish.[10] A central dimension of the Reformation also in the Nordic countries was the translation of the Bible into the national languages. In Finland, however, there was no written Finnish language before this translation. Therefore, the Finnish reformer Mikael Agricola is honored, not only as reformer, but also as the person who ensured the survival of the Finnish language. That the priests subsequently became royal civil servants, and that a centralization of the administration in the Swedish/Finnish kingdom occurred as a result, is also underlined in Finnish history. Finland became the center of the internal wars of the 1590s, leading to a re-affirmation of the Swedish Lutheran king, but also to the end of any Finnish autonomy: Finland was a Swedish region and the Church was Lutheran.

The absolutist Church Law of 1686 did not survive as long in Finland as in Sweden, where it remained unchanged until the late 1980s. The Finnish War

---

[law 1998 on the Church of Sweden] and Lag (1998:1592) om införance av lagen om Svenska kyrkan, https://www.riksdagen.se/sv/dokument-lagar/dokument/svensk-forfattningssamling/lag-19981592-om-inforande-av-lagen-19981591_sfs-1998-1592 [law on the enforcement of the law on the Church of Sweden].

8 Lag (1998:1593) om trossamfund, https://lagen.nu/1998:1593/konsolidering/1998:1593 [law on religious communities]. The law on religious communities in Sweden has been changed a number of times, the latest change is SFS 2018:1675, see the overview over changes here: http://rkrattsbaser.gov.se/sfsr?bet=1998:1593. Lag (1999:932) om stöd till trossamfunn [law on economic support to religious communities], https://lagen.nu/1999:932. Further information on the homepage of the Swedish (Government) Agency for Support for Faith Communities, accessed June 25, 2020, https://www.myndighetensst.se/en/myndigheten-for-stod-till-trossamfund.html.

9 "Kyrkoordningen," Svenska kyrkan, accessed June 25, 2020, https://www.svenskakyrkan.se/kyrkoordningen. The most recent version was published on January 1, 2020.

10 For the history of Finnish church law, see Meinander, *Finlands historia*; Juha Seppo, "Finlands Policy on Church and Religion," in *Law & Religion in the 21st Century—Nordic Perspectives*, ed. Lisbet Christoffersen, Kjell Å. Modéer, and Svend Andersen, 89-105 (Copenhagen: DJØF Publishing, 2010) and Kimmo Kääriäinen, "Religion and State in Finland," in "Legal Regulation of Religion in the Nordic Countries," Special Issue, ed. Lene Kühle, *Nordic Journal of Religion and Society* 24, no. 2 (2011): 155-71. For further analysis, see Pamela Slotte's contribution "Moving Frontiers: Configuring Religion Law and Religious Law, and Law-Religion Relations," to this volume.

during the Napoleonic era resulted in the *Russian Peace* from 1809 until the independence of 1917. As part of the continuous negotiation of internal Finnish autonomy within the Russian realm, however, the law on the Evangelical Lutheran Church of Finland was changed into a new Church Act in 1869.[11] This law acknowledged the Lutheran church as a "state church" alongside the Orthodox Church,[12] and at the same time established a synod with the power to internally self-regulate church matters within the framework of the Church Law. The Church Law, however, also stated that "final authority over the Church throughout the country is to rest with the national government."[13]

A law passed as late as in 1889 made it legal for Finnish people to belong to other churches than the Lutheran or the Orthodox. The Non-Conformity Act made the position of other Protestant churches official. Full freedom of religion was ensured in the independence-constitution of 1919, backed by legislation in 1923,[14] ensuring also the right not to belong to a religious community.

After gaining independence, the Finnish state remained the final legislative and administrative power over the Finnish Lutheran majority church. This power survived also the 1964-law on the Evangelical Lutheran church in Finland.[15] In 1993, an administrative reform passed all civil servants and all appointments of priests, bishops etc. from state hierarchy to the church authority.[16] The law also gave the Evangelical Lutheran Church of Finland the final authority over all internal matters.

While the parliament holds the legislative power when it comes to the Church Law, the Finnish parliament cannot legislate on Church Law without an initiative being taken by the Church Synod, nor can it legislate against any proposal from the synod. The new Finnish constitution of 2000, however, upheld the differentiation between the Evangelical Lutheran Church of Finland and other religious communities. Thus, the constitution states that the legislative powers of the Evangelical Lutheran Church of Finland are regulated in the law

---

11 For the historical law on the Evangelical Lutheran Church of Finland, in force 1869-1964, see "Storfurstendömet Finlands Författnings-Samling: 1869, N° 30, Kyrkolag," Markus Långin kotisivu, accessed June 25, 2020, https://www.mlang.name/arkisto/kyrkolag-1869.html.
12 For the status of the Orthodox Church and Orthodox Church Law, see the contribution by Johan Bastubacka, "Minority, Media, and Law: Reality TV, Orthodox Canon Law, Finnish and European Jurisprudence," to this volume.
13 Quoted from Seppo, "Finland's Policy on Church and Religion." See also §14 in the 1869-law on the Church of Finland, referred to in the previous footnotes.
14 https://finlex.fi/sv/laki/ajantasa/kumotut/1922/19220267
15 Kyrkolagen av den 23 december 1964.
16 Kyrkolag, 26.11.1993/1054 [law on the church], with revisions updated until June 2020; https://finlex.fi/sv/laki/ajantasa/1993/19931054

on the church.[17] Freedom of religion as such was granted in the beginning of the 2000-constituion, supplemented by new legislation in 2003.[18] The Evangelical Lutheran Church and the Orthodox Church are also covered by the general introductory chapter of the law on freedom of religion, ensuring (in §3) among other things, that the religious communities and the churches have the sole right to decide on conditions for membership of the church.

The West-Nordic Reformation took a different shape, both among the three countries (Denmark, Iceland, and Norway) and in comparison with the Reformation in Sweden/Finland. The relative lack of an ecclesiastical hierarchy marks the most central difference between East and West. The office of an archbishop was never re-introduced in the West-Nordic churches, which therefore did not have a "head of church" until the beginning of the 21st century.[19]

After a series of internal wars following the defeat to Sweden, the personally committed Lutheran King Christian III took over in 1536 as King of *Denmark* (at that time including Norway and Iceland). An early form of re-constitutionalization took place at a general political meeting on October 30, 1536, when a legal reform of state and church and their relations took place. The Catholic bishops were imprisoned and deprived of their offices. No bishops could any longer take part in state decisions, the canon law was abolished, the bishops' lands and fortunes were expropriated. The new Church Ordinance of 1537 ruled that new bishops (or "superintendents") were to be appointed by the king. Luther approved of the Danish Reformation in a letter of December in 1536, and subsequently Johannes Bugenhagen (1485-1558) came to Denmark to coronate the king according to a Philipp Melanchton-inspired version of the coronation rites in August 1537.[20] In addition, new Lutheran bishops, appointed as royal

---

17 Finlands grundlag 76 § Kyrkolagen.
18 Finlands grundlag 11 § Religions- och samvetsfrihet; Religionsfrihetslag. 6.6.2003/453; https://www.finlex.fi/sv/laki/ajantasa/2003/20030453, with later updates.
19 The Church of Norway, however, officially uses the concept *præses*, presiding bishop in the bishops' meeting, linked to the bishop of Nidaros, the seat of the last archbishop before the Reformation. Currently, the Presiding Bishop Olav Fykse; "Preses i Bispemøtet," Den norske kirke, accessed June 25, 2020, https://kirken.no/nb-NO/om-kirken/slik-styres-kirken/bispemotet/preses/.
20 Further on the Danish legal church history, see, e.g., H.J.H. Glædemark, *Kirkeforfatningsspørgsmaalet i Danmark indtil 1874: En historisk-kirkeretlig studie* (Copenhagen: Ejnar Munksgaard, 1948); Martin Schwarz Lausten, *Johannes Bugenhagen: Luthersk reformator i Tyskland og Danmark* (Copenhagen: Anis, 2011); Martin Schwarz Lausten, *Philipp Melanchton: Humanist og luthersk reformator i Tyskland og Danmark.* (Copenhagen: Anis, 2010); Martin Schwarz Lausten, *Reformationen i Danmark* (Copenhagen: Anis, 2011). Especially for the period after the constitution of 1849, see, e.g., Lisbet Christoffersen, "Church Autonomy in Nordic Law?," in *Law & Religion in the 21st Century—Nordic Perspectives*, ed. Lisbet Christoffersen, Kjell Å. Modéer, and Svend Andersen (Copenhagen: DJØF Publish-

civil servants and obliged to oversee the law of the land, were ordained by Bugenhagen for the new Lutheran church. (This meant that the apostolic succession was broken in the Danish, the Norwegian, and the Icelandic Lutheran churches). The university was restored, and finally the church was also restored by law as Lutheran in September 1537 (fully approved in 1539). Catholic rites were prohibited, monasteries closed, and Catholic pastors and teachers were to be re-schooled in the Lutheran faith.

In the discussion of whether the Reformation established a new 'state-church', the main understanding, which I endorse, is that, after 1536, the church was no different from other organizational entities in the kingdom. A royal decree from 1569 allowed access to the realm only to foreigners who acknowledged the Lutheran faith.[21] In conjunction with the Imperial Council (*Rigsråd*), the king now was the sole legislator, while canon law was abolished. This model was confirmed with the absolutist Danish Law of 1683, which underlined the Lutheran religion as the state religion and the priests as civil servants with no representation of their own. A limited freedom of religion for certain religious communities of foreigners was approved from 1685, which made room for royal acknowledgement of Jewish, Catholic, and Reformed minorities. Danes, however, were not allowed to convert to any of these minorities, and as late as the 1840s a prohibition against Catholic missionary work was upheld with reference to its canon law. The Jewish community was given citizenship after 1814, though under the condition that Danish law (and not Jewish legal norms) was followed. Other religious communities were prohibited and prosecuted as late as the 1840s.[22]

---

ing, 2010), 563-92; Lisbet Christoffersen, "A Long Historical Path towards Transparency, Accountability and Good Governance: On Financing Religions in Denmark," in *Public Funding of Religions in Europe*, ed. Francis Messner (Aldershot: Ashgate, 2015), 125-49; Marie Vejrup Nielsen and Lene Kühle, "Religion and State in Denmark," in "Legal Regulation of Religion in the Nordic Countries," Special Issue, ed. Lene Kühle, *Nordic Journal of Religion and Society* 24, no. 2 (2011): 173-88 and Niels Henrik Gregersen's contribution "Nordic Lutheranism and Secular Law: The Role of Law in the Grundtvigian Creation Theologies of K.E. Løgstrup and Regin Prenter" to this volume.

21 See the introduction to "Fremmedartiklerne af 20. september 1569," danmarkshistorien.dk, last modified April 14, 2016, https://danmarkshistorien.dk/leksikon-og-kilder/vis/materiale/fremmedartiklerne-af-20-september-1569/

22 For a more detailed analysis of the period from the Napoleonic Wars until after the Danish constitution with a special emphasis on relations between theological and legal ideology concerning legitimacy of ecclesiastical law and the impact of freedom of religion, see Lisbet Christoffersen, and Niels Henrik Gregersen, "Shaping the Danish People's Church in the Context of Freedom of Religion: A.S. Ørsted (1778-1860) and N.F.S. Grundtvig (1783-1872)," in *Law and the Christian Tradition in Scandinavia: The Writings of Great Nordic Jurists*, ed. Kjell Å. Modéer and Helle Vogt (London: Routledge, 2020).

The Danish constitution of 1849 provided full freedom of religion, including the right not to have any religion.[23] At the same time, the constitution promised to pass one single law on the People's Church (*Folkekirken*), a law that would give it an independent national structure to make decisions upon internal matters. Legislation concerning the relations between other religious communities and the state was also promised. As late as in 2017, a law on religious communities was finally passed.[24]

The promise concerning a legislation on the People's Church, however, has never been fulfilled. Instead, since the constitutional change in 1849, the parliament has legislated on the internal structure of the Church.[25] In 1903, the church was provided with an internal structure on local level, based on congregational democracy in combination with a changed model of financing (from tithes to church taxes), as well as minor economic support from the state. In 1922, legislation concerning the regional level (deans and deanery councils) was added. There are also laws on the priests as civil servants (including laws from 1948 on access for women to priesthood), laws ensuring access for all baptized to become members of the church and ensuring their rights to access to liturgical service; there are laws on other employees of the church, on the financing of the church etc. The People's Church is still understood as a branch of public state administration, with no autonomy; accordingly, general laws on public administration are in force, also within the Church, and most ministers are still civil servants of the state. As late as 2014, a public report stated that the People's Church is a state church and that the government and parliament have the sole right of legislation, including internal matters, such as rituals.[26]. The aim of this report was to pave the way for legislative changes in order for

---

23 The latest revision of the Danish constitution is from June 5, 1953. The clauses on freedom of religion and on the national majority church are unchanged. See Folketinget, *Danmarks riges grundlov af 5. Juni 1953: Tronfølgeloven* (Folketinget 2009), https://www.ft.dk/~/media/pdf/publikationer/grundloven/danmarks-riges-grundlov.ashx. An English version, provided by parliament, translates "folkekirke" with "established church", see Folketinget, *My Constitutional Act: With Explanations*, 12th. edition (The Communications Section, Danish Parliament, March 2014), https://www.ft.dk/~/media/pdf/publikationer/english/my_constitutional_act_with_explanations.ashx.

24 Lov om trossamfund uden for folkekirken, LOV nr 1533 af 19/12/2017, https://www.retsinformation.dk/eli/lta/2017/1533. The law and its background are discussed in detail in Lisbet Christoffersen, "Legal Re-Organisation of the Danish Religious Market," in *Individualisation, Marketisation and Social Capital in a Cultural Institution: The Case of the Danish Folk Church*, ed. Hans Raun Iversen et al. (Odense: University Press of Southern Denmark, 2019), 302-25.

25 "Lovstof," Kirkeministeriet, accessed June 25, 2020, https://www.km.dk/ministeriet/love-regler/.

26 Betænkning 1544/2014, chapter 9.

the Church to gain legal autonomy, at least in internal matters. However, no such piece of law has yet been proposed.

Iceland was part of the Danish kingdom from 1397 (together with Norway) and remained so after the dissolution of the Danish-Norwegian kingdom in 1814. The country, or some parts of it, was for long periods rather isolated from other parts of the realm, and in Iceland, the Reformation is understood as having been forced upon the country by the Danish king, with the last Catholic bishop fighting hard for his faith, but finally being killed. These historical experiences might have influenced legal history of the Church of Iceland by ensuring that the Christian religion could survive even under hard conditions and with no centralized leadership as long as the churches and priests were still in place, if not on a weekly then on a yearly basis.

Iceland got its own constitution in 1874. This constitution was reformulated in relation to the independence from Denmark in 1944.[27] It has been amended a number of times, last amendment being from June 1995.[28] The constitution states that the Evangelical Lutheran Church should be the People's Church in Iceland and, as such, supported and protected by the state, while at the same time granting full freedom of religion.[29] The requirement of state support to and protection of the majority church can be changed by ordinary law on the condition that the law passes a referendum.[30] The first adjustment to the system was the implementation by law of a national ecclesiastical body for the church in 1931. By law this body was given power over liturgy and other internal matters, and it became an advisory body to the parliament in ecclesiastical matters, too. In 1957, this national body was supplemented with a National Council, receiving legislative powers in internal matters, whereas the national body

---

27 Among other things, this led to a heated discussion among the Nordic bishops after World War II, see Gregersen, "Nordic Lutheranism and Secular Law," in this volume.
28 Constituton of the Republic of Iceland, with amendments, latest June 28, 1995, https://www.refworld.org/docid/3ae6b5627.html
29 Constitution of the Republic of Iceland, Article 62 & Article 63. (https://www.government.is/Publications/Legislation/Lex/?newsid=89fc6038-fd28-11e7-9423-005056bc4d74. As in the Danish constitution, the People's Church is translated into State Church, but should be translated as *by law established* church. For an analysis of the history of church law in Iceland, see Hjalti Hugason, "Isländska folkkyrkan," in *Kirkeretsantologi 2010: Bekendelse og kirkeordninger*, ed. Peter Garde et al. (Aarhus/Frederiksberg: Selskab for Kirkeret and Eksistensen, 2010); Pétur Pétursson, "Religion and State in Iceland," in "Legal Regulation of Religion in the Nordic Countries," Special Issue, ed. Lene Kühle, *Nordic Journal of Religion and Society* 24, no. 2 (2011): 189-204.
30 The constitution of Iceland, art 79 (2). An attempt to reform the Icelandic constitution took place between 2010-2013, without success. In the proposals, freedom of religion prevailed and some dimensions of disestablishment of the Lutheran church were proposed. See further Hugason, "Isländska folkkyrkan," 217-34.

was changed into an executive body. The bishops (of which there are two) are centrally placed within these bodies.

In 1997, a further change of the system was established by the law on the Church of Iceland. The state took over some of the church property and promised to fund the church accordingly. In this law, the church is defined as an independent religious organization, granted legal personality, meaning that the employees are no longer part of the state hierarchy and that the church can sue the state at the courts. The National Council is now the governing body of the church within the legislative framework, established by law. The bishop's office and the national body thereby lead the entire internal organization. On the other hand, the Icelandic president (who does not need to be a church member) is by law the formal head of the church, and represents the church externally. The president also appoints the bishops, while the government appoints the priests, though appointments are based on choices made internally within the church.

Currently, even further changes are in preparation.[31] The minister of justice is said to have negotiated and signed an agreement in September 2019 with the Church of Iceland, stipulating that the church will no longer function as another state institution. Rather, the church will come to resemble an independent religious organization, responsible for its own operations and finances. According to this source, from January 1, 2020, the Church of Iceland now processes and manages its own books.[32]

Along with the Danish and Icelandic churches, the *Church of Norway* was also forcefully reformed in 1536. Some would even argue that both the Norwegian church and the independency of the country disappeared when the Norwegian legislative body (*Norske Rigsråd*) vanished in 1536. This legal state of exception meant that the Norwegian ecclesiastical matters were not organized until 1607.[33]

---

31   The government took office on November 30, 2017. The minister of justice is Áslaug Arna Sigurbjörnsdóttir. See "About the Government," Government of Iceland, accessed June 25, 2020, https://www.government.is/government/about-the-government/. See further Ragnar Tómas, "Separation of Church and State Inevitable," Iceland review, November 4, 2019, https://www.icelandreview.com/news/separation-of-church-and-state-inevitable/.

32   The church management of books and wages builds on a lump-sum-agreement between church and state, negotiated fall 2019. According to email information from professor Hjalti Hugason, June 21, 2020, the law on the Church of Iceland is being negotiated in order to be changed, but the end result is unforeseeable.

33   For the history of Norwegian ecclesiastical law, see among others Lausten, *Philipp Melanchton*; Bernt T. Oftestad, Tarald Rasmussen, and Jan Schumacher, *Norsk Kirkehistorie*, 2nd ed. (Oslo: Universitetsforlaget, 2010); Ulla Schmidt, "State, Law and Religion in Norway," in "Legal Regulation of Religion in the Nordic Countries," Special Issue, ed. Lene Kühle, *Nordic Journal of Religion and Society* 24, no. 2 (2011): 137-53; Eivind Smith, "And they Lived Happily Together," in *Law & Religion in the 21st Century—Nordic Perspectives*,

The last Norwegian bishop tried to remain Norway Catholic and left his diocese with the archives of the Cathedral of Nidaros, before the king's troops reached him in Trondheim 1537. The Reformation was implemented through teaching and also through synods in each diocese throughout the century. However, these events do not change the general picture of the Norwegian church as increasingly under the centralized legislative and administrative power of the Danish-Norwegian king and his governmental department in Copenhagen. The introduction of the absolutist government system from 1660 and the introduction of the Norwegian Law of 1687, closely modeled on the Danish Law of 1683, further affirmed the situation.

After the Napoleonic Wars, Norway was independent for a short period in 1814 and managed to formulate its own constitution, which also became the basis for a Norwegian parliamentary governance system, until 1905 under Swedish royal ruling. Both before and after 1905, the Norwegian church was upheld under this constitutional system as a branch of the Norwegian state system with priests and bishops as civil servants and the king as the main legislator in internal matters. The local church likewise was a branch of the local governance system in the municipalities. The first half of the 20th century granted the Church of Norway bodies at the local level (congregation councils in 1920) and a yearly meeting of bishops (1934) by a royal decree, which legally speaking delegated royal power over to the bishops. Financially, the church was, however, still dependent on state and municipality financing.

On Easter Sunday in April 1942, during World War II, all bishops and 797 out of 858 pastors laid down their functions as state civil servants, though upholding their functions as ordained priests and bishops in congregations and dioceses, based on the document The Foundation of the Church (*Kirkens Grunn*).[34] After the war, many believed that this experience should lead to an independent Church of Norway, led by a national church council. However, the parliamentary majority, and especially the social democratic labor party, was against establishing the church as an independent parallel structure in society,

---

ed. Lisbet Christoffersen, Kjell Å. Modéer, and Svend Andersen (Copenhagen: DJØF Publishing, 2010), 123-44; Frank Cranmer, "Church/State Relations in Scandinavia," in *Church and State in 21st Century Britain: The Future of Church Establishment*, ed. R.M. Morris (Basingstoke: Palgrave/Macmillan, 2009), 127-50; Eivind Smith, "'… forblir Norges folkekirke': Om Grunnlovens ordvalg og dets juridiske konsekvenser," in *Folkekirke nå*, ed. Stephanie Dietrich et al. (Oslo: Verbum Akademisk, 2012), 60-71.

34 Cf. the contributions to this book by Gregersen, "Nordic Lutheranism and Secular Law," and Hans-Michael Heinig, "Neither Sacred nor Secular Law? The Self-Understanding of the Ecclesiastical Law in the Protestant Churches in Germany Before and After World War II."

in order to safeguard a liberal space within the church. The Norwegian necessity to change its constitution in order to be able to sign the European Convention of Human Rights, however, proved to the Norwegian political and administrative system that changes were necessary, also concerning the Church of Norway.

In 1969, the law established a Church Council (*Kirkerådet*). This was reformed and extended with the founding of the Assembly of the Church (*Kirkemøtet*) in 1984, which became the main representative body of the church. In 1996, a new compiled law concerning the Church of Norway appeared. The political legislature now delegated all powers of appointment and ordination to the church[35] as well as the powers of internal church regulations, including the content of liturgy[36] and the use of church buildings. At the same time, the local congregations were made independent legal subjects.

This recent legal reformation of the Church of Norway did not stop here. A series of committees, crowned with a major political compromise in 2008, led to a change of the constitution in 2012. The new text regarding freedom of religion and the Church of Norway in the constitution reads as follows: "All inhabitants of the realm shall have the right to freely practice their religion. The Church of Norway, an Evangelical Lutheran church, will remain the established Church of Norway and will as such be supported by the state. Detailed provisions as to its system will be laid down by law. All religious and belief communities should be supported on equal terms."[37] Even though the formulation "remain the Established Church of Norway" is a political translation of the concept of *folkekirke*, it is clear that the wording following: "Detailed provisions…", includes the idea of transferring further regulating powers to the church through delegation by law.

The former legitimacy for legislation on church matters, which was based on royal decrees and the king being a member of the church, is thus changed. The special legislative power in the state legislature regarding the internal structure of the Church of Norway was used in the 2016, changing the Church Law of 1996, to grant the Church of Norway legal personality as per January 1, 2017. At the same time, the Church Assembly was granted general authority over the

---

35   Apart from the appointment of bishops, which was delegated to the church in 2012.
36   See https://lovdata.no/dokument/NL/lov/1996-06-07-31, kirkeloven (the law on the church), § 24.
37   https://www.stortinget.no/globalassets/pdf/english/constitutionenglish.pdf [my translation].

Church of Norway in all matters, which were not placed elsewhere, including the authority over internal matters.[38]

The 2017 legal reformation of the Church of Norway thus established that this church was regarded as an Evangelical Lutheran church, and, as such, a *folkekirke*. The state should in the future organize this church by law. "By law established" gives a power to the state that is not granted in regard to other religious communities; at the same time, the state is obliged to support this church on an equal footing with other religious communities in the country. As part of this constitutional reform, the subsequent administrative reform resulted in legal personality for the Church of Norway, also involving the conferral of powers over all civil servants and administrative tasks in the church from the state apparatus to the church administration.

The Church of Norway is, also in the future, financed by the local municipalities and the state. Other religious communities are funded in equal amount. A national trust owns many of the church buildings. From this trust, the Church of Norway is ensured to receive what is considered ecclesiastical property, such as buildings, land etc., in the event of further legislative decisions.[39]

In sum, the Reformation in the 1500s implied a central change of legitimacy behind religious law (law both on and within religious communities) in the Nordic countries. In Sweden and Finland, double organizational standards were upheld, meaning that both external secular legitimacy within state law and internal religious legitimacy was necessary in order to establish legitimacy for ecclesiastical law. In the West-Nordic countries, the Reformation led to an organizational secularization of the legitimacy behind the law combined with a general confessionalization of the laws of the land. Subsequently, however, the powers of the state also to regulate internal church matters led, during the 20th century, to a slow secularization of the legal norms regarding internal matters within the majority churches (female priests, ordinary public law rights for individual members, etc.). In Denmark, the reformatory system is upheld, disputed, but legitimized as legal. In Norway, rapid developments since World War II show a growing tendency to base the legitimation of the internal laws and norms on human rights arguments regarding church autonomy, although it is still regulated through delegation from statutory law.

---

38 https://lovdata.no/dokument/LTI/lov/2016-05-27-17, lov-2016-05-27, law on change of the law on the Church of Norway, establishing the legal subject Church of Norway. § 24 in the Church Law was reformulated.

39 "Opplysningsvesenets fond", accessed July 1, 2020, https://www.stortinget.no/no/Saker-og-publikasjoner/Saker/Sak/?p=76671.

Regulatory Status of Nordic *by Law Established* Churches

It has been common in the literature to characterize the five Nordic majority churches as *state churches*.[40] That this is no longer a fair characteristic is argued by, for example, Frank Cranmer, who even goes so far as to identify the Church of Sweden as "disestablished," with the Church of Norway following the same pathway. However, Cranmer's view does not paint the full picture. He compares the Nordic situation to the disestablishment by law of the Church of Wales. Yet, in this comparison, it is crucial to remember that the Church of Wales, by its disestablishment, simply became part of the Anglican communion of churches with its symbolic leadership by the Archbishop of Canterbury in the Church of England.

The Nordic majority churches, on the contrary, being Lutheran by identity, do not have any such fallback position into a transnational church structure. Thus, there needs to be some sort of re-formation of these churches, and this re-formation is done by statutory law. The question in this part of the chapter is what it means to be a "by law established" church in the 21st century. The following overview will answer that question empirically by simply analyzing the content of recent legislation concerning the Nordic majority churches.

For this analysis, I take advantage of similar discussions in the English literature.[41] Cranmer in his 2009 publication considers the following areas: a) membership of the entire population; b) whether the churches are established (without fully clarifying this term); c) final legislative authority; d) national synod; e) parish councils; f) senior appointments (by state or by church); and g) financing (church tax, church fees, or direct government grants).

W. Cole Durham Jr. provided a more detailed overview in 2001, but his approach was similar: In which areas do we find Church autonomy? Where does non-establishment leave the church to its own decisions, free of interference from state legislation, state executive powers, and state judiciary? In Durham's

---

40 For an overview of the literature, see, e.g., Michael Minkenberg, "Church-State Regimes and Democracy in the West: Convergence vs Divergence," *Geopolitics, History, and International Relations* 4, no. 1 (2012): 76-106. For a discussion of the Nordic countries, compared to the United Kingdom, see Cranmer, "Church/State Relations in Scandinavia"; John Lucas (with Bob Morris), "Disestablishment in Ireland and Wales," in *Church and State in 21st Century Britain: The Future of Church Establishment*, ed. R. M. Morris (Basingstoke: Palgrave/Macmillan, 2009), 122.

41 The literature on United Kingdom majority churches is vast. I rely on Cranmer, "Church/State Relations in Scandinavia" and W. Cole Durham Jr. "The Right to Autonomy in Religious Affairs: A Comparative View," in *Church Autonomy*, ed. Gerhard Robbers (Frankfurt am Main: Peter Lang, 2001), 683-716.

view, freedom of religion and belief is the goal. Based on an interpretation of international conventions and treaty documents, Durham sees any involvement by state authorities in church affairs as problematic.

In trying to identify issues that represent the exclusive matters of a religious community, i.e. issues covered by church autonomy, Durham distinguishes between the following domains: 1) the inner domain of faith, doctrine, and policy, including legislation concerning the new formulation of church law and the authority to control and represent the community; 2) core ministry, including matters of worship, ritual and liturgy, confidential counselling, teaching the faith, and training the clergy, as well as mission and diaconal work; 3) core administration, including the right of appointment and dismissal from religious offices and secular functions; and 4) church discipline, including membership (entrance, leaving, and expulsion), territorial organization, establishment of offices, finance, church property, exemptions from labor law, religious marriage, and access to the military etc.

Against this position, I have argued that there are not only two, but rather three positions mutually relating and conflicting: (a) the state, (b) the (leadership of) the religious community, and (c) the individual citizens, being members of the majority church as well as citizens of the nation.

These three positions are mutually interrelated in different ways. We have the issue of the state versus the collective religious entity (the church). We have the position of individuals who want to belong to a religious community. But as I have argued, we also have the role of the state in protecting internal religious minorities (quite often women) within religious communities. My argument is that the position of the not-so-active members of the church (those who traditionally have taken advantage of the broadness of access to the church), is not necessarily protected by the church's internal democracy, simply because church leadership might want to ensure a hardline church discipline. That this is the case becomes clear in disciplinary cases against employees, for example.[42]

So, instead of inquiring about the extent of church autonomy (leaning to-

---

42 See Christoffersen, "Church Autonomy in Nordic Law?". My argument is that it is necessary not only to look into the relations between the two organizational levels, the state vs the church. Taking the point of departure with the individual members (or individual employees, incl. the ordained priesthood), changes the picture into three different positions that have to find a balance. See also Lisbet Christoffersen and Niels Valdemar Vinding, "Challenged Pragmatism: Conflicts of Law and Religion in the Danish Labour Market," *International Journal of Discrimination and the Law* 13, no. 2-3 (2013): 140-68, and Lisbet Christoffersen. "The Argument for a Narrow Conception of Religious Autonomy," in "Special Issue on the Ministerial Exception," ed. Pamela Slotte and Helge Årsheim, *Oxford Journal of Law and Religion* 4, no. 2 (2015): 278-302. Smith, "'… forblir Norges folkekirke',"

wards church autonomy as the absolute positive outcome), I consider the value of governance structures that ensure the rights of the individuals:

1. Which internal governance structures are established and how the faith is to be shaped?
2. How and by whom is access to membership regulated and do members have rights in the church concerning access to rituals (do ministers, or local congregations?), such as access to marriage, burial rights, to baptism, and to service, or are there elements of church discipline?[43]
3. Do all church members hold membership rights—regarding church governance, church order, and religious ideas—on an equal footing?
4. Are church employees covered by ordinary legislation in terms of employment, or is there, also regarding the employees, a degree of internal religious law regarding disciplinary questions? Are there distinct internal bodies that deal with such conflicts?
5. Are legal conflicts solved entirely internally, or is it possible to get access to ordinary courts of law to resolve legal conflicts within the church?

The answers to these questions can be found in the valid statutory law and the valid church orders for the Church of Sweden, the Evangelical Lutheran Church of Finland, the Church of Norway, and the Danish Church.[44]

---

raised a parallel question of whether there is always a common interest between those, who want a confessional church and those who want a broad church.
43 As late as in the late 19th century, all Nordic Lutheran majority churches had some sort of church discipline, barring individuals from access to church rituals or other rights. See, e.g., the Finnish church law of 1869, the 13th chapter, 100-105 §§. The disciplinary instruments were, among others, loss of the right to be a witness at baptisms and loss of election rights.
44 I do not have access to further information regarding the Church of Iceland, which is therefore not included in this overview.

1. Which internal structures are established by law and/or by internal governance orders and who decides the faith of the church?

	By statutory law	By internal governance orders
The Church of Sweden[45]	Statutory law (1998:1591) on the Church of Sweden states: 1§: The Church of Sweden is Evangelical Lutheran with congregations, dioceses, and a national organization (their main obligations and rights are described further in the law). 2§: The Church of Sweden is an open *folkekirke*, which in collaboration between a democratic organization and the ordained ministry offers ecclesial possibilities nationwide.	The Church Assembly has regulatory power regarding the faith of the church, liturgy, rituals, organization of services, membership, ordination, church organization, and the power rules at different levels (CO 10 ch, 2 §). 2/3 of the votes in the general assembly are required in cases of changes to • the faith • membership of the church • public access to information • exemptions from public access (CO 11 ch, 19 §). The Church Council (*Kyrkostyrelsen*) represents the church externally and has overall executive powers (CO 10 ch, 3 §).
The Evangelical Lutheran Church of Finland[46]	The faith as Evangelical Lutheran is decided by law (1 Ch, 1 §). The Church Order further describes the faith. The constitutional basis and the basic structure are decided by law. Governance is according to the church law decided by the General Synod in the church order (CL 2 Ch, 1 §). Election rights regarding the General Synod are decided by the Church Order. The Church Order must be published in the official collection of laws (2 Ch, 3 §). The Church Law includes • detailed regulation of how to organize the congregations (relations to municipalities, language matters etc.) (3 Ch) • delegation of powers to regulate the ecclesiastical enterprise in the Church Order; regulation of holidays (4 Ch) • detailed regulation of the organisation and powers of the local congregation (7-16 Chs)	The books used for services and for religious teaching must be in accordance with the faith (1 Ch, 2 §). The rituals etc. in the church are regulated in the Church Order, part II, ch 2 in detail.

---

45   Sources: The aforementioned law on the Church of Sweden (law 1998:1591) and the internal governance regulations, *Kyrkoordningen* (Church Order, CO) as per January 1, 2020, downloaded from the homepage of the Church of Sweden: https://www.svenskakyrkan.se/kyrkoordningen.

46   Sources: The aforementioned law on the Evangelical Lutheran Church of Finland [kyrkolagen], lag 26.11.1993/1054 and the Church Order for the Evangelical Lutheran Church of Finland, 8.11.1991/1055 år 1993 with subsequent changes, as updated per 2020: https://www.finlex.fi/sv/laki/ajantasa/1993/19931055. The Church Order is published in the official Finnish register on laws, finlex. References are to chapter and § according to this format: 1 Ch, 2 §.

The Church of Norway[47]	Constitution of Norway, article 16: an Evangelical Lutheran *folkekirke*. Church Law ch 2: Congregation councils organize local church life, while municipality-based councils are responsible for buildings, cemeteries, employees (other than priests), and the municipalities (financing the buildings and local equipment). CL ch 4: Diocesan councils. The Church Assembly (all diocesan councils together) decides on all matters that are not decided by other bodies; decides on the faith, rituals and books; takes all overall decisions, makes general internal regulations, and can delegate its powers to other bodies (CL § 24) The Church Council prepares for the Church Assembly and governs the daily work of the church on the national level (CL § 25). The bishops' meeting coordinates the work of the bishops (CL § 26). The Church Assembly can organize other bodies (CL § 27)	The overview over Church Order regulations for the Church of Norway includes 14 different chapters with a number of sections each. The religious services within the church are regulated in chapter 13, on the services, baptism, confirmation, marriage etc.

---

47   For the Church of Norway, internal governance rules are accessible on the church homepage here: https://kirken.no/nb-NO/om-kirken/slik-styres-kirken/lover-og-regler/. The internal governance rules are published in the official Norwegian register on laws (lawdata).

The Danish *folkekirke*[48]	Congregation councils are responsible for all ecclesiastical activity in the congregation, including budget decisions, maintenance of buildings, and the hiring of priests and other staff, etc. Deanery church councils (more or less comparable to the municipal organizational level, but without any influence from the secular municipality) approve of the budgets, changes to buildings, etc. They also propose the priests to be appointed by the government minister. Diocesan councils advice the bishop on ecclesiastical activity at the diocesan level. Bishops decide where to place the open position as priests. A national council on interchurch affairs decides on relations with churches abroad. A national council advices the government minister, before he/she decides the budget for the church on the national level. The government minister appoints the priests and recommends appointment of elected bishops. The queen appoints the bishops after public elections among the members of congregation councils and the priests within the diocese	Liturgy, rituals etc. are regulated by royal decree[49] on the basis of a recommendation from the government, normally backed by (a majority of) the bishops and other circles in the church. The royal decrees are published in the ordinary law data. An unofficial bishops' meeting (not regulated) clarifies matters across the church in collaboration with the government minister. An institution for further education also takes on some of these tasks on an unofficial basis.

---

48 The Danish *folkekirke* is regulated by a series of different laws on different dimensions of life in the church. I mention them here and use them in the following part of this chapter. The laws are: Law on membership of the Folkekirke: https://www.retsinformation.dk/eli/lta/2014/615. Law on congregation councils, https://www.retsinformation.dk/eli/lta/2013/771. Law on election for the congregation councils, https://www.retsinformation.dk/eli/lta/2020/12. Law on the economy within the church (including the role of deans and deanery councils), https://www.retsinformation.dk/eli/lta/2020/95. Law on election of bishops: https://www.retsinformation.dk/eli/lta/2007/608. Law on application of priests and other employees in the church: https://www.retsinformation.dk/eli/lta/2013/864. Law on civil servants: https://www.retsinformation.dk/eli/lta/2017/511. Law on the governance and use of church buildings: https://www.retsinformation.dk/eli/lta/2014/330. Law on church buildings and churchyards: https://www.retsinformation.dk/eli/lta/2016/1156. Law on funerals: https://www.retsinformation.dk/eli/lta/2020/43. Law on marriages: https://www.retsinformation.dk/eli/lta/2019/771. The *folkekirke* is also a public law institution and thus covered by the laws on public administration etc.

49 The royal decrees have been regulated between 1992 and 2012.

First, it is worth noting that these churches are all *by law established*. Their identity as Evangelical Lutheran and their obligation to cover the entire country is decided by constitution and by law. By means of legislative regulation, the legislative bodies in the country are still able to ensure these basic functions of the churches.

The Church of Sweden is regulated with a combination of a short Church Law and internal regulations in a Church Order, decided autonomously by the national body. The Church Law does not contain any delegations concerning the content of the normative regulation in the Church Order. The Church Law only requires of the church to be a *folkekirke*, democratic, national, and Lutheran. It thus seems that the internal part of the regulations, the content of the Church Order, is based on the existence of the church as such, sort of an autonomous *sui generis* competence.

It would still be possible for the legislative powers to change the law on the Church of Sweden, in case the Swedish parliament found that decisions in the Church Order, decided by the Church Assembly, would change the identity of the church away from the requirements of the law: the identity as Evangelical Lutheran, as national, as a *folkekirke,* and as democratic.

However, no other legitimacy behind interference in the internal affairs of the Church of Sweden from the legislative powers seems to exist—unless a situation of infringement based on human rights appears.

The Church of Sweden thus seems to develop towards a parallel religious legal system, partly based on church autonomy.

When looking at the very detailed Finnish regulations by law, one notes that the Finnish church law can only be changed on the initiative of the Church Assembly. It must, however, be passed through government and parliament, which means that the elements regulated by the church law are also to be approved of by the general legislative authorities. Also, the Church Order is based on delegation in the Church Law. This construction upholds Finnish law and Finnish legislative powers as united without a parallel religious legal order.

The Norwegian legislative powers have, in the revised 1996 Church Law, delegated many powers to the Church Assembly, among them the power to decide on the content of the faith (CL § 24). This is a delegation by law and could, legally speaking, be withdrawn again by the legislative powers. Until now, there is no *sui generis* in the Norwegian legislation.

Administratively speaking, regarding executive powers, it no longer seems appropriate to call the Church of Sweden, the Church of Norway, and the Evangelical Lutheran Church of Finland state churches, because their staff are employed entirely outside the state hierarchy. These churches have changed from being state churches to be by law established churches with powers to regulate themselves internally, based on delegation or on *sui generis*.

The Danish *folkekirke* is different from the other three churches in this part of the analysis. The Danish *folkekirke* does not have any regulatory body at the national level, which means that all legislative and overall administrative regulation is carried out by the legislative powers and/or the government ministry. Also, the churches in Finland, Sweden, and Norway have their own internal administrative hierarchy and all staff members—both administrative and ecclesial—are hired by the churches. In the Danish *folkekirke*, the clerical staff (priests, deans, bishops) are hired on the basis of elections by the congregation or the diocese, as civil servants of the state. The remaining staff (musicians, staff taking care of church buildings and cemeteries, etc.) are hired at the local level by the congregation councils. Thus, regarding executive powers, the Danish *folkekirke* is still to some extent a state church.

It makes quite a difference whether the normative powers within these churches are *sui generis*, for example based on legal tradition, based on a transnational legal system or on the members' decisions in an associational matter, or whether the normative power is based on delegation by law. In a *sui generis* situation, national legislative powers can only infringe if and so far as the basis for an infringement is legitimate according to international human rights. This would, for example, be the case with reference to the European Convention of Human Rights, Article 9 (2), allowing for infringement of the freedom of religion if ruled by law, necessary and proportionate in a democratic society, and the necessity is made relevant due to, for example, The freedoms and rights.

In situations where church autonomy is based on delegation by law (such as by church law, as is currently the case in Finland, and Norway), then this delegation can be withdrawn, in principle in any situation, but most likely in situations where the legislative powers do not approve of the way in which the delegated powers are used.[50]

---

50 See further on this argument for the Church of Norway, Christoffersen, "Towards Re-Sacralisation of Nordic Law?".

2. Regulation of access to membership and members' rights concerning access to rituals (baptism, marriage, burial, service)

	By Law	**By internal governance orders**
Church of Sweden	No statutory law regulates access to membership of the Church of Sweden. The Swedish marriage law (1987:230) and law on authorizing religious communities to perform marriages (1993:305) allow for the performance of marriages within authorized religious communities. The precondition is that no ceremonies taking place within the religious community lead to criminalized sexual relations (enforced, under age etc.) (SFS 2014:380) Law on Burials (1990:1144): The Church of Sweden keeps enough space at the local cemeteries for the burial of all citizens (2 ch, 1§). Payment is according to the law (SFS 2016:560).	The Church Order regulates access to membership. Previously, everyone living in Sweden, citizen or not, could become members of the church. The rules were changed in 2019 (in force July 1, 2020) (CO ch 29): A person, baptized within the church of Sweden, becomes a member. For other persons, there are 3 different possibilities: • baptized in the Church of Sweden or within a church with which the Church of Sweden has ecumenical collaboration, • baptized within another Christian church combined with education in the faith of the Church of Sweden • not yet baptized but becomes a member alongside with teaching as preparation for baptism. Services are open to everyone (CO 17:2). All members have equal access to baptism, marriage, burial, and other rituals in their congregation (CO 17:2). Children have access to baptism—adults, if they wish to live within the congregation (CO 19:2). Baptism is the only access criterion to the Eucharist (CO 20:2). Baptism, membership, and personal commitment are the access criteria for confirmation (CO 22:2). Access to marriage is based on membership, "unless certain causes hinder this access." Also non-members have in certain situations access to marriage in the Church of Sweden (CO 23:1a). The decision is taken by the priest and can be appealed. All members have access to burial service. Also non-members have access in certain situations—decisions taken by the priest can be appealed at the diocesan chapter (CO 24:1a) The church is obliged to offer one main service in all congregations each Sunday—number of services is to be decided at the diocesan level (CO 17:3-5).

The Evangelical Lutheran Church of Finland	The church law decides that membership of the church is conditioned of baptism (1 Ch, 3 §). Members leave the church by personal decision, by becoming member of another religious community, or by leaving the country (1 Ch, 4 §). Law on Burials (2003:457) obliges the local congregations of the Evangelical Lutheran Church of Finland to keep enough space in its cemeteries for all Finnish citizens, df. CL ch 17.	Access to membership is conditioned by (CO 1 Ch, 3 §): • baptism within the church • previous members can rejoin if they have passed school and want to confess the Christian belief • or want to be educated in the Christian faith and become baptized or, if they are already baptized, re-confess the faith A church member has the right to access all services (CO 1 Ch, 4 §). A church member is obliged to participate in services and to lead a Christian life, marry according to church rituals, and have his children baptized (CO 1 Ch, 5 §). The priest supervises and disciplines the church members (CO 4 Ch, 2 §). Participation in the Eucharist requires that the person is confirmed or is baptized and joined by a person who vouches (CO 2 Ch, 11 §). Marriage in the church is for members, who have participated in the confirmation teaching. If one member of the couple is not a member, he or she must be a member of another Christian church (CO 2 Ch, 18 §). All members, as well as non-members who did not directly oppose an ecclesiastical burial, have access to burial services (CO 2 Ch, 23 §).

Church of Norway	All people living in Norway as well as Norwegian citizens living abroad are seen as belonging to the church of Norway (CL § 3). Un-baptized children of members of the Church of Norway are members until baptism or turning 18. Adults must be baptized as precondition for membership. Access to rituals within a service is free for members. Payment can be demanded for rituals outside the services (CL § 20) Access to marriage within the church (or other religious communities) is conditioned on membership of the church and belonging to the congregation. Access can be denied if one member of the couple has been divorced and the former spouse still lives; or if it is a same-sex-marriage (law on marriage, § 13).[51] Access to cemeteries owned by the Church of Norway's municipality-based councils is free (law 2015 on burials, § 6)[52]	There are two different rituals for performing marriages, the older one is according to the previous constitution by the king in 2003, the recent one (for same-sex-marriages) decided by the Church Meeting in 2017.[53]

---

51 LOV-1991-07-04-47 on Marriage, https://lovdata.no/dokument/NL/lov/1991-07-04-47.
52 LOV-1996-06-07-32 on burials, https://lovdata.no/dokument/NL/lov/1996-06-07-32.
53 Rituals of 2003 for performing marriages, and rituals of 2017 for performing same-sex-marriages: https://kirken.no/globalassets/kirken.no/om-kirken/slik-styres-kirken/lover-og-regler/vigsel_alminnelige_bestemmelser.pdf

The Danish *folkekirke*	Membership is conditioned by baptism. A person, who become part of another religious community, is no longer a member of the *folkekirke* (the law on membership, § 2 (2)). All persons have the right to have their children baptized, they only have to provide Christian witnesses. All members have the right to access the rituals (baptism, confirmation, marriage, including same sex marriage, and burial, including a service), law on membership § 6. They have access to the rituals either where they live or where they belong according to other criteria (§ 7). The member, however, upholds her right to be assessed by another prior. The individual priest can refuse to perform same-sex-marriages or marriages where one of the party is divorced (medlemsskabslov § 7a) All citizens have the right to access to burial on the cemetery (law on church buildings and church yards, § 1 (2)). Members of the church have access to a service in relation to the burial (law on burials, § 7).	

What will be the result for the members if legislative powers to regulate members access to the church is decided by church bodies, either based on delegation or based on *sui generis* legislative powers? This is the question in this section.

The Church of Sweden is not bound by law in this matter. Now, 20 years after the changed relationship with the state, the Church Assembly has changed the regulation concerning its members, implying that baptism is a condition for membership. From this also follows, as in all the other Nordic majority churches, that only baptized people are eligible for elections and for positions as staff members or ordained persons within the church.

This change seems natural, and it is parallel to what is required in the other Nordic majority churches. However, less than 50% of Swedish children are baptized. The former Nordic Lutheran majority churches seem to be heading towards becoming minorities within the populations.

A central dimension of being a *folkekirke* is that the pastors are obliged to care and minister for the people and at least for the members with no distinction regarding their faithfulness. Another central dimension is that membership is easily received and not easily lost. In the Swedish transition, it was a central element to ensure that the Church of Sweden is not allowed to establish any other condition than membership of individuals asking for service (Pettersson 2011, 124).

For all these churches, membership is acquired through baptism. Interestingly, both the Norwegian and the Danish Lutheran churches give the pastors the right to deny some services to members who are not perceived to live up to certain religious requirements. It is, for example, allowed for the individual pastor to deny the re-marriage of a divorced couple, or to refuse to perform a marriage for a homosexual couple. The members, however, retain the right to access these rituals, just by another pastor, organized by the dean in the area. In Norway, two different rituals exist side by side. And in Finland, two different positions now live side-by-side within the church: the official understanding is that marriage is between man and woman. However, two persons of same gender can now be lawfully married within the church. The dioceses have different views on whether performing same-sex-marriages should lead to disciplining the pastors. A final solution has not yet been established.[54]

Only in Denmark is the right for the members to have access to rituals etc. ensured by law. In Finland, that right is ensured by the Church Order.

---

54 "Nya äktenskapslagen och kyrkan," Evangelisk-lutherska kyrkan i Finland, accessed June 25, 2020, https://evl.fi/pressrum/aktuellt-just-nu/aktenskapslagen.

3. Are there differences in voting rights vs eligibility for the church members, based on church discipline?

	By law	**By Church Orders**
Church of Sweden		All members over the age of 16 have voting rights for congregation councils etc. (CO 33 Ch, 2 §). Apart from membership, eligibility requires that the person is baptized and over the age of 18 (CO 33 Ch, 2 §)
The Evangelical Lutheran Church of Finland	The Church Assembly decides the rules on election rights and on eligibility (CL 1 Ch, 3§). The church law decides general election rights and eligibility rules (CL, chapter 23). Eligibility for church councils etc. requires the age of 18, confirmation, and that the person is well known for their Christian commitment (CL 23 Ch, 2 §) Any member of the church over the age of 16 holds electoral rights in relation to church councils etc. (CL 23 Ch, 12 §). Both men and women must be represented with at least 40% (CL 23 Ch, 8 §)	The rules on elections (*Valordningen*)[55] does not include any further regulations on election rights or eligibility.
Church of Norway	Voting rights based on membership, living in a local diocese, and being over the age of 15 (CL §4). All members are eligible to elected to congregation councils at the age of 18 (CL § 6 (3)) Membership of the church is a general condition for eligibility (CL § 29).	The Church Assembly has further regulated the election of congregation councils, church assembly etc. There are no further conditions relating to election rights and eligibility.[56]
The Danish *folkekirke*	Voting rights: membership, 18 years of age. Eligibility: membership of the church (and thus baptism) is the general requirement. An elected member can lose eligibility if the person actively, persistently, and publicly holds positions obviously against the teaching of the church (lov om valg til menighedsråd, § 3a)	

---

55 https://www.finlex.fi/sv/laki/ajantasa/2014/20140416
56 https://lovdata.no/dokument/SF/forskrift/2018-04-16-584

In the Finnish church, it is required that a person must be confirmed and also known to be a Christian person in order to be eligible in the internal elections. Simultaneously, it is ensured that both men and women must be elected. Both rules are set in the Church Law—not to be changed by the Church Assembly in internal church orders.

Only in Denmark can eligibility be lost, in the case of the person actively working against the teachings of the church.

One might wonder why rules on eligibility are interesting. However, if there were a tendency towards demanding a certain religiosity from members as a precondition for obtaining influence on church matters, it would be visible in the rules on eligibility. It is therefore central to identify increasing religious demands on church membership and thus on election rights and eligibility. It is relevant not least because the change from legitimacy through free and public elections and representation in joint democratic legislative parliaments to legitimacy within internal (church) assemblies has been argued with reference to the internal democratic elections. Therefore, eligibility rules and rules on rights to election are of general interest.

4. *Are there any religious requirements on church employees, supplementary to the general labor law? Is there a distinct internal (or maybe even external) body taking care of such cases?*

	Public law—general labor law	**Supplementary requirements (by church law or by church order)**	**Distinct body—internal or external?**
Church of Sweden		Preconditions for ordination of priests: baptism, confirmation, membership of the Church of Sweden, preparedness to serve on an equal footing with others, with no conditions regarding gender etc. (CO 25 Ch, 2 § and 31 Ch). The chapter (an internal committee at diocese level) can decide further conditions, CO 34 Ch, 9 § & 34 Ch, 11 §). There is also the right to appeal (34 Ch, 17 §). Church wardens must be baptized, members, and over the age of 16 (CO 4 Ch, 19 §). Employees must be members of the Church of Sweden (or another Lutheran church). This condition is not valid for employees, who solely work with the cemeteries. (CO 34 Ch, 7 §).	Internal body regarding the bishop's responsibilities (CO 10 Ch, 8 § & Co 14 Ch, ansvarsnämnd för biskoper) Internal body with jurisdiction to decide on petitions internally in the church (CO 10 Ch, 10 § & CO 16 Ch). Ethical guidelines (codex) for ordained ministry (Hansson, 2016)
The Evangelical Lutheran Church of Finland	Public law regulations are basic requirements for a position in the church (CL 6 Ch, 13 §)	Legal conditions for the ordination are delegated to be decided in the Church Order (CL 5 Ch, 1 (2) §). Confirmation and membership are supplementary requirements on employees with a fixed service, for employees serving at the congregational service, and for others if necessary (CL 6 Ch, 13 §). A priest can lose his position if he is not faithful to the confession or to the function (CL 5 Ch, 3 §).	Conditions for ordination as a priest are that the person (a) is known as a pious person, (b) has passed a theological exam at a university recognized by the bishops, and (c) in general is fit for the function (CO 5 Ch, 2 §).
Church of Norway		All employees must be members of the Church (CL § 29). A priest who breaks with conditions in the ordination, can be dismissed (CL § 31) The Church Assembly is by law delegated the competence to decide on further requirements for ordained ministry (CL § 31)	Conditions for service as a priest:[57] (a) member of the church; (b) passed theological exam or parallel qualifications; (c) passed exam in practical theology, and (d) capable in the Norwegian language

---

[57] Internal regulation on requirements for functioning as a priest within the Church of Norway, Forskrift om kvalifikasjonskrav for tilsetting som prest i Den norske kirke, decided by the Church Assembly, FOR-2016-04-11-1810, https://lovdata.no/dokument/SF/forskrift/2016-04-11-1810.

| The Danish *folkekirke* | General public law requirements are in force | For civil servants and thus the ministry: a general requirement to remain in accordance with the dignity of the position (tjeneste-mandsloven § 10) Dismissal of priests according to special legislation if the priest in his function or preaching is clearly beyond the Evangelical Lutheran requirements of his position (lov om domstolsbehandling af gejstlige læresager) | |

All four churches require membership (and thus baptism) of their ordained staff (priests etc.). Membership and thus baptism are also requirements for non-ordained staff members in the Swedish, the Finnish, and the Norwegian Evangelical Lutheran churches (albeit with a possible exemption for staff members working on the cemeteries), but not in the Danish church. The Finnish church requires confirmation as a precondition for ordination and in some cases also for other staff members. The Swedish church also requires confirmation of their ordained staff. All churches require as a standard a university exam of ordained staff members. The Finnish Evangelical Lutheran Church also requires that an ordained priest is known as a pious person. All churches now have rules and procedures on how to dismiss ordained and not-ordained staff members.

Regarding the standards for clergy and thus the normative basis for accusations to be considered by the Chapters/the Board of Appeal in the Church of Sweden, Hansson explains that some of the bishops have developed guidelines or ethical standards for what is inappropriate. The codex covers elements such as professional secrecy, financial transactions and gifts, advice concerning daily prayer and worship for the clergy, sexual relations with parishioners, holy matrimony, baptism of their children, and worshipping as examples of credibility. Hansson concludes that "the esteem of the ministry is more important than acts, per se, being moral or immoral."[58]

Requirements that staff members be baptized and, for example, active church members, as well as requirements for the priesthood of being known as a pious person, are useful to distinguish the jobs within the church from other jobs with the same professional dimensions. Or, put differently, such requirements make

---

58 Per Hansson, "Clergy Discipline Decisions in the Church of England and the Church of Sweden Compared," in *Church Reform and Leadership of Change*, ed. Harald Askeland and Ulla Schmidt (Eugene, OR: Pickwick Publications, 2016), 120.

the question of faith and being faithful part of the professional requirements. In a Danish context, such requirements became foreign during the 20th century, no distinctions must be made within a *folkekirke*. This is possibly the area where the Nordic Lutheran churches stand out most distinctively from each another.

5. Are legal conflicts solved entirely internally, or is it possible to get access to ordinary courts for arbitration of legal conflicts in the church?

	Internal body	**Access to court**
Church of Sweden	Disciplinary accusations are considered by the chapters and can be appealed to the Board of Appeal, Svenska Kyrkans överklagandenämnd (CO 10 Ch, 10§; CO ch 16), which takes all sorts of cases. This board is elected by the Church Assembly, presided over by a judge, and all members must have good knowledge of internal church affairs (16 ch, 2§). No further appeal is allowed (16 ch, 1§).	?
Evangelical Lutheran Church of Finland	Internal appeal bodies (chapters etc.) organized by law.	Appeals in cases concerning dismissal are referred to the court (CL 6 Ch, 68 §. Appeals concerning other decisions through the internal appeal system to the Administrative Court (CL 24 Ch, 4 §).
Church of Norway	There is no general right to administrative appeal (CL, § 38). Cases can be filed internally against a priest (CL § 31). The church can organize an internal appeal body (CL, § 27). An appeal body is established by the internal church order.[59] It has five members of which both genders must be represented; the head of the body shall be a judge, others represent competences within theology, ecclesiastical law etc. It deals with cases against priests, and other high-level dismissals.	?
The Danish *folkekirke*	The ordinary possibilities of appeal in public entities.	Access to court. Dismissal of priests requires a special session of the court.

---

59   https://lovdata.no/dokument/INS/forskrift/2016-04-11-1765?q=klagenemnd

It is rather surprising that the law on the Church of Norway does not include any regulations on internal administrative appeal. Such appellate structures and bodies are organized within the Church of Sweden and according to law in regard to the Evangelical Lutheran Church of Finland and the Danish *Folkekirke*. Lack of administrative appeal leaves the church members with no other possibilities to react against decisions than the elections every fourth year. This question is very central in order for individuals to have their rights protected, be they individual church members or staff members.

Regarding ordained staff members (priests), all churches have a system established. In Denmark, the ordinary system for civil servants is supplemented with access to a special court setting in cases of dismissal on grounds of conflict with the confession of the church. In such situations in the Evangelical Lutheran Church of Finland, ordained staff members are even ensured access to court directly by law.

It remains unclear in all countries whether other conflictual cases, for example right to membership, members' access to rituals etc., have access to court. The question can be discussed in relation to two interesting Norwegian cases.[60] The *dictum* from these two cases is that cases concerning conflict between norms within a religious community and ordinary laws (and of course especially criminal law) can be filed at the ordinary courts, without any hesitation. Cases concerning membership rights, access to rituals, and protection against exclusion might fall under the autonomy of a religious community. However, the case can be filed if it is central to the welfare of the individual and concerns procedural questions (including whether internal procedures are followed correctly), if the case concerns false facts, or if the case concerns basic norms regarding legal certainty.

The general approach in Sweden seems to be that any case of breaking the law given by parliament would go directly to the Swedish authorities (for example, a breach of the criminal law would go directly to the authorities without any internal procedure). However, it seems that only cases regulated by statutory law can be disputed at the courts. This means that the major change of formalities behind the norms in the Church of Sweden—from statutory law

---

60 The cases referred to are: (1) HR-2004-1806-A (concerning admissibility for a case on access to rituals in a mosque and access to becoming a member of the community) in which the Supreme Court formulated the aforementioned criteria for admissibility. (2) A recent case from the regional courts uses the same language; however, it is disputed as infringing the religious freedom of the Jehovah's Witnesses, see Borgarting lagmannsrett, Kjennelse—LB-2020-11024. The case might be referred to the supreme court. I thank Helge Årsheim for providing me with the cases and for a good discussion on this matter.

to internal governance orders—also in the case of Sweden constitutes a major change of final authority, moved from state administrative authority and public court to internal bodies.[61]

What is a Nordic National Church, by Law Established?

The question discussed in this section is what it means (still) to be a *by law established* national church in the Nordic countries. The material used to discuss this matter consists of the currently (June 2020) valid laws regarding the legal organization of the Nordic Lutheran majority churches. In this section, I will discuss the tendencies in the new Norwegian legislation valid from January 1, 2021 (regarding both the Church of Norway and other religious communities) in order to draw more general conclusions.

One conclusion on the development so far is that the Nordic churches need to be *by law established*, because they do not have any transnational Lutheran church order as a fallback position. One could simply argue that, since the states withdrew these churches from canon law, the states must also decide to which extent they can re-establish a sort of internal canon law. Put differently, to which extent are these churches still under the legislative, executive, and judiciary powers of the land?

The Danish *folkekirke* is still governed by the legislative and judiciary powers of the country. As for executive powers, the local congregation and deanery councils as well as pastors and bishops have been delegated executive powers by law; all other executive powers remain with the state.

The Evangelical Lutheran Church of Finland cannot legislate itself autonomously. There is only one legislative power in Finland, which also legislates the Church Law. However, the right to take initiatives regarding church law remains with the church's national bodies, which means that this dimension of executive powers lies with the church. The only executive powers that remain with the state are related to church taxes and to government approval of legislation—all further executive powers have been transferred by law to the church organization.

For the Church of Sweden and the Church of Norway, the legislator holds powers according to the constitutions to regulate the church organization. In

---

61 The analysis by Hansson, "Clergy Discipline Decisions," goes into further detail regarding which penalties are given in disciplinary cases. The analysis does not, however, provide information as to whether any of these cases are brought to the ordinary court or whether they could be so.

2000, Sweden used this legislative power to formulate the general identity and obligations of the Church of Sweden and to delegate by law further legislative powers to this church. The question regarding the protection of the rights of individual members is central. In Sweden, these protective rights are in place by statutory law as far as individual rights to access the services of the church is concerned, including rights with a civil dimension: access to marriage and burial (and the open access to services). All other membership rights are grounded only in the internally regulated Church Order, which means that conflict situations over these rights can only be settled at the internal ecclesiastical conflict resolution system.

Until the constitutional and legislative changes within the last generation, and also in the rules laid down during the internal processes regarding these changes, it has been a central task to ensure the rights of the individual church members to have access to individual and collective rituals. Also access to internal governance structures is ensured in structures that mirror membership rights in associations. Employees, however, and especially pastors, are increasingly placed under a regulatory system different from other public law employees. This trend opens for further religious disciplining, with only few possibilities of accessing ordinary courts in conflict situations. The internal bodies, organized according to Church Orders, are generally organized according to typical principles of courts. But compared with the traditional distinction of public powers, the access to a fair trial and ordinary judiciary is, for both staff and members, surprisingly un-ensured.

Given that some of the Nordic churches, those with special protection in their respective constitutions, are meant to be *folkekirke*, one could argue that statutory law ought to retain a protection of basic membership rights regarding access to rituals in those churches. And at least, one could expect that it was highlighted in the political processes that a change of legislative powers concerning membership rights and rights for staff members—from the parliament and government into internal church bodies—implies a major change of protection rights for members and staff regarding access to administrative appeal as well as regarding access to court.

All things considered, to be a *by law established* Evangelical Lutheran church in the Nordic countries is to be by law dis-established from the executive hierarchy of the state. As indicated above, the change of legislative powers leads to dis-establishment from the state court system to a higher extent than I believe people are aware of. However, the change of legal status for the churches does not include any disestablishment from ordinary legislative powers. To be a *by law established* church does not enable the church to organize itself in a parallel legal order, or to re-invent a system of canon law, based on a *sui generis* approach, maybe with an exemption in the Church of Sweden, although the state remains capable of withdrawing its delegated powers. The (other) churches are by law established, and their internal regulatory systems rely on delegation by law. Their legal systems are therefore still part of the ordinary legal systems of these countries.

As such, these churches are also characterized by being more national than confessional. One could argue that the members of these churches do not even believe in belonging to the churches.[62] That is of course not entirely correct. A core group of members are faithful Christians who want to practice their Christianity within this broad context. Other groups, however, do not want to be questioned about their individual faith but prefer to rely on the rituals in matters of faith. In general, these churches are characterized by increasing individualization while being cultural institutions that contribute to the social capital in their societies.[63] This individualization is legally supported and has also strengthened the position of the national churches vis-à-vis other religious communities in the countries.

Internationalization—Breaking up the System

In the previous analysis and conclusions, the perspective has been national and constitutional. The material for those parts of the article includes valid law in the four Nordic countries in June 2020. The material concerning the most recent legislative process, which took place in 2020 in Norway, resulting in a new law on religious communities including the Church of Norway, valid from January 2021, was however not included. In this section, I widen the perspective to

---

62   See Lisbet Christoffersen, "Not Even Believing in Belonging: States and Churches in Five North-European (Post-)Lutheran Countries," in *Law and Religion in the 21st Century: Relations between States and Religious Communities,* ed. Silvio Ferrari and Rinaldo Cristofori (Aldershot: Ashgate, 2010), 187-98. I owe the formulation "not even believing in belonging" to Grace Davie.

63   Further on this concept, see Hans Raun Iversen et al., *Individualisation, Marketisation and Social Capital in a Cultural Institution: The Case of the Danish Folk Church* (Odense: University Press of Southern Denmark, 2019) and for analysis of the legal consequences for individual members, see Lisbet Christoffersen and Karen Marie Sø Leth-Nissen, "Legally Supported Marketisation and Individualisation of the Folk Church as a Cultural Institution," in *Individualisation, Marketisation and Social Capital in a Cultural Institution: The Case of the Danish Folk Church*, ed. Hans Raun Iversen et al. (Odense: University Press of Southern Denmark, 2019), 147-73.

include the role of (European) human rights. Here, the most recent Norwegian legislation, valid from January 2021, is the case study.

The Nordic countries were among the first to sign the European Convention of Human Rights (ECHR), which came into force on September 3, 1953. The ECHR had an immediate impact on Nordic law of religion. It became obvious that the Norwegian constitution still upheld a constitutional prohibition against any immigration of Jesuits, which was in conflict with the ECHR. As a result, Norway had to delete that prohibition from its constitution. In the same vein, Norway organized by law a system of acknowledging and financing all religious communities, majority and minority, on an equal footing in 1969.[64]

Apart from that, the ECHR clauses on religion as mentioned in the first part of this chapter had little influence in the Nordic countries during the first generations. This owed mainly to the fact that the Nordic countries—who were very influential in the development, negotiations, and signature of the ECHR—in the first period decided to protect their state churches. They simply required that ECHR Article 9 could not infringe on the existing Nordic state-church systems.[65]

Therefore, it is fair to say that the first inspiration to change the national churches from state churches to *by-law-established* churches did not come from the internationalization of human rights or a Europeanization of the national governing bodies. Rather, the first inspirations came from a process of internal secularization in the Nordic societies as part of the modernization of especially the social democratic and leftist parties. It became part of the political center-left and especially the young generation of politicians from the late 1960s to rework all legislation where Lutheran Christianity still influenced the individual life of the citizens (secularization in the third meaning, as explained in the introduction

---

64   Norway had passed a law on dissenting communities in 1845, allowing for other Christian communities than the Lutheran church (Ingunn Folkestad Breistein, *Har staten bedre borgere? Dissenternes kamp for religiøs frihet 1891-1969* (Trondheim: Tapir akademisk forlag, 2003). The law on religious communities of 1969 dissolved the concept of "dissenting" (i.e., from the state church) and provided the legal ground for free right to organize religious communities, based on public funding.

65   The same was the case concerning the development of the articles on religion within the EU treaties. In spite of the development of art 17, TFEU, Denmark at least saw the state-church-arrangements as a *nole me tangere* part of the national identity, which the Union has to respect, see TEU art 5 (2). In particular, national security remains the sole responsibility of each member state. See, for a general overview, Lisbet Christoffersen, "Religion as a Factor in Multi-Layered European Union Legislation," in *Law and Religion in Multicultural Societies*, ed. Rubya Mehdi et al. (Copenhagen: DJØF Publishing, 2008), 111-30, and for an introduction to the early Danish debate on this matter, Lisbet Christoffersen, "Lovmæssigheder: Kirker og Trossamfund i EU," in *Konstellationer: Kirkerne og det Europæiske projekt*, ed. Ida Auken (Frederiksberg: Alfa-forlag, 2007), 45-68.

to this book). On this basis, marriage laws and laws on the religious identity of school as well as laws on religious instruction in schools were changed in many Nordic countries. The rights of individual members of the national churches to re-marry after divorce was disputed, but enforced.

Another inspiration, which possibly affected the political right more, was the cultural aftermath of World War II, especially the German *Barmen Declaration* and its Norwegian equivalent *The Foundation of the Church* (*Kirkens Grunn*). From the very beginning, the Norwegian School of Theology, originally lay-financed and deriving from the 19th-century lay movements, became a center for an ecclesiastical vision of the Church of Norway as a church for the people. This vision implied that not the people (and their representatives in the parliament) but "the church," by internal representation models and by the ordained priests and bishops, was responsible for the internal ideology (theology) of the church. Others, such as the Faculty of Theology at the University of Oslo, represented a broader perspective on the *Folkekirke* as the people's church. This distinction became more obvious during the last quarter of the 20th century. Also in Denmark, new private theological institutions appeared in the same period, very much based on protests against abortion legislation from the early 1970s. The Danish private theological institutions also supported ecclesiastical views of pastors as more obliged towards their theological identity than towards their identity as civil servants.[66]

It should be mentioned that the role of the majority churches in the three Scandinavian countries is linked to the role of the monarchies. Both the Norwegian and the Swedish royal houses have requested to remain bound to the Lutheran national churches. In Denmark, the discourse remains that the mon-

---

66 In Denmark, this distinction became clear in a series of cases in the 1970s, where pastors refused to baptize children of members of *folkekirken* due to a lack of church practice on the side of the parents. One of these cases even went to the European Commission on Human Rights. Here, the pastor was told that he of course had freedom of religion, namely to leave the church, but if he remained, he had to follow the legal practice. See *X. v. Denmark*, application no. 7374/76, decision on admissibility, 8 March 1976. These two positions were influenced by German legal theory on ecclesiastical law. The majority line referred to Rudolf Sohm's dictum on a sharp distinction between church as a theological and a legal entity, whereas especially Hans Dombois inspired the more conservative groups' thinking of law as grace. Dombois thus visited Denmark (Løgumkloster, the school for further education of pastors) for a seminar in 1974, organized by the conservative pastor Jørgen Glenthøj. Later cases led to the organization of the Danish association of ecclesiastical law (www.kirkeret.dk). The theoretical basis for this association has mostly been the idea of double norm systems, likewise inspired by German theory. For further details on the German theoretical approaches, see Heinig, "Neither Sacred nor Secular Law," in this volume.

arch is the head of the church, even though the constitution in Article 6 simply states that the monarch has to be a member of the church. The special role of monarchy and church in Danish society can be illustrated with reference to the 150 years celebration of the constitution in 1999, which took place at a high-level seminar in the parliament. Here, every single element of the Danish constitution of 1849 was debated. Only the intertwinement of monarchy, the Lutheran national church, and the freedom of religion remained untouchable and thus not on the agenda.

It was the Helsinki Declaration (1975)[67] that initiated a second wave of focus on human rights all over Europe. In its *decalogue,* the guiding principle for the Conference on Security and Co-operation in Europe ("respect for human rights and fundamental freedoms, including the freedom of thought, conscience, religion or belief") was one of ten basic principles. This focus became central in the fight for freedom of religion in Eastern Europe, but also raised a new argument regarding the status of former state churches: freedom was not enough, equality was required.

After the breakdown of the Soviet Union, the ECHR in a third wave again proved relevant as a foundation for processes of European collaboration. This was also the case for its provisions regarding freedom of religion in all dimensions. Of the three Copenhagen criteria regarding access to membership of the European Union (EU),[68] "stability of institutions guaranteeing democracy, the rule of law, human rights and respect for and protection of minorities" was mentioned first. In the Nordic countries as well as in the Baltic region, these criteria were also used as an argumentative basis for further development of equal treatment of religions.[69]

In the Nordic countries, the first constitutional reaction to the rising influence of human rights arguments was to refer to dualist constitutional arguments: human rights—as international law—are binding *for* the states, but not *within* the

---

67 The Final Act of the 1st CSCE Summit of Heads of State or Government, 1st August 1975, https://www.osce.org/helsinki-final-act

68 https://ec.europa.eu/neighbourhood-enlargement/policy/glossary/terms/accession-criteria_en

69 For example, that the Nordic countries still had state churches, was part of the argument regarding keeping an (Orthodox) state church in Moldova, see *Metropolitan Church of Bessarabia* v. *Moldova,* application no. 45701/99, cf. Lisbet Christoffersen, "Church Autonomy: En religionsretlig udfordring til Norden," *Retfærd: Nordisk Juridisk Tidsskrift* 27, no. 4 (2004): 87-108. See further the influential paper by Ole Espersen, *The Right to Freedom of Religion and Religious Associations: A Survey and Recommendations* (Copenhagen: the Council of the Baltic Sea States, 1999).

states. Within the states, the national constitution forms the final framework.[70] This was the basic Danish approach to EU law: EU legislation is valid law in Denmark insofar as competences have been conferred through the system behind the treaties—and only so far. The same approach is apparent in the Danish opt-outs of the EU treaties. Even though the Swedish constitutional tradition was even more dualistic, Finland and Sweden began changing their constitutions, including human rights as a central element in the normative basis for legislation, soon after their rather late 1995 EU membership with no opt-outs.

The normative question is whether statutory law—such as church laws favoring the majority churches—can be set aside as against the human rights, even though they are supported by the national constitution. This question was at the center of the so-called Folgerø-case in Norway, decided in the Grand Chamber of the European Court of Human Rights (ECtHR) by a vote of 9:8 against Norway on June 29, 2007.[71] The governmental representatives were certain of winning the case with reference to a dualist argument: the disputed law on religious instruction in schools was decided by parliament on basis of constitutional requirements. The ECtHR judgment, however, for the first time in a case concerning religion, judged a Nordic country in a violation of human rights. This result fueled the debate on balancing freedom and equality in Norwegian religion law.

Likewise, the Åke Green-case at the Swedish Supreme Court is telling: Åke Green, a pastor in the conservative Pentecostal church, wanted to show that prohibition of hate speech against homosexuals infringed his freedom of religion. In order to prove his position, which was that he was free to preach against human rights because of his freedom of religion, he published a rather harsh sermon based on scriptures from the Old Testament. A case for breaking the criminal law on hate speech was filed against him. Even though the sermon was undoubtedly against Swedish criminal law, he was acquitted at the Swedish Supreme Court. The argument was that the Swedish criminal law—in order to comply with the jurisprudence at ECtHR case law on freedom of religion and

---

[70] This position was behind, e.g., the different positions concerning the role of European and international human rights in the law of religions in Denmark. For the dualist position, see Hans Gammeltoft-Hansen, "Kommentarer til grundlovens religionsbestemmelser," in *Danmarks Riges grundlov med kommentarer*, ed. Henrik Zahle (Copenhagen: DJØF Publishing, 2005) and for an argument for including human rights in the analysis, Lisbet Christoffersen, "Europæisk perspektiv på religion i dansk forfatningsret," in *Danmarks Riges Grundlov med kommentarer*, ed. Henrik Zahle. 2nd ed. (Copenhagen: DJØF forlag, 2006), 63-76.

[71] Case of *Folgerø and Others v. Norway* [GC], application no. 15472/02, 29 June 2007.

belief—would have to make room for religious preaching, even though the religious preaching was taking the form of hate speech.[72]

Thus, human rights influenced the rapid changes of Nordic religion law in the attempt by the Nordic countries to establish not only freedom of religion, but equality among religious communities, including the majority churches that by law were dis-established from the state administrations.[73]

Only in Denmark, this transformation did not succeed. In March 2016, Heiner Bielefeldt, the then United Nations Special Rapporteur on Freedom of Religion or Belief, decided to pay a visit to a country with a Lutheran state church and therefore visited the only possible country, Denmark. In his preliminary report, he urged Denmark to move towards a more inclusive "Danishness". In his final report, however, he also admitted that no legal problems with freedom of religion were identified; the problems were more symbolical in nature, related to the principled lack of equality and especially to the dimensions of using a soft Lutheranism as a parameter of Danishness to the effect that even old non-Lutheran Christian communities could feel themselves as guests in their own country.[74]

Bielefeldt's visit was welcomed by all religious communities, including representatives from Folkekirken in Denmark, but his visit became untimely in a manner that no one could have foreseen. Just a few weeks before his visit, Danish television brought a series called *The imams behind the veil*, showing how Muslim leaders in fact prevent Muslim women from applying for divorce under Danish law in violent marriages.[75] The liberal government asked the most liberal

---

72 NJA 2005, s 805, HD 2005-11-29, mål nummer B 1050-05. The case is discussed, among others, by hl (2006), https://svjt.se/svjt/2006/213; and Eva Jagander, "Hate Speech: Två avgöranden från högsta domstolen i Sverige," *Nordisk Tidsskrift for Kriminalvidenskab* 94 (3) (2007): 236-41.

73 For more on this topic, see also the chapters by Anna-Sara Lind, "Freedom of Religion and Positive Duties of the State: The Case of Sweden," Pamela Slotte, "Moving Frontiers," Helge Årsheim, "A Minor Disturbance? Nordic Approaches to Minority Religion," and Victoria Enkvist, "Making Religion Visible in Sweden: Secular Legislation Turns Religious in the Name of Human Rights," in this volume.

74 https://www.ohchr.org/SP/NewsEvents/Pages/DisplayNews.aspx?NewsID=17201&LangID=E; https://www.ohchr.org/EN/NewsEvents/Pages/DisplayNews.aspx?NewsID=18509&LangID=E; The final report was presented to the Human Rights Council Thirty-fourth session, 27 February—24 March 2017, Agenda item 3. Available at https://ap.ohchr.org/documents/dpage_e.aspx?si=A/HRC/34/50/Add.1, https://documents-dds-ny.un.org/doc/UNDOC/GEN/G16/442/36/PDF/G1644236.pdf?OpenElement (retrieved June 2020).

75 For further on the validity of the series of programs and on the political results, see Niels Valdemar Vinding and Emil Bjørn Hilton Saggau, "Challenges of the Institutionalization of Same Sex Marriage for Religious Pluralism in Denmark," in *Islam, Religions, and Pluralism in Europe*, ed. Ednan Aslan, Ranja Ebrahim, and Marcia Hermansen (Wiesbaden:

member of government, the Minister of Culture and also of Ecclesiastical Affairs, Bertel Haarder, to lead political negotiations towards further requirements regarding adherence to democracy, human rights, equal treatment of men and women, and the rule of law within religious communities that wanted to apply for legal acknowledgement and financial support. His basic approach was: We do not want to be laughed at at our own expense.

What had changed the original, very liberal approach to the free practice of religion in Denmark was the cartoon crisis, which occurred in 2005-2006, shortly after 9/11 and the war on terror.[76] Political forces, but also broader societal and academic voices found that the burning of the Danish flag and of embassies, as well as the huge, populist reaction in the Middle East against Denmark (and Norway, by mistake of flags) was utterly unfair. Freedom of religion prevailed in Denmark, was the argument, but Muslims were not supposed to be treated any different than others; religious feelings had to be pushed back, especially if they supported the suppression of women etc. The latest development on this topic was the terror attacks in Copenhagen 2015, resulting in the murder of a public intellectual at a seminar on freedom of speech, as well as the murder of a young guard at a Jewish bar-mitzvah celebration in a Copenhagen synagogue.

These events have changed the Danish political debate. From taking freedom of religion for granted as something to be protected and supported, the majority of center-right and center-left parties now suspect religious communities (probably excepting the Lutheran majority church) of being fundamentalists, against human rights, etc. The new law on religious communities from 2017 kept clear of that development by only stating what was already enforceable law concerning acknowledgement: requirements of transparency, accountability, and good governance.[77] In this context, it has been a recurring discussion how far the political system could go in supervising religious communities.

The flip side of this discussion concerns the extent to which the political system, as framed by ECtHR, might act as a protector of religious groups and practices that by politicians are seen as potentially infringing broader societal values of human freedom, including the possibility of having established churches. Such reflections are part of the background for the second Copenhagen Declaration:

Springer, 2016). For further on the legislative development in the so-called *imam-laws*, see Christoffersen, "Legal Re-Organisation of the Danish Religious Market."

76 See, among many other introductions to this period, Lisbet Christoffersen, "The Danish Cartoons Crisis Revisited," in *Islam and Political-Cultural Europe*, ed. W. Cole Durham, Jr., David M. Kirkham, and Tore Lindholm (Farnham: Ashgate, 2012), 217-28.

77 For the relevance of that type of requirements, see Christoffersen, "A Long Historical Path."

the Council of Europe Declaration on the role of the ECtHR in protection freedoms and rights of individuals in Europe.[78] A central aspect of this declaration is the emphasis on national authorities as the first guarantors of human rights. In order to support this statement, a new principle of subsidiarity is introduced, underlining that national states enjoy a margin of appreciation in how they apply and implement the convention. This margin of appreciation is especially underlined in regard to ECHR Articles 8-11, i.e. in regard to protection of among other things freedom of religion. "Where a balancing exercise has been undertaken at the national level in conformity with the criteria laid down in the Court's jurisprudence, the Court has generally indicated that it will not substitute its own assessment for that of the domestic courts, unless there are strong reasons for doing so".[79] By this Copenhagen Declaration, the international protection of freedom of religion was severely weakened, as long as the national authorities, not least the legislative powers, ensure that they *have* considered the ECHR.

The Europeanization/internationalization, however, already impacts Nordic law on religious communities. The change of legislation from 2000 onwards implies that the Lutheran majority churches are now (in Norway, Sweden, and Finland, but not in Denmark) also covered by general legislation concerning the freedom of religion and belief and concerning how to register as a religious community. This legislation is partly influenced by the ECHR.[80] By including the majority churches under such general legislation, the systems of financing religious communities are converging in these countries. The systems of requirements from the legislator to religious communities, including the Evangelical Lutheran majority churches, are converging, too. In the same vein, a new and rather critical approach from parts of the political milieu to the religious communities appears in all the Nordic countries[81], and we can only expect more to come. In their interesting analysis of the Swedish legislation concerning religious communities, Victoria Enkvist and Per-Erik Nilsson suggest that the legal regulation of faith communities in order for them to receive economic funding

---

78 The Copenhagen Declaration of April 13, 2018 on the role of the ECtHR, accessed July 1, 2020, https://www.echr.coe.int/Documents/Copenhagen_Declaration_ENG.pdf.
79 The April 2018 Copenhagen Declaration, part 28, b) and c).
80 This has been the case since the general law on religious communities in Norway of 1969, on religious communities and on how to register as a religious community in Sweden since 1998 and 1999, and on freedom of religion in Finland since 2003.
81 See, e.g., Anna-Sara Lind, "Offentligt och privat: Regleringen av religion i Sverige," in *Sedd men osedd: Om folkkyrkans paradoxala närvaro inför 2020-talet*, ed. Anders Bäckström and Anders Wejryd (Stockholm: Verbum 2016), 152-64.

functions as a form of disciplinary system.[82] This is unquestionably the case. The burning issue in all the Nordic countries is to what extent religious communities (including majority churches) must include general rules regarding equal treatment, such as on the basis of gender and general human rights, or even must support these standards in order to be recognized, to receive rights to perform marriages, or to receive public funding.

In Sweden, the government has lost a series of cases at the Administrative Supreme Court against Jehovah's Witnesses and has consequently set up a committee, which presented new legislative proposals in the spring of 2018.[83] In Norway, the Stålsett-committee in 2013 suggested a number of principles for a politics regarding faith communities for the future, including principles regarding human rights in these communities.[84] In Denmark, a 2017 committee suggested that religious communities must stick to equality norms in their organizational rules, if they want their marriages to be legally acknowledged and receive (indirect) state funding.[85]

The scene is set for some forms of convergence among the Nordic systems. The question remains whether the states will require of the other religious communities what has been required of the majority churches during the 20th century, or whether the majority churches are now also regarded "simply" as religious communities. If the latter becomes the case, this leaves the states with just the same possibilities for regulating majority churches as for regulating minority churches, within the framework of ordinary human rights of freedom and equality. This development, of course, may change the system of "by law established churches" in the Nordic countries even more radically than what occurred during the changes around the millennium.

The most recent example of this is the political fight in the Norwegian parliament over the new law on religious communities, passed April 24, 2020.[86] Back in November 2019, the leader of the social democratic party in parliament argued

---

[82] Victoria Enkvist and Per-Erik Nilsson, "The Hidden Return of Religion: Problematizing Religion in Law and Law in Religion in the Swedish Regulation of Faith Communities," in *Reconsidering Religion, Law, and Democracy: New Challenges for Society and Research*, ed. Anna-Sara Lind, Mia Lövheim, and Ulf Zackariasson (Lund: Nordic Academic Press, 2016), 101.

[83] Cf. Enkvist and Nilsson, "The Hidden Return of Religion."

[84] NOU 2013:1: Det livssynsåpne samfunn. En helhetlig tros- og livssynspolitikk. Leading to the 2020 legislation, discussed below.

[85] Leading to law on religious communities of December 2017, however, resulting in no requirements of that kind.

[86] https://lovdata.no/dokument/NL/lov/2020-04-24-31; https://www.stortinget.no/no/Saker-og-publikasjoner/Saker/Sak/?p=76670

in an influential newspaper article that "it is the responsibility of the politicians to ensure and require of religious practice that it is not used to limit the freedoms and rights of others."[87] In response, Professor Ingunn Breistein, leader of a theological seminar for Evangelical churches, urged that economic support should not be something that can be used as an instrument of theological disciplining; it is a constitutional right for the religious communities.[88]

The new Norwegian law on religious communities, in force from January 1, 2021, aims at fulfilling the disestablishment of the Church of Norway into a complete separation between church and state. The law includes one chapter on the Church of Norway and another chapter on other religious communities and their financing. The law also includes general rules on the right of any religious community, including the Church of Norway, to set their own rules on access to membership, including membership rights (which are not at all commented on in the law). This statutory right to decide on rules for membership will also enable the religious communities to discipline their members.[89] Religious communities can register in order to obtain rights to perform marriages and to receive public funding. This right can be denied if the community, or a person acting on behalf of the community, breaks the law, is violent, does not respect rights or freedoms of others, etc.[90] The new law thus opens up for the state disciplining religious communities, which is what Breistein feared.

This law also includes the only legislative ruling concerning the Church of Norway. Chapter 3 of the law thus requires that the Church of Norway remains a national, democratic, Evangelical Lutheran church. The law decides the basic structure of the church by linking parishes and pastors as well as dioceses and bishops to the requirements in the ordination (albeit without requirements concerning the size of the parishes or the dioceses).

The only requirement is that the church shall remain national and democratic, as well as Evangelical Lutheran.[91] Within that concept, the competence to rule on the foundation and the theology of the church, on all liturgies and

---

87 Jonas Gahr Støre, "Det er politikernes ansvar å verne om—og stille krav til—religionsutøvelse," *Vårt Land*, November 27, 2019. It is the responsibility of the politicians both to guard the religious practice and to formulate requirements towards it in order to protect individuals.
88 Ingunn Folkestad Breistein, "Støre favoriserer sitt eget trossamfunn," *Vårt Land*, February 16, 2020, hoping for equal treatment without any interference into the theological questions in the religious communities; that is, equal treatment between the religious communities.
89 Law on religious communities 2020, § 12: § 2, stk. 2.
90 Law on religious communities 2020, § 12: § 6.
91 This requirement is stated in § 10.

books in use for religious services is delegated to the national church body, the Assembly.[92] This means that the rights for members to access rituals, to use hymnbooks and to explore other traditions within the church, as well as issues of equal rights, is vested only within the democratic structure of the Church. You need to obtain a majority in the elections within the church if you want to be protected in the future. The law does also not include any rules on equality rights for staff and priesthood.

The rights of the Church of Norway, as well as other religious communities, to set their own theology relies upon an understanding of church autonomy that is based on the human rights protection of freedom of religion. However, possible conflicts between autonomy for the religious community and internal disciplining of its members or staff (including the priesthood) was a central political theme in the development of the new law on religious communities—a law which came to include the Church of Norway. The very right for the individual community to register can, as mentioned, be denied, if the community or a person acting on behalf of the community breaks general laws by being violent, threatening, undermine the rights of a child, breaks with the prohibition of discrimination as formulated by law, or in any other way seriously violates the rights and freedoms of others. Also the public financing can be withdrawn in such situations. The economic support can, on the same grounds, be withdrawn from the Church of Norway.

The legislator has thus tried to find a balance between the right to church autonomy and the right of the individual to be protected against violations of his or her basic rights. The instrument is state disciplining through economic pressure, or, for other religious communities, even pressure on their legal acknowledgement according to the law.

It is not easy to formulate this balance, but it becomes clear that discrimination on basis of the gender or sex will be allowed in the future, if this discrimination is theologically argued.[93] These rules are, as mentioned, also in

---

92 Law on religious communities 2020, § 12.
93 "[T]here has to be a high level [of infringement] before the economic support is withdrawn. The right to freedom of religion and belief must not be diminished in any unfair way. The point of departure is that the communities can act on the basis of their own identity, without any interference from the state. Only if there is a conflict with other human rights, including individual rights to protection of free speech and free association, must a case be solved. Freedom of religion is also the issue if a religious community adheres to a minority position regarding e.g. same-sex-marriages or equal right of men and women. Discrimination can be accepted if it is based on the theological teaching of the religious community. Violence etc. can never be accepted with reference to theological freedom". My translation of reflections and arguments in *Forslag til forskrifter til trossamfunnsloven*,

force for the Church of Norway, who in the future will make internal decisions on its theology. So, in the future, members and staff of the Church of Norway, a majority church with around 70% of the Norwegians as members, are only given rights and protected through the internal democracy and are no longer protected from by law from discrimination.

Re-Confessionalization: Legitimacy Behind Ecclesiastical Law in the Future Nordic Majority Churches

The introduction to this book considers the epoch of *confessionalism*, in the traditional sense of a development towards inner dogmatic orthodoxy, as long gone. Instead, *re-confessionalization* is suggested as a theoretical concept to capture (a) the growing legal independence of the national churches and other religious communities from direct state involvement, and (b) the fact that legal thinking and national legislation has to deal with a considerable number of religious communities as part of a pluralistic culture.

The analysis in this chapter of the changed status of four of the five Nordic Lutheran majority churches from having been state churches into becoming *by law established*—and maybe even by law dis-established—confirms the first observation from the introduction. We are in a period of re-confessionalization, leading to growing legal independence of the former state churches. However, the analysis also shows that other religious communities do not necessarily face a growing independence from direct state involvement. On the contrary, the Nordic states, having been used to act as protectors of individual rights against religious hierarchies, also want to use their powers against other religious communities than the majority churches. The fact that the legal thinking has to deal with an increasing number of diverse religious communities only underlines that development.

On that background, it is striking that the converging control with religious practices within other religious communities exists alongside an increasing lack of control with the practices of the national churches. Even though the analysis in this chapter has shown that all the Nordic national majority churches are still by law established as Evangelical Lutheran, they also receive a rapidly growing

høringsnotat 27 maj 2020, 41-43 [proposed bylaws to the law on religious communities]. "Lov om tros- og livssynssamfunn (trossamfunnsloven) (the process leading to the new law on religious communities in Norway, valid from January 1st, 2021)," accessed June 25, 2020, https://www.stortinget.no/no/Saker-og-publikasjoner/Saker/Sak/?p=76670

independence from any legislative boundaries. This growing independence comes about by placing the national churches on par with other religious communities within the same set of laws, implying that norms are equal for the two sets of institutions without regard for the number of members, without regard for the distinction between majority and minority.

So the future implication for members and staff, including the pastors, of being a *by law established* national Evangelical Lutheran church is left for internal church bodies to decide, as long as a form of internal democracy is ensured. Thus, the new Norwegian law directly states that the church assembly will decide on rituals, liturgy, hymnbooks, and confessional grounding, and also that all religious communities, including the Church of Norway, make their own decisions on principles of membership. Basically, this change of authority implies that the Church of Norway, for example, could become a member of the Missouri synod, it could decide to abandon female priesthood, it could require active church practice as a condition for membership, and it could renegotiate the access for same-sex-couples to access the rituals in the church. All examples are relevant—this happened in the Evangelical Lutheran Church of Latvia in 1993, and those rules have recently been confirmed by the Latvian synod in 2016.

It is surprising that the new legislation does not uphold standard human rights requirements, does not uphold access to administrative appeal, does not uphold the right of members and staff of the Church of Norway to get access to courts on equal footing with members of other religious groups, does not uphold the results of the fights taken over the last 75 years concerning equal treatment between men and women and with no discrimination on the basis of sex, gender, race, etc. It seems as if the ideology of equal treatment between the religious communities and the ideology of internationalization, which implies church autonomy, has been more central to Nordic legislators than the protection of individuals' rights within their own churches. We really seem to believe that Lutheran Orthodoxy is long gone and will never return.

Bibliography[94]

Case law
European Commission of Human Rights
X. v. *Denmark*, application no. 7374/76, decision on admissibility, 8 March 1976

---

94 All legal and other official resources are retrieved June 2020.

European Court of Human Rights

Metropolitan Church of Bessarabia and others v. Moldova, application no. 45701/99, 13 December 2001

Folgerø and others v. Norway [GC], application no. 15472/02, 29 June 2007

Swedish Supreme Court

Åke Green Fallet, https://lagen.nu/dom/nja/2005s805, 29 November 2005
Norwegian Courts

Norwegian Supreme Court

Rejection of membership of a Mosqué in Norway, HR-2004-1806-A—Rt-2004-1613

Norwegian Court of Appeal

Exclusion from the Jehovas Witnesses, Borgarting lagmannsrett—Kjennelse—LB-2020-11024

Official Sources

Sweden

Kyrkoordning för Svenska Kyrkan den 1 januari 2020 Kyrkomötets beslut (SvKB 1999:1) om Kyrkoordning för Svenska Kyrkan, [the Church Order for the Church of Sweden, revised and valid from January 2020]

Lag (1998:551) om Svenska Kyrkan [the law on the Church of Sweden]

Lag (1998:1592) om införande av lagen om Svenska kyrkan [the law on implementation of the law on the Church of Sweden]

Lag (1998:1593) om trossamfund [law on religious communities]

Lag (1999:932) om stöd til trossamfund [law on economic support to religious communities]

Finland

Finlands Grundlag [the Constitution of Finland] 11.6.1999/731

Kyrkolagen av den 23 december 1964 (635/64) [the law on the Evangelical Lutheran Church of Finland, 1964-1993].

26.11.1993/1054 Kyrkolag [the valid version of this law on the Evangelical Lutheran Church of Finland with later changes]

8.11.1991/1055 år 1993 Kyrkoordning [the valid church order for the Evangelical Lutheran Church of Finland with later changes]

Lag 10.11.1922/267 Religionsfrihetslag (upphävd) [previous law on freedom of religion]

6.6.2003/453 Religionsfrihetslag [the valid law on Freedom of Religion in Finland]

8.11.2013/416 år 2014 Valordning för kyrkan [internal regulation regarding the organization of the elections internally within the Evangelical Lutheran Church of Finland]

Norway

FOR-2018-04-16-584 Regler for valg av menighetsråd, bispedømmeråd og Kirkemøtet (kirkevalgreglene) [valid law on burials with later changes], LOV-1996-06-07-31.

FOR-2016-04-11-1810 Forskrift om kvalifikasjonskrav for tilsetting som prest i Den norske kirke

Forslag til forskrifter til trossamfunnsloven, høringsnotat 27 maj 2020, 41-43 [proposed bylaws to the law on religious communities]. Accessed June 25, 2020. https://www.stortinget.no/no/Saker-og-publikasjoner/Saker/Sak/?p=76670

Kongeriket Noregs grunnlov, [the Norwegian Constitution], LOV-1814-05-17, [latest change: FOR-2020-05-29-1088 fra 14.05.2020]

Lov om Ekteskap [law on marriage], LOV-1991-97-04-47 [latest changes in 2018]

Lov om Den norske kirke (kirkeloven) [the valid law on Church of Norway with later changes] LOV-1996-06-07-31

Lov om Gravplasser, kremasjon og gravferd (gravplassloven) [Law on Burials] LOV-1996-06-07-32 FOR-2016-04-11-1765 Regler for Den norske kirkes klagenemnd

Lov om endringer i kirkeloven (omdanning av Den norske kirke til eget rettssubjekt m.m.), [legal change of the churchlaw, making the Church of Norway a legal subject], LOV-2016-05-27-17

Lov om tros- og livssynssamfunn (trossamfunnsloven) [law on religious communities], LOV-2020-04-24-31

Denmark

Betænkning 1544/2014 om Folkekirkens Styrelse [preparatory work for possible legislation on the future governance structure of the *folkekirke*]

Danmarks Riges Grundlov 5. juni 1953 (oprindelig udgave 5. juni 1849) [The Danish Constitutional Act, current valid version June 5, 1953, original version June 5, 1849].

Folketinget. *Danmarks riges grundlov af 5. Juni 1953: Tronfølgeloven.* Folketinget 2009. https://www.ft.dk/~/media/pdf/publikationer/grundloven/danmarks-riges-grundlov.ashx

LBK nr 608 af 06/06/2007 Bekendtgørelse af lov om udnævnelse af biskopper og om stiftsbåndsløsning [revised law on appointment of bishops]

LBK nr 622 af 19/06/2012, Bekendtgørelse af lov om medlemskab af folkekirken, kirkelig betjening og sognebåndsløsning [revised law on membership of the *folkekirke*]

LBK nr 771 af 24/06/2013 Bekendtgørelse af lov om menighedsråd [revised law on congregation councils]

LBK nr 864 af 25/06/2013 Bekendtgørelse af lov om ansættelse i stillinger i folkekirken m.v. [revised law on appointment to positions in the *folkekirke*]

LBK nr 330 af 29/03/2014, Bekendtgørelse af lov om bestyrelse og brug af folkekirkens kirker m.m. [revised law on governance and use of the church buildings within the *folkekirke*]

LBK nr 12 af 08/01/2020 Bekendtgørelse af lov om valg til menighedsråd [revised law on election of congregation councils]

LBK nr 95 af 29/01/2020 Bekendtgørelse af lov om folkekirkens økonomi [revised law on economic governance within the *folkekirke*]

LBK nr 1156 af 01/09/2016 Bekendtgørelse af lov om folkekirkens kirkebygninger og kirkegårde [revised law on church buildings and cemeteries within the *folkekirke*]

LBK nr 511 af 18/05/2017 Bekendtgørelse af lov om tjenestemænd [revised law on civil servants]
LBK nr 771 af 07/08/2019 Bekendtgørelse af lov om ægteskabs indgåelse og opløsning [revised law on marriages]
LBK nr 43 af 17/01/2020 Bekendtgørelse af lov om begravelse og ligbrænding [revised law on funerals]
Lov om trossamfund udenfor folkekirken, lov nr 1533 af 19/12/2017 [law on religious communities, apart from the *folkekirke*].

Iceland

Constitution of the Republic of Iceland, with later amendments, latest June 28, 1995

International Official Sources

Council of Europé. *European Convention for the Protection of Human Rights and Fundamental Freedoms, as amended by Protocols Nos. 11 and 14*, 4 November 1950, ETS 5

Literature

Andenæs, Johannes, and Arne Fliflet. *Statsforfatningen i Norge*. 10th ed. Oslo: Universitetsforlaget, 2006.

Berntson, Martin, Bertil Nilsson, and Cecilia Wejryd. *Kyrka i Sverige: Introduktion till Svensk Kyrkohistoria*. Skellefteå: Artos & Noma Bokförlag, 2012.

Breistein, Ingunn Folkestad. *Har staten bedre borgere? Dissenternes kamp for religiøs frihet 1891-1969*. Trondheim: Tapir akademisk forlag, 2003.

Breistein, Ingunn Folkestad. "Støre favoriserer sitt eget trossamfunn." *Vårt Land*, February 16, 2020.

Christoffersen, Lisbet. "Church Autonomy: En religionsretlig udfordring til Norden." *Retfærd: Nordisk Juridisk Tidsskrift* 27, no. 4 (2004): 87-108.

Christoffersen, Lisbet. "Europæisk perspektiv på religion i dansk forfatningsret." In *Danmarks Riges Grundlov med kommentarer*, edited by Henrik Zahle, 63-76. 2nd ed. Copenhagen: DJØF forlag, 2006.

Christoffersen, Lisbet. "Lovmæssigheder: Kirker og Trossamfund i EU." In *Konstellationer. Kirkerne og det Europæiske projekt*, edited by Ida Auken, 45-68. Frederiksberg: Alfa-forlag, 2007.

Christoffersen, Lisbet. "Religion as a Factor in Multi-Layered European Union Legislation." In *Law and Religion in Multicultural Societies*, edited by Rubya Mehdi, Hanne Petersen, Erik Reenberg Sand, and Gordon R. Woodman, 111-30. Copenhagen: DJØF Publishing, 2008.

Christoffersen, Lisbet. "Church Autonomy in Nordic Law?" In *Law & Religion in the 21st Century—Nordic Perspectives*, edited by Lisbet Christoffersen, Kjell Å. Modéer, and Svend Andersen, 563-92. Copenhagen: DJØF Publishing, 2010.

Christoffersen, Lisbet. "Not Even Believing in Belonging: States and Churches in Five North-European (Post-)Lutheran Countries." In *Law and Religion in the 21st Century: Relations between States and Religious Communities*, edited by Silvio Ferrari and Rinaldo Cristofori, 187-98. Aldershot: Ashgate, 2010.

Christoffersen, Lisbet. "The Danish Cartoons Crisis Revisited." In *Islam and Political-Cultural Europe,* edited by W. Cole Durham, Jr., David M. Kirkham, and Tore Lindholm, 217-28. Farnham: Ashgate, 2012.

Christoffersen, Lisbet. "A Long Historical Path towards Transparency, Accountability and Good Governance: On Financing Religions in Denmark." In *Public Funding of Religions in Europe*, edited by Francis Messner, 125-49. Aldershot: Ashgate, 2015.

Christoffersen, Lisbet. "The Argument for a Narrow Conception of Religious Autonomy." In "Special Issue on the Ministerial Exception," edited by Pamela Slotte and Helge Årsheim, *Oxford Journal of Law and Religion* 4, no. 2 (2015): 278-302.

Christoffersen, Lisbet. "Legal Re-Organisation of the Danish Religious Market." In *Individualisation, Marketisation and Social Capital in a Cultural Institution: The Case of the Danish Folk Church,* edited by Hans Raun Iversen, Lisbet Christoffersen, Niels Kærgård, and Margit Warburg, 302-25. Odense: University Press of Southern Denmark, 2019.

Christoffersen, Lisbet. "Transnational Religious Law: Exemplified by the United Methodist Church." In *Transnationalisation and Legal Actors: Legitimacy in Question*, edited by Bettina Lemann Kristiansen, Katerina Mitkidis, Louise Munkholm, Lauren Neumann, and Cécile Pelaudeix, 201-216. London and New York: Routledge, 2019.

Christoffersen, Lisbet. "Towards Re-Sacralisation of Nordic Law?" In *Formatting Religion: Across Politics, Education, Media, and Law,* edited by Marius Timmann Mjaaland, 175-204. London and New York: Routledge, 2020.

Christoffersen, Lisbet, and Karen Marie Sø Leth-Nissen. "Legally Supported Marketisation and Individualisation of the Folk Church as a Cultural Institution." In *Individualisation, Marketisation and Social Capital in a Cultural Institution: The Case of the Danish Folk Church,* edited by Hans Raun Iversen, Lisbet Christoffersen, Niels Kærgård, and Margit Warburg, 147-73. Odense: University Press of Southern Denmark, 2019.

Christoffersen, Lisbet, Kjell Å. Modéer, and Svend Andersen, eds. *Law & Religion in the 21st Century—Nordic Perspectives*. Copenhagen, DJØF Publishing, 2010.

Christoffersen, Lisbet, and Niels Henrik Gregersen. "Shaping the Danish People's Church in the Context of Freedom of Religion: A.S. Ørsted (1778-1860) and N.F.S. Grundtvig (1783-1872)." In *Law and the Christian Tradition in Scandinavia: The Writings of Great Nordic Jurists*, edited by Kjell Å Modéer and Helle Vogt. London: Routledge, 2020.

Christoffersen, Lisbet, and Niels Valdemar Vinding. "Challenged Pragmatism: Conflicts of Law and Religion in the Danish Labour Market." *International Journal of Discrimination and the Law* 13, no. 2-3 (2013): 140-68.

Cranmer, Frank. "Church/State Relations in Scandinavia." In *Church and State in 21st Century Britain: The Future of Church Establishment*, edited by R.M. Morris, 127-50. Basingstoke: Palgrave/Macmillan, 2009.

Durham, W. Cole, Jr. "The Right to Autonomy in Religious Affairs: A Comparative View." In *Church Autonomy,* edited by Gerhard Robbers, 683-716. Frankfurt am Main: Peter Lang, 2001.

Enkvist, Victoria. *Religionsfrihetens rättsliga ramar*. Uppsala: Iustus förlag, 2013.
Enkvist, Victoria, and Per-Erik Nilsson. "The Hidden Return of Religion: Problematizing Religion in Law and Law in Religion in the Swedish Regulation of Faith Communities." In *Reconsidering Religion, Law, and Democracy: New Challenges for Society and Research*, edited by Anna-Sara Lind, Mia Lövheim, and Ulf Zackariasson, 93-103. Lund: Nordic Academic Press, 2016.
Espersen, Ole. *The Right to Freedom of Religion and Religious Associations: A Survey and Recommendations*. Copenhagen: the Council of the Baltic Sea States, 1999.
Folketinget. *My Constitutional Act: With Explanations*. 12th. edition. The Communications Section, Danish Parliament, March 2014. https://www.ft.dk/~/media/pdf/publikationer/english/my_constitutional_act_with_explanations.ashx
Gammeltoft-Hansen, Hans. "Kommentarer til grundlovens religionsbestemmelser." In *Danmarks Riges grundlov med kommentarer*, edited by Henrik Zahle. Copenhagen: DJØF Publishing, 2005.
Glædemark, H.J.H. *Kirkeforfatningsspørgsmaalet i Danmark indtil 1874: En historisk-kirkeretlig studie*. Copenhagen: Ejnar Munksgaard, 1948.
Hansson, Per. "Clergy Discipline Decisions in the Church of England and the Church of Sweden Compared." In *Church Reform and Leadership of Change*, edited by Harald Askeland and Ulla Schmidt, 117-134. Eugene, OR: Pickwick Publications, 2016.
Hugason, Hjalti. "A Case Study of the Evolution of a Nordic Lutheran Majority Church." In *Law & Religion in the 21st Century—Nordic Perspectives*, edited by Lisbet Christoffersen, Kjell Å. Modéer, and Svend Andersen, 107-22. Copenhagen: DJØF Publishing, 2010.
Hugason, Hjalti. "Isländska folkkyrkan." In *Kirkeretsantologi 2010: Bekendelse og kirkeordninger*, edited by Peter Garde, Zacharias Balslev-Clausen, Peter Christensen, Lisbet Christoffersen, Anders Jørgensen, and Kirsten Busch Nielsen, 217-34. Aarhus and Frederiksberg: Selskab for Kirkeret and Eksistensen, 2010.
Iversen, Hans Raun, Lisbet Christoffersen, Niels Kærgård, and Margit Warburg, eds. *Individualisation, Marketisation and Social Capital in a Cultural Institution: The Case of the Danish Folk Church*. Odense: University Press of Southern Denmark, 2019.
Jagander, Eva. "Hate Speech: Två avgöranden från högsta domstolen i Sverige," *Nordisk Tidsskrift for Kriminalvidenskab* 94(3) (2007): 236-41.
Kühle, Lene. "Concluding Remarks on Religion and State in the Nordic countries." In "Legal Regulation of Religion in the Nordic Countries," Special Issue, edited by Lene Kühle, *Nordic Journal of Religion and Society* 24, no. 2 (2011): 205-13.
Kühle, Lene, ed. "Legal Regulation of Religion in the Nordic Countries," Special Issue, *Nordic Journal of Religion and Society* 24, no. 2 (2011).
Kääriäinen, Kimmo. "Religion and State in Finland." In "Legal Regulation of Religion in the Nordic Countries," Special Issue, edited by Lene Kühle, *Nordic Journal of Religion and Society* 24, no. 2 (2011): 155-71.
Lausten, Martin Schwarz. *Johannes Bugenhagen: Luthersk reformator i Tyskland og Danmark*. Copenhagen: Anis, 2011.
Lausten, Martin Schwarz. *Philipp Melanchton: Humanist og luthersk reformator i Tyskland og Danmark*. Copenhagen: Anis, 2010.

Lausten, Martin Schwarz. *Reformationen i Danmark*. Copenhagen: Anis, 2011.

Lucas, John (with Bob Morris). "Disestablishment in Ireland and Wales." In *Church and State in 21st Century Britain: The Future of Church Establishment*, edited by R.M. Morris, 111-26. Basingstoke: Palgrave/Macmillan, 2009.

Lind, Anna-Sara. "Offentligt och privat: Regleringen av religion i Sverige." In *Sedd men osedd: Om folkkyrkans paradoxala närvaro inför 2020-talet*, edited by Anders Bäckström and Anders Wejryd, 152-64. Stockholm: Verbum, 2016.

Meinander, Henrik. *Finlands historia. linjer, strukturer, vändpunkter*. Helsingfors: Schildt & Söderströms, 2006.

Minkenberg, Michael. "Church-State Regimes and Democracy in the West: Convergence vs Divergence." *Geopolitics, History, and International Relations* 4, no. 1 (2012): 76-106.

Modéer, Kjell Å. "The Long Way towards Traditional Autonomy." In *Law & Religion in the 21st Century—Nordic Perspectives*, edited by Lisbet Christoffersen, Kjell Å. Modéer, and Svend Andersen, 81-88. Copenhagen: DJØF Publishing, 2010.

Nielsen, Marie Vejrup, and Lene Kühle. "Religion and State in Denmark." In "Legal Regulation of Religion in the Nordic Countries," Special Issue, edited by Lene Kühle, *Nordic Journal of Religion and Society* 24, no. 2 (2011): 173-88.

Oftestad, Bernt T., Tarald Rasmussen and Jan Schumacher. *Norsk Kirkehistorie*. 2nd ed. Oslo: Universitetsforlaget, 2010.

Pettersson, Per. "State and Religion in Sweden: Ambiguity between Disestablishment and Religious Control." In "Legal Regulation of Religion in the Nordic Countries," Special Issue, edited by Lene Kühle, *Nordic Journal of Religion and Society* 24, no. 2 (2011): 119-35.

Pétursson, Pétur. "Religion and State in Iceland." In "Legal Regulation of Religion in the Nordic Countries," Special Issue, edited by Lene Kühle, *Nordic Journal of Religion and Society* 24, no. 2 (2011): 189-204.

Seppo, Juha. "Finland's Policy on Church and Religion." In *Law & Religion in the 21st Century—Nordic Perspectives*, edited by Lisbet Christoffersen, Kjell Å. Modéer, and Svend Andersen, 89-105. Copenhagen: DJØF Publishing, 2010.

Schmidt, Ulla. "Church Reforms and Public Reforms." In *Church Reform and Leadership of Change*, edited by Harald Askeland and Ulla Schmidt, 38-55. Eugene, OR: Pickwick Publications, 2016.

Schmidt, Ulla. "State, Law and Religion in Norway." In "Legal Regulation of Religion in the Nordic Countries," Special Issue, edited by Lene Kühle, *Nordic Journal of Religion and Society* 24, no. 2 (2011): 137-53.

Smith, Eivind. "And they Lived Happily Together." In *Law & Religion in the 21st Century—Nordic Perspectives*, edited by Lisbet Christoffersen, Kjell Å. Modéer, and Svend Andersen, 123-44. Copenhagen: DJØF Publishing, 2010.

Smith, Eivind. "'… forblir Norges folkekirke': Om Grunnlovens ordvalg og dets juridiske konsekvenser." In *Folkekirke nå*, edited by Stephanie Dietrich, Hallgeir Elstad, Beate Fagerli, and Vidar L. Haanes, 60-71. Oslo: Verbum Akademisk, 2015.

Støre, Jonas Gahr. "Det er politikernes ansvar å verne om—og stille krav til—religionsutøvelse." *Vårt Land*, November 27, 2019.

Vinding, Niels Valdemar, and Emil Bjørn Hilton Saggau. "Challenges of the Institutionalization of Same Sex Marriage for Religious Pluralism in Denmark." In *Islam, Religions, and Pluralism in Europe*, edited by Ednan Aslan, Ranja Ebrahim, and Marcia Hermansen, 173-92. Wiesbaden: Springer, 2016.

Österdahl, Inger. "Åke Green och missaktande men inte hatiskt tal." *Svensk Juristtidning* 91, no. 3 (2006): 213-26.

Webpages

Danmarkshistorien.dk. "Fremmedartiklerne af 20. september 1569 (regulation on access to the Danish Kingdom for foreigners)." Last modified April 14, 2016. https://danmarkshistorien.dk/leksikon-og-kilder/vis/materiale/fremmedartiklerne-af-20-september-1569/.

Den norske kirke. "Lover og regler (homepage of the Church of Norway with an overview over the valid statutory laws and internal regulations in the Church of Norway)." Accessed June 25, 2020. https://kirken.no/nb-NO/om-kirken/slik-styres-kirken/lover-og-regler/.

Den norske kirke. "Preses i Bispemøtet (on the presiding bishop in the Church of Norway)." Accessed June 25, 2020. https://kirken.no/nb-NO/om-kirken/slik-styres-kirken/bispemotet/preses/.

European Court of Human Rights. *Guide on Article 9 of the European Convention of Human Rights: Freedom of Thought, Conscience and Religion*. Last modified 30 April, 2020, https://www.echr.coe.int/Documents/Guide_Art_9_ENG.pdf.

Evangelisk-lutherska kyrkan i Finland. "Nya äktenskapslagen och kyrkan (on same-sex-marriage within the Evangelical Lutheran Church of Finland)." Accessed June 25, 2020. https://evl.fi/pressrum/aktuellt-just-nu/aktenskapslagen.

Kirkeministeriet. "Lovstof (overview over laws on the Danish *folkekirke*)." Accessed June 25, 2020. https://www.km.dk/ministeriet/love-regler/.

Markus Långin kotisivu. "Storfurstendömet Finlands Författnings-Samling: 1869, N° 30, Kyrkolag (The historical law on the Evangelical Lutheran Church of Finland, in force 1869-1964)." Accessed June 25, 2020. https://www.mlang.name/arkisto/kyrkolag-1869.html.

Government of Iceland. "About the Government." Accessed June 25, 2020. https://www.government.is/government/about-the-government/.

Stortinget. "The Constitution." Accessed June 25, 2020. https://www.stortinget.no/en/In-English/About-the-Storting/The-Constitution/.

Stortinget. "Lov om tros- og livssynssamfunn (trossamfunnsloven) (the process leading to the new law on religious communities in Norway, valid from January 1st, 2021)." Accessed June 25, 2020. https://www.stortinget.no/no/Saker-og-publikasjoner/Saker/Sak/?p=76670.

The Swedish (government) Agency for Support for Faith Communities. Accessed June 25, 2020. https://www.myndighetensst.se/en.

Tómas, Ragnar. "Separation of Church and State Inevitable." Iceland review, November 4, 2019. https://www.icelandreview.com/news/separation-of-church-and-state-inevitable/.

11. Recognition, Religious Identity, and Populism: Lessons from Finland

Risto Saarinen and Heikki J. Koskinen[1]

The period from 1945 to 1990 has often been regarded as the time of universalism and globalization. International organizations such as the United Nations and legal charters such as the Universal Declaration of Human Rights were created to steer global developments in a coherent and responsible manner. Increasing travel, trade, and communication opportunities brought about a new global awareness. For the first time in human history, not only political rulers but also educated citizens of very different countries were conscious of what was happening in the entire world. Within Christianity, the Ecumenical Movement and the Second Vatican Council contributed to this overall wave of globalization.

After the end of the Cold War, however, new discussions on national and religious identities emerged. In many cases, for instance, in the rise of Islam in the Middle East and in the new prominence of the Orthodox Church in Russia and the Catholic Church in Poland, these national and religious identities replaced the earlier attitudes of universalism. In politics, this meant that the trend of increasing globalization came to be accompanied by new trends of nationalism, separatism, and regional self-interest. In addition, political, religious, and ethnic minorities became visible in a new manner after 1990.[2]

Recognition and Identity—from Liberals to Populists

Charles Taylor's 1995 essay on the politics of recognition captured the new political and philosophical situation particularly well. Taylor argues that the so-called politics of universalism, in which equality and toleration are practiced, is not sufficient to guarantee the good life for minorities and neglected

---

1 RS has written parts 1 and 2. Part 3 was written jointly.
2 For this periodization, see Risto Saarinen, "Ecumenism," in *Global Dictionary of Theology*, ed. William Dyrness and Veli-Matti Kärkkäinen (Nottingham: IVP Press, 2008), 263-69.

parties. In addition, minorities need conscious recognition by others. With the help of such recognition, they become visible members of the society and can in turn affirm others so that a mutual recognition and a multicultural society can emerge. Sometimes such recognition also implies positive discrimination, that is, particular opportunities for the minority.[3]

Especially in American settings, the strong connection between recognition procedures and the civil rights of the African American and the Native American peoples as well as of sexual minorities prompted the rise of so-called identity politics. In addition to the distribution of wealth and promotion of tolerance and peace, politics can be employed to promote the rights of different minorities in the society at large.[4] Through recognizing the rights of African Americans, gays and lesbians, the state can give a distinct identity to these groups. Due to such conscious identity politics, these groups become equal to all others. In addition, they receive a distinct identity which characterizes them as a group. After twenty years of identity politics, two problems or worries (A and B) continue to appear in this context.

A. While civil rights movements normally promote the creation of distinct identities, they are also aware that this implies a compromise with the democratic state. If gays and lesbians, for instance, let themselves become defined by the democratic majority, they may lose some of their original autonomy. Typically, this worry is formulated by theorists.[5] In practice, most minorities and neglected parties seek recognition from the democratic majority, with the expectation that their autonomy is not at stake.

B. There is also an opposite worry which is the main theme of the present chapter. Given that we affirm and practice identity politics, which identities qualify as "good" or at least unproblematic in the eyes of a democratic multicultural state? After Taylor's essay, identity politics has become a tool of progressive and liberal pressure groups, especially on the American scene. In Europe, however, the term "identity" has been adopted by the nationalist "identitarian" movements which claim their right to a homogenous identity and turn against multiculturalism.[6]

---

3 Charles Taylor, "The Politics of Recognition," in *Philosophical Arguments* (Cambridge MA: Harvard University Press, 1995), 225-56.
4 Simon Thompson, *The Political Theory of Recognition: A Critical Introduction* (Cambridge: Polity, 2006).
5 Lois McNay, *Against Recognition* (Cambridge: Polity, 2008).
6 José Pedro Zúquete, *The Identitarians: The Movement against Globalism and Islam in Europe* (Notre Dame, IN [Indiana]: Notre Dame University Press, 2018). This work contains uniquely rich documentation of the ideological developments until 2018.

For American liberals, such movements do not qualify as identity politics. After the 2016 American presidential election, the theoretical discussion is nevertheless turning towards also using the phrase "identity politics" with regard to conservative and populist movements. More importantly, these movements claim a recognition of their distinct identity in terms which resemble earlier discussions on multiculturalism.

The present chapter argues that recent developments in the Finnish conservative religious scene participate in the larger trend of conservative or "identitarian" politics. Through digital media, new ideas can be exchanged and new positions adopted very rapidly. Digital platforms and social media enable new rhetorical strategies which shape and reconstitute religious identities. Achieving recognition through social media is very important. However, bad publicity and liberal misrecognition may also bring new conservative supporters, if the public realm as a whole is polarized. We use Finnish conservatives as a test case to help us understand the complex dynamics of recognition in the digital era.

As the field of identity politics and identitarian movements is rather recent and keeps changing, we will first (1) outline some new American and European discussions to show in which sense identity politics is shifting from liberalism towards conservatism and populism. With the help of this outline, we can then (2) proceed to the Finnish religious conservatives and their relationship to populism. After providing some introductory features, we focus our attention on one recent case. Finally (3), this case is compared with the theoretical concepts of recognition and identity.

In the American progressive camp, the recognition of otherness and identity politics are often seen as alternatives to such a universalist view which is unable to respect differences among different groups. This camp interprets identity politics as an instrument in the struggle for civil rights and multiculturalism which continues to emerge. The *Stanford Encyclopedia of Philosophy*'s entry "Identity Politics" can be regarded as an influential codification of this progressive variant in the U.S. The last update of the entry (2016) defends the legacy of radical multiculturalism, although it also pays attention to the academic criticism presented to the politics of recognition.

In the entry, identity politics is described as "activity and theorizing founded in the shared experiences of injustice of members of certain social groups".[7] As particular instances of this kind, gender and feminism, gay, lesbian and queer

---

7   Cressida Heyes, "Identity Politics," in *Stanford Encyclopedia of Philosophy,* Stanford University, 1997. Article published July 16, 2002; last modified March 23, 2016, https://plato.stanford.edu.

people, as well as different issues of race and ethnicity are discussed. According to the entry, identity politics emerged with new feminism and African American civil rights debates in the second part of the 20th century.

The connection between identity politics and recognition theory is argued as follows:

> What makes identity politics a significant departure from earlier, pre-identarian forms of the politics of recognition is its demand for recognition on the basis of the very grounds on which recognition has previously been denied: it is qua women, qua blacks, qua lesbians that groups demand recognition. The demand is not for inclusion within the fold of 'universal humankind' on the basis of shared human attributes; nor is it for respect 'in spite of' one's differences. Rather, what is demanded is respect for oneself as different.[8]

The word "identarian" is employed in this quote as a positive and progressive term that depicts the radically liberal politics of recognition. While such identity politics may be critical of some forms of universalism, the entry situates it firmly within a progressive liberal democracy. A conventional liberal democracy may, however, need new forms of social inclusion and affirmation of minorities in order to enable a truly progressive multiculturalism. The different ethnic groups should therefore have a higher profile in order for their identity to be visible. Some examples will make European readers raise their eyebrows. The *Stanford Encyclopedia* considers the issue of who counts as white as follows:

> That a US citizen of both Norwegian and Ashkenazi Jewish heritage will check that they are white on a census form says relatively little … about their experience of their identity, or indeed of their very different relationship to anti-Semitism.[9]

This quote is awkward already because of what it insinuates about the Norwegians. Even more awkward is the assumption that the Jews are very different from other people. Let it here only be stated that the quoted passage represents a variant of radically progressive multiculturalism which may lack some universalist values of liberalism.

When the *Stanford Encyclopedia* entry is compared with other recent texts dealing with identity politics, very different meanings can be gathered. The

---

8   Heyes, "Identity Politics," quoting Sonia Kruks, *Retrieving Experience: Subjectivity and Recognition in Feminist Politics* (Ithaca, NY: Cornell University Press, 2001), 85.
9   Kruks, *Retrieving Experience*, 85. Heyes, "Identity Politics."

phrase "identity politics" has taken completely new dimensions in newspaper use as well as in official documents. Already in 2014, the Finnish Foreign Ministry defined identity politics as "political movement based on ethnic, racial, or religious identity that is striving for power in the state".[10] Dictionary meanings of the phrase are often fairly close to this definition. While the definition may be technically compatible with the *Stanford Encyclopedia*, in the European scene it alludes more to the current nationalist politics in Poland or Hungary than to the liberal scene in the U.S.

A typical conversation reflecting this shift in the term "identity politics" is reported in *The New Yorker*. Here, the reporter David Remnick interviews the author Mark Lilla on the occasion of his new book on identity politics. They discuss the populist Steve Bannon's remark that the Democratic Party lost the presidential election because they advocated progressive identity politics, thus chasing the majority away to the Republican camp.[11]

Lilla is himself a liberal democrat, but he agrees with Bannon's remark. Identity politics can be a trend, but it can hardly win majority votes since it appeals mostly to minorities with a high degree of academic awareness. To be successful with majorities once again, Lilla finds that the Democrats should abandon identity discourses and return to normal, more universal politics. In addition, the Republicans with Donald Trump developed a new version of identity politics which appeals to ordinary people much more than the academic discourse of the liberals does.[12]

In Europe, the word "identity" is currently prominently employed by the conservative and nationalist-populist movements. The French group *Bloc Identitaire* was established in 2003 and its German counterpart *Identitäre Bewegung* in 2014. The younger French identitarian group, *Génération Identitaire*, was founded in 2012 and the post-Trumpian Euro-American fraternity, Identity Evropa (sic!), in 2016.[13] While these movements remain fairly small in terms of their number adherents, they offer ideological support for the larger political parties such as the *Front (Assemblée) Nationale* in France and *Alternative für Deutschland* in Germany. Identitarian movements also normally embrace the term populist.[14]

---

10   The original Finnish text (as of October 20, 2014) is quoted in Risto Saarinen, "Identiteettipolitiikka, toisen tunnustaminen ja teologia," in *Uskonto ja identiteettipolitiikka,* ed. Elina Hellqvist, Minna Hietamäki, and Panu Pihkala (Helsinki: STKS, 2015), 12-13.
11   David Remnick, "A Conversation with Mark Lilla on His Critique of Identity Politics," *New Yorker*, August 25, 2017; Mark Lilla, *The Once and Future Liberal: After Identity Politics* (New York: HarperCollins, 2017).
12   Lilla, *The Once and Future Liberal*.
13   Zúquete, *Identitarians*, 20-30, 307-08.
14   Zúquete, *Identitarians*, 127.

The identitarian populists are not simply listening to the voice of the "little people." Their ideology is based on a considerable literary production which to a large extent has been written by the French intellectuals of so-called New Right (*Nouvelle Droite*). Alain de Benoist's and Jean-Claude Valla's writings on European civilization are formative for the New Right. Pierre Vial and his identitarian magazine *Terre et Peuple* define European identity in ethnic terms.[15]

The New Right makes many claims regarding its own longer history, from the ancient city-state of Sparta to the nationalism of the 19th and the politically conservative movements of the 20th century. Friedrich Nietzsche, Ezra Pound, and Ernst Jünger are often quoted as intellectual allies of the identitarians.[16] From our outsider perspective, however, the French (and to some extent Italian) New Right is the actual seedbed of identitarian thinking since the 1980s.

Guillaume Faye's *Why We Fight* (2001) establishes the identitarian turn of the New Right. Faye's *The New Jewish Question* (2007) claims that the struggle for white survival is necessary because of massive Muslim immigration to Europe. Renaud Camus's *The Great Replacement* (2011) argues that the entire European population will be replaced in two or three generations because Muslim immigrants have so many children. The historian Dominique Venner has provided an identitarian view of French and European civilization. After his ostentatious suicide in 2013 at the altar of Notre Dame cathedral in Paris (imitating the seppuku of Japanese writer Yukio Mishima), Venner has become the martyr and saint of European identitarians.[17]

Through his Arktos Publishing, nowadays located in Budapest, the Swedish identitarian activist Daniel Friberg publishes English editions of the seminal French works, exercising a pan-European influence on the so-called "True Right". In Scandinavia, Friberg is also one of the founders of *Nordisk Alternativhöger* (Nordic Alt Right).[18] While Friberg is the most influential North European identitarian, Kai Murros in Finland, Ruuben Kaalep in Estonia, and Aurelija Aniulyte in Denmark have received some fame in their international networks.[19]

While people like Murros remain fairly unknown in their home countries, they can exercise a considerable international influence in the digital world. Moreover, Sweden and Denmark are considered by some European identitarian authors to be the first actual battlefields between liberal multiculturalism

---

15 Zúquete, *Identitarians*, 7-17.
16 Zúquete, *Identitarians* provides rich documentation of this.
17 Zúquete, *Identitarians*, 11-25, 145, 312.
18 Zúquete, *Identitarians*, 99-100, 301; Daniel Friberg, *The Real Right Returns* (Budapest: Arktos, 2015).
19 Zúquete, *Identitarians*, 89, 249, 334.

and Islamic invasion.[20] For such reasons, Northern European countries play a distinctive role in various identitarian and populist visions.

Among the identitarians, the word "identity" means predominantly a homogenous cultural and national profile, closed borders, and opposition to the European Union and other allegedly universalist political ventures. The origins of the identitarian movement can be expressed with the slogan: "In the beginning … there was anti-universalism"[21] The identitarian meaning is quickly becoming the new primary sense of identity politics also in the English-language media. In the *Guardian* newspaper, Sheri Berman argues that identity politics benefits the right more than the left. Like Lilla, she maintains that the left needs to help citizens see what unites them, instead of focusing on their differences.[22]

Berman argues that both progressives and conservatives have a predisposition towards intolerance. These predispositions take power when a sufficient external stimulus arises. Trump's presidency provides such a stimulus for the liberals, whereas increased immigration may be a stimulus for the conservatives. In both camps, or in all camps, this psychological dynamics creates intolerance rather than tolerance. For such reasons, identity politics should not operate with differences but rather with increased universalism. Berman quotes Karen Stenner's psychological research, indicating that the exposure to difference aggravates intolerance instead of alleviating it. At the same time, "nothing inspires greater tolerance from the intolerant than an abundance of common and unifying beliefs, practices, rituals, institutions and processes."[23] While the *Stanford Encyclopedia* defends a radically pluralist politics of recognition, Berman points to the benefits of actual uniformity.

On the one hand, Christianity is a universalist religion. On the other hand, it often relies on traditionalism, with all kinds of particularities and differences. How does Christianity fit into the framework of identitarian developments? Initially, the French New Right was secularist, preferring ethnic traditions to Christian universalism. This preference changed considerably with the debates related to the new marriage law in France in 2012-2014. The identitarians opposed homosexual marriage and became allied with Christian conservatives in

---

20 Zúquete, *Identitarians*, 333-34 (the international role of Murros), 354-56 (Sweden and Denmark in the texts of Julian Langness and Georges Feltin-Tracol).
21 Zúquete, *Identitarians*, 105.
22 Sheri Berman, "Why Identity Politics Benefits the Right More Than the Left," *Guardian*, August 14, 2018.
23 Berman, "Identity Politics"; Karen Stenner, *The Authoritarian Dynamic* (Cambridge: Cambridge University Press, 2005).

this venture. The so-called *"La Manif pour tous"* demonstrations against the new marriage law united Catholic traditionalists with the identitarians.[24]

After these events, there are diverse connections between the identitarian movement and the traditionalist Catholic program of a "Christian comeback" after the liberal times of the Second Vatican Council. In many ways, Catholic identitarians are a minority in the church, opposing Pope Francis's liberal stance towards asylum seekers. However, in France, Poland, and Hungary, the identitarians can also count on considerable support from traditionalist Catholic circles.[25] In Russia, the Orthodox Church clearly supports nationalist causes and Russia is also seen as a positive model country in some identitarian circles.[26]

The links between conservative Protestants and identitarians remain poorly studied. In the following, it will be shown that such a link exists in today's Finland. Recently, the liberal Nordic countries have seen an uprise in populist and nationalist parties which oppose universalist and globalist values. As these countries have established Lutheran churches which are predominantly liberal, one may ask whether the conservative Christians in these churches see their anti-liberal stance also in political and even identitarian terms. In the following, this question will be approached with the help of one particular case. It is too early to say whether it is symptomatic of a more general phenomenon.

The Right Media: How Religious and Populist Causes Coincide in Finland

Some demographic background is necessary in order to describe the case at hand. The Evangelical Lutheran Church of Finland (ELCF) had four million members in 2017, comprising about 70 % of the entire population of Finland. While the overall leadership and membership of this church represents liberal mainline Lutheranism, a considerable number of conservatives are also active within the church. For the most part, the conservatives stem from the traditional Pietistic movements that have operated in Finland since the 19th century. Nowadays, they have strong ties with Anglo-American evangelicalism. At the same time, most Finnish conservatives emphasize their strongly confessional Lutheranism.

While in Sweden and Norway many conservative movements have left the

---

24 Zúquete, *Identitarians*, 220-22.
25 Zúquete, *Identitarians*, 218-26.
26 Zúquete, *Identitarians*, 231-32.

established church, most Finnish conservatives remain members of the ELCF. They have links with Pentecostals and small free churches through the Christian Democratic Party (CDP), which is represented in the parliament with an electorate of 4-5% of all votes. The longtime leader of the CDP, Päivi Räsänen, was the Minister of the Interior from 2011 to 2015. She is a confessional Lutheran who is against women's ordination and criticizes the liberal abortion laws of Finland. The ELCF as a whole does not share the conservative interests of the CDP, which therefore remains a minor party of conservative evangelicals.

As key minister for immigration, Räsänen promoted fairly liberal policies. Thus, her political stance in this matter deviated significantly from the populist conservative party, the so-called Finns Party (perussuomalaiset), earlier also known as the "True Finns".[27] In the major European refugee crisis of 2015-2016, the positions of liberal and conservative Christians in Finland were remarkably similar, advocating an increased responsibility and openness towards asylum seekers. This is important because Finns in general have restrictive attitudes towards immigrants and because the Finns Party has been victorious in two parliamentary elections (2011 and 2015) with its anti-immigrant and anti-EU agenda.

In many other respects, Finnish conservative Lutherans feel marginalized in religious and public life. Because they do not accept women's ordination, their young theologians cannot normally become ordained as pastors of the ELCF. This has led to complex double structures in church and worship life. On moral issues, the conservatives' positions often differ from Finnish liberal and permissive stances. They nowadays tacitly approve divorce but are against gay marriage, which has recently been approved by the state and is currently finding its way into the liberal church life as well.

Lutheranism is an interesting denomination from the perspective of recognition theory, because Lutheran identity is typically defined with a view to a larger party that is regarded as problematic. Lutheran confessional writings define church identity relationally, pointing out how Lutherans deviate from the Roman Catholic Church. Confessional Lutherans in Finland typically construct their identity in terms of difference from the established church that is regarded as too liberal and accommodating. In this manner, Lutheran group identity is deeply heteronomous in its dependence on the point of comparison.[28]

---

27 "The Finns" and "The Finns Party" are nowadays the more common English translations of the party's name. The older translation "True Finns" can also be found in English sources.
28 For a general introduction, see, e.g., Eric Gritsch, *A History of Lutheranism* (Minneapolis, MN: Fortress, 2002).

Finnish conservatives do not want to leave the established church, but say that they aim at renewing it in their own fashion. The dilemma of leaving or remaining is very complex and also connected to financial and social benefits. One practical consequence of this dilemma is that the conservatives are openly critical of the bishops and other mainline church leaders. Leaving the church, however, would end this criticism and, as a consequence, end the process of creating identity in terms of relational heteronomy. As this process is the standard way of defining identity in Lutheranism, it is still preferred today to other ways.

As our test case deals with the links between the Finns Party and religious conservatives, one needs to emphasize that before the digital era such links were not programmatic but accidental. While for a long time the Finns Party has included many committed Christians, one cannot discern any earlier institutional links between Finnish conservative Christians and the Finns Party. The CDP continues to be the political wing of conservative evangelicals.

This state of affairs resembles the relationship between Trump and conservative evangelicals in America. On the one hand, the non-religious populism of Trump remains very different from Christian causes. On the other hand, political mechanisms can be created through which conservative evangelicals can support Trump. Is it possible to construct similar mechanisms in a Nordic country like Finland? If evangelicals feel marginalized and cannot subscribe to the liberal values of the Finnish state and the established church, populist writers can develop a mechanism to channel conservative religious feelings towards populist political goals.

If conservative Christians feel that they are positively recognized by the populists, they can be made to support their causes as well. Our following test case considers this possibility. At the same time, the test case shows that nothing is clear and straightforward in the digital world. We are operating with ad hoc communities which give weak signals. As scholars, we should listen to these weak signals and consider their significance.

On July 27, 2018, a conservative evangelical professor of education at the University of Jyväskylä, Tapio Puolimatka, lamented on the populist digital media *Oikea Media* (oikeamedia.com, "the right media" in Finnish) that the recent increase in gay rights meant that paedophilia, another trait of permissive society, would also soon be legalized.[29] When the Rector of the University, Keijo Hämäläinen, said that he had to discuss such statements with Puolimatka, on

---

29 Tapio Puolimatka, "Kampanja pedofilian laillistamiseksi," *Blogi, Oikea media*, July 27, 2018, https://www.oikeamedia.com/o1-75907.

August 1 *Oikea Media* published a defense of Puolimatka, stating that "political persecution is happening at the University of Jyväskylä."[30]

Räsänen rushed to defend Puolimatka's academic freedom. On August 7, she presented in parliament an official question to the Finnish government, stating that the freedom of speech of Professor Puolimatka had been jeopardized through the actions of Rector Hämäläinen. She urged the Finnish government to take action to secure the freedom of academic research.[31]

On August 13, *Oikea Media* published an extensive defense of Puolimatka with the headline "Does the University of Jyväskylä promote the legalization of paedophilia?" A byline of the same article states that "the red-green sexual-radical campaign is an open attack against true academic freedom". In this article, Päivi Räsänen's defense of Puolimatka was supported by the extensive comments of Juha Ahvio, a conservative pastor and Docent in Dogmatics at the University of Helsinki.[32]

Oikea Media was established in January 2017 and in the meantime has become the leading alternative populist media in Finland. Looking at the stories, advertisements and blogs available in this webzine, one can see its proximity to the Finns Party. With regard to our topic, it is important to note that *Oikea Media* frequently deals with religious, moral, and academic issues.

In the summer of 2017, the Finns Party was split into two factions, the moderate ones leaving the party and establishing a new political group.[33] The most vocally Christian leaders were among those who left the party. The current leader of the Finns Party, Jussi Halla-aho, describes himself as a non-religious agnostic. Because of his vehement criticism of Islam, Halla-aho has sometimes been regarded as hostile to all kinds of religious views. The populist nationalism of the Finns Party is thus fairly secular in its general outlook.

In the Puolimatka case, however, *Oikea Media* often emphasizes Christian values. Learned theologians contribute actively to *Oikea Media*, defending its positions. While Halla-aho's Finns Party continues to be hostile to asylum seekers, it is remarkable that Päivi Räsänen of the CDP supports *Oikea Media*'s writings

---

30   Jukka Rahkonen, "Jyväskylän yliopistolla muhii poliittiset vainot," *Oikea media*, August 1, 2018, https://www.oikeamedia.com/o1-76812.
31   Päivi Räsänen, "Kirjallinen kysymys korkeimman opetuksen ja tutkimuksen sananvapauden turvaamisesta," accessed January 21, 2019, https://www.eduskunta.fi/FI/vaski/Kysymys/Documents/KK_309+2018.pdf.
32   Tytti Salenius, "Onko Jyväskylän yliopistossa meneillään monitahoinen kampanja pedofilian laillistamiseksi?," *Oikea media*, August 13, 2018, https://www.oikeamedia.com/o1-78809.
33   For this and the following, see, e.g., Lauri Nurmi, *Perussuomalaisten hajoamisen historia* (Helsinki: Into, 2017).

regarding the Puolimatka case. Obviously, Puolimatka does not speak about Islam, but about sexual ethics. In this manner, *Oikea Media* seeks support from those conservative Christians who do not oppose immigration but who are most certainly against paedophilia. With the help of the Puolimatka case, *Oikea Media* and the Finns Party can appear as defenders of traditional Christain values.

The Puolimatka case created a snowball effect in the larger Finnish newspapers and on television channels. The position of Rector Hämäläinen was supported by, among others, the University of Jyväskylä Students' Union, the Finnish Union of University Professors, the Finnish Academy of Science and Letters, and the Sexpo Foundation that attends to human sexual rights. Among numerous individual supporters of Hämäläinen were Björn Vikström, the ELCF Bishop of Porvoo, and Petri Luomanen, Vice-Dean for Research at the Faculty of Theology in the University of Helsinki. Puolimatka's rights to present his case were defended, in addition to *Oikea Media*, by a few professors and pastors.[34]

Reading this documentation, one cannot escape the impression that Puolimatka lost his case completely in the public sphere. Even Räsänen does not say that she agrees with him but states only that Puolimatka's freedom of speech must be respected. However, this complete misrecognition of Puolimatka meant an increased recognition of *Oikea Media* in the Finnish media scene and among conservative Christians. Through the Puolimatka case, this alternative media became much better known in Finland. Thus, the Puolimatka case is a model example of what is in the populist discourse called "liberal tears". According to this strategy, you aim at creating negative reactions from people whom your own potential supporters count as their adversaries. If liberal academics shed tears over your opinions, then those opinions can more easily be embraced by conservatives.

Most importantly, the Puolimatka case displays conspicuous similarities with the above-mentioned French case of 2012-2014, referred to as "*La Manif pour tous*". In the French case, the New Right and the identitarians joined religious conservatives in their opposition to the legalization of homosexual marriage in France. Joint mass protests were called with the slogan "manifestation for

---

34 "Kohu kirjoituksesta 'Kampanja pedofilian laillistamiseksi'," *ApoWiki*, accessed January 2019, https://apowiki.fi/wiki/Kohu_kirjoituksesta_%22Kampanja_pedofilian_laillistamiseksi%22. This website collects the entire debate and presents it from the perspective of conservative Christians but recording also the non-conservative contributions fairly and in detail. For a large-scale overview of the entire Finnish debate, see also Petri Jääskeläinen, "Jumala, Trump ja Putin," *Kirkko ja kaupunki*, August 20, 2018, https://www.kirkkojakaupunki.fi/-/jumala-trump-ja-putin-kristillisen-konservatiivioikeiston-toiminta-suomessa-kulkee-samoilla-raiteilla-kuin-yhdysvaltain-evankelikaaleilla.

everyone". The protests did not halt the legislation, but they initiated a new "Christian populism" and "Catholic identitarianism".[35] As in the Puolimatka case, sexual ethics was instrumental in creating this new alliance. As in the Puolimatka case, the failure of the actual case was nevertheless a victory for those who intended to win Christians for the identitarian cause.

In Finland, similar legislation took effect in 2017. It was opposed by a conservative Christian coalition, *aito avioliitto* (True Marriage). The Finnish *Aito avioliitto* employs the same logo as *La Manif pour tous* in France, depicting a husband, a wife, a son, and a daughter holding each other's hands. *Aito avioliitto* was initiated by Jukka-Pekka Rahkonen. He is today the editor-in-chief of *Oikea Media*. Because of all these similarities, one can draw the conclusion that the Puolimatka case was not merely spontaneous. It repeats a pattern which was earlier employed in France. While one cannot find hard evidence of it having been politically steered by the Finns Party or the CDP (or both), the activism of *Oikea Media* was carefully planned.

In sum, the snowball effect of liberal criticism gave *Oikea Media* the golden opportunity to present itself and the Finns Party as friends and supporters of conservative Christians. Neither Puolimatka nor Räsänen are known as the Finns Party adherents, but they are well-known religious conservatives who are often mocked by the liberals. As a skilled politician, the CDP's Räsänen immediately seized the opportunity to form a new kind of conservative coalition with the Finns Party in the field of sexual ethics and religion.

Among *Oikea Media* blog writers, the theologian Juha Ahvio in particular has been busy creating this new constellation of values.[36] Ahvio uses the title Research Director of the Patmos Mission Foundation, a conservative evangelical association. In his blogs, Ahvio takes up political topics and gives them a Christian coloring. He praises the Brazilian President Jair Bolsonaro, the Hungarian Prime Minister Viktor Orban, the Swedish populist party *Sverigedemokraterna* and the Dutch populist leader Geert Wilders. Like the European identitarians, Ahvio supports Donald Trump, associating him with Christian values.[37]

---

35 Zúquete, *Identitarians*, 220.
36 For this and the following, see Juha Ahvio's *blogi* at *Oikea media*, accessed January 21, 2019, https://www.oikeamedia.com/blogit.
37 Ahvio, "Kansalliskonservatiiviset Ruotsidemokraatit nousevat Ruotsissa," *Blogi, Oikea media*, September 1, 2018, https://oikeamedia.com/o1-80812?fbclid=IwAR2qjBIsDd6C9eXsIOEYJKaUBtTykUIo_GfNjiFH2dU5OXqMNWXqyzmDrDI; "Dosentti Markku Ruotsilan pätevän kattava analyysi USA:n sydänmaiden konservatiivien kapinasta," *Blogi, Oikea media*, November 2, 2018, https://oikeamedia.com/o1-87716?fbclid=IwAR0mLDYfOVFFMLRCRFO6vU2YKmDaq4_Sk8HL6C1HQLJdwdY7ndr0bmOjbco; "Trump ja republikaanit saivat strategisen torjuntavoiton USA:n välivaaleissa," *Blogi, Oikea media*, Novem-

On his blog of December 21, 2018, titled "What Is Permitted to Say about Islam and the European Union", Ahvio takes up the basic identitarian doctrine regarding the "great replacement". Mentioning Camus by name, Ahvio presents the entire population of Europe as about to be replaced with Africans. The European Union is actually realizing a "politics of population replacement". Emanuel Macron has a positive expectation, according to Ahvio, that 200 million Africans will come to Europe in next twenty years.[38]

Some of Ahvio's blogs have devotional content, giving *Oikea Media* a distinctly religious flavor. In his Christmas blog of 2018, Ahvio describes the doctrines of the Trinity, the incarnation, and the virgin birth. In the human nature of God-man Jesus, "the x-chromosome comes from Mary and the genes of the y-chromosome from God". While this blog is otherwise traditional and orthodox, it thus highlights the particular masculinity of God.[39] In Ahvio's Christianity, the y-chromosome has theological significance.

The identitarians criticize "effeminate Euro men" and see feminine modernity in terms of problematic weakness. Their own Christian faith is regarded as "proud, combatant, chivalrous, sacral and aesthetic", whereas modern liberal faith represents "effete Christianity, desacralized and soft."[40] Western liberals suffer from "devirilization", in which "feminist, xenophile, homophile, and humanitarian values" are exaggerated and "the idea of war and the figure of the soldier" are neglected.[41]

Ahvio has a twofold mission. He proclaims an anti-liberal, masculine Christianity in this identitarian sense. At the same time, he attempts to persuade atheist and secularist identitarians to see how Christianity can contribute to the anti-universalist cause of the Finns Party.

Another active theologian and blogger at *Oikea Media* is Arto Luukkanen,

---

ber 8, 2018, https://oikeamedia.com/o1-88317; "Presidentti Jair Bolsonaro ja Brasilian konservatiivinen vastavallankumous," *Blogi, Oikea media*, November 25, 2018, https://oikeamedia.com/o1-90006; "GCM-sopimus edistää globalistista YK-radikalismia," *Blogi, Oikea media*, January 5, 2019, https://oikeamedia.com/o1-94416. For Trump and identitarians, see Zúquete, *Identitarians*, 261-62.

38 Ahvio, "Mitä islamista ja Euroopan unionista saa Suomessa sanoa?," *Blogi, Oikea media*, December 21, 2018, https://www.oikeamedia.com/o1-92711.

39 Ahvio, "Jumalan Pojan inkarnaatio on joulun ydinsanoma myös vuonna 2018," *Blogi, Oikea media*, December 23, 2018, https://www.oikeamedia.com/o1-92906. This is my hermeneutical interpretation of Ahvio's intention. A biologist might remark that the divine origin of the y-chromosome would mean a lack of masculinity in Jesus.

40 Zúquete, *Identitarians*, 219, 342.

41 Zúquete, *Identitarians*, 341, referring to Guillaume Faye.

Lecturer in Russian and Eastern European Studies at the University of Helsinki.[42] Luukkanen is also the Chair of the Executive Board of Suomen Perusta Foundation, a political think tank allied with the Finns Party. He does not proclaim conservative Christianity in the fashion of Ahvio but writes as an academic expert on history and values. Luukkanen appeared on the television channel Alfa TV together with Puolimatka on August 8, 2018, defending the freedom of speech. At the same time, he appealed to common sense and moderation.[43] On the pro-Christian spectrum of *Oikea Media*, one can find both moderate academic expertise (Luukkanen) and ardent identitarianism (Ahvio), suiting in different electoral tastes.

Oikea Media blog writers like to use academic titles. Several professors, docents, and Ph.Ds write regular blogs. There is even an anonymous blog, "Professor's Thoughts," which gives expert opinions on many issues, often on an almost daily basis.[44] An occasional reader of *Oikea Media* receives the impression that the webzine is predominantly run by academic experts. In this regard, *Oikea Media* displays a certain affinity to Vial, Venner, and other prominent ideologists of the French New Right and identitarian movement. While the content of their message often remains populist, their argumentation is based on the values of European civilization as understood by historians and other professional academics. Such values include the freedom of speech and a conservative-masculine family ethos.

From Populism to Recognition Theories

Our interest in identitarian movements derives from our long-term research work on the project "Reason and Religious Recognition", funded by the Academy of Finland at the University of Helsinki. In this project, we focus on the significance of so-called recognition procedures in the history of ideas as well as in contemporary Western society.[45]

---

42 Arto Luukkanen, *Blogi, Oikea media*, accessed January 21, 2019, https://www.oikeamedia.com/blogit.
43 *AlfaTV*, accessed January 21, 2019, http://www.permanto.fi/fi/web/alfatv/player/vod?assetId=10763988%20.
44 Anonymous, "Professorin ajatuksia," *Blogi, Oikea media*, accessed January 21, 2019, https://www.oikeamedia.com/blogit.
45 For this work, see Risto Saarinen, *Recognition and Religion: A Historical and Systematic Study* (Oxford: Oxford University Press, 2016) and Maijastina Kahlos, Heikki Koskinen & Ritva Palmén, eds., *Recognition and Religion: Contemporary and Historical Perspectives* (London: Routledge, 2019).

Current recognition theory is often considered to have emerged after Charles Taylor's influential essay mentioned above. Recognition theory can thus be interpreted as lending support to non-universalist views of society. The emergence of identitarian movements shows, however, that anti-universalism can also lead to significant problems. Therefore, we need to ask in this last part of our paper how recognition procedures, identity politics and universalism can coexist in social theory.

After dealing with the Finnish example above, let us think about the relationship between recognition procedures and identitarian politics more generally. While liberal U.S. identity politics employs recognition theory, no such historical connection can be observed with regard to French identitarian writers. De Benoist often mentions Taylor and the communitarian philosophers[46], and obviously, a generally anti-universalist thinking can make such connections. Nevertheless, the French origins of the movement are historically independent of Taylor's recognition theory.

Since the 1990s, Axel Honneth has developed a theory of recognition, which can cope with different social phenomena in greater detail than Taylor's rather general outline. Honneth considers, for instance, that the so-called "respect" dimension of recognition is universal and concerns all citizens alike. The dimensions of "love" and "esteem" are more individual and distinct. Universal and distinctive variants of interhuman recognition coexist in different spheres of human life.[47]

In his 2018 book, Honneth reflects on so-called pathologies of recognition. In his Hegelian terminology, "pathology" means false or problematic psychological and social reactions in which one can nevertheless see traces of that "healthy" interaction which establishes social recognition.[48] While Honneth advocates Hegel's view of recognition, he is ready to admit that this view also includes certain pathologies. He treats Hegel's view of family, marriage and women as an example. Honneth grants that the Hegelian tradition does not take the equality of women seriously enough, and that a male-centered societal recognition is a blind spot of this tradition.[49]

To some extent, the strong connection between recognition, identity politics, and multiculturalism may have been prompted by Taylor's above-mentioned considerations on the politics of recognition. Honneth's social and political

---

46 So Zúquete, *Identitarians*, 11.
47 Axel Honneth, *Kampf um Anerkennung* (Frankfurt: Suhrkamp, 1992).
48 Axel Honneth, *Anerkennung: Eine europäische Ideengeschichte* (Berlin: Suhrkamp, 2018), 214-15.
49 Honneth, *Anerkennung*, 219-23.

thought, on the other hand, is not restricted to distinctive identities.[50] His version of recognition theory, particularly where the dimension of "respect" is concerned, is compatible with universalism. Thus, in a conceptual sense, Taylor's move from the politics of universalism to a politics of recognition is not a necessary one. In particular, the radical variant of such a move available in recent identity politics is only one very specific option available within the larger theory of recognition.

In our view, the identitarian developments discussed above clearly manifest a "pathological" variant of identity formation. While they apply a non-universalist politics of recognition, this application does not enhance social cohesion, but rather evokes reactions that create polarization and exclusion in a democratic society. For recognition theory and identity politics based on such theory, this means a certain vulnerability. One cannot easily separate healthy identities from pathological ones. Very different people can construct very different identities by applying procedures of recognition and misrecognition. For such reasons, identity politics can also take identitarian and populist forms. Several problems must be avoided here. On the one hand, we cannot simply distinguish between "good" and "bad" identities. On the other hand, some procedures are arguably more harmful and manipulative than others.

If universal and unproblematic recognition is not content-determined, can it produce any kind of identity? Let us distinguish between generic and qualitative identity. Generic identity has to do with what we fundamentally are: human beings, persons, and autonomous agents. Qualitative identity has to do with who we are in the sense of the more specific qualities, features, and properties that we happen to instantiate.

When universalist policies and our universal sameness are under discussion, it is the generic sense of identity that is in play. When distinctive cultural, ethnic, religious or sexual identities are the issue, it is rather the qualitative sense of identity that is meant. Such forms of qualitative identity can also be seen as contingent in nature, and as something historically, socially, and psychologically constructed. Thus, there is no necessary connection to a supposed "metaphysical givenness". If any such givenness is assumed for qualitative identities, then this is an additional assumption and should be treated accordingly. With "given" differences, we easily end up with problematic identitarian stances.

Let us briefly focus on the structural functions of distinctive qualitative identities. They are important for us because they provide an understanding of who we are and of our defining characteristics as human beings. With their help,

---

50   For comparisons between Taylor and Honneth, see Thompson, *Political Theory*.

we construct our lives as men and as women, as Christians and as Muslims, as religious persons and as non-religious persons, as liberals and as conservatives, as Democrats and as Republicans. To thus speak of living-as-something is precisely to talk about identities in a qualitative sense. The narrative of "living-as-something" need not be metaphysiclly given, but it has the risk of becoming that.

Collective identities that equip us with this sense of "living-as-something" provide norms or models which play a role in shaping plans of our lives. They effectively function as kinds of narratives that individual persons (and in an extended sense also groups and institutions) can use in shaping their projects and in telling their life stories. The identitarian movement is a warning case of a "metaphysically given" narrative which becomes outwardly hostile and creates its identity through strict exclusion. In socially pathological cases, homogenous identity profiles can become outwardly hostile and inwardly too tightly scripted, which connects the topic of identity with the themes of social oppression and political power.

The theoretical lesson to be learned from this case is that our identity narratives, our "living-as-something," need to avoid both shapeless universalism and exclusively given identity profiles. Within a pluralistic global context as well as within multicultural societies defined by narrower national borders, the empirical reality of "living-as-something" gives rise to the need for human beings to somehow coexist despite their differences of opinion and regardless of their conflicts over various beliefs and practices. This reality does not call for identitarian solutions but rather for attitudes in which both sameness and difference can coexist. How might this be possible?

Building on the theoretical work of Honneth and Rainer Forst,[51] let us claim that the attitude and dimension of *respect*, on the one hand, is related to the universal sameness of all humans as members of the same community, fellow citizens, and legal subjects. The dimension of *esteem*, on the other hand, is related to qualitative identity. Although esteem is important to individuals' self-relations and communities of expertise, it is a more demanding conception of recognition than respect. This is because it may be challenging or impossible to directly esteem identities that one takes to be somehow bad or false.

Moreover, recognizing our differences or distinctive identities instead of our commonalities or universal sameness may not always be a good idea, as this would mean an esteem that we are not ready to grant. This does not mean,

---

51 Honneth, *Kampf um Anerkennung* and Rainer Forst, *Toleranz im Konflikt* (Frankfurt: Suhrkamp, 2003). For interactions between respect and esteem, cf. also Thompson, *Political Theory*.

however, that granting esteem to views different from one's own is impossible. A universalist way of providing positive recognition for different "living-as-something" identities can be based on taking the right to identity-formation as a universal right in itself, without incorporating any requirements for esteeming any particular identities. Other chapters in this book, dealing with group rights and minority rights, can provide legal models of recognition to achieve this moderately universalist end.

In concrete terms, we may find it valuable that there are conservative religious persons although we do not agree with them. Or, from a different perspective, we may find the so-called "red-green" liberals valuable discussion partners even when we want to remain traditionalists ourselves. Granting such "content-undetermined" esteem to others means that we avoid polarizations and affirm both "living-as-something" and some kind of a multicultural democratic setting. In terms of our above-mentioned examples, this means that the Puolimatka case manifests a problematic identitarian way of constructing "given" enemies. The contrast between Norwegians and Jews in the *Stanford Encyclopedia of Philosophy* can also lead to harmfully polarized "given" identities. While identitarians manifest the problem of "given" pathological identities particularly well, liberals are not immune to the problem of exaggerated polarization.

For Lutherans in particular, such polarization may also mean that the Lutheran concept of confessional identity cannot be merely heteronomous and relational. One needs to esteem some qualitative features not because they are for "us" and against "them" but because they instantiate the universal right to identity-formation. What Honneth calls the primacy of the individual[52] may offer a way of granting esteem also to those others whose views we do not share. The trick is to avoid polarization between us and them. In this manner, universalism and recognition can be meaningfully combined.

We have not employed the term "reconfessionalization" in our analysis. As the populist movements often represent somewhat extreme versions of the late modern fragmentation and polarization of opinions, this term may have more adequate uses in some other contexts. As the identitarian movement is currently extending its influence to religious and theological matters, we nevertheless need to be aware of this influence when different variants of reconfessionalization are being discussed.

A striking example of this kind of influence is provided by Juha Ahvio's March 17, 2019 blog on *Oikea Media*. On this blog, titled "Why does a Christian need to be a patriot with nationalist spirit?", Ahvio argues that "our Protestant

---

52   Honneth, *Anerkennung*, 70-71, 226-27.

evangelical faith gives us a duty to have nationalist spirit". He also says that the Bible obliges us to nationalism.[53] Such rhetoric could be labeled as religious renationalization, an idea that would have been unthinkable in Northern European countries before the most recent identitarian turn.

Bibliography

Literature

Berman, Sheri. "Why Identity Politics Benefits the Right More Than the Left." *Guardian*, August 14, 2018.

Forst, Rainer. *Toleranz im Konflikt*. Frankfurt: Suhrkamp, 2003.

Friberg, Daniel. *The Real Right Returns*. Budapest: Arktos, 2015.

Gritsch, Eric. *A History of Lutheranism*. Minneapolis, MN: Fortress, 2002.

Heyes, Cressida. "Identity Politics." In *Stanford Encyclopedia of Philosophy*. Stanford University, 1997. Article published July 16, 2002; last modified March 23, 2016. https://plato.stanford.edu.

Honneth, Axel. *Anerkennung: Eine europäische Ideengeschichte*. Berlin: Suhrkamp, 2018.

Honneth, Axel. *Kampf um Anerkennung*. Frankfurt: Suhrkamp, 1992.

Jääskeläinen, Petri. "Jumala, Trump ja Putin." *Kirkko ja kaupunki*, August 20, 2018. https://www.kirkkojakaupunki.fi/-/jumala-trump-ja-putin-kristillisen-konservatiivioikeiston-toiminta-suomessa-kulkee-samoilla-raiteilla-kuin-yhdysvaltain-evankelikaaleilla.

Kahlos, Maijastina, Heikki Koskinen, and Ritva Palmén, eds. *Recognition and Religion: Contemporary and Historical Perspectives*. London: Routledge, 2019.

Kruks, Sonia. *Retrieving Experience: Subjectivity and Recognition in Feminist Politics*. Ithaca, NY: Cornell University Press, 2001.

Lilla, Mark. *The Once and Future Liberal: After Identity Politics*. New York: HarperCollins, 2017.

McNay, Lois. *Against Recognition*. Cambridge: Polity, 2008.

Nurmi, Lauri. *Perussuomalaisten hajoamisen historia*. Helsinki: Into, 2017.

Remnick, David. "A Conversation with Mark Lilla on His Critique of Identity Politics." *New Yorker*, August 25, 2017.

Räsänen, Päivi. "Kirjallinen kysymys korkeimman opetuksen ja tutkimuksen sananvapauden turvaamisesta." Accessed January 21, 2019. https://www.eduskunta.fi/FI/vaski/Kysymys/Documents/KK_309+2018.pdf.

---

53 Ahvio, "Vuosi 2019 totuuden valossa: Miksi kristityn tulee olla kansallismielisen isänmaallinen?," *Blogi, Oikea media*, March 17, 2019, https://www.oikeamedia.com/o1-102312. During the spring of 2019, the connection between nationalism and Christian conservativism was discussed in Finland. For this, see Risto Saarinen, "Finnish New Right and Religious Right Converge," University of Helsinki, last modified April 15, 2019, https://www.helsinki.fi/en/news/nordic-welfare-news/finnish-new-right-and-religious-right-converge.

Saarinen, Risto. "Ecumenism." In *Global Dictionary of Theology*, edited by William Dyrness and Veli-Matti Kärkkäinen, 263-69. Nottingham: IVP Press, 2008.

Saarinen. Risto. "Identiteettipolitiikka, toisen tunnustaminen ja teologia." In *Uskonto ja identiteettipolitiikka*, edited by Elina Hellqvist, Minna Hietamäki, and Panu Pihkala, 9-33. Helsinki: STKS, 2015.

Saarinen, Risto. *Recognition and Religion: A Historical and Systematic Study*. Oxford: Oxford University Press, 2016.

Stenner, Karen. *The Authoritarian Dynamic*. Cambridge: Cambridge University Press, 2005.

Taylor, Charles. "The Politics of Recognition." In *Philosophical Arguments*, 225-56. Cambridge, MA: Harvard University Press, 1995.

Thompson, Simon. *The Political Theory of Recognition: A Critical Introduction*. Cambridge: Polity, 2006.

Zúquete, José Pedro. *The Identitarians: The Movement against Globalism and Islam in Europe*. Notre Dame, IN: Notre Dame University Press, 2018.

Webpages

Ahvio, Juha. "Kansalliskonservatiiviset Ruotsidemokraatit nousevat Ruotsissa." *Blogi, Oikea media*. September 1, 2018. https://oikeamedia.com/o1-80812?fbclid=IwAR2qjBIsDd6C9eXsIOEYJKaUBtTykUIo_GfNjiFH2dU5OXqMNWXqyzmDrDI.

Ahvio, Juha. "Dosentti Markku Ruotsilan pätevän kattava analyysi USA:n sydänmaiden konservatiivien kapinasta." *Blogi, Oikea media*. November 2, 2018. https://oikeamedia.com/o1-87716?fbclid=IwAR0mLDYfOVFFMLRCRFO6vU2YKmDaq4_Sk8HL6C1HQLJdwdY7ndr0bmOjbco.

Ahvio, Juha. "Trump ja republikaanit saivat strategisen torjuntavoiton USA:n välivaaleissa." *Blogi, Oikea media*. November 8, 2018. https://oikeamedia.com/o1-88317.

Ahvio, Juha. "Presidentti Jair Bolsonaro ja Brasilian konservatiivinen vastavallankumous." *Blogi, Oikea media*. November 25, 2018. https://oikeamedia.com/o1-90006.

Ahvio, Juha. "Mitä islamista ja Euroopan unionista saa Suomessa sanoa?" *Blogi, Oikea media*. December 21, 2018. https://www.oikeamedia.com/o1-92711.

Ahvio, Juha. "Jumalan Pojan inkarnaatio on joulun ydinsanoma myös vuonna 2018." *Blogi, Oikea media*. December 23, 2018. https://www.oikeamedia.com/o1-92906.

Ahvio, Juha. "GCM-sopimus edistää globalistista YK-radikalismia." *Blogi, Oikea media*. January 5, 2019. https://oikeamedia.com/o1-94416.

Ahvio, Juha. "Vuosi 2019 totuuden valossa: Miksi kristityn tulee olla kansallismielisen isänmaallinen?," Blogi, Oikea media, March 17, 2019, https://www.oikeamedia.com/o1-102312.

AlfaTV. Accessed January 21, 2019. http://www.permanto.fi/fi/web/alfatv/player/vod?assetId=10763988%20.

Anonymous. "Professorin ajatuksia." *Blogi, Oikea media*. Accessed January 21, 2019. https://www.oikeamedia.com/blogit.

ApoWiki. "Kohu kirjoituksesta 'Kampanja pedofilian laillistamiseksi'." Accessed January 2019. https://apowiki.fi/wiki/Kohu_kirjoituksesta_%22Kampanja_pedofilian laillistamiseksi%22.

Luukkanen, Arto. *Blogi, Oikea media*. Accessed January 21, 2019. https://www.oikeamedia.com/blogit.

Puolimatka, Tapio. "Kampanja pedofilian laillistamiseksi." *Blogi, Oikea media*. July 27, 2018. https://www.oikeamedia.com/o1-75907.

Rahkonen, Jukka. "Jyväskylän yliopistolla muhii poliittiset vainot." *Oikea media*, August 1, 2018. https://www.oikeamedia.com/o1-76812.

Saarinen, Risto. "Finnish New Right and Religious Right Converge." University of Helsinki. Last modified April 15, 2019. https://www.helsinki.fi/en/news/nordic-welfare-news/finnish-new-right-and-religious-right-converge.

Salenius, Tytti. "Onko Jyväskylän yliopistossa meneillään monitahoinen kampanja pedofilian laillistamiseksi?" *Oikea media*, August 13, 2018. https://www.oikeamedia.com/o1-78809.

III

Internationalization

12. Constitutional Identity in the Nordic Countries 1950-2015

Helle Krunke

Introduction

In this chapter, I will analyze how the Nordic constitutional systems have developed during the period after World War II until the present, in light of legal Europeanization and internationalization.[1] What role constitutional identity plays in a Nordic context will be discussed, and how it is influenced by Europeanization and internationalization, including in the field of religion.

Research Questions, Concepts, Method, and Delimitation

I will seek to answer the following research questions: How have the processes of internationalization and Europeanization in general impacted the Nordic constitutional systems and the Nordic constitutional identity? And how have they impacted the field of religion? Referring to the introduction to this volume, this chapter will primarily focus on the management of the religion-secular divide in the organizational and structural dimensions of social life (secularity$^{\text{meaning1-2}}$).

This research will be carried out in three steps, moving from the more general levels toward the more specific levels. The reason for this approach is partly to place the more specific question of religion within a broader context in order to deepen the understanding of the developments we find in that particular field. Partly, the purpose relates to the relationship between the concepts of constitutional law, constitutional identity, and specific elements of constitutional values and identity. One might say that they form a Russian *babushka doll*—in order to look at the smallest doll we have to open the bigger dolls that surround it.

---

[1] The author would like to thank research student Benjamin Vynne Muschinsky for a thorough search of sources for this chapter.

This naturally leads to my explainations of the concepts "constitutional law" and "constitutional identity". When defining *constitutional law* I take inspiration from the following definition:[2]

> Constitutional Law is part of the general legislation and it is different from politics, economy etc. Danish Constitutional Law is the part of Danish law, which concerns the political structure in Denmark. This includes 1) legislation concerning the political authorities, especially the parliament and government and their relationship to the courts and other authorities, 2) the relationship between the mentioned authorities and private parties, and 3) the human rights, which apply in Denmark.

In this definition, "Danish" and "Denmark" can be substituted with the name of any other Nordic state.

The term "constitutional identity" exists both outside of European Union (EU) law and within it. In this essay, *constitutional identity* is understood as the core or fundamental elements or values of a particular state's constitutional order as the expression of its individuality[3] and in light of Article 4, Part 2, of the Treaty of the European Union (TEU), which refers to national identity that can be found in the fundamental structures, political and constitutional, inclusive of regional and local self-government. The two main questions regarding constitutional identity are: Who defines it, and who communicates it to the EU?

Nordic constitutions do not refer to constitutional identity, Nordic courts have not directly defined what falls under constitutional identity and very little literature exists on constitutional identity in the Nordic countries. This does not mean that the Nordic countries do not have a constitutional identity, but it means that we will have to extract it ourselves from an interpretation of the constitution, from case law, and perhaps other sources as well.

From the above definitions of constitutional law and constitutional identity, it is clear that constitutional identity must be sought within constitutional law, since it can be defined as the core or fundamental elements or values of a particular state's constitutional order, as the expression of its individuality. As mentioned, this relationship between the two concepts supports our choice of the babushka-approach.

---

2   This is a translation of the definition of constitutional law by Henrik Zahle. See Henrik Zahle, *Dansk forfatningsret: Institutioner og regulering* (Copenhagen: Christian Ejlers' Forlag, 2001), 19.

3   See Christian Calliess and Gerhard van der Schyff, eds., *Constitutional Identity* (Cambridge: Cambridge University Press, 2019).

In order to answer our research questions, I will apply a comparative constitutional method and more specifically a contextualized functional approach.[4] The babushka-approach goes well with the choice of a contextualized comparative method since the outer layers provide the contextual understanding of the inner layers. I have selected the following key features in my comparative functional approach, in which I particularly focus on the impact of Europeanization and internationalization on the Nordic constitutional texts: the institutional structure and division of powers, judicial review of legislation, and human rights.[5] However, it should be emphasized that since I only have one chapter available to cover such a broad theme, this overview will be broad.

With regard to theory, I will draw on two other research projects. First, I will be able to stand on the shoulders of a new comparative and contextual study of Nordic constitutions published in 2018, which has a special focus on the impact of international human rights conventions and EU law on the Nordic constitutional systems.[6] Second, I take inspiration from a comparative study on constitutional identity in different European countries, which was published in 2019.[7]

The Development of Internationalization and Europeanization of the Legal Systems from 1950-2015—An Overview

In reaction to World War II, a number of international organizations were established in the 1940s and 1950s. The purpose of these organizations was to prevent new wars and crimes against humanity and human dignity. Some of these organizations were European, such as the European Council (established 1949) and the European Coal and Steel Community (established 1952). Others were international, such as the United Nations (UN, established 1945). Some initiati-

---

4   See Vicki C. Jackson, "Comparative Constitutional Law: Methodologies," in *The Oxford Handbook of Comparative Constitutional Law*, ed. Michel Rosenfeld and András Sajó (Oxford: Oxford University Press, 2012), 72. The main characteristics of a contextualized functional approach are that a number of constitutional functions (e.g., the legislative function) are chosen as the object of comparison, and that they are studied in light of the context (for instance, a political context), in which they exist (as opposed to a black-letter comparison where only the wording of the constitutional texts are compared).
5   This is to some extent in accordance with the comparative study in Helle Krunke and Björg Thorarensen, eds., *The Nordic Constitutions: A Comparative and Contextual Study* (Oxford: Hart Publishing, 2018), which I will draw on in the present study.
6   See Krunke and Thorarensen, *The Nordic Constitutions*.
7   See Calliess and Schyff, *Constitutional Identity*.

ves, such as the International Criminal Court, share the same background and purpose, though established at a later point of time (establishment of the ICC was decided in 1998 and it entered into force in 2002). While some organizations aimed at drafting human rights conventions, such as the European Convention of Human Rights (ECHR, 1950), others aimed at cooperation on raw materials used in war and on trade: for instance, the European Coal and Steel Community (which much later turned into the European Union as we know it today). Some organizations later broadened their scope. Although human rights were not part of the cooperation within the European Coal and Steel Community from the beginning, already in the 1960s the European Court of Justice (CJEU) started to develop a protection of human rights and general principles of EU law in its case law.[8] Eventually, the EU Charter of Fundamental Rights appeared: first as a political document and later as a legally binding document, when the Lisbon Treaty was adopted and came into effect in 2009.

Viewed from a legal perspective, this new European and international cooperation took different legal forms, and in some cases it revolutionized international cooperation. From a constitutional law point of view, the most interesting examples are: the ECHR, the UN's Universal Declaration of Human Rights (and other UN conventions on human rights), and treaties of the European cooperation starting with the Coal and Steel Community which later turned into the European Community and finally the European Union (and the European Economic Area (EEA)). While the ECHR is an internationally binding document which has been ratified by the member states and incorporated into their national legal systems, the UN's Universal Declaration of Human Rights is an international declaration which is not binding for the member states. Finally, what we know today as the European Union has had a supranational element since the beginning, meaning that legislation could be binding for the member states without any incorporation into national law. Later on, the CJEU formulated, among other things, the principle of supremacy of EU law over national legislation and constitutions, and the principle of direct effect.[9]

This brings us to another interesting feature of the European and international cooperation. The international conventions and treaties sometimes also establish international courts, such as the European Court of Human Rights

---

8   See for instance Gráinne de Búrca, "The Evolution of EU Human Rights Law," in *The Evolution of EU Law*, ed. Paul Craig and Gráinne de Búrca (Oxford: Oxford University Press, 2011), 477-80.
9   See C-6/64, *Costa v ENEL*, ECLI:EU:C:1964:66, and C-26/62, *NV Algemene Transporten Expeditie Onderneming van Gend & Loos v Netherlands Inland Revenue Administration*, ECLI:EU:C:1963:1.

(ECtHR), the CJEU and the International Court of Justice. Some of these courts, especially the ECtHR and the CJEU, share a dynamic interpretation style[10], which we are not used to in the Nordic countries. In the Nordic countries, the courts traditionally apply a quite narrow textual approach in their interpretation of legal texts, with a strong focus on the original intent of the legislator. Furthermore, legal principles (EU constitutional principles) play a more important role both in the EU treaties and in the case law of the CJEU than we are used to in the Nordic legal systems. In this way, a new "legal world order" was slowly created after World War II. Naturally, we sometimes experience legal clashes between national constitutional and legal systems and international or European legal systems.[11] Such clashes can relate to substance and/or to the form of legal reasoning and style. The Nordic countries all have a so-called dualistic legal system.

The Impact of Internationalization and Europeanization on the Nordic Constitutional Systems from 1950 to 2015: Developments, Similarities, Differences, Explanations

The development of international and European legal systems described above has had an impact on the Nordic constitutional systems, though not necessarily the same impact on all of them.[12] Actually, the Coal and Steel Community, established in 1952, had an impact on the design of the Danish Constitution already in 1953, even though Denmark did not join the European Community until 1973. Thus, in the revision of the Constitution it was considered that Denmark might one day want to join the new type of supranational cooperation which had been invented with the Coal and Steel Community. Therefore, Article 20 was inserted into the Constitution of 1953, making it possible for Denmark to transfer sovereignty to an international organization without amending the Constitution. The idea was that since the amendment procedure is among the

---

10   Dynamic interpretation is characterized by a purpose-oriented free interpretation style in which the treaty is interpreted as a living instrument (as opposed to a narrow text-oriented interpretation style).
11   See for instance the quite recent Ajos case: C-441/14, *Dansk Industri (on behalf of Ajos A/S) v Estate of Karsten Eigil Rasmussen*, ECLI:EU:C:2016:278, and the judgment 15/2014 by the Danish Supreme Court of Justice of December 6, 2016, available in English at https://domstol.dk/media/2udgvvvb/judgment-15-2014.pdf.
12   For a detailed comparative analysis of the impact of Europeanization and internationalization on the Nordic constitutional systems, see Krunke and Thorarensen, *The Nordic Constitutions*.

most comprehensive in the world and includes among other things an election and a referendum, Article 20 would make it possible to cede sovereignty through a less comprehensive procedure, which mandates a referendum only if it is not possible to gain a 5/6 majority in parliament in favor of a transfer of sovereignty. Since the Constitution has not been revised since 1953, Article 20 is still in force; it has been applied several times in relation to European cooperation, beginning in 1972.

Sweden and Finland joined the EU in 1995 and both constitutions now have provisions on the transfer of sovereignty: in Chapter 10, Article 6, of the Swedish Instrument of Government, and in Section 94 of the Finnish Constitution. Norway and Iceland, on the other hand, are only members of the EEA. Whereas Norway has a provision on the transfer of sovereignty in Article 115 of its constitution, this is not the case in the Icelandic Constitution. Since 1953, the international vision and outlook characterizing the 1953 revision of the Danish Constitution have fallen behind, and the Danish Constitution is now the only constitution of a Nordic EU Member State that does not reflect EU membership. The Swedish and Finnish constitutions both mention the EU in their text. In the Finnish case, EU membership is already mentioned in the first provision of the Constitution, which also mentions other forms of international cooperation and Finland's dedication to human rights in general. The Swedish Constitution mentions the EU is in the first chapter of The Instrument of Government on International Relations.

Ironically, Denmark, which became a member of the EU more than 45 years ago and more than 20 years before Sweden and Finland, has chosen to have a constitution with no trace of the EU in the text, even though in reality the EU has a huge impact on Denmark. With regard to Norway and Iceland, there is no trace of the EEA. This might formally speaking make sense in light of the distinction between the EU being a supranational organization and the EEA being an international organization. In reality, however, both Norway and Iceland are much affected by the EEA, and in many areas the legal situation is the same as for EU member states. For instance, the Court of Justice of the European Free Trade Association (EFTA) has established a quasi-direct effect principle (Case E-1/94) and a quasi-primacy principle (Case E-1/01).

In general, the EU legal system significantly impacts the national legal systems of its member states, including Denmark, Sweden, and Finland. A large majority of new legislation is initiated in Brussels. Through the development of principles of supremacy, direct effect and state liability, and with the assistance of national courts, which are required to apply EU law and interpret in accordance with EU law and case law from the CJEU, the EU legal system has managed to secure effective enforcement and thereby an impact which no other international organization can compete with. Among other factors, the preliminary ruling system supports a uniform interpretation of EU law in the member states.

How does the mentioned development affect the competences of the political and judicial institutions and, not least, the systems of separation of powers in the Nordic countries? Starting with the political institutions, to a certain extent political debate on new legislation has shifted from the national parliaments to the EU legislature. Since the national governments represent their countries when new EU legislative initiatives are discussed in the Council, in reality power is transferred from parliaments to governments. Compared to other EU member states, the Nordic countries led by the Danish parliament have managed to exert a very strong parliamentary influence on national EU policy and new EU bills through strong scrutiny procedures and mandate procedures in the European Policy Committees. However, although Nordic parliaments might be strong compared to many other parliaments, differences also exist, which are reflected in the use of the Early Warning System[13] and the Barroso Initiative[14]. Interestingly, while Sweden is the member state in the EU which has submitted the most reasoned opinions, Denmark has submitted an average number of opinions and Finland is among the member states with the fewest submitted opinions.[15] According to Anna Jonsson Cornell, this might be explained by the fact that the Danish mandate procedure is stronger and more binding for the

---

13 The Early Warning System (EWS) was introduced with the Lisbon Treaty. See Consolidated Version of the Treaty on the European Union (TEU) [2008] OJ C115/13, Art. 5, Part 2, and the Protocol on the application of the principles of subsidiarity and proportionality. National parliaments may object to Commission proposals within eight weeks of their publication on the grounds that it breaches the principle of subsidiarity. These objections are referred to as "reasoned opinions". If they represent at least 1/3 of the votes allocated to national parliaments and their chambers, the Commission must review the draft legislation. The Commission can decide to maintain, amend or withdraw its proposal. For a more thorough description, see the aforementioned Protocol.
14 The Barroso Initiative was introduced in 2006 with the aim of facilitating a more direct dialogue with the national parliaments. Documents are sent directly to the parliaments and they can comment on them to the Commission. These comments from the parliaments are not binding for the Commission. Compared to the EWS, the Barroso Initiative allows a parliament to make comments beyond the principle of subsidiarity. See *A Citizens Agenda: Delivering results for Europe,* Commission Communication to the European Council COM (2006) 211, 10 May 2006.
15 See Anna Jonsson Cornell, "Similar but Different: Comparing the Scrutiny of the Principle of Subsidiarity within the EWM in Denmark, Finland and Sweden," in *National and Regional Parliaments in the EU-Legislative Procedure Post-Lisbon*, ed. Anna Jonsson Cornell and Marco Goldini (Oxford: Hart Publishing, 2017), 201.

government than is the case in Sweden and Finland. This means that the Swedish parliament has more interest in using the opinions available for influencing EU legislation. In Finland, there is a tradition for speaking with one voice on EU policy through the government; therefore, the Finnish parliament is the least active in submitting opinions.[16] Moving on to the substance of the opinions, in the Nordic opinions there seems to be a special focus on Nordic values such as democracy, openness, strong welfare systems with many social rights financed by the public taxation system, and protection of the environment.[17] This reflects the fact that common Nordic values exist, and the fact that not only does the EU impact the Nordic countries, the Nordic countries also impact the EU. With regard to Norway and Iceland, the national parliaments might be said to have less influence on the EEA since, formally, their cooperation is normally international and not supranational cooperation, although in reality Norway and Iceland are significantly impacted by the EEA.[18]

This brings us to how the EU/EEA impacts the national courts and their relation to national political institutions. Even though in some cases the Nordic courts have emphasized the special Nordic separation of powers model, with strong parliaments and reticent courts (the Norwegian Supreme Court being the strongest and most active Nordic court followed by the Icelandic Supreme Court),[19] it is fair to say that the Nordic courts have gained power through the EU/EEA. As mentioned above, the national courts play an important role in the enforcement of EU law. Furthermore, in Finland and Sweden, the Nordic EU member states with the traditionally weakest courts, the courts have gained more competence with regard to judicial review of constitutionality of legislation and thereby in relationship to the parliaments. This tendency is most significant in Finland. Traditionally, the Finnish courts have not had the competence to review the constitutionality of legislation. However, after joining the EU in 1994 and under the influence of the stronger European and international human rights focus, such a competence for the courts was introduced in 2000 as Article 106 of

---

16 See Cornell, "Similar But Different," 201-23.
17 See Helle Krunke, "Impact of EU/EEA on the Nordic Constitutional Systems," in *The Nordic Constitutions: A Comparative and Contextual Study*, ed. Helle Krunke and Björg Thorarensen (Oxford: Hart Publishing, 2018), 187-88.
18 See Björg Thorarensen, "Mechanisms for Parliamentary Control of the Executive," in *The Nordic Constitutions: A Comparative and Contextual Study*, ed. Helle Krunke and Björg Thorarensen (Oxford: Hart Publishing, 2018), 67-105.
19 See Eivind Smith, "Judicial Review of Legislation," in *The Nordic Constitutions: A Comparative and Contextual Study*, ed. Helle Krunke and Björg Thorarensen (Oxford: Hart Publishing, 2018), 107-08.

the constitution.[20] In Finland, a strong *ex ante* review of bills exists, carried out by the Constitutional Law Committee under the Finnish parliament. Since the courts have not traditionally had the competence to review the constitutionality of legislation, while parliament had the Constitutional Law Committee, from the perspective of the separation of powers, parliament has been strong and the courts weak. Since the Constitutional Law Committee still carries out *ex ante* review, it seems that in reality the Finnish courts will still be weakened to a certain extent.

If we move on to the field of human rights, the ECHR in particular has had a significant impact on the constitutional texts of the Nordic countries apart from Denmark. The human rights chapter of the Icelandic Constitution was amended in 1995, adding new rights and modernizing old ones. The bill accompanying the Act referred to the ECHR and among other instruments UN human rights instruments.[21] This was the first time since 1874 that the constitutional human rights catalogue was amended. When the Norwegian Constitution was revised in 2014, the ECHR and the International Covenant on Civil and Political Rights impacted the amendments of its human rights provisions. According to Article 92, the state authorities must respect and ensure human rights as expressed in the constitution and in human rights treaties binding for Norway.[22] Through the amendments, many international human rights in treaties binding for Norway were included in the text of the constitution (Part E). Article 1 of the Finnish Constitution already refers to international human rights treaties. In 1995, the human rights catalogue was modernized with a broad range of economic, social, cultural rights and provisions on protection of the environment and the right to good administration.[23] Sweden has a long and strong tradition in support of human rights, especially regarding freedom of the press and access to public documents. The human rights provisions of the constitution were amended in 1974 in Chapter 2 of the Instrument of Government. Chapter 2 was amended in 1976, 1979, 1994, and 2011. The latest amendment led to new provisions on the protection of personal privacy and a prohibition of discrimination on the basis

---

20 See Juha Lavapuro, Tuomas Ojanen, and Martin Scheinin, "Rights-Based Constitutionalism in Finland and the Development of Pluralist Constitutional Review," *International Journal of Constitutional Law* 9, no. 2 (2011): 505-31.
21 See Tuomas Ojanen, "Human Rights in Nordic Constitutions and the Impact of International Obligations," in *The Nordic Constitutions: A Comparative and Contextual Study*, ed. Helle Krunke and Björg Thorarensen (Oxford: Hart Publishing, 2018), 141.
22 See Ojanen, "Human Rights in Nordic Constitutions," 142.
23 See Ojanen, "Human Rights in Nordic Constitutions," 142. See also the chapter by Pamela Slotte, "Moving Frontiers: Configuring Religion Law and Religious Law, and Law-Religion Relations," in this volume.

of sexual orientation.[24] The Danish Constitution has not been amended since 1953, and some provisions date back to 1849. The ECHR and other international human rights instruments have not affected the constitutional text. However, because the ECHR has been incorporated into Danish law, the Convention has had a significant impact in Denmark—especially in light of the fact that the human rights protection in the constitutional text has not been modernized and the Convention therefore provides a more modern protection of human rights in Denmark.[25] The difference is that, in Denmark, such rights are only protected at the legislative level of ordinary law, while in the other Nordic countries where the impact of the ECHR and other international human rights instruments have found their way to the constitutional text, they provide protection at the constitutional level. This means that the national legislature cannot violate them in legislation.

Traditionally, the Nordic constitutions have not mentioned general principles and human rights in their first provisions, a tradition which exists also in Germany. However, mentioning general principles and human rights in preambles and preliminary provisions of treaties is a strong tradition in EU treaties and human rights treaties such as the ECHR. This tradition seems to have rubbed off on some of the Nordic constitutions. Hence, the Finnish Constitution, section 1:2, the Norwegian Constitution, Article 2, and the Swedish Instrument of Government, Article 2, now all set out general principles and rights.[26] Although such provisions are normally not directly enforceable in the courts, this development reflects how the Nordic legal systems are changing as a result of inspiration from the European and international legal systems.

When it comes to general legal principles, the general EU legal principles formulated by the CJEU in the field of rights have had an even more serious impact on the Nordic constitutional systems. Such principles are given the same legal weight as the EU treaties, though they are not mentioned in the treaties themselves. The CJEU deduces such principles from Art. 6 (1) and (3) of the TEU. A general EU legal principle on the prohibition of age discrimination was introduced in the famous Mangold case and given direct effect between two private parties.[27] Even though this was much debated in the legal literature, the CJEU defined a prohibition against discrimination based on religion as a

---

24 See Ojanen, "Human Rights in Nordic Constitutions," 141.
25 See Helle Krunke and Björg Thorarensen, "Concluding Thoughts," in *The Nordic Constitutions: A Comparative and Contextual Study*, ed. Helle Krunke and Björg Thorarensen (Oxford: Hart Publishing, 2018), 203-18.
26 See Ojanen, "Human Rights in Nordic Constitutions," 143.
27 See C-144/04, *Werner Mangold v Rüdiger Helm*, ECLI:EU:C:2005:709.

general EU principle in the recent Vera Egenberger case,[28] giving it effect in the relationship between two private parties. This development of defining unwritten general principles at the EU treaty level, meaning that they have primacy over national legislation and constitutions according to EU law, contradicts the Nordic legal tradition. This clash of legal traditions was clear in the Ajos case.[29] In this case, legal certainty and the Nordic separation of powers model were at stake. The Danish Supreme Court refused to follow a preliminary ruling from the CJEU according to which the general EU principle on the prohibition of age discrimination was to be given effect between two private parties.

In relation to the impact of Europeanization and internationalization on the Nordic courts, there seems to be a tendency of courts to be more dynamic in their interpretation style, inspired by the dynamic interpretation style of the CJEU and the ECtHR. This is especially true for Finland and Norway: in Norway, the described development has led to a debate on whether judges should be politically appointed, as is the case in the United States, in the future.[30] This tendency is less marked in Denmark. The impact of the EU legal system on the Nordic legal systems is not only related to a substantial amount of EU law entering the Danish legal system, but also to legal method, reasoning, and interpretation. Nordic courts are inspired to apply more dynamic interpretation methods and to be less positivistic in their legal reasoning than has traditionally been the case.[31]

The Impact of Internationalization and Europeanization on Nordic Constitutional Identity

In the section entitled "Research questions, concepts, method, and delimitation", constitutional identity was defined as the core or fundamental elements or values of a particular state's constitutional order as the expression of its individuality,[32] and in light of Article 4, Part 2, of the TEU, which refers to the

---

28 See C-414/16, *Vera Egenberger v Evangelisches Werk für Diakonie und Entwicklung eV*, ECLI:EU:C:2018:257.
29 See C-441/14, *Dansk Industri (on behalf of Ajos A/S) v Estate of Karsten Eigil Rasmussen*, ECLI:EU:C:2016:278, and the judgment 15/2014 by the Danish Supreme Court of Justice of December 6, 2016, available in English at https://domstol.dk/media/2udgvvvb/judgment-15-2014.pdf.
30 See Smith, "Judicial Review of Legislation," 107-32.
31 See Krunke and Thorarensen, "Concluding Thoughts," 214.
32 See Calliess and Schyff, *Constitutional Identity*.

national identity that can be found in the fundamental structures, political and constitutional, inclusive of regional and local self-government.

Interestingly, the term "constitutional identity" is almost nonexistent in the Nordic constitutions, constitutional literature of the Nordic countries, and case law from the Nordic courts. Thus, there has not existed a self-consciousness with regard to constitutional identity. Ironically, viewed from the outside, the Nordic constitutional systems often stand out in their containing particular features not found in other constitutional systems. Constitutional identity is not a new term in international constitutional theory. We find the term in, for instance, Michel Rosenfeld's "Constitutional Identity."[33] A new consciousness of our Nordic constitutional identity has appeared as an effect of EU integration.[34] In particular, Article 4, Part 2 of the TEU has driven such a focus:

> The Union shall respect the equality of Member States before the Treaties as well as their national identities, inherent in their fundamental structures, political and constitutional, inclusive of regional and local self-government. It shall respect their essential State functions, including ensuring the territorial integrity of the State, maintaining law and order and safeguarding national security. In particular, national security remains the sole responsibility of each Member State.

This provision can be found among the "common provisions" of the treaty. Even before Article 4, Part 2 was introduced, there was a protection of national identity in the Maastricht Treaty and the Amsterdam Treaty.[35] There already exists quite an extensive body of case law from the CJEU in this field. Obviously, it is an advantage for a member state to be able to define and express its constitutional identity. In this regard, constitutional courts such as the German Constitutional Court have been rather active, while the Nordic courts have been silent. As mentioned above, there are two main questions regarding constitu-

---

33   Michel Rosenfeld, *The Identity of the Constitutional Subject: Selfhood, Citizenship, Culture, and Community* (New York: Routledge, 2010).
34   In 2014, the first Nordic academic conference on Nordic constitutional identity was held at the University of Turku (Finland). The conference papers were later published in a special issue of the Nordic legal journal *Retfærd*: see *Retfærd* 37, no. 4 (2014).
35   See Armin von Bogdandy and Stephan Schill. "Overcoming Absolute Primacy: Respect for National Identity under the Lisbon Treaty," *Common Market Law Review* 48, no. 5 (2011): 1427. According to the authors, the difference between protection of national identity in the Lisbon Treaty and in the former treaties is the new "link between national identity and the 'fundamental political and constitutional structures.' This distances the notion of national identity in Article 4 (2) TEU from cultural, historical, or linguistic criteria and turns to the content of domestic constitutional orders."

tional identity: Who defines it, and who communicates it to the EU? In countries such as Germany, the constitutional courts do both.

However, in the Nordic countries with their tradition of quite reticent courts, Nordic courts do not find it natural to engage in defining a constitutional identity that is not defined in the written sources. This is, of course, a challenge since Article 4, Part 2, also mentions the importance of equality of the member states before the treaties. The problem is very well illustrated by the Danish Ajos case, in which the Danish government referred to Article 4, Part 2, and defined the principle of the separation of powers in the Nordic sense with reticent courts and strong parliaments and the principle of the rule of law as part of Danish constitutional identity.[36] On the other hand, the Supreme Court did not refer to Article 4, Part 2 or constitutional identity, although it did mention the role of the Danish courts as an argument for not following the preliminary reference from the CJEU[37] in its own judgment.[38] The Ajos case illustrates the unwillingness of the courts to take upon themselves this role of defining and referring to constitutional identity. Furthermore, the case reflects the fact that the courts resist the judicialization of Europeanization in this field. Perhaps this will change in the future because of the impact of the EU legal systems and the international human rights systems on the Nordic constitutional systems, including the role of general constitutional principles and rights.

As mentioned earlier, the Finnish, Swedish, and Norwegian constitutions have adopted introductory provisions with such general principles. Furthermore, the supreme courts of all the Nordic countries except Denmark have adopted a style in their judgments which has characteristics from the case law of the CJEU and the ECtHR and, even more important, a slightly more activist approach in their rulings. Such a development could mean that, over time, the traditional Nordic separation of powers system, with quite reticent

---

36   See Ministry of Foreign Affairs of Denmark written submission of December 19 2014 to the Court of Justice, para. 51.
37   See C-441/14, *Dansk Industri (on behalf of Ajos A/S) v Estate of Karsten Eigil Rasmussen*, ECLI:EU:C:2016:278. According to the CJEU, it was possible for the Danish Supreme Court to interpret Danish legislation in accordance with the EU principle against age discrimination, and hence apply EU law to the case. However, in its judgment, the Danish Supreme Court insisted that it was a *contra legem* situation and that the Court was not able to apply EU law to the case; instead, Danish law was applied. See Helle Krunke and Sune Klinge "The Danish Ajos Case: The Missing Case from Maastricht and Lisbon," *European Papers* 3, no 1 (2018): 157-82.
38   See the judgment in Case 15/2014 by the Danish Supreme Court of Justice of December 6 2016, available in English at https://domstol.dk/media/2udgvvvb/judgment-15-2014.pdf.

courts and strong parliaments, will slowly embrace a more active role for the courts. Since the Danish government has defined the traditional relationship between courts and parliament as a part of Danish constitutional identity—which is probably true for all the Nordic countries—this could also mean that constitutional identity in this field might slowly change in the future in the Nordic countries. Some Nordic countries are further along in this process than others. Obviously, many values such as democracy, human rights, and rule of law are shared by the Nordic countries and the EU. This means that the impact of Europeanization is not so strong in these fields. At the same time, in practice, conflicts can arise between the two legal systems, causing challenges with regard to the rule of law and legal certainty. This is the case, even though such principles exist in both legal systems—as we have seen in the mentioned Ajos case.

The influence of Europeanization and internationalization on the Nordic constitutional systems is reflected at several levels, including substance (for instance, new rights), legal style (for instance, legal argumentation and the role of general legal principles), and constitutional identity (for instance, the role of courts). Referring to Kaarlo Tuori's theory on the three levels of law, we find that the Nordic constitutional systems are impacted by Europeanization and internationalization at all three levels: surface law, legal culture, and deep structure.[39]

While the Nordic countries are slowly acquiring a consciousness of constitutional identity as a concept and of what Nordic constitutional identity is, the European academic debate on constitutional identity has turned a corner with a new focus on some Eastern European countries' use of constitutional identity as one tool among others applied to protect their national legal systems against EU principles on rule of law and court independence. Thus, constitutional identity has suddenly become a problematic and debated concept in EU law, since it might legitimize populist governments' elimination of basic European values such as democracy and human rights.[40]

---

39 See Kaarlo Tuori, *Critical Legal Positivism* (Aldershot: Ashgate, 2002), 147, 150, 154-55, 157, 165-66, 169, 173-74, 177, 183-84, 186-88, 191-92.

40 See the Horizon2020 research project on varieties of populism: "DEMOS—Democratic Efficacy and the Varieties of Populism in Europe," *ECAS*, accessed April 11, 2019, https://ecas.org/projects/demos/.

Tying up the Loose Ends: Religion, Constitutional Law, and Constitutional Identity

The foreign reader of Nordic constitutions might be surprised, since some Nordic states are both monarchies and democracies, and some Nordic states have a state church but also freedom of religion and a tradition of secularism.[41] Thus, the Nordic constitutional systems seem to uphold rather old-fashioned institutions, while at the same time embracing modern values of democracy and human rights. Below, I will discuss how the previously described impact of Europeanization and internationalization on the Nordic constitutional systems plays out in the field of religion. My focus will be on broader perspectives, rather than an extensive legal dogmatic analysis of the interplay of specific provisions within national law, EU law, and the ECHR.

According to Markku Suksi, when searching for common roots of Nordic constitutional law, one of few historically rooted elements is the constitutional position of the Evangelical Lutheran Church or at least of the faith.[42] Suksi emphasizes this feature as something which has been (and to some extent still is) a common denominator between the Nordic countries, and which has its common historical roots in the Protestant Reformation.[43] While Denmark, Norway, and Iceland all have a state church, this is no longer the case in Sweden, which carried out a full separation of church and state in 2000. In Finland, no formal state church has been in place since 1869. The Evangelical Lutheran Church, which is the majority church, and the Finnish Orthodox Church, are today both recognized as national churches.[44]

Turning to the EU, in the search for the EU constitutional identity in the field of religion, a good place to start is the interesting debate which took place at the time of the drafting and adoption of the Constitutional Treaty. Catholic states such as Italy, Poland, Lithuania, Malta, Portugal, the Czech Republic, and Slovakia pushed for an explicit reference to "the Christian roots of Europe", while member states such as France, which is secular, and the Nordic countries, pushed in the opposite direction. In the EU Parliament, eleven Danish members

---

41   Thus, for instance, the Danish Constitution has a provision on the State Church in Article 4, and a provision on freedom of religion in Article 67.
42   See Markku Suksi, "Common Roots of Nordic Constitutional Law?," in *The Nordic Constitutions: A Comparative and Contextual Study*, ed. Helle Krunke and Björg Thorarensen (Oxford: Hart Publishing, 2018), 38.
43   See Suksi, "Common Roots," 32-37. Another common historically rooted element is a very strong local decision-making power. A more current common constitutional root is citizenship. Suksi, "Common Roots," 41-42.
44   See the chapters by Johan Bastubacka and Pamela Slotte in this volume.

voted against mentioning "Judaeo-Christian roots", while two voted in favor, and altogether the EU Parliament rejected the proposition by 283 votes to 211. In the end, the following wording was adopted for the preamble:

> DRAWING INSPIRATION from the cultural, *religious* and humanist inheritance of Europe, from which have developed the universal values of the inviolable and inalienable rights of the human person, freedom, democracy, equality and the rule of law [emphasis added by author].

As it is well known, the Constitutional Treaty never entered into force. Instead, the Lisbon Treaty was drafted, adopted, and came into effect in 2009. The Lisbon Treaty adopted the abovementioned wording on religious inheritance, Article 1, and this was inserted into the preamble of the TEU. The impact of the new wording has been described as follows:[45]

> This approach involves, in contrast to strictly secular public orders, the recognition of a religious element to the Union's constitutional values and public morality. On the other hand, the reference to religion is balanced by references to cultural and humanist influences, the latter of which have, as Taylor has argued, functioned so as to reduce the influence of religion over public life in Europe. Furthermore, these religious and humanist influences are recognised in their instrumental capacity as contributors to the emergence of values such as respect for individual rights, democracy, equality etc.

And further:[46]

> In contrast to religiously based constitutions such as the Irish Constitution which defines its ultimate notion of the good in explicitly religious terms, the Preamble to the Lisbon Treaty portrays democracy and respect for individual rights as the ultimate good to which Europe's cultural, religious and humanist influences have contributed. Thus, the role accorded to Europe's religious inheritance is substantially counterbalanced by ideas which owe much to humanist notions of human self-government. As the text of the Preamble makes clear, this balance between religious and humanist influences is also influenced by cultural factors.

---

45 See Ronan McCrea, "The Recognition of Religion within the Constitutional and Political Order of the European Union," *LEQS Paper*, no. 10 (September 2009), 6.
46 See McCrea, "The Recognition of Religion," 6.

Viewed from a Nordic perspective, it is interesting that the Nordic countries together with secular countries such as France pushed and voted against directly including Europe's Christian roots in the EU treaties.

Turning to the CJEU, a recent judgment is extremely interesting in relation to the EU constitutional identity. In the Vera Egenberger judgment, Case C-414/16 of April 17, 2018, the CJEU stated that prohibition of discrimination based on religion is a general principle of EU law:[47]

> *The prohibition of all discrimination on grounds of religion or belief is mandatory as a general principle of EU law.* That prohibition, which is laid down in Article 21(1) of the Charter, is sufficient in itself to confer on individuals a right which they may rely on as such in disputes between them in a field covered by EU law (see, with respect to the principle of non-discrimination on grounds of age, judgment of 15 January 2014, Association de médiation sociale, C-176/12, EU:C:2014:2, paragraph 47).
>
> As regards its mandatory effect, Article 21 of the Charter is no different, in principle, from the various provisions of the founding Treaties prohibiting discrimination on various grounds, even where the *discrimination derives from contracts between individuals* (see, by analogy, judgment of 8 April 1976, Defrenne, 43/75, EU:C:1976:56, paragraph 39; of 6 June 2000, Angonese, C-281/98, EU:C:2000:296, paragraphs 33 to 36; of 3 October 2000, Ferlini, C-411/98, EU:C:2000:530, paragraph 50; and of 11 December 2007, International Transport Workers' Federation and Finnish Seamen's Union, C-438/05, EU:C:2007:772, paragraphs 57 to 61) [emphasis added by author].[48]

Since prohibition of discrimination based on religion is a general principle of EU law, it has the same legal effect as the treaties, including primacy over national legislation and constitutions (seen from an EU law perspective). Furthermore, as mentioned in paragraph 77, the principle also applies to cases which involve two private parties or individuals. Until now, only the principle against age discrimination has been accorded such a status in the Mangold case, Mangold C-144/04. However, the CJEU also states:

---

[47] See Luísa Lourenço, "Religion, Discrimination, and the EU General Principles' Gospel: Egenberger," *Common Market Law Review* 56, no. 1 (2019): 193-208 and Sune Klinge, "'Religion is the new black'—et farvel til fagbevægelsens kampdag?," *Rule of Law* (blog), http://www.ruleoflaw.dk/sune-klinge-om-mangold-ajos-doktrinen-religion-is-the-new-black-et-farvel-til-fagbevaegelsens-kampdag/.

[48] C-414/16, *Vera Egenberger v Evangelisches Werk für Diakonie und Entwicklung eV*, paras. 76-77.

> In the light of those considerations, the answer to Question 3 is that Article 4 (2) of Directive 2000/78 must be interpreted as meaning that the genuine, legitimate and justified occupational requirement it refers to *is a requirement that is necessary and objectively dictated, having regard to the ethos of the church or organisation concerned, by the nature of the occupational activity concerned or the circumstances in which it is carried out,* and cannot cover considerations which have no connection with that ethos or with the right of autonomy of the church or organisation. That requirement must comply with the *principle of proportionality* [emphasis added by author] [49]

This means that the national courts must balance the prohibition against discrimination with requirements necessary and objectively dictated regarding the ethos of the church. In a comment to a blog on the Egenberger judgment by Sune Klinge,[50] Lisbet Christoffersen has emphasized that not only is this practice in accordance with case law from the ECtHR, it is also in accordance with Article 70 of the Danish Constitution, which prohibits discrimination based on religion.[51] According to Ronan McCrea in a 2016 article:[52]

> there is a high degree of convergence but that the broader remit of the Luxembourg Court means that its approach to religion will not be restricted to following that of the ECtHR. In particular there is scope for significant differences between the two courts on the question of a "ministerial exemption" in relation to the protection of the rights of employees of religious bodies and the question of indirect discrimination on grounds of religion or belief. These differences highlight the degree to which restricting indirect discrimination on religious grounds draws on ideas of collective disadvantage which are distinct from (and somewhat in tension with) the right to freedom of religion and belief as interpreted by the ECtHR which has seen religious freedom as primarily an individual right that applies equally to all forms of belief.

---

49 C-414/16, *Vera Egenberger v Evangelisches Werk für Diakonie und Entwicklung eV*, para. 69. [Emphasis added by author.]
50 Klinge, "'Religion is the new black'."
51 Klinge, "'Religion is the new black'."
52 See Ronan McCrea, "Singing from the Same Hymn Sheet? What the Differences between the Strasbourg and Luxembourg Courts Tell Us about Religious Freedom, Non-Discrimination and the Secular State," *Oxford Journal of Law and Religion* 5, no. 2 (2016): 183-210. See also Lourenço, "Religion, Discrimination and the EU General Principles' Gospel," 193-208.

Interestingly, the line set out by the CJEU in the Egenberger case has since been followed in the IR case, C-68/17, and the very recent Cresco Investigation case, C-193/17.[53] These cases confirm that the prohibition against discrimination based on religion is a general EU principle, that the national courts must balance the prohibition against discrimination with requirements necessary and objectively dictated having regard to the ethos of the religious community[54], and that the principle can be applied in cases concerning two private parties.

Having looked briefly at EU constitutional identity in the field of religion, we move on to cast a glance at whether EU member states can protect their constitutional identity in the field of religion. Article 4, Part 2, on constitutional identity, can be relevant in cases concerning religion. For instance, in the Samira Achbita case, Case C-157/15, General Advocate Kokott expressed the following opinion:

> Finally, it is important, when interpreting and applying the principle of equal treatment, to have regard also to the national identities of Member States inherent in their fundamental structures, both political and constitutional (Article 4(2) TEU). In relation to an issue such as that under consideration here, this may mean that, in Member States such as France, where secularism has constitutional status and therefore plays an instrumental role in social cohesion too, the wearing of visible religious symbols may legitimately be subject to stricter restrictions (even in the private sector and generally in public spaces) than in other Member States the constitutional provisions of which have a different or less distinct emphasis in this regard.[55]

The CJEU did not refer to Article 4, Part 2. Seen from a Nordic perspective, it is interesting that Kokott refers to the fact that secularism has constitutional status in France, in contrast to member states *where the constitutional provisions have a different or less distinct emphasis in this regard*. This is also in line with Bogdandy and Schill: "Thus, only elements somehow enshrined in national constitutions

---

53 See C-193/17, *Cresco Investigation GmbH v Markus Achatzi*, ECLI:EU:C:2019:43, and C-68/17, *IR v JQ*, ECLI:EU:C:2018:696, and Sune Klinge, "Er helligdagsbetaling kun for (ret)troende? Om Cresco-dommen og juridisk frihåndstegning," *Rule of Law* (blog), January 22, 2019, http://www.ruleoflaw.dk/er-helligdagsbetaling-kun-for-rettroende-om-cresco-dommen-og-juridisk-frihaandstegning/.
54 This applies to all registered religions, both minority and majority religions. Egenberger considered atheists, while the IR-case considered Catholics, and Cresco considered a minority religion (2% of the population).
55 C-157/15, *Samira Achbita, Centrum voor gelijkheid van kansen en voor racismebestrijding v G4S Secure Solutions NV*, ECLI:EU:C:2017:203, para. 125.

or in domestic constitutional processes can be relevant for Article 4(2) TEU".[56] The constitutional provisions, however, only give a first indication of what national identity means for each member state. What also needs to be looked at is the jurisprudence of national constitutional courts. In this context, decisions on the relationship between EU law and domestic constitutional law play a particularly important role. They illustrate best the areas of actual and potential conflict. After all, it was often the challenge of European integration that brought to the fore the issue of national identity.[57] With regard to Germany, in the German Lisbon judgment the German Constitutional Court has emphasized the status of churches, religion, and ideological communities as having partly democratic self-determination:[58]

> Finally, democratic self-determination relies on the possibility to assert oneself in one's own cultural area, especially relevant in decisions made concerning the school and education system, family law, language, certain areas of media regulation, and the status of churches and religious and ideological communities.

The need for a clear expression of constitutional identity also indirectly follows from Commission v Poland, Case C-165/08. The CJEU stated that

> it is sufficient to hold that the Republic of Poland, upon which the burden of proof lies in such a case, has failed, in any event, to establish that the true purpose of the contested national provisions was in fact to pursue the religious and ethical objectives relied upon.[59]

Bogdandy and Schill interpret the judgment in the following way: Even though the CJEU explicitly reserved for itself the right to rule on the question of whether moral or ethical considerations could allow a member state to derogate from an obligation under secondary EU law, at the very least the citation above indicates

> an openness of the Court to consider possibilities for Member States to derogate from secondary EU law if this serves to protect certain fundamental principles affected but not considered by the content of the secondary EU measure in question.

---

56   See Bogdandy and Schill, "Overcoming Absolute Primacy," 1430.
57   Bogdandy and Schill, "Overcoming Absolute Primacy," 1433.
58   See the judgment from the German Federal Constitutional Court of June 30, 2009, para. 260: www.bundesverfassungsgericht.de/SharedDocs/Downloads/EN/2009/06/es20090630_2bve000208en.pdf?__blob=publicationFile&v=1.
59   C-165/08, *Commission v Poland*, ECLI:EU:C:2009:473, para. 51.

> If the values invoked by Poland had formed part of Poland's national identity, the duty to respect that national identity under Article 4(2) TEU could in our view have provided a legal basis for Poland to derogate from the obligation to implement the Directive in question, provided that non-compliance with the EU Directive was proportionate in view of the conflicting principles.[60]

Interestingly, the general principle of a prohibition against discrimination based on religion, which the CJEU formulated in the Egenberger case, is hierarchically on the same level as the treaties and not just part of secondary EU legislation.

Given this background, it seems that, if the Nordic countries want to strengthen their chances of protecting "Nordic secularism" or other Nordic positions with regard to religion as part of Nordic constitutional identity, they must make the Nordic identity clear in the constitutional texts, and/or the Nordic Supreme Courts must become more active in defining such identity in their judgments on the relationship between EU law and domestic Constitutional Law. Such a development might not be in accordance with the way in which the role of religion in society is described in all the Nordic constitutions and with how the role of courts is viewed in the Nordic countries. However, not only with regard to the role of religion in society, but also regarding other features of constitutional identity which the Nordic countries might want to protect, they will need to consider whether the constitutional texts and the judgments from the Supreme Courts express these values clearly enough. This is necessary when the national constitutional systems encounter the EU legal system. Otherwise, the Nordic countries will not gain the same protection and influence as other national constitutional orders in the EU. Some of the Nordic constitutions refer directly to a state church or a majority church. However, what this precisely means in relation to Nordic constitutional identity has not (yet) been defined by the Nordic Supreme Courts.

As we have seen in the previous sections of this chapter, some of the Nordic constitutional systems seem to be increasingly influenced by Europeanization and internationalization with regard to substance (for instance, new rights), legal style (for instance, legal argumentation and the role of general legal principles), and constitutional identity (for instance, the role of courts). Over time, this might draw the legal systems closer to each other; thus, the clash between legal systems might not appear as often as in the earlier days of EU integration. However, to imagine that the problem will disappear because of the above-mentioned development is unrealistic. We are looking at a slow process and we cannot

---

60   See Bogdandy and Schill, "Overcoming Absolute Primacy," 1445.

know how far or in which fields it will play out. A final comment might be that it is simply part of the multi-level constitutional order that we have to live with the constant interplays between different national and European legal systems which sometimes seem to clash, sometimes go hand in hand, and sometimes move closer to each other. This also applies to the field of law and religion.

Conclusion

In conclusion, as mentioned above, national constitutional identity as expressed in Article 4, Part 2, TEU, can be derived primarily from the constitution and judgments from the constitutional court and the supreme court, especially on the relationship between EU law and domestic constitutional law. On the one hand, this means that the Nordic countries must be clear regarding their constitutional identity in such sources; of course, this includes the field of religion. On the other hand, it also means that national constitutional identity originates from national sources in the form of the constitution and the judgments from the supreme court. Thus, constitutional identity is not substantively impacted by Europeanization or internationalization itself. European and international law must be accepted into the national legal systems by means of amendments of the constitutional text or by case law from the supreme court. If the Nordic countries inspired by European and international legal systems choose to amend their constitutions to reflect European and international law, for instance by adopting new human rights into their constitutions, or if the Nordic Supreme Courts become more activist, then the constitutional identity of the Nordic countries might be impacted. This also applies to the role of religion in society.

Bibliography

Court of Justice of the European Union
C-26/62, *NV Algemene Transport- en Expeditie Onderneming van Gend & Loos v Netherlands Inland Revenue Administration*, ECLI:EU:C:1963:1.
C-6/64, *Costa v ENEL*, ECLI:EU:C:1964:66
C-144/04, *Werner Mangold v Rüdiger Helm*, ECLI:EU:C:2005:709
C-165/08, *Commission v Poland*, ECLI:EU:C:2009:473
C-441/14, *Dansk Industri (on behalf of Ajos A/S) v Estate of Karsten Eigil Rasmussen*, ECLI:EU:C:2016:278
C-157/15, *Samira Achbita, Centrum voor gelijkheid van kansen en voor racismebestrijding v G4S Secure Solutions NV*, ECLI:EU:C:2017:203

C-68/17, *IR v JQ*, ECLI:EU:C:2018:696

C-414/16, *Vera Egenberger v Evangelisches Werk für Diakonie und Entwicklung eV,* ECLI:EU:C:2018:257

C-193/17, *Cresco Investigation GmbH v Markus Achatzi,* ECLI:EU:C:2019:43

Danish Supreme Court of Justice

Judgment 15/2014, December 6, 2016, available in English at https://domstol.dk/media/2udgvvvb/judgment-15-2014.pdf.

German Federal Constitutional Court

Judgment of June 30, 2009: www.bundesverfassungsgericht.de/SharedDocs/Downloads/EN/2009/06/es20090630_2bve000208en.pdf?__blob=publicationFile&v=1.

Official sources

A Citizens Agenda: Delivering results for Europe, Commission Communication to the European Council COM (2006) 211, 10 May 2006.

Consolidated Version of the Treaty on the European Union (TEU) [2008] OJ C115/13

Ministry of Foreign Affairs of Denmark written submission of 19 December 2014 to the Court of Justice.

Literature

Bogdandy, Armin von, and Stephan Schill. "Overcoming Absolute Primacy: Respect for National Identity under the Lisbon Treaty." *Common Market Law Review* 48, no. 5 (2011): 1417-54.

de Búrca, Gráinne. "The Evolution of EU Human Rights Law." In *The Evolution of EU Law*, edited by Paul Craig and Gráinne de Búrca, 465-97. Oxford: Oxford University Press, 2011.

Calliess, Christian, and Gerhard van der Schyff, eds. *Constitutional Identity in a Europe of Multilevel Constitutionalism*. Cambridge: Cambridge University Press, 2019.

Cornell, Anna Jonsson. "Similar but Different: Comparing the Scrutiny of the Principle of Subsidiarity within the EWM in Denmark, Finland and Sweden." In *National and Regional Parliaments in the EU-Legislative Procedure Post-Lisbon*, edited by Anna Jonsson Cornell and Marco Goldini, 201-24. Oxford: Hart Publishing, 2017.

Jackson, Vicki C. "Comparative Constitutional Law: Methodologies." In *The Oxford Handbook of Comparative Constitutional Law*, edited by Michel Rosenfeld and András Sajó, 54-74. Oxford: Oxford University Press, 2012.

Krunke, Helle. "Impact of EU/EEA on the Nordic Constitutional Systems." In *The Nordic Constitutions: A Comparative and Contextual Study*, edited by Helle Krunke and Björg Thorarensen, 167-202. Oxford: Hart Publishing, 2018.

Krunke, Helle, and Sune Klinge. "The Danish Ajos Case: The Missing Case from Maastricht and Lisbon." *European Papers* 3, no 1 (2018): 157-82.

Krunke, Helle, and Björg Thorarensen, eds. *The Nordic Constitutions: A Comparative and Contextual Study*. Oxford: Hart Publishing, 2018.

Krunke, Helle, and Björg Thorarensen. "Concluding Thoughts." In *The Nordic Constitutions: A Comparative and Contextual Study*, edited by Helle Krunke and Björg Thorarensen, 203-18. Oxford: Hart Publishing, 2018.

Lavapuro, Juha, Tuomas Ojanen, and Martin Scheinin. "Rights-Based Constitutionalism in Finland and the Development of Pluralist Constitutional Review." *International Journal of Constitutional Law* 9, no. 2 (2011): 505-31.

Lourenço, Luísa. "Religion, Discrimination, and the EU General Principles' Gospel: Egenberger." *Common Market Law Review* 56, no. 1 (2019): 193-208.

McCrea, Ronan. "The Recognition of Religion within the Constitutional and Political Order of the European Union." *LEQS Paper*, no. 10 (September 2009).

McCrea, Ronan. "Singing from the Same Hymn Sheet? What the Differences between the Strasbourg and Luxembourg Courts Tell Us about Religious Freedom, Non-Discrimination and the Secular State." *Oxford Journal of Law and Religion* 5, no. 2 (2016): 183-210.

Ojanen, Tuomas. "Human Rights in Nordic Constitutions and the Impact of International Obligations." In *The Nordic Constitutions: A Comparative and Contextual Study*, edited by Helle Krunke and Björg Thorarensen, 133-66. Oxford: Hart Publishing, 2018.

Retfærd 37, no. 4 (2014).

Rosenfeld, Michel. *The Identity of the Constitutional Subject: Selfhood, Citizenship, Culture, and Community*. New York: Routledge, 2010.

Smith, Eivind. "Judicial Review of Legislation." In *The Nordic Constitutions: A Comparative and Contextual Study*, edited by Helle Krunke and Björg Thorarensen, 107-32. Oxford: Hart Publishing, 2018.

Suksi, Markku. "Common Roots of Nordic Constitutional Law?" In *The Nordic Constitutions: A Comparative and Contextual Study*, edited by Helle Krunke and Björg Thorarensen, 9-42. Oxford: Hart Publishing, 2018.

Thorarensen, Björg. "Mechanisms for Parliamentary Control of the Executive." In *The Nordic Constitutions: A Comparative and Contextual Study*, edited by Helle Krunke and Björg Thorarensen, 67-106. Oxford: Hart Publishing, 2018.

Tuori, Kaarlo. *Critical Legal Positivism*. Aldershot: Ashgate, 2002.

Zahle, Henrik. *Dansk forfatningsret: Institutioner og regulering*. Copenhagen: Christian Ejlers' Forlag, 2001.

Webpages

ECAS. "DEMOS—Democratic Efficacy and the Varieties of Populism in Europe." Accessed April 11, 2019. https://ecas.org/projects/demos.

Klinge, Sune. "'Religion is the new black'—et farvel til fagbevægelsens kampdag?" *Rule of Law* (blog). May 1, 2018. http://www.ruleoflaw.dk/sune-klinge-om-mangold-ajos-doktrinen-religion-is-the-new-black-et-farvel-til-fagbevaegelsens-kampdag/.

Klinge, Sune. "Er helligdagsbetaling kun for (ret)troende? Om Cresco-dommen og juridisk frihåndstegning." *Rule of Law* (blog). January 22, 2019. http://www.ruleoflaw.dk/er-helligdagsbetaling-kun-for-rettroende-om-cresco-dommen-og-juridisk-frihaandstegning/.

13. A Minor Disturbance? Nordic Approaches to Minority Religion

Helge Årsheim

Introduction

At the Northern extremes of Europe, Iceland, Norway, Finland, Sweden, and Denmark have long been colloquially known as "Norden", or the Nordic region. To the rest of the world, differences between these countries tend to be negligible or non-existent, boundaries between states are often mistaken or simply ignored. This is not surprising: from the outside, the region appears to be relatively homogenous and harmonious, politically stable, and thriving in social, material, and economic terms. While these characteristics can be backed up by statistical evidence, they can also sometimes obscure the inter-Nordic diversity that exists in parallel to these overarching similarities. These differences are located on numerous fronts, from the more obvious, such as the difference in population size, with Iceland at 348 450 (2018)[1] and Sweden at 10 151 588 inhabitants (2018),[2] to differences in political orientation. The western states of Iceland, Norway and Denmark were founding members of NATO, while Sweden and Finland have been neutral and non-affiliated. These differences can be traced to their divergent histories as Great Powers (Denmark and Sweden) or as colonial possessions and relative peripheries (Iceland, Norway, and Finland).

One of the lesser known and less-researched aspects of Nordic diversity concerns the role of ethnic, religious, and linguistic minorities. Like so much else in the region, the social, political, and legal management of such minorities has been doubly marked by convergence and divergence. Convergences have

---

1 "Population—key figures 1703-2018," Statistics Iceland, accessed June 22, 2018, http://px.hagstofa.is/pxen/pxweb/en/Ibuar/Ibuar__mannfjoldi__1_yfirlit__yfirlit_mannfjolda/MAN00000.px.
2 "Population Statistics," Statistics Sweden, accessed June 22, 2018, http://www.scb.se/en/finding-statistics/statistics-by-subject-area/population/population-composition/population-statistics/#_Keyfigures.

occurred as consequences of larger social changes that have affected all the countries in the region simultaneously, such as rising numbers of immigrants and refugees in the last two decades, and by inter-Nordic cooperation in policymaking towards groups like the indigenous Sami in the North. Divergences, on the other hand, have occurred due to country-specific, internal conditions that range from different orientations at the international level to domestic political expediency.

Across the region, the composition and interrelationship of majorities and minorities have changed in tandem with the terms and criteria used to set minorities apart from the mainstream. These changes have occurred in interaction with the growth of international regulatory regimes to which the countries in the region have become part. The Council of the League of Nations was responsible for the agreement in 1923 that Swedish would be the official language of the Åland islands as a safeguard against Finnish assimilationist policies following the formal recognition of the islands as parts of the Finnish nation-state after the conclusion of World War I. Similarly, the Danish understanding that the state could and should exercise "custodianship" of the indigenous population in Greenland originates not only in domestic political decisions, but in the exclusion of the overseas territories from the Treaty of Kiel after the Napoleonic Wars granted the Danish state full sovereignty over the island. This sovereignty was confirmed by the International Court of Justice (ICJ) in its decision to deny Norwegian claims of sovereignty over East Greenland in 1933.[3]

In the decades following World War II, Nordic approaches to the management of minorities have developed in ever closer interaction with their participation in international regulatory regimes. From the explicit protections for the rights of minorities in the *International Covenant on Civil and Political Rights* (1966, ICCPR) and the *International Convention on the Elimination of Racial Discrimination* (1965, ICERD) to the ILO *Indigenous and Tribal Peoples Convention* (1989) and the Council of Europe *Framework Convention for the Protection of National Minorities* (1995), policies and legislation on the rights and entitlements of minorities have been shaped in conversation with legislation and jurisprudence developed at the regional and international levels. The incorporation of these rights and entitlements have happened in fits and starts: while Nordic states have signed and ratified most of these instruments, their approaches to the adoption and implementation of binding legislation to give effect to their provisions has been marked by differing priorities and approaches.

---

3   Permanent Court of International Justice, *Legal Status of Eastern Greenland (Denmark v Norway)*, 1933 [1933] P.C.I.J. Ser. A/B, No. 53, 71.

This chapter takes as its starting point the adoption and implementation of international standards that regulate the relationship between religious minority communities and the wider society in the Nordic region in order to address the larger question of whether a more or less unified approach that favors the "secularity of law" can be detected in the legal systems of these countries. More specifically, the chapter explores whether the characteristics of "secularity$^{\text{meaning3}}$" in the tripartite definition of secularity developed by Charles Taylor are evident in laws on minority rights in the Nordic region. While Taylor has conceded that this assertion is limited to the region dominated by "Latin Christendom", he has also acknowledged that this region, which is mostly centered around the "North Atlantic world" contains considerable diversity,[4] and the Nordic region would appear to be one of the sub-units of this division that may differ from the majority. Under secularity$^{\text{meaning3}}$, the conditions for personal belief have changed distinctively from those of earlier ages, as the "buffered self", perceiving itself as a bounded entity distinct from its surroundings, has taken center stage, replacing an earlier, more "porous" self that was more vulnerable to external, mythical forces.[5] Consequently, under secularity$^{\text{meaning3}}$, the primary locus of "religion" is in the minds of believers, and if the legal frameworks in place in the Nordic region for the protection of minority religion were to be fully in line with secularity$^{\text{meaning3}}$, they would have to take the personal beliefs of individual members of minority communities as their starting point.

The question of how well Nordic legal protection for minority religions is aligned with the concept of secularity$^{\text{meaning3}}$ will be explored in this chapter by examining how these countries have adopted and implemented legal rules that regulate the religious identity, beliefs, and practices of minority communities. Importantly, these processes are not singular or unidirectional within each country, but take place through the continued interaction between and beyond the Nordic region, at the European and at the international levels of governance, all of which provide different standards for the management of religious minorities. While this chapter draws on earlier research on the interaction between international and domestic norms in general[6] and specifically in the Nordic region,[7] it also elaborates and expands upon these analyses, discussing patterns of legislative change in relation to the question of the secularity of law.

---

4   Charles Taylor, *A Secular Age* (London: The Belknap Press, 2007), 29.
5   Taylor, *A Secular Age*, 38.
6   Will Kymlicka, "The Internationalization of Minority Rights," *International Journal of Constitutional Law* 6, no. 1 (2008): 1-32.
7   Lauri Hannikainen, "The Status of Minorities, Indigenous Peoples and Immigrant and Refugee Groups in Four Nordic States," *Nordic Journal of International Law* 65, no. 1 (1996):

Notably, the minority concept is not indigenous to the legal systems of the Nordic region, but has been imported from abroad as part of the large-scale internationalization of law that took place over the course of the 19th and 20th centuryies. Although the term "minority" in itself was lacking in the legal lexicon of the Nordic countries, several initiatives to regulate and manage a variety of different groups that diverged from the perceived "majority" of citizens were devised in the region prior to the introduction of the term "minority." From the Protestant Reformations onwards, communities adhering to other religious traditions, such as Catholics and Jews, were subject to measures regulating everything from their religious dress and practices to their access to the territories under state jurisdiction.[8]

Other groups subject to regulatory measures included the travelers in the region: the Roma, Romani, and Gypsy and Tater communities, all of which were targeted by aggressive laws against vagrancy well into the 20th century. The substantial migration westward of Finnish citizens settling in Sweden and the eastern parts of Norway led to suspicions of a gradual demographic invasion, which in turn led to repressive measures against these minorities, particularly in terms of denying them access to formal ownership of land. Finally, the Sami in Northern Norway, Sweden, and Finland and the Inuit in Greenland were subject to a combination of missionary and assimilatory measures from the 18th century onwards, eradicating local religious beliefs, languages, customs, and cultural expressions in the process. In the modern era, the majority of these regulations have been adjusted or rolled back in their entirety. Parallel to the dwindling regulatory interest in these "old" and established minorities, however, all the Nordic states have begun strictly regulating the access of "new" minorities in their jurisdictions, primarily refugees and asylum seekers, whose influx has steadily increased since the 1990s.

Although the tokens that set some segments of society apart from the rest to form distinctive minorities have shifted over time according to local and regional conditions, the rapid internationalization of law that followed in the years after World War II has led to the development, dissemination, and implementation of a global lexicon of minority characteristics. The relative attention paid to each of these characteristics and their internal relationships can be traced through the increased willingness among states to sign and ratify international treaties

---

1-71.

8   For a general overview of the management of minorities in the Nordic region, see Sven Tägil, ed., *Ethnicity and Nation Building in the Nordic World* (Carbondale, IL/ Edwardsville, IL: Southern Illinois University Press, 1995).

that provide some form of minority protection. In the following section, this chapter traces the evolution of the global lexicon of minority characteristics, summarizing its main features and how it has travelled to the Nordic region through local legal adjustments. Following this overview, the "secularity" of this lexicon as it has been developed in the Nordic region will be discussed critically, followed by a summary and conclusion.

Discrimination

Despite the exclusion of minorities as rights-holders in the *Universal Declaration of Human Rights* (1948), the gradual decolonization of African and Asian countries and the increased criticism against racial segregation in South Africa and the United States helped propel racial discrimination to the forefront of the international legislative efforts in the 1960s, culminating in the adoption of the *International Convention on the Elimination of Racial Discrimination* (ICERD) in 1965.

ICERD was the first major international instrument to influence Nordic legislation on minorities directly. The treaty, which was ratified throughout the region by 1971, requires all states to "bring to an end" racial discrimination by any persons, groups, or organizations, using "all appropriate means, including legislation".[9] The convention originated in a resolution adopted by the UN General Assembly in 1960 in response to "manifestations of racial, religious and national hatred".[10] While the original draft convention circulated at the General Assembly concerned both religious and racial hatred, the resulting convention was limited to covering racial discrimination.[11]

The implementation of the ICERD represented a new challenge to the Nordic countries, whose policy cooperation, particularly at the international level, was already extensive by the time the instrument was signed and ratified.[12] In order to coordinate their implementation efforts, a Nordic commission was established

---

9   See United Nations General Assembly, *International Convention on the Elimination of Racial Discrimination,* A/RES/2106(XX)A-B, 21 December 1965, Article 2(d).
10 United Nations General Assembly, *Manifestations of racial and national hatred*, A/RES/1510(XV), 12 December 1960.
11 See Malcolm D. Evans, *Religious Liberty and International Law in Europe* (Cambridge: Cambridge University Press, 1997) and Brice Dickson, "The United Nations and Freedom of Religion," *International and Comparative Law Quarterly* 44, no. 2 (1995): 327-57.
12 In 1962, the five countries entered into a cooperative treaty, colloquially known as the "Helsingfors treaty", regulating cooperation across a broad range of issues. It was signed on March 23 1962 and entered into force July 1 1962. See "Samarbeidsavtale mellom Norge,

in 1966 to review existing legislation and propose amendments and new legislation where needed. Norway, Sweden, and Denmark already had legislation prohibiting racial hatred on their books: Norway amended §135 of the 1902 *Penal Act* in 1960, as a direct response to the same incidents of anti-Semitism that inspired the ICERD, while Denmark and Sweden had similar provisions in place by 1939 and 1948, respectively.[13]

Nordic prohibitions against expressions of hatred have never shed the religious component that became impossible at the international level, retaining prohibitions against both racial and religious hatred that remain on the books to this day. Significantly, from the earliest iterations of prohibitions against religious and racial hatred, several of the Nordic countries relied on a "declaration of faith"[14] as the object of protection, rather than the more generic term "religion", which caused so much consternation during the negotiations towards the ICERD. This specific terminology has a long prehistory in Nordic legislation and jurisprudence, as the legal protection of the declaration of faith was coterminous with the protection of the monarchy during the centuries of absolutism that followed in the region in the wake of the Protestant Reformations.[15] It would also seem to bring the Nordic legal approach to religion in discrimination law in line with the conditions that prevail under the notion of "secularity^{meaning3}" developed by Taylor, in which the "buffered self" is empowered to determine his or her religion quite autonomously.

Danmark, Finland, Island og Sverige [Helsingforsavtalen]," *Lovdata,* accessed June 25, 2018, https://lovdata.no/dokument/NL/lov/1962-03-23-2.

13 Per Haave, "Ingen rasediskriminering av "tatere"? Om Norges ratifisering av FNs rasediskrimineringskonvensjon i 1970," in *Assimilering og motstand: Norsk politikk overfor taterne/romanifolket fra 1850 til i dag; Vedlegg til NOU 2015:7* (Oslo: Kommunal- og moderniseringsdepartementet, 2015), 34.

14 *Trosbekjennelse* (Norwegian).

15 Sweden remained absolutist until 1809, Denmark until 1848. In Sweden, the 1593 Uppsala Synod laid down the foundations of the Swedish confession of faith, later to be confirmed in the 1686 *Church Law.* In Denmark-Norway, a similar statement of the foundations of the faith was laid out in the Church Ordinances of 1537 and 1539, later to be confirmed in the *Danish* (1683) and *Norwegian* (1687) *Law* of King Christian V. These laws spelled out the conditions for absolutism quite clearly, and the preeminence of the declaration of faith within this system is evident. The religion to be allowed within the dominion must be based on the "Holy Biblical Scripture, the Apostolic, Nicene and Athanasian Creeds, and the unchanged Augsburg Confession, given in 1530, and Luther's Small Cathechism" (*Hellige Bibelske Skrift, det Apostoliske, Nicænishe og Athanasii Symbolis, og den Uforandrede Aar et tusind fem hundrede og tredive overgiven Augsburgiske Bekiendelse, og Lutheri liden Catechismo*). The provision in *Norwegian Law* 2-1 remains valid law in Norway, albeit only as a statement of the theological foundations of the Church of Norway. See also Bo Stråth, "Nordic Modernity: Origins, Trajectories and Prospects." *Thesis Eleven* 77, no. 1 (2004): 5-23.

With the demise of absolutism in the 19th century, legal protections for declarations of faith were severed from their intimate connection to the monarchies of the Nordic region, but were resurrected in the form of regulations that targeted blasphemy and the defamation of religion. Across the region, these laws targeted the denigration or belittlement of God, and/or more general expressions of faith.[16] Importantly, these provisions were moved from the basic laws and constitutional acts of the countries to the category of criminal laws. Punishments for transgressions were gradually reduced from the death penalty during the period of absolutism to smaller fines and strictly limited terms of imprisonment in the 19th century. Over the course of the 20th century, laws against blasphemy and defamation have gradually been expanded from the sole protection of the majority religion to protections available for all religious communities. With the sole exception of Finland, which has seen some jurisprudence on this topic in recent decades, these laws have now been abolished across the region. Protections offered by anti-hate speech legislation have been considered sufficient.[17]

In current anti-hate speech legislation, the criminal law in Sweden offers protection for "declarations of faith", while Danish and Finnish criminal law offers protection for "belief" and "religion". The Norwegian law was revised from "declaration of faith" in 2006 in order to offer protection for "religion or belief" in order to bring the terminology of the law better in line with the language used in international human rights law. Although this switch may seem superfluous, as the protections available for religion within international human rights law also tend to be limited to matters of belief, this change of terminology potentially widens the scope of protected persons: As a wider and more inclusive concept, the category of "religion" can be construed as protecting religious identity and group membership, not least due to the upturn in the amount of legal theory and jurisprudence dealing with the "intersectionality" between different forms of identity.[18] Additionally, the "religion" under protection by the different provisions of international human rights law has too long been dominated by the "freedom of religion or belief umbrella", which tends to

---

[16] For an overview of contemporary Nordic blasphemy laws, see Jeroen Temperman and András Koltay, eds., *Blasphemy and Freedom of Expression. Comparative, Theoretical and Historical Reflections after the Charlie Hebdo Massacre* (Cambridge: Cambridge University Press, 2017), especially chapters by Årsheim, Äystö, and Binderup and Lassen.

[17] Despite this region-wide development, there have been suggestions both in Sweden and Norway to expand hate speech legislation in order to offer protection against the "defamation" of religion.

[18] Nazila Ghanea, "Intersectionality and the Spectrum of Racist Hate Speech: Proposals to the UN Committee on the Elimination of Racial Discrimination," *Human Rights Quarterly* 35, no. 4 (2013): 935-54.

boil down complicated matters of religious adherence and group membership to an individual elective (see below).[19]

Minorities

With the entry into force of the *International Covenant on Civil and Political Rights* (ICCPR) in 1976, the Nordic countries were required to review their legislation on minorities from a more comprehensive point of view than the ICERD, as Article 27 of the ICCPR provided that ratifying states "in which ethnic, religious or linguistic minorities exist" were obliged to make sure that "persons belonging to such minorities shall not be denied the right, in community with the other members of their group, to enjoy their own culture, to profess and practise their own religion, or to use their own language". Unlike the ICERD, which is strictly limited to racial and ethnic discrimination, the ICCPR required states to accommodate a broader set of rights for a larger section of society: According to the UN Human Rights Committee (HRC), which has been tasked with the oversight of the ICCPR, Article 27 "is distinct from, and additional to, all the other rights which, as individuals in common with everyone else, they are already entitled to enjoy under the Covenant".[20] The protections required by the article cannot be limited to nationals, nor can they be exclusive to groups with longer residency. Crucially, this means that refugees, immigrants, and even visitors with shorter stays fall within the scope of the article, as long as they belong to a recognizable minority united by a distinct religion, culture, or language.

At the time when the ICCPR entered into force, the general approach among the Nordic countries to the role of minorities within their countries remained one of integration and assimilation, rather than the accommodation and recognition required under the ICCPR. The Nordic drive towards integration and assimilation of minorities, which began a steady decline following the conclusion of World War II, was mostly centered on language as the key factor distinguishing minority communities from majority society. While minorities like the Sami and the Inuit were religiously distinct from the majority population until the 18th century, missionary and colonizing policies practically eradicated their

---

19   Nazila Ghanea, "Are Religious Minorities Really Minorities?," *Oxford Journal of Law and Religion* 1, no. 1 (2012): 57-79.
20   United Nations Human Rights Committee (HRC), *General Comment Adopted by the Human Rights Committee under Article 40, Paragraph 4 of the International Covenant on Civil and Political Rights*. General Comment No. 23 (50) (art.27). CCPR/C/21/Rev.1/Add.5. 26 April 1994.

beliefs and practices, of which only scattered remnants now exist. Cultural practices, on the other hand, occupied a sort of middle position, with the non-sedentary lifestyles of communities like the Travelers, Roma, Tatar, and Sami being frowned upon and sought amended through policy measures, although never eradicated in practice.

Although specific provisions for the protection of the rights of minorities had no established counterpart in the legislation of the Nordic countries, the protections required by Article 27 of the ICCPR have gradually although unevenly become recognized in the Nordic region. Domestic legal guarantees have been implemented in order to support the linguistic and cultural rights of specific minorities, in particular the Sami and Inuit, who have become subject to broad-ranging legislation which also grants these groups a certain degree of autonomy in their traditional territories.[21] These concessions have been strongest in relation to language rights, more intermediate in terms of cultural rights, and virtually non-existent in the area of religious rights. The unevenly distributed protections available for different types of minority groups is not unique to the Nordic region, but represents something of an international norm, as the pre-eminence of belief-based notions of religious rights have eclipsed and largely replaced more identity-based protections for religious belonging.[22]

Indigenous Peoples

While the minority issue was reintroduced to international human rights law through the ICCPR in 1976, the rights of indigenous peoples developed along a parallel track under the auspices of the International Labor Organization (ILO), which began adopting standards to protect indigenous peoples' rights in the 1920s as a subset of its larger work of protecting labor rights globally. Recognizing the particular challenges faced by the exploitation of workers belonging to indigenous peoples, the ILO continued working with indigenous rights issues through the interwar years, acting as the lead agency in the "Andean Indian Program", a large-scale development project in Latin America conducted from

---

21 Sami law is a relatively new field of research. For an overview, see Christina Allard and Susann Funderud Skogvang, *Indigenous Rights in Scandinavia: Autonomous Sami Law* (London and New York: Routledge, 2015).
22 The paramount importance of belief-centered notions of religion has prevailed, despite the "comeback" of minority rights through the ICERD and the ICCPR.

the 1950s to the 1970s.[23] One of the outcomes of this project was the 1957 *Convention concerning the Protection and Integration of Indigenous and Other Tribal and Semi-Tribal Populations in Independent Countries*. This convention, while important in providing a new vocabulary for the notion of indigeneity as a subject of international law, is today widely regarded as assimilationist and insufficiently cognizant of the right to self-determination among indigenous peoples.[24] The specific rights of indigenous peoples were spelled out in greater detail more than 30 years later, with the passing of the landmark 1989 *Indigenous and Tribal Peoples Convention*, which remains the most ambitious and far-reaching binding legal instrument for the protection of indigenous peoples' rights.

Unlike minorities, for whom the characteristics that set them apart from majority society tend to be language, culture, or religion, the notion of indigeneity is more open-ended, yet also more comprehensive. Article 1 of the ILO Convention[25] identifies self-identification as indigenous as the core criterion, while also establishing that the term applies to "tribal peoples in independent countries whose social, cultural and economic conditions distinguish them from other sections of the national community, and whose status is regulated wholly or partially by their own customs or traditions or by special laws or regulations". Under this definition, indigeneity is not limited to peoples that have become subject to colonizing efforts, but the term also encompasses groups that have otherwise been set apart for cultural, social, or economic reasons. Although religion does not play a decisive role in the recognition of indigeneity in this instrument, Article 5 specifies that "a) the social, cultural, religious and spiritual values and practices of these peoples shall be recognised and protected". Unlike protections for minorities and the general population, however, the religious and spiritual values of indigenous peoples are specifically tied up with their collective relationship with the territories they habitually inhabit, a relationship that is spelled out and protected in Article 13: "governments shall respect the special importance for the cultures and spiritual values of the peoples concerned of their relationship with the lands or territories".

In the Nordic region, the ILO Convention has been ratified only by Norway and Denmark, both of which have granted their indigenous populations a sem-

---

23 Lee Swepton, "A New Step in the International Law on Indigenous and Tribal Peoples: ILO Convention No. 169 of 1989," *Oklahoma City University Law Review* 15, no. 3 (1990): 677-714, 680.
24 Benedict Kingsbury, "Indigenous Peoples," *Max Planck Encyclopedia of Public International Law Online*, last modified November 2006, http://opil.ouplaw.com/home/EPIL.
25 International Labor Organization. *Indigenous and Tribal Peoples Convention*, (No. 169), June 27, 1989.

blance of autonomy. While Denmark introduced home rule and an independent parliament in Greenland in 1979, Norway passed its *Sami Act* in 1987, which led to the creation of the Sami Parliament in 1989. Although both the Swedish and the Finnish constitutions recognize the specific rights of the Sami and maintain Sami parliaments, neither has ratified the ILO Convention.

The rights of indigenous peoples were further elaborated at the international level in 2007 when the UN General Assembly adopted the *Declaration on the Rights of Indigenous Peoples* (UNDRIP).[26] Expanding on the protections for the religion of indigenous populations in the ILO Convention, the UNDRIP Article 11 establishes the right to redress "with respect to their cultural, intellectual, religious and spiritual property taken without their free, prior and informed consent or in violation of their laws, traditions and customs". On the religious and spiritual rights of indigenous peoples, Article 12 of the UNDRIP provides that

> Indigenous peoples have the right to manifest, practise, develop and teach their spiritual and religious traditions, customs and ceremonies; the right to maintain, protect, and have access in privacy to their religious and cultural sites; the right to the use and control of their ceremonial objects; and the right to the repatriation of their human remains.

Article 25 further expands on the special relationship between indigenous peoples and their traditional territories, granting their right "to maintain and strengthen their distinctive spiritual relationship with their traditionally owned or otherwise occupied and used lands, territories, waters and coastal seas". Although the UNDRIP is not a legally binding document, it has become a rallying cry for indigenous activists globally and provides the roadmap for the monitoring work being done at the UN Expert Mechanism on the Rights of Indigenous Peoples. All the Nordic countries voted in favor of the declaration in the General Assembly, indicating their will to offer the kinds of protection fleshed out in the instrument.

In their domestic legislation, however, none of the countries have adopted the kinds of guarantees listed in Article 12 in order to provide protection for the rights of indigenous peoples to manifest their religious and spiritual traditions. In the Nordic countries, the rights of indigenous peoples have been primarily related to the maintenance of certain significant cultural practices, notably in hunting and reindeer husbandry, the preservation of indigenous languages,

---

26   United Nations General Assembly, *United Nations Declaration on the Rights of Indigenous Peoples*, A/RES/61/295, 13 September 2007.

and to the autonomy of indigenous communities over their traditional lands. This set of priorities is recognizable in the self-government act concerning the status of Greenland as an autonomous region of Denmark[27] and in the legislative frameworks governing the Sami in Norway, Sweden, and Finland. These three countries have also been negotiating a Nordic Sami Convention since 2011, with signatures and ratification still pending. The draft convention emphasizes the importance of preserving the language, culture, and way of life of the Sami, while also securing their right to a limited degree of autonomy and a right to consultations in matters that concern their affairs.[28]

National Minorities

While the implementation of ICERD and the ICCPR represented the gradual amalgamation of international and domestic legal rules on the rights of minorities, the *Framework Convention for the Protection of Minorities* adopted by the Council of Europe in 1995 required the introduction of a new category of legal regulation. Throughout the convention, the protection offered is directed towards "national minorities", prompting the explicit recognition of a set of minority groups distinct from other, presumably "non-national", minorities, in contrast to the more open-ended and inclusive understanding of minorities under the ICCPR. The convention details a list of rights and entitlements for minorities and encompasses a broad and inclusive notion of both "culture" and "religion". Notably, unlike the ICCPR, Article 5 of the convention stresses that religion is an "essential element of ... identity", while Article 8 safeguards the right to "manifest ... religion or belief". In this way, both the belief-centered notion and the more broadly conceived notion of "religion" are preserved and protected under the instrument.

At the time of ratification, none of the Nordic countries had enacted legislation that protected "national minorities" as a distinctive category. In their reporting to the committee overseeing the implementation of the convention, the states have chosen different paths. Denmark stated upon ratification that the convention would singularly apply to the German minority in South Jutland,

---

27   For an English translation of the act, see *Act on Greenland Self-Government*, Act no. 473 of 12 June 2009, accessed January 14, 2019, https://naalakkersuisut.gl//~/media/Nanoq/Files/Attached%20Files/Engelske-tekster/Act%20on%20Greenland.pdf
28   For an English translation of the convention, see Nordic Saami Convention, 13 January 2007, accessed January 14, 2019, https://www.regjeringen.no/globalassets/upload/aid/temadokumenter/sami/sami_samekonv_engelsk.pdf

comprising of 15-20 000 people. The government of Finland, on the other hand, emphasized that "the existence of a minority does not depend on a declaration by the Government but on the factual situation in the country". Relying on this factual situation, the Finnish government listed Swedish-speaking Finns, Roma, Sami, Jews, Tatars, and Old Russians as sizeable minorities with a presence in Finland, numbering approximately 300 000.

Prompted by the language used in the Framework convention, the Norwegian government devised a new definition of "national" minorities which required a "long-term connection" with the state in question, more specifically a connection of at least 100 years. Under this definition, Norwegian authorities have designated Jews, Kven, Roma/Gypsies, Romani/Travellers, and Skogfinn (i.e., "Forest Finns") as official "national minorities" eligible for the protection in the convention. While the Norwegian government has yet to adopt legislation targeting these groups specifically, it has adopted a range of policy measures addressing the specific challenges of members of these communities. Notably, the Sami are not considered to be a "national minority" due to their status as an indigenous people (see above). Like Norway, Sweden responded to the ratification of the convention by adopting a specific definition of a "national" minority, which also emphasized the duration of the connection between the minority and the state. In Government Bill 1998/99:143 *National Minorities in Sweden*, the government fleshed out the specific rights and entitlements of such minorities. Under this bill, the recognized minorities are the Sami, the Swedish Finns, the Jews, the Roma, and the Tornedalers.

The Multiple Religions of Minority Rights

The development of legal guarantees for the protection of minorities has come in fits and starts, with continuous interaction and adaptation between international trends and domestic legal guarantees. While the absence of minority protections in the UDHR (1948) was formulated in stark opposition to the crucial role of minority rights in the incipient international law in preceding centuries, their ostensible "comeback" in the ICCPR (1966) indicated the perceived need for some form of protection for vulnerable communities that could not be satisfied by the individually oriented protection offered by the UDHR. The further expansion of protection for indigenous peoples against racial discrimination and, more recently, for "national minorities," underscores the perception that law can and should provide specific protection for vulnerable communities that are additional to the protection of human rights law.

The continued strengthening of the rights of minorities has provided domestic legal systems with conceptual and jurisprudential challenges in order to keep pace with international ambitions. In the Nordic region, these challenges have been met with a mixture of enthusiasm and reluctance. While all the countries of the region have implemented the minimum safeguards for minorities required by international law, local adaptations have been notable, with Sweden and Finland not yet opting into the ILO framework for the protection of indigenous peoples, and all the countries of the region choosing different paths in their understanding of what constitutes "national" minorities under the 1995 framework convention.

Among the challenges for the realization of minority rights both at the international level and at the level of domestic adaptations made in order to implement international law, the religion of minorities stands out as one of the most vexing and complicated. Unlike other characteristics that tend to set minorities apart from the mainstream and have become subject to legal protection, such as language, nationality, or ethnicity, religion is frequently considered to be an individual choice, whose realization and practice is preceded by deeply held thoughts, convictions, or beliefs. This distinctive conception of religion as primarily an intellectual, individual concept can be found not only in the UDHR, but also in the European convention on Human Rights (1950) and in the ICCPR. Throughout these instruments, "religion" is primarily a set of beliefs which can never be legitimately limited, complemented by a range of "manifestations" of this belief, such as "worship, observance, practice and teaching," whose limitations are strongly circumscribed.[29]

Despite the expanded notion of religion inherent to subsequent instruments and jurisprudence, the conception of religion as primarily a matter of personal belief is hard to square with provisions that secure the "religious rights" of minorities. This is particularly the case in the so-called "minority within a minority" issue, in which the issuing of rights to collectives risks undermining the same rights of individual members within the collective who may disagree with one or more aspects of how the religious identity in question should be managed and negotiated. The minority-within-minority issue has particularly been raised as a concern for marginalized women within recently arrived migrant communities, but similar tensions can also be traced among historical

---

[29] The eligible limitations listed in the ICCPR include: "Freedom to manifest one's religion or beliefs may be subject only to such limitations as are prescribed by law and are necessary to protect public safety, order, health, or morals or the fundamental rights and freedoms of others."

minorities with regard to decisions on who gets to determine the boundaries of their key characteristics.

In the Nordic context, the question of minority religion has long been ignored, surpassed in recognition and importance by protection based on language and ethnicity. One part of this disinterest became evident during the incorporation of international protections against racial discrimination, where several of the Nordic countries opted for protection that combined racial discrimination and discrimination based on "declarations of faith". Hence, the "religion" eligible for protection in the Nordic region was derived from the individualist, belief-centered notion of religion already protected under provisions in place to secure the freedom of religion or belief for everyone. Similarly, the protection available for minorities under Article 27 of the ICCPR has been applied exclusively to protect the rights of ethnic and linguistic minorities, as have the provisions safeguarding the rights of indigenous peoples and national minorities. As a result of this situation, access to religion-based protection among the many "new" minorities that have settled in the Nordic region is precarious, as religious identity, beliefs, and practice are considered to be a private, individual affair.

Minority Rights and the Secularity of Law

Legal protection for the religious identities and practices of minority communities in the Nordic region are all ostensibly "secular" in the sense of Taylor's "secularity^{meaning3}," whereby citizens are free to choose their own beliefs and identities without state interference (see above). However, given the variety of legal guarantees on offer for the religious expressions and identities of minorities which are additional to the erstwhile robust protection for religious freedom and non-discrimination available for everyone,[30] minorities can choose from a range of different framings of their right claims and corresponding avenues of litigation. They can choose to frame their case as an issue of general religious discrimination, of a specific minority right, of an indigenous rights issue, or of a national minority issue. Depending on which set of rights is activated, different communities of activists, lobbyists, politician and sectors of society may

---

30 All the Nordic countries have ratified the ECHR and the ICCPR and have enacted legislation that turns their provisions on the freedom of religion or belief into binding domestic law. For an overview of the guarantees in question, see Heiner Bielefeldt, Nazila Ghanea, and Michael Wiener, *Freedom of Religion or Belief: An International Law Commentary* (Oxford: Oxford University Press, 2016) and Paul M. Taylor, *Freedom of Religion: UN and European Human Rights Law and Practice* (Cambridge: Cambridge University Press, 2005).

be enlisted for support or may resist the utilization of instruments perceived to be developed for other purposes. The wide selection of jurisprudential options on offer invites "strategic litigation," whereby minorities seeking protection are presented with a wide range of choices that come with different pros and cons for success. These choices are further conditioned by the prevalence of language and ethnicity as the primary markers of minority identity in the Nordic region, further jeopardizing religion-based claims.

Although the diversity of potential frames for rights claims and their attendant supporting communities provide minorities with a degree of self-determination, such diversity also destabilizes the ostensible "secularity" of legislation. By providing minorities with different avenues and frames of reference for the formulation of their claims to equality, lawmakers and the judiciary invite introspective debates within minority communities regarding the self-perception of their religion. A legal claim based on a religious belief, identity, practice, or institution will necessarily be developed and litigated using different categories and procedures, depending on the set of rights chosen. Because of the indeterminacy of these choices, the emancipatory freedom envisaged by Taylor under secularity^{meaning3} may be undermined by the sheer variety of available legal options, inviting in-group debates in which technical know-how and political connections may become more decisive for the final choice of rights set than the perceived "fit" between religious and legal categories. The growing importance of such a technocratically-informed approach to jurisprudence risks leading down the road towards the "colonization of the lifeworld" lamented by Jürgen Habermas as one of the problematic aspects of the ongoing "juridification" of society.[31] According to Habermas, the increasing remit and power of legal and bureaucratic regulations represents a shift away from informal conflict-resolution mechanisms within the communities affected by legislation, which are replaced by the decisions of bureaucrats without the contextual and situational information necessary to make an informed decision at their disposal.[32]

The variety of legal options available for minority communities to gain recognition may not only lead to in-group hostilities and competition but can also jeopardize the efficiency of the legislation adopted. As Robert M. Cover has observed, if the legal categories of regulations are perceived to be too distant

---

31 Jürgen Habermas, *The Theory of Communicative Action*, vol. 2 (Boston: Beacon Press, 1987).
32 For a discussion of juridification and its perceived colonizing force, see Daniel Loick, "Juridification and Politics: From the Dilemma of Juridification to the Paradoxes of Rights," *Philosophy & Social Criticism* 40, no. 8 (2014): 757-78.

from the *nomos* or "normative universe" subscribed to within the minorities under regulation, their binding power will be correspondingly diminished. This binding power will be particularly precarious, according to Cover, if the divide between the founding narratives and mythologies of the majority and minorities of a society becomes too wide—leading not only to the inefficiency of law, but to the loss of legal meaning.[33]

Additionally, legal rights and guarantees introduced to provide minorities with robust protections and increased freedom and equality may be self-defeating, repeating the cyclical "paradox of recognition" identified by Wendy Brown. According to Brown, such paradoxes occur whenever legislators introduce highly specific legislation targeting precarious subgroups in society. Singling out these subgroups as eligible for special protection, they risk encoding and solidifying the very subordination sought to be eliminated.[34] Hence, emancipatory legislation based on identity can potentially end up in a paradox:

> while [rights based on identity] may entail some protection from the most immobilizing features of that designation, it reinscribes the designation as it protects us, and thus enables our further regulation through that designation[35]

Taken together, the critical perspectives offered by Habermas, Cover, and Brown challenge the recognition of minority rights at the conceptual level, unsettling the capacity of law to adhere to a strictly defined notion of "secularity," whether in the sense indicated by Taylor or in a broader sense. Through the development of a set of overlapping and intersecting rules on minority rights that provide different protections for religious beliefs, identities, and practices according to which minority group one belongs to, Nordic approaches to minority rights appear to be unable to live up to the conditions under which "secularity$^{\text{meaning3}}$" can be in effect, as members of minority groups are effectively barred from developing the kind of autonomous "buffered selves" imagined by Taylor.

Importantly, neither of these critical perspectives invalidate, nor refute the notion of minority rights as such—rather, they offer critical tools for the assessment and further refinement of such provisions. More specifically, in the development of minority rights provisions, lawmakers and adjudicators must pay attention to the compatibility between the life worlds of citizens and the

---

33 Robert M. Cover, "The Supreme Court, 1982 Term Foreword: Nomos and Narrative," *Harvard Law Review* 97 (1983): 4-68.
34 Wendy Brown, "Suffering Rights as Paradoxes," *Constellations* 7, no. 2 (2000): 230-41.
35 Brown, "Suffering Rights as Paradoxes."

technical governance required by bureaucracies criticized by Habermas, to the delicate balancing act between state-made norms and the "normative universes" inhabited by different communities stressed by Cover, and to the risk of solidifying and further exoticizing the minority traits sought protected by legislation, as identified by Brown.

Governing Minority Religion in the Nordic Countries

In the decades following World War II legislative and political change in the Nordic region has increasingly taken place in interaction with a large and growing set of international norms and institutions. In this process, the Nordic countries have balanced their domestic legislative frameworks against the norms they have agreed to implement under international law. Despite their long history of regional cooperation in legal matters, the Nordic countries diverge considerably over how they have implemented and applied the international norms that govern the rights of religious minorities. These divergences appear not only in terms of which minorities are eligible for which kinds of protection and how different minorities have fared in the legal systems of each country, but also in the ways in which "religion" as a category of legal regulation is conceptualized and becomes subject to legal regulation and jurisprudence. These differences are evident in how some Nordic countries have retained the term "declaration of faith" in hate speech and anti-discrimination law, in the differing forms of accommodation of the religious practices of minorities, and in their management of indigenous peoples like the Sami and the Inuit. Despite the shared legal culture and institutional frameworks for cooperation in the Nordic countries, members of religious minorities crossing national borders within the region become subject to different sets of rights with each border crossing.

Because of the tendency in both international and Nordic law to consider religion primarily as a matter of personal beliefs, the religions of minorities in the Nordic region have generally not been subject to the kind of additional protection that has been developed for linguistic and ethnic rights. While the question of how minority religions are expressed and played out is of course not determined entirely in the legal sphere, the lack of a unified and coherent legal policy on which aspects of minority religion should be eligible for additional protections crucially affects the ways in which minority religion can gain legal recognition. These effects are evident both in material terms, in which the legal guarantees for minority religion are weak and largely overlooked both by legislators, activists, and the minorities themselves, and in more overarching, conceptual terms, as the minority concept in the Nordic sphere has been almost exclusively tied to language and ethnicity. So far, this state of affairs has not led to significant challenges in the Nordic region, as most resident minorities have relied on the linguistic and ethnic markers that are most efficient in the legal domain, not least because over time many of the minorities in question have adopted the religion of the majority. However, with the considerable influx of recently arrived migrants whose markers of difference from majority society represent a new and unfamiliar assemblage of language, ethnicity, and religion, only time will tell how well developed Nordic legal guarantees for minority rights are to accommodate these kinds of differences.

Bibliography

Permanent Court of International Justice

Legal Status of Eastern Greenland (Denmark v Norway), 1933 [1933] P.C.I.J. Ser. A/B, No. 53, 71.

Official Sources

Act on Greenland Self-Government Act no. 473 of 12 June 2009, accessed January 14, 2019, https://naalakkersuisut.gl//~/media/Nanoq/Files/Attached%20Files/Engelske-tekster/Act%20on%20Greenland.pdf.

International Labor Organization. *Indigenous and Tribal Peoples Convention* (No. 169), 27 June 1989.

Lovdata. "Samarbeidsavtale mellom Norge, Danmark, Finland, Island og Sverige [Helsingforsavtalen]." Accessed June 25, 2018. https://lovdata.no/dokument/NL/lov/1962-03-23-2.

Nordic Saami Convention, 13 January 2007. Accessed January 14, 2019, https://www.regjeringen.no/globalassets/upload/aid/temadokumenter/sami/sami_samekonv_engelsk.pdf.

United Nations General Assembly. *International Convention on the Elimination of Racial Discrimination*, A/RES/2106(XX)A-B, 21 December 1965.

United Nations General Assembly. *Manifestations of racial and national hatred*, A/RES/1510(XV), 12 December 1960.

United Nations General Assembly. *United Nations Declaration on the Rights of Indigenous Peoples*, A/RES/61/295, 13 September 2007.

United Nations Human Rights Committee (HRC), *General Comment Adopted by the Human Rights Committee under Article 40, Paragraph 4 of the International Covenant on Civil and Political Rights*. General Comment No. 23 (50) (art.27). CCPR/C/21/Rev.1/Add.5., 26 April 1994.

Literature

Allard, Christina, and Susann Funderud Skogvang. *Indigenous Rights in Scandinavia: Autonomous Sami Law*. London and New York: Routledge, 2015.

Bielefeldt, Heiner, Nazila Ghanea, and Michael Wiener. *Freedom of Religion or Belief: An International Law Commentary*. Oxford: Oxford University Press, 2016.

Brown, Wendy. "Suffering Rights as Paradoxes." *Constellations* 7, no. 2 (2000): 230-41.

Cover, Robert M. "The Supreme Court, 1982 Term Foreword: Nomos and Narrative". *Harvard Law Review* 97 (1983): 4-68.

Dickson, Brice. "The United Nations and Freedom of Religion." *International and Comparative Law Quarterly* 44, no. 2 (1995): 327-57.

Evans, Malcolm D. *Religious Liberty and International Law in Europe*. Cambridge: Cambridge University Press, 1997.

Ghanea, Nazila. "Are Religious Minorities Really Minorities?" *Oxford Journal of Law and Religion* 1, no. 1 (2012): 57-79.

Ghanea, Nazila. "Intersectionality and the Spectrum of Racist Hate Speech: Proposals to the UN Committee on the Elimination of Racial Discrimination." *Human Rights Quarterly* 35, no. 4 (2013): 935-54.

Haave, Per. "Ingen rasediskriminering av "tatere"? Om Norges ratifisering av FNs rasediskrimineringskonvensjon i 1970." In *Assimilering og motstand: Norsk politikk overfor taterne/romanifolket fra 1850 til i dag; Vedlegg til NOU 2015:7*, 29-61. Oslo: Kommunal- og moderniseringsdepartementet, 2015.

Habermas Jürgen. *The Theory of Communicative Action*. Vol. 2. Boston: Beacon Press, 1987.

Hannikainen, Lauri. "The Status of Minorities, Indigenous Peoples and Immigrant and Refugee Groups in Four Nordic States." *Nordic Journal of International Law* 65, no.1 (1996): 1-71.

Kymlicka, Will. "The Internationalization of Minority Rights." *International Journal of Constitutional Law* 6, no. 1 (2008): 1-32.

Loick, Daniel. "Juridification and Politics: From the Dilemma of Juridification to the Paradoxes of Rights." *Philosophy & Social Criticism* 40, no. 8 (2014): 757-78.

Stråth, Bo. "Nordic Modernity: Origins, Trajectories and Prospects." *Thesis Eleven* 77, no. 1 (2004): 5-23.

Swepton, Lee. "A New Step in the International Law on Indigenous and Tribal Peoples: ILO Convention No. 169 of 1989." *Oklahoma City University Law Review* 15, no. 3 (1990): 677-714.

Taylor, Charles. *A Secular Age*. London: The Belknap Press, 2007.

Taylor, Paul M. *Freedom of Religion: UN and European Human Rights Law and Practice*. Cambridge: Cambridge University Press, 2005.

Temperman, Jeroen, and András Koltay, eds. *Blasphemy and Freedom of Expression Comparative, Theoretical and Historical Reflections after the Charlie Hebdo Massacre*. Cambridge: Cambridge University Press, 2017.

Tägil, Sven, ed. *Ethnicity and Nation Building in the Nordic World*. Carbondale, IL/ Edwardsville, IL: Southern Illinois University Press, 1995.

Webpages

Kingsbury, Benedict. "Indigenous Peoples." *Max Planck Encyclopedia of Public International Law Online*. Last modified November 2006. http://opil.ouplaw.com/home/EPIL.

Statistics Iceland. "Population—key figures 1703-2018." Accessed June 22, 2018. http://px.hagstofa.is/pxen/pxweb/en/Ibuar/Ibuar__mannfjoldi__1_yfirlit__yfirlit_mannfjolda/MAN00000.px.

Statistics Sweden. "Population Statistics." Accessed June 22, 2018. http://www.scb.se/en/finding-statistics/statistics-by-subject-area/population/population-composition/population-statistics/#_Keyfigures.

14. Moving Frontiers: Configuring Religion Law and Religious Law, and Law-Religion Relations

Pamela Slotte

The Constitution of 1919 (*Regeringsformen* 94/1919) of the newly independent Finnish republic formally recognized individual and collective religious freedom and established state neutrality in relation to religion.[1] How things actually looked in practice, however, is another thing. The first Act on the Freedom of Religion (267/1922) came into effect in 1923. According to Leena Sorsa, negative and positive understandings of religious freedom, freedom "from" and "to"

---

1 Pekka Hallberg et al., eds., *Perusoikeudet*, Online library Alma Talent, 2011, accessed May 29, 2019, http://fokus.almatalent.fi/teos/FAIBCXJTBF; *PeVL 12/1982 vp*: Perustuslakivaliokunnan lausunto. According to Juha Seppo, religious freedom as a collective freedom was also guaranteed at the constitutional level through the so-called "church-paragraph" (83§), which mentioned the majority church and confirmed its special legal status. See Juha Seppo, *Uskonnonvapaus 2000-luvun Suomessa* (Helsinki: Edita, 2003), 38-39. In fact, Finland had four "constitutions", or as Markku Suksi has called it, "a multi-documentary formal Constitution" comprising the 1919 Instrument of Government (Constitution) (*Regeringsformen* 94/1919), the 1922 Ministerial Responsibility (Constitution) Act (*Lag angående rätt för riksdagen att granska lagenligheten av medlemmarnas av statsrådet och justitiekanslerns ämbetsåtgärder*), the 1922 Court of the Realm (Constitution) Act (*Lag om riksrätten*), and the 1928 Parliament (Constitution) Act (*Riksdagsordning*). See Markku Suksi, "Common Roots of Nordic Constitutional Law?," in *The Nordic Constitutions: A Comparative and Contextual Study*, ed. Helle Krunke and Björg Thorarensen (Oxford: Hart Publishing, 2018), 27. The 1919 Instrument of Government was the "main" constitution. Through the constitutional reform at the end of the 20th century, this legislation was merged into one law. *KM 1997:13*: Perustuslaki 2000—komitean mietintö, 10; *PeVM 10/1998 vp*: Perustuslakivaliokunnan mietintö, Hallituksen esitys uudeksi Suomen Hallitus-muodoksi, 3-5; *HE 1/1998 vp*: Hallituksen esitys Eduskunnalle uudeksi Suomen Hallitusmuodoksi, 32-33. For an overview of the various stages of the work to thoroughly renew the constitution, the beginnings of which can be traced back to the end of the 1960s, see Ilkka Saraviita, *Perustuslaki 2000: Kommentaariteos uudesta valtiosäännöstä Suomelle* (Helsinki: Lakimiesliiton Kustannus, 2000), 1-45. This chapter has been written as part of the author's academy research fellow project "Management of the Sacred: A Critical Inquiry", funded by the Academy of Finland 2013-2018 (grant number: 265887) and work as vice-director of the Centre of Excellence in Law, Identity and the European Narratives, Academy of Finland 2018-2025 (grant number: 312430).

religion, cross swords throughout the period of independence.[2] Throughout the 20th century, the Act on the Freedom of Religion of 1922 met with resistance from so-called "free thinkers". In addition, various religious minorities have been dissatisfied with the Act from an equality perspective.[3]

The more specific background for the new Act on the Freedom of Religion (453/2003) that was elaborated at the turn of the 21st century is, however, the basic rights reform that was carried out in 1995, the section on freedom of religion and conscience of the new Constitution (731/1999, in force 2000), as well as the international human rights treaties that Finland has ratified, including the European Convention on Human Rights and Fundamental Freedoms which came into effect in 1990.[4] The key considerations pertaining to the new Act on the Freedom of Religion 2003 relates to this.[5] The work to reform basic rights protection formed part of a more comprehensive effort to renew the constitution, an endeavor that included addressing questions about societal power relations, religion-state relations, and the religious freedom of churches and other religious communities.[6]

This chapter focuses on the last part of the 20th century and the beginning of the 21st century, when these major legal reforms took place in Finland and the new 2000 Constitution and the new Act on the Freedom of Religion were developed. More specifically, the chapter studies the new legal framework of religious freedom (broadly understood, including the new constitutional guarantees) and the deliberations accompanying its elaboration (including parliamentary debates, the input of majority and minority religious communities at different times in the legislative process, etc.). Broadly speaking, the aim is to investigate how international and European human rights law (legal trans-

---

2 Leena Sorsa, *Kansankirkko, uskonnonvapaus ja valtio: Suomen evankelis-luterilaisen kirkon kirkolliskokouksen tulkinta uskonnonvapaudesta 1963-2003* (PhD diss., Tampere: Kirkon tutkimuskeskus, 2010), 71.
3 Seppo, *Uskonnonvapaus*, 58-59.
4 *HE 309/1993 vp*: Hallituksen esitys Eduskunnalle perustuslakien perusoikeussäännösten muuttamisesta, 39.
5 *KM 1999:5*: Uskonnonvapauskomitean välimietintö, 15-16; *KM 2001:1*: Uskonnonvapauskomitean mietintö, 19-20; Seppo, *Uskonnonvapaus*, 80.
6 Seppo, *Uskonnonvapaus*, 56. The membership of the Council of Europe (1989) and the European Union (1995) are also important for the increased importance of basic rights and human rights in Finland. Before the 1980s, basic and human rights played a more minor role in the Finnish legal context. Basic rights were basically seen as setting limits to the power of the legislator. Tuomas Ojanen, *Johdatus perus- ja ihmisoikeusjuridiikkaan* (Helsinki: Helsingin yliopiston oikeustieteellisen tiedekunnan julkaisuja, 2009), 10-11.

plants[7]) affected the law of the land, in particular the understanding thereof, as well as the legal perception of and regulation of religion (and belief) with regard to minority and majority religious positions in Finland.[8] The following sections will offer an overview of previous research with regard to the theme of the chapter, as well as present the theoretical framework for the analysis conducted, after which the research aim will be specified in more detail.

Previous Research

The following overview of previous research primarily concentrates on monographs. The renewal of Finnish religious freedom legislation and fundamental rights protection with regard to freedom of religion or belief around the turn of the last century has engaged scholars of law, ecclesiastical law, and church history, as well as (to some extent) religious studies. The studies by Juha Seppo are to be counted among the more important works, for example his *Uskonnonvapaus 2000-luvun Suomessa*. Likewise of importance as regards the more general legal reforms are, for example, Ilkka Saraviita's *Perustuslaki 2000: kommentaariteos uudesta valtiosäännöstä Suomelle* (2000), *Perusoikeudet* (2011) by Pekka Hallberg et al., *Uusi perustuslakimme* (2000) by Antero Jyränki, and *Uusi perustuslakikontrolli* (2010) by Juha Lavapuro.[9]

The position of the Evangelical Lutheran Church of Finland vis-à-vis religious freedom in a broad sense, and the standpoints of the church on proposed reforms of Finnish religion law during the latter part of the 20th century, was the object of Sorsa's doctoral dissertation in church history, *Kansankirkko, uskonnonvapaus ja valtio: Suomen evankelis-luterilaisen kirkon kirkolliskokouksen tulkinta uskonnonvapaudesta 1963-2003* (2010).[10]

Different religious minority positions in relation to the new Act on the Freedom of Religion 2003 was the object of the article by Tuula Sakaranaho, "Kohti moniuskontoista Suomea? Vähemmistönäkökulma uuteen uskonnonvapaus-

---

7   Terminology from Kaarlo Tuori, *Critical Legal Positivism* (Aldershot: Ashgate, 2002), 164, who in turn refers readers to the concept of legal transplants in Alan Watson, "Legal Transplants and Law Reform," *The Law Quarterly Review* 92, no. 1 (1976): 79-84; Alan Watson, "Comparative Law and Legal Change," *Cambridge Law Journal* 37, no. 2 (1978): 313-36.
8   See also the chapters by Helle Krunke and Helge Årsheim in this volume.
9   Seppo, *Uskonnonvapaus*; Saraviita, *Perustuslaki*; Hallberg et al. eds., *Perusoikeudet*; Antero Jyränki, *Uusi perustuslakimme* (Turku: Iura Nova, 2000); Juha Lavapuro, *Uusi perustuslakikontrolli* (Helsinki: Suomalainen Lakimiesyhdistys, 2010).
10 Sorsa, *Kansankirkko*.

lakiin" in the edited volume *Kirkko ja usko tämän päivän Suomessa* (2007).[11] Also relevant in this context is the article by Johannes Heikkonen "Yhdenvertaisen uskonnon- ja omantunnonvapauden kipupisteitä Suomessa" (2012), and the article by Matti Kotiranta, "The Recent Developments in the Relationship between State and Religious Communities in Finland" in Wilhelm Rees et al., *Neuere Entwicklungen im Religionsrecht europäischer Staaten* (2013).[12]

The nature of the law of the Evangelical Lutheran Church of Finland and its relation to the general law of the land and, to a lesser extent, international law has been extensively researched by Pekka Leino in his books *Kirkkolaki vai laki kirkosta* (2002), *Kirkko ja perusoikeudet* (2003), and *Endast kyrkans egna angelägenheter* (2012).[13] Questions pertaining to the autonomy of the Evangelical Lutheran Church was also the topic of Arto Seppänen's doctoral dissertation in law, *Tunnustus kirkon oikeutena* (2007).[14]

The previous research listed above partly represents diverging views on religio-political questions. For example, conservative Lutheranism in legal garb comes up against a more comprehensive freedom of religion or belief perspective, in which issues of equality call for a redefinition of the legal and wider societal status of the majority faith. The latter research, to the extent it is legal research, is predominantly legal dogmatic, focusing on what Kaarlo Tuori calls the "surface level" of law.[15] The theological (church historical) research is, as far as concrete religion law goes, largely descriptive. While some references can be found, on the whole the above-mentioned contributions do not draw

---

11 Tuula Sakaranaho, "Kohti moniuskontoista Suomea? Vähemmistönäkökulma uuteen uskonnonvapauslakiin," in *Kirkko ja usko tämän päivän Suomessa*, ed. Aku Visala (Helsinki: Suomalainen teologinen kirjallisuusseura, 2007), 124-59.

12 Johannes Heikkonen, "Yhdenvertaisen uskonnon- ja omantunnonvapauden kipupisteitä Suomessa," *Oikeus* 41, no. 4 (2012): 554-63; Matti Kotiranta, "The Recent Developments in the Relationship between State and Religious Communities in Finland," in *Neuere Entwicklungen im Religionsrecht europäischer Staaten*, ed. Wilhelm Rees, María Roca, and Balázs Schanda (Berlin: Dunker & Humblot, 2013), 303-31. Kotiranta also has other publications documenting Finnish religion-state relations, e.g. Matti Kotiranta, "The Application of Freedom of Religion Principles of the European Convention on Human Rights in Finland," in *Religious Freedom in the European Union: The Application of the European Convention on Human Rights in the European Union*, ed. Achilles Emilianides (Leuven: Peeters, 2011), 129-52.

13 Pekka Leino, *Kirkkolaki vai laki kirkosta: Hallinto-oikeudellinen tutkimus kirkon oikeudellisista normeista ja niiden synnystä* (PhD diss., Helsinki: Suomalainen Lakimiesyhdistys, 2002); Pekka Leino, *Kirkko ja perusoikeudet* (Helsinki: Suomalainen Lakimiesyhdistys, 2003); Pekka Leino, *"Endast kyrkans egna angelägenheter": En kyrkorättslig undersökning av kyrkans egna angelägenheter i kyrkolagstiftningen om Evangelisk-lutherska kyrkan i Finland* (PhD diss., Turku: Åbo Akademis förlag, 2012).

14 Arto Seppänen, *Tunnustus kirkon oikeutena* (PhD diss., Rovaniemi: Lapin yliopisto, 2007).

15 Tuori, *Critical Legal Positivism*, 147.

extensively on, nor enter into a discussion with, a wider international academic law and religion discussion and theoretical framework. Accordingly, the present chapter aims to complement previous research by adopting a more theoretical approach that for its theoretical framework draws its inspiration from a broader international scientific conversation within the field of law and religion for the purpose of conducting a "multi-layered" study of Finnish religion law and its foundational assumptions at the turn of the 21st century.[16] The following section will explain the theoretical framework of this chapter in more detail.

Theoretical Framework

Zachary Calo has observed that the statement that (modern) law is secular by and large suggests that the speaker presumes that law has freed itself from a theological economy (in a "jurisdictional" and "ontological" sense[17]).[18] Thus the meaning of law exists unconstrained by religion, even if law is not void of value commitments.[19] But law has no substance apart from what we choose to fill it with. The frame of reference of law is immanent, and meaning is produced according to an internal logic.[20] Added to this, alternative strong narratives ("thick forms of meaning", "strong moralities"), including religious ones that challenge the law, are considered problematic.[21]

In both this and other volumes resulting from the project *Protestant Legacies in Nordic Law*, we have sought to deepen the understanding of the sense in which the above claim—i.e., law's meaning being wholly detached from

---

[16] An exception to the research that is usually either legal or historically focused is a chapter by the systematic theologian Hans-Olof Kvist. According to Kvist, his chapter has a more systematic-theological focus. However, it mostly presents a historical overview from the time of the early Church, and only on its penultimate page mentions in passing the new 2000 Constitution and its section on freedom of religion and conscience. Hans-Olof Kvist, "Kirkon omimmista lähtökohdista nousevien perustavien struktuurien teologista reflektointia kirkkoa, valtiouskontoa, valtiokirkkoa ja tunnustuksetonta valtiota koskevassa asiakentässä," in *Julkisoikeudellinen yhteisö vai Kristuksen kirkko?*, ed. Tapani Ihalainen and Antti Laato (Kaarina: Fonticulus, 2008), 15-77.

[17] Zachary R. Calo, "Christianity, Islam, and Secular Law," *Ohio Northern Law Review* 39, no. 3 (2013): 881.

[18] Zachary R. Calo, "Constructing the Secular: Law and Religion Jurisprudence in Europe and the United States," in Robert Schuman Centre for Advanced Studies Research Paper No. RSCAS 2014/94 (2014): 2-3, 23.

[19] Calo, "Constructing the Secular," 23.

[20] Calo, "Christianity," 880; referring to Rémi Brague, *The Law of God: The Philosophical History of an Idea* (Chicago: University of Chicago Press, 2005), 1.

[21] Calo, "Constructing the Secular," 11.

religion—is or is not the case as far as Nordic law is concerned. We are particularly interested in the "legal turn"[22] that followed in the wake of the Protestant Reformations and in how a Protestant legacy has had a bearing on Nordic law and the understanding of the same—to the extent that it has—and how this impact has changed through the centuries as a consequence of external and internal factors. As far as this volume goes, the focus is on the second half of the 20th century until today, a time marked *inter alia* by "juridification" in the sense of a growth and diversification of the international legal framework, more supervisory bodies including supranational human rights courts, and increased litigation in matters of religion and belief.[23]

Calo emphasizes the necessity of not getting stuck in a binary way of thinking that contrasts religion with secularism and views it as a zero sum game in which "every gain for religion comes at the expense of secularism and vice-versa".[24] Something is either secular or religious. Calo is obviously not alone in raising this critical point.[25] To study history can be a way of pointing to alternative ways of thinking about and realizing the relation between the "religious" and the "secular" with respect to law. This can also take place, for example, by showing how religion persists in informing the law in partly indirect ways: for example, by studying concrete legislation and adjudication and the ideas that in such cases make themselves known about the division of power and spheres of competence, and "legality".[26]

Likewise, in this and other volumes resulting from this research project, we present "theological accounts of the secular as a challenge to the secular/religious binary"[27], including in the matter of law. In a broad sense, law can form part of "external" religious organization and thus of "practice". "Secular" law can be something one engages with and relates to, for example, through litigation or by giving input, including upon request, in legislative processes. This is

---

22 Terminology borrowed from John Witte Jr., "From Gospel to Law: The Lutheran Reformation and Its Impact on Legal Culture," *Ecclesiastical Law Journal* 19, no. 3 (2017): 275.
23 For a discussion of juridification in relation to religion, see Helge Årsheim and Pamela Slotte, "The Juridification of Religion?," *Brill Research Perspectives in Law and Religion* 1, no. 2 (2017): 1-89.
24 Calo, "Constructing the Secular," 22-23. See also Calo, "Christianity," 880.
25 See, e.g., Silvio Ferrari, "Law and Religion in a Secular World: A European Perspective," *Ecclesiastical Law Journal* 14, no. 3 (2012): 356.
26 Topics such as spheres of competence and division of powers between "secular" and "religious" actors have occupied Leinonen and Seppänen. Mentioned above in their research into the law of the Evangelical Lutheran Church of Finland.
27 Zachary R. Calo, "Law in the Secular Age," *European Political Science Review* 13, no. 3 (2014): 308.

not necessarily seen as alien to one's own faith.[28] In the context of discussing the laws of churches, Norman Doe talks about religious law as "applied theology".[29] However, depending on the religious community in question, a strict division between religious law and religion law cannot necessarily be made. Perhaps better said, religion law may also form part of the "internal" regulation of a religious community. In light of what I have noted thus far, it is already not far-fetched to draw the conclusion that this can be the case with relation to a majority religious community in a particular context.

Calo proposes that the relations between "religious" and "secular" values in law should be seen as dialectic rather than binary.[30] Certainly, it is worthwhile inquiring into the particular dialectics at play, shifting the focus from ascertaining that something either is or is not "religious" or "secular", to illuminating how these kinds of labels are employed, the underlying assumptions steering their employment, and what they thus "*do*".

∼

In the book *The Origins of Political Order*, Francis Fukuyama underlines the importance of the idea that political leaders are also subordinate to the law.[31] According to Fukuyama, functional democracy is dependent on the rule of law, a state centralized power, and a government that is accountable to the the people.[32] The idea that also those holding political power are subordinate to the law is a prerequisite for the rule of law.[33] In his book, Fukuyama traces "instances where religious ideas played an independent role in shaping political outcomes."[34] As far as Western Europe is concerned, the roots of rule of law are to be located in the particular shape Western European Christendom took on in premodernity.[35]

---

28 For an overview of how a number of contemporary Christian and Islamic thinkers seek to formulate constructive understandings of "the secular" and of "secular law", with a point of departure in the perspective of their own theological traditions, and of the relations between theology and secular modern law, see Calo, "Christianity."
29 Norman Doe, *Christian Law: Contemporary Principles* (Cambridge: Cambridge University Press, 2013), 384-85.
30 Calo, "Constructing the Secular," 3.
31 Francis Fukuyama, *The Origins of Political Order: From Prehuman Times to the French Revolution* (New York: Farrar, Straus and Giroux, 2011), 15-16.
32 I am grateful to Kimmo Ketola for drawing my attention to this idea in the writings of Fukuyama. Fukuyama, *The Origins of Political Order,* 15-16.
33 Fukuyama, *The Origins of Political Order*, 246.
34 Fukuyama, *The Origins of Political Order*, 444.
35 Fukuyama, *The Origins of Political Order*, 262, 275. He notes that: "While comparable independent religious institutions existed in India, the Middle East, and the Byzantine

Furthermore, Fukuyama maintains that the Scandinavian countries—and in his book he *de facto* presents Denmark as a kind of ideal type—have taken the lead when it comes to developing an understanding of rule of law and "accountability". Hereby he gives prominence to the Protestant Reformation, among other things.[36] The start of the Reformation as it pertains exactly to this was perhaps not that promising. As John Witte, Jr observes:

> The Lutheran reformers removed the Pope … But the reformers ultimately anointed the secular prince as the new vice-regent of God on earth, the *summus episcopus*, with too few constitutional safeguards against his tyrannical excesses and too few intellectual resources to support civil disobedience, let alone political revolt.[37]

Simultaneously, Witte underlines that *reconstruction* became a very important task for Lutheran theologians and jurists of 1530s Germany onwards: "reconstruction of the civil law on the strength of the gospel".[38] The two kingdoms doctrine came to be of importance in the redefinition of the understanding of authority, government, and the division of power between the church and the state, between canon law and civil law.[39]

Other volumes of the *Protestant Legacies in Nordic Law* project study how this reconstruction came to be expressed both in Germany and in the Nordic countries at the time of the Reformation and during the subsequent centuries.[40] As far as this chapter goes, I will limit myself to noting that the rule of law forms a cornerstone of modern law. By zeroing in on it, we move from what can be seen as the *surface level* of law (notably statutes and other legal regulations, court decisions, statements of legal science), down through the layer of the *legal culture* (professional culture, general doctrines of different fields of law, and the doctrine of the sources of law), to the study of what Tuori has called the *deep*

Empire, none succeeded to the extent of the Western church in institutionalizing an independent legal order. Without the investiture conflict and its consequences, the rule of law would never have become so deeply rooted in the West." Fukuyama, *The Origins of Political Order*, 444.
36 Fukuyama, *The Origins of Political Order*, 432-34.
37 Witte, "From Gospel," 288.
38 Witte, "From Gospel," 274.
39 Witte, "From Gospel," 276, 278-79.
40 See Tarald Rasmussen and Jørn Sunde, eds., *Protestant Legacies of Nordic Law: The Early Modern Period* (Paderborn: Brill-Schönningh, *forthcoming*); Anna-Sara Lind and Victoria Enkvist, eds., *Constitutionalisation and Hegemonisation: Exploring the Boundaries of Law and Religion 1800-1950* (Odense: University Press of Southern Denmark, *forthcoming*).

structure of law (basic categories, fundamental principles and "a fundamental type of rationality"). This slowly-transforming layer of law, "the *longue durée* of the law", which together with the legal culture both renders possible and sets bounds to what takes place at the surface level, carries a legacy that only slowly changes or is phased out.[41] The surrounding culture, in a broad sense and not limited to national borders, has contributed to the development of the foundational categories, principles and the understanding of the "type of law" we are dealing with today: "mature modern law" as Tuori calls it.[42]

According to Tuori, modern law is about change and renewal. However, in talking about law's different layers, Tuori wants to underscore law's historicity, among other things[43]:

> the purposive rationality of modern law—the conscious aspiration to achieve social changes through legislation—entails a tendency to disengage the past from the future ... not even as positive law does the law wholly lose its memory or sever all its ties to its past. With respect to the continuous alternations at the law's surface level, the legal culture represents the memory of the law and keeps alive the connection to the past of the law; when the legal culture encounters new legislation, the past encounters the future, and this cannot but leave traces in the law, primary oriented towards the future.[44]

Moreover, the slowly transforming deep structure of law can bear a legacy from earlier types of law. With reference to Michel Foucault, and drawing attention to a crucial focal point of the project *Protestant Legacies in Nordic Law*, Tuori talks of "continuities in the *epistemes* of successive epochs, for instance in

---

41 Tuori, *Critical Legal Positivism*, 147, 150, 154-55, 157, 165-66, 169, 173-74, 177, 183-84, 186-88, 191-92. Tuori wants to make us aware of the fact that law is more than its surface level. He is flexible as to how many "layers" we may want to attribute to law, and what to locate at each level, but in principle he identifies three layers. Tuori, *Critical Legal Positivism*, 154, 196. He allocates basic and human rights to the different levels in different ways. See, e.g., Tuori, *Critical Legal Positivism*, 190, 240.
42 Tuori, *Critical Legal Positivism*, 154, 194.
43 Tuori, *Critical Legal Positivism*, 197.
44 Tuori, *Critical Legal Positivism*, 162-63. The memory of which he speaks is the "practical knowledge" of the culture of professional lawyers. Tuori, *Critical Legal Positivism*, 163. Both the level of legal culture and the level of deep structure are present in actors of the legal community in *sensu stricto* in the form of an internalized practical knowledge. Tuori, *Critical Legal Positivism*, 133, 161, 163. For a study of how a Protestant legacy is kept alive in the professional Nordic legal culture in an era that emphasizes the secularity of law, see Kjell Å. Modéer's chapter "Christian Torchbearers in the Dark of Positivism: Survivors and Catalysts within Nordic Law and Religion 1950—2000," in this volume.

their constitutive concepts" and infers that such is the case, for example, as far as some of the categories at law's deep structure are concerned.[45] Returning to Fukuyama, we could think of *rule of law* here.

∼

In the writings of Hussein Ali Agrama, we encounter a way of formulating an understanding of "religious" and "secular" beyond binary oppositions and which at a theoretical level connects this, among other things, to a discussion of legality, rule of law, and the relation between law and the surrounding (majority) culture.[46] The concrete context in which he writes is primarily Egypt, but the following basic theoretical points of his are of broader relevance.[47]

In a manner that echoes Calo, Agrama notes that we cannot answer the "binary" question of whether a given state is religious or secular. Simultaneously, it is not a false question. "[I]t is rather a question whose persistence, force, and inability to be resolved expresses the peculiar *intractability* of our contemporary secularity."[48] Hence, while the question cannot be answered, it at once constitutes an inescapable aspect of what Agrama calls our "modern secularity". Another basic feature of this secularity is the central position attributed to the modern state and its legal powers, embodied in the rule of law.[49] In fact, according to Agrama, "a rule of law is indispensible to how secular power works".[50]

Secular power makes possible "state sovereign capacity", by which Agrama means the capacity to regulate "over and within social life". This should not be mistaken for actual control. Rather, it is about the state's "in-principle right and responsibility to regulate should this be deemed necessary."[51] Moreover, sovereignty does not solely allude to the capacity to regulate our lives when this is needed. It also refers to how this concept structures the understanding of reality. "It is also a central organizing concept of contemporary life. As such it brings together commonplace concerns into a specific constellation of desire

---

45 Tuori, *Critical Legal Positivism*, 189.
46 Hussein Ali Agrama, *Questioning Secularism: Islam, Sovereignty, and the Rule of Law in Modern Egypt* (Chicago: University of Chicago Press, 2012).
47 In addition, as Agrama notes, the Egyptian legal system is to a large extent based on European, in particular French, law. Agrama, *Questioning Secularism*, 2.
48 Agrama, *Questioning Secularism*, 71.
49 Agrama, *Questioning Secularism*, 30.
50 Agrama, *Questioning Secularism*, 35.
51 Agrama, *Questioning Secularism*, 31.

and anxiety."⁵² This includes the visualization and regulation of the place of religion in society.

> The state's authority to decide what counts as religious and what scope it can have in society is crucially vested in a rule of law, and thus the law is always entangled in the question of religion and politics.⁵³

A legal key concept "at the heart of the rule of law, and which it is responsible to protect" is "public order". Historically, this concept developed concurrently with understandings of the modern state, its sovereignty and regulative power. According to Agrama, it obtains its distinctive shape during the mid and late-19th century in connection with the development of European private law to handle legal pluralism.

> Within this doctrine, public order is defined as those laws and values that are essential to a state's social and legal cohesion and that are usually held by the majority of its citizens. As an international law concept, public order is understood to consist of the general principles that underlay liberal legality—such as procedural fairness and formal liberal equality. But as a concept bound by the state, it is also understood to consist of the *particular* values and laws specific states deem to be foundational to their own social and legal cohesion. The public order is therefore seen as an intrinsically flexible concept whose contents, because they change over time and between states, are for judges to decide.⁵⁴

That is, "public order" is thought to comprise general principles that are key to liberal legality. The purpose is to uphold the rule of law. However, this simultaneously confirms state sovereignty. It is the state that decides, at least in the first instance, when there is a threat to public order and when the protection of public order *de facto* demands the limitation or suspension of valid law.⁵⁵

---

52   Agrama, *Questioning Secularism*, 32.
53   Agrama, *Questioning Secularism*, 33.
54   Agrama, *Questioning Secularism*, 95.
55   Agrama, *Questioning Secularism*, 38, 97. It is not far-fetched to draw a connection here to Carl Schmitt's analysis the nature of law and his observation that "Sovereign is he who decides on the exception", by which he means the particular moment when it is appropriate to step outside the rule of law in the interest of the public. Carl Schmitt, *Politiche Theologie: Vier Kapitel zur Lehre von der Souveränitet*, 2nd ed. (Munich: Leipzig Verlag von Duncker & Humblot, 1934). Agrama also mentions Schmitt in a presentation of Giorgio Agamben's ideas of law and the sovereign as being simultaneously both within and outside law, "simultaneously legal and nonlegal". Agrama, *Questioning Secularism*, 142-43;

Agrama hereby identifies a space for interpretation as well as an indeterminacy at the heart of key categories.[56]

Further, it is important to note that, as the concept of public order is connected to the state, it is also made up of the values and laws that the state in question considers essential for social and legal cohesion. We are dealing here with a flexible concept with changing content, at least in some sense. "Public order" conveys "the principles and sensibilities of particularist narratives, putatively rooted in majority sentiments, but that are also deemed foundational to the state."[57] Majoritarian values and perceptions, for example pertaining to religion and the boundaries of freedom of religion or belief, are alterable (something which for purposes of this chapter below will be connected explicitly with the internationalization of religion law). Accordingly, the legal notion of public order "blurs division between legal equality and majority values".[58] Formal equality before the law concretely takes on a shape influenced by majoritarian views.

> Thus the rule of law, through its connection to public order, becomes firmly attached to majority-minority relations even though it is supposed to promote formal equality between citizens of the state. And because of this, legal entanglements with theological questions can also become attached to majority-minority relations.[59]

Giorgio Agamben, *Homo Sacer: Sovereign Power and Bare Life* (Stanford, CA: Stanford University Press, 1998).

56 Agrama, *Questioning Secularism*, 98. In relation hereto, it is worth noting that, in relation to all layers of law, Tuori underscores the role of actors (judges, lawyers, legal experts, and scholars) in interpreting and applying the law, and in systematizing, construing and reconstructing, and renewing the law. Tuori, *Critical Legal Positivism*. According to Witte, Luther considered the question of equity as central in all rule application, both with regard to legal rules and other rules. The result could be to strictly apply or not apply a rule, while the rule as such was not to be undermined. Witte, "From Gospel," 283-84; WA, TR 3, no. 4178: Martin Luther, *D. Martin Luthers Werke*. Kritische Gesamtausgabe. *Tischreden*, 6 vols (Weimar: Hermann Böhlaus Nachfolger, 1912-21); *LW* 54:43-44, 325; Martin Luther, *Luther's Works*, ed. Jaroslav Pelikan, Helmut T. Lehmann, and Christopher Boyd Brown, 75 vols (Philadelphia, PA/St. Louis, MO: Concordia Publishing House, 1955-); WA, TR 1, no. 315: Martin Luther, *D. Martin Luthers Werke*. Kritische Gesamtausgabe. *Tischreden*, 6 vols (Weimar: Hermann Böhlaus Nachfolger, 1912-21); WA 14: 667ff: Martin Luther, *D. Martin Luthers Werke*. Kritische Gesamtausgabe. 73 vols (Weimar: Böhlau, 1883-2009); *LW* 46:100: Martin Luther, *Luther's Works*, ed. Jaroslav Pelikan, Helmut T. Lehmann, and Christopher Boyd Brown, 75 vols (Philadelphia, PA/St. Louis, MO: Concordia Publishing House, 1955-).
57 Agrama, *Questioning Secularism*, 38.
58 Agrama, *Questioning Secularism*, 98.
59 Agrama, *Questioning Secularism*, 98.

In the second part of this chapter, I will make use of the theoretical framework presented above for the purpose of examining how, in a Finnish context, ideas of rule of law, legality, public order, and so forth, have been connected to issues of religion (regulation of religion and religious regulation), when a movement "downwards" from the international level through legal transplants[60] encounters a movement "upwards" from the local level.

The Internationalization of Finnish Religion Law

The concrete empirical context is the legislative changes in Finland pertaining to freedom of religion or belief at the turn of the last century. According to Talal Asad, state power has always been unstable; he asks where the margins of the state are, those places where state law and order continuously have to be reestablished.[61] Asad further notes that "the origins of the modern (secular) state are connected to the concern for agreement among 'reasonable' men and thus to the creation of a margin to which 'religion' (and other forms of uncertain belief) properly belonged."[62] Legislative processes are places where such reestablishment by agreement takes place.

In the following, I offer an account of the concrete reforms carried out, and the discussions accompanying them, at the end of the 20th and beginning of the 21st centuries and which were explicitly legitimized, *inter alia*, by reference to the need of the Finnish state to live up to its international legal obligations as regards human rights. What is it that takes place? What becomes an issue at all? What ends up being the focus of the reforms as far as freedom of religion or belief goes? Hereby, how is the state interpretative prerogative conceptualized within the structure of a secular frame narrative and unremitting majoritarian sensibilities when it comes to looking at law and the relation between religion and politics? What understanding of religion and its boundaries thereby emerges? How and when can freedom of religion or belief be limited? When and how are questions of "rule of law", "legality" and "public order" actualized? When an

---

60 For example, legality (in the sense of "prescribed by law") and "public order" are mentioned in Article 9(2) of the European Convention on Human Rights and Fundamental Freedoms as legitimate grounds for restricting manifestations of religion or belief and these notions play key roles in the jurisprudence of the European Court of Human Rights.
61 Talal Asad, "Where Are the Margins of the State?," in *Anthropology in the Margins of the State*, ed. Veena Das and Deborah Poole (Santa Fe, NM: School of American Research Press, 2004), 281.
62 Asad, "Where Are the Margins of the State?," 285.

aim is to strengthen the autonomy of religious communities, as the committee established to draft the new Act on the Freedom of Religion notes,[63] what is this autonomy taken to encompass? To what extent does one discuss internal regulation and religious law in this context? More generally, what does one consider necessary to regulate, and where? Who should be responsible for what (regulation)? And what does all this tell us about the "secularity" of contemporary Finnish law of the land, how it is constructed and reconstructed (to refer back to Witte's terminology), and thus hov it deals (or not) with a religious legacy?

Until the 1980s, fundamental rights and human rights did not play a key role in Finnish legal reality.[64] But international human rights treaties came to serve as a guide for the fundamental rights committee that was appointed in 1989 and completed its work in 1992, with the fundamental rights reform taking place in 1995.[65] In addition, the membership of the Council of Europe (1989) and the European Union (1995) were important for the increased importance of basic rights and human rights in Finland.[66] Legal transplants thus affected the understanding and regulation of freedom of religion or belief in Finland.

The Finnish fundamental rights reform emphasizes the state's "positive" obligations to promote or guarantee the actual realization of fundamental and human rights alongside the "negative" obligation to respect these rights.[67] A key feature of the reform is also the aspiration to expand the substantial reach of fundamental rights. No longer is it almost solely about "classic" freedom rights but also about social, economic, and cultural rights (albeit not always phrased in the form of subjective individual rights), which up to that point had been inconsistently regulated in the 1919 Constitution.[68] In this and other ways,

---

63 KM 1999:5, 19; KM 2001:1, 1, 22.
64 Ojanen, *Johdatus*, 10. As mentioned earlier, basic rights are primarily seen as setting limits to the power of the legislator. Ojanen, *Johdatus*, 10.
65 KM 1992:3: Perusoikeuskomitean mietintö, 13; HE 309/1993 vp, 5-6; Jyränki, *Uusi perustuslakimme*, 277; Seppo, *Uskonnonvapaus*, 53; Ojanen, *Johdatus*, 49. The work of thinking through fundamental rights had been ongoing through the 1870s but had not really taken off. The work was done in committees and working groups, but no agreement was reached; in the 1980s, fundamental rights was above all the subject of expert opinions. KM 1992:3, 13; Perusoikeustyöryhmä, *Perusoikeustyöryhmä 1992 mietintö*, Oikeusministeriön lainvalmisteluosaston julkaisu, 2/1993 (Helsinki: Oikeusministeriö, 1993), 3; HE 309/1993 vp, 36; Jyränki, *Uusi perustuslakimme*, 277; Seppo, *Uskonnonvapaus*, 53.
66 KM 1992:3, 13; HE 309/1993 vp, 8-9, 40-41.
67 KM 1992:3, 117-19, 373-74.
68 KM 1992:3, 13-18, 46, 90-91; HE 309/1993 vp, 1, 5, 14, 16; Ojanen, *Johdatus*, 12; Tuomas Ojanen, "Human Rights in Nordic Constitutions and the Impact of International Obligations," in *The Nordic Constitutions: A Comparative and Contextual Study*, ed. Helle Krunke and Björg Thorarensen (Oxford: Hart Publishing, 2018), 142. The fundamental rights committee linked this emphasis on social, cultural, and economic rights explicitly to the

the 1919 Constitution and the Finnish fundamental rights system is considered outdated.[69] International human rights treaties play an important role here.[70]

More specifically, the fundamental rights reform also brought with it a broader concept of religious freedom as "conviction", which was introduced as a separate category alongside religion after a lack had been identified at the preparatory stage.[71] "Conviction" is taken to encompass both religious and other kinds of convictions.[72] The new set of fundamental rights norms as such was moved to the new constitution.[73] This placement is seen as underlining the notion that fundamental rights are naturally linked to issues of division and the use of state power and should inform the interpretation of the latter, and the fact that many other regulations in the constitution are of importance for the functioning of the fundamental rights system.[74]

The Special Status of the Evangelical Lutheran Church Remains

Interestingly enough, when the work on the new constitution commenced, the first draft did not include mention of the so-called "church-paragraph", Section 83 of the 1919 Constitution, which specifically mentioned the majority

---

welfare state, which was considered to be the current form of a state governed by the rule of law (*oikeusvaltio*). KM 1992:3, 46.
69 *HE 309/1993 vp*, 14. A further task highlighted during the fundamental rights reform was to more generally ponder what role and emphasis to give to collective rights, including the right of minorities to uphold and develop their language and culture. KM 1992:3, 92, 110.
70 Ojanen, *Johdatus*, 48.
71 *HE 309/1993 vp*, 14, 18, 55; Seppo, *Uskonnonvapaus*, 10-11. However, also the right to leave a religious community had exsisted; thus, other convictions than religious ones had been recognized in practice. Perusoikeustyöryhmä, *Perusoikeustyöryhmä 1992 mietintö*, 7; KM 1992:3, 289. For an overview of discussions pertaining to "conviction" during the preparatory work, see *PeVM 25/1994 vp*: Perustuslakivaliokunnan mietintö n:o 25 hallituksen esityksestä perustuslakien perusoikeussäännösten muuttamisesta, 8-9; *PeVM 25/1994 vp*, Liite 3 Eduskunnan Sivistyslautakunnan Lausunto n:o 3, 38-39; KM 1992:3, 286; Tuula Majuri, *Lausunnot Perusoikeuskomitean mietinnöstä: Tiivistelmä* (Helsinki: Oikeusministeriö, 1992), 72-75.
72 Perusoikeustyöryhmä, *Perusoikeustyöryhmä 1992 mietintö*, 79; KM 1992:3, 95.
73 Pekka Hallberg, "Johdanto," in *Perusoikeudet*, ed. Pekka Hallberg et al., Online library Alma Talent, 2011, accessed May 29, 2019, http://fokus.almatalent.fi/teos/FAIBCXJTBF. The new set of fundamental rights included in the 2000 Constitution also includes Section 1 proclaiming the inviolability of human dignity and the obligation to promote justice in society. In addition, an explicit prohibition of discrimination was added (in Section 5). For a discussion of the latter, see Perusoikeustyöryhmä, *Perusoikeustyöryhmä 1992 mietintö*, 16, 54-57.
74 Perusoikeustyöryhmä, *Perusoikeustyöryhmä 1992 mietintö*, 50; KM 1992:3, 95.

church and confirmed its special legal status. The working group *Perustuslaki 2000* ("Constitution 2000") chose to omit it on the grounds that the constitution should not mention the Evangelical Lutheran Church or any other churches or religious communities. The working group also wanted to dispense with the legislative procedure for enactment of church law that had been regulated in the Church Act 1993/1054: namely, that it is up to the Evangelical Lutheran Church itself to propose new legislation in everything pertaining to its own internal affairs, changes to the Church Act, and the abolishment of the Church Act.[75] As Seppo sees it, the working group wanted to extend the powers of the parliament at the expense of the church's own institutions.[76] However, it is worth remembering that a key aspect of the overall reform indeed was to strengthen parliamentarism.[77]

However, the subsequent *Perustuslaki 2000* ("Constitution 2000") committee was receptive to the criticism that these proposals were encountered from the church. The committee included in its proposed bill a section stating that it was the Church Act which regulated the organization and administration of the Evangelical Lutheran Church. The proposed bill also affirmed the legislative procedure for enacting the Church Act.[78] Both aspects found expression in what became Section 76 ("The Church Act") of the 1999 Constitution: "Provisions on the organisation and administration of the Evangelical Lutheran Church are laid down in the Church Act. The legislative procedure for enactment of the Church Act and the right to submit legislative proposals relating to the Church Act are governed by the specific provisions in that Code." However, contrary to what was the case in Section 83:3 of the 1919 Constitution, mention of other religious communities and their right to establish themselves in Finland is omitted. The committee report PeVM 10/1998 observed that other communities were covered by Section 13:2-3 of the Constitution, on the freedom of assembly and freedom of association, as well as by the Associations Act 503/1989.[79]

---

75 Perustuslaki 2000-työryhmä, *Perustuslaki 2000: Yhtenäiset perustuslain tarve ja keskeiset valtiosääntöoikeudelliset ongelmat; Työryhmän mietintö*, Oikeusministeriön lainvalmisteluosaston julkaisu, 8/1995 (Helsinki: Oikeusministeriö), 1996.
76 Seppo, *Uskonnonvapaus*, 56. This can be related to Sorsa's observation that the working group *Perustuslaki 2000* wanted to tone down the collective role and meaning of religion, emphasizing instead increased protection of individual understandings of religion. Sorsa, *Kansankirkko*, 229.
77 *HE 1/1998 vp*, 5; *HE 232/1988 vp*: Hallituksen esitys Eduskunnalle tasavallan presidentin vaalitavan muuttamista ja eräiden valtaoikeuksien tarkistamista koskevaksi lainsäädännöksi; *KM 1997:3*, 70.
78 *KM 1997:13*, 229-30.
79 *PeVM 10/1998 vp*, 13. One explanation is that, given that the new constitution was systematized in a different way and its headings did not mention institutions, the subsec-

Hence, *de facto* the Evangelical Lutheran Church was afforded more exclusive explicit attention in the new constitution. This is the case even though the fundamental rights reform underlined the principle of non-discrimination that was subsequently included in Section 5:2 of the 2000 Constitution, and which is said to require that public power treat all religious communities and world views even-handedly.[80] Yet, it was conceded during the preparatory work of the fundamental rights reform that this did not require making changes to state-church relations or taking measures with regard to Section 83 of the 1919 Constitution, or other rules regulating the relations between the state and religious communities, even if there is an indirect link to freedom of religion or conviction.[81]

Against this backdrop, the new Act on the Freedom of Religion (453/2003) also leaves intact the basic structure when it comes to religion law in Finland. That is, one continues to distinguish between national churches (the Evangelical Lutheran Church of Finland and the Finnish Orthodox Church) and other registered religious communities with corresponding legal status. As Seppo sees it, the reason is that the constitution did not demand anything else. The government proposal for the new Act on the Freedom of Religion also maintained that there was no need to change state-church relations.[82] According to Seppo, it was also not part of the government proposal for the new Act on the Freedom of Religion and other related laws to examine the legal status of the national churches. Thus, this was not seen as necessary for the purpose of safeguarding religious freedom,[83] nor as a hindrance to formal or substantial equality. Indeed, the government proposal for the new Act of Freedom of Religion observes that it is a testimony to the state's wish to treat registered religious communities evenhandedly that the new Act regulates them specifically in Chapter 2, while the activities of the Evangelical Lutheran Church of Finland and the Finnish Orthodox Church are regulated in their respective special laws.[84]

---

tion mentioning other religious communities was omitted. Martin Scheinin, "Uskonnon ja omantunnon vapaus (PL 11 §)," in *Perusoikeudet*, ed. Pekka Hallberg et al. (Helsinki: Werner Söderström lakitieto, 1999), 355; Sorsa, *Kansankirkko*, 253.

80 Perusoikeustyöryhmä, *Perusoikeustyöryhmä 1992 mietintö*, 79; *HE 309/1993 vp*, 55. This prohibition of discrimination, including on grounds of religion, rendered obsolete the earlier Section 9 of the 1919 Constitution that had prohibited discrimination on the basis of membership of a particular religious community. *HE 309/1993 vp*, 44.

81 Perusoikeustyöryhmä, *Perusoikeustyöryhmä 1992 mietintö*, 79; *HE 309/1993 vp*, 55.

82 *HE 170/2002 vp*: Hallituksen esitys eduskunnalle uskonnonvapauslaiksi ja eräiksi siihen liittyviksi laeiksi, 7, 24; Seppo, *Uskonnonvapaus*, 81.

83 Seppo, *Uskonnonvapaus*, 216-17.

84 *HE 170/2002 vp*, 30.

The New Section on Freedom of Religion and Conscience

As mentioned above, the new set of fundamental rights norms as such was moved to the new constitution. As far as freedom of religion or belief is concerned, Section 11 ("Freedom of religion and conscience") of the new constitution includes the following:

> Everyone has the freedom of religion and conscience.
>
> Freedom of religion and conscience entails the right to profess and practice a religion, the right to express one's convictions and the right to be a member of or decline to be a member of a religious community. No one is under the obligation, against his or her conscience, to participate in the practice of a religion.[85]

For the purposes of this chapter, it is also worth mentioning Section 2 of the Constitution, entitled "Democracy and the rule of law": "The powers of the State of Finland are vested in the people, who are represented by the Parliament. Democracy entails the right of the individual to participate in and influence the development of society and his or her living conditions. The exercise of public powers shall be based on an Act. In all public activity, the law shall be strictly observed." This section reaffirms that Finland is a representative democracy. The parliament is the highest state organ and all exercise of public power has to be democratically grounded, as well as grounded in and strictly following the law. The rule of law forms part of the Finnish system of government.[86] The Evangelical Lutheran Church is considered part of the public power and has to respect the law in all its activities.[87] Also important is Section 22 of the Constitution, entitled "Protection of basic rights and liberties": "The public authorities

---

85 To be sure, the question of whether the concept of "conscience" is legally viable or not—because of its Christian legacy—was the topic of discussion during the fundamental rights reform. Tuomas Ojanen and Martin Scheinin, "Uskonnon ja omantunnon vapaus (PL 11 §)," in *Perusoikeudet*, ed. Pekka Hallberg et al., Online library Alma Talent, 2011, accessed May 29, 2019, http://fokus.almatalent.fi/teos/FAIBCXJTBF; *PeVM 25/1994 vp*, 8-9.

86 *KM 1997:13*, 24, 134-35; *HE 1/1998 vp*, 74.

87 *HE 309/1993 vp*, 26; Jyränki, *Uusi perustuslakimme*, 68; Ojanen, *Johdatus*, 32. See also Perusoikeustyöryhmä 1992, 37-8. I will not enter here into a more comprehensive discussion of how this is to be interpreted. Interestingly, according to case law, public law bodies (*julkisoikeudellinen yhteisö*) do not enjoy fundamental rights protection. Perusoikeustyöryhmä, *Perusoikeustyöryhmä 1992 mietintö*, 33, as well as e.g. *PeVL 18/1982 vp*: Perustuslakivaliokunnan lausunto; *PeVL 6/1990 vp*: Perustuslakivaliokunnan lausunto; *PeVL 7/1990 vp*: Perustuslakivaliokunnan lausunto.

shall guarantee the observance of basic rights and liberties and human rights." This is interpreted as supplying the basis—at the constitutional level—for a "human rights friendly" interpretation of law.[88]

The renewed section on freedom of religion and conscience differs from its predecessor in various ways. It applies to everyone residing in Finland and not only to Finnish citizens.[89] The earlier section did not explicitly speak in terms of freedom of conscience, but the new version does. Freedom of conscience is taken to cover both religious and other worldviews or life stances.[90] Moreover, influenced by international human rights treaties, a distinction is made between the freedom to have a religion and the right to practice religion, as well as between the freedom to have a conviction and the right to express one's convictions.[91]

The New Act on the Freedom of Religion: Focus on Positive Freedom and Enhanced Religious Autonomy

The Act on the Freedom of Religion (453/2003) regulates in more detail the practice of freedom of religion and conscience as protected in the new constitution.[92] The Ministry of Education, which appointed a committee to develop the new Act on the Freedom of Religion, observed that the fundamental rights reform that had taken place had broadened the concept of freedom of religion to encompass freedom of religion and conviction, and that the new rule was more comprehensive, as it covered both religions and other worldviews and life stances. One also notes, again, the way in which the ratification by Finland of a number of international human rights treaties entailing freedom of thought, conscience, and religion had altered the situation, requiring action.[93] In addition,

---

88 Ojanen, *Johdatus*, 49.
89 Here also, international human rights law has an impact. Ojanen, *Johdatus*, 48-49. See also KM 1992:3, 46; HE 309/1993 vp, 2, 5, 21. In general, it is a basic rule today that fundamental rights belong to all natural persons under Finnish jurisdiction. HE 308/1993 vp, 23; Jyränki, *Uusi perustuslakimme*, 285; Ojanen, *Johdatus*, 21. Indirectly, fundamental rights protection is extended to legal persons as some fundamental rights are of direct importance to legal persons. This is because many of these rights are such that they cannot be seen as simply "individual". Some rights can only be fully realized in community with others. Jyränki, *Uusi perustuslakimme*, 286; Ojanen, *Johdatus*, 24-25, 30.
90 HE 170/2002 vp, 7. See also PeVM 25/1994 vp, 8-9, as well as e.g. KM 1992:3, 104, 110.
91 HE 170/2002 vp, 7; Seppo, *Uskonnonvapaus*, 55.
92 Ojanen and Scheinin, "Uskonnon ja omantunnon vapaus."
93 Opetusministeriö, project number OPM0610:00/30/06/1998. See also HE 170/2002 vp, 5, 20.

certain specific problems were mentioned as reasons for the need for a new Act on the Freedom of Religion: the way in which the old act was organized was considered outdated and leading to administrative problems and problems related to the drafting of law; the way in which age limits related to the religious affiliation of children were determined; the question of how persons could cease to be members of religious communities (only by visiting a public authority); out-of-date rules for registration of a religious community; topical issues related to graveyards and burial places.[94]

In turn, the appointed committee observed in its so-called middle-report that, in relation to the Act on the freedom of religion (267/1922), the new version would have the same scope of application. However, the committee found it necessary to revise concrete regulation considered outdated with regard to its structure and style of writing. The old Act had obvious flaws and left unnecessary room for interpretation. It had to be revised in the new context of the present day.[95] Furthermore, as the committee noted in its reports, a basic feature of the reforms was to strive to increase the autonomy and improve the conditions for the operating of religious communities, and to survey which parts of the Associations Act 503/1989 that were or were not applicable to religious communities given their special status as legal subjects.[96]

The emphasis placed on autonomy is a consequence of the importance afforded to the positive freedom to practice religion in light of present-day and international human rights treaties. It is assumed that this positive freedom to practice religion requires that individuals and religious communities are afforded maximum autonomy as far as freedom to practice one's religion goes. The role of the state is only to "create the general external constitutional conditions for religious practice, but leave all decisions that truly concern substance to the parties concerned".[97] What this autonomy would include in more detail is explicated in rather standard terms by Seppo in his comment on the position of the constitutional committee during the legislative process: the cult, the

---

94 Seppo, *Uskonnonvapaus*, 60.
95 *KM 1999:5*, 15-16; *KM 2001:1*, 19-20; Seppo, *Uskonnonvapaus*, 64. See also *HE 170/2002 vp*, 20, 22.
96 *KM 1999:5*, 47-49; Seppo, *Uskonnonvapaus*, 77-78. See also *HE 170/2002 vp*, 5.
97 Seppo, *Uskonnonvapaus*, 80-81 [my translation]. As the committee observes, the aim is to get rid of unnecessary regulation of registered religious communities and promote evenhanded treatment by public power, while still retaining the possibility for public authorities to intervene when a religious community is violating human dignity, fundamental rights, or otherwise acts in opposition with the foundations of the legal order. *KM 2001:1*, 22.

choice of leaders, the establishment of religious educational institutions, and religious publications.[98]

Among other things, this emphasis on autonomy led to the suggestion of a period of transition allowing religious communities an opportunity to regulate internally issues that the committee suggested should form part of the new Act on the Freedom of Religion. More to the point, the committee wanted to give individuals the opportunity to be members of more than one religious community, something which was prohibited under the Act on the Freedom of Religion of 1922.[99] Hence, the state wanted to regulate the matter in accordance with what it understood religious autonomy to encompass. Yet simultaneously and for reasons of consistency, the state wished to give communities a chance to react in time so that they articulated in the form of own regulation their theological position on the matter in a way that safeguarded their autonomy. It was up to the churches and religious communities themselves to set the criteria for membership.[100]

Where to Regulate What?

The work carried out resulted in a new Act on the Freedom of Religion as well as changes to a number of other laws relating to religious freedom such as the *Basic Education Act* 628/1998, the *Act on General Upper Secondary Education* 629/1998 and the *Accounting Act* 1336/1997. In addition, entirely new legislation, a *Burial Act* 457/2003, was enacted. Section 1 of the *Burial Act* in addition to spelling out the scope of the act, defers also to the *Church Act* and the *Act on the Orthodox Church* 521/1969 (and, following later revisions, to the *Act on the Orthodox Church* 985/2006 and also to the *Church Order of the Orthodox Church* 174/2006) and what there is prescribed regarding funeral activities in a burial ground of one of these churches.

---

98 Seppo, *Uskonnonvapaus*, 191; *PeVM 10/2002 vp*: Perustuslakivaliokunnan mietintö, Hallituksen esitys uskonnonvapauslaiksi ja eräiksi siihen liittyviksi laeiksi, 2-3, making reference also to the preparatory work of the fundamental rights reform, *HE 309/1993 vp*, 55. See further also e.g. *KM 1992:3*, 287-88.
99 *KM 1999:5*, 31.
100 The committee ended up proposing a period of transition of three years after the entry into force of the new Act on the Freedom of Religion (before the prohibition of multiple membership of the old Act on the Freedom of Religion was overturned) so that the national churches and other religious communities had time to reflect and take a stand on the question of dual membership. The Church Act and the Act on the Orthodox Church of that time did not take a stand on the issue. *KM 2001:1*, 29-30; Seppo, *Uskonnonvapaus*, 81-82.

This tells us something about what one considers ought to be regulated where, and about who is or should be responsible for what. Quite concretely, it was suggested that certain matters should be moved from one piece of legislation to another. The reports of the committee as well as the governmental proposal mention funerals, taxation, marriage, and religious education as such matters,[101] and as noted above, changes were made. Moreover, as has been said, certain things were supposed to be left completely to so-called "internal regulation".

In general, one goal was a slimmed down Act. The previous Act had been too detailed. It was not considered appropriate that the Act on the Freedom of Religion regulate such matters that with regard to substance were regulated elsewhere. To give a further example, in the desire to escape overlapping (double) legislation, it was considered worthwhile to only regulate in the Act on the Freedom of Religion those matters which were specific to religious communities, while issues which united religious communities and non-profit associations were to be regulated in the Associations Act 503/1989.[102] However, in order to know what needed to be regulated in the Act on the Freedom of Religion, the committee concluded that one had to define what is meant by the terms "religion" and the "practice of religion", as this would make it easier to distinguish religious communities from other voluntary associations whose activities were likewise regulated by the Associations Act.[103] These considerations are reflected in the explications of what is the "purpose and forms of activity of a registered religious community" in Section 7 of the new Act:

> The purpose of a registered religious community is to organise and support individual, communal and public activities relating to the profession and practise of religion that are based on a creed, religious texts regarded as sacred, or another specified and established basis for activities regarded as sacred.[104]

---

101 *KM 1999:5*, 17-18; See also *KM 2001:1*, 21-22, 28; *HE 170/2002 vp*, 22-23, 30.
102 *KM 1999:5*, 17-22, 48-49; *KM 2001:1*, 22-24, 28; Seppo, *Uskonnonvapaus*, 19, 190. See also *HE 170/2002 vp*, 50-54.
103 *KM 1999:5*, 26-27: "Within the context of the new act on the freedom of religion, confessing and practicing religion would mean activities that are expressed in the cult and other private, communal, and public forms of religious practice and which are based on a creed, writings considered holy, or other individualized religious grounds." [My translation]. See also *KM 2001:1*, 35; *HE 170/2002 vp*, 38.
104 Translation by the Ministry of Education and Culture, available at URL [accessed June 1, 2020]: https://www.finlex.fi/fi/laki/kaannokset/2003/en20030453.pdf.

Hence, we can conclude from this that, while there is a push for the broadest possible collective religious autonomy, and it is underscored that what is aimed for is a slimmed down Act that also leaves certain things to be regulated solely by the religious communities or national churches themselves, "secular" national law beyond the Act on the Freedom of Religion is also still very much (in a non-problematic way) considered "religion law". A slimmed-down Act on the Freedom of Religion does not by definition equal less external regulation of matters of concern to churches and other religious communities. Moreover, for purposes of deciding what should be regulated where, religion actually has to be defined for the purposes of the law (even if the constitution itself does not define "religion" or "conviction").

Legal Limits to Freedom of Religion and Conscience

The new Act on the Freedom of Religion is ordinary law, and all ordinary law and its application must conform to the constitution, including the section on freedom of religion and conscience. However, as a part of Finnish law, neither fundamental rights nor human rights are *absolute*. When it comes to fundamental rights, this is discernible from the legal text itself.

An aim of the fundamental rights reform at the end of the 20th century was to dispose of outdated and overly general formulations that made possible too far-reaching restrictions on fundamental rights.[105] The 1919 Constitution had given the legislator ("*laadittu lainvarainen*") broad scope to limit fundamental rights in ordinary law.[106] The designation "in law" served the purpose of signalling that a matter that previously had been an administrative matter or dealt with at a lower level in the rule hierarchy should now be reserved for the legislator. Several of the so-called legal reservations (*lakivaraus*) were "simple" ones, however, that did not specify further the criteria for the discretion of the legislator. This had resulted in a situation in which establishing the boundary between acceptable and inadmissible legislative limits to fundamental rights had become ambiguous.[107]

Further, the position at the time of the fundamental rights reform was that the 1919 Constitution model with its extensive use of generally phrased legal

---

[105] *HE 309/1993 vp*, 17.
[106] *KM 1992:3*, 59-60; Perusoikeustyöryhmä, *Perusoikeustyöryhmä 1992 mietintö*, 9.
[107] *HE 309/1993 vp*, 7, 14; *PeVM 25/1994*, 4. See also *KM 1992:3*, 56-57, 133; Perusoikeustyöryhmä, *Perusoikeustyöryhmä 1992 mietintö*, 45.

reservations did not go well with the idea that fundamental rights ought to be binding for the legislator. As explicated in detail during the preparatory work, the general conditions were that any limitation must have a basis in an act of parliament.[108] It must also be based on acceptable grounds that are clearly delimited, precise, and discernible from the law itself.[109] It should not be allowed to regulate about extensive, summary, and unusual limitations to fundamental rights in ordinary law.[110] Any justified limitation must answer to a pressing societal need or general interest and be necessary for the attainment of the acceptable goal in question.[111] Finally, any limitation must not affect the essential core of a fundamental right, nor be out of tune with Finland's obligations under international human rights law.[112] Simultaneously, flexibility is also underscored as important, meaning that the fundamental rights and their limitations have to be formulated in a "timeless" manner so as to be applicable for some time into the 21st century and under changed circumstances.[113]

The result is that several provisions of the new set of fundamental rights contain a so-called regulation reservation (*regleringsförbehåll*). This means that the legislator has the power to regulate in ordinary law in more detail regarding the use of the fundamental right, including limiting the right in question, as long as the right is not "weakened". It also *de facto* means that the lawmaker is obliged to regulate about reservations in law. Some fundamental rights provisions, in turn, include a so-called qualified legal reservation (*kvalificerat lagförbehåll*). This

---

108 *HE 309/1993 vp*, 29. See also *PeVM 25/1994 vp*, 5; *KM 1992:3*, 380. This follows, as Ojanen points out, from "the rule of law principle". Ojanen, "Human Rights," 146. An aim of the overall constitutional reforms was to strengthen the principle of the rule of law, among other things by specifying the matters having to be regulated in law. *KM 1997:3*, 86-87.
109 *HE 309/1993 vp*, 23; *PeVM 25/1994 vp*, 5. See also *KM 1992:3*, 138-39.
110 *HE 309/1993 vp*, 30. An additional general limitation clause, as proposed by the *Perusoikeuskomitea* (see, e.g., *KM 1992:3*, 138) was discarded by the *Perusoikeustyöryhmä*, and also does not appear in the resulting government proposal. Perusoikeustyöryhmä, *Perusoikeustyöryhmä 1992 mietintö*, 29, 47. See also *HE 309/1993*, 38; *PeVM 25/1994 vp*, 4.
111 *PeVM 25/1994 vp*, 5. See also *KM 1992:3*, 385-86.
112 *HE 309/1993*, 46; *PeVM 25/1994 vp*, 5. See also *KM 1992:3*, 19, 116, 139-40, 381-84; Perusoikeustyöryhmä, *Perusoikeustyöryhmä 1992 mietintö*, 17. More comprehensive limitations should be prohibited under normal circumstances. *KM 1992:3*, 19; Perusoikeustyöryhmä, *Perusoikeustyöryhmä 1992 mietintö*, 17. I will not here enter into a discussion about the possibility to derogate from fundamental rights during times of so-called public emergency. It was a topic, however, during the fundamental rights reform and constitutional reform. See, e.g., Perusoikeustyöryhmä, *Perusoikeustyöryhmä 1992 mietintö*, 122; *KM 1992:3*, 148-51, 158, 390-98. Ojanen notes that Section 23 of the 2000 Constitution here closely follows international human rights law (ICCPR, Article 4 and ECHR, Article 15). Ojanen, "Human Rights," 147.
113 *HE 1/1998 vp*, 31; *PeVM 25/1994 vp*, 4; *KM 1997:3*, 69.

means that the provision in question in an exhaustive manner stipulates the grounds on which the fundamental right can be limited.[114]

Section 11 of the 2000 Constitution, on freedom of religion and conscience, does not include a limitation clause.[115] This means that it is possible in law to set limits to this fundamental right in keeping with the general requirements that pertain to limitations to fundamental rights and freedoms. Any limit has to have been legislated about in a law passed by parliament (the criterion of legality) and may not come into conflict with Finland's human rights obligations. In the case of freedom of religion and conscience, this means that the limitation clauses in ICCPR Art. 18 and ECHR Art. 9 have to be taken into account insofar as "the practice or expression of freedom of religion and conscience" goes.[116] The memorandum of the constitutional committee in connection with the fundamental rights reform offers guidance as to what this means more concretely[117] and, as commentators have pointed out, shows close affinity with the criteria used by the European Court of Human Rights to determine whether or not a limitation is legitimate.[118] As far as ECHR Article 9 goes, the justified limitations listed in paragraph 2 are as follows: "freedom to manifest one's religion or beliefs shall be subject only to such limitations as are prescribed by law and are necessary in a democratic society in the interests of public safety, for the protection of public order, health or morals, or for the protection of the rights and freedoms of others."[119]

---

114 *HE 309/1993 vp*, 27-30; *PeVM 25/1994 vp*, 4-6; Jyränki, *Uusi perustuslakimme*; 292-93; Saraviita, *Perustuslaki*, 110-11; Ojanen, *Johdatus*, 37. See also Perusoikeustyöryhmä, *Perusoikeustyöryhmä 1992 mietintö*, 41; *KM 1992:3*, 119-20.

115 During the fundamental rights reform, it was observed that the lack of a limitation clause would underline the "heightened protection of this freedom amongst other fundamental rights", notwithstanding the fact that the freedom can be limited on certain grounds. *KM 1992:3*, 286.

116 Ojanen and Scheinin, "Uskonnon ja omantunnon vapaus," [my translation]. See also *HE 309/1993 vp*, 40; *PeVM 25/1994 vp*, 5; Perusoikeustyöryhmä, *Perusoikeustyöryhmä 1992 mietintö*, 80-81.

117 *PeVM 25/1994 vp*, 5; Ojanen and Scheinin, "Uskonnon ja omantunnon vapaus." *PeVM 25/1994 vp*, 5, calls for an "interpretative harmonization of fundamental rights and human rights".

118 Veli-Pekka Viljanen, "Perusoikeuksien rajoittaminen," in *Perusoikeudet*, ed. Pekka Hallberg et al., Online library Alma Talent, 2011, accessed May 29, 2019, http://fokus.almatalent.fi/teos/FAIBCXJTBF; Jukka Viljanen, "Euroopan ihmisoikeussopimuksen rajoituslausekkeen tulkinnan yhteys perusoikeusuudistukseen—kohti yleistä perus- ja ihmisoikeuksien rajoituskriteeristöä," *Oikeus*, no. 4 (1995): 377-79; Jukka Viljanen, "Euroopan ihmisoikeussopimus perustuslakivaliokunnan tulkintakäytännössä," in *Oikeustiede—Jurisprudentia* XXXVIII, ed. Leena Hallila (Helsinki: Suomalainen Lakimiesyhdistys, 2005): 461-520.

119 See also *HE 170/2002 vp*, 8.

In practice, this suggests that there is an inviolable core to the freedom: the inner freedom of thought of the individual, the freedom to have and adopt a faith or conviction or to abstain from such, freedom from coercion in matters of faith, as well as the right not to have to participate in foreign religious practice. What can legitimately be limited on certain grounds are the "external forms" of manifestation, of practice of the freedom of religion or conscience, including collective action (practice).[120]

Additionally, during the fundamental rights reform it was stated in the government proposal for the fundamental rights reform that the lack of an explicit limitation clause in relation to freedom of religion and conscience does not authorize activities that violate "human dignity, other human rights, or are against the foundations of the legal order [oikeusjärjestys]".[121] Among these activities outlawed are counted: mutilation of the human body, under any circumstances, including female circumcision, as well as polygamy—which is seen as "not compatible with the Finnish legal order". Furthermore:

> the constitutional protection of freedom of religion and conscience does not hinder the enacting of legislation related to peace and order [järjestysluonteinen] that are expressive of generally accepted moral and ethical values in society, legislation which different religious movements must take into consideration in their religious and related practice.[122]

This statement echoes Agrama's observation that what is public order falls back on particular (majoritarian) values and that the purpose to uphold the rule of law simultaneously confirms state sovereignty. Moreover, according to the government proposal, the perspective of other people's fundamental rights has to be taken into account when interpreting the scope of fundamental rights, including the concept of practicing religion. According to the government proposal, the fundamental rights of children, including their right to life and personal integrity, cannot be violated by referring to someone else's freedom of religion and conscience.[123]

---

120 Ojanen and Scheinin, "Uskonnon ja omantunnon vapaus." See also e.g. *KM 1992:3*, 286-87.
121 *HE 309/1993 vp*, 56 [my translation]. The same observation was made during the reform of the Freedom of Religion Act by the committee appointed to draft the new Act and is also included in the governmental proposal. *KM 1999:5*, 28; *KM 2001:1*, 7, 35-36; *HE 170/2002 vp*, 7, 9.
122 *HE 309/1993 vp*, 56 [my translation]. See also e.g. *KM 2001:1*, 35-36.
123 *HE 309/1993 vp*, 56; Ojanen and Scheinin, "Uskonnon ja omantunnon vapaus."

To Follow the Law and Respect Fundamental and Human Rights

This relates to a further dimension of the limits of freedom of religion and conscience. Section 8 of the 1919 Constitution states that: "A Finnish citizen has the right to practice religion in public and in private as long as this does not violate the law or good habits, publicly and privately practice religion, and also, in a way that is regulated separately, withdraw from the religious community to which he belongs, and the freedom to join another religious community."[124] The new 2000 Constitution does not mention the prohibition of violating the law or good habits. Likewise, Section 1 of the 1922 Act on the Freedom of Religion states: "In Finland it is allowed to practice religion in public and in private, as far as law and good habit are not violated."[125] No such limitation clause can be found in the 2003 Act on the Freedom of Religion. Section 1 of that Act states: "The purpose of this Act is to safeguard the exercise of the freedom of religion as provided in the Constitution of Finland. In addition, this Act lays down provisions on the founding of registered religious communities and the basis for their activities".

It is clear from an examination of the preparatory work that "good habits/customs" (*hyvät tavat*) is considered "too vague and subjective in a pluralistic society".[126] Moreover, the committee elaborating the new act found that the criterion of legality, that law sets limits to the practice of freedom of religion and conviction, was covered by other legislation (and we have seen above how this plays out) and that a separate mention was therefore superfluous.[127] Likewise, the subsequent government proposal for the new Act on the Freedom of Religion states that it is not necessary to include a limitation clause spelling out that the law has to be obeyed.[128] In addition, the Evangelical Lutheran Church is counted as part of public power and in accordance with Section 2 of the new Constitution must observe the law in all its public activities.[129]

---

124 My translation. See also *HE 309/1993 vp*, 7.
125 My translation.
126 *KM 1999:5*, 53; *KM 2001:1*, 21, 35; *HE 170/2002 vp*, 22 [my translation]. The same limitation clause also appeared elsewhere than in Section 1: e.g., in relation to the registration of religious communities.
127 *KM 1999:5*, 4, 28-29, 53; *KM 2001:1*, 7, 21, 35. See also *HE 170/2002 vp*, 22. In the old Act, Section 4), acts of private religious practice that violated the law or good habits could result in a fine (unless stricter punishment was called for). The committee found this provision outdated, recognizing also the right to privacy and the difficulty of proving a violation of such kind. *KM 1999:5*, 28-29.
128 *HE 170/2002 vp*, 39.
129 Ojanen, *Johdatus*, 32.

On the other hand, added to the new Act on the Freedom of Religion is the requirement in Section 7 ("Purpose and forms of activity of a registered religious community"), that a registered religious community "shall fulfil its purpose with respect for fundamental and human rights". We can view this as an expression of the internationalization of religion law. What does this mean more concretely, in addition to what has been spelled out in the previous section? Section 25 ("Dissolution of a community and warning") of the new Act states that:

> The competent court of first instance of the municipality in which a registered religious community has its registered office may, upon action brought by the Ministry of Education, a public prosecutor or a member of the religious community, declare the community dissolved if the community acts *materially against the law* or its purpose laid down in the community by-laws.
>
> If the *public interest* does not require that the community be dissolved, a warning may be issued to the community instead of dissolution.[130]

According to Seppo, who was a member of the committee, the dissolution of a community is a very exceptional case. That a registered religious community must have acted in a way that in a material—substantial—way breaks the law means that the unlawful behavior must have been continuous, and it has to be proven that the community has clearly been indifferent to the legal rules. The other basis for dissolution, that the community acts against "its purpose as laid down in the community by-laws", refers to the criterion of importance ("materially").[131] In addition, it is worth mentioning the reference to public interest in Section 25, which Seppo does not mention, but which offers a link back to the discussion in the first part of this chapter.

Concluding Remarks

At the end of the 20th century, a culture of fundamental rights and human rights took root in the Finnish legal context in a different way than before. The purpose of this chapter has been to examine how this concretely works together with—

---

130 Translation by the Ministry of Education and Culture, accessed June 2, 2020, https://www.finlex.fi/fi/laki/kaannokset/2003/en20030453.pdf. My emphasis.

131 Seppo, *Uskonnonvapaus*, 205; KM 2001:1, 46; HE 170/2002 vp, 49. Seppo further notes that dissolution would mean a limitation to a fundamental right and that, in such cases, the rules that govern how fundamental rights can be limited must be followed. Seppo, *Uskonnonvapaus*, 205.

reaffirms and reconfigures—ideas about religious freedom, and "deep structure" ideas about rule of law and legality. What we encounter is an expansion of the substantial basic rights protection, including an expanded concept of freedom of religion and a stronger emphasis on positive freedom of religion, and on collective religious autonomy (which the introduction to this volume identifies as an aspect of "re-confessionalization"). The perception of what this collective religious autonomy is supposed to include seems standard.

Another key concern of the reform, alongside the expansion of the scope of fundamental rights, was to clarify the grounds for the limitation of rights.[132] It is interesting to notice that key clauses on freedom of religion and conscience in the Constitution (Section 11) and the Act on the Freedom of Religion (Section 1) no longer include a limiting clause referring to the need to follow (ordinary secular) law. From the perspective of the wider Finnish legal context, however, it is clear that this should not be taken to mean that individual and collective religious freedom cannot be restricted or limited on legal grounds. The examination of the wider legal context has also shown the influence of international human rights law when it comes to the interpretation of the grounds of limitation—including public order—and the way in which this further affirms secular power (to refer back to Agrama), and indeed to Section 22 of the new Finnish Constitution. "Deep structure" ideas of rule of law and legality are affirmed, with the state as the guarantor.[133]

Moreover, looking at the concrete legislative changes that took place, the legal reforms come across very much as being about the harmonization of law, of international law with national law and within the context of national law: of different pieces of legislation with each other.[134] Or perhaps, in the latter case, we could also say that the reforms very much emphasized clarification and simplification: in rethinking what should go where, and in getting rid of overlapping legislation. It appears that much of this work fell back on an understanding of the law of the land as "one" (albeit not totally). We encounter

---

132 *HE 309/1993 vp*, 14.
133 The new Constitution opens with an affirmation of state sovereignty in Section 1, which includes internal sovereignty in the sense of supreme domestic legislative power. Jyränki, *Uusi perustuslakimme*, 54.
134 See, e.g., *HE 1/1998 vp*, 30-32; *KM 1997:3*, 69. The aim of the overall constitutional reforms was not to change the basic constitutional principles, including the rule of law, parliamentarism, and the division of power, but about achieving new clarity, intelligibility, coherence, and up-to-date legal provisions. *HE 1/1998 vp*, 22; *KM 1997:3*, 70, 72. Ojanen ascribes "harmonisation of constitutional and international protection of human rights" via the impact of international human rights treaties on constitutional reforms, e.g., also to the other Nordic countries. Ojanen, "Human Rights," 143.

an "uncomplicated" view on religion law. For the changes seem to have been not simply of a principled nature (as we might have expected) and about having a law that is up-to-date, but also to a large extent legal technical, as, for example, when regulations concerning to churches and religious communities are inserted into those laws where they are considered to make most sense with regard to their substance.[135]

To sum up, the basic system was thus kept intact, including the fundamental distinction between national churches and registered religious communities with resulting different legal status. Perhaps we see here to some extent the remnants of Protestant hegemony, including the seemingly persistent understanding of the law of the land as secular—both in the sense of "secularity[meaning1]" and "secularity[meaning2]" as identified in the introduction to this volume.

Bibliography

Official sources

Religionsfrihetslag (Act on the Freedom of Religion) 6.6.2003/453. Translation by the Ministry of Education and Culture. Finlex Data Bank. Accessed June 2, 2020, https://www.finlex.fi/fi/laki/kaannokset/2003/en20030453.pdf.

Council of Europe. *European Convention for the Protection of Human Rights and Fundamental Freedoms, as amended by Protocols Nos. 11 and 14*, 4 November 1950, ETS 5

HE 170/2002 vp: Hallituksen esity eduskunnalle uskonnonvapauslaiksi ja eräiksi siihen liittyviksi laeiksi.

HE 1/1998 vp: Hallituksen esitys Eduskunnalle uudeksi Suomen Hallitusmuodoksi

HE 309/1993 vp: Hallituksen esitys Eduskunnalle perustuslakien perusoikeussäännösten muuttamisesta

HE 232/1988 vp: Hallituksen esitys Eduskunnalle tasavallan presidentin vaalitavan muuttamista ja eräiden valtaoikeuksien tarkistamista koskevaksi lainsäädännöksi

KM 2001:1: Uskonnonvapauskomitean mietintö

KM 1999:5: Uskonnonvapauskomitean välimietintö

KM 1997:13: Perustuslaki 2000—komitean mietintö

KM 1992:3: Perusoikeuskomitean mietintö

Lag angående rätt för riksdagen att granska lagenligheten av medlemmarnas av statsrådet och justitiekanslerns ämbetsåtgärder (Ministerial Responsibility Act) 25.11.1922/274, repealed. Finlex Data Bank. Accessed June 1, 2020. https://www.finlex.fi/sv/laki/alkup/1922/19220274

---

135 Cf. Saraviita, *Perustuslaki*, 27, who observes that the overall constitutional reforms were marked by a sense of urgency and the reasons given for the need for reform were of a more practical, functional nature, with restraint shown with regard to broader questions of a principled nature.

Lag om riksrätten (Court of the Realm Act) 25.11.1922/273, repealed. Finlex Data Bank. Accessed June 1, 2020. https://www.finlex.fi/sv/laki/alkup/1922/19220273

PeVL 7/1990 vp: Perustuslakivaliokunnan lausunto

PeVL 6/1990 vp: Perustuslakivaliokunnan lausunto

PeVL 18/1982 vp: Perustuslakivaliokunnan lausunto

PeVL 12/1982 vp: Perustuslakivaliokunnan lausunto

PeVM 10/2002 vp: Perustuslakivaliokunnan mietintö, Hallituksen esitys uskonnonvapauslaiksi ja eräiksi siihen liittyviksi laeiksi

PeVM 10/1998 vp: Perustuslakivaliokunnan mietintö 10/1998 vp, Hallituksen esitys uudeksi Suomen Hallitus-muodoksi

PeVM 25/1994 vp: Perustuslakivaliokunnan mietintö n:o 25 hallituksen esityksestä perustuslakien perusoikeussäännösten muuttamisesta

Regeringsform för Finland (Instrument of Government) 17.7.1919/94, repealed. Finlex Data Bank. Accessed June 1, 2020. https://www.finlex.fi/fi/laki/alkup/1919/19190094001

Riksdagsordning (Parliament Act) 13.1.1928/7. Finlex Data Bank, repealed. Accessed June 1, 2020. https://www.finlex.fi/sv/laki/alkup/1928/19280007

Literature

Agamben, Giorgio. *Homo Sacer: Sovereign Power and Bare Life*. Stanford: Stanford University Press, 1998.

Ali Agrama, Hussein. *Questioning Secularism: Islam, Sovereignty, and the Rule of Law in Modern Egypt*. Chicago: University of Chicago Press, 2012.

Asad, Talal. "Where Are the Margins of the State?" In *Anthropology in the Margins of the State*, edited by Veena Das and Deborah Poole, 279-88. Santa Fe, NM: School of American Research Press, 2004.

Brague, Rémi. *The Law of God: The Philosophical History of an Idea*. Chicago: University of Chicago Press, 2005.

Calo, Zachary R. "Constructing the Secular: Law and Religion Jurisprudence in Europe and the United States." In *Robert Schuman Centre for Advanced Studies Research Paper*, No. RSCAS 2014/94 (2014): 1-24.

Calo, Zachary R. "Christianity, Islam, and Secular Law." *Ohio Northern Law Review* 39, no. 3 (2013): 879-900.

Calo, Zachary R. "Law in the Secular Age." *European Political Science Review* 13, no. 3 (2014): 306-10.

Doe, Norman. *Christian Law: Contemporary Principles*. Cambridge: Cambridge University Press, 2013.

Ferrari, Silvio. "Law and Religion in a Secular World: A European Perspective." *Ecclesiastical Law Journal* 14, no. 3 (2012): 355-70.

Fukuyama, Francis. *The Origins of Political Order: From Prehuman Times to the French Revolution*. New York: Farrar, Straus and Giroux, 2011.

Hallberg, Pekka. "Johdanto." In *Perusoikeudet*, edited by Pekka Hallberg, Heikki Karapuu, Tuomas Ojanen, Martin Scheinin, Kaarlo Tuori, and Veli-Pekka Viljanen. Online library Alma Talent, 2011. Accessed May 29, 2019. http://fokus.almatalent.fi/teos/FAIBCXJTBF.

Hallberg, Pekka, Heikki Karapuu, Tuomas Ojanen, Martin Scheinin, Kaarlo Tuori, and Veli-Pekka Viljanen, eds. *Perusoikeudet*. Online library Alma Talent, 2011. Accessed May 29, 2019. http://fokus.almatalent.fi/teos/FAIBCXJTBF.

Heikkonen, Johannes. "Yhdenvertaisen uskonnon- ja omantunnonvapauden kipupisteitä Suomessa." *Oikeus* 41, no. 4 (2012): 554-63.

Jyränki, Antero. *Uusi perustuslakimme*. Turku: Iura Nova, 2000.

Kotiranta, Matti. "The Application of Freedom of Religion Principles of the European Convention on Human Rights in Finland." In *Religious Freedom in the European Union: The Application of the European Convention on Human Rights in the European Union*, edited by Achilles Emilianides, 129-52. Leuven: Peeters, 2011.

Kotiranta, Matti. "The Recent Developments in the Relationship between State and Religious Communities in Finland." In *Neuere Entwicklungen im Religionsrecht europäischer Staaten*, edited by Wilhelm Rees, María Roca and Balázs Schanda, 303-31. Berlin: Dunker & Humblot, 2013.

Kvist, Hans-Olof. "Kirkon omimmista lähtökohdista nousevien perustavien struktuurien teologista reflektointia kirkkoa, valtiouskontoa, valtiokirkkoa ja tunnustuksetonta valtiota koskevassa asiakentässä." In *Julkisoikeudellinen yhteisö vai Kristuksen kirkko?*, edited by Tapani Ihalainen and Antti Laato, 15-77. Kaarina: Fonticulus, 2008.

Lavapuro, Juha. *Uusi perustuslakikontrolli*. Helsinki: Suomalainen Lakimiesyhdistys, 2010.

Leino, Pekka. *"Endast kyrkans egna angelägenheter": En kyrkorättslig undersökning av kyrkans egna angelägenheter i kyrkolagstiftningen om Evangelisk-lutherska kyrkan i Finland*. PhD diss., Turku: Åbo Akademis förlag, 2012.

Leino, Pekka. *Kirkko ja perusoikeudet*. Helsinki: Suomalainen Lakimiesyhdistys, 2003.

Leino, Pekka. *Kirkkolaki vai laki kirkosta: Hallinto-oikeudellinen tutkimus kirkon oikeudellisista normeista ja niiden synnystä*. PhD diss., Helsinki: Suomalainen Lakimiesyhdistys, 2002.

Lind, Anna-Sara, and Victoria Enkvist, eds. *Constitutionalisation and Hegemonisation: Exploring the Boundaries of Law and Religion 1800-1950*. Odense: University Press of Southern Denmark, *forthcoming*.

Majuri, Tuula. *Lausunnot Perusoikeuskomitean mietinnöstä: Tiivistelmä*. Helsinki: Oikeusministeriö, 1992.

Ojanen, Tuomas. "Human Rights in Nordic Constitutions and the Impact of International Obligations." In *The Nordic Constitutions: A Comparative and Contextual Study*, edited by Helle Krunke and Björg Thorarensen, 133-66. Oxford: Hart Publishing, 2018.

Ojanen, Tuomas. *Johdatus perus- ja ihmisoikeusjuridiikkaan*. Helsinki: Helsingin yliopiston oikeustieteellisen tiedekunnan julkaisuja, 2009.

Ojanen, Tuomas, and Martin Scheinin. "Uskonnon ja omantunnon vapaus (PL 11 §)." In *Perusoikeudet*, edited by Pekka Hallberg, Heikki Karapuu, Tuomas Ojanen, Martin Scheinin, Kaarlo Tuori, and Veli-Pekka Viljanen. Online library Alma Talent, 2011. Accessed May 29, 2019. http://fokus.almatalent.fi/teos/FAIBCXJTBF.

Perusoikeustyöryhmä. *Perusoikeustyöryhmä 1992 mietintö*. Oikeusministeriön lainvalmisteluosaston julkaisu, 2/1993. Helsinki: Oikeusministeriö, 1993.

Perustuslaki 2000-työryhmä. *Perustuslaki 2000: Yhtenäiset perustuslain tarve ja keskeiset valtiosääntöoikeudelliset ongelmat; Työryhmän mietintö.* Oikeusministeriön lainvalmisteluosaston julkaisu, 8/1995. Helsinki: Oikeusministeriö, 1996.

Rasmussen, Tarald, and Jørn Øyrehagen Sunde, eds. *Protestant Legacies of Nordic Law: The Early Modern Period* (forthcoming).

Sakaranaho, Tuula. "Kohti moniuskontoista Suomea? Vähemmistönäkökulma uuteen uskonnonvapauslakiin." In *Kirkko ja usko tämän päivän Suomessa*, edited by Aku Visala, 124-59. Helsinki: Suomalainen teologinen kirjallisuusseura, 2007.

Saraviita, Ilkka. *Perustuslaki 2000: Kommentaariteos uudesta valtiosäännöstä Suomelle.* Helsinki: Lakimiesliiton Kustannus, 2000.

Scheinin, Martin. "Uskonnon ja omantunnon vapaus (PL 11 §)." In *Perusoikeudet*, edited by Pekka Hallberg, Heikki Karapuu, Martin Scheinin, Kaarlo Tuori, and Veli-Pekka Viljanen, 353-86. Helsinki: Werner Söderström lakitieto, 1999.

Schmitt, Carl. *Politiche Theologie: Vier Kapitel zur Lehre von der Souveränitet*, 2nd ed. Munich: Leipzig Verlag von Duncker & Humblot, 1934.

Seppo, Juha. *Uskonnonvapaus 2000-luvun Suomessa.* Helsinki: Edita, 2003.

Seppänen, Arto. *Tunnustus kirkon oikeutena.* PhD diss., Rovaniemi: Lapin yliopisto, 2007.

Sorsa, Leena. *Kansankirkko, uskonnonvapaus ja valtio: Suomen evankelis-luterilaisen kirkon kirkolliskokouksen tulkinta uskonnonvapaudesta 1963-2003.* PhD diss., Tampere: Kirkon tutkimuskeskus, 2010.

Suksi, Markku. "Common Roots of Nordic Constitutional Law?" In *The Nordic Constitutions: A Comparative and Contextual Study*, edited by Helle Krunke and Björg Thorarensen, 9-42. Oxford: Hart Publishing, 2018.

Tuori, Kaarlo. *Critical Legal Positivism.* Aldershot: Ashgate, 2002.

Viljanen, Jukka. "Euroopan ihmisoikeusopimuksen rajoituslausekkeen tulkinnan yhteys perusoikeusuudistukseen—kohti yleistä perus- ja ihmisoikeuksien rajoituskriteeristöä." *Oikeus*, no. 4 (1995): 372-82.

Viljanen, Jukka. "Euroopan ihmisoikeussopimus perustuslakivaliokunnan tulkintakäytännössä." In *Oikeustiede—Jurisprudentia XXXVIII*, edited by Leena Hallila, 461-520. Helsinki: Suomalainen Lakimiesyhdistys, 2005.

Viljanen, Veli-Pekka. "Perusoikeuksien rajoittaminen." In *Perusoikeudet*, edited by Pekka Hallberg, Heikki Karapuu, Tuomas Ojanen, Martin Scheinin, Kaarlo Tuori, and Veli-Pekka Viljanen. Online library Alma Talent, 2011. Accessed May 29, 2019. http://fokus.almatalent.fi/teos/FAIBCXJTBF.

Watson, Alan. "Legal Transplants and Law Reform." *The Law Quarterly Review* 92, no. 1 (1976): 79-84.

Watson, Alan. "Comparative Law and Legal Change." *Cambridge Law Journal* 37, no. 2 (1978): 313-36.

Witte, John, Jr. "From Gospel to Law: The Lutheran Reformation and Its Impact on Legal Culture." *Ecclesiastical Law Journal* 19, no. 3 (2017): 271-91.

Årsheim, Helge, and Pamela Slotte. "The Juridification of Religion?" *Brill Research Perspectives in Law and Religion* 1, no. 2 (2017): 1-89.

Other Sources

LW: Luther, Martin. *Luther's Works*, edited by Jaroslav Pelikan, Helmut T. Lehmann, and Christopher Boyd Brown, 75 vols. Philadelphia, PA/St. Louis, MO: Concordia Publishing House, 1955-.

WA: Luther, Martin. *D. Martin Luthers Werke*. Kritische Gesamtausgabe, 73 vols. Weimar: Böhlau, 1883-2009.

WA TR: Luther, Martin. *D. Martin Luthers Werke*. Kritische Gesamtausgabe. *Tischreden*, 6 vols. Weimar: Böhlau, 1912-21.

List of abbreviations

HE: hallituksen esitys [government proposal]

KM: komiteanmietintö [committee report]

PeVL: perustuslakivaliokunnan lausunto [statement of the Constitutional Law Committee]

PeVM: Perustuslakivaliokunnan mietintö [report of the Constitutional Law Committee]

vp: valtiopäivät [Parliament]

15. Freedom of Religion and Positive Duties of the State: The Case of Sweden

Anna-Sara Lind

Introduction and Points of Departure

This contribution investigates current challenges that the realization of the positive duties of human rights, especially freedom of religion, poses. Traditionally, freedom of religion has been regarded as a negative right, i.e. a right in relation to which the state abstains from taking actions.[1] Positive rights are the demands put on the state to act in order to realize a specific right. With regard to positive rights, the state is required to act so that it ensures that individuals can enjoy their rights. These positive duties vary from article to article in the international conventions, especially in the European Convention on Human Rights (ECHR). The aim of this contribution is to investigate what the theoretical bases for positive obligations are and therefore take as the point of departure the case law of the European Court of Human Rights (ECtHR) as well as European Union (EU) law. A basic illustration of the ideas that were put forth by the so-called Uppsala School, a theory on philosophy of law developed in the Nordic countries in the early 20th century, will also be included. The ideas of the Uppsala School will be included here because the aim of this chapter is to see how these thoughts currently interact with human rights law when it comes to the positive obligations of the state and municipalities in their work of realizing freedom of religion for faith organizations, churches, and individuals.

The case of insurance has been chosen as the focus of this chapter in order to be able to view different perspectives on freedom of religion and to be able to illustrate certain points in the current contribution: the scope and application of human rights in the national context, as well as the duties of the state and private entities. Over the course of the last decade we have seen that, for religious communities that are not Christian, it has become increasingly difficult to rent

---

1 Iain Cameron, *An Introduction to the European Convention of Human Rights*, 8th ed. (Uppsala: Iustus förlag, 2018), 52.

a flat, a basement, or other space. The choice of insurance as the focus of this chapter has been made for two reasons: a) the Uppsala School (and its reluctance toward values and human rights) and b) the recent Swedish Inquiry Report SOU 2018:18. It is not possible to understand the deeper position of human rights and fundamental rights in the Scandinavian countries without understanding the Uppsala School. A basic assumption is that there are difficulties if you are not part of the majority religion, but at the same time there is a wish from society to assist, although such assistance is not always feasible in practice. The concept of the layers of legal culture, as expressed in the research of Kaarlo Tuori, has guided this contribution as it has other contributions to the present volume.[2] We will have the opportunity to come back to this later on when exploring today's presence of the Uppsala school in relation to the realization of human rights. From the beginning of the 20th century, the secularity of the law in the Nordic countries has been intimately linked to the Uppsala School. Accordingly, the Uppsala School has had a more general impact on how the Nordic countries have related to fundamental rights and human rights.[3]

There are also societal, not just scientific or legal reasons, for studying the matters presented in this chapter. Religion is a sensitive matter in Sweden today. It tends to pop up in different contexts, in different settings, and in different forms. The religion of "the others" has become a topic of political debate with extreme right-wing populists who have entered the parliament (the Sweden Democrats party).[4] From a more practical point of view, decisions indirectly having an impact on the exercise of freedom of religion are taken by national and local authorities every day,[5] and the debate involving civil society and individuals is as strong as ever.[6]

---

[2] See the introduction to this current volume but also to Anna Sara Lind and Victoria Enkvist, "Introduction: Deep structures of power; Theoretical points of departures," in *Constitutionalisation and Hegemonisation: Exploring the Boundaries of Law and Religion 1800-1950*, ed. Anna-Sara Lind and Victoria Enkvist (Odense: University Press of Southern Denmark, *forthcoming*).

[3] The focus of this contribution is, however, not to study how human rights can be understood from emotivist, Kantian, or natural law perspectives; on these issues, see e.g. Pamela Slotte, *Mänskliga rättigheter, moral och religion: Om de mänskliga rättigheterna som moraliskt och juridiskt begrepp i en pluralistisk värld*, Åbo: Åbo Akademi Förlag, 2005.

[4] Compare with the contribution by Risto Saarinen and Heikki Koskinen, "Recognition, Religious Identity, and Populism: Lessons from Finland," in this volume.

[5] See the contribution by Victoria Enkvist, "Making Religion Visible in Sweden: Secular Legislation Turns Religious in the Name of Human Rights", in this volume.

[6] Mia Lövheim, "Culture, Conflict and Constitutional Right: Representations of Religion in the Daily Press," in *Religion and European Society: A Primer*, ed. Benjamin Schewel and Erin K. Wilson (Hoboken, NJ: John Wiley & Sons, 2020), 69-81.

Setting the Scene

Freedom of religion has accordingly been vividly discussed in cases relating to school and education,[7] housing issues, freedom of conscience for health personnel,[8] and younger persons being radicalized.[9] The case of insurance has been chosen as the focus of this chapter as it serves as a good case for highlighting different perspectives on freedom of religion that might fall a bit outside the scope of what we find at the very heart of the public sphere. As we will see later in this chapter, this case will in turn illustrate and articulate certain points. But insurance is also relevant in relation to the Uppsala School and its reluctance toward values, including fundamental values. Insurance, as it is presented here, is a legal construction that has very much a private law character and could at first sight be seen as distant from human rights such as freedom of religion. Nevertheless, as we will see, insurances is a tool for realizing the freedom of religion in practice.

But insurance is also relevant for the work of the governmental committee[10] that was given the task of investigating new conditions and options regarding state support for religious communities. The committee presented its proposal in spring 2018 in an inquiry report.[11] As the committee was given the overall task of increasing the realization of freedom of religion, it also presented a dense inquiry. Its proposal was a thorough regulation of how to recognize faith communities. This means that more criteria are to be met in order for a faith organization to get financial support.[12] As we will see, on the surface, each rule is neutral but risks shaping the faith communities in a firm way.

In relation to this recent inquiry, why is the issue of insurance interesting?

---

7   Lotta Lerwall, "Förbud mot konfessionella skolor?," *Svensk Juristtidning*, no. 7 (2018): 523-41. See also Dir. 2019:25 *Tilläggsdirektiv till Utredningen om konfessionella inslag i skolväsendet* where a national inquiry is asked by the government to investigate the matter further.
8   Kavot Zillén, *Hälso- och sjukvårdspersonalens religions- och samvetsfrihet: En rättsvetenskaplig studie om samvetsgrundad vägran och kravet på god vård*, Uppsala: Uppsala Universitet, 2016.
9   SOU 2017:67 Våldsbejakande extremism—En forskarantologi
10 Committee investigating state support for religious communities (*Utredningen om översyn av statens stöd till trossamfund*).
11 SOU 2018:18 Statens stöd till trossamfund i ett mångreligiöst Sverige.
12 Victoria Enkvist and Per-Erik Nilsson, "The Hidden Return of Religion Problematising Religion in Law and Law in Religion in the Swedish Regulation of Faith Communities," in *Reconsidering Religion, Law, and Democracy: New Challenges for Society and Research*, ed. Anna-Sara Lind, Mia Lövheim, and Ulf Zackariasson (Lund: Nordic Academic Press, 2016), 93-108. Compare with Victoria Enkvist and Per-Erik Nilsson, "Techniques of Religion-Making in Sweden: The Case of the Missionary Church of Kopimism," *Critical Research on Religion* 4, no. 2 (2016): 141-55.

Today, many faith organizations are prevented from exercising and living out their religious beliefs because they are not able to get renting contracts. They have difficulties getting contracts because of difficulties getting insurance. This is not a problem for the Christian faith communities but for "the others". We can conclude that not having the possibility of renting is a problem if you are not part of the majority, although there could be a wish for the majority to assist and support. Insurance concerns issues relating to theft, fire, damage of goods in the building, criminal offences, etc. On the surface, the rules and conditions of insurances are expressed in a neutral manner. Such insurance becomes difficult for these minorities to get, because insurance providers do not consider the faith organizations as eligible for meeting the different conditions that they are required to respect.

The structure of this chapter is as follows: A brief section on Scandinavian Realism, in general and more specifically, the Uppsala School, follows the introduction. This section is necessary because it is not possible to understand the deeper position of human and fundamental rights in the contemporary Scandinavian countries without understanding the Uppsala School. The section on *Freedom of Religion – Elements of positive obligations* [see p. 424], presents basic features of the freedom of religion as part of the ECHR. The section, *EU law – Beyond human rights?* [p. 431], analyzes newer trends or at least indications of changes in the field of non-discrimination and religion. In order to explore the current legal developments and traces of change in how freedom of religion currently is evolving, the following section gives us more information about how the situation in Sweden. This section is entitled *A room of one's beliefs – a new architecture of freedom?* and serves a double purpose. It explains suggested changes regarding financial support for faith communities and describes how Muslim faith communities view their own situation. The chapter ends with a section with concluding remarks, where we ask ourselves if there is in fact a renaissance of the Uppsala School.

Lastly, a few words on the perspectives governing the work of this anthology. The current volume covers decades that have seen major changes relating to law and religion. In a short period of time, major issues have been discovered, experienced, and debated in all the countries touched upon in this project. As this volume proposes re-confessionalization as its overall concept, the secularity of law is studied at organizational, structural, and personal levels. As expressed in the "Introduction", differences between these levels of secularity are investigated from the perspective of different disciplines.[13]

---

13 See Pamela Slotte, Niels Henrik Gregersen, and Helge Årsheim, "Introduction: Internationalization and Re-Confessionalization: Law and Religion in the Nordic Realm 1945-2017,"

Scandinavian Realism—the Uppsala School

To a great extent, the legal traditions of the Nordic countries are similar: not too theoretical, but rather oriented towards practical solutions and considerations.[14] This is something that can be traced back to the 19th century, although that period was more oriented towards natural law and positivism. In Sweden, church law had become more and more similar to a sort of a secularized administrative law for the Swedish state church, and in the 1950s the field had entirely vanished from legal education at the Swedish universities.[15] In Sweden and Denmark, a new form of legal philosophy began to develop in the 1920s, a legal philosophy that had its roots in this Nordic legal tradition. The main and initial group of this movement was the Uppsala School.[16] The founder of this legal philosophy was Axel Hägerström (1868-1939).

Others were to follow Hägerström,[17] for example Vilhelm Lundstedt (1882-1955), Alf Ross (1899-1979), Karl Olivecrona (1897-1980), and Per Olof Ekelöf (1906-1990). After the end of World War II, Swedish lawyers were trained in this tradition, greatly inspired by Hans Kelsen (1881-1973) and claiming to be neutral in regards to fundamental values.[18] Thus the Uppsala School had a significant impact on the thinking and argumentation of many Nordic lawyers, most strongly in Sweden and Denmark where its development and application could easily be fulfilled.[19] The point of departure for the Uppsala School was the idea that there are no absolute rights. Furthermore, the Uppsala School held

---

    in this volume. Compare with Lind and Enkvist, "Introduction."

14 See also Pamela Slotte's contribution to this volume, in which she points to the major reforms that have taken place in Finland the last 30 years: a new bill of rights, a new constitution, and a new Act on freedom of religion. See Slotte, "Moving Frontiers: Configuring Religion Law and Religious Law, and Law-Religion Relations."

15 Kjell Å. Modéer, "Kyrkans rätt framför dess lag: Europé och jurist i den svenska folkkyrkans tjänst; Göran Göransson (1925-1998)—en kyrkorättshistorisk biografi," *Kyrkohistorisk årsskrift* 119 (2019): 153.

16 Stig Strömholm, *Rätt, rättskällor och rättstillämpning: En lärobok i allmän rättslära*, 5th ed. (Stockholm: Norstedts Juridik, 1996), 101.

17 For a recent study on Axel Hägerström, see Patricia Mindus, *A Real Mind: The Life and Work of Axel Hägerström* (New York: Springer, 2017) as well as Johan Strang, "Scandinavian Legal Realism and Human Rights: Axel Hägerström, Alf Ross and the Persistent Attack on Natural Law," *Nordic Journal of Human Rights* 36, no. 3 (2018): 202-18. In his inauguration lecture, Hägerström underlined that metaphysics was dead and that there are no objective rights or duties, this is grounded in a suspicious metaphysics that needs to be erased once and for all. See: Modéer, "Kyrkans rätt framför dess lag," 153.

18 Modéer, "Kyrkans rätt framför dess lag," 153.

19 In Norway, natural law perspectives also came to play a role. In Finland, legal thought remained closer to that of German legal scholars.

that general values should be denied and that a judge must always act to create law in order to serve the good of society. Values, in themselves constructed by man and highly dependent on their context, however, may be given a role in relation to a legal context where the law ought not to go beyond its frames in order to be valid. The philosophers of the Uppsala School were also convinced that every legal problem had more than one possible and legally correct answer. As for the connection to "realism", the Uppsala School stressed that their theory was hesitant in terms of recognizing the importance of general legal concepts for argumentation. They thought that reflection on how the courts actually reached their decisions was the proper object of the law.[20] In this connection, the concept of "the nature of the matter" or "real considerations" became the basis of the Danish and Swedish doctrine of legal sources. Law was also considered an instrument of "social engineering"; this was viewed as a core element of Scandinavian Realism. And for the development of the Swedish welfare state, law as a tool of change was crucial.[21]

To some extent the view was different in Norway (where natural law remained an important factor) and even more so in Finland. In Finland, the dominance of German jurisprudence was strong and only began to diminish from the 1950s with the more contemporary influences from Analytical Philosophy and the so-called Analytical School of Law. Analytical criticism focused mainly on "conclusions from concepts". We can conclude that, in Finland today, legal and fundamental principles have become important, but concepts are still the focus: they prepare the way for principles-based legal argumentation.

The positions of the Uppsala School are not easy to combine with the idea of a strong written constitution, nor with a strong position of international human rights. It is no surprise that what we call Scandinavian Realism became a strong phenomenon in Denmark and Sweden in the 20th century. These countries, which possessed constitutions of long standing, had not had to fight for freedom nor to win over any external power. Nor has the position of human rights been strongly rooted in the constitutional framework nor in the legal tradition. At the time of the beginning of the Uppsala School, the constitutions of these two countries were already old and neither politically nor judicially

---

20   Tormod Otter Johansen, *Förvaltning som verksamhet: Bidrag till offentligrättens allmänna läror*, Juridiska institutionens skriftserie 31 (JD diss., Gothenburg: Göteborgs Universitet, 2019), 69-71.

21   Mats Kumlien, *Professorspolitik och samhällsförändring: En rättshistorisk undersökning av den svenska förvaltningsrättens uppkomst* (Stockholm: Jure AB, 2019), 226-28.

important.²² On the contrary, in Finland and Norway the constitutions had served as symbols of a fight against an external supreme power, a weapon in fighting against oppression.²³ In Finland, a more legalistic tradition evolved. Older constitutions, with roots going back to ancient times, also pointed towards a more political and careful constitutional interpretation.²⁴

In relation to the ECtHR, an ambiguity becomes relevant. This became clear from the beginning of the 1980s, when the ECtHR began ruling against the Nordic convention states. But already when the Nordic countries began to ratify the ECHR in the 1950s, one should understand that the contemporary situation reflected some ambiguity. By then, Sweden had become more secular and the Uppsala School had gained more influence. Not surprisingly, the first Act on Freedom of Religion was enacted in Sweden, stating a negative right from religion (necessary in order to meet the requirements of the ECHR). As Modéer puts it, at that time, the struggle between the old idealistic and metaphysically oriented legal perspectives had been replaced with a more positivist pragmatic and realistic legal concept.²⁵ The implication became clearer and clearer the more significant the ECHR's constitutional status became. How is one to deal with the fact that the ECtHR has opinions relating to the interpretation of (constitutional) rights? And, if the ECHR is to be interpreted in a dynamic way, should this interpretation also count for the way the constitution is perceived? This has not been easy for legislators to handle. In the case of Sweden, we can see some reluctance that still remains in the constitution itself. When Sweden entered the EU, the ECHR was implemented as an Act of Parliament. It was added to Chapter 2, Section 19 of the Swedish Constitution that no Act or decision should go against the ECHR. At the same time, from the beginning of the 1980s, there has existed a clause stating that a court or an authority which finds a written

---

22 In Sweden, the Constitution Instrument of Government (IG) (SFS 174:152 *Regeringsformen*) was considered outdated in some respects. For decades, the new parliamentary system and equal and universal suffrage were not regulated in the constitution. See Mats Kumlien, *Professorspolitik*, 199. See also Fredrik Sterzel, "Författningens föränderlighet: Från 1809 till 1974," in *Författning i utveckling: Tjugo studier kring Sveriges författning*, 2nd ed. (Uppsala: Iustus förlag 2009), 70-91.
23 On Norway, see Eivind Smith, *Konstitusjonelt demokrati*, 4th ed. (Bergen: Fagbokforlaget, 2017). On Finland, see Markku Suksi, *Finlands statsrätt* (Turku: Åbo Akademis förlag, 2002). See also Pia Letto-Vanamo, Ditlev Tamm and Bent Ole Gram, eds., *Nordic Law in European Context* (New York: Springer, 2019).
24 Ross also questioned how the Constitution of Denmark ought to be interpreted. See Alf Ross, *Dansk statsforfatningsret* (Copenhagen: Nyt Nordisk Forlag Arnold Busck, 1959-1960) and Alf Ross, *Ret og retfærdighed: En indførelse i den analytiske retsfilosofi* (Copenhagen: Nyt Nordisk Forlag Arnold Busck, 1953).
25 Modéer, "Kyrkans rätt framför dess lag," 155.

rule that is contradictory to the constitution or any higher rule or that has been decided in a manner that is not correct, must disregard this rule and not apply it. For rules that have been decided by the parliament or the government, this should be the case if the contradiction is manifest (Swedish *uppenbart*), or manifestly contradictory. The "manifest-criterion" was interpreted in a narrow way, especially for rules that had been enacted by the parliament.[26] At the beginning of 2000s, one started to see a new development: the rules and decisions stemming from EU law or referring to the ECHR were not affected by this constitutional clause. In the constitutional revision of 2010, the clause was changed. Today, it mentions that one should be especially careful if parliament has decided the rule.[27]

Freedom of Religion—Elements of Positive Obligations

Freedom of religion as expressed in the ECHR and through the case law of the ECtHR has been extensively analyzed in the legal literature of the last decade.[28] Here, we must outline how this right is protected in Article 9 of the ECHR to the extent needed in order to further study and understand the implications of the right in relation to the Swedish case that is the focus of this chapter.

The freedom of religion as expressed in Article 9 of the ECHR is a right that, as is the case with other rights, varies in strength and content depending on context and case, since it is a right in which state parties also have a rather large margin of appreciation underlines this observation. First and foremost, it includes the right to have a specific belief or faith. It includes the absolute right to have a faith or belief but also the right to live and exercise one's religion or faith through, for example, ceremonies and rituals. We can accordingly say that freedom of religion includes a certain core: the right to have a belief or faith. But there is also an external sphere of the freedom that is possible to limit: the right to exercise one's belief.[29] The ECHR protects first of all the core of the freedom of religion. The right to have an individual, personal belief is part of the freedom of religion in Article 9 of the ECHR that cannot be limited. This right

---

26 Karin Åhman, *Normprövning: Domstols kontroll av svensk lags förenlighet med regeringsrätten och europarätten* (Stockholm: Norstedts Juridik, 2011).
27 See Chapter 11 Section 14 and Chapter 12 Section 10 of the IG.
28 Prop. 2009/10:80 En reformerad grundlag, 145-47.
29 See, e.g., *Darby v. Sweden*, application no. 11581/85, 187 ECHR (Ser. A) (Annex) 9 May 1989, 44. See also Victoria Enkvist, *Religionsfrihetens rättsliga ramar* (Phd. diss. Uppsala: Iustus förlag, 2013), 108-9.

includes the freedom to choose freely, keep and change one's belief or faith.[30] Accordingly, the scope and application of this absolute right is very narrow. Examples of situations in which the right to have a belief or a faith have been seen as violated include when people are forced to change, abandon, or alter their religion or belief, when people are punished due to their conviction, or when they are forced to state what their conviction is. Not all forms of beliefs are included in Article 9, a fact illustrated by the ECtHR in the case *Pretty v. the United Kingdom*.[31] This conclusion is confirmed in later cases as well.[32] All the world religions and different forms of these, such as the Jehovah's Witnesses, are viewed as beliefs worthy of protection.[33] But newer forms have also been included and are protected by the article, as is non-religion.

As we shall see below, core concepts for understanding the scope of the freedom of religion include "faith", "belief", "manifestation", and "limitation." The convention states possess a limited possibility to determine whether or not a manifestation should be protected. It is not for the state to decide if a conviction is true or not or if it should be seen as socially accepted, nor is it the ECtHR's task to judge if a belief is true or legitimate.[34] In the case *Campbell and Cosans v. the United Kingdom*, the ECtHR concluded that the expression "beliefs" in Article 9 of the ECHR "denotes views that attain a certain level of cogency, seriousness, cohesion and importance".[35] In this description is not included a right to decide if the belief is legitimate or not. A belief worthy of protection is always something that has to do with individuals' subjective experiences, and this creates complicated decisions relating to how and where to draw the line. Consequently, the ECtHR has been very generous in its rulings on how to decide whether a belief is worthy of protection according to Article 9 of the ECHR.

Defining the Outer Limits—The Right to Live One's Religion

The relative right to *exercise* one's religion or belief includes the broad field of the freedom of religion and, accordingly, is possible to limit. Article 9 of the ECHR includes a non-exhaustive list of possible limitations. This is because in some cases a manifestation of one's belief can be difficult to reconcile with the

---

30   *Kjeldsen, Busk Madsen and Pedersen v. Denmark*, application nos 5095/71, 5920/72, 5926/72, 7 December 1976.
31   *Pretty v. the United Kingdom,* application no. 2346/02, 29 April 2002.
32   See *S.A.S. v. France* [GC], application no. 43835/11, 1 July 2014.
33   See, e.g., *Kokkinakis v. Greece*, application 14307/88, 25 May 1993.
34   *Manoussakis and others v. Greece,* application 18748/91, 26 September 1996, para. 47; *Hasan and Chaush* v. *Bulgaria*, application no. 30985/96, 26 October 2000, para. 78.
35   *Campbell and Cosans v. the United Kingdom,* application nos 7511/76, 7743/76, 25 February 1982, para. 36.

fundamental rights of others. Over time, this vagueness has changed in the case-law of the ECtHR. In older case-law, criteria were decided upon regarding what could be seen as a manifestation of religion worthy of protection (manifestation). One such criterion is the link between belief and expression first stated by the European Commission in the decision *Arrowsmith v. the United Kingdom*.[36] In this case, the Commission differentiated between actions that are motivated and influenced by a belief and those which are manifested by a belief.[37] The actions of the first category normally fall outside the protected area of freedom of religion, while the second category falls within. According to the Commission, the conduct or action must be closely related to the belief in question. Over time, the ECtHR has ceased giving importance to what can be considered a manifestation worthy of protection. Today, attention is given to the question of whether the manifestation can be limited through the wording of Article 9.2 of the ECHR and the individual's view on the question of what should be a religious manifestation. Consideration of the link between the action and the belief seems to occur if the link is unclear or doubtful. This is illustrated by the case *Leyla Şahin v. Turkey*, in which the ECtHR emphasized finding out whether there were legitimate reasons for limiting the manifestation of freedom of religion according to Article 9.2 of the ECHR.[38] In the case *Leyla Şahin v. Turkey*, the link between manifestation and belief was further explored. In the judgment *Eweida and Others v. the United Kingdom*, the ECtHR stated that the requirement of a link should be decided by taking into consideration the circumstances of the individual case, and that one could not ask that the individual should have an obligation to show that the action was done in order to fulfil a religious duty.[39] Accordingly, the ECtHR has come to the conclusion that the question of what counts as "manifestation" for purposes of Article 9 should be handled more generously. This is a reasonable development, as the Court is given the option to decide immediately if a certain measure has led to a limitation of the individual's freedom of religion and if this limitation has been legitimate; i.e., whether the measure has been necessary due to the interests listed in Article 9.2 of the ECHR.

---

36 *Arrowsmith v. the United Kingdom*, application no. 7050/75, 19 DR 5, 12 October 1978; *Pretty v. the United Kingdom*, para. 82. Compare with *Eweida and Others v. the United Kingdom*, applications no. 48420/10, 59842/10, 51671/10 and 36516/10, 15 January 2013, para. 82.
37 *Arrowsmith v. the United Kingdom*, para. 71.
38 *Leyla Şahin v. Turkey* [GC], application no. 44774/98, 10 November 2005, para. 78. See also *Ahmet Arslan and Others v. Turkey*, application no. 41135/98, 23 February 2010.
39 *Eweida and Others v. the United Kingdom*, para. 82, "there is no requirement on the applicant to establish that he or she acted in fulfilment of a duty mandated by the religion in question."

Limiting the Freedom of Religion

In some cases, the area belonging to the outer, external sphere of freedom of religion can be limited. It follows from Article 9.2 of the ECHR that the freedom to live and manifest one's religion or belief can be limited to some extent. When it has been determined that the manifestation falls within and is protected by Article 9.1 of the ECHR and that the manifestation has been limited by a convention state, it must be decided if the manifestation is *legitimate* and *allowed*. A convention state can limit the right to manifest one's religion if the limitation is prescribed by law (law, regulations, *travaux préparatoires*, or case law: sufficiently clear, precise, accessible, and foreseeable) and necessary in a democratic society due to public safety, for the benefit of public order, health or morals, or for protecting the individual freedoms and rights of others. The different legitimate aims listed in Article 9.2 are limited and should not be supplemented with other criteria.[40] In order to decide if a limitation is legitimate or not, the public interest in limiting the right to manifest one's religion or belief is weighed against the individual interest of being allowed to manifest one's belief. The question of whether a limitation is necessary in a democratic society has been considered more important than that of the interest behind the limitation. In the cases in which the convention states have limited individuals' rights, in general the ECtHR has maintained a restrictive interpretation of the "necessary" requirement.[41]

In order for a limitation to be necessary in a democratic society, there must be a *pressing social need*,[42] and the limitation must be proportionate in relation to the protected interest. The ECtHR has explained that a contract of employment cannot mean that individuals are denied their rights. A worker's freedom to conclude a contract cannot be used as an argument for allowing fundamental human rights to be ignored. In the case *Eweida and Others* v. *the United Kingdom*, the ECtHR explains that:

> Given the importance in a democratic society of freedom of religion, the Court considers that, where an individual complains of a restriction on freedom of religion in the workplace, rather than holding that the possibility of changing job would negate any interference with the right, the better approach would be to weigh that possibility in the overall balance when considering whether or not the restriction was proportionate.[43]

---

40 Enkvist, *Religionsfrihetens rättsliga ramar*, 101-3.
41 *Silver and Others v. the United Kingdom*, applications no 5947/72, 6205/73, 7052/75, 7061/75, 7107/75, 7113/75 and 7136/75, 25 March 1983, para. 97 d.
42 *Handyside* v. *the United Kingdom*, application no. 5493/72, 7 December 1976, para. 48.
43 *Eweida and Others* v. *the United Kingdom*, para. 83.

The ECtHR has first and foremost taken into consideration the employee's possibility of choosing when considering whether the limitation has been necessary in a democratic society. It can be questioned if a concluded employment contract is always voluntary, and if employees have at all a genuine option of quitting their position. The possibility for an employee to refrain from entering into an employment contract or having the option to resign for religious reasons can be influenced by economic or social circumstances. The same reasoning can be employed for a job-seeker where the social vulnerability can be considered even stronger.

Here, the center of attention is the positive obligations that rise from the ECHR in relation to the realization of the freedom of religion. National agencies and authorities are obliged to act in order for freedom of religion to mean something, to have value. The ECtHR has explained that it is important for a faith community to be able to hold ceremonies in an appropriate building.[44] On another occasion, limitations of this right have been explained as reasonable.[45] As an example, the ECtHR upheld sending a person to prison for using premises for a ceremony without having official permission.[46] The ECtHR has also dealt with matters relating to permission to build a place of worship.[47] In several of these cases, the rights of others and constitutional values are important when denying a faith community something that relates to the premises of their faith.

The freedom of religion as stated in Article 9 of the ECHR is indeed an interesting right and its scope is depending on how one approaches the right. As we have seen, the core of the right is one thing, the external dimension another. And this is also true dependent on whether one considers the positive or negative duties involved in the right. Is it the case that the state has a duty to ensure that individuals and faith organizations have a genuine possibility of realizing their rights, and if so, to what extent? In reality, rules relating to insurance can be the point that closes the possibility of realizing one's freedom of religion. And if we study the cases *Vergos* v. *Greece*[48] *and Johannische Kirche and Peters* v. *Germany*,[49] we can see that the ECtHR gives us some guidance when it comes to the matter of religious groups having the right to meet in premises for the purpose of realizing their religion.

---

44 Hans Danelius, *Mänskliga rättigheter i europeisk praxis*, 5th ed. (Stockholm: Norstedts Juridik, 2015), 362.
45 *Vergos* v. *Greece*, application no. 65501/01, 24 June 2004.
46 *Manoussakis and others v. Greece*.
47 *Johannische Kirche and Peters v. Germany*, application no. 41754/98, decision of 10 July 2001.
48 *Vergos* v. *Greece*.
49 *Johannische Kirche and Peters* v. *Germany*.

But there are other rights that are also relevant. The right to property and the right to conduct a business raise similar questions as to where the line of the state's responsibility should be drawn. In cases relating to rent issues, the right to property has been limited for the general public's good, but the ECtHR has also needed to decide upon what kinds of measures a state can decide to take in order to protect tenants or landlords. In this regard, social justice, being a politically important matter, has been considered to be a very important value.[50]

Lastly, the prohibition of discrimination is established in Article 14 ECHR and as such should be linked to other articles in the ECHR. The situation at hand in our Swedish case study involves more rights and freedoms than are covered solely by Article 9. It seems that the case studied here involves *both* religion and ethnicity when it is difficult to obtain insurance and find premises for religious ceremonies. This will be explained in more detail in the following text, but for now we suggest that Article 14 of the ECHR can be relevant in combination with Article 9, 10 and/or additional protocol 1 Article 1.

EU Law—Beyond Human Rights?

The presence of EU law in the Swedish setting adds yet another layer of complexity to the judicial matters surrounding the realization of the freedom of religion. Today, constitutional patterns are more complex than ever. One can speak of a pluralization of law, in which different jurisdictions, although existing in the same country, overlap and engage with each other. In Sweden, this is the case: EU law and national law are more intertwined that ever, and the ECHR has been granted the status of national law. We can conclude that there are several layers of law in different fields, several legislators being active, and more interpreters of the law than has ever been the case before.[51]

The project of the EU was not a constitutional project from the beginning, but a strong collaboration between states to increase wealth and strengthen finances in order to realize stability in Europe. The last decades have seen the EU legal order, being *sui generis*, become its own constitutional order but not without tensions in relation to the member states. Important in these different changes is the Court of Justice of the European Union (CJEU). This Court

---

50   *Mellacher et al. v. Austria*, application nos 10522/83, 11011/84 and 11070/84, 19 December 1989.
51   Anna-Sara Lind, "Social rights and EU Citizenship," in *Bridging the Prosperity Gap in the EU: The Social Challenge Ahead*, ed. Ulf Bernitz, Moa Mårtensson, Lars Oxelheim, and Thomas Persson (Cheltenham: Edward Elgar, 2018), 22-45.

presented and introduced human rights to the European Communities and has tried to evoke these rights as principles in order to avoid clashes with the constitutional systems of the member states. Eventually, the ECHR was referred to in the core treaties of the EU. Today, the EU is struggling with a heterogeneous and diverse group of 28 member states. Globalization, migration, and populism are challenges for all these member states although in different forms and strengths. The EU has slowly begun to change its language in order to be more constitutional, adapting to national perspectives, and less international. In the CJEU's rulings we can see a constitutional language moving away from human rights: fundamental rights are not human rights, but EU rights. Some state that the CJEU is undermining the rights nationally, in its practical realization, and forcing the member states to adjust their system in a way that is not "rights friendly".[52]

The EU system is currently, despite its EU Charter on Fundamental Rights, starting to show less understanding for adapting to the ECHR and its margin of appreciation.[53] We are now seeing that the CJEU has begun to change its position regarding how to balance the responsibility for realizing fundamental rights. In the case of *Google v. Spain*, it has opened up for the realization of fundamental rights through private parties who also have the responsibility of doing so.[54] This development is in line with the development of some cases from the ECtHR relating to privacy,[55] but contradicts the national constitutional traditions and cultures. The political strength of the EU and its Court, as well as the EU's position as *sui generis* for half a century, open up for rulings that do not depend upon assessing any margin of appreciation or searching for criteria such as "manifest". Rulings and legislation have become more legally detailed than was the case earlier, and fewer alternative solutions are possible. This also means that other rights than those initially considered become important.

In the last decade, religion in particular has begun to emerge in cases before

---

52 Iain Cameron, "Freedom of Religion and Competing Human Rights Systems," in *Freedom of Religion in the 21st Century: A Human Rights Perspective on the Relation between Politics and Religion*, ed. Hans-Georg Ziebertz and Ernst Hirsch Ballin (Leiden: Brill, 2016), 44.
53 Cf. Cameron, *Freedom of Religion*, 43.
54 Google v. Spain deals with issues relating to privacy as a fundamental right within the EU system. See Cecilia Magnusson Sjöberg, "Safeguarding Freedom of Information in a Privacy Protection Society: The Interplay with Public Records Management," in *Information and Law in Transition: Freedom of Speech, Privacy, Democracy and the Internet in the 21st Century*, ed. Anna-Sara Lind, Jane Reichel, and Inger Österdahl (Stockholm: Liber förlag, 2015), 100-14.
55 See, e.g., *Hatton and Others v. the United Kingdom*, application no 36022/97, 2 October 2001.

the CJEU.⁵⁶ Article 10 of the EU Charter on Fundamental Rights (the Charter) regulates freedom of religion. It is based on the wording of Article 9 of the ECHR and cannot be derogated from.⁵⁷ However, the legal development has not been as rapid as one might have guessed from following public debate. In cases C-71/11 and C-99/11, *Y and Z v. Germany*, the CJEU's attention turned toward the definition of religion for asylum seekers. The distinction of external/internal freedom of religion seemed less important in this case, which focused on understanding how Directive 2004/83 should be understood in relation to the risk of being put in danger once a religious person is sent back to his country of origin.⁵⁸

Article 10 of the Charter has been relevant in more cases. The case C-157/15, *Samira Achbita v. G4S Secure Solutions NV*, concerns issues relating to discrimination and to publicly showing religious symbols and clothing. The complaint dealt with the situation of a Muslim woman who worked for a private company and who wore a headscarf. The employer had decided to have internal rules forbidding the visible wearing of any political, philosophical, or religious sign in the workplace. The question in the case was whether this could be said to be in violation of Directive 2000/78 which states a general framework for combating discrimination on the grounds of religion or belief, disability, age, or sexual orientation as regards employment and occupation. The CJEU referred once again to the ECHR and explained that the Charter uses the term 'religion' in a broad sense, as the freedom of persons to manifest their religion is included. Therefore, the EU legislature must be considered to have intended to take the same approach when adopting Directive 2000/78. Accordingly, the concept of 'religion' in Article 1 of that directive should be interpreted as covering both the *forum internum*, that is, the fact of having a belief, and the *forum externum*, that is, the manifestation of religious faith in public.⁵⁹ The CJEU then concluded that it was for the national court to rule in the case. It also explained that it could

---

56 See, e.g., C-426/16, *Liga van Moskeeën en Islamitische Organisaties Provincie Antwerpen VZW and Others v. Vlaams Gewest*, ECLI:EU:C:2018:335, which is about religious slaughter and animal welfare legislation within the European Union. In this case (para. 79) the Court concluded that a disproportionate financial burden due to the animal welfare legislation was not enough to say that the legislation in question had infringed upon the freedom of religion. In C-74/16, *Congregación de Escuelas Pías Provincia Betania v. Ayuntamiento de Getafe*, ECLI:EU:C:2017:496, state aid rules were discussed in relation to special rules.
57 The rights from which there can be no derogation under Article 15(2) of the ECHR are those enshrined in Articles 2, 4, 5(1) and 49 of the Charter. See cases C-71/11 and C-99/11, *Y and Z v. Germany*, ECLI:EU:C:2012:518, para. 8.
58 Cases C-71/11 and C-99/11, *Y and Z v. Germany*, para. 72.
59 C-157/15, *Samira Achbita, Centrum voor gelijkheid van kansen en voor racismebestrijding v. G4S Secure Solutions NV*, ECLI:EU:C:2017:203, para. 28.

not decide anything in relation to the issue of discrimination, as not enough evidence had been shown in that regard. However, the CJEU indicated another issue for the national court to bear in mind. The CJEU underscored that an employer's wish to project an image of neutrality towards customers relates to the freedom to conduct a business as stated in Article 16 of the Charter. In principle, it is legitimate, notably where the employer, in pursuit of that aim, involves only those workers who are required to come into contact with the employer's customers.[60] The CJEU also admitted that an interpretation to the effect that the pursuit of that aim allows, within certain limits, a restriction to be imposed on the freedom of religion is, moreover, borne out by the caselaw of the ECtHR in relation to Article 9 of the ECHR (para. 39). The prohibition of workers from wearing visible signs of political, philosophical, or religious beliefs is appropriate for the purpose of ensuring that a policy of neutrality is properly applied, provided that that policy is genuinely pursued in a consistent and systematic manner (para. 40).[61]

The case C-25/17, *Tietosuojavaltuutettu*, deals with the practice of door-to-door preaching by the Jehovah's Witnesses. In Finland, the National Data Protection Board had raised concerns about how data and personal information was handled in these situations. The CJEU concluded that a religious community is a controller, jointly with its members who engage in preaching, for the processing of personal data carried out by the latter in the context of door-to-door preaching organized, coordinated, and encouraged by that community. This was said without it being necessary that the community has access to those data, or to establish that that community has given its members written guidelines or instructions in relation to the data processing. In Article 17 TFEU, the principle of the organizational autonomy of religious communities is stated. However, the CJEU stated that the obligation of every person to comply with the rules of EU law on the protection of personal data cannot be regarded as an interference in the organizational autonomy of those communities.[62]

One of the most recent cases is C-414/16, *Vera Egenberger v. Evangelisches Werk für Diakonie und Entwicklung eV*, in which the claimant had applied for a job in a church. She had been asked to indicate that she was a member of a Christian church. As she had not done so, she supposed that her application had been

---

60 C-157/15, *Samira Achbita, Centrum voor gelijkheid van kansen en voor racismebestrijding v. G4S Secure Solutions NV*, para. 38.
61 See also the case C-188/15, *Asma Bougnaoui, Association de défense des droits de l'homme (ADDH) v. Micropole SA, formerly Micropole Univers SA*, ECLI:EU:C:2017:204, in which there was no internal rule at the workplace.
62 C-25/17, *Tietosuojavaltuutettu*, ECLI:EU:C:2018:551, para. 74.

rejected because she did not belong to any denomination. The case turned out to be complicated as it involved national rules, religious organizational rules, EU law as expressed in Directive 2000/78 and in the fundamental treaties, and the Charter. The prohibition of all discrimination on grounds of religion or belief is mandatory as a general principle of EU law and is laid down in Article 21(1) of the Charter. The CJEU underlined that it is sufficient in itself to confer on individuals a right which they may rely on in disputes within a field covered by EU law. This prohibition is valid also for contracts between individuals.[63]

A Room of One's Beliefs – A New Architecture of Freedom?

Freedom of religion is a legal construction with implications for individuals and organizations. It has inner implications and external expressions. Part of this freedom is that a place for worship is necessary. Until the present time, it has been a requirement that faith organizations are requested to have a place of worship (house, church, etc.) in order to receive funding. In the Swedish Inquiry Report SOU 2018:18 (hereafter the Inquiry), it is suggested that having a place of worship should no longer be a criterion for receiving funding. The proposal does not, however, completely solve the problem of funding.

The Inquiry explains that an express aim of its work is to give the freedom of religion a stronger position as a human right and through the state's support to strengthen the democratic principles in important parts of civil society. It is evident that these two interests can easily contradict each other. The wish to maintain a strong position for the freedom of religion is explained as follows: The state should make sure that all registered faith communities receive the same state support in the exercise of their respective traditions. This should be done while at the same time following up and controlling the communities' activities. The control easily comes with a risk of limiting and restraining the faith communities' freedom of expression.[64] Two issues then become important to reflect upon: firstly, what are the clear conditions that the state can ask for regarding the religious expressions of the faith communities so that these conditions and the religious expressions do not contradict the democratic principles? Secondly, do these criteria respect the constitutional demands of Chapter 2 section 21 in

---

63 C-414/16, *Vera Egenberger v. Evangelisches Werk für Diakonie und Entwicklung eV*, ECLI:EU:C:2018:257, para. 78.
64 Compare with Tuomas Ojanen, "Human Rights in Nordic Constitutions," in *The Nordic Constitutions*, ed. Helle Krunke and Bjørg Thorarensen (Oxford: Hart publishing, 2018), 146.

the Swedish Instrument of Government (IG, *Regeringsformen*)? These criteria are: that the limitation should be necessary in a democratic society, that it must never go beyond what is necessary with regard to the purpose which occasioned it, and that it not be carried so far as to constitute a threat to the free shaping of opinion as one of the foundations of democracy. Finally, no limitation may be imposed solely on grounds of a political, religious, cultural, or other such opinion. The democratic criterion suggested in the Inquiry appears to follow from a wish that the state should combat situations in which financial support is paid to faith communities seeking to establish undemocratic values. The criterion does not follow from or refer to the constitutional system as such.

A suggestion to restrain or even limit the freedom of religion can have an impact on adherents of many forms of religion. The larger the range of options for limiting support, the greater the risk that those who are not part of the majority religion do not receive support. This is especially true if the Act is not designed to respect minority expressions of religion. If it is worded in a general manner but mostly takes into account the majority's perspective, minorities risk not being heard. In the long run, a too-narrow way of viewing the democracy criteria risks having an impact on the realization of other rights, including not only those groups who (unconsciously) work for undemocratic values. The limitation of a right risks engendering unwanted and unproportioned effects. In Sweden, one example that can be mentioned is the suggested Act prohibiting the wearing of masks during demonstrations.[65] The Council on Legislation reacted strongly as it took into consideration the effect the suggested Act would have on all sorts of demonstrations and freedoms of opinion.[66]

At several points, the Inquiry refers to what it calls "our fundamental values" (*våra grundläggande värderingar*)[67]. This concept is supposed to establish the basis for the democracy criterion that the Inquiry intends to develop and present. At the same time, the Inquiry underlines that such a criterion should not be a pretext for testing or performing a value judgment on the faith community's belief.[68] The Inquiry also set forth that Chapter 1 Section 2 states the fundamental values that are especially important for Swedish society, and for which all agencies and public servants should strive when realizing their missions and tasks. This constitutional statement was introduced into the Constitution in the late 1970s and is the constitutional expression of the welfare

---

[65] This was in 2005. See Prop. 2005/06:11 Maskeringsförbud.
[66] Council on Legislation, 29 September 2004. See Prop. 2005/06:11, bilaga 5.
[67] See SOU 2018:18, 28.
[68] Compare with Prop. 1998/99:124 Staten och trossamfunden—stöd, medverkan inom totalförsvaret, m.m., 66, see SOU 2018:18, 276-77.

state. In it we find the following elements: social rights formulated as goals; the freedom and dignity of every person; sustainable development; everyone's right to private and family life; the ideas of democracy, equality, and the prohibition of discrimination; the right of the Sami people and other minorities to preserve and develop a cultural and social life of their own; children's rights. How have these fundamental values been communicated in other contexts? One problem for everyone given the task of interpreting and applying the law is to know what fundamental values are and how they should be interpreted. It has been shown in the field of school legislation that this task has been difficult, to say the least.[69] To focus only on one section of Chapter 1 IG without taking into account the basis for the rule of law in the Swedish legislation (stated in Chapter 1 Section 9 IG) risks placing the issue in a strange light. The statement of Chapter 1 Section 2 is an important component of the democratic *rechtsstaat* that Sweden is today and that is communicated through Chapter 1 of the IG. To those fundamental values are normally added the right to access public documents (principle of transparency) and the freedom of expression as stated in the constitutional acts the Freedom of the Press Act and the Fundamental Law on Freedom of Expression. In the case HFD 2017 ref. 4, the Jehovah's Witnesses applied for financial support from the National Agency on financial support for faith communities. The Agency and later the Government denied the application, stating that the Act in question must be interpreted in the of fundamental rights and values. It was explained that the right to health and hospital care is set forth as a fundamental dimension of Swedish society. Furthermore, the Jehovah's Witnesses would not be eligible for the support as the organization does not accept blood transfusions and have specific rules for their members on how they should receive—and not receive—health care. However, this ruling was reached without any reference to Chapter 1 Section 2 of the IG. The Supreme Administrative Court overturned these decisions.

The reference to Chapter 1 Section 2 of the IG also gives us the chance to reflect upon what the terms "striving for" and "promote" mean. Their meaning in public international law and in Chapter 1 Section 2 is not automatically the same. Chapter 1 Section 2 is often described as indicating a goal for the public sphere to achieve; as such, it is not justiciable in court. It serves as an interpretative tool in court and indicates what the legislator should achieve.

---

69 See Victoria Enkvist, "Realising Religion through the Lens of the Swedish School," in *Constitutionalisation and Hegemonisation: Exploring the Boundaries of Law and Religion 1800-1950*, ed. Anna-Sara Lind and Victoria Enkvist (Odense: University Press of Southern Denmark, *forthcoming*). A comparison with other fields would potentially give further insights.

It is relevant to note that this section is set forth by the Inquiry while many other fundamental rights are not, although they are highly relevant in relation to religion. Freedom of expression, assembly, manifestation, and organization are all rights that create a solid ground for the freedom of expression to thrive. Moreover, minorities' and national minorities' rights are only briefly mentioned and not problematized or analyzed further.

An important point to make here is the method chosen by the Inquiry. Human rights seem to be rather difficult to handle. Several conventions are mentioned but not dealt with in depth.[70] Today, the ECHR is part of Swedish national law, as it is implemented by an Act of Parliament.[71] Sweden is a dualist country[72] but has now decided also to implement the Convention on the Rights of the Child. This in turn leads to new legal issues relating to how this convention should be realized in a Swedish context.[73] A narrow view on how to handle fundamental rights and human rights commitments risks leading the legislator down the wrong path, risking the creation of a weaker protection for the freedom of religion. The more isolated the perspective relating to freedom of religion is, the weaker its basis and the greater the risks of narrowing its potential scope.

Let us return to the Inquiry and its mission. The Government asked the Inquiry to stress that the idea behind the support is that the financial support contributes to an active and durable religious activity and through this to promote the freedom of religion. But the Inquiry focuses to a large extent on the definition of "religious activity" as described through a broader understanding of the term "faith community". Such activities include religious activities such as ceremonies, sermons, prayers, meditation, or similar rituals. Also, the social missions of the faith communities are mentioned. However, it is not clear from the text if these missions are linked to the religious activity of the members of the faith community.

---

70 E.g, the United Nations *International Covenant on Economic, Social and Cultural Rights*; the United Nations *Convention on the Rights of the Child*; and the *European Social Charter* (the Council of Europe).
71 Act (1994:1219) on the European Convention on the Protection of Human Rights and Fundamental Freedoms. See also Prop. 1993/94:117 Inkorporering av Europakonventionen och andra fri- och rättighetsfrågor.
72 Constitutionally speaking, conventions ratified by a state can become part of the national legal system in two ways. If a state is monist, the international convention automatically takes its place in the national hierarchy of norms as soon as the state has ratified it. In a dualist country, the national parliament needs to act in order to implement the convention.
73 See Prop. 2017/18:186 Inkorporering av FN:s konvention om barnets rättigheter.

One example illustrating how difficult it can be to interpret the democracy criterion is the rather controversial case concerning an application for financial support from the organization Sweden's Young Muslims (SUM). The national agency in charge (*Myndigheten för ungdoms- och civilsamhällesfrågor*, MUCF) decided to decline the application for the year 2017. The agency was convinced that the organization did not organize activities that respected the ideas of democracy as expressed in the Government's ordinance (2011:65) on financial support to children's and youth's organizations. This decision in turn was overruled by the Stockholm administrative court, which stated that SUM in its activities respects the ideas of democracy, including "equality and prohibition of discrimination".[74] We can conclude that it is not easy to interpret the law when it is a matter for an agency to decide upon financial support to a civil society organization dealing with religious activities.

The view that the state should be neutral in relation to faith communities is set forth at several points. When the state or one of its agencies is striving towards neutrality it is important to reflect upon what a declined application could mean.[75] This is especially true for the effects the financial support is meant to have, but also for its legitimacy. State financial support to faith communities, as described by the Inquiry, is formulated in a vague manner, leaving an opening for various interpretations. Accordingly, one could reflect upon how the state remains neutral in relation to faith communities or rather how the framing of the legislation and the definition of freedom of religion, freedom of speech, democracy, and other features of the rule of law is done.

As a building, a mosque can take different shapes; this is especially true of those in Sweden. It is often the case that the buildings are not constructed for service primarily as a mosque. In Sweden, only five cities have mosques that were built in order to serve as mosques. All the other Muslim faith communities have access to buildings that they rent or own and that have served as churches, private homes, warehouses, etc. before being turned into mosques. A study performed by the Centre of Multidisciplinary Studies on Racism (Cemfor, Uppsala University) explains that 24 % of the mosques are to be found in basements, 26 % in apartments or office apartments, 18 % in larger halls of buildings in the industrial area of the city, office buildings, or family houses. 30 % of the mosques in Sweden are located in individual buildings.[76] More than 50 % of

---

74 Case nr 192-17.
75 SOU 2018:18, 29.
76 Mattias Gardell, *Moskéers och muslimska församlingars utsatthet och säkerhet i Sverige 2018* (Uppsala: Uppsala Universitet, 2018), 7-8.

the Muslim faith communities expressed in the survey that it was hard or very hard to find a place that could serve as a mosque. These faith communities have very limited financial resources and, in turn, this means that 83 % of the communities rent the place of their mosque's location.[77]

The study also explains that renting the location means that the Muslim faith organization is exposed to several difficult and even dangerous situations. It is difficult to find a place to rent, but it can also be difficult to keep a place once you have found it. The owners and the neighbors do not always welcome the presence of a mosque, and the prayers taking place at different hours, sometimes in the middle of the night, are not appreciated by the non-Muslim surroundings. Several faith organizations had received warnings from the landlords and have feared losing their lease.[78]

As to the possible dangerous dimensions of this situation, one should note that blunt threats are common. As it is presented in the survey conducted by Cemfor, anti-Muslim threats and attacks on mosques (some sort of physical attack) had increased from 29 % in 2010 to 41 % in 2014. In 2018, yet another great increase had taken place as 59 % of Muslim organizations gave a positive answer to a survey question regarding physical attacks.[79]

These numbers are relevant to the questions explored in this chapter. And the statistics become even more interesting when one notes that only 57 % of Muslim organizations in Sweden have a valid insurance for their mosque. 27 % of faith organizations report that they have not found an insurance company willing to insure them or that the ones they have found do not give them a reasonable premium or conditions. Around 20 % report that they cannot afford any insurance. And for a faith organization not having financial resources, being run on a non-profit basis, already facing higher rents than others, the difficulties of getting insurance at a level equivalent to other faith communities are real. As soon as an insurance company realizes that the question of obtaining insurance originates from a Muslim faith organization, they withdraw or increase the premium.[80]

---

77   Gardell, *Moskéers och muslimska församlingars utsatthet*, 8.
78   Gardell, *Moskéers och muslimska församlingars utsatthet*, 9.
79   Gardell, *Moskéers och muslimska församlingars utsatthet*, 15.
80   Gardell, *Moskéers och muslimska församlingars utsatthet*, 23-24.

Concluding Remarks—A Renaissance for the Uppsala School?

Human rights as expressed in public international law are often said to be rooted in natural law, as they state rights that people already have in their capacity as human beings. On several occasions, authors have claimed that this proves that natural law has experienced a renaissance in the 20th century. However, I suspect that this is not entirely true; the right of the freedom of religion illustrates this suspicion very well.

Freedom of religion is a very diverse and complex right. As we have seen in this chapter, it touches upon different sorts of rights in its realization. According to the international conventions, it is not an absolute right and it can be limited. It is not a right that is equal for everyone, as it can be limited; and in the European setting it can also be differentiated in relation to foreigners residing in a convention state.[81] It contains positive and negative elements; freedom from and freedom to religion are both important features of the right as are the individual and collective dimensions of it.

Returning to the situation in Sweden, the sceptical attitude of Scandinavian Realism as expressed in the Uppsala School has resulted in a very slow development in relation to constitutionally granted fundamental rights. As to human rights in international treaties ratified by Sweden, Sweden still holds firmly to its dualist approach and avoids directly implementing the conventions.[82] In this chapter, we have seen that the realization of the freedom of religion necessitates an active legislator who explains the content of and outer limits of a right. This is especially true when the caselaw is not fully developed. Recent developments in caselaw also evince a reluctance on the part of the courts to take on the responsibility of deciding what should count as freedom of religion. This is true for the CJEU, where the religious dimension of a case is decided through other, more material, rules in secondary legislation. This way of reasoning is fully in line with the beliefs of the Uppsala School. In the Nordic countries, and especially in Sweden, the tendency has not been to follow the constitutional discourse of other European countries. Instead of linking to the concepts of "human dignity" and natural law as other countries (especially the ones with Catholic roots) have done in their constitutional development, Nordic lawyers have shown themselves reluctant to do so.[83]

---

81 Not treating everyone alike does not necessarily mean that the measure is discriminatory. Discrimination is when the difference in treatment is not legally justiciable.
82 The ECHR was implemented in 1995, and the United Nations Convention on the Rights of the Child was implemented as late as January 1, 2020. See Prop. 2017/18:186.
83 Modéer, "Kyrkans rätt framför dess lag," 155-56.

The example of "housing religion" in this chapter shows that the realization of a human right can seldom be done just by reading the text of a certain article in a certain convention. Needless to say, the duties of a convention state depend on how institutions and legislators act. If the state does not demand from private parties that they be just and act in order to ensure that unjustified inequalities are handled, then the state is not living up to its responsibility, hence it is not fully respecting the complex mechanisms surrounding the realization of human rights.

Perhaps the Uppsala School represents a way of reconciling the past and the future. As a reaction to natural law and plain positivism, it showed at its birth flexibility and adaptability at a time where social change and challenges were important. The legal philosophy behind the legislation and the courts' decisions became a way of reconciling a fragmented and unequal era. Today, social engineering has difficulties encountering the human rights paradigm, especially in the field of religion. Internationalization and re-confessionalization are social changes most likely to stay in this globalized world. There have never been so many rights (human, constitutional, European, legal) as there are today, and the freedom of religion has never been as protected in Europe as it is today. Nevertheless, as is shown in the case of insurances for religious housing studied here, the local rules and the interpretation at different levels in the national context become key for the realization of the freedom of religion. The scope and the content of the right in question depends on the wish of the authorities to act in order to realize the right. This gives an additional perspective that contextualizes "law" as well as "religion". We need to be able to understand the two phenomena jointly as they develop together in political, institutional, and cultural frameworks. Not acting, avoiding taking measures will ultimately lead to a non-realization of the human rights. This would in the longer run mean that the basic point of departure for respecting the ECHR is not met; the convention state needs to secure everyone within their jurisdiction the rights and freedoms defined in the ECHR. In order to do so, more attention should be paid to the interpretation of rights. And more understanding of the fact that crucial parts of the realization of rights are embedded in material national law and in local rules. The administrative structure and often, in the case of realizing the freedom of religion, private parties are setting the frame for how to understand the right locally. Interpreting the rules and enacting decisions that realize human rights accordingly need to be done with all legal tools applicable. This conclusion is well in line with the heritage of the Uppsala school.

Bibliography

Swedish Courts

Supreme Administrative court
HFD 2017 ref. 4

Stockholm Administrative Court
Case nr 192-17

European Commission on Human Rights
Darby v. Sweden, application no. 11581/85, 187 ECHR (Ser. A) (Annex), 9 May 1989
Arrowsmith v. the United Kingdom, application no. 7050/75, 19 DR 5, 12 October 1978

European Court of Human Rights
Kjeldsen, Busk Madsen and Pedersen v. Denmark, application nos 5095/71, 5920/72, 5926/72, 7 December 1976
Campbell and Cosans v. the United Kingdom, application nos 7511/76, 7743/76, 25 February 1982
Mellacher et al. v. Austria, application nos 10522/83, 11011/84 and 11070/84, 19 December 1989
Darby v. Sweden, application no. 11581/85, 23 October 1990
Kokkinakis v. Greece, application 14307/88, 25 May 1993
Manoussakis and others v. Greece, application 18748/91, 26 September 1996
Hasan and Chaush v. Bulgaria, application no. 30985/96, 26 October 2000
Johannische Kirche and Peters v. Germany, application no. 41754/98, decision of 10 July 2001
Pretty v. the United Kingdom, application no. 2346/02, 29 April 2002
Vergos v. Greece, application no. 65501/01, 24 June 2004
S.A.S. v. France [GC], application no. 43835/11, 1 July 2014
Eweida and Others v. the United Kingdom, applications no. 48420/10, 59842/10, 51671/10 and 36516/10, 15 January 2013
Leyla Şahin v. Turkey [GC], application no. 44774/98, 10 November 2005
Ahmet Arslan and Others v. Turkey, no. 41135/98, 23 February 2010
Silver and Others v. the United Kingdom, application nos 5947/72, 6205/73, 7052/75, 7061/75, 7107/75, 7113/75 and 7136/75, 25 March 1983
Handyside v. the United Kingdom, application no. 5493/72, 7 December 1976
Hatton and Others v. the United Kingdom, application no. 36022/97, 2 October 2001

Court of Justice of the European Union
C-71/11 and C-99/11, *Y and Z v. Germany*, ECLI:EU:C:2012:518
C-157/15, *Samira Achbita, Centrum voor gelijkheid van kansen en voor racismebestrijding v. G4S Secure Solutions NV*, ECLI:EU:C:2017:203.
C-188/15, *Asma Bougnaoui, Association de défense des droits de l'homme (ADDH) v. Micropole SA, formerly Micropole Univers SA*, ECLI:EU:C:2017:204

C-74/16, *Congregación de Escuelas Pías Provincia Betania v. Ayuntamiento de Getafe*, ECLI:EU:C:2017:496

C-414/16, *Vera Egenberger v. Evangelisches Werk für Diakonie und Entwicklung eV*, ECLI:EU:C:2018:257

C-426/16, *Liga van Moskeeën en Islamitische Organisaties Provincie Antwerpen VZW and Others v. Vlaams Gewest*, ECLI:EU:C:2018:335

C-25/17, *Tietosuojavaltuutettu*, ECLI:EU:C:2018:551

Official sources

Act (1994:1219) on the European Convention on the Protection of Human Rights and Fundamental Freedoms

Council of Europe. *European Social Charter (Revised)*, 3 May 1996, ETS 163

Dir. 2019:25 Tilläggsdirektiv till Utredningen om konfessionella inslag i skolväsendet

Prop. 1993/94:117 Inkorporering av Europakonventionen och andra fri- och rättighetsfrågor

Prop. 1998/99:124 Staten och trossamfunden—stöd, medverkan inom totalförsvaret, m.m.

Prop. 2005/06:11 Maskeringsförbud

Prop. 2009/10:80 En reformerad grundlag

Prop. 2017/18:186 Inkorporering av FN:s konvention om barnets rättigheter

SFS 174:152 Regeringsformen (Instrument of Government)

SOU 2017:67 Våldsbejakande extremism—En forskarantologi

SOU 2018:18 Statens stöd till trossamfund i ett mångreligiöst Sverige

United Nations General Assembly. *International Covenant on Economic, Social and Cultural Rights*, 16 December 1966, A/RES/2200A (XXI)

United Nations General Assembly. *Convention on the Rights of the Child*, 20 November 1989, A/RES/44/25

Literature

Borevi, Karin, Anette Leis-Pieters, and Anna-Sara Lind. "Layers of Inconsistency: A Multidisciplinary analysis of the Swedish National Agency on Education's Guidelines on Muslim Headscarf." In *Reconsidering Religion, Law, and Democracy: New Challenges for Society and Research*, edited by Anna-Sara Lind, Mia Lövheim, and Ulf Zackariasson, 179-98. Lund: Nordic Academic Press, 2016.

Cady, Linell E., and Elizabeth Shakman Hurd. *Comparative Secularisms in a Global Age*. London: Palgrave Macmillan, 2010.

Cameron, Iain. "Freedom of Religion and Competing Human Rights Systems." In *Freedom of Religion in the 21st Century: A Human Rights Perspective on the Relation between Politics and Religion*, edited by Hans-Georg Ziebertz and Ernst Hirsch Ballin, 26-51. Leiden: Brill, 2016.

Cameron, Iain. *An Introduction to the European Convention of Human Rights*. 8th ed. Uppsala: Iustus förlag, 2018.

Christoffersen, Lisbet, Kjell Å. Modéer, and Sven Andersen, eds. *Law and Religion in the 21st Century—Nordic Perspectives*, Copenhagen: Djøf Publishing, 2010.

Danelius, Hans. *Mänskliga rättigheter i europeisk praxis*. 5th ed. Stockholm: Norstedts Juridik, 2015.

Enkvist, Victoria. "Realising Religion through the Lens of the Swedish School." In *Constitutionalisation and Hegemonisation: Exploring the Boundaries of Law and Religion 1800-1950*, edited by Anna-Sara Lind and Victoria Enkvist Odense: University Press of Southern Denmark, *forthcoming*.

Enkvist, Victoria. *Religionsfrihetens rättsliga ramar*. Phd. diss. Uppsala: Iustus förlag, 2013.

Enkvist, Victoria, and Per Erik Nilsson. "The Hidden Return of Religion Problematising Religion in Law and Law in Religion in the Swedish Regulation of Faith Communities." In *Reconsidering Religion, Law, and Democracy: New Challenges for Society and Research*, edited by Anna-Sara Lind, Mia Lövheim, and Ulf Zackariasson, 93-108. Lund: Nordic Academic Press, 2016.

Enkvist, Victoria, and Per-Erik Nilsson. "Techniques of Religion-Making in Sweden: The Case of the Missionary Church of Kopimism." *Critical Research on Religion* 4, no. 2 (2016): 141-55.

Gardell, Mattias. *Moskéers och muslimska församlingars utsatthet och säkerhet i Sverige 2018*. Uppsala: Uppsala Universitet, 2018.

Helin, Markku. "Om rättsfakta i civilrätten." In *Law and Society. Contributions by the Honorary Doctors*, edited by Mattias Dahlberg, 129-47. Uppsala: Iustus förlag, 2019.

Johansen, Tormod Otter. *Förvaltning som verksamhet: Bidrag till offentligrättens allmänna läror*. Juridiska institutionens skriftserie 31. JD diss., Gothenburg: Göteborgs Universitet, 2019.

Kumlien, Mats. *Professorspolitik och samhällsförändring: En rättshistorisk undersökning av den svenska förvaltningsrättens uppkomst*. Stockholm: Jure AB, 2019.

Lerwall, Lotta. "Förbud mot konfessionella skolor?" *Svensk Juristtidning*, no. 7 (2018): 523-41.

Letto-Vannamo, Pia, Ditlev Tamm, and Bent Ole Gram, eds. *Nordic Law in European Context*. New York: Springer, 2019.

Lind, Anna-Sara. "Social rights and EU Citizenship." In *Bridging the Prosperity Gap in the EU: The Social Challenge Ahead*, edited by Ulf Bernitz, Moa Mårtensson, Lars Oxelheim, and Thomas Persson, 22-45. Cheltenham: Edward Elgar, 2018.

Lind, Anna-Sara, and Victoria Enkvist. "Introduction: Deep structures of power; Theoretical points of departures." In *Constitutionalisation and Hegemonisation: Exploring the Boundaries of Law and Religion 1800-1950*, edited by Anna-Sara Lind and Victoria Enkvist. Odense: University Press of Southern Denmark, *forthcoming*.

Lind, Anna-Sara, Mia Lövheim, and Ulf Zackariasson, eds. *Reconsidering Religion, Law, and Democracy: New Challenges for Society and Research*. Lund: Nordic Academic Press, 2016.

Lövheim, Mia. "Culture, Conflict and Constitutional Right: Representations of Religion in the Daily Press." In *Religion and European Society: A Primer*, edited by Benjamin Schewel and Erin K. Wilson, 69-81. Hoboken, NJ: John Wiley & Sons, 2020.

Magnusson Sjöberg, Cecilia. "Safeguarding Freedom of Information in a Privacy Protection Society: The Interplay with Public Records Management." In *Information and Law in Transition: Freedom of Speech, Privacy, Democracy and the Internet in the*

21st Century, edited by Anna-Sara Lind, Jane Reichel, and Inger Österdahl, 100-14. Stockholm: Liber förlag, 2015.

Mindus, Patricia. *A Real Mind: The Life and Work of Axel Hägerström*. New York: Springer, 2017.

Modéer, Kjell Å. "Kyrkans rätt framför dess lag: Europé och jurist i den svenska folkkyrkans tjänst; Göran Göransson (1925-1998)—en kyrkorättshistorisk biografi." *Kyrkohistorisk årsskrift* 119 (2019): 153-73.

Ojanen, Tuomas. "Human Rights in Nordic Constitutions." In *The Nordic Constitutions*, edited by Helle Krunke and Bjørg Thorarensen, 133-66. Oxford: Hart publishing, 2018.

Ross, Alf. *Dansk statsforfatningsret*. Copenhagen: Nyt Nordisk Forlag Arnold Busck, 1959-1960.

Ross, Alf. *Ret og retfærdighed: En indførelse i den analytiske retsfilosofi*. Copenhagen: Nyt Nordisk Forlag Arnold Busck, 1953.

Slotte, Pamela. *Mänskliga rättigheter, moral och religion: Om de mänskliga rättigheterna som moraliskt och juridiskt begrepp i en pluralistisk värld*. Åbo: Åbo Akademis Förlag, 2005.

Smith, Eivind. *Konstitusjonelt demokrati*. 4th ed. Bergen: Fagbokforlaget, 2017.

Sterzel, Fredrik. "Författningens föränderlighet: Från 1809 till 1974." In *Författning i utveckling: Tjugo studier kring Sveriges författning*, 70-91. 2nd ed. Uppsala: Iustus förlag 2009.

Strang, Johan. "Scandinavian Legal Realism and Human Rights: Axel Hägerström, Alf Ross and the Persistent Attack on Natural Law." *Nordic Journal of Human Rights* 36, no. 3 (2018): 202-18.

Strömholm, Stig. *Rätt, rättskällor och rättstillämpning: En lärobok i allmän rättslära*. 5th ed. Stockholm: Norstedts Juridik, 1996.

Suksi, Markku. *Finlands statsrätt*. Turku: Åbo Akademi förlag, 2002.

Zillén, Kavot. *Hälso- och sjukvårdspersonalens religions- och samvetsfrihet: En rättsvetenskaplig studie om samvetsgrundad vägran och kravet på god vård*. Uppsala: Uppsala Universitet, 2016.

Åhman, Karin. *Normprövning: Domstols kontroll av svensk lags förenlighet med regeringsrätten och europarätten*. Stockholm: Norstedts Juridik, 2011.

16. Making Religion Visible in Sweden: Secular Legislation Turns Religious in the Name of Human Rights

Victoria Enkvist

Introduction

Sweden is often said to be one of the most secular countries in the world. But even though most Swedes are said not to be religious, 57.7 % were members of the Church of Sweden at the end of 2018.[1] How this affects the perceived notion that Sweden is a very secular society, built on secular values, is interesting and deserves a deeper investigation. What do we mean by secular, post-secular, and neutral societies? How do these concepts relate and function together with democracy and human rights such as freedom of religion?

Among other things, the increased scope of freedom of religion regulations has opened the door to religion once again from a judicial point of view. How does this development relate to secular legislation and the application of the same?

In this context, it is important to explain the underlying aim of this chapter. The point of departure for the ProNoLa project[2], of which this essay is a part, is how religion has affected the secular legislation that developed during the period of modernity and how religion has affected secular legislation today. The ProNoLa project also studies how religion has affected our understanding of the law of the land as secular and the results of the internationalization of the Nordic law.

In this essay, the religious aspect is represented by human rights law because it is through freedom of religion that religion has entered domestic secular leg-

---

1   "Medlemmar i Svenska kyrkan i förhållande till folkmängd den 31.12.2018 per församling, pastorat och stift samt riket," Svenska kyrkan, accessed February 15, 2020, https://www.svenskakyrkan.se/statistik.
2   The overarching goal of Protestant Legacies in Nordic Law: Uses of the Past in the Construction of the Secularity of Law (ProNoLa) is to examine the relations between Lutheran majority traditions and the development of secular law in the Nordic region in the course of the last 500 years.

islation in Sweden. This development is new and unprecedented in Swedish history, which makes it an important subject to study from a multidisciplinary perspective. This chapter attempts to frame some of the important judicial questions concerning this development.

As mentioned above, human rights and the scope and understanding of human rights have increased in importance during the 21st century. The role of religion has changed and gained importance or at least become more present in public during the same period.[3] Freedom of religion and the way in which we interpret this right is often debated in media and politics.

In the 20th century, religion and human rights were viewed as having shared values, to a certain degree. Both were seen as means of the striving for a better world.[4] In the 21st century, religion is sometimes described as a counterpart to democracy and human rights.[5]

When talking about freedom of religion in Sweden, understanding, or at least having knowledge of, the concepts of neutrality and secularity is equally important as understanding religion. Such understanding is important because these concepts are connected to each other in modern Western societies.

A good point of departure for describing and discussing neutrality and secularity in a Swedish context is analysis of the preparatory works regarding the division of state and church. There are several preparatory works regarding this issue and the question was debated over a period as long as fifty years. The preparatory works define "neutral" as the state refraining from taking a stand in matters concerning philosophy of life, and the state remaining passive toward all forms of expressions for religion and non-religious beliefs.[6]

Besides this form of neutrality, other forms of neutrality were identified, such as positive and negative neutrality. This concept means that a state can have a positive or negative attitude towards different religious groups.[7] The state's treatment of religions may show its negative or positive attitude towards

---

3   Questions concerning religious symbols in the public has increased during the last decade.
4   Joseph Runzo, "Secular Rights and Religious Responsibilities," in *Human Rights and Responsibilities in the World Religions*, ed. Nancy M. Martin, Joseph Runzo, and Arvind Sharma (Oxford: Oneworld, 2003), 9. Mahatma Gandhi and Martin Luther King can serve as examples.
5   See, e.g., *Dahlab v. Switzerland*, application no. 42393/98, decision 15 February 2001. In this case, the ECtHR remarks that it appears difficult to reconcile the wearing of an Islamic headscarf with the message of tolerance, respect for others, and, above all, equality and non-discrimination that all teachers in a democratic society must convey to their pupils.
6   SOU 1972:36 Samhälle och trossamfund: slutbetänkande, 49. See also Victoria Enkvist, *Religionsfrihetens rättsliga ramar* (Phd. diss. Uppsala: Iustus förlag, 2013), 77-79, 252-53.
7   SOU 1972:36, 49. See also Enkvist, *Religionsfrihetens rättsliga ramar*, 77-79, 252-53.

them. A society can be negatively disposed towards some groups and positively disposed towards others, which means that the society is built on negative neutrality. An active, positive attitude from society means that society promotes the activities of religious groups.[8]

In the secular Swedish society, religion was considered something belonging to the private sphere. Public space strove to be a religiously neutral place with secular values. What these secular values really meant is difficult to deduce, but the visible signs of religion became less visible during the 20th century. The near eradication of visible signs of religion from the public sphere raises the question of whether the underlying values that affected secular legislation, as well as its application, also changed.[9]

Today, in the post-secular society we can see a return of religion into public space. This return can partly be explained by the increased importance of human rights. The application of all forms of legislation must take human rights, and thus freedom of religion, into consideration. In this process, different religious values may come into conflict with what people tend to call secular values; these conflicts must sometimes be solved judicially. Thus, it is important to identify how these conflicts are resolved, and to identify the legal principles that come into play when problems arise. It can show us how religion affects the interpretation of secular law.

One religion that has been a focus of political debate in Sweden in recent years is Islam, and different manifestations of Islam have been questioned, such as the wearing of hijab and the building of mosques. Both have been debated in several European countries and can be discussed from a variety of legal perspectives. The main legal question in this chapter concerns the freedom of religion and its relation to the legislation that surrounds the building process. This essay can be seen as a supplement to the other essays in this volume because it concentrates on lower regulations in the norm hierarchy, for example, the Planning and Building Act (*Plan- och Bygglagen*, PBL) and its relation to freedom of religion in different human rights systems.

The framework for the following discussion is the concept of freedom of religion as found in the Swedish Instrument of Government (IG) and the European Convention on Human Rights (ECHR). The main reasons for choosing the IG and ECHR is that the IG is a constitutional legislation while the ECHR has

---

8   SOU 1972:36, 49.
9   About different layers in the legal culture, see Kaarlo Tuori, *Critical Legal Positivism* (Aldershot: Ashgate, 2002).

been law in Sweden since 1995. In chapter 2 article 19 of the IG it is stipulated that a law or other regulation may not be issued in conflict with the ECHR.

For example, when new legislation is proposed, the legislator is bound by article 2:19 of the IG to make sure that the legislation is consistent with the human rights in the ECHR. Existing legislation is expected to be interpreted in a manner consistent with Sweden's international obligations.[10]

Freedom of Religion According to the Human Rights Instruments

Freedom of religion is seemingly the same right in the IG and the ECHR. In line with the wording in the articles, it gives everyone the right to hold and manifest their religion. At the same time, the regulations are constructed in different ways in each instrument and the protected area for the rights differs due to the fact that freedom of religion is interpreted and thus applied in different ways. The right in the IG cannot be limited unless the manifestation in reality concerns any of the opinion rights, such as for example freedom of expression or freedom of assembly.[11] Freedom of religion in the ECHR can be limited, but the core of the right is absolute.

The differences in interpretation can partly be explained by the construction of the regulations themselves but also by differences in culture and tradition and the role of religion in different jurisdictions. Another important cause of the varying interpretations is the position of minorities. It seems to be an important question whether minority groups or religious minorities are seen as a threat to or as an asset for society.[12] The minority perspective is important when studying the actual law of the land. If only the majority perspective is highlighted, important parts of law of the land will be overlooked.

As for the building of mosques, the mosque is one of the most visible signs of Islam and an important place where Muslims can gather to manifest their religion.[13] One reason for the political debate is this: the presence of mosques in Sweden and the call to prayer issued from the minarets.

Besides that, there has been some commotion regarding the building of

---

10 Iain Cameron, *An Introduction to the European Convention on Human Rights* (Uppsala: Iustus förlag, 2006), 178-84.
11 SOU 1975:75, 326.
12 See e.g. *Dahlab* v. *Switzerland*.
13 Simon Sorgenfrei, *Islam i Sverige: De första 1300 åren* (Bromma: Myndigheten för stöd till trossamfund, 2018), 233.

mosques. The building process in Sweden is quite complex and it is not necessary to explain it in depth in this text. The interesting part is that it is considered to be a neutral and universal legislation that can be applied in the same manner for all citizens. Religion is not mentioned in the legislation, nor in the preparatory works. The latter is important when interpreting legislation in Sweden.

However, according to the human rights systems, it is mandatory for those applying Swedish legislation, for example public servants, to consider human rights when applying the law at hand.

The case law relating to the ECHR is important when trying to understand the different articles in the ECHR. The case law concerning building restrictions is limited, which makes it difficult to draw general conclusions, but I will present some of the case law in this chapter in order to show the arguments of the European Court of Human Rights (ECtHR) in cases concerning religious buildings related to Article 9.

Manoussakis and others v. *Greece*[14] is a case concerning obstructions posed by the need for planning authorization for the use of a rented room as a place for worship under Article 9 of the ECHR. The complaint made by the applicants in that case was based on the argument that the restrictions imposed on Jehovah's Witnesses by the Greek government prevented them from exercising their right to freedom of religion. The applicants stated that, in terms of the legislation and administrative practice, their religion did not enjoy the safeguards guaranteed to it in all the other member states of the Council of Europe. The ECtHR came to the conclusion that the imposed restriction, in this case the impugned conviction, had such a direct effect on the applicants' freedom of religion that it could not be regarded as proportionate to the legitimate aim pursued, nor, accordingly, as necessary in a democratic society. The ECtHR also remarked:

> As a matter of case-law, the Court has consistently left the Contracting States a certain margin of appreciation in assessing the existence and extent of the necessity of an interference, but this margin is subject to European supervision, embracing both the legislation and the decisions applying it. The Court's task is to determine whether the measures taken at national level were justified in principle and proportionate.[15]

In delimiting the extent of the margin of appreciation, the ECtHR took regard to what was at stake, namely the need to secure true religious pluralism, ac-

---

14 *Manoussakis and others* v. *Greece*, application no. 18748/91, 26 September 1996.
15 *Manoussakis and others* v. *Greece*, para. 44.

cording to ECtHR an inherent feature of the notion of a democratic society. In this part, the ECtHR referred to the *Kokkinakis* v. *Greece* judgment. Further, the ECtHR emphasized that considerable weight has to be attached to the need when it comes to determining, pursuant to Article 9.2, whether the restriction is proportionate to the legitimate aim pursued. The ECtHR came to the conclusion that the restrictions imposed on the freedom to manifest religion by the provisions of the Greek law calls for very strict scrutiny by the court.[16]

The Universal Declaration of Human Rights (UDHR) served as an inspiration in the construction of the ECHR. Article 9 of the ECHR is inspired by Article 18 of the UDHR. Freedom of thought, conscience, and religion is stipulated in Article 18 of the UDHR. It is also mentioned in Article 18 in the International Covenant on Civil and Political Rights (ICCPR). According to the committee, "the concept of worship extends to ritual and ceremonial acts giving direct expression to belief, as well as various practices integral to such acts, including the building of places of worship".[17]

The UN Special Rapporteur investigated the question of legislation concerning planning and construction of buildings; a brief comment on the Rapporteur's findings will follow this analysis.

The UN Special Rapporteur found the potential for planning restrictions to operate as a preventive measure against religious minorities. A similar study made by an NGO, The International Helsinki Federation for Human Rights, has also examined the use of planning restrictions in Germany and Macedonia and came to the same conclusion as the UN Special Rapporteur in its investigation of several countries. From a human rights perspective, the relation between the legislation concerning building restrictions and freedom of religion is interesting and of great importance because it has a huge impact on the scope and meaning of freedom of religion. In the case of the Islamic community in *Bosnia and Herzegovina* v. *The Republica Srpska*, the Human Rights Chamber for Bosnia and Herzegovina emphasized that European institutions have a positive obligation to protect the rights enshrined in the ECHR by effective, reasonable, and appropriate measures. They also stressed the importance of removing the climate of fear in order to allow the practice of religion in genuine freedom.[18]

The apparently neutral requirement of an authorization to operate a place of worship can be transformed from a formality into a restriction against the right

---

16 *Manoussakis and others* v. *Greece*, para. 44.
17 United Nations Human Rights Committee (HRC), *CCPR General Comment No. 22 article 4. Article 18 (Freedom of Thought, Conscience or Religion)*, 30 July 1993, CCPR/C/21/Rev.1/Add.4.
18 Paul M. Taylor, *Freedom of Religion* (Cambridge: Cambridge University Press, 2005), 244.

to freedom of religion depending on the way in which the right is interpreted. It depends on the context and the interpretation of the national legislation as well as the surrounding human rights systems. If human rights are not taken into consideration in the application of ordinary legislation, the concept of human rights becomes a dead letter. So, the important question is not only whether legislation exists that holds the member states to their obligations, but also whether the already existing legislation is interpreted in a way that fulfills the rights contained in the human rights instruments.

In the case *Metropolitan Church of Bessarabia* v. *Moldova*, the applicants alleged that the Moldovan authorities' refusal to recognize the Metropolitan Church of Bessarabia infringed upon their freedom of religion, since only religions recognized by the Moldovan government could be practiced in Moldova. In this case, the ECtHR observed that, not being recognized, the applicant church could not operate. In order to determine whether that interference was a breach of the ECHR, the ECtHR had to decide whether the infringement was prescribed by law, pursued a legitimate aim, and whether the provision on which the refusal was grounded was necessary in a democratic society.

In the same case, the ECtHR referred to its case law in Articles 8 to 11 of the ECHR concerning the terms "prescribed by law" and "in accordance with the law". According to the case law cited, the articles not only require that the impugned measures have some basis in domestic law, but also that the quality of the law in question must be sufficiently accessible and foreseeable. The law must be formulated with sufficient precision to enable the individual to regulate his conduct. In *Hasan and Chaush* v. *Bulgaria*,[19] the ECtHR stated that, in order to meet the requirements, domestic legislation must afford a measure of legal protection against arbitrary interference by public authorities with the rights guaranteed by the ECHR. The law must indicate with sufficient clarity the scope of any such discretion and the manner of its exercise.[20]

In conclusion, in the Moldova case, the ECtHR considered whether the refusal to recognize the applicant church was proportionate to the legitimate aim pursued. The ECtHR found that it was not proportionate and legitimate. Neither could the refusal be considered necessary in a democratic society. In other words, a breach of Article 9 of the ECHR had been committed.

The law requirement differs between the IG and the ECHR when it comes to infringement of human rights. In the IG, the law requirement is static and

---

19 *Hasan and Chaush* v. *Bulgaria*, application no. 30985/96, 26 October 2000.
20 *Metropolitan Church of Bessarabia* v. *Moldova*, application no. 45701/99, 13 December 2001, para. 109.

means legislation in its "real" meaning: it requires norms that are established by the parliament. According to the ECHR, it is sufficient if the norms meet the requirements about foreseeability and clarity as stated above. Consequently, the former is a formal requirement and the latter is more of a substantial demand.

While religious freedom has been seen primarily as a matter of individual conscience, at least according to the Swedish IG, among other things it also implies freedom to "manifest [one's] religion" alone and in private or in community with others, in public and within the circle of those whose faith one shares. Article 9 of the ECHR lists a number of forms of manifestation that one's religion or belief may take, including worship, teaching, practice, and observance. However, the article does not protect every act motivated or inspired by a religion or belief. In *Kokkinakis* v. *Greece*, the ECtHR remarked that, in a democratic society within which several religions coexist, it may be necessary to place restrictions on this freedom in order to reconcile the interests of the various groups and ensure that everyone's beliefs are respected.[21] In *Sidiropoulos and Others* v. *Greece* and in *Canea Catholic Church* v. *Greece*, the ECtHR ruled that one of the means of exercising the right to manifest one's religion, especially for a religious community, was the possibility of ensuring judicial protection of the community, its members, and its assets. In order to do that, Article 9 must be seen in light of Article 11 and Article 6.[22]

According to the margin of appreciation, the ECtHR leaves it up to the member states to decide whether and to what extent an interference is necessary, although the ECtHR supervises both the existence of a relevant legislation and how the legislation is applied. The ECtHR asserts that the measures taken at a national level are justified in principle and proportionate. Paragraph 2 of Article 9 requires the ECtHR to determine whether the interference corresponds to a "pressing social need" and is "proportionate to the legitimate aim pursued". In order to determine the scope of the margin of appreciation, the ECtHR takes into account what is at stake.

If a religiously neutral legislation is interpreted in such a way that it limits freedom of religion in practice, such limitation must be done in accordance with the prerequisites that are given for limitations for each given article in the ECHR. This means that application of the legislation concerning planning regulations in Sweden must take into consideration the case law from the

---

21 *Kokkinakis* v. *Greece*, application no. 14307/88, 25 May 1993, para. 33.
22 *Sidiropoulos and Others* v. *Greece*, application nos 57/1997/841/1047, 10 July 1998 para. 40; and *Canea Catholic Church* v. *Greece*, application no. 25528/94, 16 December 1997, paras. 33, 40-41.

ECtHR. The freedom of religion clause in the IG does stipulate a freedom to hold and to manifest one's religion, either by oneself or together with others. The preparatory works give no guidance regarding how to interpret situations that involve the regulations concerning planning restrictions when it comes to religious buildings. This is because such regulations are considered secular and neutral legislation. The aims of this legislation point in the opposite direction to freedom of religion. In this case, a secular value base may come into conflict with a religious value base.

Planning Regulations, Human Rights, and Interpretation in Sweden

In Sweden, several cases concerning building of mosques have been tried. However, not all of them are tried in court. Construction of all buildings must be in accordance with the prerequisites found in the Planning and Building Act (PBL) and in the detailed development plan (*detaljplan*). The municipalities set up the development plan.

One important requirement is found in 2.1 of PBL, which says that, when examining matters under PBL, account must be taken of both general and individual interests. This wording can and must be interpreted; in order to do so, one has to turn to legal sources such as preparatory works and, of course, the surrounding regulations. I will not discuss the deeper and more detailed regulation and procedure of the application process. Instead, it is important to emphasize the room for interpretation that the wording in this article makes possible and what this means from a human rights perspective and what it says about the nature of Swedish law. Interpretation of this article must consider not only the article itself and the legal sources surrounding it, but also human rights such as freedom of religion. In considering Article 9 of the ECHR, it is necessary to discuss how the national legislation and its construction, as well as its application, corresponds to the prerequisites in Article 9, paragraph 2. What is the quality of the law, and is it sufficiently accessible and foreseeable? Is the legislation formulated with sufficient precision to enable the individual to regulate his conduct? One must perform a balancing act between the fact that, in a democratic society in which several religions coexist, it may be necessary to place restrictions on freedom of religion in order to reconcile the interests of the various groups and at the same time ensure that everyone's beliefs are respected. This is a difficult balancing act, but the regulations in the Swedish PBL would probably be considered to be legitimate and foreseeable in the formal sense according to the requirements in Article 9.2 in the ECHR. The application part can also be discussed. Do those who apply the legislation and make the decisions balance those decisions in relation to the IG and the ECHR?

Several legal questions can arise in cases concerning the planning and construction of religious buildings besides the regulation in the PBL. One example is a case that was tried in court which concerned a piece of land in Fyllinge in Halmstad that was dedicated to the Islamic Children's and Cultural Association through an agreement between the association and the municipality. The association wanted to build a mosque on the ground. An agreement was concluded between the municipal council's building committee and the Islamic group. The complainants argued that the decision was so important to the residents of the municipality that the decision should have been made by the municipal council. However, the Administrative Court ruled that there had been no errors in the agreement and rejected the appeal. The matter was appealed to the District Court of Gothenburg.

The Court of Appeal agreed with the Administrative Court's assessment in all parts except with respect to the power of the committee to approve the reservation agreement in light of the delegation ban found in Aticle 6.34 of the old municipal legislation (*Kommunallag*, KL) (1991:900). The Court of Appeal stated that the amount of the purchase price itself fell within the scope of what the committee could decide, in accordance with the delegation scheme for the Municipal Board of Halmstad Municipality.

The Court of Appeal expressed that the approval of the reservation agreement should have been decided at a higher municipal political level than that of the community building committee. In the Court of Appeal's opinion, the case could be considered of significant general interest and of high social relevance. Furthermore, the Court of Appeal thought that the decision could be regarded as affecting the direction of the municipal operations. Decisions in such cases, the court said, must be made in accordance with 6.34 of the KL and could not be delegated to a committee.

The judicial question in this case is not a religious one, at least not at first glance. The court never mentioned freedom of religion, nor did it discuss if the interpretation and application of the KL was in accordance with the ECHR, even though the case concerned the possibility of meeting and manifesting their religion for those who purchased the land.

There are specific circumstances regarding the agreement in the above-mentioned case. Other cases concerning the building of mosques may actualize the PBL and other judicial questions may be considered. But the overarching question concerning human rights and freedom of religion is the same. Is the interpretation and application of the legislation in accordance with the rights at the heart of the matter?

The aim of human rights systems is that human rights must be taken into consideration in the different systems when ordinary legislation is applied by public servants. However, in reality this demands time and knowledge that may not be possible to sustain within the public system. On the other hand, it is necessary for the realization of human rights.

The political system in Sweden is a democratic system, with the majority ruling the minority. However, in order to constrain the majority from oppressing minorities, the constitution contains a built-in system with, among other things, a human rights chapter that aims to protect minorities. Human rights (for example, free speech) is intended for all citizens, but such protection is most important for those with a divergent opinion, for reasons that are obvious. Human rights is, in other words, a way for power to limit itself and a way for the minority to retain their unique features.

Human rights are often seen as a fundamental part of a well-functioning democracy, but in some democratic theories human rights are not included because they put a restraint on the public will, the will of the majority.[23] With regard to this, human rights are not unproblematic. The necessity will always exist of balancing between the protection of minorities and the will of the majority. The balancing of these interests is not always easy to achieve. It presupposes a legislator and an interpreter of judicial norms who take seriously the limitations they have imposed upon themselves.

Interpretation and the Importance of a Mutual Language

The discourse about freedom of religion often employs concepts such as democracy, religion, and secularism. Definitions, or perhaps the understandings of these concepts that sometimes can be seen as buzzwords, must be explained in order to have a common language and common starting points. A common language is also important when it comes to the impact of legislation. Legislation is an expression of values and norms and a tool for changing societies. This means that legislation is a powerful tool in itself, but for legislation to have an impact on a deeper level, the people must understand and approve of the

---

23 Eivind Smith and Olof Petersson, "Konstitutionell demokrati som begrepp och som ideal," in *Konstitutionell demokrati*, ed. Eivind Smith and Olof Petersson (Stockholm: SNS förlag, 2004), 29ff.

legislation.[24] As a prerequisite for legislation having an impact, it is important that the language is common and the words, as for example "religion" in different human rights instruments, mean the same. Freedom of religion is an example of this issue. The words "religion" and "manifestation" can be interpreted in many different ways; the way in which the words are interpreted determines the scope of the right.

How human rights are interpreted and applied is decisive for the impact of these rights. From a judicial point of view, human rights are a bit problematic because they are often constructed in a way that makes them open to a variety of interpretations and these interpretations are themselves often founded on earlier interpretations, which sometimes makes the concretization of rights seem untimely. The need for interpretation is not unique to human rights: all judicial norms are subject to interpretation. However, the constructions of human rights are often compromises between different political parties or states, which creates a broad space for interpretation. Sometimes the comprehension of rights seems unclear.

The context in which human rights operate is crucial for their interpretation. The constitution, and accordingly human rights, was not regarded as an important part of the judicial system in Sweden during the first half of the 20th century.[25] But in the latter part of the 20th century and in the 21st century, the importance of human rights has developed and become significant, not only in the legislation process but also for those working in public organizations. Whenever legislation comes into force and public servants are about to apply legislations or judicial norms, human rights have to be taken into consideration. When a legal norm is about to be applied by the public servant, he or she has to determine if the application at hand is in accordance with the human rights instruments to which Sweden has committed itself. If it is found not to be in accordance with the human rights regulations in the IG or in the ECHR, the norm is not to be applied.

The religious demographic landscape in Sweden has changed in the last decade. There are several reasons for this: the secularization process is one possible reason, as is immigration. Immigration is a powerful demographic

---

24 See e.g. Antoni Gramsci, *Selections from the Prison Notebooks* (London: Lawrence & Wishart, 1995), xx in the introduction and 376-77. See also Antonio Santucci, *Antonio Gramsci 1891-1937: Intellektuell och politisk biografi* (Lund: Celanders Förlag, 2014), 36.
25 Fredrik Sterzel, *Författning i utveckling: Konstitutionella studier*, Rättsfondens skriftserie 33 (Uppsala: Iustus förlag, 1998), 14.

phenomenon with a formative effect upon our societies and the regulations and systems upholding society.[26]

For a long time, human rights have focused mainly on the individual and the individual's right to have and to hold his or her rights. Today, claims are being made for the rights of groups. The reasons for this development can be many, but one explanation is that society has changed. It is no longer only a question about the individual rights of immigrants; it has become a question of citizens belonging to minority groups.[27] This development has actualized questions about political and religious participation in the public space. In this context, the question about forming an identity as an individual or as a member of a collective is important, and is also related to the question of being a migrant on the move or a permanent citizen. The difference between these ways of identifying ourselves may have an impact on the way we claim our rights. The collective identity can in some cases come into conflict with other conceptions in a society and in terms of political identity this can be problematic.[28]

In other words, this can be said to be a question regarding assimilation, toleration, and respect. When we look upon the "others" as an individual or as a group, it tends to be easier to demand and expect the individual to assimilate to the majority society than to ask the group of "others" to do the same. This dynamic may have an impact on how seemingly secular and neutral legislation is interpreted.

The discipline of sociology of religion sometimes utilizes the concepts of *the return of religion* and *the new visibility of religion*. These are two different points of departure when it comes to analyzing the role of religion in our modern societies. These concepts set the boundaries for theories concerning secularization and are based on the belief that religion disappeared when the modern secular societies emerged and placed religion and politics in different spheres: the former in the private sphere and the latter in the public sphere. Sweden has been labelled a secular society in which religion has no role or part in the public sphere.

---

26 Albert Bastenier, "Islam in Belgium Contradictions and Perspectives," in *The New Islamic Presence in Western Europe*, ed. Tomas Gerholm and Yngve Georg Lithman (London: Mansell Publishing Limited, 1988), 134.
27 Bastenier, "Islam in Belgium," 134.
28 Charles Taylor, "Why We Need a Radical Redefinition of Secularism," in *The Power of Religion in the Public Sphere*, ed. Eduardo Mendieta and Jonathan VanAntwerpen (New York: Colombia University Press, 2011), 45.

These assumptions have been questioned of late because empirical research reveals another reality. Nevertheless, even though the role of religion cannot be fully explained within these categories, they can be helpful in order to shed light on the development of the relation between religion and presumably secular legislation in Sweden.

Perhaps the *new visibility of religion* in the public sphere can be explained in terms of the idea that for a large number of people religion has never disappeared, but that these people have not had power and space in the public sphere. Access to the public space is a crucial element when ensuring individuals their rights. The definition and concretization of rights are important. Who is setting the frames for rights and why?

Sweden today can be described as a post-secular society in the sense that it cannot be identified as a straightforwardly religious society or a completely secular society.

According to Jürgen Habermas, the challenge for religious groups and other minorities as well is to translate religious language into secular language to gain access to the larger group and to those in power. Habermas states:

> What I have in mind is the task of translating not from a religious discourse but from presentations in a religious language to public language, which allows us to arrive at reasons that are more general than the ones in the original language. This wider accessibility and appeal of reasons is the idea I connect with the secular reasons which are secular in the sense of transcending the semantic domains of particular religious communities.[29]

The increasing religious pluralism in Sweden and many Western states has made it more difficult for states and political parties to exclude arguments based on religion and demands related to religion.[30]

If Muslims or other religious minority groups are marginalized through what on the surface seems like neutral legislations, it probably will affect the legitimacy of the rulers and the legislation will be less effective.

---

29 Judith Butler, Jürgen Habermas, Charles Taylor, and Cornel West, "Concluding Discussion," in *The Power of Religion in the Public Sphere*, ed. Eduardo Mendieta and Jonathan VanAntwerpen (New York: Colombia University Press, 2011), 114.

30 Anders Bäckström, "Religion mellan det privata och det offentliga: Om religion och välfärd," in *Religionens offentlighet: Om religionens plats i samhället*, ed. Hanna Stenström (Skellefteå: Artos & Norma bokförlag, 2013), 33.

Some Concluding Remarks

How religion is formulated and described matters. For a long time, religion has been considered something that in Sweden belongs to the private sphere; religion is both described as a fundamental part of life and also as dangerous and extreme. Adherents of Islam are sometimes seen as a threat due to the fact that the core of the religion does not comply with the modern division of private and public spheres. Can that division be made? What is private and what is public?[31]

Freedom of religion has become a question of freedom from something, the secular argument, and freedom to something, the religious argument. This way of viewing freedom of religion actualizes questions concerning the visibility of religion. Different expressions such as the wearing of headscarves and the building of religious buildings serve as examples of sources of conflict between religion and secular values.

Tensions occur when religion makes its way into the public arena and the state is forced to handle questions about demarcation lines, such as what religion is and what it is not, and which parts of religion can and must be protected.

The context in which human rights are situated, and in which human rights are used and interpreted, have changed during the past decade. Today, human rights is a legal tool that is recognized from a legal perspective.

The development from only taking into account the negative obligations according to the human rights instruments, to a focus on positive obligations, has changed and enlarged the scope of several human rights over the course of the last decade. Positive obligations can be described as the state having not only the responsibility to ensure its citizens that existing legislation complies with human rights, but the state also has the responsibility to apply legislation in compliance with the human rights instruments. This has proved to be of great significance when it comes to cases concerning the right to privacy according to Article 8 of the ECHR. The question is one of whether and how positive obligations are used under Article 9. Article 9 has a wide margin of appreciation, and this may pose a problem when it comes to positive obligations. What can be expected of the state when great consideration is accorded the traditions and culture of the state?

The scope of the freedom of religion is very narrow if there is no possibility of manifesting that religion. For example, if you have a right to manifest your religion either by yourself or together with others to meet and have sermons,

---

31 Bäckström, "Religion mellan det privata och det offentliga," 35.

but you do not have a place where you can gather, this will have a negative effect on the possibility of exercising your freedom of religion.

Bibliography

European Court of Human Rights
Canea Catholic Church v. *Greece*, application no. 25528/94, 16 December 1997
Dahlab v. *Switzerland*, application no. 42393/98, decision 15 February 2001
Hasan and Chaush v. *Bulgaria*, application no. 30985/96, 26 October 2000
Kokkinakis v. *Greece*, application no. 14307/88, 25 May 1993
Manoussakis and others v. *Greece*, application no. 18748/91, 26 September 1996
Metropolitan Church of Bessarabia v. *Moldova*, application no. 45701/99, 13 December 2001
Sidiropoulos and Others v. *Greece*, application no. 57/1997/841/1047, 10 July 1998

Official sources
SOU 1972:36 Samhälle och trossamfund: slutbetänkande
United Nations Human Rights Committee. *CCPR General Comment No. 22 article 4. Article 18 (Freedom of Thought, Conscience or Religion)*, 30 July 1993, CCPR/C/21/Rev.1/Add.4.

Literature
Bastenier, Albert. "Islam in Belgium Contradictions and Perspectives." In *The New Islamic Presence in Western Europe*, edited by Tomas Gerholm and Yngve Georg Lithman, 133-45. London: Mansell Publishing Limited, 1988.
Butler, Judith, Jürgen Habermas, Charles Taylor, and Cornel West. "Concluding Discussion." In *The Power of Religion in the Public Sphere*, edited by Eduardo Mendieta and Jonathan VanAntwerpen, 109-17. New York: Colombia University Press, 2011.
Bäckström, Anders. "Religion mellan det privata och det offentliga: Om religion och välfärd." In *Religionens offentlighet: Om religionens plats i samhället*, edited by Hanna Stenström, 27-46. Skellefteå: Artos & Norma bokförlag, 2013.
Cameron, Iain. *An Introduction to the European Convention on Human Rights*. Uppsala: Iustus förlag, 2006.
Claesson, Urban. "Habermas, kyrka och offentlighet: Ett historiskt perspektiv på religionens återkomst." In *Religionens offentlighet: Om religionens plats i samhället*, edited by Hanna Stenström, 47-60. Skellefteå: Artos & Norma bokförlag, 2013.
Enkvist, Victoria. *Religionsfrihetens rättsliga ramar*. PhD diss. Uppsala: Iustus förlag, 2013.
Gramsci, Antonia. *Selections from the Prison Notebooks*. London: Lawrence & Wishart, 1995.

Runzo, Joseph. "Secular Rights and Religious Responsibilities." In *Human Rights and Responsibilities in the World Religions*, edited by Nancy M. Martin, Joseph Runzo, and Arvind Sharma, 9-25. Oxford: Oneworld, 2003.

Santucci, Antonio. *Antonio Gramsci 1891-1937: Intellektuell och politisk biografi*. Lund: Celanders Förlag, 2014.

Smith, Eivind, and Olof Petersson. "Konstitutionell demokrati som begrepp och som ideal." In *Konstitutionell demokrati,* edited by Eivind Smith and Olof Petersson, 7-41. Stockholm: SNS förlag, 2004.

Sorgenfrei, Simon. *Islam i Sverige: De första 1300 åren*. Bromma: Myndigheten för stöd till trossamfund, 2018.

Sterzel, Fredrik. *Författning i utveckling: Konstitutionella studier*. Rättsfondens skriftserie 33. Uppsala: Iustus förlag, 1998.

Taylor, Charles. "Why We Need a Radical Redefinition of Secularism." In *The Power of Religion in the Public Sphere,* edited by Eduardo Mendieta and Jonathan VanAntwerpen, 34-59. New York: Colombia University Press, 2011.

Taylor, Paul M. *Freedom of Religion*. Cambridge: Cambridge University Press, 2005.

Tuori, Kaarlo. *Critical Legal Positivism*. Farnham: Ashgate, 2002.

Webpages

Svenska kyrkan. "Medlemmar i Svenska kyrkan i förhållande till folkmängd den 31.12.2018 per församling, pastorat och stift samt riket." Accessed February 15, 2020. https://www.svenskakyrkan.se/statistik.

Index of Subjects

A

Anti-nazi resistance 28, 41-42, 45-46, 49, 51-53, 59-61, 64-65, 71-72, 75, 89, 96, 110, 118, 140, 189, 197

Autonomy
– Church autonomy 261, 273-276, 280-281, 305, 307
– Religious autonomy 223-224, 403, 405, 407, 413

B

Barmen Declaration 67-69, 72, 118, 132, 145, 169, 176, 297

Bible 117, 124, 168, 183, 186, 188, 190-191, 196, 199, 264, 334

C

Château Bossey ecumenical institute 116

Christian tradition 101, 131, 148, 183, 188, 190-191, 196

Church of Iceland 181, 269-270

Church of Norway 46, 140, 181-183, 189, 191, 259, 262, 270-274, 276, 278, 280, 284, 287, 289, 291-293, 295, 297, 304-307

Church of Sweden 16, 44, 181, 260, 262-264, 274, 276-277, 280, 282, 285-287, 289-295, 447

Church synod 184-185, 189, 194, 265

Confessing Church 42, 49, 53, 56, 67, 72, 117, 145, 169-171

Confessional culture 17-19

Confessionalization 16-17, 21, 227, 273

Conservative 17-19, 137, 147, 152, 154, 186, 196, 198, 200, 238, 243-245, 247, 253, 299, 317, 319-327, 329, 332-333, 388

Constitution 29, 31-33, 37, 51-52, 79, 93, 99-100, 103, 131-132, 135-136, 149, 169-171, 175-176, 181-183, 221, 233, 249, 265, 268-269, 271-272, 278, 280, 284, 293-294, 296, 298-299, 340, 342-344, 347-349, 351, 353-355, 356, 360, 373, 385-386, 398-403, 407, 409, 411, 413, 424-426, 436, 457-458

Constitutional identity 339-341, 349-353, 355, 357-360

Constitutional law 70, 96, 100, 124, 175, 221-222, 263, 339-340, 342, 347, 353, 358-360

Council of Europe 25-26, 302, 364, 374, 398, 451

Court of Justice of the European Union (CJEU)/European Court of Justice 27, 251, 342-344, 348-351, 355, 357-359, 431-435, 441

Creation theology 42, 55, 76, 82, 94, 118

D

Danish Folk Church 124, 181, 193

Dansk Samling (political party) 51, 66
Denmark/Danish 14-19, 22, 24-25, 27-30, 34, 41-54, 57-65, 67, 69-77, 79, 88-90, 95, 98, 100-101, 104, 110, 118, 124, 181, 184, 189, 192-194, 233-241, 244-246, 248-251, 253-254, 260, 262, 266-271, 273, 276, 279, 281, 285-288, 290-293, 297-303, 320, 340, 343-345, 347-349, 351, 353, 356, 363-364, 368-369, 372-374, 392, 423-424

E

Eastern Canon Law 204, 214
Ecclesiastical law 17, 23, 26, 30, 31, 43, 48, 65, 78, 87, 101, 115-117, 120-122, 131, 139, 164-166, 169, 171-177, 209, 212, 240, 243, 251, 259, 261-263, 273-274, 281, 291, 293-296, 298, 302-303, 306-307, 316, 319-320, 328, 353-354, 363, 387, 391, 431, 442
Equal rights 188, 195, 203, 220, 242, 305
European Convention on Human Rights (ECHR) 25-27, 119, 222 223, 272, 281, 296, 298, 302, 342, 347, 348, 353, 376, 386, 409, 419, 422, 425-434, 438, 442, 449-456, 458, 461.
European Court of Human Rights (ECtHR) 25-27, 119-120, 122-223, 251-252, 296, 298-299, 302, 342, 347-348, 353, 409, 419, 422, 425-434, 438, 442, 449-456, 458, 461

Europeanization 31-32, 203, 296, 302, 339, 341, 343, 349, 351-353, 359-360
Evangelical 15-16, 20, 52-53, 68-69, 133, 141, 143, 169-171, 175-176, 181-183, 259-260, 263, 265-266, 269, 272-273, 276-278, 280, 283, 287, 289-294, 302, 304, 306-307, 322-324, 327, 334, 353, 387-388, 399-402, 411
Evangelical Church of Germany 141
Evangelical Lutheran Church of Denmark 14-19, 22, 24-25, 27-30, 34, 41-54, 57-65, 67, 69-77, 79, 88-90, 95, 98, 100-101, 104, 110, 118, 124, 181, 184, 189, 192-194, 233-241, 244-246, 248-251, 253-254, 260, 262, 266-271, 273, 276, 279, 281, 285-288, 290-293, 297-303, 320, 340, 343-345, 347-349, 351, 353, 356, 363-364, 368-369, 372-374, 392, 423-424
Evangelical Lutheran Church of Finland (ELCF) 16, 20, 182, 260, 265-266, 276-277, 280, 283, 287, 289-293, 322-323, 326, 353, 387-388, 399-402, 411

F

Finland/Finnish 15, 16, 19-20, 24-27, 30, 32-34, 41, 43-44, 47-48, 123-124, 181-182, 203-208, 210-212, 214, 216-222, 224-229, 260, 262, 264-266, 273, 276, 280-281, 283, 286-293, 299, 302, 315, 317, 319-320, 322-327, 329-330, 344-349, 351, 353, 355, 363-364, 366, 369, 373-376, 385-389, 397-403, 407, 410-413, 424-425, 434

Finns Party 323-329
Freedom of religion / religious
    freedom 22-24, 27, 31-33, 107,
    119-120, 175, 222, 225, 227, 233,
    237, 260-261, 263, 265-269, 272,
    275, 281, 298-302, 305, 353,
    356, 369, 377, 385-388, 396-399,
    401-407, 409-413, 419-422, 425-431,
    433-436, 438-439, 441-442, 447-458,
    461-462
Fundamental rights 26, 33, 220, 342,
    387, 398-399, 401-403, 407-410,
    412-413, 420, 422, 428, 432-433,
    437-438, 441
Fundamentalism 156, 238, 247

G
Gender equality 181, 190, 195
German Christians 56, 68, 117, 146,
    169-171, 175
Group rights 333
Grundtvigianism 52-55

H
Hague Convention 42, 72-76, 110
Human dignity 112-113, 115, 117, 149,
    154, 174, 341, 410, 441
Human rights 25, 27, 30, 33, 78,
    80-81, 107-108, 114, 117, 119-120,
    122, 149-151, 164, 174, 187,
    191, 203-204, 216, 220, 222, 227,
    229, 237, 244, 246, 251-252,
    261, 272-273, 280-281, 296,
    298-303, 305, 307, 315, 340-342,
    344, 346-348, 351-353, 360, 367,
    369-371, 375-376, 386, 390,
    397-399, 403-404, 407-413, 419-422,
    424, 429, 431-432, 438, 441-442,
    447-453, 455-459, 461

Humanism 50-51, 54, 56, 66, 237

I
Iceland/Icelandic 14-16, 24, 26, 41,
    43-44, 47, 181, 262, 266, 269-270,
    273, 344, 346, 353, 363
Idealism, legal 76
Identitarian 316-317, 319-322, 326-334
Identity 27, 31-32, 203, 233, 235,
    246-247, 250, 252-253, 260, 274,
    280, 294, 297, 315-321, 323-325,
    327, 330-333, 339-341, 349-353,
    355, 357-360, 365, 369, 371, 374,
    376-379, 459
Indigenous 364, 366, 371-377, 380
Internationalization 13-14, 24, 28,
    31-32, 125, 187, 203, 259, 261,
    295-296, 302, 307, 339, 341,
    343, 349, 352-353, 359-360, 366,
    396-397, 412, 442, 447
Islam 23, 222, 233-253, 315, 325-326,
    328, 449-450, 461
Islamism 235-236, 238-239, 246, 248,
    254

J
Jews/Jewish 45-46, 53, 58-59, 68-70,
    72, 74, 92, 110, 267, 301, 318, 320,
    333, 366, 375
Judicial dialogue 242, 431, 447-449,
    456, 458
Jurisprudence 13, 21, 23, 26, 77,
    95-96, 163, 165-169, 172-175,
    203-204, 209, 212, 214, 216-221,
    224-225, 227, 229, 254, 299, 302,
    358, 364, 368-369, 376, 378, 380,
    424
Justification by faith 90, 138

L

Laws of life 42, 58-59, 61-63, 76, 79
Legal culture 22, 29, 43, 76, 109-110, 112, 119, 121, 164, 203-204, 216-217, 225, 229, 352, 380, 392-393, 420
Legislation 13, 16, 19-20, 22-24, 26, 33, 63, 65, 74, 76, 110, 117, 119, 121, 123-124, 149, 203-204, 216-222, 224-226, 228, 233, 244, 249-250, 260-263, 265-266, 268, 272, 274-276, 280, 290, 293, 296-297, 299, 302, 306-307, 327, 340-342, 344-349, 355, 359, 364, 367-371, 373-375, 378-380, 387, 390, 393, 400, 405-406, 410-411, 413, 432, 436-437, 439, 441-442, 447, 449-461
Legal Realism 29, 33, 43, 76-80, 96-97, 109, 119
Legal systems 164, 295, 341-344, 348-349, 351-352, 359-360, 365-366, 376, 380
Legality 175, 390, 394-395, 397, 409, 411, 413
Lex naturalis 28, 42, 47, 77
Lutheran World Foundation 113
Lutheranism 14-15, 19, 41, 43, 48-49, 300, 322-324, 388

M

Manifestation 169, 171, 247, 326, 367, 376, 410, 427-429, 433, 438, 449-450, 454, 458
Margin of appreciation 302, 426, 432, 451, 454, 461
Marriage 17, 22, 30, 57, 142, 204, 208, 212-218, 220, 225-227, 229, 240, 242-243, 275-276, 278, 282-286, 294, 297, 300, 303-304, 321-323, 326-327, 330, 406
Media 113, 197, 203-206, 210, 224-225, 227, 229, 236, 240-241, 249, 251, 317, 321-322, 324-329, 333, 358, 448
Ministry
– State's ministry 184-185
– Women's ministry 183, 185-186, 188, 190-193, 195, 198-200
Minorities 23, 25, 27, 31-34, 234, 248, 252, 267, 275, 285, 298, 315-316, 318-319, 363-367, 370-372, 374-381, 386, 422, 436-438, 450, 452, 457, 460
Mosques 245, 439-440, 449-451, 455-456
Multicultural 316, 332-333
Multiculturalism 233, 316-318, 320, 330
Muslims 30, 34, 233-242, 245-247, 249-254, 301, 332, 439, 450, 460

N

Natural law
– as ethics 11, 18, 28, 42, 75, 80-82, 93, 98, 117-119, 166, 441-442
– as legal theory 11, 13, 17, 28, 42, 78, 80-82, 94, 96, 103, 112, 117, 119, 163, 166, 172, 174, 423-424, 441-442
– in ecclesiastical jurisprudence 172
– Renaissance 117, 172, 441
Naturalism 76-77
Nazism 49, 51-53, 56-59, 65, 71-72, 89, 96

Neutrality 33, 41, 44, 46, 223, 385, 434, 439, 448-449
Non-discrimination 27, 355, 377, 401, 422
Norden, East (Finland, Sweden) 14, 43, 262
Norden, West (Denmark, Iceland, Norway) 14-15, 43-44, 262, 266, 273
Nordic Democracy 29, 51, 87, 100-101, 104
Norway/Norwegian 14-17, 19-20, 22, 24-25, 30, 41, 43-48, 61, 67-69, 71-72, 75, 101, 110-111, 114, 123, 132, 140, 181-185, 187-193, 195-197, 200, 228, 259-262, 266-267, 269-274, 276, 278, 280-281, 284, 286-287, 289-293, 295-297, 299, 301-307, 318, 322, 344, 346-348, 349, 351, 353, 363-364, 366, 368-369, 372-375, 424-425

O

Oeconomia 11, 18-19, 62-63, 68
Orders of creation 57-58, 79, 144
Orthodox/orthodoxy 30, 101, 203-204, 206, 208-222, 224-229, 234, 239, 244, 260, 265-266, 306-307, 315, 322, 328, 353, 401, 405

P

Pastoral Letter 46-47, 69-71
Polarization 247, 331, 333
Populism 315, 317, 324, 327, 329, 432
Positive obligations 398, 419, 422, 426, 430, 452, 461

Postwar Germany 92, 132, 135, 140, 145
Priesthood 102, 209-210, 213-214, 218, 220-222, 226, 268, 290, 305, 307
Protestantism 18, 53, 66, 134, 148-149, 164
Public order 33, 45, 73, 236-237, 354, 395-397, 409-410, 413, 429

R

Reality TV 203, 205-207, 209-210, 216, 221, 225
Rechtstheologie 108, 118, 122, 125
Recognition 20, 23, 25, 30-32, 34, 102, 141, 190, 315-318, 321, 323, 326, 329-333, 354, 364, 370, 372, 374, 377-380
Re-confessionalization 11, 13-14, 16, 20-21, 23-24, 28, 30, 32, 147, 181, 195-196, 199-200, 228, 254, 259, 262, 306, 413, 422, 442
Reformism 15, 25, 49, 52, 119, 121, 123-124, 147, 186, 189, 236, 239-241, 244-245, 263-266, 272-273, 386-387, 397-401, 403-404, 407, 409-410, 413
Religion law 11, 32, 34, 261, 299-300, 385, 387-389, 391, 396-397, 401, 407, 412, 414
Religious law 13, 30, 164, 203, 224, 226, 229, 273, 276, 385, 391, 398
Replacement 320, 328
Rule by law 31, 49, 65-67, 72, 75-77, 103, 259-263, 267, 269-270, 272-274, 277, 280-282, 285-287, 289, 291-296, 300, 303, 305-307, 409, 429, 453
Rule of law 28, 30, 77, 150, 173, 237, 246-247, 254, 298, 301, 351-352,

354, 391-392, 394-397, 402, 410, 413, 437, 439

S

Scandinavian creation theology 55, 76, 82, 94, 118

Scandinavian Legal Realism 33, 76-80, 96, 109, 109, 112, 119, 419-425, 441-442

Secular 13, 17-20, 22-23, 27-31, 33-34, 41-44, 47, 62, 67, 70, 72-73, 76, 87, 90, 93, 102-104, 107-108, 117, 120, 124-125, 131-134, 141, 147, 149, 155, 163-164, 169, 171-172, 174-175, 177, 181, 185-187, 191, 193, 195, 198-199, 204, 226, 233-237, 242, 244, 248, 251-253, 264, 273, 275, 279, 325, 339, 353-355, 377, 389-392, 394, 397, 407, 413-414, 425, 447, 449, 455, 459-461

Secularism 50, 66, 140, 235-239, 241-242, 249-250, 253-254, 353, 357, 359, 390, 457

Secularization 14, 20, 23, 31, 66, 107, 109, 115, 118, 120, 122, 139, 142-144, 198, 200, 262, 273, 296, 458-459

Separation between Church/religion and State 26-27, 44, 63, 120, 171, 238, 242, 304, 353

Social democrats 88

Sweden/Swedish 14-16, 19-20, 24-25, 27, 29-30, 32-33, 41, 43-49, 52, 101, 107, 108-116, 118-125, 181, 184, 189, 191, 193-196, 198, 200, 205, 210, 228, 250, 260, 262-264, 266, 271, 273-274, 276-277, 280-282, 285-287, 289-295, 297, 299, 302,

303, 320, 322, 327, 344-348, 351, 353, 363-364, 366, 368-369, 373-376, 419-420, 422-426, 431, 435-441, 447-451, 454-455, 457-461

T

Three Estates, doctrine of 11, 18-19, 22, 62

Totalitarianism 88-89, 91, 103, 132, 137, 139, 143, 148, 150-151, 153-154

Traditionalism 235, 321

Transitional justice 45-46, 60, 64

Two Kingdoms Doctrine 155, 173, 392

Two Regiments, doctrine of 18, 62, 67, 69, 77, 173

W

Welfare state 52, 103-104, 107, 112, 123, 247, 424

World Council of Churches(WCC) 113, 115-116, 125

World War II 15, 19, 28-30, 41, 43-45, 47, 49, 51, 56, 58, 66, 78, 87, 100, 107, 110, 112-113, 116-117, 132, 135, 137, 145-146, 148, 163, 176, 187, 227, 271, 273, 297, 339, 341, 343, 364-365, 370, 380, 423

Index of Names

A

Afanasiev, Nicholas 215
Agrama, Hussein Ali 33, 237, 394-396, 410, 413
Agricola, Mikael 264
Ahrén, Per Olov 123
Ahvio, Juha 325, 327-329, 333
Al-Nabhani, Taqiuddin 248-249
Al-Qaradawi, Yousuf 244
Andersen, Johanne 193-194
Andræ, Tor 110
Aniulyte, Aurelija 320
Anselm, Reiner 133
Arabi, Ibn 240
Arvidson, Stellan 110
Askildsen, Arne 191
Augustine 90
Aulén, Gustaf 49, 110

B

Baer, Katarina 224
Balanos, Demetrios S. 228
Balsamon, Theodore 214
Bannon, Steve 319
Barth, Karl 49, 53, 55, 57, 67, 117-118, 122, 155, 173
Benoist, Alain de 320, 330
Berggrav, Eivind 47, 52, 68, 110, 114, 132, 140-142, 189
Berman, Harold J. 18
Berman, Sheri 321
Best, Werner 60, 71
Bielefeldt, Heiner 300

Bjerkås, Ingrid 197-200
Björkquist, Manfred 184
Bjørnson, Erling 186
Bogdandy, Armin von 357-358
Bohlin, Torsten 109-110, 113
Bolsonaro, Jair 327
Bonhoeffer, Dietrich 118
Brandby-Cöster, Margareta 194
Breistein, Ingunn 304
Brenneche-Petersen, Edith 194
Brilioth, Yngve 116
Brown, Wendy 379-380
Brunstädt, Friedrich 168, 171
Buber, Martin 56
Bugenhagen, Johannes 14-15, 266-267, 312
Bultmann, Rudolf 49, 55, 58
Böckenförde, Ernst-Wolfgang 175

C

Calo, Zachary R. 389-391, 394
Calvin, Jean 146
Camus, Renaud 320, 328
Cervin, Andreas 111
Christian III 14, 44, 266
Christian X 45
Cover, Robert M. 378-380
Cranmer, Frank 274

D

Dahrendorf, Ralf 149
Dibelius, Otto 137, 141-145
Doe, Norman 391

Dombois, Hans 173-174
Dressler, Markus 23
Durham, W. Cole Jr. 274-275

E
Eichmann, Adolf 163
Eidem, Erling 47
Ekelöf, Per Olof 423
Erlander, Tage 101
Espersen, Preben 124
Etchemendy, Matthew X. 76

F
Faye, Guillaume 320
Fischer, Agnethe 197
Florovsky, Georges 228
Fogh, Mogens 94
Forst, Rainer 332
Foucault, Michel 393
Friberg, Daniel 320
Fuglsang-Damgaard, Hans 47, 50
Fukuyama, Francis 391-392, 394

G
Gerhardsen, Einar 101
Giertz, Bo 195-196
Glynn, Kevin 204
Gogarten, Friedrich 56
Gollwitzer, Helmut 138, 146, 153
Graf, Friedrich Wilhelm 133
Green, Åke 299
Groes, Ebbe 100
Groes, Lis 100
Grotius, Hugo 81
Grundt, Gulla M. 186
Grundtvig, N. F. S. 52-54, 56, 63, 89, 94
Grønn-Hagen, Karen 192
Gullaksen, Per-Otto 123

Gullberg, Hjalmar 111-112, 119
Gustav Vasa 15, 262
Göransson, Göran 29, 108-110, 112-125

H
Habermas, Jürgen 242, 378-380, 460
Halla-aho, Jussi 325
Hallberg, Pekka 387
Hammarskjöld, Dag 24, 116
Hanneken, Herman von 73
Hanson, Kristian 68
Hautala, Anni 208, 213
Heckel, Johannes 172-173
Heckel, Martin 18
Hedenius, Ingemar 110
Hedtoft, Hans 101
Hegel, Georg Wilhelm Friedrich 330
Heidegger, Martin 56-58, 62
Heikkonen, Johannes 388
Helweg-Larsen, Else-Merete 95
Hemmingsen, Niels 19
Henriksen, Anna J. 186
Heuser, Stefan 32, 34
Hirsch, Emanuel 49, 144
Hirsi Ali, Ayaan 237, 239
Hitler, Adolf 49-50, 96, 117, 142, 154, 169
Holberg, Ludvig 17
Holm, Bo Kristian 19
Holstein, Günther 167-168
Honecker, Martin 133
Honneth, Axel 330, 332-333
Hussain, Waseem 243
Hussein, Tarek Ziad 236, 245-247, 253-254
Husserl, Edmund 57
Hägerström, Axel 76, 95, 423
Hämäläinen, Keijo 324-326
Høyland, Ola 192

Haakon VII 46
Haarder, Bertel 301

I
Inacker, Joachim 133
Indrebø, Ragnvald 188

J
Jensen, Anne 213
Jhering, Rudolf von 111
Johansen, Birgitte Schepelern 239
Jonsson Cornell, Anna 345
Jünger, Ernst 320
Jyränki, Antero 387
Jørgensen, Jørgen 94

K
Kallio, Maaret 208
Kant, Immanuel 50
Kaufmann, Thomas 17-19
Kavka, Misha 205, 225
Kelsen, Hans 95, 423
Kern, Kyprian 214, 216
Khankan, Sherin 236, 240-243, 245, 253
Kierkegaard, Søren 56
Klinge, Sune 356
Koch, Hal 29, 45, 47, 52-53, 59-64, 78-79, 81, 87-95, 98, 100-104
Koch, Hans 88
Koch, L. 88
Koefoed, Nina J. 19
Kokott, Juliane 357
Korpela, Jukka 208, 212, 224-225
Koskinen, Seppo 224
Kotiranta, Matti 388
Kristina(queen) 262
Kruse, Frederik Vinding 50
Kücükakin, Sami 243

Künneth, Walter 137
Kaalep, Ruuben 320

L
Laban, Abu 245
Larsen, Malik 245
Lavapuro, Juha 224, 387
Leino, Pekka 388
Leiter, Brian 76
Leo (Archbishop) 203, 209, 212
Lie, Trygve 24
Liermann, Hans 168
Lilla, Mark 319, 321
Lipps, Hans 56
Lundstedt, Vilhelm 423
Luomanen, Petri 326
Luther, Martin 14-15, 34, 56, 69, 77, 90, 96, 103, 118, 138, 144, 146, 148, 155, 266
Luukkanen, Arto 328-329
Løgstrup, K. E. 28, 41-43, 45, 48-49, 52-67, 71-72, 76, 78-81, 118
Løgstrup, Rosemarie, 58

M
Macciavelli, Nicholo 140
Macron, Emanuel 328
Arvind-Pal S. Mandair 23
Mangold, Werner 348, 355
McCrea, Ronan 356
Melanchton, Philipp 266
Mishima, Yukio 320
Mowinckel, Johan Ludwig 185
Moxter, Michael 176
Munk, Kaj 70, 110
Murros, Kai 320
Mussolini, Benito 88
Müller, Ludwig 169
Myrdal, Alva 120

N
Nawaz, Nazreen 251
Niebuhr, Reinhold 114
Niemöller, Martin 114
Nietzsche, Friedrich 55, 112, 320
Nilsson, Per-Erik 302
Norton, Anne 233
Nygren, Anders 49, 113
Nørregaard, Jens 88
Nørvig, Anne-Marie 100

O
Olivecrona, Karl 76-78, 81, 423
Orban, Viktor 327

P
Palme, Olof 120
Peter of Rome 43
Petersen, Fredrik 195
Petrén, Gustaf 120
Petrén, Sture 120
Pettersen, Jakob 191
Plato 88
Põder, Christine Svinth-Værge 72
Pope Francis 322
Poulsen, Thorvald 194
Pound, Ezra 320
Prenter, Regin 28, 41-43, 45, 48-49,
    51-57, 65-66, 67, 71-77, 81, 118
Puchta, Georg Friedrich 167
Pufendorf, Samuel von 17, 81
Puolimatka, Tapio 324-327, 329, 333

Q
Quisling, Vidkun 46, 68-69, 140

R
Radbruch, Gustav 172
Rahkonen, Jukka-Pekka 327

Ramadan, Tariq 240
Rasmussen, Tarald, 43
Rees, Wilhelm 388
Reinhard, Wolfgang 16
Remnick, David 319
Rendtorff, Trutz 132, 134-135
Robberstad, Knut 187
Rosemarie (born Pauly) 58
Rosenfeld, Michel 350
Ross, Alf 29, 76-77, 87, 93, 95-104, 423
Roy, Olivier 23, 247-248
Räsänen, Päivi 323, 325-327

S
Sakaranaho, Tuula 387
Saraviita, Ilkka 387
Savigny, Friedrich Carl von 166-167
Scavenius, Erik 60
Scheliha, Arnulf von 133
Schelsky, Helmut 149
Scheurl, Adolf von 167
Schill, Stephan 357-358
Schilling, Heinz 16-17
Schjelderup, Kristian 190, 197
Schleiermacher, Friedrich 168
Schmidt, Erik Ib 100
Schmitt, Carl 172
Schoen, Paul 172
Schweitzer, Wolfgang 138, 148-149,
    152
Seip, Henrik Aubert 110
Sendstad, Olav Valen 68
Seppo, Juha 387, 400-401, 404, 412
Seppänen, Arto 388
Seweriin, Rakel 192
Sigismund 15
Sigurdson, Ola 118
Sigurðsson, Sigurgeir 47
Skard, Bjarne 188, 190

Smemo, Johannes 188
Smend, Rudolf 149, 172
Smidt, Johannes 188, 192
Sohm, Rudolf 165-166, 168, 297
Sorouch, Abdol Karim 242
Sorsa, Leena 385, 387
Spengler, Oswald 111
St. Basil the Great 214
Stalin, Joseph 50
Stange, Carl 49
Stauning, Thorvald 49-50
Stendal, Synnøve Hinnaland 182
Stenner, Karen 321
Storeide, Hjalmar 191
Strandberg, Carl 119
Suksi, Markku 353
Sundberg, Halvar 121
Sundby, Olof 113, 116
Svenningsen, Niels 60
Söderblom, Nathan 109, 116
Södling, Maria 195-196
Sørensen, Arne 51

T
Tavakoli, Jaleh 236-239, 253-254
Taylor, Charles 21, 315-316, 330-331, 354, 365, 368, 377-379
Terboven, Josef 46, 111
Thastum, Bodil 88
Thielicke, Helmut 137, 146, 150, 152
Trillhaas, Wolfgang 137, 148, 152-153
Trump, Donald 319, 321, 324, 327
Träskman, Gunnar 123-124
Tuori, Kaarlo 22, 352, 388, 392, 393, 420
Tönnies, Ferdinand 149

U
Undén, Östen 119

V
Valla, Jean-Claude 320
Venner, Dominique 320, 329
Vermehren, Ruth 193-194
Vial, Pierre 320, 329
Vikström, Björn 326
Vold, Agnes 192, 197-198

W
Weber, Max 149
Wendland, Heinz-Dietrich 148
Wiig, Alf 190
Wilders, Geert 327
Wingren, Gustaf 49, 55-56, 118
Witte, John Jr. 18, 392, 398
Wolf, Erik 117, 173
Wolf, Ernst 53, 138, 146, 149-150, 152-153

Z
Zahle, Henrik 124
Zayd, Nasr Hamid Abou 240

Ø
Ørsted, Anders Sandøe 96

Å
Aalen, Leiv 198-199
Aarflot, Andreas 123